ARTIFICIAL INTELLIGENCE IN THEORY AND PRACTICE

IFIP – The International Federation for Information Processing

IFIP was founded in 1960 under the auspices of UNESCO, following the First World Computer Congress held in Paris the previous year. An umbrella organization for societies working in information processing, IFIP's aim is two-fold: to support information processing within its member countries and to encourage technology transfer to developing nations. As its mission statement clearly states,

> *IFIP's mission is to be the leading, truly international, apolitical organization which encourages and assists in the development, exploitation and application of information technology for the benefit of all people.*

IFIP is a non-profitmaking organization, run almost solely by 2500 volunteers. It operates through a number of technical committees, which organize events and publications. IFIP's events range from an international congress to local seminars, but the most important are:

• The IFIP World Computer Congress, held every second year;
• Open conferences;
• Working conferences.

The flagship event is the IFIP World Computer Congress, at which both invited and contributed papers are presented. Contributed papers are rigorously refereed and the rejection rate is high.

As with the Congress, participation in the open conferences is open to all and papers may be invited or submitted. Again, submitted papers are stringently refereed.

The working conferences are structured differently. They are usually run by a working group and attendance is small and by invitation only. Their purpose is to create an atmosphere conducive to innovation and development. Refereeing is less rigorous and papers are subjected to extensive group discussion.

Publications arising from IFIP events vary. The papers presented at the IFIP World Computer Congress and at open conferences are published as conference proceedings, while the results of the working conferences are often published as collections of selected and edited papers.

Any national society whose primary activity is in information may apply to become a full member of IFIP, although full membership is restricted to one society per country. Full members are entitled to vote at the annual General Assembly, National societies preferring a less committed involvement may apply for associate or corresponding membership. Associate members enjoy the same benefits as full members, but without voting rights. Corresponding members are not represented in IFIP bodies. Affiliated membership is open to non-national societies, and individual and honorary membership schemes are also offered.

ARTIFICIAL INTELLIGENCE IN THEORY AND PRACTICE

IFIP 19th World Computer Congress,
TC 12: IFIP AI 2006 Stream, August 21-24, 2006,
Santiago, Chile

Edited by

Max Bramer
University of Portsmouth, UK

 Springer

Artificial Intelligence in Theory and Practice

Edited by M. Bramer

p. cm. (IFIP International Federation for Information Processing, a Springer Series in Computer Science)

ISSN: 1571-5736 / 1861-2288 (Internet)

ISBN: 13: 978-1-4419-4188-6
Printed on acid-free paper

eISBN: 10: 0-387-34747-X
eISBN: 13: 978-0-387-34747-9

9 8 7 6 5 4 3 2 1
springer.com

Contents

Paper Sessions

Knowledge and Information Management

Agents 1

Knowledge Acquisition and Data Mining

Evolutionary Computation

Foreword

The papers in this volume comprise the refereed proceedings of the conference 'Artificial Intelligence in Theory and Practice' (IFIP AI 2006), which formed part of the 19th World Computer Congress of IFIP, the International Federation for Information Processing (WCC-2006), in Santiago, Chile in August 2006.

The conference is organised by the IFIP Technical Committee on Artificial Intelligence (Technical Committee 12) and its Working Group 12.5 (Artificial Intelligence Applications).

All papers were reviewed by at least two members of our Programme Committee. The best papers were selected for the conference and are included in this volume. The international nature of IFIP is amply reflected in the large number of countries represented here.

The conference featured invited talks by Rose Dieng, John Atkinson, John Debenham and myself. IFIP AI 2006 also included the Second IFIP Symposium on Professional Practice in Artificial Intelligence, organised by Professor John Debenham, which ran alongside the refereed papers. I should like to thank the conference chair, Professor Debenham for all his efforts in organising the Symposium and the members of our programme committee for reviewing an unexpectedly large number of papers to a very tight deadline.

This is the latest in a series of conferences organised by IFIP Technical Committee 12 dedicated to the techniques of Artificial Intelligence and their real-world applications. The wide range and importance of these applications is clearly indicated by the papers in this volume. Further information about TC12 can be found on our website http://www.ifiptc12.org.

Max Bramer
Chair, IFIP Technical Committee on Artificial Intelligence

Acknowledgements

Conference Organising Committee

Conference General Chair

John Debenham (University of Technology, Sydney, Australia)

Conference Program Chair

Max Bramer (University of Portsmouth, United Kingdom)

Executive Programme Committee

Max Bramer (University of Portsmouth, United Kingdom)
John Debenham (University of Technology, Sydney, Australia)
Vladan Devedzic (University of Belgrade, Serbia and Montenegro)
Eunika Mercier-Laurent (KIM, France)

Programme Committee

Agnar Aamodt (Norwegian University of Science and Technology,
    Norway)
Analia Amandi (ISISTAN Research Institute, Argentina)
Lora Aroyo (Eindhoven University of Technology, The Netherlands)
Stefania Bandini (University of Milan, Italy)
Max Bramer (University of Portsmouth, United Kingdom)
Krysia Broda (Imperial College London, United Kingdom)
Zdzislaw Bubnicki (Wroclaw University of Technology, Poland)
Luigia Carlucci Aiello (Università di Roma La Sapienza, Italy)
Monica Crubezy (Stanford University, USA)
John Debenham (University of Technology, Sydney, Australia)
Joris Deguet (CNRS - IMAG Institute, France)
Evangelos Dellis (Inst. of Informatics & Telecommunications, NCSR,
    Athens, Greece)
Yves Demazeau (CNRS - IMAG Institute, France)
Vladan Devedzic (University of Belgrade, Serbia and Montenegro)

Tharam Dillon (University of Technology, Sydney, Australia)
John Domingue (The Open University, United Kingdom)
Anne Dourgnon-Hanoune (EDF, France)
Gintautas Dzemyda (Institute of Mathematics and Informatics, Lithuania)
Henrik Eriksson (Linköping University, Sweden)
Matjaz Gams (Slovenia)
Ana Garcia-Serrano (Technical University of Madrid, Spain)
Daniela Godoy (ISISTAN Research Institute, Argentina)
Fedja Hadzic (University of Technology, Sydney, Australia)
Andreas Harrer (University Duisburg-Essen, Germany)
Timo Honkela (Helsinki University of Technology, Finland)
Werner Horn (Medical University of Vienna, Austria)
Tony Jan (University of Technology, Sydney, Australia)
Kostas Karpouzis (National Technical University of Athens, Greece)
Dusko Katic (Serbia and Montenegro)
Ray Kemp (Massey University, New Zealand)
Dr. Kinshuk (Massey University, New Zealand)
Joost N. Kok (Leiden University, The Netherlands)
Stasinos Konstantopoulos (Inst. of Informatics & Telecommunications, NCSR, Athens, Greece)
Jasna Kuljis (Brunel University, United Kingdom)
Daoliang Li (China Agricultural University, Beijing)
Ilias Maglogiannis (University of Aegean, Samos, Greece)
Suresh Manandhar (University of York, United Kingdom)
Ramon Lopez de Mantaras (Spanish Council for Scientific Research)
Brian Mayoh (University of Aarhus, Denmark)
Dimitri Melaye (CNRS - IMAG Institute, France)
Eunika Mercier-Laurent (KIM, France)
Tanja Mitrovic (University of Canterbury, Christchurch, New Zealand)
Riichiro Mizoguchi (Osaka University, Japan)
Zsolt Nagy (Budapest University of Technology and Economics, Hungary)
Pavol Navrat (Slovak University of Technology in Bratislava, Slovakia)
Erich Neuhold (RSA-DME)
Bernd Neumann (University of Hamburg, Germany)
Daniel O'Leary (University of Southern California, USA)
Andrea Omicini (Alma Mater Studiorum–Università di Bologna, Italy)
Mihaela Oprea (University of Ploiesti, Romania)
Stavros Perantonis (Inst. of Informatics & Telecommunications, NCSR, Athens, Greece)
Guillaume Piolle (CNRS - IMAG Institute, France)
Alun Preece (University of Aberdeen, United Kingdom)
Abdel-Badeeh M. Salem (Ain Shams University, Egypt)
Demetrios Sampson (University of Piraeus & CERTH, Greece)

Can Common Sense uncover cultural differences in computer applications?

Junia Anacleto[1], Henry Lieberman[2], Marie Tsutsumi[1],Vânia Neris[1],
Aparecido Carvalho[1], Jose Espinosa[2], Muriel Godoi[1] and Silvia Zem-
Mascarenhas[1]

1 Advanced Interaction Laboratory - LIA
UFSCar – Rod. Washigton Luis KM 235 – São Carlos – SP – Brazil
{junia, marie_tsutsumi, vania, fabiano, muriel_godoi}@dc.ufscar.br;
silviazem@power.ufscar.br
WWW home page: http://lia.dc.ufscar.br
2 MIT Media Laboratory
20 Ames St., 384A Cambridge MA 02139
{lieber, jhe}@media.mit.edu
WWW home page: http://www.media.mit.edu

Abstract. Cultural differences play a very important role in matching
computer interfaces to the expectations of users from different national and
cultural backgrounds. But to date, there has been little systematic research as
to the extent of such differences, and how to produce software that
automatically takes into account these differences. We are studying these
issues using a unique resource: Common Sense knowledge bases in different
languages. Our research points out that this kind of knowledge can help
computer systems to consider cultural differences. We describe our
experiences with knowledge bases containing thousands of sentences
describing people and everyday activities, collected from volunteer Web
contributors in three different cultures: Brazil, Mexico and the USA, and
software which automatically searches for cultural differences amongst the
three cultures, alerting the user to potential differences.

1. Introduction

The answer to the title question, according to our preliminary results, is yes.
However, to uncover cultural differences is not a simple task. Many researchers have
pointed that cultural differences should be considered in the design of interactive
systems [13, 7]. Culture is a shared meaning system which forms a framework for
problem solving and behavior in everyday life. Individuals communicate with each
other by assigning meaning to messages based on their prior beliefs, attitudes, and
values [7].

Please use the following format when citing this chapter:

Anacleto, J., Lieberman, H., Tsutsumi, M., Neris, V., Carvalho, A. et.al., 2006, in IFIP International Federation for Information Processing, Volume 217, Artificial Intelligence in Theory and Practice, ed. M. Bramer, (Boston: Springer), pp. 1–10.

The cultural differences express the "world vision" a group of people have. This vision is expressed in the simple activities that people do everyday. Arguably the most general and widely applicable kind is knowledge about the everyday world that is possessed by most people in a given culture — what is widely called 'common sense knowledge'. While 'common sense' to the ordinary people is related to 'good judgment' as a synonymous, the Artificial Intelligence community uses the term 'common sense' to refer to the millions of basic facts and understandings that most people have. For example, the lemon is sour; to open a door, you must usually first turn the doorknob; if you forget someone's birthday, they may be unhappy with you.

Common sense knowledge, thus defined, spans a huge portion of human experience, encompassing knowledge about the spatial, physical, social, temporal and psychological aspects of typical everyday life. Common sense is acquired from the interaction with the environment. Changing the environment changes the perception of common sense and is one of the reasons why different and diverse cultures exist. This conception of common sense is building ontology about everyday life based on the shared experiences of a community [12].

The challenge is to try to represent cultural knowledge in the machine, and have interfaces that automatically and dynamically adapt to different cultures. While fully implementing this goal is still out of reach, this paper takes some first steps.

We have collected large knowledge bases representing Commonsense knowledge in three cultures: Brazil, Mexico and the USA. Comparison between these knowledge bases gives us a basis for automatically discovering differences between cultures, and finding analogies from one culture to another. Software for cultural comparison is useful in many contexts. For example, by those who want to develop systems focusing on a specific user group (e.g. a teacher who consults the common sense database to prepare a specific instructional content); by those who want to develop systems which use the cultural knowledge stored in the knowledge bases (e.g search engines that consider the context); and by those who want to facilitate communication between people, providing mutual knowledge about their cultures.

In this context, the main purpose of this work, partially supported by TIDIA-Ae FAPESP project, proc no. 03/08276-3, and by CAPES, is to evaluate how the cultural differences can be recognized in the databases that store common sense. For that, we select a theme that frequently appeared in the Brazilian knowledge base – food. Considering that eating habits express culture (F1) and common sense affects eating habits (F2), we could say that common sense expresses culture. F1 is taken as true and so we should demonstrate F2.

It is important that the reader understands that we make no claim to have fully described a national culture, or to have fully captured cultural differences. Instead, the goal is simply to get some useful representation of culture and common knowledge, where otherwise the computer would have none. We believe that our contribution is the first attempt to systematically study the extent and nature of cultural differences; to represent cultural differences in machine-readable form; and to present an example of software that searches for such differences and provides inter-cultural translations automatically.

The next section presents how data are collected in the Open Mind Common Sense (OMCS) knowledge bases. To give the reader some idea of how knowledge in the various databases compares, we present some example comparisons for the food domain. We then discuss the prototype agent for finding cultural differences, followed by conclusion and future work.

2. The Open Mind Common Sense Approach for Gathering and Using Common Sense Facts

Arguably the most general and widely applicable kind of knowledge about the everyday world is the knowledge we typically assume is possessed by ordinary people in a given culture — what is widely called 'common sense knowledge'. One way that AI has used to represent this knowledge is by simple sentences asserting such facts (pioneered by Doug Lenat's CYC project). For example, a lemon is sour; to open a door, you must usually first turn the doorknob; if you forget someone's birthday, they may be unhappy with you. Common sense knowledge, thus defined, spans a huge portion of human experience, encompassing knowledge about the spatial, physical, social, temporal and psychological aspects of typical everyday life.

Since every ordinary person has the common sense that computers lack, why not involve everyone in building the knowledge base that is necessary to give computers what they need to be able of common sense reasoning? Nowadays, it is easy to reach lots of people through the Internet. For gathering the common sense data some Open Mind Common Sense websites were built. As the name suggests, the Open Mind Common Sense (OMCS) sites are open. Everyone who wishes to help can contribute with his or her knowledge.

The data are stored in the OMCS database as simple statements in natural language. However, for machine use, it is necessary to put them in a representation that allows machines to make practical inferences and analogies. For that, the data are submitted to a natural-language parser that generates a set of normalized nodes that are semantically related, composing a semantic network. A better understanding about how this semantic network is generated is presented by Liu [12].

Once the semantic network is ready, applications can be developed using the common sense knowledge provided by different users.

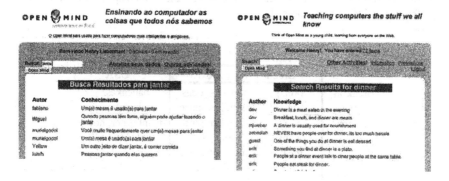

Figure 1. Common Sense sentences from Portuguese- and English-speaking contributors

3. Common Sense and Eating Habits

In this section, we give the reader a glimpse of what can be compared between the sites. Again, the idea is *not* to present a definitive scientific survey about such issues as what people actually eat for breakfast in Brazil versus the USA. The knowledge, after all, comes from members of the general public who may have legitimate disagreements or differing experiences about these issues. The idea is that Common Sense collects *plausible* (rather than completely accurate) answers about these questions, which can lead to *plausible* assumptions about cultural differences.

Considering the redundancies in our data, we selected categories that appeared in higher frequency in each base. Some of these data were presented in [1]. The categories are presented bellow.

Time for meals
One of the most common themes in the knowledge bases is time for meals. Table 1 shows what is considered common sense for most of the collaborators.

Table 1. Time for meals.

	Brazil	Mexico	USA
Lunch	11:30 to 13:00	14:00 to 16:00	12:00 to 14:00
Dinner	18:30 to 20:00	20:00 to 21:00	18:00 to 19:00

Here it is interesting to note that meals in Mexico are the latest ones. Although in Brazil and the USA, meals happen at a similar hour, in Mexico it seems to be common to have lunch after 14:00.

What do people eat in each meal?
Differences between what is eaten in each meal also can be noticed. Table 2 shows what seems to be considered common sense about what to eat in each meal.

It is possible to notice that Brazilian people prepare lighter food at breakfast. Also Mexican people seem to like food make with flour. Concerning desserts, Brazilian people associate ice cream as something cooling, and are reluctant to eat it in Brazil's (relatively mild) winter. On the other hand, American people seem to prefer pies and other baked desserts.

Table 2. What do they eat in each meal?

	Brazil	Mexico	USA
Breakfast	bread	tamales, eggs with hot sauce	pancakes, bagels
Lunch	rice, beans, meat, salad, egg	chicken with mole, roast meat, pastries, chilaquiles, barbacoa, tacos	hamburger, hot dog, pizza, sandwiches
Dinner	rice and beans,	tamales and atole,	steak and eggs, baked chicken,

	soup, salad, sandwich	quesadillas, coffee and cookies, bread with bean	clam chowder, mashed potatoes
Dessert	ice cream, fruit, candy	rice with milk, churros with chocolate, nuts with honey (crowbar), sweet coconut	pumpkin pie, apple pie, ice cream, cheese cake

Food for special occasions

Christmas and parties were topics that collaborators remembered too. Table 3 shows the main types of food cited for this occasions. It is interesting to notice that in Brazil and México it seems to be common have salty food for Christmas while in the USA sweet dishes seem to be more appreciated. On the other hand, beer seems to be appreciated at parties in all three countries.

Table 3. Food for special occasions.

	Brazil	Mexico	USA
Party	snack, candy, cake, meat, beer	beer, tequila	beer, vodka
Christmas	turkey, pork, lamb	romeritos, codfish, spaghetti	cranberry sauce, pineapple salad, frozen Christmas Pudding

4 Using Cultural Knowledge in Interactive Applications

We believe the cultural differences stored in the common sense bases can be helpful in (a) helping those who want to consider these differences in the development of interactive systems; (b) facilitating the interaction of different users by applications that use this common sense; and (c) facilitating the communication between people. Here we point out how developers involved in the situations cited above can use the cultural differences stored in common sense knowledge bases.

Developing systems considering cultural differences: Human Computer Interaction research raises further questions about how to understand culture and how it can and should affect user-interface design. Attributes as attraction, dynamism, activity, level of expertise, faith, intentions, locality, social validation, preferences, and scarcity have different weightings in different cultures [2]. Consequently, user-interface developers face further challenges [13]. Many questions still persist while talking about considering cultural differences in the design of interactive systems. Marcus [13] raises some questions: Are our notions of usability culturally biased? How should culture differences relate to persuasion and establishment of trust in Web sites and Web-based applications? How should culture dimensions relate to established dimensions of intelligence and change your thinking about online help, documentation, and training? How do culture differences relate to new insight about cognition differences? Do these differences change your thinking about user search strategies, mental models, and navigation? The only consensus seems to be that these attributes have different values and are key characteristics of the cultures to which they belong [4]. Despite the importance of these questions, some developers still face an uphill battle to get budgets for culture-oriented research and development accepted, to find and allocate the human resources, and to achieve project success [13]. In this context, collecting these "world views" and making them available for everyone that wants to develop a user-interface, can be expensive and laborious. The use of the Internet and the collaboration of millions of people allow knowledge bases to reflect actual cultural knowledge without cost, as anyone can have access to the database at the sites.

Developing systems which consider cultural differences: As the complexity of computer applications grows, it may be that the only way to make applications more helpful and avoid stupid mistakes and annoying interruptions is to make use of common sense knowledge. Cellular telephones should know enough to witch to vibrate mode if you're at the symphony. Calendars should warn you if you try to schedule a meeting at 2 AM or plan to take a vegetarian to a steak house. Cameras should realize that if you took a group of pictures within a span of two hours, at round the same location, they are probably of the same event [8]. In the web context, the necessity of using common sense knowledge becomes even more evident. The number of web pages available on Internet increases day after day, and consequently, finding relevant information becomes more and more a difficult task [3]. Also, Web Search tools do not do a very good job of discerning individuals' search goals [16]. However, when we consider communities of people with common interests, it is possible to improve the quality of the query results using knowledge extracted from common sense databases and observing behaviors of people of same culture. When a user submits a query, the cultural aspects suggest specific information exploiting previous observations about the behavior of other users when they asked similar queries. Different users may merit different answers to the same query [3]. As cultural differences can be detected in common sense bases, search engines that attempt to leverage common sense have a great opportunity to reflect cultural differences in their results.

Developing systems which facilitate communication between people by showing cultural differences: Communication between people from different cultures is a field which presents many interesting aspects. To show that common sense can help showing the cultural differences, a prototype of a mail client was developed. The application has an agent that keeps watching what the user is typing, while makes commentaries on the differences in the grounding that can lead to possible misunderstandings. The system also uses these differences to calculate analogies for concepts that evoke the same social meaning in those cultures. We focus this prototype on the social interaction among people in the context of eating habits, but it could scale to other domains. The system's interface has three sections, as can be seen in Figure 2. The first one – at the upper left – is the information for the email addresses and the subject, the second one – at the upper right – is where the agent posts its commentaries about the cultural differences and the third part – the lower part – is the body of the message. The second section has four subsections: the upper one shows the analogies that the agent found and the other three show the data that are not suitable for analogy. For example, in our screen shot, the third label for the Mexican culture – Mexicans thinks that dinner is coffee and cookies – and the second for American culture – Americans think that dinner is baked chicken – cannot make a meaningful analogy even if they differ only in one term.

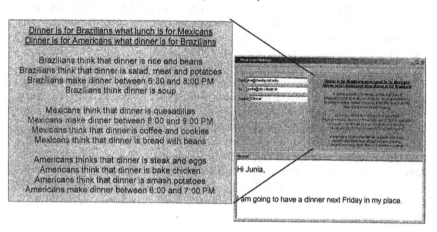

Figure 2. A screen shot of the system.

In order to make the cultural analogies, the system uses four semantic networks. The OMCSNet [10] semantic network (OMCSNet.OM), which was mined from the Open Mind corpus, is used as the core engine because it provides tools for context expansion and is especially designed for working with Open Mind Common Sense databases. The other three databases are culturally specific; they have knowledge about the Brazilian, Mexican and North-American culture – these semantic networks are called OMCSNet.BR, OMCSNet.MX and OMCSNet.US respectively. The OMCSNet.BR was built from data mined from the Brazilian Open Mind Common Sense database. In the American and Mexican cases, the statements were already in English language. In the Brazilian case, the statements were originally in Portuguese. For this project, a small group of statements related to eating habits were selected and freely translated to English to be parsed.

The calculation of cultural analogies is divided into eight steps.

Data retrieval (step 1): The first thing that the system does is to use the NLP package MontyLingua [9] to get the relevant concepts of the mail. This information is presented as tuples of (verb subject direct_object indirect_object). In the example above, the NLP tool produces the output ("have" "I" "dinner" "my place").

Context retrieval (step 2): Then, we use each direct and indirect object of the tuples from the previous step to query the OMCSNet.OM for the relevant concepts. Querying this network first gives us some query expansion of "culturally independent" relations. That is, the base OMCSNet.OM, as our largest and most diverse collection, is taken as the "standard" to which the other databases are compared. Since OMCSNet.OM itself has some cultural bias, it would be better, once we have collected enough knowledge bases in other languages, to create a "worldwide" knowledge base by removing all culturally-specific statements, as a basis for comparison. The result of this query is used to get the context in the culturally specific nets. At the end of this stage the output was ranked using two criteria: the first one prefers the concepts resulting for the cultural databases, and the second is to rank first the concepts that come from the part of the email that the user has just written. This helps to address the relevance effectively by giving preference to the important topics of each culture, and in the recent topics of the mail. This process brings concepts as *lunch, food, meal,* and *salad,* that are in the semantic neighborhood of *dinner.*

Node retrieval (step 3): In this step, we get the tuples whose nodes are in the context of the mail from OMCSNet.MX and OMCSNet.US. The output of this step is the pieces of common sense knowledge for the Mexican and American culture (see Figure 3). At this point we have everything the databases have about the eating habits in both cultures. For example: the output from OMCSNet.MX has the following, among others: ['TakeTime', 'dinner', 'between 8:00 PM and 9:00 PM'], ['KindOf', 'dinner', 'light meal'], ['IsA', 'dessert', 'rice with milk'], ['IsA' 'food' 'chocolate']; and from OMCSNet.US has: ['TakeTime', 'dinner', 'between 6:00 PM and 7:00 PM'], ['KindOf', 'dinner', 'heavy meal'], ['IsA', 'dessert', 'pumpkin pie'], ['IsA' 'food' 'chocolate'].

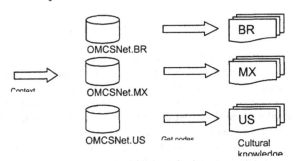

Figure 3. The node retrieval operation.

Relevance of the nodes (step 4): By comparing each node with the cultural sets of knowledge in the previous step we can get its relevance. For this operation, the SIM operation from Cohen's WHIRL [12] is used, as in Figure 4. The interesting part about WHIRL is that it is a system that effectively interleaves inference with retrieval. This operation allows getting the similarity for each node in one set with all the elements of the other set and always maps to a number between zero and one.

Calculation of analogies (step 5): If the value of one node and the semantic relations in the tuples of one set are equal to the tuples of the other cultural set, then the unmatching concept is an analogy between the two cultures that are being considered. In addition, the semantic relation is analyzed in order to avoid irrelevant analogies. These analogies are ranked using the similarity between the two nodes. If two different pairs of tuples allow the same analogy, the values of the relevance scores are added. In our example set, the only nodes that are suitable for analogy are the nodes that talk about the 'KindOf' meal the dinner is in both cultures. This process is similar to Dedre Gentner's classic Structure Mapping analogy method.

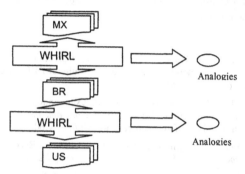

Figure 4. Calculation of the relevance and the analogies.

Calculate the nodes to display (step 6): The nodes are sorted using the relevance of their context and their similarities produced by the SIM operator.

Chose the information to display (step 7): The nodes ranked higher are chosen to be displayed. First, we choose the nodes to calculate analogies and then the rest of the nodes, the former nodes give information about things that are different, but do not have a counterpart in the other culture, or are grounding information that makes no sense for an analogy [6].

Map the concept to English (step 8): For each semantic relation in the net, a custom template that maps its information to English sentences was created and applied before displaying the information. For the analogies, an additional template is used to explain why the system made this analogy. In Figure 2 we show only the top four concepts that are displayed after applying the template.

5. Conclusions and Future Works

This work has presented some first steps in the modeling and use of cultural differences in interactive applications. This way, we answer affirmatively to the question proposed in the title of this paper. We model cultural differences by comparing knowledge bases of Commonsense statements collected from volunteer Web contributors in various cultures. We explore applications by those who want to focus on a specific user group; by those who want to develop systems which use the cultural knowledge stored in the knowledge bases; and by those who want to facilitate communication between people, providing mutual knowledge about their cultures. This work is part of a larger effort to model Commonsense knowledge. In [8], we present many applications that have built using the OMCS, ConceptNet, and related tools, for providing intelligent defaults in interactive systems and mapping from user goals to actions. Future work will also include the investigation of cultural expressions in Open Mind Common Sense considering a larger number of facts. Also other domains will be studied in order to verify the cultural differences besides eating habits domain. While we have not yet conducted formal user tests with the email application, informal feedback from users shows that, while the absolute accuracy of suggestions is not high, users do appreciate the occasional useful suggestion and it is not excessively distracting even when suggestions are not relevant. We hope developers of interactive systems use the knowledge about culture stored in Open Mind Common Sense databases in order to facilitate the interaction between humans and computers.

References

1. Anacleto, J.; Lieberman, H; Tsutsumi, M.; Neris, V.; Carvalho, A.; Espinosa, J.; Zem-Mascarenhas, S. Using Common Sense to Recognize Cultural Differences. Submitted as a work-in-progress paper to *CHI 2006*.

2. Bailey, B.P., Gurak, L.J., and Konstan, J.A. An examination of trust production in computer-mediated exchange. *Proc. 7th Human Factors and the Web 2001 Conference* www.optavia.com/hfweb/7thconferenceproceedings.zip/bailey.pdf. Last visited in Jan, 06.

3. Birukov, A., Blanzieri, E, Giorgini, P. Implicit: An AgentBased Recommendation System for Web Search. *Proc. AAMAS'05 (July 25-29,2005, Utrecht, Netherlands).*

4. Choi, B., Lee, I., Kim, J., Jeon, Y. A Qualitative Cross-National Study of Cultural Influences on Mobile Data Service Design. *Proc. CHI 2005.*

5. Cohen, William W. WHIRL: A word-based information representation language. Artificial Intelligence (2000) 163-196.

6. Falkenhainer, B., Gentner, D. The Structure-Mapping Engine. *Proceedings of the Fifth National Conference on Artificial Intelligence. (1986)*

7. Khaslavsky, J. Integrating Culture into Interface Design. *Proc CHI 1998* p 365-366.

8. Lieberman, L., Liu, H., Singh, P., Barry, B. Beating Common Sense into Interactive Applications. American Association for Artificial Intelligence, Winter 2005, p 63-76

9. Liu, Hugo. MontyLingua: An End-to-End Natural Language Processor for English. (2003)

10. Liu, Hugo and Singh, Push. OMCSNet: A Commonsense Inference Toolkit. MIT Media Lab Society Of Mind Group Technical Report SOM02-01. (2002) 272-277.

11. Liu, H.; Singh, P. Commonsense Reasoning in and over Natural Language. Proc. 8th KES 04. http://web.media.mit.edu/~push/CommonsenseInOverNL.pdf. Last visited in Jan, 06.

12. Liu, H; Singh P. ConceptNet: A Practical Commonsense Reasoning Toolkit. BT Technology Journal, v. 22, n. 4, p. 211-226, 2004. http://web.media.mit.edu/~push/ConceptNet-BTTJ.pdf. Last visited in Jan, 06.

13. Marcus, A. Culture Class vs. Culture Clash. *Proc. Interactions 2002 (June, 2002)*, 25 p.

14. Singh, P. The OpenMind Commonsense Project. KurzweilAI.net, 2002. Available in: :< http://web.media.mit.edu/~push/OMCSProject.pdf>. Last visited in Jan, 06.

15. Spink, A., Ozmutlu S., Ozmutlu H.,Jansen B. J. U.S. VERSUS EUROPEAN WEB SEARCHING TRENDS. SIGIR Forum. Fall 2002, Vol. 36, No. 2, p 32-38

16. Teevan, J., Dumais, S. T., Horvitz, E. Personalizing Search via Automated Analysis of Interests and Activities. *Proc. SIGIR '05 (August 15–19, 2005, Salvador, Brazil).*

ARTIFICIAL INTELLIGENCE AND KNOWLEDGE MANAGEMENT

Hugo Cesar Hoeschl[1]; Vânia Barcellos[2] [3]

[1]WBSA Intelligent Systems S.A., [2]Research Institute on e-Gov, Juridical Intelligence and Systems – IJURIS ; [3]Federal University of Santa Catarina - Program of Post-Graduation in Engineering and Knowledge Management

hugo@wbsa.com.br; vania@ijuris.org

http://www.ijuris.org

Abstract. This article intends to make an analysis about the Artificial Intelligence (AI) and the Knowledge Management (KM). Faced with the dualism mind and body how we be able to see it AI? It doesn't intent to create identical copy of human being, but try to find the better form to represent all the knowledge contained in our minds. The society of the information lives a great paradox, at the same time that we have access to an innumerable amount of information, the capacity and the forms of its processing are very limited. In this context, institutions and centers of research devote themselves to the finding of ways to use to advantage the available data consistently. The interaction of the Knowledge Management with Artificial Intelligence makes possible the development of filtering tools and pre-analysis of the information that appear as a reply to the expectations to extract resulted optimized of databases and open and not-structuralized source, as the Internet.

1. INTRODUCTION

For Castells [1] the technology does not decide to society and neither the society writes the course of the technological transformation, since factors, including creativity and enterprising initiative, intervene in the trial of scientific discovery, technological innovation and social application, so that the final result depends on a complex interactive standard. While the technologies of the information advance, the gears,

Please use the following format when citing this chapter:

Hoeschl, H.C., Barcellos, V., 2006, in IFIP International Federation for Information Processing, Volume 217, Artificial Intelligence in Theory and Practice, ed. M. Bramer, (Boston: Springer), pp. 11–19.

persons and technologies, go altering their objectives and originating an endless cycle of renewal. Inside that cycle presents-itself of clear form the dizzy evolution of the technology of the data processing, that has amount of studies dedicated to the reproduction of abilities and human capacities such the manuals, as much as the intellectuals, that is the Artificial Intelligence (AI). The intelligence is more than the faculty of learn how, apprehend or understand, interpret and, mainly adapt itself to the situations.

The present study search flow through about the dualism mind and body and the paper of the AI in his incessant search of automation of man (mind and body) (item 2), right away we are going to show an join between AI and Knowledge Management (item 3), showing the present importance of itself to automate the knowledge in the companies. We will show at the end (item 4) the evolution of the studies in AI carried by the Author and his Team and its application.

2. AI AND DUALISM: MIND AND BODY

Suppose a robot in a factory of cars and that we be able to ask it what is his opinion about mind and body. Evidently that creature will not be able to answer promptly, therefore it will have that to inspect before its models, as is programmed for carry out determined functions, for example adapting some piece or performming the painting of the vehicle that is passing over the caterpillar, probably will not obtain no answer.

There have been many discutions about questions of philosophical order and epstemological, questioning any possibility of Artificial Intelligence (AI). It would be possible the construction of an intelligence or similar conscience of human being in a machine? Human intelligence in its biological and animal concepts?

Many authors as John Searle, says that despite a machine could speak chinese language by resources as examining and comparing data table and binary references this doesn't grant that this machine can really understand and speak the language. It means that whether the machine can realize Turing Tests doesn't grant that it is as conscious as any human being.

The possibility of translating human intelligence to plastic artificial base has a clear limit: If intelligence can be generated from these elements, it must be necessarilly different from human one, because results happen from different human elements.

However they have not been trying to replace human being or to create artificial mind and body, but to replicate special activities and jobs using human being way, as using special robots to save life in a burning , earthshake or anyother place dangerous for human staff get.

Because of discussion of possibility of generate artificial intelligence scientists have being gathering many knowledge since early 50th, these studies have being getting more and more interests because of commercial applications.

Researches in AI are related to areas of application that involve human reasoning, trying to imitate it and performing inferences. As Savory [22] these areas of application that are generally enclosed in the definitions of AI include, among others: intelligent systems or systems based on knowledge; intelligent / learning systems; understanding / translation from natural language; understanding / voice generating; analysis of image, scene in real time and automatic programming.

Notice, then, an introductory and superficial vision, about how artificial intelligence can be defined Pfaffenberger [10]: "Artificial intelligence - The field of the computer sciences that intends to perfect the computers endowing them with some peculiar characteristics of human intelligence, as the capacity to understand natural language and to simulate the reasoning in uncertainty conditions."

The following are important aspects of AI, as Rabuske [11], among others: development of heuristical methods for the solution of problems; representation of knowledge; treatment of natural language; acquisition of knowledge; artificial reasoning and logics and tools. Amongst its main applications, we have the following: mastering systems; processing of natural language; recognition of standards; robotics; intelligent databases; test of theorems and games.

Using of intelligent techniques and trying to develop computer applications provided of logical or structured cases database, to help in the task of the study of facts involves a difficult work.

For Nonaka [7], the cartesian dualism between subject and object or mind and body started from the budget of that the essence of a human being is the rational thoughtful. This thoughtful life seeks the knowledge isolating itself off the remainder of the world and off the others human being. But the imposed contemporary challenges to the cartesian dualism emphasized the importance of some forms of interaction between the self and the external world in the search of the knowledge.

For Choo [2] the needs of information are many times understood like the cognitives necessities of a person: faults or weakness of knowledge or comprehension that can be expressed in questions or topics set to a system or source of information. Then to satisfy cognitive necessity, would be to store the information that answers to what was asked. Then, returning back to our robot in a factory of cars, if a machine in which was installed some system of intelligent search, the answer would be immediate and satisfactory. In that case, the techniques and models of AI are necessary for an emotional and affectionate search of the humanity that seeks the knowledge.

3. AI AND KNOWLEDGE MANAGEMENT

The Italian sociologist, Domenico di Masi, in his book "O Ócio Criativo", speaks about the war between the companies, in that dispute the concurrent commercially want destroy each other, but when a company is defeated, will not be destroyed, but assimilated. This means, search the patrimony of know-how, of men and of ideas, so that is powerfull to improve the productive units instead of eliminate-her.

The knowledge became to be the focus of the business leaders, that seek way of increasing the performance of its organizations. They will assure the viability and the supported success. Methods and techniques to acquire, represent, share and maintain the knowledge did itself necessary, therefore is in all of the places (software, persons, organizations, nature, among others), and in all the forms, as for example, in a base of facts, in the person, in an organizational practice shared tacitly, or to even in a robot.

In that sense, Choo [2] emphasizes that the creation of extensive knowledge the capacities of the organizations elevating the level of specialization of his own members and learning with persons of outside of his scopes. The same author says that the external and internal ways of creation of knowledge occur in a broader organizational context, defined by an evaluation of the new knowledge regarding the strategic purpose of the organization, an appreciation of his essential capacities, an estimate of the technological potential and of the market, and the recognition that the operational innovations demand the support of new social systems of information.

Like this arose the Knowledge Engineering in late 70th, before sight barely as a discipline of the AI with the objective of creating approaches and tools to build systems based in the knowledge. It researches carried out in that area permitted the knowledge models structures construction, their systematization and, mainly, to their reuse.

In the early the Knowledge Engineering was involved with the art of build specialists systems, systems based in the knowledge and intensive knowledge information systems, summarizing everything, systems based in the knowledge. The systems based in the knowledge are arising from of the AI.

For Muñoz-Seca [8] despite of intangibility of the knowledge, to be able to handle it physically, needs its transformation in structures stuff. The knowledge must be incorporated to a physical structure that is able to be transformed by very well established physical methods and from the which can be extracted off new ones by sensorial methods. The knowledge in pure form is not sufficient to satisfy all the needs of the economy. The support for the mind should be supplemented with the support for the body. Consequently, the knowledge should be transformed also in fit entities inside the basic trials of the company and of the society. The materialization of the knowledge should be translated in a form that can be manipulated, stored, transmitted, restrored and used easily, without have of appeal to the person that originated it.

To capture all the knowledge process it, store it and reuse it became the big challenge of the technology that has been finding in the techniques of AI intelligent solutions over of the last decades.

4. RESEARCHES IN AI - EVOLUTION AND APPLICATIONS

We will illustrate the application of AI through some empirical procedures adopted by the author and his team.

The team has a multidisciplinary character, built by researchers with expressive scientific and technical qualification, with formation in distinct areas of the knowledge, such as: Science of the Computation, Right, Administration, Engineering of Output, Systems of Information, Psychology, Science of the Information, and other, graduated as post doctorate, doctorate and master. It produces since 1999 methodologies, software, everybody with techniques and approaches of AI accepted by the national scientific community and international. Of that output, detach the following:

Starting with the methodology CBR – Case Based Reasoning is used in parts with techniques of retrieval of literal information, presenting a superior performance to the traditional data bases. For in such a way, had been developed two new technologies for the team the Structured Contextual Search – SCS and the Dynamically Contextualised Knowledge Representation (DCKR).

CSS® is a methodology that allows the search in natural language through the context of the information contained in the knowledge base, thus breaching, the search paradigm by means of key words and connectors, making it possible for the user to describe a number of characters presented by each consultation, allowing thus, a more elaborated conception of the search. The research is considered ' contextual ' and ' structured ' because of the following reasons: 1. We take into consideration the context of documents stored at the formation of the rhetorical structure of the system 2. This context guides the process of adjustment of the entrance as well as the comparison and election of documents; 3. At the moment of the elaboration of the consultation, the entrance is not limited to a set of words, or the indication of attributes, being able to assume the format of a question structured by the set of a long text is added to the possibility of operating dynamic weights on specific attributes, that work as ' filters ' and make a preliminary election of documents to be analyzed.

DCKR® consists of a dynamic process of analysis of the general context that involves the problem focused. It makes comparisons between the context of documents, enabling the accomplishment of a more precise search and with a better quality. Moreover, the documents are retrieved through pre-determined indexes, that can be valuated by the user when consulting. This technique implies a significant increment in the performance in knowledge structured systems.

Digesto® – Site of legal search (www.digesto.net), that enables to the user the recuperation of documents regarding doctrine, jurisprudence, legislation and legal articles. It is a tool for searching in the web, that use techniques of databases textuais and DCKR®.

Alpha Themis® - Intelligent software for the retrieval of the knowledge contained in the "resolutions" of the national courts. It is a system of legal technology, one of the first ones in Brazil to unite Artificial Intelligence and Law. It uses techniques of textual Data base and CBR.

Jurisconsulto® - Innovative system to retrieve sentences in computerized data bases through CBR. It uses techniques of textual Data Base and CBR.

Olimpo®- The system has its performance centered in the combination of aspects derived from CBR and from the representation of added literal information to an suitable organization of knowledge the referring to the resolutions of the Security Council of the ONU, what allows the retrieval of texts with characteristics similar to the information supplied by the user in natural language. New documents are automatically enclosed in the knowledge base through the extraction of relevant information through a technique called DCKR®. Concepts of CBR and techniques of information retrieval have been applied for a better performance of the system, resulting in the methodology called SCS®.

And the last, the sytem that fusing the Management of the Knowledge and Artificial Intelligence, called System KMAI. It will be discoursing about the incorporation of this revolutionary model of analysis of information, that it initiates with a methodology called Dynamically Contextualised Knowledge Representation (DCKR) supported by specific tools to the technology quoted and finishes with intelligent algorithms of recovery of information called Structured Contextual Search (SCS). Other already spread out cutting-adge technologies which collaborate for the transformation of information in knowledge will also be approached.

The present story intends to demonstrate system KMAI, as well as its tools and respective phases: engineering of the knowledge, collecting and storage of information, final analysis and diffusion.

KMAI- Knowledge Management with Artificial Intelligence is, before anything, a concept. It aims at being a strategical differential in the organizations of the knowledge that intend to acquire competitiveness through the processing of information for decision taking.

This concept initially integrates the Knowledge Management with the Intelligence of symbiotic form, considering that, in a systemic form, the last one belongs to the first one. To produce intelligence alone is possible with the processes of management of the knowledge or, still, to produce strategical information (knowledge) the rude information (data) must be organized. The catalytic element of the reaction of this fusing of references is Artificial Intelligence, which adds value to the pre-analyses and the discovery of occult knowledge (knowledge discovery), through its capacity of mathematical processing, computational and simulation of analytical human functions.

To complete the output of the last years, was thrown recently in the internet the ONTOWEB® (www.ontoweb.com.br) that is an information analysis system that enables a research contextualised in the sources accessed. The kernel of this technology is focused in the new era of the internet, in the which semantic and ontologies work together to increase the prominent information search trial in documents of the web. The utilization of ontologies permits to the ONTOWEB® activate a systematic completely innovative one in the location of documents by considering the context of the matter that is being researched. The ontologies build a pre existing net of concepts inter-related that expand the concept used, driven the system to the setting that it fits. It lets the ONTOWEB ® locate, automatically, which records in their base have more resemblance with the text digitated.

Using modern techniques of Artificial Intelligence, following down are described some of ONTOWEB® differentials:

- Possibility of using over more than 10.000 words for analysis: the field of research is not limited to the key words or to simple expressions of search;
- Lines graphic generation in the answer: It is possible to get visual accompany of the variation of the matter researched in

the time, generating subsidies for a more efficient qualitative analysis;

- Utilization of ontology contextualized in the trial of recuperation expanding the concepts used in the research and identifying its context is possible locate the best documents fit to the demand requested;
- Presentation of the result based in similarity: its answers organization criterion is purely technical, guaranteeing that the records will be presented in decreasing order of resemblance with the matter researched.

5. CONCLUSION

We tried in this work, even in synthetic way, flow about the importance of the AI, therefore many critics arise, many times by absence of knowledge to what is being done of research in that area.

The researches in IA opened a true fan of systems that use its techniques, that are since games, systems specialists, neural nets, recognition of hand writing, graphic computation, multiagents systems, translator and Chatter Bots (robots of software for conversation) among others.

Upon trying to join AI and Knowledge Management the Authors had the intention of showing how much the techniques of AI are able to help in this task. There are needs of information in the economic world, the information are spread, the knowledge is contained in persons and documents, then the application of techniques of AI to acquire, store, prosecute and reuse, generating more and more innovations in the world of the business is necessary.

For Goswami [3] one of the biggest problems for the computer is to work with the creativity, therefore are competent in the remixing of objects inside contexts supplied by the programmer, but cannot discover news contexts. However humans can do that because of our not local conscience, jumps outside from the system, and like this we generate something news in an entirely new context. The creativity is, fundamentally, not local way of cognition. The application developed by the Author and his team is an example of innovation, because started from techniques and models of AI, created intelligent systems to manage the knowledge, therefore will not have loses of time seeking information or digital and physical files, the information, graphic and analyses, are in the screen just waiting to get a choice, giving a jump outside of the system using all its creativity.

REFERENCES

1. CASTELLS, Manuel. A sociedade em rede (A era da informação: economia, sociedade e cultura; v.1). São Paulo, Paz e Terra, 1999.
2. CHOO, Chun Wei. A Organização do Conhecimento. São Paulo: Ed. SENAC, 2003.
3. GOSWAMI, Amit.O Universo Autoconsciente como a consciência cria o mundo material. Trad. Ruy Jungmann. 3ª ed.; Ed. Rosa dos Tempos; 2000.
4. HAMIT, Francis. A realidade virtual e a exploração do espaço cibernético. Rio de Janerio: Berkley, 1993.
5. HOESHL, Hugo Cesar. Tecnologia da Informação Jurídica para o Conselho de Segurança da ONU. Ed. Papel Virtual; Rio de Janeiro; 2002.
6. HOESHL, Hugo Cesar et al. SAEI Management, an application of KMAI - Knowledge Management with Artificial Intelligence. 34th Argentine Conference on Informatics and Operational Research http://www.cerider.edu.ar/jaiio34/inicio.html
7. NONAKA, Ikujiro; TAKEUCHI, Hirotaka. Criação de Conhecimento na Empresa: Como as grandes empresas japonesas geram a dinâmica da inovação. Rio de Janeiro: Campus, 1997.
8. MASI, Domenico de. O Ócio Criativo. Entrevista a Maria Serena Palieri; tradução de Lea Manzi; Rio de Janeiro: Sextante, 2000.
9. MUÑOZ-SECA, Beatriz.; Riverola Josep. Transformando conhecimento em resultados: a gestão do conhecimento como diferencial na busca de mais produtividade e competitividade. Trad. Carlos Racca. São Paulo: Clio Editora; 2004.
10. PFAFFENBERGER, Bryan. Dicionário dos usuários de micro computadores. Rio de Janeiro: Campus, 1993.
11. RABUSKE, Renato Antonio. Inteligência Artificial. Florianópolis: Ed. Ufsc, 1995.
12. SAVORY, S. E.(editor), "Some Views on the State of Art in Artificial Intelligence" em "Artificial Intelligence and Expert Systems", Ellis Horwood Limited, 1988, pp. 21-34, Inglaterra .

The *IONWI* Algorithm: Learning when and when not to interrupt

Silvia Schiaffino and Analía Amandi
ISISTAN Research Institute – Facultad de Cs. Exactas – UNCPBA –
Campus Universitario, Paraje Arroyo Seco, Tandil, 7000, Bs As, Argentina
Also CONICET, Consejo Nacional de Investigaciones Científicas y
Técnicas, Argentina
{sschia,amandi}@exa.unicen.edu.ar

Abstract. One of the key issues for an interface agent to succeed at assisting a user is learning when and when not to interrupt him to provide him assistance. Unwanted or irrelevant interruptions hinder the user's work and make him dislike the agent because it is being intrusive and impolite. The *IONWI* algorithm enables interface agents to learn a user's preferences and priorities regarding interruptions. The resulting user profile is then used by the agent to personalize the modality of the assistance, that is, assisting the user with an interruption or without an interruption depending on the user's context. Experiments were conducted in the calendar management domain, obtaining promising results.

Keywords: intelligent agents, user profiling, human-computer interaction

1. Introduction

As intelligent agents take on more complexity, higher degrees of autonomy and more "intelligence", users start to expect them to play by the same rules of other complex, autonomous and intelligent entities in their experience, namely, other humans [16]. Our previous studies [19] demonstrated that the way in which an interface agent assists a user has an impact on the competence of this agent and it can make the interaction between user and agent a success or a failure. This is the

Please use the following format when citing this chapter:

Schiaffino, S., Amandi, A., 2006, in IFIP International Federation for Information Processing, Volume 217, Artificial Intelligence in Theory and Practice, ed. M. Bramer, (Boston: Springer), pp. 21–30.

concern of a recent research area within Human-Computer Interaction (HCI) that studies the "etiquette" of human-computer relationships [3; 17; 18]. We agree with the researchers in this area on that the ability to adapt to the way in which a user wants to interact with the agent is almost as important as the ability to learn the user's preferences in a particular domain.

As pointed out in [14], one of the problems with the interface agents developed thus far is their incorrect estimates of the user's task priorities, which makes information to be introduced at inappropriate times and with unsuitable presentation choices. Although agents are well-intentioned, they do not consider the impact an interruption has on the user. Research has found that interruptions are harmful. They are disruptive to the primary computing task and they decrease users' performance. However, interruptions are necessary in interface agent technology since agents need to communicate important and urgent information to users.

To solve this problem, when the agent detects a (problem) situation relevant to the user it has to correctly decide if it will send him a notification without interrupting the user's work, or if it will interrupt him. On the one hand, the user can choose between paying attention to a notification or not, and he can continue to work in the latter case. On the other hand, he is forced to pay attention to what the agent wants to tell him if it interrupts him abruptly.

Not to disturb the user, the agent has to base its decision on various factors, such as: the relevance and the urgency the situation has for the user; the relationship between the situation to be notified or the assistance to be provided and the user's goals; the relevance the situation underlying the interruption has to the current user tasks; how tolerant the user is of interruptions; and when he does not want to be interrupted no matter how important the message is. In summary, the interface agent has to learn which situations are relevant and which are irrelevant so that no unwanted interruptions occur.

In this work we present a user profiling algorithm named *IONWI* that learns when a user can or should be interrupted by his agent depending on the user's context. In this way, the agent can provide personalized assistance to the user without hindering his work.

This article is organized as follows. Section 2 presents our proposed profiling algorithm. Section 3 shows the results we have obtained when assisting users of a calendar management system. Section 4 describes some related works. Finally, Section 5 presents our conclusions and future work.

2. The *IONWI* Algorithm

In order to assist a user without hindering his work, an interface agent has to learn the user's interruption needs and preferences in different contexts. In this work we propose an algorithm, named *IONWI* (acronym for Interruption Or Notification Without Interruption), capable of learning when to interrupt a user and when not from the observation of the user's interaction with a computer application and with the agent.

The algorithm learns when a situation that may originate an interruption is relevant to the user's needs, preferences and goals, and when it is irrelevant. In addition, this algorithm also considers the relationship and relevance the situation originating the interaction has with the user's current task.

2.1 Algorithm inputs and outputs

The input for our learning algorithm is a set of user-agent interaction experiences. An interaction experience *Ex* is described by seven arguments <*Sit, Mod, Task, Rel, UF, E, date*>: a problem situation or situation of interest *Sit* is described by a set of features and the values these features take, *Sit={(feature$_i$,value$_j$)}*; the modality *Mod* that indicates whether the agent interrupted the user or not to provide him assistance; the *Task* the user was executing when he was interrupted or notified, which is described by a set of features and the values these features take *Task={(feature$_i$,value$_j$)}*; the relevance *Rel* the interruption has for the *Task*; the user feedback *UF* (regarding the assistance modality) obtained after assisting the user; an evaluation *E* of the assistance experience (success, failure or undefined); and the *date* when the interaction experience was recorded.

For example, consider that the user is scheduling a meeting with several participants and he is interrupted by his agent to remind him about a business meeting that will take place the next day. The user does not pay attention to the message being notified and presses a button to tell the agent not to interrupt him in these occasions. From this experience the agent learns that reminders of this kind of meetings are not relevant to the user, and it will send him a notification in the future without interrupting him. In this example, the different components of the assistance experience are:

Sit ={(type, event reminder), (event-type, business meeting), (organizer, boss), (participants, [Johnson, Taylor ,Dean]), (topic, project A evolution), (date, Friday), (time, 5p.m.), (place, user's office)}

Mod = interruption

Task = {(application, calendar management system),(task, new event), (event type, meeting), (priority, high), ...}

Rel = irrelevant, unrelated

UF = {(type, explicit), (action, do not interrupt)}

E = {(type, failure), (certainty, 1.00)} (interruption instead of notification)

Date = {(day, 18), (month, December), (year, 2005)}

The output of our algorithm is a set of facts representing the user's interruptions preferences. Each fact indicates whether the user needs an interruption or a notification when a given situation occurs in the system. Facts constitute part of the user profile. These facts may adopt one of the following forms: "in problem situation *Sit* the user should be interrupted", "in situation *Sit* the user should not be interrupted", "in situation *Sit* and if the user is performing the task *T*, he should not be interrupted", "in situation *Sit* and if the user is performing the task *T*, the agent can interrupt him". Each fact *F* is accompanied by a certainty degree *Cer(F)* that indicates how certain the agent is about this preference. Thus, when an interface agent has to decide whether to interrupt the user or not given a certain problem situation, the agent uses the knowledge it has acquired about a user's interruption preferences to choose the assistance modality it supposes the user expects in that particular instance of a given situation. Once the assistance has been provided, the agent obtains explicit and/or implicit user feedback. This new interaction is recorded as an assistance experience, which will be used in the future to incrementally update the knowledge the agent has about the user.

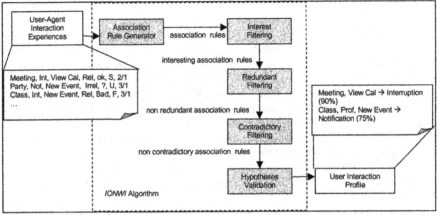

Fig. 1. *IONWI* Overview

2.2 *IONWI* Overview

The *IONWI* algorithm uses association rules to obtain the existing relationships between situations, current user tasks and assistance modalities. Classification techniques have been discarded since we cannot always label an interaction as a success or a failure, and we need a group of interactions to draw a conclusion about the user's preferences.

As shown in Figure 1, the first step of our algorithm is generating a set of association rules from the user-agent interaction experiences. Then, the association rules generated are automatically post-processed in order to derive the user profile from them. Post-processing steps include: detecting the most interesting rules according to our goals, eliminating redundant and insignificant rules, pruning out contradictory weak rules, and summarizing the information in order to formulate the hypotheses about a user's preferences more easily. Once a hypothesis is formulated, the algorithm looks for positive evidence supporting the hypothesis and negative evidence rejecting it in order to validate it. The certainty degree of the hypothesis is computed taking into account both the positive and the negative evidence. This calculus is done by using metrics from association rule discovery. Finally, facts are generated from the set of highly supported hypotheses; facts compose the user interaction profile.

The following subsections describe in detail each step of the algorithm.

2.3 Mining Association Rules from User-Agent Interaction Experiences

An association rule is a rule that implies certain association relationship among a set of objects in a database, such as occur together or one implies the other. Association discovery finds rules about items that appear together in an event (called transactions), such as a purchase transaction or a user-agent interaction experience. Association rule mining is commonly stated as follows [1]: Let $I=\{i_1,...,i_n\}$ be a set of items, and D be a set of data cases. Each data case consists of a subset of items in I. An association rule is an implication of the form X→Y, where $X \subset I$, $Y \subset I$ and $X \cap Y = \varnothing$. X is the antecedent of the rule and Y is the consequent. The support of a rule X→Y is the probability of attribute sets X and Y occurring together in the same transaction. The rule has support s in D if $s\%$ of the data case in D contains $X \cap Y$. If there are n total transactions in the database, and X and Y occur together in m of them, then the support of the rule X→Y is m/n. The rule X→Y holds in D with confidence c if $c\%$ of data cases in D that contain X also contain Y. The confidence of rule X→Y is defined as the probability of occurrence of X and Y together in all transactions in which X already occurs. If there are s transactions in which X occurs, and in exactly t of them X and Y occur together, the confidence of the rule is t/s.

Given a transaction database D, the problem of mining association rules is to find all association rules that satisfy: minimum support (called *minsup*) and minimum confidence (called *minconf*). There has been a lot of research in the area of association rules and, as a result, there are various algorithms to discover association rules in a database. The most popular is the Apriori algorithm [1], which is the one we use to find our association rules.

2.4 Filtering Out Uninteresting and Redundant Rules

In this work, we are interested in those association rules of the form "situation, modality, task → user feedback, evaluation"; "situation, modality → user feedback, evaluation"; "situation, modality, relevance → user feedback, evaluation" and "situation, modality, task, relevance → user feedback, evaluation", having appropriate support and confidence values. We are interested in these rules since they provide us information about the relationships between a situation or problem description and the modality of assistance the user prefers, which have received a positive (negative) evaluation. They also relate a situation and the current user task with an assistance modality, as well as a situation, the current user task and the relevance of the situation to the task with a certain assistance modality. To select these types of rules, we define templates [10] and we insert these templates as restrictions in the association mining algorithm. Thus, only interesting rules are generated (steps 1 and 2 in Figure 1 are then merged).

Once we have filtered out those rules that are not interesting for us, we will still have many rules to process, some of them redundant or insignificant. Many discovered associations are redundant or minor variations of others. Thus, those spurious and insignificant rules should be removed. We can then use a technique that removes those redundant and insignificant associations [13]. For example, consider the following rules:

R1: Sit{(Type, Event Reminder)(Event-Type = doctor))} (Task=View Calendar), (Mod =interruption) → (UF = do not interrupt), (Ev = failure) [sup: 0.4, conf: 0.82]

R2: Sit{(Type, Event Reminder)(Event-Type = doctor)}, (Task=View Calendar), (Event-Priority = high)), (Mod =interruption) → (UF= do not interrupt), (Ev = failure) [sup:0.4, conf: 0.77]

If we know R1, then R2 is insignificant because it gives little extra information. Its slightly higher confidence is more likely due to chance than to true correlation. It thus should be pruned. R1 is more general and simple.

In addition, we have to analyze certain combinations of attributes in order to determine if two rules are telling us the same thing. For example, a rule containing the pair "interruption, failure" and another containing the pair "notification, success" are redundant provided that they refer to the same problem situation and they have similar confidence values. As well as analyzing redundant rules, we have to check if there are any contradictory rules. We define that two rules are contradictory if for the same situation and, eventually for the same user task, they express that the user wants both an interruption and a notification without interruption.

2.5 Building Facts from Hypotheses

The association rules that have survived the pruning processes described above are those the *IONWI* algorithm uses to build hypotheses about a user's interruption preferences. A hypothesis is obtained from a set of association rules that are related because they refer to the same problem situation but are somewhat different: a "main" association rule; some redundant association rules with regards to the main rule, which could not be pruned out because they did not fulfill the similar confidence restriction; and some contradictory rules with regards to the main rule, which could be not pruned away because they did not meet the different confidence requirement. The main rule is chosen by selecting from the rule set the rule that has the greatest support value, whose antecedent is the most general, and whose consequent is the most specific.

$$Cer(H) = \alpha Sup(AR) + \beta \frac{\sum_{k=1}^{r} Sup(E+)}{\sum_{k=1}^{r+l} Sup(E)} - \gamma \frac{\sum_{k=1}^{l} Sup(E-)}{\sum_{k=1}^{r+l} Sup(E)}$$

Equation 1

Once the *IONWI* algorithm has formulated a set of hypotheses it has to validate them. The certainty degree of a hypothesis H is computed as a function of the supports of the rule originating the hypothesis and the rules considered as positive and negative evidence of H. The function we use to compute certainty degrees is shown in Equation 1, where: α, β and γ are the weights of the terms in the equation (we use $\alpha=0.8$, $\beta=0.1$ and $\gamma=0.1$), $Sup(AR)$ is the support of the rule originating H, $Sup(E^+)$ is the support of the rules being positive evidence, $Sup(E^-)$ is the support of the rules being negative evidence, $Sup(E)$ is the support value of an association rule taken as evidence (positive or negative), r is the amount of positive evidence and t is the amount of negative evidence.

2.6 Incremental Learning

The database containing interaction experiences is not static, because updates are constantly being applied to it. On the one hand, new interaction experiences are added since the agent keeps observing a user's behaviour. On the other hand, old experiences are deleted because they become obsolete. In consequence, new hypotheses about a user's interruption preferences may appear and some of the learned hypotheses may become invalid.

We address this problem from the association rule point of view, that is, as the database changes new association rules may appear and at the same time, some existing association rules may become invalid. The incremental version of *IONWI* uses the FUP2 algorithm [5] to update the association rules and the DELI algorithm [12] to determine when it is necessary to update the rules. The DELI algorithm uses a sampling technique to estimate the difference between the old and new association rules. This estimate is used as an indicator for whether the FUP2 algorithm should be applied to the database to accurately find out the new association rules. If the estimated difference is large enough (with respect to some user specified threshold), the algorithm signals the need of an update operation, which can be accomplished by using the FUP2 algorithm. If the estimated difference is small, then we do not run FUP2 immediately and we can take the old rules as an approximation of the new rules. Hence, we wait until more changes are made to the database and then re-apply the DELI algorithm.

3. Experimental Results

We tested our algorithm with a set of 26 datasets[1] containing user-agent interactions in the calendar management domain. Each database is composed of the attributes that describe the problem situation or situation of interest originating the interaction, the primary user task, the modality of the assistance, the relationship between the situation and the user task, the user feedback, and the evaluation of the interaction experience. The sizes of the datasets vary from 30 to 120 interactions.

To evaluate the performance of an agent using our learning algorithm we used one of the metrics defined in [4]. The precision metric measures an interface agent's ability to accurately provide assistance to a user. As shown in Equation 2, we can define our precision metric as the ratio of the number of correct interruption preferences to the total number of interruption preferences generated by *IONWI*. Similarly, as shown in Equation 3, we can define the recall metric (i.e. what the agent could not learn) as the ratio of the number of correct interruption preferences to the number of preferences indicated by the user.

---

[1] The datasets can be found at http://www.exa.unicen.edu.ar/~sschia

Figure 2 presents the results we have obtained. The graph in Figure 2(a) plots the percentage of interruption preferences correctly identified by the *IONWI* algorithm (with respect to the total number of preferences obtained); the number of incorrect interruption preferences; and the number of "hidden" preferences, that is those preferences that were not explicitly stated by the user but are correct. Each figure shows the percentage values obtained when averaging the results we got with the different users. The graph in Figure 2(b) shows the percentage of correct interruption preferences (with respect to the number of preferences specified by the user) and the percentage of missing interruption preferences, that is those that the algorithm could not detect. Each graphic shows the average percentage values of the results obtained with the different datasets.

$$IONWI_{precision} = \frac{number\ of\ correct\ preferences}{number\ of\ preferences}$$

Equation 2

$$IONWI_{recall} = \frac{number\ of\ correct\ preferences}{number\ of\ preferences\ for\ user}$$

Equation 3

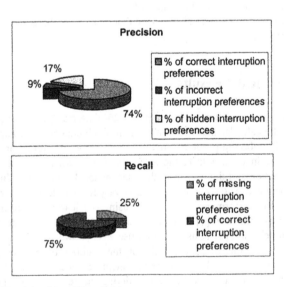

Fig. 2. *IONWI* Precision (a) and Recall (b)

We can observe in the figures that the percentage of incorrect interruption preferences is small (9% in average), and that the percentage of correct preferences plus the percentage of hidden preferences is considerably high. The percentage of correct interruption preferences plus the percentage of hidden preferences can be considered as the precision of the algorithm. This value is approximately 91%. Thus, we can state that the learning capability of the *IONWI* algorithm is good.

Regarding the algorithm recall, 25% of the interruption preferences specified by the user were not discovered by our algorithm. Although not observable in the graphic, this value was smaller for those datasets containing more than 50 records.

4. Related Work

Interruptions have been widely studied in the HCI area[2], but they have not been considered in personal agent development. These studies revealed that the disruptiveness of an interruption is related to several factors, including complexity of the primary task and/or interrupting task, similarity of the two tasks [8], whether the interruption is relevant to the primary task [6], stage of the primary task when the interruption occurs [7], management strategies for handling interruptions [15], and modalities of the primary task and the interruption [2, 11].

People at Microsoft Research have deeply studied the effects of instant messaging (IM) in users, mainly on ongoing computing tasks [6, 7, 9]. These authors found that IM that were relevant to ongoing tasks were less disruptive than those that were irrelevant. This influence of relevance was found to hold for both notifications viewing and task resumption times, suggesting that notifications that were unrelated to ongoing tasks took longer to process.

As we have already said, related studies on interruptions come from different research areas in which interface agents are not included. Nevertheless, the results of these studies can be taken into account by interface agents to provide assistance to users without affecting users' performance in a negative way and, thus, diminishing the disruptiveness of interruptions. None of the related works we have discussed has considered the relevance of interruptions to users, or the relevance the situation originating the interruption has for the user. This issue and the relevance of interruptions to user tasks are two aspects of interruptions that our learning algorithm considers.

5. Conclusions and Future Work

We have presented a profiling algorithm that learns when and when not to interrupt a user, in order to provide him assistance. We have evaluated our proposal in the calendar management domain and the results we have obtained are quite promising. Experiments with personal agents assisting users with our approach in other domains are currently being carried out.

As a future work, we are planning to enhance the representation of a user's context in order to take other aspects into account.

[2] Bibliography on this topic: http://www.interruptions.net/literature.htm

References

[1] Agrawal, R., Srikant, R. - Fast Algorithms for Mining Association Rules – In Proc. 20th Int. Conf. Very Large Data Bases (VLDB) – 487 – 499 – (1994)

[2] Arroyo, E., Selker, T, Stouffs, A. – Interruptions and multimodal outputs: Which are less disruptive? – In IEEE International Conference on Multimodal Interfaces ICMI 02 – 479 - 483 (2002)

[3] Bickmore, T. Unspoken rules of spoken interaction. Communications of the ACM, 47 (4): 38 – 44 – (2004)

[4] Brown, S. and Santos, E. - Using explicit requirements and metrics for interface agent user model correction. In Proc. 2nd International Conference on Autonomous Agents – (1998)

[5] Cheung, D., Lee, S., Kao, B. A general incremental technique for maintaining discovered association rules. In Proc.5th Int. Conf. on Database Systems for Advanced Applications – (1997).

[6] Czerwinski, M., Cutrell, E., Horvitz, E. Instant messaging and interruption: Influence of task type on performance. In Proc. OZCHI2000 – 2000.

[7] Czerwinski, M., Cutrell, E., Horvitz, E. Instant Messaging: Effects of Relevance and Timing. People and Computers XIV: Proceedings of HCI 2000 – 71 – 76 (2000)

[8] Gillie T., Broadbent, D. What Makes Interruptions Disruptive? A Study of Length, Similarity and Complexity - Psychological Research, Vol. 50, 243 – 250 (1989)

[9] Horvitz, E., Jacobs, A., Hovel, D. Attention-Sensitive Alerting - Proceedings of UAI 99, Conference on Uncertainty and Artificial Intelligence – 305 - 313 (1999)

[10] Klementinen, M., Mannila, H., Ronkainen, P., Toivonen, H., Verkamo, A. I. - Finding interesting rules from large sets of discovered association rules. In 3rd Int. Conf. on Information and Knowledge Management – (1994) 401 – 407

[11] Latorella, K. Effects of Modality on Interrupted Flight Deck Performance: Implications for Data Link - Proceedings of the Human Factors and Ergonomics Society 42nd Annual Meeting (1998)

[12] Lee, S., Cheung, D. Maintenance of discovered association rules: When to update? In Proc. SIGMOD Workshop on Research Issues in Data Mining and Knowledge Discovery – (1997)

[13] Liu, B., Hsu, W., Ma, Y. - Pruning and summarizing the discovered associations - In Proc. 5th ACM SIGKDD – (1999)

[14] Mc. Crickard, S., Chewar, C. Attuning notification design to user goals and attention costs. Communications of the ACM, 46 (3): 67 – 72 – (2003)

[15] Mc Farlane, D. Coordinating the interruption of people in human-computer interaction. INTERACT 99, 295 – 303 – (1999)

[16] Miller, C. Definitions and dimensions of etiquette. In Proc. AAAI Fall Symposium on Etiquette and Human-Computer Work – (2002)

[17] Miller, C. Human-computer etiquette: Managing expectations with intentional agents. Communications of the ACM, 47 (4): 31 – 34 – (2004)

[18] Nass, C. Etiquette equality: Exhibitions and expectations of computer politeness. Communications of the ACM, 47 (4): 35 – 37 – (2004)

[19] Schiaffino, S., Amandi, A. – User – Interface Agent Interaction: Personalization Issues – International Journal of Human – Computer Studies, 60 (1): 129 – 148 – (2004)

Formal Analysis of the Communication of Probabilistic Knowledge

João Carlos Gluz[1,2,3], Rosa M. Vicari[1], Cecília Flores[1], Louise Seixas[1]

1 Instituto de Informática, UFRGS,95501-970, Porto Alegre, RS, Brasil,
{jcgluz,rosa,dflores}@inf.ufrgs.br, seixasl@terra.com.br
2 ESD, UERGS, Guaíba, RS, Brasil, joao-gluz@uergs.edu.br
3 FACENSA, Gravataí, RS, Brasil, jcgluz@facensa.com.br

Abstract. This paper discusses questions about communication of probabilistic knowledge in the light of current theories of agent communication. It will argue that there is a semantic gap between these theories and research areas related to probabilistic knowledge representation and communication, that creates very serious theoretical problems if agents that reason probabilistically try to use the communication framework provided by these theories. The paper proposes a new formal model, which generalizes current agent communication theories (at least the standard FIPA version of these theories) to handle probabilistic knowledge communication. We propose a new probabilistic logic as the basis for the model and new communication principles and communicative acts to support this kind of communication.

1   Introduction

This paper will present a theoretical study about which kind of meaning can be assigned to the communication of probabilistic knowledge between agents in Multiagent Systems (MAS), at least when current theories for agent communication are considered. The work starts in section 2, presenting several considerations showing that exists a semantic gap between current agent communication theories and research areas related to probabilistic knowledge representation and communication. This gap creates very serious theoretical problems if the designer of agents that reason probabilistically tries to use the communication framework provided by these theories to model and implement all agent's communication tasks.

To minimize this gap we propose a new formal model in section 3, which generalizes the formal model, used in FIPA agent communication standards [6], to handle probabilistic knowledge communication. We propose a new probabilistic logic, called *SLP*, as the basis for the new model. The *SLP* logic is compatible with the logic used as the foundation of FIPA standards (the *SL* logic) in the sense that all valid formulas (theories) of *SL* are also valid formulas of *SLP*. The axiomatic system of *SLP* is correct. It is also complete, if the axiomatic system of *SL* is complete.

Please use the following format when citing this chapter:

Gluz, J.C., Vicari, R.M., Flores, C., Seixas, L., 2006, in IFIP International Federation for Information Processing, Volume 217, Artificial Intelligence in Theory and Practice, ed. M. Bramer, (Boston: Springer), pp. 31–40.

Based on *SLP* logic we propose a minimum set of new communication principles in section 4 that are able to correlate probabilistic reasoning with communication related inference tasks. Two new communicative acts are proposed that would allow agents to communicate basic probabilistic propositions without having to agree previously on a probabilistic content format.

This is the most important result of the paper. To our knowledge, this is the first work that tries to integrate in a single probabilistic-logical framework two entirely different approaches to understand and model communication. What we have done, after have carefully isolated formal axiomatic agency and communication theories used by FIPA, was to define the minimum set of new axioms necessary and sufficient to support an probabilistic form of assertive and query communicative acts. We also maintain the principles, acts and axioms as simple as possible to be able to easily assess how much we were departing from classical Speech Act theory. We believe, that given the circumstances, albeit a conservative approach, this is the correct approach. The result was a clear and simple generalization of current FIPA axiomatic communication and agent theories that is able to handle basic probabilistic communication between agents.

A secondary, but interesting, result of the paper is the (relative) completeness of *SLP* logic. To our knowledge, there is no other axiomatization for an epistemic and temporal modal logic, which allow probabilities for first order modal sentences, and is proved complete.

2   Motivation

This work has started with a very practical and concrete problem, which was how to model (and implement) the communication tasks of all agents from a real MAS: the AMPLIA system [13,8]. We have decided to use only standard languages and protocols to model and implement these tasks in order to allow reusability of the agent's knowledge and to allow an easier interoperation of AMPLIA with others intelligent learning systems. To this purpose we decided to use FIPA standards based on two assumptions: (a) the standards are a good way to ensure MAS knowledge reusability and interoperability; (b) the formal basis of FIPA standards offer an abstract and architecture independent way to model all communication tasks of the system, allowing a high level description of the communication phenomena. However, we have found that it was impossible to meet even most basic communication requirements of AMPLIA using only FIPA standards. All AMPLIA's agents use and communicate probabilistic (bayesian) knowledge, but FIPA standards assigns no meaning to probabilistic knowledge representation or communication.

Of course it is possible to try to "hide" all probabilistic knowledge in a special new content format, allowing, for example, that Bayesian Networks (BN) should be "encoded" in this format and then embedded as contents of FIPA Agent Communication Language (ACL) communicative acts. The knowledge to be passed as contents of assertive acts like FIPA's **inform**, can be considered as a logical proposition that the agent believe it is true. In being so, it is possible to assume that, from a communication point of view, it is only necessary that the agent believe that the "hidden" probabilistic knowledge transported by the act be true. Any other meaning related the probabilistic knowledge do not need be "known" by the agent in respect to communication tasks or in any reasoning related to these tasks.

2.1   The Research Problem

The approach to "hide" probabilistic knowledge solves some basic implementation problems if theoretical or formal aspects of this kind of communication are not considered. However, when analyzed more carefully this approach does not seem to be very sound.

The first problem is related to the fact that formal semantics of FIPA ACL is based on axiomatic logical theories of intention and communication [4,5,11,12]. Besides particular pre and pos-conditions (expressed as logical axioms) for some act, these theories will define clearly when the act should be emitted, what are the intentions of the sender agents when it send the act, which effects this act should cause in the receiver agent and so on. The knowledge transported in these acts are only logical propositions, but these propositions are related to internal beliefs, intentions and choices of the agents and must be used in reasoning process that will decides when to emit some act or how the act received should be understood. This imply that even if you have some probabilistic knowledge "hidden" in the contents of a communicative act, then this knowledge *cannot be used* in any internal reasoning process related to communication tasks, because formal model and theories that fundament this reasoning (at least in FIPA standards) are purely logical and do not allow reasoning about probabilities. This generates a strange situation when you have an agent with probabilistic reasoning abilities: the agent can "think" probabilistic in all internal reasoning, but never can "think" probabilistically when talking, listening and trying to understand (i.e. communicating) other agents, at least when purely logical theories are used to fundament the communication. It has the additional consequence that an agent that reason only by probabilistic means cannot "use" FIPA acts, languages and protocols if it wants to keep theoretical consistency.

The second question arises from epistemological and linguistic considerations, when we take into account agents that can reason probabilistically. We will assume that the agent uses subjective (bayesian) reasoning and can assign probabilities to his beliefs, that is, the agent can reason with degrees of belief. Assuming only basic rationality for this kind of agent, then, if it has some probabilistic belief and needs to inform this belief to another agent it will need to be sure that the proper degree of belief be also correctly informed. For instance, if it strongly believes (90% of chance) that it will rain tomorrow and need to inform this belief to another agent to change his behavior (for example, to cancel some encounter), then it will need to convince the other agent to have the same strong belief about the possibility to rain tomorrow. Some appropriate locus for the transportation of this kind of probability needs to be found in current theories of communication. The problem is that the Speech Act Theory of Searle and Grice, which provides the epistemological and linguistic basis for formal communication theories, simply do not consider the possibility of agents to communicate knowledge of probabilistic nature because the most basic semantic "unit" of knowledge that is considered by the theory is a logical proposition. Consequently, all formal theories of communication (including, the Theory of Action, Intention and Communication of Cohen, Levesque [4,5] and Sadek [11,12]) have adopted this point of view and do not consider probabilistic knowledge communication as a real possibility.

Together both questions create a very interesting dilemma: if an agent use probabilistic reasoning and need to inform some probabilistic belief to another agent it will have serious problems to do this task, because current linguistic theories say that there is no means to accomplish it (according to these theories there is no *locus* to communicate probabilities). These theories, at least in their formal counterpart, say even more, stating that even if you can send this probabilistic knowledge there is no way to consider this knowledge when reasoning about communication tasks. This surely is not a good situation from a theoretical point of view, and our work will try to start to correct this problem, at least in the limited sense of FIPA formal agent communication model.

2.2   Related Work

The problems expressed in previous sub-section are not addressed in recent research literature about ACLs (see [3]). Research in this area and related areas of agent societies and social interaction is more focused in the study about logical aspects of social institutions, including trust relationship, intentional semantics for social interaction and similar concepts, but not in checking the role of probabilities in these concepts. A similar situation also occurs in the research area of probabilistic knowledge representation for MAS. Main papers in those areas are focused on the question of how to communicate and distribute BN probabilistic knowledge between agents [14], keeping the inference processes consistent, efficient and epistemologically sound. These pieces of research offer a separate form of knowledge representation and communication not related to ACL research. Our work intends to start to bridge this gap, by showing how probabilistic knowledge can be included in the FIPA communication framework in an integrated and uniform way.

Our approach to formalize the communication of probabilistic knowledge is based on the idea that the best way to do this, in a way that is integrated and compatible with current agent communication theories (at least in the FIPA case), is to use a modal logic that can handle probabilities, that is, to use a *probabilistic logic*. In terms of Artificial Intelligence research, probabilistic logics were first described by Nilsson [10], already using a possible-worlds model to define the semantic of his logic. The initial work of Nilsson was profoundly extended, in the beginnings of 1990, by the works of Halpern [9], Abadi [1] and Bacchus [2] mainly related to epistemic (or doxastic) probabilistic modal logics. Currently there is also an active line of research based on probabilistic extensions to the CTL* temporal logic from Emerson and Srinavan, like the PCTL logic of Segala. However, due to the nature of the theories of agent communication, that require BDI modal operators, we focused our research only on epistemic probabilistic modal logics.

3   SLP Probabilistic Logic

3.1   FIPA's SL Logic

The *SL* (*Semantic Language*) is a BDI-like modal logic with equality that fundaments FIPA communication standards. This logic was defined by Sadek's work [11,12], which attributes a model-based semantics for *SL* logic. In *SL*, there is no means of attributing any subjective probability (or degree of belief) to a particular belief of some agent, so it is not possible to represent or reason about probabilistic knowledge in this logic.

Besides the usual operators and quantifiers of the predicate logic with equality, *SL* contains modal operators to express the beliefs ($B(a,\varphi)$), choices $C(a,\varphi)$ and intentions ($I(a,\varphi)$) of an agent a. *SL* also has a relatively obscure modal operator that defines an "absolute uncertainty" that an agent can have about some belief. The $U(a,\varphi)$ operator, however, does not admit any kind of degree or uncertainty level. There is no clear connection between probability theory and U operator. It is also possible to build action expressions that can be connected in series $e_1;e_2;...;e_n$, in alternates $e_1|e_2$ or verified by an agent a $(a,e)?$. Temporal and possibility assertions can be made based on the fact that an action or event has happened (***Done***(*e*, φ)), on the possibility that an action or event may happen (***Feasible***(*e*, φ)) and on which agent is responsible for an action (***Agent***(*a*,*e*,φ)).

3.2   The *SLP* Logic

The extension of the *SL* logic is called *SLP*, for *Semantic Language with Probabilities*, and it is defined through the extension of the *SL* formal model. For such purpose, *SLP* will incorporate numerical operator, relations and expressions, and terms that denote probabilities expressing the subjective probability (degree of belief) of a given sentence or statement being true.

The probabilistic term ***BP***(*a*,φ) is specific for *SLP* and informs the probability of a proposition φ be true with respect to the beliefs of agent *a*, that is, it defines the subjective probability assigned to φ by *a*. For example, ***BP***(*a*,∃(*x*)(P(*x*)) ≤ **1** express the fact that the subjective probability assigned by agent *a* to the possibility that some element of the domain satisfies P(*x*) is less than **1**.

The model-based semantics for formulas of *SLP* is defined over a set Φ of symbols for variables, functions, predicates, primitive actions, agents and constants through models *M* with the following structure:

$$M = <W, Agt, Evt, Obj, B, C, E, AGT, \sigma, RCF, \mu >$$

The elements *W*, *Agt*, *Obj*, *Evt*, *B*, *C*, *E*, *AGT* and *σ* are part of the formal model originally defined for *SL* by Sadek [12]. They define the set of possible worlds (*W*), agents (*Agt*), primitive events (*Evt*), objects (*Obj*) and causative agent for primitive events (*AGT*) of *SLP*. They also define the set of accessibility relations for beliefs (*B*), choices (*C*) and future worlds (*E*) of *SLP*. The mapping *σ* denotes a standard first-order logic interpretation that attributes, for each possible world, function and predicate symbol in Φ a correspondent element in *Agt* ∪ *Obj* ∪ *Evt* (the logical domain of *SLP*).

The elements *μ* and *RCF* are new elements specifically defined to *SLP*. The set *μ* is a set of mappings that attributes to each agent *a* a discrete probability distribution function *μ_a* on the set of possible-worlds *W*. The basic restriction to this set of mappings is that any mapping *μ_a* must respect the restrictions for any discrete probability function. The symbol *RCF* denotes the (up to isomorphism) closed field of real numbers. *RCF* it is the domain for the purely numerical formulas of *SLP* and includes addition and multiplication operations on real numbers, the neutral elements of these operations, the partial ordering ≤_{ref} and it satisfies all properties of real closed fields.

The formal semantics of *SLP* expressions, that are not probabilistic, are identical to the semantics given for *SL* in [12]. The presentation of the semantic for the entire *SLP* logics is out of the scope of present work (it is defined in [7]), however, here we will define the formal semantics of the basic belief relation *B*(*a*,φ) and of the new probabilistic term ***BP***(*a*,φ), to show the correlation between these two constructions.

Definition 1. *The modal operator B(a, φ) expresses the fact that the agent a beliefs that the sentence φ is true in a model M, world w and evaluation function v if and only if φ is true in any world w' which can be reached from w using B_a the belief accessibility relation for the agent a:*

$M,w,v \models B(a,\varphi)$ iff $M,w',v \models \varphi$,   for all w' such that $w\,\mathcal{B}_a\,w'$.

Definition 2. *The semantic of the probabilistic term $BP(a,\varphi)$ is the probability estimated by agent a that φ is true. This probability is calculated summing up the distribution function μ_a over the worlds where agent a believe that φ is true:*

$$[BP(a,\varphi)]_{M,w,v} = \mu_a(\{w' \mid w\mathcal{B}_aw' \text{ and } M,w',v \models \varphi\})$$

Besides these definitions, we add two assumptions to the formal model of *SLP*.

Assumption 3. *The following equivalences are valid in SLP:*

$B(a, \varphi) \Leftrightarrow BP(a, \varphi)=1$

$U(a, \varphi) \Leftrightarrow BP(a, \varphi)=0.5$

This assumption states the basic relationship between probabilistic and non-probabilistic (i.e. purely logical) beliefs in *SLP* and between "absolute" uncertainties and probabilistic beliefs.

Assumption 4. *Any formula φ inside $BP(a,\varphi)$ terms must be a sentence (a closed formula) of the logic. Numerical constants or variables cannot be used as arguments of logical predicates (and vice-versa).*

The axiomatic system of *SLP* was built over the axiomatic system of *SL*. It incorporates all axioms and inference rule from *SL*. To support probabilities were added the axiomatic system for the real closed field of numbers and axioms and inference rules equivalent to Kolmogorov axioms for Probability Theory.

3.3   Properties of SLP Logic

The basic properties of SLP are enunciated in the following propositions.

Proposition 5. *Any valid formula of SL is also a valid formula of SLP and any purely logical valid formula of SLP is a valid formula of SL.*□

The proof of this proposition is not so simple because of assumption 3 which forces that every world with nonzero probability from a *M* model can be reached by any other world of this model through the $\mathcal{B}$ relation, something that is not required in *SL* (or in other epistemic modal logics). Even so, it was possible to prove in [7], that any valid model of *SL* is also a valid model of *SLP* and *vice-versa* and thus proves the proposition 5.

Proposition 6. *The axiomatic system of SLP is correct.*□

The new axioms and inference rules of *SLP* are derived from the axiomatic theory of probabilities from Kolmogorov and from the axiomatic theory of the real field, both proved correct axiomatic systems.

In our proposed extension to *SL*, we have taken special care to avoid the problem of undecidability of probabilistic logics described in [1]. We have found a very interesting result, showing that there is a simpler and intuitive set of restrictions, not so strong as the restrictions proposed by Halpern and Bacchus that keep the resulting axiomatic system complete.

Proposition 7. *The axiomatic system of SLP is complete if the axiomatic system of SL is also complete.*□

The basic insight that lead us to the (relative) completeness proof of *SLP* was based on the observation that the incompleteness proof for probabilistic logics made by Abadi and Halpern [1] relied on the fact that the same variables can be "shared" by terms inside probabilistic operator and logical formulas outside these operators, i.e., it is possible to have expressions like $P(x,y) \land BP(Q(x))=r$, where the variable x is shared by $P(x,y)$ and $Q(x)$ inside the *BP* operator. The consequence is that if we not allow shared variables between probabilistic terms and logical formulas, then Abadi technique will not work. This is not the

istic terms and logical formulas, then Abadi technique will not work. This is not the same to say that the corresponding axiomatic system is complete, but it shows that this should be possible. Indeed, if we do not allow this kind of sharing, as is the case of *SLP* because of assumption 4, it is possible to use proof techniques developed by Halpern [9] and separate the probabilistic and non-probabilistic parts of some formula. This is the basic method employed on the completeness proof of *SLP*. In [7] it was shown that the validity of any formula φ of *SLP* can be reduced to the validity of an equivalent formula $\psi \wedge \pi$, where ψ is a purely logical formula containing no numerical or probabilistic term and π is a purely numerical formula containing no logical predicate/term neither any probabilistic term.

In this case, the validity of formula ψ is entirely dependant on the original *SL* axiomatic system and the validity of π depends on the first order axiomatic theory of real closed fields that, by a well-known result of Tarski, is a decidable problem. This result was proved using a finitary generalization of the Halpern techniques presented in [9] to substitute probabilistic terms that contain closed first order modal formulas with universally quantified numerical variables.

4 Communication of Probabilistic Knowledge

4.1 Principles for Probabilistic Communication

The FIPA ACL semantic depends on several logical axioms that define principles for agency and communication theories (see [11,12] for details). The theory of agency employed by FIPA includes rationality, persistency and consistency principles for beliefs, choices and intentions of agents defined as *SL* axioms and theorems. The theory of communication is formed by several axioms that define communication principles like the belief adjustment, sincerity, pertinence and cooperation principles besides the 5 basic communication properties stated in FIPA ACL specification [6]. These principles are generally sufficient to handle reasoning needs for communication purposes in any rational BDI agent that is FIPA compliant (at least when the sender's agent centered semantics used by FIPA ACL is appropriate for the application or domain in question). In being so, our first principle can be stated as the following assumption.

Assumption 8 *Agents that need to communicate probabilistic knowledge and intend to use FIPA-ACL should also respect the theory of agency and the theory of communication proposed in FIPA standards.*

This assumption is perfectly reasonable because of compatibility between *SL* and *SLP* assured by proposition 5, that implies that any valid theory of *SL* is a valid theory of *SLP*. However, when agents use probabilistic reasoning and need to use this kind of knowledge for communication purposes, then the purely logical theories of agency and communication are not much useful. To handle these situations we propose that these theories be extended by two new principles that will be able to bridge the gap between purely logical considerations and probabilistic reasoning, in terms of agent's communication decisions. We will propose only a minimum set of new principles, strictly necessary to correlate probabilistic knowledge used by the agent to decision and inference processes related to communication tasks.

One fundamental property of FIPA theory is the principle that assures the agreement between the mental state of some agent and their beliefs [12]. Using this principle is possible to assert propositions like $B(a, \varphi) \leftrightarrow B(a, B(a, \varphi))$ and $BP(a,\varphi)=1 \leftrightarrow B(a,BP(a,\varphi)=1)$, if all propositions and predicate symbols in φ appears in the scope of a modal operator formalizing a mental attitude of agent a:

This is an interesting fact but is very limited in the case of probabilistic communication. The principles of FIPA's theory of communication assume that the agent must believe non-probabilistically in some fact, before the communication starts. Therefore, what we need is some principle that will allow us to correlate probabilistic beliefs with non-probabilistic beliefs. This is assured by the following proposition of *SLP*.

Proposition 9. *Principle of Probabilities and Beliefs Agreement: if some agent a assume that the probability of proposition φ is p, then this is equivalent to state that it also believe in this fact*:

$$\models BP(a, \varphi){=}p \leftrightarrow B(a, BP(a, \varphi){=}p\,) \;\square$$

This principle allows agents to put any probabilistic beliefs "inside" epistemic belief operators and then to use any other axioms and theorems of communication or agency theories to make communication related reasoning.

The proposition 9 is necessary but is not enough. We need some kind of reason to effectively start some new communicative act. In FIPA this is assured by the principle of belief adjustment [12] that states that if some agent a believe in φ, believe that is competent in this belief and thinks that another agent b do not believe in φ, then it adopts the intention to make b believe in φ.

$$\models B(a, \varphi \wedge B(b, \neg\varphi) \wedge Comp(a, \varphi)) \rightarrow I(a, B(b, \varphi))$$

The predicate *Comp(a,φ)* states the competence of agent a about φ.

The belief adjustment principle also falls in the same limiting situation of the mental state and belief agreement principle when applied to the probabilistic case. Therefore, we need another principle stated in the following proposition.

Proposition 10. *Principle of Probabilities Adjustment: if some agent a believe that the probability of proposition φ is p, believe that it is competent in this belief and also believe that another agent b have different estimation for the probability of φ, then it should adopt the intention to make agent b also believe that the probability of φ is p*:

$$\models BP(a,\varphi){=}p \wedge BP(a,BP(b,\varphi){=}p){<}1 \wedge B(a,Comp(a,BP(a,\varphi){=}p))) \rightarrow I(a, BP(b, \varphi){=}p) \;\square$$

This principle is derived from belief adjustment principle, using the proposition 9 stated before (see [7] for details). It will have the same function of belief adjustment principle for the probabilistic reasoning case, providing agents with intentions to solve perceived differences between probabilistic beliefs shared by several agents.

4.2   Communicative Acts for Probabilities

Like *SL*, *SLP* also can be used as a content representation language for FIPA-ACL communicative acts. This allows the representation and distribution of probabilistic knowledge like BN between agents using standard assertive (**inform**) acts. However, to do this is necessary to assume a particular structure in the contents of these acts. The assertive acts defined in Speech Act theory (and the equivalent **inform** FIPA-ACL acts) do not assume any particular internal structure in the propositions passed as contents of these acts. So, in the general case of probabilistic communication not seem reasonable to always assume a particular structure in the content of assertive act used to communicate probabilities. To handle this we propose that the strength (or weakness) of the assertive force of some speech act should be measured by a probability. In this way, any kind of propositions can be used as contents of these probabilistic assertive acts, because the (subjective) probability of the proposition will be transmitted as a graduation of the force. This graduation is a numerical coefficient that represents the subjective probability of the proposition (i. e., the graduation of the assertive force is directly related to the belief degree on the proposition). Two new probabilistic communicative acts were defined. They are considered extensions to the FIPA-ACL, creating the *Probabilistic Agent Communication Language* (PACL).

The acts **inform-bp** and **query-bp** acts are defined, respectively, to allow that the information about subjective probabilities of an agent to be shared with other agents and to allow that a given agent could query the degree of belief of another agent. Using the notation employed by FIPA-ACL [6] the **inform-bp** act is formalized as follows:

$<a,$ **inform-bp** $(b, <\varphi, p>)>$

   $FP: BP(a,\varphi){=}p \wedge BP(a, BP(b,\varphi){=}p){<}1$

   $RE: BP(b,\varphi){=}p$

This act informs the probability for some closed formula φ. The feasibility precondition of the act (*FP*) requires only that an agent to believe that the subjective probability of φ is p and that another agent b has the chance of not believing in this fact. In this case, if the other necessary conditions are fulfilled (see [6]), then the **inform-bp** act will be emitted. The rational effect (*RE*) that is expected with the act emission is that agent b also comes to believe that the probability of φ is p.

The **query-bp** act was also modeled after an analysis of the **query-if** act, which is its similar when dealing with truth-values. This directive act is used to retrieve the probabilistic information associated to a particular proposition.

4.3 Examples

The use of **inform-bp** acts is straightforward. Assume that some agent a believe that agent b have a different estimation of the probability of φ and also believe that his estimation is competent:

$$BP(a,\varphi){=}p \wedge B(a, BP(b,\varphi){\neq}BP(a,\varphi)) \wedge B(a,Comp(a,BP(a,\varphi){=}p))) \qquad (1)$$

Using the axioms and inference rules of *SLP* it is possible to infer, from $B(a, BP(b,\varphi){\neq}BP(a,\varphi))$ and $BP(a,\varphi){=}p$, that $\neg B(a, BP(b,\varphi){=}p)$. But this is equivalent to $BP(a,BP(b,\varphi){=}p){<}1$, resulting:

$$BP(a,\varphi){=}p \wedge BP(a,BP(b,\varphi){=}p){<}1 \wedge B(a,Comp(a,BP(a,\varphi){=}p))) \qquad (2)$$

Then, by (2) and proposition 10 the agent a need to assume the intention to inform b about the probability of φ. By the communication theory of FIPA this intention and beliefs stated in (2) are enough to cause the emission of the **inform-bp** act from a to b agent informing the probability of φ.

If we force that agents a and b use *SLP* as content language and require that agent a be completely unsure if agent b knows the probability of φ, then it is also possible to use the **inform** acts of FIPA. The principle stated in proposition 9 allows to infer, from $BP(a,\varphi){=}p$, that:

$$B(a,BP(a,\varphi){=}p). \qquad (3)$$

In FIPA **inform** act, the feasibility precondition (*FP*) also requires that agent a be completely unsure if the agent b knows some proposition ψ is stated as:

$$\neg B(a, B(b, \psi) \vee B(b,\neg \psi) \vee U(b, \psi) \vee U(b,\neg \psi)) \qquad (4)$$

Substituting ψ in (4) by $BP(b,\varphi){=}p$ we have:

$$\neg B(a,B(b,BP(b,\varphi){=}p) \vee B(b,\neg BP(b,\varphi){=}p) \vee U(b,BP(b,\varphi){=}p) \vee U(b,\neg BP(b,\varphi){=}p)) \qquad (5)$$

So, agent *a* believes in (3) and if it also believes in (5) it can emit an **inform** act to agent *b*, with the proposition $BP(a,\varphi)=p$ as the content of the act.

5 Future Works

Several interesting developments can follow our work. A direct possibility it is to check the influence of probabilistic knowledge and reasoning in other types of communicative acts and interaction protocols. Particularly interesting and related to our ongoing research it is the application of probabilistic knowledge and reasoning to model formally negotiation protocols, mainly when these protocols are related to the pedagogical negotiation, which is a very complex form of interaction that occurs in intelligent learning environments (and classrooms) [8]. Another possibility is to use the logical representation schemes for BN (like the schemes presented in [2] and [7]) as a starting point for the research of shared ontologies for probabilistic knowledge. The considerable research work already done for logical based ontologies, can be applied to this new research.

7 Acknowledgments

The authors gratefully acknowledge the Brazilian agencies CAPES, CNPq and FAPERGS for the partial support to this research project

8 References

[1]   M. Abadi and J. Halpern. Decidability and Expressiveness for First-Order Logics of Probability. In *Procs of IEEE Symp. on Foundations of Computer Science*, 30, 1989.

[2]   F. Bacchus. Lp, a Logic for Representing and Reasoning with Statistical Knowledge. *Computational Intelligence*, 6:209-301, 1990.

[3]   B. Chaib-Draa and F. Dignun. Trends in Agent Communication Language. *Computational Intelligence* v. 2, n. 5. Cambridge, MA: Blackwell Publ., 2002

[4]   P. Cohen and H. Levesque. Rational Interaction as the Basis for Communication, In P. Cohen, J. Morgan and M. Pollack (Ed.). *Intentions in Communication*. Cambridge, MA: MIT Press, 1990.

[5]   P. Cohen and H. Levesque. Communicative Actions for Artifical Agents. In *Procs of ICMAS-95*. San Francisco. Cambridge: MIT Press, 1995.

[6]   FIPA. FIPA Communicative Act Library Specification, Std. SC00037J, FIPA, 2002.

[7]   J. C. Gluz. Formalization of the Communication of Probabilistic Knowledge in Multiagent Systems: an approach based on Probabilistic Logic (In Portuguese). *PhD Thesis*. Instituto de Informática, UFRGS, Porto Alegre, 2005.

[8]   J. C. Gluz, C. Flores, L. Seixas and R. Viccari, R. Formal Aspects of Pedagogical Negotiation in AMPLIA System. In: *Procs of TISE-2005*. Santiago, Chile, 2005.

[9]   J. Y. Halpern. An Analysis of First-Order Logics of Probability. *Artificial Intelligence*, 46: 311-350, 1990.

[10]   N. J. Nilsson. Probabilistic Logic. *Artificial Intelligence, Amsterdam*, 28: 71-87, 1986.

[11]   M. D. Sadek. Dialogue Acts are Rational Plans. In: *Procs. of ESCA/ETRW Workshop on the Structure of Multimodal Dialogue*, Maratea, Italy, 1991.

[12]   M. D. Sadek. A Study in the Logic of Intention.'In: *Procs. of KR'92*, p. 462-473, Cambridge, USA, 1992.

[13]   R. M. Vicari, C. D. Flores, L. Seixas, A. Silvestre, M. Ladeira, H. A. Coelho. Multi-Agent Intelligent Environment for Medical Knowledge. *Artificial Intelligence in Medicine*, 27(3): 335-366, March 2003.

[14]   Y. Xiang, A probabilistic framework for cooperative multi-agent distributed interpretation and optimization of communication. *Artificial Intelligence*, 87: 295-342, 1996

Detecting and Repairing Anomalous Evolutions in Noisy Environments: Logic Programming Formalization and Complexity Results

Fabrizio Angiulli[1], Gianluigi Greco[2], and Luigi Palopoli[3]

[1] ICAR-CNR, Via P. Bucci 41C, 87030 Rende, Italy
   angiulli@icar.cnr.it
[2] Dept. of Mathematics - Univ. della Calabria, Via P. Bucci 30B, 87030 Rende, Italy
   ggreco@mat.unical.it
[3] DEIS - Univ. della Calabria, Via P. Bucci 41C, 87030 Rende, Italy
   palopoli@deis.unical.it

Summary. In systems where agents are required to interact with a partially known and dynamic world, sensors can be used to obtain further knowledge about the environment. However, sensors may be unreliable, that is, they may deliver wrong information (due, e.g., to hardware or software malfunctioning) and, consequently, they may cause agents to take wrong decisions, which is a scenario that should be avoided. The paper considers the problem of reasoning in noisy environments in a setting where no (either certain or probabilistic) data is available in advance about the reliability of sensors. Therefore, assuming that each agent is equipped with a background theory (in our setting, an extended logic program) encoding its general knowledge about the world, we define a concept of detecting an anomaly perceived in sensor data and the related concept of agent recovering to a coherent status of information. In this context, the complexities of various anomaly detection and anomaly recovery problems are studied.

1 Introduction

Consider an agent operating in a dynamic environment according to an internal background theory (the agent's trustable knowledge) which is enriched, over time, through sensing the environment. Were sensors completely reliable, in a fully observable environment, the agent could gain a perfectly correct perception of environment evolution. However, in general, sensors maybe unreliable, in that they may deliver erroneous observations to the agent. Thus, the agent's perception about environment evolution might be erroneous and this, in turn, might cause that wrong decisions are taken.

In order to deal with the uncertainty that arises from noisy sensors, probabilistic approaches have been proposed see, e.g., [5, 6, 7, 14, 16, 21]) where evolutions are represented by means of dynamic systems in which transitions among possible states

Please use the following format when citing this chapter:

Angiulli, F., Greco, G., Palopoli, L., 2006, in IFIP International Federation for Information Processing, Volume 217, Artificial Intelligence in Theory and Practice, ed. M. Bramer, (Boston: Springer), pp. 41–50.

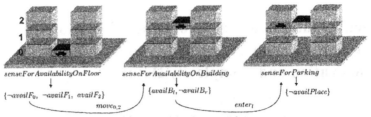

$sense For AvailabilityOnFloor$ $senseForAvailabilityOnBuilding$ $senseForParking$
                    ↓   ↓   ↓
$\{\neg availF_0, \ \neg availF_1, \ availF_2\}$ $\{availB_l, \neg availB_r\}$ $\{\neg availPlace\}$
                    $move_{0,2}$ $enter_l$

Fig. 1. Parking lot example.

are determined in terms of probability distributions. Other approaches refer to some *logic* formalization (see, e.g., modal logics, action languages, logic programming, and situation calculus [2, 11, 12, 20]) in which a logical theory is augmented to deal quantitatively and/or qualitatively with the reliability of the sensors.

In this paper we take a different perspective instead, by assuming that no information about reliabilities of sensors is available in advance. Therefore, in this context, neither probabilistic nor qualitative information can be exploited for reasoning with sensing. Nonetheless, it is in any case relevant to single out faulty sensor data in order for the agent to be able to correctly maintain a correct perception about the status of the world. To this aim, we introduce a formal framework good for reasoning about anomalies in agent's perception of environment evolutions, that relies on the identification of possible discrepancies between the observations gained through sensors and the internal trustable knowledge of the agent.

In order to make the framework clearer, we next introduce a running example.

1.1 Example of Faulty Sensors Identification

Consider an agent who is in charge of parking cars in a parking lot (see Figure 1). The parking lot consists of two buildings, each with several floors. The floors are reached via a single elevator which runs in the middle in between the two buildings (so, there is a building to *left* and one to the *right* of the elevator door). A number of sensors are used to inform the agent about parking place availability at different levels of the two buildings. In particular, the sensors tell the agent: (a) if there is any available parking place at some level in any of the two buildings (sensor s_1); (b) given the floor where the agent is currently located, if there is any available parking place in the left and/or the right building at that floor (sensor s_2); (c) given the floor and the building (left or right) where the agent is currently located, whether parking places are available at that floor in that building (sensor s_3) – let us assume that there are a total of n parking places at each level of each of the two buildings. Also, the agent uses a background theory that tells him that if he is at floor i of the building x and sensors s_1, when queried, signalled parking availability at level i and sensor s_2, when queried, signalled a parking availability in building x then there must be indeed at least one parking place available at his current position.

Now, assume that, in fact, the agent senses sensor s_3 and the sensor returns the information that no place is available at the current agent's position. This clearly disagrees with the internal state of the agent that tells that there should be indeed at least one place available in that position. Such disagreement implies that some anomalies came into play somehow.

In particular, the agent might doubt about the reliability of sensor s_3 (that is, there actually are available parking places at the agent position, but s_3 tells that none is available). Similarly, the agent might suspect that sensor s_1 is reliable while s_2 is not, thereby inferring that there is a place to park at the very floor where he is currently located, but on the opposite building.

1.2 Contribution and Organization

Within the framework outlined above, the contribution of the paper is as follows.

In Section 2, we introduce some preliminaries on extended logic programming which shall constitute the basic formalism exploited for modelling agents background knowledge. Then, in Section 3, we formally propose a concept of anomaly in state evolutions of a dynamic environment, as perceived by an agent sensing that environment through (possibly) noisy sensors. Moreover, we define a suitable concept of recovering the agent internal mental state from anomalies.

After that the framework has been introduced, we turn to the study of the computational complexity of some basic relevant problems related to state evolution anomaly detection and recovery. The results are proved and discussed in Section 4. We considered background knowledge bases modelled by means of not-free extended logic programs as well as general logic programs under both the brave and the cautious semantics. We point out here that, depending on the complexity of the agent background knowledge, anomaly checking may be characterized by a quite varied degree of difficulty, ranging from simple checking for the occurrence of complementary literals in sensor data and in the agent background knowledge (which is basically the case for our running example above) to quite complex tasks. The capability of characterizing computational complexity sources in knowledge representation frameworks is important both for gaining knowledge of the structure of the problems the framework comprises and, above all, to be able to realize effective rewriting and optimizations needed to efficiently implement them [10]. This justifies our interest in analyzing the complexity of anomaly detection and repair in agent evolutions, which will accounted for in the paper.

We believe that our investigation is a step towards providing capabilities for dynamic plan monitoring and repairing in noisy environment, where it can be useful for an agent that is trying to achieve its goals to be able to monitor, identify anomalies and fix a plan while evolving [3, 4, 8]. In this respect, it deserves of further work the possibility of prototypically implementing anomalies identification primitives for agent evolutions on top of some available answer set engine (e.g., [13, 17]), and subsequently made them available to conditional planning environments (e.g., [15, 19, 22]).

2 Preliminaries on Extended Logic Programs (ELPs)

We briefly recall here that a propositional ELP is a set of rules of the form $L_0 \leftarrow L_1, \ldots, L_m, not\ L_{m+1}, \ldots, not\ L_n$ $(n \geq m \geq 0)$, where the symbol "not" denotes negation by default, and each L_i is a literal, i.e. an expression of the form p or $\neg p$ with p a propositional letter and the symbol "$\neg$" denotes classical negation. By $\mathbf{h}(r)$ we denote the head L_0 of the rule r, and by $\mathbf{b}(r)$ its body $L_1, \ldots, L_m, not\ L_{m+1}, \ldots, not\ L_n$. An ELP is *positive* if classical negation does not occur in the program.

In the following, we consider the *answer set* semantics for ELPs [9]. *Answer sets* of an ELP P are defined as follows. Let $Lit(P)$ denote the set of all the literals obtained using the propositional letters occurring in P. Let a *context* be any subset of $Lit(P)$. Let P be a *negation-by-default-free* ELP. Call a context S *closed under P* iff for each rule $L_0 \leftarrow L_1, \ldots, L_m$ in P, if $L_1, \ldots, L_m \in S$, then $L_0 \in S$. An *answer set* of P is any minimal context S such that (1) S is closed under P and (2) if S is inconsistent, that is if there exists a propositional letter p such that both $p \in S$ and $\neg p \in S$, then $S = Lit(P)$. An answer set of a general ELP is defined as follows. Let the *reduct of P w.r.t the context S*, denoted by $Red(P, S)$, be the ELP obtained from P by deleting (i) each rule that has $not\ L$ in its body for some $L \in S$, and (ii) all subformulae of the form $not\ L$ of the bodies of the remaining rules. Any context S which is an answer set of $Red(P, S)$ is an *answer set* of P. By ANSW(P) we denote the collection of all consistents answer sets of an ELP P. An ELP P is ANSW-consistent iff ANSW$(P) \neq \emptyset$.

An ELP P *cautiously* entails a literal l, written $P \models_c l$, iff for each $S \in$ ANSW(P), $l \in S$. An ELP P *bravely* entails a literal l, written $P \models_b l$, iff there exists $S \in$ ANSW(P) such that $l \in S$.

3 Formal Framework

In this section, we introduce a simple framework to model environment state evolutions with sensing, and we formally state the problem of reasoning about possibly faulty sensors. In this respect, we present some techniques that an agent might exploit to identify 'anomalous' observations (and, hence, faulty sensors), and a 'repair approach' in execution monitoring accommodating the uncertainty on the outcome of the sensors.

3.1 Sensors, Agents, and Transitions

Let $\mathcal{F}$ be a set of propositional variables. We denote by $\neg f$ the negation of any $f \in \mathcal{F}$, and by $\mathcal{F}^{\neg}$ the set $\{\neg f \mid f \in \mathcal{F}\}$.

We distinguish two (disjoint) sets of variables: (i) *beliefs B*, denoting the agent beliefs about the status of the world; (ii) *observables O*, modelling the actual status of the world as returned by a set S of environment sensors. Specifically, for each sensor $s \in \mathcal{S}$, $\lambda(s) \subseteq \mathcal{O}$ denotes the set of propositional variables that are sensed by

$$\mathcal{B}: \begin{cases} floor_0, \ floor_1, \ floor_2 \\ building_l, \ building_r \end{cases} \qquad \mathcal{S}: \begin{cases} \lambda(s_1) = \{availF_0, \ availF_1, \ availF_2\} \\ \lambda(s_2) = \{availB_l, \ availB_r\} \\ \lambda(s_3) = \{availPlace\} \end{cases}$$

$$\mathcal{O}: \begin{cases} availF_0, \ availF_1, \ availF_2 \\ availB_l, \ availB_r \\ availPlace \end{cases} \qquad \mathcal{K}: \begin{cases} availPlace \leftarrow availF_i, \ availB_j, \\ \qquad\qquad floor_i, \ building_j. \end{cases}$$

$$\begin{cases} senseForAvailabilityOnFloor: & \langle floor_0, \ s_1\rangle \\ senseForAvailabilityOnBuilding: & \langle \emptyset, \ s_2\rangle \\ senseForParking: & \langle \emptyset, \ s_3\rangle \\ move_{i,j}: & \langle floor_i, \{\neg floor_i, \ floor_j\}\rangle \\ enter_j: & \langle \emptyset, \{building_j\}\rangle \end{cases}$$

Fig. 2. Formalization of the parking lot example.

s. Moreover, at any time instant, we assume that the value of the sensor is returned by a function $val : \mathcal{S} \mapsto \lambda(\mathcal{S}) \times \lambda(\mathcal{S})^\neg$ producing a consistent set of observables (literals which the sensor evaluates to 'true').

Example 1. In the *parking lot* application, the sensors $\mathcal{S}$, the observables $\mathcal{O}$ and the beliefs $\mathcal{B}$ are reported in Figure 2, where, for instance, $availF_i$ means that there are parking places available at level i, $availB_l$ that at the current floor there are places available in the left building, and $building_r$ that the car is currently in the building on the right.   ◁

Each agent is characterized by a *background knowledge* $\mathcal{K}$ expressed as an extended logic program over $\mathcal{F}$, and, over time, by a current *state* represented as a pair of sets $S = \langle S_B, S_O \rangle$, where $S_B \subseteq B \times B^\neg$ and $S_O \subseteq O \times O^\neg$, such that both S_B and S_O are consistent. In the following, S_B (resp. S_O) will be denoted by $\mathcal{B}(S)$ (resp. $\mathcal{O}(S)$). In order to achieve its goals, the agent operates by executing *operators* that cause *transitions* between states, that is, they cause the environment to evolve together with the agent mental state. In particular, a transition usually changes the agent's beliefs; yet, it may change the observables if the corresponding operator includes a *sensing*.

Several ways to define transitions between states in the presence of sensing actions have been proposed in the literature, accounting, e.g., for non-deterministic effects, causal effects, probabilities, and so on (see, e.g., [20, 18, 14, 12, 21] and references therein). In the foregoing, we decided to refer to a particularly simple approach, since the results we are going to present are largely independent of the chosen formalization of transitions and associated operators. Hence, in order to make the exposition clearer we resume to a quite simple model which allows to specify preconditions, multiple-effects and *sensing actions*. So, in our context, an operator t for an agent A is simply a pair $\langle c, e \rangle$ such that c is a logic formula over the set $B \cup O$ denoting the preconditions, and e is the effect of the operator which can be either *(i)* a consistent subset e_B of $B \times B^\neg$, or *(ii)* a sensor $e_s \in \mathcal{S}$. We denote by $con(t)$ the precondition c, and by $eff(t)$ the effect e of t. See Figure 2 for the theory $\mathcal{K}$ and the set of operators in our parking lot application.

In the following, given a precondition c and an answer set S we will assume that the entailment $S \models c$ is polynomial time decidable. An ELP P *cautiously* entails a condition c, written $P \models_c c$, iff for each $S \in \text{ANSW}(P)$, $S \models c$. An ELP P *bravely* entails a condition c, written $P \models_b c$, iff there exists $S \in \text{ANSW}(P)$ such that $S \models c$.

We next define the semantics of applying operators to agent's states.

Definition 1. Let A be an agent and $\langle S_B, S_O \rangle$ be a state for it. An operator $t = \langle c, e \rangle$ is *applicable* in $\langle S_B, S_O \rangle$ if $(\mathcal{K} \cup S_B \cup S_O) \models c$, and the *result of its application* is the state $\langle S'_B, S'_O \rangle$ defined as:

- $\langle S_B, (S_O \setminus v^-) \cup v \rangle$, with $v = val(e_s)$, if $e = e_s \in S$, and
- $\langle S_B \setminus e_B^- \cup e_B, S_O \rangle$, if $e = e_B \subseteq B \times B^-$.

In the case above, we also write $\langle S_B, S_O \rangle \rightarrow_t \langle S'_B, S'_O \rangle$. $\square$

Example 2. Consider again Figure 2, and in particular, the set of operators reported in the bottom part of it: Given the state $\langle \{floor_0\}, \emptyset \rangle$, we can easily see that the operator $move_{1,2}$ is not applicable. Conversely, the agent might apply the operator $senseForAvailabilityOnFloor$ and a possible outcome is $\langle \{floor_0\}, \{\neg availF_0, \neg availF_1, availF_2\} \rangle$. Figure 1 shows an example of transitions between states exploiting such operators.   ◁

3.2 Reasoning on Evolutions

The repeated application of operators define an evolution for the agent. Formally, an evolution H for A is a succession of states of the form $\langle S_B^0, S_O^0 \rangle \rightarrow_{t_1} \langle S_B^1, S_O^1 \rangle \rightarrow_{t_2} \ldots \rightarrow_{t_n} \langle S_B^n, S_O^n \rangle$, such that (*i*) each transition t_i is applicable in the state $\langle S_B^{i-1}, S_O^{i-1} \rangle$ and (*ii*) each state $\langle S_B^i, S_O^i \rangle$ is the result of the application of t_i in $\langle S_B^{i-1}, S_O^{i-1} \rangle$. Intuitively, H represents an actual plan that the agent is performing in order to achieve a given goal starting from the initial state $\langle S_B^0, S_O^0 \rangle$.

In the following, $len(H)$ denotes the number of transitions occurring in the evolution H; $state_i(H)$ denotes the ith state of the evolution H; $state(H)$ denotes $state_{len(H)}(H)$; $tr_i(H)$ denotes the ith transition occurred in the evolution; $H[i]$ denotes the evolution $state_0(H) \rightarrow_{tr_1(H)} \cdots \rightarrow_{tr_i(H)} state_i(H)$.

As previously pointed out, while dealing with noisy sensors, there might be evolutions in which the agent finds some discrepancies between its mental beliefs (plus its trustable knowledge) and the observations at hand. The following definition formalizes such a notion of 'disagreement'.

Definition 2. Let H be an evolution for the agent A with knowledge $\mathcal{K}$. A set of observations $W \subseteq \mathcal{O}(state(H))$ is an *anomaly* for A in H if $\forall w \in W$, $th(A, H) \setminus W \models \neg w$, where $th(A, H)$ denotes the theory $\mathcal{K} \cup \mathcal{B}(state(H)) \cup \mathcal{O}(state(H))$. $\square$

Example 3. Let H be the evolution: t_1 : $senseForAvailabilityOnFloor$; t_2 : $move_{0,2}$; t_3 : $senseForAvailabilityOnBuilding$; t_4 : $enter_l$; and t_5 : $senseFor$ $Parking$.

Assume, now, that sensed values are such that $\mathcal{O}(state_1(H)) \supseteq \{\neg availF_0, \neg availF_1, availF_2\}$, $\mathcal{O}(state_3(H)) \supseteq \{availB_l, \neg availB_r\}$, and $\mathcal{O}(state_5(H)) \supseteq \{\neg availPlace\}$ – see, again, Figure 2. Intuitively, the agent is planning to park at the second floor in the left building after sensing s_1 and s_2. But, the result of sensing s_3 is anomalous, as it disagrees with its mental beliefs (in $\mathcal{K}$) according to which $availPlace$ should be true there. ◁

The agent employed in our running example has a unique possible view of the world, being its knowledge a positive program. In general, an agent may have several possible worlds. Thus, in the following we will distinguish between the cautious and the brave semantics. In particular, while anomaly existence under the cautious semantics expresses that no possible world is consistent with the sensor readings, under the brave semantics a set of sensor readings is anomalous if each sensor reading is inconsistent with some possible world in which all sensors of the set are simultaneously kept quiet.

Given an anomaly, we are interested in finding possible fixes for it, i.e., "alternative" evolutions defined over the same set of transitions in which, however, the result of the sensing actions may differ from the evolution in which the anomaly has been singled out. This is formalized next with the notion of *repair* for an evolution.

Definition 3. An evolution H' for A is a *repair* for H w.r.t. an anomaly W if:
1. $len(H) = len(H')$,
2. $tr_i(H) = tr_i(H')$, for each $1 \leq i \leq len(H)$, and
3. $\forall w \in W \cap \mathcal{O}(state(H'))$, $th(A, H') \setminus W \not\models \neg w$.

Moreover, H' is *non trivial* if $W \cap \mathcal{O}(state(H'))$ is not empty. □

Example 4. For instance, a repair for our running example is obtained by replacing the value returned by sensor s_2 with $\{\neg availB_l, availB_r\}$ while keeping the values returned by s_1 and s_3. This represents the scenario in which the available place is in the opposite building of the same floor. ◁

4 Reasoning with Noisy Sensors

Now that we have defined our formal framework for anomaly detection and repairing of an agent's mental state evolution, we turn to the problem of defining relevant agent's reasoning tasks. Moreover, as already stated in the Introduction, is it important to pinpoint the computational complexity characterizing such tasks, since this is a fundamental premise to devising effective and optimized implementations of our framework.

Specifically, we shall next consider the following relevant problems:

- ANOMALY-EXISTENCE: Given an agent A and an evolution H for it, does there exist an anomaly W for A in H?
- REPAIR-EXISTENCE: Given an agent A and an anomaly W for A in an evolution H, does there exist a (non trivial) repair H' for H w.r.t. W?

	not -free	cautious	brave
ANOMALY-EXISTENCE	P-c	Σ_2^P-c	NP-c
REPAIR-EXISTENCE	NP-c	Σ_2^P-c	Σ_2^P-c
REPAIR-CHECKING	NP-c	Σ_2^P-c	Σ_2^P-c
ANOMALY&REPAIR-CHECK.	P-c	D^P-c	D^P-c

Fig. 3. Complexity of Basic Problems.

- REPAIR-CHECKING: Given an agent A and evolutions H and H', is H' a repair for H w.r.t. some anomaly W for A?
- ANOMALY&REPAIR-CHECKING: Let A be an agent and H an evolution. Given an evolution H' and a set of observables $W \subseteq \mathcal{O}(state(H))$, is W an anomaly for A in H, and H' a repair for H w.r.t. W?

Complexity results concerning problems defined above are depicted in Figure 3. In the following, the complexity of the ANOMALY-EXISTENCE problem for a particular semantics of general logic programs is investigated.

Let T be a truth assignment of the set $\{x_1, \ldots, x_n\}$ of boolean variables. Then, we denote by Φ the boolean formula $\Phi = C_1 \wedge \ldots \wedge C_m$ in conjunctive normal form, with $C_j = t_{j,1} \vee t_{j,2} \vee t_{j,3}$, where each $t_{j,k}$ is a literal on the set of boolean variables $X = x_1, \ldots, x_n$. Recall that deciding the *satisfiability* of Φ is a well-known NP complete problem.

Theorem 1. ANOMALY-EXISTENCE *for ELPs under brave semantics is* NP-*complete.*

Proof:

(Membership) The problem can be solved by a polynomial time nondeterministic Turing machine that guesses a subset $W \subseteq \mathcal{O}(state(H))$ together with $n = |W|$ contexts $S_1, \ldots, S_n$ of $th(A, H) \setminus W$ such that $\neg w_i \in S_i$, and then checks in polynomial time that each S_i is an answer set of the reduct of $th(A, H) \setminus W$ w.r.t. S_i and, hence, of $th(A, H) \setminus W$.

(Hardness) Given the boolean formula Φ, consider the set of observables $\mathcal{O}(\Phi) = \{x_0, x_1, \ldots, x_n\}$, the sensor $s(\Phi)$ with $\lambda(s(\Phi)) = \mathcal{O}(\Phi)$, and the agent $A(\Phi)$ with knowledge $\mathcal{K}(\Phi)$:

$$r_0 : sat \leftarrow c_1, \ldots, c_m.$$
$$r_{1,j} : c_j \leftarrow \sigma(t_{j,1}). \qquad (1 \leq j \leq m)$$
$$r_{2,j} : c_j \leftarrow \sigma(t_{j,2}). \qquad (1 \leq j \leq m)$$
$$r_{3,j} : c_j \leftarrow \sigma(t_{j,3}). \qquad (1 \leq j \leq m)$$
$$r_{4,i} : \neg x_i \leftarrow not\ x_i, sat. \quad (0 \leq i \leq n)$$

where $\sigma(x_i) = x_i$ and $\sigma(\neg x_i) = not\ x_i$, the operator $t(\Phi) = \langle \emptyset, s(\Phi) \rangle$, and the evolution $H(\Phi) = \langle \emptyset, \emptyset \rangle \rightarrow_{t(\Phi)} \langle \emptyset, \mathcal{O}(\Phi) \rangle$. Now we prove that there exists an anomaly $W \subseteq \mathcal{O}(\Phi)$ for $A(\Phi)$ in $H(\Phi)$ iff Φ is satisfiable.

($\Rightarrow$) Assume that there exists an anomaly W for $A(\Phi)$ in $H(\Phi)$. Then $th(A(\Phi), H(\Phi)) \setminus W \models \neg w, \forall w \in W$. As the negation of some observable x_i can be implied only by rule $r_{4,i}$, then it is the case that there exists an answer set M of $th(A(\Phi), H(\Phi))$ such that $sat \in M$. Consequently, $T(x_i) = \textbf{true}, \forall x_i \in X \setminus W$, and $T(x_i) = \textbf{false}, \forall x_i \in W$, is a truth assignment to the variables of Φ that makes the formula satisfied.

($\Leftarrow$) Assume that Φ is satisfiable, and let T_X be a truth value assignment to the variables in X that makes Φ true. Then $W = \{x_0\} \cup \{x_i \mid T_X(x_i) = \text{false}\}$ is an anomaly for $A(\Phi)$ in $H(\Phi)$.

According to the theorem above, negation by default makes ANOMALY-EXISTENCE intractable. Moreover, under the cautious semantics the problem is more difficult than under the brave (see Figure 3), unlike most cases in which a kind of symmetry holds between the complexity of the two semantics (within the same level of the polynomial hierarchy).

5 Conclusions

In this paper we have defined a formal framework good for reasoning about agents' mental state evolution about environments sensed through possibly unreliable sensors. In our framework, no information (neither certain nor probabilistic) is assumed to be available in advance about the reliability of sensors. The agent's perception can however be maintained to encode a correct perception of the world through the identification and the resolution of discrepancies occurring between sensor delivered data and the agent's internal trustable knowledge, encoded in the form of an ELP under answer set semantics. After having defined the formal framework, in order to pinpoint main computational complexity sources implied in the implementation of the anomaly detection and repairing agent's mental state evolution, several reasoning problem have been considered and their complexity have been studied.

We note that the problem of *belief change* is only loosely related to work here done. Indeed, rather than being interested in revising the agent theory in order to entail the new information provided by the environment, we are interested in singling out environmental manifestations to be doubted about. The notion of minimal repair is indeed relevant in order to rank different possible repairs. We point out that several relations of preference between repairs can be embedded in the basic framework here introduced. Indeed, a natural form of preference relies in the number of agent observations the repair should change in order to recover its mental consistency, while it is also interesting to rank repairs depending on the number of anomalies they are able to fix. Furthermore, while sensors under consideration can only report binary states, the framework is not limited to the management of binary environmental measures, as many-valued discrete signals can be indeed simulated by sets of binary signals. Investigating the impact of enriching the framework with sensors delivering real-valued data is also of interest. Finally, it is interesting to explore how the presented framework could be embedded within a full-fledged conditional agent planning system. All those issues discusses above will be the topics of future investigation, while we are currently involved with the implementation of our system on top of the DLV system [13].

References

1. F. Angiulli, R. Ben-Eliyahu-Zohary, and L. Palopoli. Outlier detection using default logic. *in Proc of IJCAI'03*, pp. 833-838.
2. F. Bacchus, J.Y. Halpern, and H.J. Levesque. Reasoning about noisy sensors and effectors in the situation calculus. *Artificial Intelligence*, 111(1-2): 171-208, 1999.
3. M. Balduccini and M. Gelfond. Diagnostic reasoning with a-prolog. *TPLP*, 3(4-5): 425-461, 2003.
4. C. Baral, S.A. McIlraith, and T.C. Son. Formulating diagnostic problem solving using an action language with narratives and sensing, *in Proc of KR'02*, pp. 311-322.
5. C. Baral, N. Tran, and L.C. Tuan. Reasoning about actions in a probabilistic setting. *in Proc. of AAAI/IAAI'02*, pp. 507-512.
6. C. Boutilier, R. Dean, and S. Hanks. Planning under uncertainty: structural assumptions and computational leverage. *JAIR*, 11: 1-94, 1999.
7. C. Boutilier, R. Reiter, and B. Price. Symbolic dynamic programming for first-order MDPs. *IJCAI'01*, pp. 690-700.
8. M. Fichtner, A. Großmann, and M, Thielscher. Intelligent execution monitoring in dynamic environments, *Fundamenta Informaticae*, 57(2-4):371-392. 2003.
9. M. Gelfond and V. Lifschitz. Classical Negation in Logic Programs and Disjunctive Databases. *New Generation Comput.*, 9(3-4): 365-386, 1991.
10. G. Gottlob. Complexity and Expressive Power of Disjunctive Logic Programming. *in Proc of ILPS'94*, pp. 453-465.
11. E. Giunchiglia, J. Lee, V. Lifschitz, N. McCain, and H. Turner. Nonmonotonic Causal Theories. *Artificial Intelligence*, 153(1-2): 49-104, 2004.
12. L. Iocchi, T. Lukasiewicz, D. Nardi, and R. Rosati. Reasoning about Actions with Sensing under Qualitative and Probabilistic Uncertainty. *in Proc of ECAI'04*, pp. 818-822.
13. N. Leone, G. Pfeifer, W. Faber, F.Calimeri, T.Dell'Armi, T. Eiter, G. Gottlob, G.Ianni, G.Ielpa, C.Koch, S.Perri, and A.Polleres. The dlv system for knowledge representation and reasoning. *in Proc. of JELIA'02*, pp. 537-540.
14. M.L. Littman, J. Goldsmith, and M. Mundhenk. The Computational Complexity of Probabilistic Planning. *JAIR* 9:1-36, 1998.
15. J. Lobo. COPLAS: a COnditional PLannner with Sensing Actions. *FS-98-02*, AAAI, 1998.
16. S.M. Majercik and M.L. Littman. Contingent planning under uncertainty via stochastic satisfiability. *Artificial Intelligence*, 147(1-2):119-162, 2003.
17. I. Niemelä and P. Simons. Smodels: An implementation of the stable model and well-founded semantics for normal LP. *in Proc. of LPNMR'97*, pp. 420-429.
18. J. Rintanen. Expressive Equivalence of Formalisms for Planning with Sensing. *in Proc. of ICAPS'03*, pp. 185-194.
19. J. Rintanen. Constructing conditional plans by a theorem prover. *JAIR*, 10:323-352, 2000.
20. T.C. Son, P.H. Tu, and C. Baral. Planning with Sensing Actions and Incomplete Information Using Logic Programming. *in Proc of LPNMR'04*, pp. 261-274.
21. T.C. Son and C. Baral. Formalizing sensing actions A transition function based approach. *Artificial Intelligence*, 125(1-2):19-91, 2001.
22. M. Thielscher. Programming of Reasoning and Planning Agents with FLUX. *in Proc. of KR'02*.

Adding Semantic Web Services Matching and Discovery Support to the MoviLog Platform

Cristian Mateos   Marco Crasso   Alejandro Zunino   Marcelo Campo

ISISTAN Research Institute - Also CONICET
Facultad de Cs. Exactas, Departamento de Computación y Sistemas, UNICEN
Campus Universitario - Paraje Arroyo Seco - (B7001BBO) - Bs. As., Argentina
email: azunino@exa.unicen.edu.ar

Summary. Semantic Web services are self describing programs that can be searched, understood and used by other programs. Despite the advantages Semantic Web services provide, specially for building agent based systems, there is a need for mechanisms to enable agents to discover Semantic Web services. This paper describes an extension of the MoviLog agent platform for searching Web services taking into account their semantic descriptions. Preliminary experiments showing encouraging results are also reported.

1 Introduction

Once a big repository of Web pages, images and others forms of static data, the Web is evolving into a worldwide network of *Web Services*, paving the way to the so-called Semantic Web [1]. A Web Service [2] is a distributed piece of functionality that can be published, located and accessed through standard Web protocols. The goal of Web services is to achieve automatic interoperability between Web applications by providing them with an infrastructure to use Web-accessible resources.

Several researchers agree that mobile agents will have a fundamental role to materialize this vision [3, 4]. A mobile agent is a computer program which is able to migrate between network sites to perform tasks and interact with resources. Mobile agents have good properties that make them suitable for exploiting the potential of the Web [5]: support for disconnected operations, robustness and scalability.

Despite the advantages mobile agents offer, many challenges remain to glue them with Web services. Most of these challenges are a result of the nature of the Web. From its beginnings the Web has been mainly designed for human use and interpretation. Hence, mobile agents cannot autonomously take advantage of Web resources, thus forcing developers to write hand-coded solutions that are difficult to extend, reuse and maintain. Besides, the inherent complexity of mobile code programming with respect to traditional non-mobile systems, has dwindled the massive adoption of mobile agent technology, limiting its usage to small applications and prototypes.

In this sense, we believe there is a need for a mobile agent development infrastructure that addresses these problems and, at the same time, preserve the key benefits of mobile agents for building distributed applications. To this end, we have developed MoviLog [6], a platform for building Prolog-based mobile agents on the WWW.

Please use the following format when citing this chapter:

Mateos, C., Crasso, M., Zunino, A., Campo, M., 2006, in IFIP International Federation for Information Processing, Volume 217, Artificial Intelligence in Theory and Practice, ed. M. Bramer, (Boston: Springer), pp. 51–60.

MoviLog encourages the usage of mobile agents by supporting a novel mechanism for handling mobility named RMF (Reactive Mobility by Failure). It allows programmers to easily build mobile agents on the Semantic Web without worrying about Web services location or access details. Furthermore, to take into account the semantics of services, we have extended MoviLog with support for semantic matching and discovery of Web services. The extension, called Apollo, enables an automatic interoperation between mobile agents and Web services with little development effort.

This paper is organized as follows. The next section introduces semantic Web services. Sect. 3 presents the MoviLog platform. Sect. 4 describes Apollo. Sect. 5 explains an example. Sect. 6 reports experimental results. Sect. 7 discusses the most relevant related work. Finally, Sect. 8 draws conclusions.

2 Semantic Web Services

Web services are a suitable model to allow systematic interactions of programs across the WWW. To hide the diversity of resources hosted by the WWW, Web services technologies mostly rely on XML, a structured language that extends and formalizes HTML. In this sense, the W3C Consortium has developed SOAP [1], a communication protocol based on XML. Besides, languages for describing Web services have been developed. An example is WSDL[2], an XML-based language for describing services as a set of operations over SOAP messages. From a WSDL document, a program can find out the specific services a Web site provides, and how to use and invoke these services.

UDDI [3] defines mechanisms for searching and publishing Web services. By means of UDDI, Web service providers register information about the services they offer, thus making it available to potential clients. The information managed by UDDI ranges from WSDL files describing services to data for contacting providers.

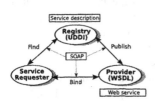

Fig. 1. Web services architecture

Fig. 1 shows the conceptual architecture of Web services. A Web service is defined by a WSDL document describing a set of operations. A provider creates WSDLs for its services and publish them in an UDDI registry. A requester can browse registries to find services matching his needs. Then, the requesters can bind to the provider by invoking any of the operations defined by the WSDLs.

The weakest point of the architecture shown above is that it does not consider the semantics of services. To achieve an automatic interaction between agents and Web services, each service must be described in a nonambiguous and computer-understandable way. In this sense, some languages for Web services metadata annotation have emerged, such as RDF [4] and OWL [7], whose goal is to provide a formal

---

[1] SOAP (Simple Object Access Protocol): http://www.w3.org/TR/soap/

[2] WSDL (Web Service Description Language): http://www.w3.org/TR/wsdl

[3] UDDI (Universal Description, Discovery and Integration): http://www.uddi.org

[4] RDF (Resource Description Framework): http://www.w3.org/RDF/

model for describing the concepts involved in services. In this way, agents can *understand* and reason about the functionality a Web service performs, thus enabling the automatization of Web applications. Finally, a step towards the creation of a standard ontology of services is OWL-S [8]. The next section introduces MoviLog.

3 MoviLog

MoviLog [6] is a platform for programming mobile agents. The execution units of MoviLog are Prolog-based mobile agents named *Brainlets*. MoviLog uses strong mobility, where Brainlets execution state is transferred transparently on migration. Besides providing basic mobility primitives, the most interesting aspect of MoviLog is the notion of Reactive Mobility by Failure (RMF), a novel mobility model that reduces the effort for developing mobile agents by automating decisions such as when or where to migrate upon a *failure*. A failure is defined as the impossibility of an executing agent to obtain some required resource at the current site.

Roughly, each Brainlet possess Prolog code that is organized in two sections: *predicates* and *protocols*. The first section defines the agent behavior and data. The second section declares rules that are used by RMF for managing mobility. RMF states that when a predicate declared in the protocols section of an agent fails, MoviLog moves the Brainlet along with its execution state to another site that contains definitions for the predicate. Indeed, not all failures trigger mobility, but only failures caused by predicates declared in the protocols section. The idea is that normal predicates are evaluated with the regular Prolog semantics, but predicates for which a protocol exists are treated by RMF so that their failure may cause migration. The next example presents a simple Brainlet whose goal is to solve an SQL query given by a user on a certain database:

```
PROTOCOLS
   protocol(dataBase, [name(X), user(U), passwd(P)]).
CLAUSES
   doQuery(DBName, Query, Res):-
      dataBase([name(DBName), user('default'), passwd('')], Conn),
      doQuery(Conn, Query, Res), closeConnection(Conn).
   ?-sqlQuery(DBName, Query, Res):- doQuery(DBName, Query, Res).
```

PROTOCOLS section declares a protocol stating that the evaluation of *database(...)* predicate must be handled by RMF. In other words, the RMF mechanism will act whenever an attempt of connecting to the given database with the supplied username and password fails at the current site. As a result, RMF will transfer the agent to a site containing a database named *DBName*. After connecting to the database, the Brainlet will execute the query, and then return to its origin. Note that the protocol does not specify any particular value of the properties of the requested connection, which means that all unsuccessful attempts to access locally *any* database with *any* username-password combination will trigger reactive mobility.

Despite the advantages RMF has shown, it is not adequate for developing Web-enabled applications because it lacks support for interacting with Web resources. To overcome this limitation, RMF and its runtime support have been adapted to provide a tight integration with Web Services [9]. Also, to take advantage of services semantics, an infrastructure for managing and reasoning about Web services metadata named Apollo has been built. The rest of the paper focuses on Apollo.

4 Semantic Matching in MoviLog

Semantic matching allows agents to take advantage of ontologies by using inference capabilities. An ontology represents the meaning of terms in vocabularies and the relationships between these terms [1]. Reasoners are often used to infer knowledge from ontologies. We have developed a Prolog-based reasoner as a set of rules and facts for describing and manipulating ontologies. In addition, the reasoner includes matchmaking rules to determine semantic similarity between any pair of concepts.

4.1 Representing ontologies in Prolog

We have developed a reasoner on top of the OWL-Lite language [7]. Unfortunately, OWL-Lite only supports classification hierarchy and simple constraints, thus offering less expressiveness than other languages belonging to the OWL family. However, OWL-Lite ensures inference completeness and decidability.

Table 1. OWL to Prolog correspondence

OWL-Lite	Prolog	Description
Class	class(X)	X is a class.
rdfs:subClassOf	subClassOf(X,Y)	X is a subclass of class Y.
rdf:Property	property(X)	X is a property.
rdfs:subPropertyOf	subPropertyOf(X,Y)	X is a subproperty of property Y.
Individual	individualOf(X,Y).	X is an instance of class Y.
inverseOf	inverseOf(X,Y)	X is inverse to property Y.
equivalentProperty	equivalentProperty(X,Y)	X is equivalent to property Y.
equivalentClass	equivalentClass(X,Y)	X is equivalent to class Y.
Properties	triple(X,Y,Z).	X is related to Z by property Y.

Interestingly, OWL-Lite can be translated to first order logic [10]. Table 1 shows the Prolog counterpart for some of the OWL-Lite sentences supported by our reasoner. OWL-Lite classes and properties are represented as simple facts; relationships are expressed as RDF triples. An RDF triple is a structure with the form *triple(subject, property, object)* which indicates that *subject* is related by *property* to *object* value. OWL-Lite features such as cardinality, range and domain constraints over properties are represented as triples. For example, *triple(author, range, person)* states that property *author* must be an instance of the class *person*. In addition, equality, inequality and transitive sentences of OWL-Lite may indirectly relate a concept to another. Our reasoner defines the following set of rules for dealing with these relationships:

```
triple(X,E,Y):- equivalentProperty(P,E), triple(X,P,Y).
triple(Y,O,X):- inverseOf(P,O), triple(X,P,Y).
triple(X,T,Z):- transitive(T), triple(X,T,Y), triple(Y,T,Z).
```

The first rule states that X is related to Y by property E, if E is equivalent to P and X is related to Y by P. For example, if *author* and *writer* were equivalent properties, then *triple(article, writer, person)* holds. The second rule states that Y is related to X by property O whenever *inverseOf(P,O)* is true and X is related to Y by P. For example, if *hasPublication* and *author* were inverse properties, then *triple(person, hasPublication, article)* holds. The last rule handles transitive relationships between concepts: if *John* is *Paul*'s *advisor*, and *Paul* is *George*'s *advisor*, then *John* is *George*'s *advisor*.

Fig. 2 shows an ontology for documents. It defines that a *thesis* and an *article* are *documents*, both having one or more authors. A *thesis* has an *advisor*. Both *author* and *advisor* are properties with range *person*. A document has a title, a language and some *sections*. Finally, a section has a

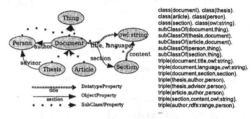

Fig. 2. An ontology for generic documents

content. In the rules two new concepts appear: *Thing* and *owl:string*. Thing is the parent class of all OWL classes. Also, OWL includes some built-in datatypes.

4.2 Matching concepts

Ontologies can be used to describe data and services in a machine-understandable way. Automated data migration systems use ontologies to semantically describe their data structures. A process may then migrate a record from a source database to a sufficiently similar record in a target database. In automated Web services discovery systems, agents usually try to locate a sufficiently similar service to accomplish their current goal. Indeed, the problem to define what "sufficiently similar" means.

The degree of match between two concepts depends on their distance in a *taxonomy tree*. A taxonomy may refer to either a hierarchical classification of things or the principles underlying the classification. Almost anything can be classified according to some taxonomic scheme. Mathematically, a taxonomy is a tree-like structure that categorizes a given set of objects. We have defined four degrees of matching according to [11]. The rational to compute the similarity between two concepts X and Y is:

- **exact** if X and Y are individuals belonging to the same or equivalent classes, we label similarity as **exact**.
- **subsumes** if X is a subclass of Y we label similarity as **subsumes**.
- **plug-in** if Y is a subclass of X we label similarity as **plug-in**.
- **fail** occurs when none of the previous labels could be stated.

We have enhanced this scheme by considering the distance between any pair of concepts in a taxonomy tree (see Fig. 3). From the diagram, it can be clearly stated that *c2* is more similar to *b1* than *a1*: their similarity has been labeled as **plug-in**, but *c2* is hierarchically closer to *b1* than *a1*.

The matchmaking algorithm consists of a set of Prolog rules for calculating the distance between concepts within a taxonomy. The rule *match(C0, C1, Label, Dist)* returns the distance between *C0* and *C1* under *Label*. For example, the rule for equivalent classes is:

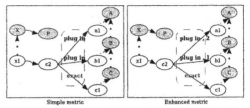

Fig. 3. Enhanced degree of match

```
match(X,Y,exact,0):- equivalentClass(X,Y).
```

The distance between two concepts is defined recursively as:

```
isSubClassOf(X,Y,1):- subClassOf(X,Y).
isSubClassOf(X,Y,N):- subClassOf(X,Z), isSubClassOf(Z,Y,T), N is T+1.
```

Applying the previous rules with X=article produces: *isSubClassOf(article,document,1)* and *isSubClassOf(article,thing,2)*. Matching rules for subsumes and plug-in labels use *isSubClassOf(X,Y,Z)* to compute distance as shown below:

```
match(X,Y,subsumes,N):- isSubClassOf(X,Y,N).
match(X,Y,plugin ,N):- isSubClassOf(Y,X,N).
```

For space reasons, matchmaking support for properties is omitted. Nevertheless, the scheme previously discussed applies when computing distance between properties.

4.3 Semantic Web Services Discovery

In order to perform a semantic search of a Web service instead of a less effective keyword based search, an agent needs computer processable descriptions of services. Ontologies can be used for representing such descriptions. In this sense, OWL-S [8] aims at creating a standard service ontology. OWL-S consist of a set of predefined classes and properties for

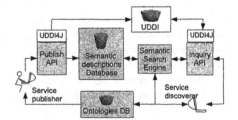

Fig. 4. The Apollo System

representing services. However, OWL-S is intended to describe services and how they must be invoked, but not how to semantically locate them. We combined OWL-S descriptions with UDDI registries to build a semantic Web services discovery system called Apollo. Fig. 4 shows its architecture.

Apollo allows a Web service publisher to annotate services by using concepts from a shared OWL-S ontology database. Apollo is based on an OWL-S subset named Service Profile, which offers support for semantic description of services functionality, arguments, preconditions and effects. In this way, a publisher can describe services and its parameters in terms of concepts from the shared database. WSDL documents are stored in UDDI nodes by using UDDI4J[5]. Finally, each WSDL document and its concepts are associated through the *Semantic Descriptions Database*.

A search request contains a concept describing the desired service functionality, and two sets of concepts for in/out parameters. To perform a more effective search, service requests are forwarded both to UDDI registries and to the Semantic Search Engine. Data resulting from an UDDI search are transformed to concepts from the *Ontology Database* by a component that extends the UDDI Inquiry API.

The main component of the *Semantic Search Engine* is the semantic reasoner. It uses a matchmaking scheme and a simple algorithm for sorting the results of a service search according to the degree of match. The algorithm first tries to contact a Web service that semantically matches the requested conceptual output. If there are more than one Web service with the same degree of match for their output, the algorithm examines inputs to check that the requester is able to invoke the service. The pseudo code for the Web service rating algorithm is:

```
exact = 2; subsumes = 1; plug_in= 0;
MatchResult compare(MatchResult mr0, MatchResult mr1) {
    if (mr0.output.label > mr1.output.label) return mr0;
    else if (mr0.output.label < mr1.output.label) return mr1;
    else { if (mr0.output.distance < mr1.output.distance) return mr0;
        else if (mr0.output.distance > mr1.output.distance) return mr1;
    }
    /* Outputs match... Now compare input parameters. */
}
```

5 A sample scenario

Suppose we are deploying a network composed of sites that accepts Brainlets for execution. Some of these sites offers Web services for translating different types of documents (articles, forms, theses, etc.) to a target language. Every time a client wishes to translate a document, an agent is asked to find the service that best adapts to the kind of document being processed. In order to add semantics features to the model, all sites publish and search for Web services by using Apollo, and services are annotated with concepts from the ontology presented in Sect. 4.1 (see Fig. 2).

We assume the existence of different instances of Web services for handling the translation of a specific type of document. For example, translating a plain document may differ from translating a thesis, because a smarter translation can be done in this latter case: a ser-

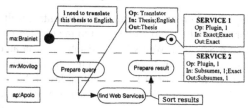

Fig. 5. A Brainlet for thesis translation

vice can take advantage of a thesis' keywords to perform a context-aware translation. Nevertheless, note that a thesis could be also translated by a Web service which expects a Document concept as an input argument, since Thesis concept specializes Document according to our ontology.

When a Brainlet gets a new document for translation, it prepares a semantic query. In this case, the agent needs to translate a thesis to English. Fig. 5 shows the activities

---

[5] UDDI for JAVA: http://www-124.ibm.com/developerworks/oss/uddi4j/

performed by each actor involved in the translation process. Before sending the service query, the Brainlet sets the service desired output as a Thesis. Also, the Brainlet sets the target language as english and the source document kind as Thesis, and then the semantic search process begins. Apollo uses semantic matching capabilities to find all existing Translation services. Let us suppose two services are obtained: a service for translating theses (*s1*) and a second service (*s2*) for translating any document.

After finding a proper list of translation Web services, Apollo sorts them according to the degree of match computed between the semantic query and services descriptions, and returns this new list back to the client. In the example, the degree of match for *s1* is greater than for *s2*, because *s1* outputs a Thesis (**exact**) while *s2* was labeled as **subsumes** with distance one.

```
PROTOCOLS
    protocol(webService, [ name(translate), input([thesis,english]), output(thesis) ]).
CLAUSES
    % The Prolog structure representing some thesis
    thesis([ title('A_title'), author('An_author'), language(spanish),
            advisor('An_advisor'), sections([...])}).
    ?-translate(TargetLang, Res):-
        webService([ name(translate), input([thesis,TargetLang]),
            output(thesis) ], WSProxy), thesis(Th), executeService(WSProxy,
            [Th, TargetLang], Res).
```

The previous code shows the implementation of the Brainlet discussed so far. As explained before, when the *webService(...)* predicate is executed, RMF contacts Apollo to find candidate services that semantically match the Brainlet's request. The evaluation of the predicate returns a proxy to the resulting service, which is used to effectively access it. The way the service is actually contacted (i.e. migrate to the service location or remotely invoke it) depends on access policies based on current execution conditions (network load, agent size, etc.) managed by the underlying platform.

6 Experimental results

In this section we report some experimental results. Particularly, we evaluated the performance of Apollo with regard to the number of published Web services. We generated a Semantic Web services database in an automatic fashion and we published it into Apollo. Both Apollo and all test applications were deployed on a Pentium 4 2.26 GHz with 512 MB of RAM, running Java 1.4.2 on Linux.

The Semantic Web services database was created by using two ontologies: a stock management domain and a car selling domain. Each service description was composed of five properties: input, output, category, preconditions and effects. Therefore, its input would be instantiated as a *cs:sportcar* concept, its output as a *cs:quote* concept, and finally its functionality as a *cs:car quoting* concept. Furthermore, another Web service can do the same for a "Sedan" car. In this case, since both *cs:sport* car and *cs:sedan* are *cs:vehicles*, service input would be instantiated as *cs:sedan*. Finally, searches have been simulated by using randomly generated conditions and expected results.

The resulting average response time for 600 random searches were: 2.37 ms (100 services), 12.65 ms (1000 services) and 149.33 ms. (10000 services). From this we can conclude that Apollo performance is good. Note that the overall response time is less than 200 ms for 10000 Web services descriptions.

Fig. 6 shows the relationship between database size and the time for processing 200 different searches. It can be seen that the worst response time is less than 600 ms. Note that the peaks of the curves are caused by the JAVA garbage collector.

7 Related work

Some related approaches are [12, 13, 14]. Most of them describe services by means of ontologies and a discrete scale of semantic similarity based on [11]. One limitation of these approaches is that their matching scheme do not consider the distance between concepts within a taxonomy tree. Hence, similarity related to different specializations of the same concept are wrongfully computed as being equal.

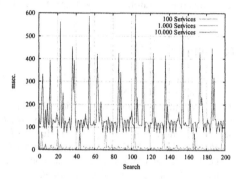

Fig. 6. # of searches vs. response time

The OWL-S Matchmaker [8] is a semantic Web service discovery and publication system. It includes a semantic matching algorithm based on service functionality and data transformation descriptions written in OWL-S. Data transformation descriptions are made in terms of service input and output arguments. Moreover, service search requests are enriched with concepts for describing the list of services that match a required data transformation. The OWL-S Matchmaker does not support taxonomic distance between concepts either.

In [15], a Web service is described by an OWL-S Service Profile instance or an extension of an existing profile. Semantic similarity between two services is computed by comparing their profiles' metadata instead of input/output concepts. A service request must contain the class associated to the *ideal* service profile (i.e. the one preferred by the requester), which is matched against published profiles. The drawback of this approach is its lack of support for finding available service profiles extensions.

Some interesting advances towards the integration of agents and Web services are ConGolog [16] and IG-JADE-PKSLib [17]. However, these approaches present the following problems: bad performance/scalability (IG-JADE-PKSLib), no/limited mobility (IG-JADE-PKSLib, ConGolog). In addition, none of the previous platforms provide support for semantic matching and discovery of Web services.

8 Conclusion and future work

This paper introduced Apollo, an infrastructure for semantic matching and discovery of Web services. Unlike previous work, Apollo defines a more precise semantic matching algorithm, implemented on top of a Prolog reasoner which offers inference capabilities

over OWL-Lite to a semantic Web services search engine. In addition, the integration
of MoviLog with Apollo enables the development of mobile agents that interact with
Web-accessible functionality. This leads to the creation of an environment where sites
can publish their capabilities as Semantic Web services, so that agents can use them.

In the context of Apollo, some issues remain to be solved. First, OWL-Lite needs
to be replaced by a more powerful and expressive language, such as OWL DL or OWL
Full. Second, the Ontologies Database content must be enhanced in order to provide
a framework to describe, publish and discover other types of semantically-annotated
Web resources (pages, blogs or agents), and not just Web services. Thereby an agent
would be able to autonomously interact with Web services or Web content.

References

1. T. Berners-Lee, J. Hendler, and O. Lassila, "The semantic Web," *Scientific American*,
   vol. 284, pp. 34–43, May 2001.
2. S. J. Vaughan-Nichols, "Web services: Beyond the hype," *Computer*, vol. 35, Feb. 2002.
3. J. Hendler, "Agents and the semantic web," *IEEE Intelligent Systems*, vol. 16, Mar. 2001.
4. M. N. Huhns, "Software agents: The future of Web services," in *Agent Technology Work-shops 2002*, vol. 2592 of *Lecture Notes in Artificial Intelligence*, pp. 1–18, 2003.
5. D. B. Lange and M. Oshima, "Seven good reasons for mobile agents," *Communications of the ACM*, vol. 42, pp. 88–89, Mar. 1999.
6. A. Zunino, C. Mateos, and M. Campo, "Reactive mobility by failure: When fail means move," *Information Systems Frontiers*, vol. 7, no. 2, pp. 141–154, 2005. ISSN 1387-3326.
7. G. Antoniou and F. van Harmelen, "Web Ontology Language: OWL," in *Handbook on Ontologies in Information Systems* (S. Staab and R. Studer, eds.), Springer-Verlag, 2003.
8. M. Paolucci and K. Sycara, "Autonomous semantic Web services," *IEEE Internet Computing*, vol. 7, no. 5, pp. 34–41, 2003.
9. C. Mateos, A. Zunino, and M. Campo, "Integrating intelligent mobile agents with Web services," *International Journal of Web Services Research*, vol. 2, no. 2, pp. 85–103, 2005.
10. J. de Bruijn, A. Polleres, and D. Fensel, "Deliverable D20v0.1 OWL Lite, WSML Working Draft." http://www.wsmo.org/2004/d20/v0.1/, June 2004.
11. M. Paolucci, T. Kawamura, T. Payne, and K. Sycara, "Semantic matching of Web services capabilities," in *First International Semantic Web Conference*, vol. 2342, Springer, 2002.
12. K. Sivashanmugam, K. Verma, A. P. Sheth, and J. A. Miller, "Adding semantics to Web services standards," in *IEEE International Conference on Web Services*, June 2003.
13. I. Horrocks and P. F. Patel-Schneider, "A proposal for an owl rules language," in *The 13th international conference on World Wide Web*, pp. 723–731, ACM Press, Jan. 01 2004.
14. L. C. Chiat, L. Huang, and J. Xie, "Matchmaking for semantic Web services," in *IEEE International Conference on Services Computing (SCC'04)*, pp. 455–458, IEEE, 2004.
15. L. Li and I. Horrocks, "A software framework for matchmaking based on semantic Web technology," *International Journal of Electronic Commerce*, vol. 8, no. 4, pp. 39–60, 2004.
16. S. A. McIlraith and T. C. Son, "Adapting golog for programming the semantic Web," in *Fifth Symposium on Logical Formalizations of Commonsense Reasoning)*, May 20–22 2001.
17. E. Martínez and Y. Lespérance, "IG-JADE-PKSlib: An Agent-Based Framework for Advanced Web Service Composition and Provisioning," in *Workshop on Web Services and Agent-Based Engineering*, pp. 2–10, July 19–23 2004.

Learning Browsing Patterns
for Context-Aware Recommendation

Daniela Godoy and Analía Amandi

ISISTAN Research Institute, UNICEN University
Campus Universitario, CP 7000, Tandil, Argentina
Also at CONICET, Argentina
{dgodoy,amandi}@exa.unicen.edu.ar

Abstract. The success of personal information agents depends on their capacity to both identify relevant information for users and proactively recommend context-relevant information. In this paper, we propose an approach to enable proactive context-aware recommendation based on the knowledge of both user interests and browsing patterns. The proposed approach analyzes the browsing behavior of users to derive a semantically enhanced context that points out the information which is likely to be relevant for a user according to its current activities.

1 Introduction

The main goal of personal information agents is to present relevant information to users based on the knowledge of their interests. In order to enable the adaptation and personalization of information delivered to users, personal agents learn and represent long-term interests into user profiles. Thus, user profiling addresses the issue of modeling interests to determine the relevance of a new, previously unseen piece of information.

In addition to merely choosing the right information, personal agents should also be aware of the user context in order to provide information in the time and in the place it is more relevant to users. User profiles are frequently seen as a way to disambiguate search topics. Even though this use of profiles supports interactive context-aware information retrieval in which relevant documents are gathered upon a direct user request, because of the lack of knowledge about the active goals, it fails at supporting proactive context-aware retrieval in which relevant documents are presented to users according to their activities [3].

In order to enable proactive context-aware information retrieval and recommendation, user behavior patterns as regards interests have to be explicitly modeled into profiles. The extraction of such patterns is fostered by semantically enriched profiles which provide a hierarchical organized view of the concepts a user is interested in. Either ontology-based profiling [8] or conceptual clustering [7] allow agents to obtain these hierarchies starting from examples.

In this paper, we present an approach to augment a hierarchical representation of user interests obtained by conceptual clustering with user behavior patterns extracted from observing the browsing activity. This enables proactive

Please use the following format when citing this chapter:

Godoy, D., Amandi, A., 2006, in IFIP International Federation for Information Processing, Volume 217, Artificial Intelligence in Theory and Practice, ed. M. Bramer, (Boston: Springer), pp. 61–70.

and adaptable behavior of personal agents which become able to predict and
anticipate user information needs. Section 2 describes this approach. Experimental results are summarized in Section 3. Section 4 compares this work with
related ones. Finally, concluding remarks are stated in Section 5.

2 Learning and Using Browsing Patterns

The browsing behavior of users is an important resource for inferring contextual
information. It can be seen as a sequence of activities that are related to one
another not only through evolving information interests that can be described at
conceptual level, but also through proximity in time. By activity it is understood
a page visit which takes place during the course of browsing, while groups of
these activities can be referred to as sessions.

Information agents can take advantage of the knowledge gained from observing user browsing in conjunction with long-term user interests to retrieve
context-relevant information. If an agent detects the user is browsing through
certain interest categories, it can anticipate the categories in the same session
the user is likely to be interested in. The goal of activity-awareness is, therefore,
to proactively retrieve Web pages matching the user interests and compute a
set of recommendations for the current or active user session.

To accomplish this goal, browsing patterns referring to categories in the user
profile that are usually accessed together serve as the basis for recommendation and are mined starting from observation of frequent associations among
browsing activities. For extracting navigational patterns, the existence of a conceptual hierarchy constituting the user profile is assumed, so that it can be used
to characterize Web pages, i.e. to describe pages in terms of interest categories.

A conceptual clustering algorithm that carries out incremental, unsupervised concept learning over Web documents was used in this work to obtain
such hierarchical descriptions of user interests. However, other approaches can
be applied within this framework. Hierarchies of concepts produced by this algorithm, named *WebDCC* [7], are classification trees in which internal nodes
represent concepts and leaf nodes represent clusters of examples.

In user profiles, browsing habits are represented by association of the form
$A \Rightarrow B$, where A and B are groups of categories and the association indicates
that, if the user current activities include visiting pages about the categories in
A, the next activities are likely to include visiting pages about B.

2.1 Client-Side Sessionization

A browsing session is a set of page references that takes place during one logical
period, e.g. the sequence of page accesses that takes place from a log in to a log
out of the browser. By identifying the session boundaries, it is ensured that the
information collected from one session is within the same context, which provides a good foundation for inferring and applying context in recommendation.

In contrast to Web usage mining, which focuses on extracting patterns of
multiple users within server logs, a more accurate and complete picture of a
user Web activity can be obtained from client side data. User actions can be

recorded in an activity log by applications monitoring Web browsers. Thus, the content of Web pages, the access time, the time spent on each page and other information is available for analysis. Furthermore, actions such as opening or closing the browser can be used to start and finish browsing sessions.

From client-side observation, it is possible to reliably recognize sessions in the user activity log to evaluate the user interests as well as to understand user frequent browsing patterns. A session S_j is a list of pages a user accessed to ordered by time-stamp as follows:

$$S_j = \{(p_1, time_1), (p_2, time_2), \ldots, (p_n, time_n)\}$$

where $time_i$ is the time the user accessed the page p_i such that $time_i \leq time_j, \forall i \leq j$. Then, the user browsing activities are partitioned into a set of sessions $S = \{S_1, S_2, \ldots, S_k\}$ containing individual page references.

The process of segmenting the activity of a user into sessions is performed using a time-oriented heuristic in which a time-out establishes a period of inactivity that is interpreted as a signal that the session has ended. If the user did not request any page for a period longer than max_time (30 min. is used as default time-out) subsequent requests are considered to be in another session. In addition, the active session is finished when the browser is closed and a new session is started when the browser is re-opened.

2.2 Transaction Identification

The notion of session can be further abstracted by selecting a subset of pages that are significant or relevant for analysis. Each semantically meaningful subset of pages belonging to a user session is referred to as a transaction. Transaction identification assumes that user sessions have already been identified. Hence, the input to this process consists in the page references for a given user session. In Web usage mining there is no convenient method of clustering page references into transactions smaller than an entire user session [6].

To identify semantically meaningful transactions, content pages are considered as those belonging to one or more categories in the profile, unlike content pages in other approaches which are identified simply based on the time spent on a page or on backtracking during the user navigation [5]. Pages not belonging to any category in the profile are considered irrelevant for usage mining since they do no entail information about the user habits regarding interests. Then, a content-only transaction is formed by all the content pages in a session. Figure 1 illustrates the formation of these transactions.

The resulting transactions are further divided using the time window approach, which divides each transaction into time intervals no longer than a specified threshold. This approach assumes that meaningful transactions have an overall average length associated with them. For a large enough specified time window, each transaction will contain an entire user session. If W is the length of the time window, then two pages p_i and p_j are in the same session if:

$$p_i.time - p_j.time \leq W$$

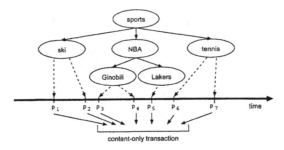

Fig. 1. Example of a content-only transaction

In this way, the set of pages $P = \{p_1, p_2, \ldots, p_n\}$, each with its associated $time_i$, appearing in the set of sessions S are partitioned into a set of m user transactions $T = \{t_1, t_2, \ldots, t_m\}$ where each $t_i \in T$ is a subset of P. The problem of mining association rules is defined over these collection of subsets from the item space where an item refers to an individual page reference.

To incorporate the knowledge of the user interests in pattern extraction, further processing of user activities is needed to map individual Web page references to one or more user interest categories. The enriched version of transactions leads to set of rules that includes categories. Thus, recommendations can be broaden to include any Web page belonging to the involved categories. To integrate content and usage data, each page p_i in a transaction t_j is considered to have an associated set of categories it belongs to, denoted $C_i = \{c_1, c_2, \ldots, c_p\}$, where C_i is extensionally defined by all the categories c_j in the path from the root of the hierarchy to the leaf cluster in which the page p_i was classified into.

If only the cluster a page belongs to is used to describe sessions, the discovered association rules will relate clusters but not categories. Instead, the inclusion of the ancestors in the path from the cluster the page was classified into until the root, makes it possible to find rules at different levels. The result of replacing the elements of the transactions in T by categories in the user profile is a set of transactions $T' = \{t'_1, t'_2, \ldots, t'_m\}$ where each $t'_i \in T'$ is a subset of C. The algorithm for transaction identification can be outlined as follows:

1. For each session $S_i \in S$, create a new transaction t_i in T
2. For each page $p_j \in S_i$, find the set C_j by classifying the page into the current user interest hierarchy
3. If $C_j \neq \emptyset$, add p_j to the transaction t_i since the page is a content page
4. Repeat steps 2 and 3 until all page references have been either added to the transaction or discarded
5. Repeat steps 1 to 4 until all sessions in S have been processed
6. Use the time window approach to partition each $t_i \in T$ into transactions smaller than W
7. For each resulting transaction $t_i \in T$, create the transaction t'_i in T' replacing each page $p_j \in t_i$ by the corresponding C_j

2.3 Mining Association Rules

The association rule mining problem was stated in [1]. Let $\mathcal{I} = \{I_1, I_2, \ldots, I_m\}$ be a set of literals called items, a subset $X \subseteq \mathcal{I}$ is called an itemset and a k-itemset is an itemset that contains k items. Let $\mathcal{D}$ be a database of transactions, where each transaction T is a set of items such that $T \subseteq \mathcal{I}$. Each itemset has a certain statistical significance called support such that an itemset has *support s* in the transaction set $\mathcal{D}$ if $s\%$ of the transactions in $\mathcal{D}$ contain X. An association rule is an implication of the form $X \Rightarrow Y$, where $X \subset \mathcal{I}$, $Y \subset \mathcal{I}$, and $X \cap Y = \emptyset$. The rule $X \Rightarrow Y$ holds in the transaction set $\mathcal{D}$ with *confidence c* if $c\%$ of the transactions in $\mathcal{D}$ that contain X also contain Y.

The problem of mining association rules in $\mathcal{D}$ consists in finding all rules $X \Rightarrow Y$ that have support greater than a user-specified minimum support, called *minsup*, and confidence, called *minconf*. For each rule, the support threshold describes the minimum percentage of transactions containing all items that appear in the rule, whereas the confidence threshold specifies the minimum probability for the consequent to be true if the antecedent is true.

In a hierarchical description of user interests, associations or access patterns may contain interesting regularities at different levels of abstraction including categories or clusters that are related according to the user habits. The problem of mining multiple-level or generalized association rules assumes a hierarchy or taxonomy $\mathcal{T}$ on the items instead of a flat itemset $\mathcal{I}$. A generalized association rule is an implication of the form $X \Rightarrow Y$, where $X \subset \mathcal{I}$, $Y \subset \mathcal{I}$, $X \cap Y = \emptyset$ and no item in Y is an ancestor of any item in X as this would be a trivially valid association. The rule $X \Rightarrow Y$ holds in the transaction set $\mathcal{D}$ with confidence c and support s if $c\%$ of the transactions in $\mathcal{D}$ that support X also support Y and $s\%$ of transactions in $\mathcal{D}$ support $X \cup Y$. These rules are called generalized association rules because both X and Y can contain items from any level of the taxonomy $\mathcal{T}$.

If the problem of determining if a transaction T support an itemset X is considered, for each item $x \in X$ it is necessary to check whether x or some descendant of x is present in the transaction. To simplify this task, all the ancestors of each item in T are added to this transaction to form an extended transaction T'. A straightforward method to find generalized association rules is to run any association rule algorithm on the extended transactions since T supports X if and only if T' is a superset of X. For empirical evaluation of the proposed approach, we used the *Apriori* algorithm over the set of extended transactions obtained as pages are classified in the concept hierarchy.

2.4 Activity-Based Recommendation

From user browsing sessions, patterns representing the user navigational behavior are extracted in the form of association rules, which relate sets of categories or concepts in the user profile. Information agents, therefore, become able to proactively retrieve relevant information to generate recommendations for a user by matching the current user activity against the discovered patterns.

To gather a set of possible recommendations, an agent can perform a Web search to retrieve pages belonging to the concepts the user is interested in. For example, the agent can retrieve pages from some fixed sites (e.g. a newspaper Web site) or find the nearest neighbors of a page in the profile used as query.

A fixed-size sliding window is used over the active session to capture the current user activity. For a sliding window of size n, the active session ensures that only the last n visited pages influence recommendation. The use of a window is important in discovering context since most users go back and forth while browsing to find the desired information so that earlier portions of the browsing history may refer to no longer valid information needs.

In the recommendation phase, the active session is compared with the discovered rules. If the active session matches the antecedent of an association rule, recommendations are finding by retrieving Web pages belonging to the categories in the rule consequent.

3 Experimental Results

To evaluate the activity-base recommendation approach, a client-side log of visited Web pages in a number of topics a user is interested in and the location of the pages on the user interest hierarchy are needed. Unfortunately, available datasets belong to individual Web sites and record the accesses of several users.

In the absence of client-side data, the content and logs of the *Music Machines*[1] Web site were used for experimentation. In these logs users are anonymized with respect to originating machine, i.e. all hits from one machine on a particular day have the same label. Thus, the browsing behavior of individual users can be interpreted respecting their interest categories within the site. *Music Machines* contains 4582 distinct pages about various kind of electronic musical equipment grouped by manufacturers.

Each access log consists of the user label, request method, accessed URL, data transmission protocol, access time and browser used to access the site. The server logs were filtered to remove those entries that are irrelevant for analysis and those referring to pages that do not exist in the available site copy.

From all users who entered the site after 20/8/98, when the copy of the site was made, the five users having the longest sessions were selected. Then, the experimental procedure simulates users browsing the *Music Machines* site and obtaining recommendations. For each user a profile was built based on both the content of Web pages from the site and the user behavior regarding interest categories. Experiments for each user proceed as follows:

1. Identify the user entries in the log files
2. Extract the URLs of the visited pages and run *WebDCC* algorithm over these pages using the available copy of the *Music Machines* site
3. Identify user sessions in the logs using *max_time*=30 minutes
4. Partition user sessions into transactions and mapping Web page references to categories in the profile

---

[1] http://www.cs.washington.edu/ai/adaptive-data/

ID	duration	# entries	# filtered entries	# sessions	# pages	# clusters	# filtered clusters
1	11:55:29	31404	938	9	1669	115	100
2	23:19:57	3639	2511	23	2427	229	145
3	13:18:47	3511	589	11	1663	129	91
4	21:28:38	3347	1087	10	1782	176	97
5	12:22:52	2862	2114	14	2851	312	176

Table 1. Summary of user data and experimental results

5. Divide the resulting set of transactions into a training (approx. 70%) and a testing set (approx. 30%) for experiments
6. Use the training set to mine association rules regarding categories
7. Use the testing set to simulate active session windows and recommend pages
8. Evaluate the recommendations in terms of precision and coverage

To assess quantitative values of recommendation performance, we used the adaptations of precision and coverage measures proposed by [9]. Given a transaction t and a set of recommendations R produced using a window w such that $w \subseteq t$, the precision and coverage of R with respect to t are defined as:

$$precision(R,t) = \frac{|R \cap (t-w)|}{|R|} \qquad coverage(R,t) = \frac{|R \cap (t-w)|}{|t-w|}$$

Thus, precision measures the degree to which recommendations are accurate for the active session and coverage measures its ability to recommend all the items that are likely to be visited by the user in the active session.

For a given transaction t in the testing set and an active session window of size n, we randomly chose $|t| - n + 1$ groups of items, each having size n, from the transaction as the surrogate active session windows. For each of these active sessions, a set of recommendations are produced based on the extracted rules. The recommendations are compared to the remaining items in the transactions, i.e. $t - w$, to compute performance measures. For each measure, the final score of the transaction t is the average over all of the $|t| - n + 1$ surrogate active sessions associated with this transaction.

The entries remaining after cleaning the logs were used to extract the documents each user accessed in the site. Table 1 summarizes the number of entries, sessions and unique pages accessed in the site. *WebDCC* algorithm was run over the documents each user accessed to identify the interest categories. These documents were partitioned into several clusters although no concepts were extracted by the clustering algorithm. This was mainly due to the site content and structure. It contains few pages referred to many manufacturers, so that different clusters are created for each of them and no generalization is possible.

From the total number of clusters resulting from running the algorithm, meaningless clusters containing a single instance were filtered out before association rule mining. Then, the pages in each session were partitioned into

W	# transactions	# items	# rules	# recom.	precision	coverage
3	120.20 ± 92.96	13.85 ± 3.62	247.20 ± 199.11	2.34 ± 2.06	75.79 ± 17.31	6.84 ± 6.85
			15423.00 ± 17533.67	3.87 ± 3.61	68.94 ± 20.90	10.13 ± 8.71
5	101.80 ± 98.05	19.73 ± 4.60	486.40 ± 409.05	4.87 ± 5.24	66.15 ± 21.81	8.67 ± 8.20
			16135.80 ± 15442.15	6.10 ± 5.61	59.73 ± 17.71	10.51 ± 8.49
10	45.60 ± 31.19	32.97 ± 6.41	920.00 ± 567.92	5.84 ± 5.48	63.97 ± 18.36	16.02 ± 13.07
			37223.60 ± 39060.43	7.81 ± 5.35	57.83 ± 13.69	19.34 ± 12.42
15	32.00 ± 20.02	46.73 ± 9.38	1255.60 ± 424.38	9.32 ± 4.04	62.32 ± 15.54	17.11 ± 6.90
			47948.40 ± 8319.91	11.44 ± 2.71	55.96 ± 9.32	17.89 ± 4.08

Table 2. Effect of time window in recommendation

transactions and, in turn, the pages in each transaction were mapped into clusters obtaining a set of content-enhance transactions.

There are several parameters influencing the results of recommendation, including the size of the time window W, the size of the sliding window n, the confidence threshold and the size of the itemsets.

The length of the time window W affects primarily the number of transactions obtained from a given session and, consequently, the number of rules and the quality of recommendations. In the first experiment, we investigated the impact of different values of W on the number of rules and the quality of the resulting recommendations for the five users by testing the values 3, 5, 10 and 15 minutes. In association rule mining, all rules having a support greater than 2% were extracted. For recommendation, we used a fixed active window of size 3 and a minimum confidence of 90%. Table 2 summarizes the average and standard deviation of values obtained for the five users in: number of transactions, items per transaction, extracted rules, recommendations, precision and coverage of recommendations. For each value of W in the table, the the results for rules having 1-itemsets and 2-itemsets are shown.

The higher the value W, the lower the number of transactions and the longer its size in terms of the average number of items. Fewer transactions lead to more rules since they are supported by the data, but the quality of these rules is inferior to the quality of rules extracted when more information is available. Indeed, the precision in recommendation decreases from $W = 3$ to $W = 15$. For further experiments we set $W = 3$ min. since the dropping in precision for the immediately next value $W = 5$ is significant (approx. 9%), but the improvement in coverage is rather small (approx. 2%).

The results of 1-itemsets and 2-itemsets, on the other hand, show the same relationship between precision and coverage. The values of precision diminish when 2-itemsets are considered, increasing the coverage of recommendations. In this case, not only the improvement in coverage can be considered small given the loss in precision, but also the number of rules rises drastically. The on-line analysis of such high number of rules becomes too expensive.

To investigate the effect of window size, the portion of the active window session used to produce recommendations, experiments were performed using

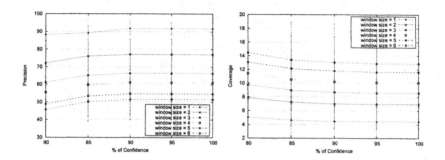

Fig. 2. Impact of window size on precision and coverage of recommendations

window sizes from 1 to 6. Figure 2 shows the impact of window size on precision and coverage of recommendations. In the figures, the results summarize the average and standard deviation of the scores achieved for the five users involved in the experiments varying the confidence threshold.

From both figures, it can be concluded that the smaller the size of the time window, the higher the precision of recommendation and the lower its coverage. Indeed, the best precision was obtained with a window of size one, but the coverage of recommendations was the poorer too. As the size of the window is enlarged, there are more rules matching the pages inside the window, increasing the number of recommendations and, consequently, their coverage.

There is a trade-off between enlarging enough the window size to recommend most of the pages that are relevant to the current activity context but not enlarge it too much to start recommending pages that were relevant to the previous context of the user in the browsing session. However, precision can be sacrificed in this decision for the sake of an increase in coverage since a lower precision means that the agent is recommending pages which are not contextually relevant but are still content relevant to the user interests.

4 Related Work

Efforts in building user profiles representing user interests have been frequently seen as a method of gathering contextual information since the knowledge contained in a profile persists across retrieval sessions and can be automatically added to queries. However, user profiles by themselves have not means to anticipate information needs given the user current activities and, therefore, do not support proactive context-aware recommendation. In our approach, the current activities act as trigger for retrieval of information matching long-term interests.

WordSieve [2] and *Watson* [4] are systems that use context for information seeking. *WordSieve* is an algorithm to build context profiles which distinguish sets of documents that users tend to access in groups. *Watson* observes the use of standard software tools and generates queries to seek context-relevant information. Instead of retrieving documents based solely on words extracted from recently consulted documents, our approach extracts information about how users tend to access documents regarding long-term interests to determine what kind of documents are likely to be interesting in a certain context.

The proposed approach differs from Web usage mining techniques in two aspects. First, server-side usage mining provides information about a specific Web site based on correlations among the pages that multiple users have visited. By contrast, our approach extracts rules from the observation of a single user browsing the Web. Second, most Web usage mining approaches obtain association rules that relate single Web pages. By capturing navigational patterns at conceptual level our approach provides more flexibility in recommendation.

5 Conclusions

The user context is an important aspect to take into account in recommendation which, however, has received little attention in personal agents. Most agents are concerned with estimating the interest of new pieces of information, instead of trying to place the relevant information in the right contexts. In this paper, we have described an approach to consider the activity context during profiling to enable context-aware recommendation. Experimental results showed that the extraction of association rules describing browsing patterns at conceptual level helps to predict part of the interests which are relevant to the user in a session.

References

1. R. Agrawal, T. Imielinski, and A. Swami. Mining association rules between sets of items in large databases. In *Proceedings of the 1993 ACM SIGMOD International Conference on Management of Data*, pages 207–216, 1993.
2. T. Bauer and D. Leake. WordSieve: A method for real-time context extraction. In *Proceedings of the Third International and Interdisciplinary Conference on Modeling and Using Context*, pages 30–44, 2001.
3. P. Brown and G. Jones. Context-aware retrieval: Exploring a new environment for information retrieval and information filtering. *Personal and Ubiquitous Computing*, 5(4):253–263, 2001.
4. J. Budzik, K. Hammond, and L. Birnbaum. Information access in context. *Knowledge based systems*, 14(1-2):37–53, 2001.
5. M-S. Chen, J. S. Park, and P. Yu. Efficient data mining for path traversal patterns. *IEEE Transactions on Knowledge and Data Engineering*, 10(2):209–221, 1998.
6. R. Cooley, B. Mobasher, and J. Srivastava. Grouping web page references into transactions for mining world wide web browsing patterns. In *Proceedings of the IEEE Knowledge and Data Engineering Exchange Workshop*, pages 2–9, 1997.
7. D. Godoy and A. Amandi. Modeling user interests by conceptual clustering. *Information Systems*, 31(4-5):247–265, 2006.
8. S. Middleton, N. Shadbolt, and D. Roure. Ontological user profiling in recommender systems. *ACM Transactions on Information Systems*, 22(1):54–88, 2004.
9. B. Mobasher, H. Dai, T. Luo, and M. Nakagawa. Discovery and evaluation of aggregate usage profiles for Web personalization. *Data Mining and Knowledge Discovery*, 6(1):61–82, 2002.

Applying Collaborative Filtering to Reputation Domain: a model for more precise reputation estimates in case of changing behavior by rated participants

Alexandre Lopes, Ana Cristina Bicharra Garcia

Instituto de Computação - Universidade Federal Fluminense (UFF)

Rua Passo da Pátria, 156 Bloco E Sala 350 - 24.210-240 – Niterói – RJ.

alexcflopes@gmail.com, bicharra@ic.uff.br

Abstract. Automated Collaborative Filtering (CF) techniques have been successfully applied on Recommendation domains. Dellarocas [1] proposes their use on reputation domains to provide more reliable and personalized reputation estimates. Despite being solved by recommendation field researches (e.g. significance weighting [2]), the problem of selecting low-trusted neighborhoods finds new roots in the reputation domain, mostly related to different behavior by the evaluated participants. It can turn evaluators with similar tastes into distant ones, contributing to poor reputation rates. A Reputation Model is proposed to minimize those problems. It uses CF techniques adjusted with the following improvements: 1) information of evaluators taste profiles is added to the user evaluation history; 2) transformations are applied on user evaluation history based on the similarities between the taste profiles of the active user and of the other evaluators to identify more reliable neighborhoods. An experiment is implemented through a simulated electronic marketplace where buyers choose sellers based on reputation estimates generated by the proposed reputation model and by a model that uses traditional CF. The goal is to compare the proposed model performance with the traditional one through comparative analysis of the data that is created. The results are explained at the end of the paper.

1 Introduction

The goal of online reputation reporting systems and models applied in e-commerce systems [1, 3] is to restrain the participation of agents who have a poor-quality service history in electronic marketplaces. These models can combine both direct and indirect [4] information sources to better estimate their participants' reputation. The direct sources contain information on past encounters between the client and the rated

Please use the following format when citing this chapter:

Lopes, A., Garcia, A.C.B., 2006, in IFIP International Federation for Information Processing, Volume 217, Artificial Intelligence in Theory and Practice, ed. M. Bramer, (Boston: Springer), pp. 71–80.

supplier. The indirect one contain information indirectly acquired through other clients' witnesses [1, 3, 5] or through the analysis of their social relationship network, which is kept by the suppliers [4]. Even though reputation models based on direct sources are considered to be the most reliable way of estimating the supplier's reputation, there is a higher amount of available information through indirect sources, which should be used in case there's little probability of any two participants having a history of past encounters [4]. The problem with models based on indirect sources is the possibility that the reputation estimate will not be as reliable as desired, because it is difficult to measure precisely subjective aspects like quality of service. The reputation estimate is based on aggregates that do not reflect the differences in the client's taste or the context of the interaction [1, 3]. If it is poorly calculated, the reputation estimate can cause clients to interact with suppliers who they wouldn't choose to transact with otherwise.

1.1   Automated Collaborative Filtering applied to Reputation Models

For more reliable calculation of reputation estimates, Dellarocas [1], proposes the incorporation of the Automated Collaborative Filtering (CF) technique to the reputation model. The CF has been used in Recommendation and Information Filtering Systems [6]. It identifies similarities between an active user and other users based on the similarities in past ratings on common items, and uses this similarity to generate recommendations about items not yet rated by the active user. The neighbor users are the ones who have higher similarity factor with the active user.

The goal of incorporating the CF to reputation domains is to estimate the reputation of a supplier in a personalized way, calculating it based on the ratings of clients that have similar tastes with those of the active client.

1.2   The "False Good Neighbor" Problem

This problem is described in the Recommendation Systems literature as being a situation in which clients calculated as having greatest similarity with the active client are, in fact, not that similar [2, 7]. It can happen because of coincident ratings and because of a low number of common ratings between the clients. The very work of Herlocker [2] already proposes solutions for this issue, however, there are other factors in the reputation domain that can contribute to situations of false neighborhood, such as changes in the supplier's behavior from one encounter to another and rating manipulation by clients with bad intentions. In this paper we intend to explore the changes in the supplier's behavior. Suppliers who change their behavior from one encounter (and rating) to another may cause deviations in the similarity detection between clients, causing clients with similar preferences not to be considered neighbors, or inversely, causing clients with different preferences to be considered neighbors. It is important to notice that these problems do not happen in conventional Recommendation Systems because the rated items are products and not rational entities (humans or computers). Products don't have behavior, their characteristics and looks are normally maintained after each rating, while a supplier has goals, which influence his actions and behavior [4]. Apart from timely aspects, if two clients disagree on a product's rating, it is safe to say that it's because they have different tastes. In the case of supplier's rating, if they disagree on a rating, there are no guarantees that the suppliers maintain the same behavior with each client.

2   Proposed Model

This paper proposes a way of minimizing this problem adjusting the CF technique to calculate more precisely the similarity between users, considering, besides the ratings they enter, their preferences, which are presented through reputation rating issues (price, quality, etc.), that have been used as base for the rating. The model also aims to be applied on application domains as Electronic Marketplaces and partially decentralized P2P information sharing systems.

2.1   Automated Collaborative Filtering applied to Reputation Models

An example of a matrix of ratings in the reputation domain is presented in table 1.

Table 1. Matrix of ratings in a reputation system

Item rated / Rater	Client 1	Client 2
Supplier X	3.8	3.8
Supplier Y	1.1	3

To minimize the negative effects of a supplier's behavior change on the reliability of the recommendations, we propose a rating history adjustment based on taste similarity between the clients, which general scheme is presented in the following algorithm.

2.2   Proposed model's high level algorithm:

1. The active client chooses one of two operational modes [8]: the Prediction Mode – in which you estimate the reputation value of a supplier with whom to interact; or the Recommendation Mode – in which you generate a list of recommendations sorted by the highest reputation values of the estimated suppliers; in the first case, a premise is that the client can use any mediation resource available to locate suppliers and negotiate with them. In the second case, choosing the supplier is made based on the recommendation list generated.
2. The Reputation Service recovers all common rating history between the active client and other clients (neighbors), creating an Active Client Matrix of Ratings;
3. Before calculating the similarity with each neighbor, and to minimize the problems of changing behavior, the Reputation Service adjusts the Active Client Matrix of Ratings, with each cell being recalculated as described in the "Matrix of Ratings Transformation" section;

4. It is applied the traditional CF algorithm over the transformed matrix, which will generate the chosen supplier's predictive reputation value, or a recommendation list.
5. The client decides if he/she will start a transaction according to the recommendations or predictions generated.
6. At the end of the transaction, the client writes a testimonial on the supplier's reputation. Besides the general reputation, every testimonial must have the reputation values rated for each rating issue and the preferences of the client (more details in the following section).

2.3   Matrix of Ratings Transformation and reputation calculation

Extended Matrix of Ratings

In order for the transformation indicated in step 3 to take place, it is necessary to work with an Extended Matrix of Ratings (table 3) that contemplates, besides the General Reputation Ratings, the client's tastes and the reputation values given by rating issue (contract clause). The client's tastes are represented in the model as "Reputation Preferences", which are data structures inspired in the Behavioural Aspects φ and Ontological Structures defined in the ReGreT [9] model. The conceptual representation of the Extended Matrix of Ratings, as well as of the Reputation Preferences, can be seen in the class diagram, Fig.1, and described below.

Each and every Reputation Rating is associated to a Contract and to the Client's current Reputation Preference. The Reputation Preferences change as time goes by and are used in the supplier's reputation rating task. They are composed of Rating Issues. Each contract clause is related to a Rating Issue that has a weight and a rating formula. The Rating Issues indicate how deviations of the final values in relation to the agreed values influence (negatively or positively) the Behavioural Aspect. In this sense, they have similar function to the Ground Relations defined in the ReGreT model. Such influence must be calculated through a domain-dependent formula that is described in the Expression attribute of the RatingFormula class. The proposed model shares the ReGreT's premise that reputation is a complex concept (Complex Behavioural Aspects) rated through the combination of various simpler rating dimensions (Simple Behavioural Aspects), table 2. Thus, every Reputation Preference is made up of various Rating Issues, which, combined with its weight, would determine the general reputation value.

Table 2. Example of Rating Issues combinated into a Reputation Preference

Reputation Preferences (Complex Behavioural Aspect)	Rating Issue (Simple Behavioural Aspect)	Issue	Weight	Influence
Good-seller	Offers_High_Price	Price	0,6	Negative
	Offers_Good_Quality	Quality	0,4	Positive

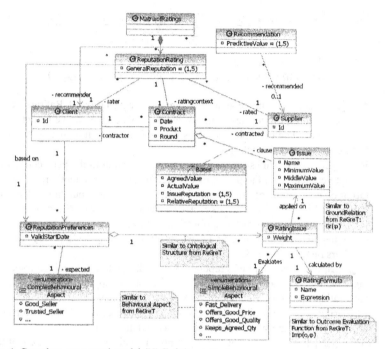

Fig. 1. Complete conceptual model (UML 2.0 notation)

Table 3 is an Extended Matrix of Ratings from table 1. The reputation preferences are in the "weight" line, while the reputation values given by rating issues are in the "Rating" line. The relative rating is the product of the weight of the issue and the reputation rating of the issue.

Table 3. Example of Extended Matrix of Ratings

	Rater	Client 1				Client 2			
Rated	**Issue**	**Quality**	**Price**	**Date**	**General**	**Quality**	**Price**	**Date**	**General**
Supplier X	Weight	0.3	0.2	0.5		0.2	0.3	0.5	
	Rating	5	4	3		4	5	3	
	Relative Rating	1.5	0.8	1.5	3.8	0.8	1.5	1.5	3.8
Supplier Y	Weight	0.3	0.2	0.5		0.3	0.2	0.5	
	Rating	3	1	0		4	4	2	
	Relative Rating	0.9	0.2	0	1.1	1.2	0.8	1	3

2.4   How to perform the adjustments over the Extended Matrix?

The equations (1) (2) and (3) implement the necessary calculations for reputation rating as well as the Matrix of Ratings adjustments shown in step 3 of the proposed model's high level algorithm.

$$(1) \qquad Ar_{neighbor,supplier} = R_{activeclient,supplier} * sf_{activeclient,neighbor,supplier}$$

(2) $R_{activeclient,supplier} = \dfrac{\sum_{issue} (rt_{supplier,issue} * w_{activeclient,issue})}{\sum_{issue} (w_{activeclient,issue})}$

(3) $sf_{activeclient,neighbor,supplier} =$
        $cosine\ (preferences_{activeclient,supplier}\ ,\ preferences_{neighbor,supplier})$

Where,

$Ar_{neighbor,supplier}$ – is the reputation value of each Matrix of Ratings cell, adjusted accordingly to the similarity factor between the Active Client and the Neighbor. The examples in tables 4 and 5 illustrate how the Matrix of Ratings transformation takes place.

$R_{activeclient,supplier}$ - is the supplier's reputation according to the perspective of the active client. It is the pondered average of the active client's reputation rating on every issue of the contract and not in only one reputation value, as it happens in other systems like eBay (www.ebay.com). The calculation formula is independent of the application domain and the quantity of issues of the negotiated contracts, and always result of growing scale values of real numbers between 1 and 5.

$rt_{supplier,issue}$ - is the supplier's reputation accordingly to a determined issue of the contract. The calculation format depends on the application domain and the rating of the Behavioural Aspect (examples described in the "Experiment" section), but it must produce values between 1 and 5 so as to not compromise the supplier's reputation calculation (eq. 2).

$w_{activeclient,issue}$ – is the weight and the importance given by the active client to the issue. The weight is a real number between 0 and 1 given by the client, which may vary as time goes by. The sum of the issue's weights must always total 1.

$sf_{activeclient,neighbor,supplier}$ - represents the similarity factor between the active client and a determined neighbor. It is determined through a cosine function, which calculates the distance between the rating issues' weight vectors, and so, identifying similarities in the reputation preferences applied by the active client and its neighbors when rating a common supplier's reputation.

2.5   Example of the Matrix of Ratings transformation

Considering Client 1 as being the active client, and applying the equations (1) (2) and (3) on a Matrix of Ratings from table 3 (and simplified table 4), we have the results in the Adjusted Matrix from table 5. This Matrix is used as input to step 4 of proposed model's high level algorithm.

Table 4. Active client 1's Matrix of Ratings

Rated	Rater	
	Client 1	Client 2
Supplier X	3.8 (R)	3.8
Supplier Y	1.1 (R)	3

Table 5. Adjusted Matrix of Ratings

Rated	Rater	
	Client 1	Client 2
Supplier X	3.8	3.7 (Ar)
Supplier Y	1.1	1.1 (Ar)

3 Experiment

The experiment's goal is to prove that the proposed model minimizes the effects on the seller's behavior change. It was assembled so it could be possible to compare the performance of the proposed model accordingly to a model based on traditional CF technique, through a system that simulates an e-commerce product marketplace, and that registers the effects of the rated seller's changing behavior. The experiment was inspired in the work conducted in [10], incorporating its organization and way of measuring the performance of the tested models. However, the system's architecture is different because the proposed reputation model is based exclusively on witnesses recovery by collaborative filtering mechanisms.

The simulation is made of 16 buyers and 64 sellers. Half of the buyers receive seller's recommendations based on the proposed CF algorithm, and the other half, based on the traditional algorithm. The transactions occur in 64 rounds, being 51 training rounds and 13 test rounds. The goal of the training rounds is to prepare the reputation database and to prevent the low dispersion of ratings from damaging the tested CF algorithm performance. During these rounds, the reputation module does not provide recommendation (sellers are randomly selected), it is only fed by the buyer's ratings. The test rounds are for monitoring buyer performance and for complementing the comparative analysis between the tested reputation models. Buyers select sellers with the highest reputation prediction value in the recommendation lists generated by the reputation module. In each round, it is possible to occur up to 16 transactions, totaling 1024 transactions per simulation. The maximum number each buyer can close per round is one transaction. Each seller can participate in one or more transactions per round.

The system has modules that simulate buyers and sellers, and a reputation service capable of generating recommendation based in the traditional CF technique and in the proposed technique. The reputation service implements two CF algorithms with user-to-user correlation developed from the algorithm originally proposed by Resnick in [6]. They share common configurations, like similarity calculation between neighbors through Pearson's coefficient, and the usage of a neighborhood selection method by a maximum amount of neighbors (best-n-neighbors) [2, 7] (configured to 30 neighbors).

When starting a transaction, both buyer and seller agree on the price and the quality of the product. The initial agreement is established based on the middle values (30,00 for price and 3 for quality). During the transaction, the seller can change the agreed values with the buyer according to his/her behavior, what will influence in the outcome of the transaction. There are three types of behavior:

Bad– During training rounds, in 60% of the transactions they increase the initially agreed price in ¼ and decrease quality in ¼. In the rest of the transactions, they present a similar behavior than the Good one. The originally defined percentage in the experiment with ReGreT was 75%, however, in this case, it makes more sense to define it as 60% so as to make the behavior changes more frequent. During test rounds, they increase price and decrease quality in 100% of the rounds. The sellers are configured like this to reproduce the false neighborhood situations in which other buyers with similar preferences are not considered neighbors, and vice-versa.

Good - Along all rounds, this type of seller increases the quality of product in ¼, and decreases its price in ¼. They are configured this way so as to benefit buyers who effectively receive the best recommendations, and then, represent a counterpoint relative to the disappointment of a buyer in case he/she receives a bad recommendation.

Neutral– There are no changes on the agreement of the contract in any of the rounds.

When closing a transaction, the buyers rate the seller's reputation, and update their cash. The seller's reputation is rated in a growing scale of real numbers which go from 1 to 5, being calculated as the ratings' pondered average of the issues of the product, as shown in the simplified equation (1):

$$(1)\ R_{b,s} = \frac{(rt_{s,qual} * w_{b,qual}) + (rt_{s,price} * w_{b,price})}{(w_{b,qual} + w_{b,price})}$$

The weight w is chosen randomly to each buyer in the beginning of the simulation, and remains unchanged during the whole simulation.

The Rating Issue formula specific in this domain are:
Quality Issue: (4) $rt_{s,qual} = fv_{s,qual}$ **Price Issue:** (5) $rt_{s,price} = 6 - (fv_{s,price}/10)$

where $fv_{s,price}$ represents the final selling price, and $fv_{s,qual}$ the final quality value.

Each buyer initiates the simulation with 5000,00 in cash, which are updated at the end of each transaction, as shown in equations 6 and 7:
$$(6)\ cb_t = cb_{t-1} - fv_{s,price} + rp$$

where *cb* represents the buyer's cash (cb_t the current round cash and cb_{t-1} the previous round cash) and *rp* the resale price. It was defined that, in test rounds, the buyers should resell the acquired products, with the resale price being determined by the quality of the acquired product: (7) $rp = fv_{s,qual} * 10$

The resale is lucrative every time the buyer transacts with a seller who has good behavior, and prejudicial every time he transacts with a seller who has bad behavior. With this premise, there is a performance comparison between the two tested reputation models. The buyers are separated in two groups: the ones who select sellers based on the given recommendations according to the proposed reputation model (ACF1); and the ones who select their partners based on the recommendations generated by the traditional CF technique (ACF). At the end of each round the average cash value is collected between the buyers by group, and after the closing of the simulation, the distribution of averages by round can be analyzed so as to verify if the proposed method is better than the traditional one and if this difference is statistically significant.

3.1 Performed tests

Several test scenarios were anticipated in the simulation, representing different proportions of buyers according to their behavior. We applied statistical analysis in all of the scenarios (the "t" test, the unilateral, for independent samples, using significance level α of 5%). Each sample refers to one of the buyer's groups, and is formed by the distribution of averages of cash per test round. We tested the following hypothesis:

H_0 – The performance of the proposed reputation model (called ACF1) is like the one in the model that uses the traditional CF technique (called ACF) in scenarios where buyers will change their behavior from one rating to another, noted as:

$$H_0: \mu_{acf1} = \mu_{acf}$$

H_1 - The performance of the proposed recommendation method tends to be better than the originally proposed CF method, in scenarios where the buyers will change their behavior from one rating to another:

$$H_1: \mu_{acf1} > \mu_{acf}$$

The performance of the proposed model (ACF1) was superior to the traditional model (CF) in every test, being statistically significant in 5 of the 7 tested scenarios. The average of buyer's cash who used ACF1 was superior after the execution rounds on every test scenario executed. We present a summary of the results in table 6 and in Fig. 2.

Table 6. Summary of test results

	Scenario I	Scenario II	Scenario III	Scenario IV	Scenario V	Scenario VI	Scenario VII
Summary of results							
Bad	40%	50%	50%	55%	60%	65%	75%
Good	50%	40%	50%	35%	30%	25%	25%
Neutral	10%	10%	0%	10%	10%	10%	0%
Best performance	ACF1	ACF1	ACF1	ACF1	ACF1	ACF1	ACF1
Significance probability	0.005	0.004	0.007	0.008	0.018	0.057	0.139

As the number of Bad buyers increase, the significance probability decreases. Even with the ACF1 model keeping better performance in relation to ACF, the difference between both is no longer statistically significant as the proportion of Bad Buyers is higher or equal to 65%.

Due to space constraints, we show only one of the comparative performance graphics of the test scenarios.

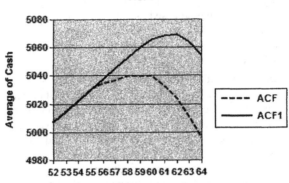

Fig. 2. 40% Bad, 50% Good and 10% Neutral Scenario

4   Conclusions

In this paper, we propose a model so that personalized reputation ratings based on CF can work adequately in case of changing behavior from the rated participants. The good results obtained in described simulations allow us to continue this work, performing field experiments so as to ratify the preliminarily results obtained.

5   References

1.   C. Dellarocas, Immunizing Online Reputation Reporting Systems Against Unfair Ratings and Discriminatory Behavior, in: Proceedings of the Conference on Electronic Commerce, (Minneapolis, Minnesota, 2000), pp. 150-157.

2.   J.L. Herlocker, J.A. Konstan, A. Borchers and J. Riedl, An algorithm framework for performing collaborative filtering, in: Proceedings of the 22nd Annual International ACM SIGIR Conference on Research and Development in Information Retrieval, (1999).

3.   P. Resnick, R. Zeckhauser, E. Friedman and K. Kuwabara, Reputation Systems, *COMMUNICATIONS OF THE ACM*, **43**(12), 45-48 (2000).

4.   J. Sabater and C. Sierra, Reputation and Social Network Analysis in Multi-Agent Systems, in: AAMAS'02, (Bologna, Italy, 2002), pp. 475-482.

5.   T.D. Huynh, N.R. Jennings and N.R. Shadbolt, On Handling Inaccurate Witness Reports, in: 8th Int. Workshop on Trust in Agent Societies, (Utrecht, The Netherlands, 2005), pp. 63-77.

6.   P. Resnick, N. Iacovou, M. Suchak, P. Bergstrom and J. Riedl, GroupLens: An Open Architecture for Collaborative Filtering of Netnews, in: CSCW, (1994), pp. 175-186.

7.   R. Torres, *Personalização na Internet* (Novatec Editora, São Paulo, 2004).

8.   S.T.K. Lam and J. Riedl, Shilling Recommender Systems for Fun and Profit, in: Proceedings of the 13th international conference on World Wide Web, (2004), pp. 393-402.

9.   J. Sabater. Trust and reputation for agent societies *Institut d'Investigació en Intel.ligència Artificial*, Consell Superior d'Investigacions Científiques, Catalonia, Spain. (2003).

10.   J. Sabater, Evaluating the ReGreT system, Applied Artificial Intelligence, **18**(9/10), 797-813 (2004).

Combine Vector Quantization and Support Vector Machine for Imbalanced Datasets

Ting Yu, John Debenham, Tony Jan and Simeon Simoff
Institute for Information and Communication Technologies
Faculty of Information Technology, University of Technology, Sydney,
PO Box 123, Broadway, NSW 2007, Australia
Capital Markets Cooperative Research Centre, Australia
{yuting, debenham, jant, simeon}@it.uts.edu.au

Abstract. In cases of extremely imbalanced dataset with high dimensions, standard machine learning techniques tend to be overwhelmed by the large classes. This paper rebalances skewed datasets by compressing the majority class. This approach combines Vector Quantization and Support Vector Machine and constructs a new approach, VQ-SVM, to rebalance datasets without significant information loss. Some issues, e.g. distortion and support vectors, have been discussed to address the trade-off between the information loss and undersampling. Experiments compare VQ-SVM and standard SVM on some imbalanced datasets with varied imbalance ratios, and results show that the performance of VQ-SVM is superior to SVM, especially in case of extremely imbalanced large datasets.

1 Introduction

The class imbalance problem typically occurs when, in classification problem, there are many more instances of some classes than other. In cases of extremely imbalanced (skewed) dataset with high dimensions, standard classifier tends to be overwhelmed by the large classes and ignore the small ones. Therefore, machine learning becomes an extremely difficult task, and performances of normal machine learning techniques decline dramatically. In practical applications, the ratio of the small to the large classes can be drastic such as 1 to 100, or 1 to 1000 [1] .

The recent Sigkdd explorations published a special issue on learning from imbalanced data sets [1], which summarized some well-known methods for dealing with problems with the imbalanced data: at the data level, undersampling and oversampling; at the algorithms level, one-class learning (cost-sensitive learning) and boasting etc.

Please use the following format when citing this chapter:

Yu, T., Debenham, J., Jan, T., Simoff, S., 2006, in IFIP International Federation for Information Processing, Volume 217, Artificial Intelligence in Theory and Practice, ed. M. Bramer, (Boston: Springer), pp. 81–88.

Random undersampling can potentially remove certain important examples, and random oversampling can lead to overfitting. In addition, oversampling can introduce an additional computational task if the data set is already fairly large but imbalance.

A few researches of combining data compression techniques and machine learning have been done: Jiaqi Wang el at [2] combines K-means clustering and SVM to speed up the real-time learning; Smola el at [3] discussed the combination between VQ and SVM in their book.

At the algorithms level, for SVMs, cost-sensitive learning [5, 6, 7] aims to incorporate into the SVMs the prior knowledge of the risk factors of false positives and false negatives. Gang Wu el at [8] implemented KBA, Kernel Boundary Alignment to imbalanced datasets. Rehan Akbani el at [4] implemented SMOTE, a derivative of Support Vector Machine, to imbalanced datasets and discussed the drawbacks of random undersampling. Being different from the random undersampling, VQ compresses datasets by clustering them instead of simply eliminating instances.

2 Support Vector Machine

Support Vector Machine and other kernel methods were maturated and implemented broadly in 1990s, after Vapnik [9]. Support Vector Machine transforms (approximates) the nonlinear problem within a lower dimension space (input space) into a linear problem within a higher dimension space (feature space). Within this linear feature space, SVM could be treated as a linear learning machine, which finds a maximum margin hyper-plane to separate the given data with some tolerance (slack variables) to the noise. Vapnik-Chervonenkis (VC) dimension restricts the degree of approximations (generalization).

Decision Function of support vector classification (pattern reorganization):

$$f(x) = \text{sgn}(\sum_{i=1}^{m} y_i \alpha_i \langle \Phi(x), \Phi(x_i) \rangle + b) = \text{sgn}(\sum_{i=1}^{m} y_i \alpha_i k(x, x_i) + b) \qquad (1)$$

and the following quadratic program:

$$\max_{\alpha \in R} W(\alpha) = \sum_{i=1}^{m} \alpha_i - \frac{1}{2} \sum_{i,j=1}^{m} \alpha_i \alpha_j y_i y_j k(x_i, x_j) \qquad (2)$$

subject to $\alpha_i \geq 0$ for all $I=1, ..., m$, and $\sum_{i=1}^{m} \alpha_i y_i = 0$

3 Vector Quantization

Vector quantization (VQ) is a lossy data compression method based on the principle of block coding. According to Shannon's theory of data compression, lossy data compression, better known as rate-distortion theory, the decompressed data does not have to be exactly the same as the original data. Instead, some amount of distortion, D, is tolerated. Moreover the lossless compression is no distortion, i.e. D=0.

In 1980, Linde, Buzo, and Gray (LBG) [10] proposed a VQ design algorithm based on a training sequence. The use of a training sequence bypasses the need for multi-dimensional integration required by previous VQ methods. A VQ that is designed using this algorithm are referred to in the literature as an LBG-VQ, which can be stated as follows. Given a vector source with its statistical properties known, given a distortion measure, and given the number of codevectors, find a codebook (the set of all red stars) and a partition (the set of blue lines) which result in the smallest average distortion [11].

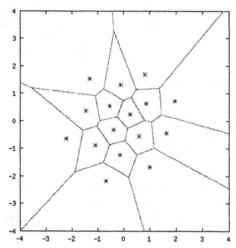

Fig. 1. A simple example of two-dimensional LBG-VQ [11]

Suppose a training sequence consisting of M vectors: $T = \{x_1, x_2, ..., x_M\}$, and N codevectors $C = \{c_1, c_2, ..., c_N\}$, then the whole region is partitioned by the codevectors into a set of sub-regions, so-called "Voronoi Region", $P = \{S_1, S_2, ..., S_N\}$. Vectors within a region S_n are represented by their codevector $Q(x_m) = c_n$ if $x_m \in S_n$, and the average distortion can be given by:

$$D_{ave} = \frac{1}{Mk} \sum_{m=1}^{M} \| x_m - Q(x_m) \|$$

which measures the information loss. Thus, the design problem can be stated as: to find C and P such that D is minimized.

If C ad P are a solution to the above minimization problem, then is must satisfy two criteria: Nearest Neighbour Condition, $S_n = \{x \mid \| x - c_n \|^2 \leq \| x - c_{n'} \|^2 \ \forall n' = 1, 2, ..N\}$, and Centroid Condition:

$$c_n = \frac{\sum_{x_m \in S_n} x_m}{\sum_{x_m \in S_n} 1}, \ n=1, 2, .., N.$$

The LBG VQ design algorithm is an iterative algorithm, which alternatively solves the above two optimality criteria. The algorithm requires an initial codebook. This initial codebook is obtained by the *splitting* method. In this method, an initial codevector is set as the average of the entire training sequence. This codevector is then split into two. The iterative algorithm is run with these two vectors as the initial codebook. The final two codevectors are splitted into four and the process is repeated until the desired number of codevectors is obtained [11].

4. VQ-SVM to Rebalance Dataset

VQ-SVM combines Vector Quantization and Support Vector Machine for dealing with extreme imbalance datasets, in which standard Support Vector Machine losses its accuracy dramatically. Here Vector Quantization could be treated as another way for incorporating domain knowledge into Support Vector Machine. In this case, the domain knowledge is the imbalance ratio and distribution of the majority group. Similar research can be found at authors' other papers [12, 13].

Pseudo-code of the algorithm VQ-SVM:

```
/* Step 1: Set parameters of VQ-SVM */
Float g;  //the kernel parameter g
Int number_of_undersampling;  // the number of code-vectors
```

/* LBG-VQ compresses the majority group and reduces the number of instances down to the given number, and then the new group and the minority group are combined to construct a balanced training dataset */
```
Balanced_Majority = LBGvq(Majority, number_of_undersampling);
New_training_data = combine(Balanced_Majority, Minority);
```

/* SVM based on the new balanced data*/
```
Model = SVM (New_training_data, g);
```

Under-sampling the frequency of the majority class, e.g. random undersampling, has its drawbacks and results in information loss. Support Vector Machine selects a subset of instances along the hyper-plane, so-called support vectors, and used them as the set of x_i within the decision function (1). These support vectors lie within the margin, and their α_is are non-zero, $0 < \alpha_i < C$. That is: as the hyperplane is completely determined by the instances closest to it, the solution should no depend on the other examples [3].

The random undersampling inevitably reduces the number of support vectors, and thus potentially losses information with these removed support vectors. According to the theory of data compression, vector quantization is superior to random undersampling in term of the information loss, but both of them suffer from another risk of information loss within the majority group: Vector Quantization replaces some original SVs by their corresponding codevectors, which become new SVs and push the optimal hyperplane away from the original one trained by imbalanced data (cf. figure 2). Rehan Akbani el at [4] and Gang Wu el at [8] found that in case of imbalanced dataset, SVM always pushes the hyperplane towards minority group, which causes that the learning machine is overwhelmed by the majority group and minority group losses its information completely.

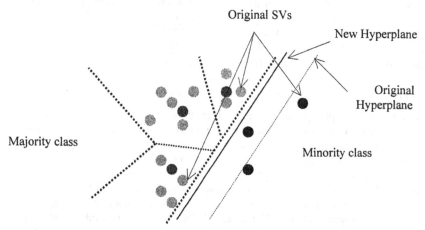

Fig. 2 VQ replaces the observations (yellow points) of majority group by codevectors (red points), the number of which is more equal to the number of observations (grey points) of the minority group. However, the imbalanced maximum margin hyperplane (dashed line) is pushed towards a new position (solid line), which is much closer to the majority group.

Throughout reducing the number of SVs of the majority group, VQ-SVM pulls the biased hyperplane away from the minority group. That is more close to the underlying "real" boundary.

VQ-SVM sacrifices the information held by the majority group to retrieval the information contained by the minority group. This is very important in many real life practices, which focus on the minority group. On the other hand, the compression ratio is tuned by the VQ-SVM to minimize the information loss of majority group. Therefore the optimal model is a trade-off between the compression rate and improved data balance, classification accuracy (i.e. g-means).

5. Experiments

For this evaluation, we used four UCI datasets. Those UCI datasets we experimented with are *abalone* (abalone19), *yeast* (yeast5) *glass* (g7), and letter (letter26). The number in the parentheses indicates the target class we chose. Table 1 shows the characteristics of these six datasets organized according to their negative-positive training-instance ratios. The top dataset (abalone 19) is the most imbalanced (the ratio is about 1:130). The four datasets mostly consist of continuous data instead of categorical data.

Table 1. Four UCI datasets with different compression rates: in the letter (26) dataset, the results of two compression rates demonstrate the effect of "over-compression". Through the initial exploration, the minority class is not linearly separated, and that is said, the minority class randomly scatters within the majority class.

Dataset	Positive Insts	Negative Insts	Imbalance Ratio	Insts after under-sampling
Abalone (19)	32	4145	1:129.54	32
Yeast (5)	47	1437	1:30.5	64
Letter (26)	734	19266	1:26.28	299 (1024) 550(2048)
Glass (7)	29	185	1:6.3	32

Because it is expected that undersampling at high rates generate a trade-off between improved data balance and loss of important information, we examined whether different compression rate could lead to a further enhancement of results.

The machine learning community use two metrics the sensitivity and the specificity, when evaluating the performance of various tests. Sensitivity can be defined as the accuracy on the positive instances: True Positives /(True Positives + False Positives), while specificity can be defined as the accuracy on the negative instances: True Negatives / (True Negatives + False Positives) [4]. Kubat et al [14] suggest the g-means, $g = \sqrt{acc^+ acc^-}$, which combines specificity and sensitivity. In our experiments, the g-means replaces the standard accuracy rate, which losses its functions in imbalanced datasets.

Table 2. Test Result

Dataset	SVM			VQ-SVM		
	Se	Sp	G-means	Se	Sp	G-means
Abalone (19)	0	1	0	1	0.88356	0.93998
Yeast (5)	0	1	0	0.9	0.7561	0.8249
Letter (26)	0.3537	1	0.5948	1	0.1871	0.4326
				0.7007	0.9995	0.8368
Glass (7)	0.6667	1	0.8165	0.6667	1	0.8165

These experiments use LibSVM C code [15] to test the performance of c-SVM with RBF of the gamma values from 0.5 to 2. VQ-SVM consists of the Support Vector Classification by the Spider Machine Learning toolbox [16] and the Vector Quantization by the DCPR Matlab toolbox [17].

The results of experiments show that the g-means of VQ-SVM are rather better or equal to ones of standard SVM. In detail, the specificities of SVM are better than VQ-SVM, but SVM predicts all of instances as negative. Thus the specificities of standard SVM do not make any sense. In the dataset, Letter (26), while VQ-SVM compresses the number of negative instances to an extremely low level, a new imbalanced dataset is produced, and the predictive results of this dataset show that the positive group overwhelms the learning machine.

In case that the imbalance ratio is not high and rather small dataset (e.g. Glass (7) 1:6.3 and 185 instances), the impact of VQ is not significant, e.g. almost equal value of g-means between SVM and VQ-SVM.

6. Conclusion

The results of experiments have proved the theoretic part: SVM is highly sensitive to the balance ratio between the numbers of the vectors of classes, and majority group often overwhelms the learning machine. In case of the large amount of training data with imbalance classes, oversampling increases the number of minority class, but at the same time introduces more computation costs, especially with respect to SVM. Instead of a step of the data pre-process, within the VQ-SVM, VQ optimises directly the predictor performance in case of imbalanced datasets. The previous results show the significant improvement in case of binary classification.

In the further works, more precious controls and methods are necessary to be investigated. Especially the compression to only support vectors instead of all of vectors may enhance the controllability of the algorithm of VQ-SVM and manage the information loss caused by compression.

Acknowledge:

The work has been supported by Capital Markets CRC, and the authors would like to thank Prof Donald Stokes for his support and datasets.

Reference:

1. Chawla, N.V., N. Japkowics, and A. Kolcz, *Editorial: special issue on learning from imbalanced data sets.* SIGKDD Explorations, 2004. 6(1).
2. Wang, J., X. Wu, and C. Zhang, *Support vector machines based on K-means clustering for real-time business intelligence systems.* International Journal of Business Intelligence and Data Mining, 2005. 1(1).
3. Scholkopf, B. and A.J. Smola, *Learning with Kernels, Support Vector Machines, Regularization, Optimization, and Beyond.* 2002: MIT Press.
4. Akbani, R., S. Kwek, and N. Japkowicz. *Applying Support Vector Machines to Imbalanced Datasets.* in *Proceedings of the 15th European Conference on Machine Learning (ECML).* 2004.
5. Veropoulos, K., C. Campbell, and N. Cristianini. *Controlling the Sensitivity of Support Vector Machines.* in *the International Joint Conference on Artificial Intelligence (IJCAI99), Workshop ML3.* 1999. Stockholm, Sweden.
6. Karakoulas, G. and J. Shawe-Taylor. *Optimizing classifiers for imbalanced training sets.* in *Advances in neural information processing systems.* 1998: MIT Press, Cambridge, MA, USA.
7. Lin, Y., Y. Lee, and G. Wahba, *Support Vector Machines for Classification in Nonstandard Situations.* Machine Learning, 2002. 46(1-3): p. 191 - 202.
8. Wu, G. and E.Y. Chang, *KBA: kernel boundary alignment considering imbalanced data distribution.* IEEE Transactions on Knowledge and Data Engineering, 2005. 17(6): p. 786 - 795.
9. Vapnik, V., *The Nature of Statistical Learning Theory.* 1995, New York: Springer-Verlag.
10. Linde, Y., A. Buzo, and R.M. Gray, *An Algorithm for Vector Quantizer Design.* IEEE Transactions on Communications, pp., 1980: p. 702--710.

11. Gersho, A. and R.M. Gray, *Vector Quantization And Signal Compression*. 1992: Kluwer Academic Publishers.
12. Yu, T., T. Jan, J. Debenham, and S. Simoff. *Incorporating Prior Domain Knowledge in Machine Learning: A Review*. in *AISTA 2004: International Conference on Advances in Intelligence Systems - Theory and Applications in cooperation with IEEE Computer Society*. 2004. Luxembourg.
13. Yu, T., T. Jan, J. Debenham, and S. Simoff. *Incorporate Domain Knowledge into Support Vector Machine to Classify Price Impacts of Unexpected News*. in *The 4th Australasian Conference on Data Mining*. 2005. Sydney, Australia.
14. Kubat, M. and S. Matwin. *Addressing the Curse of Imbalanced Data Sets: One-Sided Sampling*. in *Proceedings of the Fourteenth International Conference on Machine Learning*. 1997.
15. Chang, C.-C. and C.-J. Lin, *LIBSVM: a Library for Support Vecter Machine*. 2004, Department of Computer Sicence and Information Engineering, National Taiwan University.
16. Weston, J., A. Elisseeff, G. Baklr, and F. Sinz, *SPIDER: object-orientated machine learning library*. 2005.
17. Jang, J.-S.R., *DCPR MATLAB Toolbox*. 2005.

Ontology Support for Translating Negotiation Primitives

Maricela Bravo[1], Máximo López[1], Azucena Montes[1], René Santaolaya[1],
Raúl Pinto[1], and Joaquín Pérez[1]

[1]Centro Nacional de Investigación y Desarrollo Tecnológico
Interior Internado Palmira S/N, Cuernavaca, Mor. 62490, México
{mari_clau, maximo, amr, rene, rpinto, jperezo}@cenidet.edu.mx,
WWW home page: http://www.cenidet.edu.mx

Abstract. In this paper we present an ontology solution to solve the problem of language heterogeneity among negotiating agents during the exchange of messages over Internet. Traditional negotiation systems have been implemented using different syntax and semantics. Our proposal offers a novel solution incorporating an ontology, which serves as a shared vocabulary of negotiation messages; and a translation module that is executed on the occurrence of a misunderstanding. We implemented a service oriented architecture for executing negotiations and conducted experiments incorporating different negotiation messages. The results of the tests show that the proposed solution improves the interoperability between heterogeneous negotiation agents.

1 Introduction

Negotiation plays a fundamental role in electronic commerce activities, allowing participants to interact and take decisions for mutual benefit. Recently there has been a growing interest in conducting negotiations over Internet, and constructing large-scale agent communities based on emergent Web service architectures. The challenge of integrating and deploying negotiation agents in open and dynamic environments is to achieve effective communications.

Traditional negotiation systems have been implemented in multi-agent systems (MAS), where agents exchange messages using an agent communication language (ACL) based on a specification like KQML [1] or FIPA [2]. These specifications provide a set of negotiation primitives based on speech act theory, and provide semantics for these primitives usage during communication. In order to facilitate effective communication, agents must be designed to be compliant with one of these

Please use the following format when citing this chapter:

Bravo, M., López, M., Montes, A., Santaolaya, R., Pinto, R., Pérez, J., 2006, in IFIP International Federation for Information Processing, Volume 217, Artificial Intelligence in Theory and Practice, ed. M. Bramer, (Boston: Springer), pp. 89–98.

ACL specifications. But the implementations of these negotiation primitives in real systems, differs in syntax and usage, because is based on proprietary program code produced by developers.

The problem of communication between negotiation agents is that even if two agents are following the same ACL, they may still suffer misunderstandings due to the different syntax and semantics of their vocabularies. In table 1, we can see that some of the reported communication languages in negotiation systems are based on FIPA, and some use a different ACL not compliant with any particular specification.

Table 1. Negotiation primitives used in different systems

Authors	ACL	Negotiation Primitives	
Jin Baek Kim, Arie Segev [7]	FIPA	Initial_offer RFQ Accept Reject Offer Counter-offer	
Stanley Y. W. Su, Chunbo Huang, Joachim Hammer [8]	FIPA	CFP Propose Accept Terminate Reject Acknowledge Modify Withdraw	
Anthony Chavez, Pattie Maes [10]	Uses a predefined set of methods, not compliant with any ACL specification.	accept-offer?(agent, from-agent, offer) what-is-price?(agent, from-agent) what-is-item?(agent, from-agent) add-sell-agent add-buy-agent add-potential-customers(sell-agent, potential-customers) add-potential-sellers(buy-agent, potential-sellers) agent-terminated(marketplace, agent) deal-made(marketplace, sell-agent, buy-agent, item, price)	
Sonia V. Rueda, Alejandro J. García, Guillermo R. Simari [11]	Based on speech act theory, not compliant with any ACL specification.	Requests_Add(s, h, p) Authorize_Add(s, h, p) Require(s, h, p) Demand(s, h, p) Accept(s, h, p)	Reject(s, h, p) Unable(s, h, p) Require-for(s, h, p, q) Insist_for(s, h, p, q) Demand_for(s, h, p, q)

Haifei Li, Chunbo Huang and Stanley Y.W Su [12]	Superset of FIPA	Call for proposal Propose proposal Reject proposal Withdraw proposal		Accept proposal Modify proposal Acknowledge message Terminate negotiation	
Jürgen Müller [6]	Based on speech act theory, not compliant with any ACL specification	Initiators: Propose, Arrange, Request, Inform, Query, Command, Inspect	Reactors: Answer, Refine, Modify, Change, Bid, Send, Reply, Refuse, Explain	Completers: Confirm, Promise, Commit, Accept, Reject, Grant, Agree.	

To solve the communication problem between heterogeneous agents, we selected a translation approach based on the implementation of a shared ontology. In this ontology we explicitly describe and classify negotiation primitives in a machine interpretable form. Negotiation agents should not be forced to commit to a specific syntax. Instead, the ontology provides a shared and public vocabulary that the translator module uses to help agents to communicate during negotiation processes. We have implemented a negotiation system based on Web services technologies, into which we have incorporated the translator module and the shared ontology. Our approach acknowledges that agents may use different negotiating languages.

The rest of the document is organized as follows. In section 2, we present the translator architecture. In section 3, we describe the design of the ontology. In section 4, the general architecture of the system for executing negotiation processes is presented. In section 5, we describe the results of experiments. Finally in section 6, we present conclusions.

2 Architecture of the Translator

The translator acts as an interpreter of different negotiation agents. In figure 1, we present the architectural elements involved in translation. This architecture consists of the following elements: multiple negotiation agents, the message transport, the translator module, and the shared ontology. Each negotiation agent in turn consists of a local ACL, decision making strategies to determine the preferences, and the negotiation protocol.

For example, suppose that agents A and B initiate a negotiation process, using their own local ACL, sending messages over the message transport. If happens that agent A misunderstands a message from agent B, it invokes the semantic translator module sending the message parameters (sender, receiver, message). The translator interprets the message based on the definitions of the sender agent and converts the message into an interlingua. Then the translator converts the interlingua representation to the target ACL based on the receiver agent definitions. Finally sends the message back to the invoking agent A and they continue with execution of negotiation. The translator is invoked only in the occurrence of a misunderstanding, assuring interoperability at run time.

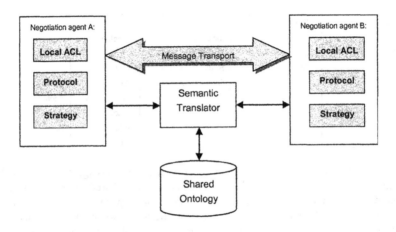

Fig. 1. Translator architecture

3 Shared Ontology

The principal objective in designing the ontology was to serve as an *interlingua* between agents during exchange of negotiation messages. According to Müller [6], negotiation messages are divided into three groups: initiators, if they initiate a negotiation, reactors, if they react on a given statement and completers, whether they complete a negotiation. We selected this classification to allow the incorporation of new negotiation primitives from the local agent ACL. Figure 2 shows the general structure of our ontology.

Based on the concepts and negotiation primitives we built our ontology. To code the ontology we decided to use OWL as the ontological language, because it is the most recent development in standard ontology languages from the World Wide Web Consortium (W3C)[1]. An OWL ontology consists of classes, properties and individuals. We developed the ontology using Protégé [14, 15], an open platform for ontology modeling and knowledge acquisition. Protégé has an OWL Plugin, which can be used to edit OWL ontologies, to access description logic reasoners, and to acquire instances of semantic markup.

---

[1] http://www.w3.org

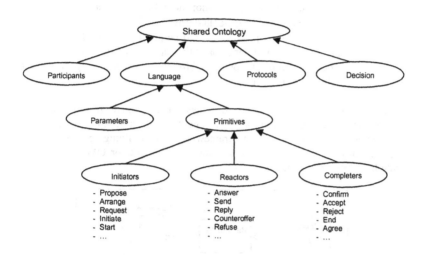

Fig. 2. General structure of the negotiation ontology

4 Implementation of the Negotiation System

The general architecture for the execution of negotiation processes is illustrated in figure 4. In this section we briefly describe the functionality and implementation techniques for each component.

a. The matchmaker is a Java module which is continuously browsing buyer registries and seller descriptions, searching for coincidences.

b. The negotiation process module is a BPEL4WS-based engine that controls the execution of negotiation processes between multiple agents according to the predefined protocols. BPEL4WS provides a language for the formal specification of business processes and business interaction protocols. The interaction with each partner occurs through Web service interfaces, and the structure of the relationship at the interface level is encapsulated in what is called a partner link.

c. Seller and buyer agents are software entities used by their respective owners to program their preferences and negotiation strategies. For example, a seller agent will be programmed to maximize his profit, establishing the lowest acceptable price and the desired price for selling. In contrast, a buyer agent is seeking to minimize his payment. On designing the negotiation agents, we identified three core elements, strategies, the set of messages and the protocol for executing the negotiation process. The requirements for these elements were specified as follows:

- Strategies should be private to each agent, because they are competing and they should not show their intentions.
- Messages should be generated privately.
- The negotiation protocol should be public or shared by all agents participating, in order to have the same set of rules for interaction. The negotiation protocol establishes the rules that agents have to follow for interaction.

d.   The translator module is invoked whenever the agent misunderstands a negotiation message from another agent. The translator module was implemented using Jena2, a framework for building Semantic Web applications. It provides a programmatic environment for OWL, including a rule-based inference engine.

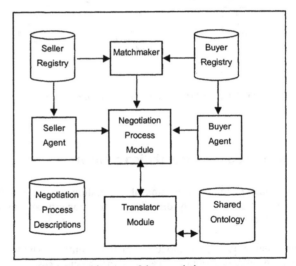

Fig. 3. Architecture of the negotiation system

5 Experimentation

In this section we describe the methodological steps that we followed for the execution of experiments.

a.   Identify and describe negotiation agent's characteristics
Table 2 shows the characteristics of agents A and B, specifying their language definitions: names of primitives and a description.

---

[2] http://jena.sourceforge.net

Table 2. Characteristics of agents A and B

Agent A	Language definitions
	(CFP, "Initiate a negotiation process by calling for proposals"), (Propose, "Issue a proposal or a counterproposal"), (Accept, "Accept the terms specified in a proposal without further modifications"), (Terminate, "Unilaterally terminate the current negotiation process"), (Reject, "Reject the current proposal with or without an attached explanation"), (Acknowledge, "Acknowledge the receipt of a message"), (Modify, "Modify the proposal that was sent last"), (Withdraw, "Withdraw the last proposal")

Agent B	Language definitions
	(Initial_offer, "Send initial offer"), (RFQ, "Send request for quote"), (Accept, "Accept offer"), (Reject, "Reject offer"), (Offer, "Send offer"), (Counter-offer, "Send counter offer") (Withdraw, "Withdraw the last proposal")

b.   Classify negotiation primitives in the ontology classes

For each negotiation primitive we need to analyze its semantics and usage. According to this description we can identify to which class it belongs. Table 3 shows the classification of the primitives provided by agents A and B.

Table 3. Classification of negotiation primitives

Agent	Starter	Reactor	Completer
A (Buyer)	CFP	Propose	Accept
		Modify	Reject
		Withdraw	Terminate
		Acknowledge	NotUnderstood
B (Seller)	RFQ	Initial_Offer	Accept
		Offer	Reject
		Counter_Offer	NotUnderstood

c.   Align primitives in a finite state machine

Alignment is necessary to verify and clarify the intended usage of negotiation primitives.

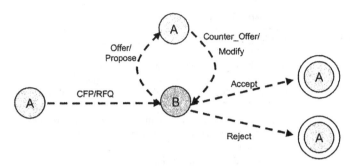

Fig. 4. Finite state machine

d.   Identify and establish the relations between different primitives
Based on the classification of primitives and their allocation in the finite state
machine, we can identify the relations between negotiation primitives.

A		**B**
CFP	isSynonymOf	RFQ
Propose	isSynonymOf	Offer
Propose	isSynonymOf	Inicial_Offer
Modify	isSynonymOf	Counter_Offer
Withdraw	isSynonymOf	Counter_Offer
Terminate	isSimilarOf	Reject

e.   Publish and code primitives in the ontology
This step consists of populating the ontology with the primitive's definitions and
relations.

f.   Execute negotiation
When primitives have been published, the process of negotiation between these
agents can be started. We executed 15 negotiation tests with these agents. The results
of these experiments were registered in a log file. Table 4 shows the results.

Table 4. Experimental results

Test	LastPrice	MaxPay	Iterations	Quantity	FinalPrice	Result
1	$ 1,750.00	$ 1,000.00	12	1500	$ -	Reject
2	$ 774.00	$ 1,760.00	3	887	$ 1,674.00	Accept
3	$ 1,788.00	$ 128.00	12	1660	$ -	Reject
4	$ 1,058.00	$ 110.00	12	1270	$ -	Reject
5	$ 761.00	$ 77.00	2	1475	$ -	NotUnderstood
6	$ 621.00	$ 446.00	12	56	$ -	Reject
7	$ 114.00	$ 704.00	7	8	$ 614.00	Accept

Test	LastPrice	MaxPay	Iterations	Quantity	FinalPrice	Result
8	$ 1,837.00	$ 2,199.00	9	53	$ 2,137.00	Accept
9	$ 1,665.00	$ 2,047.00	9	56	$ 1,965.00	Accept
10	$ 1,920.00	$ 286.00	12	81	$ -	Reject
11	$ 172.00	$ 1,553.00	2	41	$ 1,172.00	Accept
12	$ 980.00	$ 1,541.00	2	67	$ -	NotUnderstood
13	$ 1,276.00	$ 500.00	2	43	$ -	Reject
14	$ 1,500.00	$ 1,108.00	2	110	$ -	NotUnderstood
15	$ 1,400.00	$ 1,520.00	3	4	$ 1,452.00	Accept

The results of experiments showed that there were some negotiations that ended the process with a *NotUnderstood* message. This was due to the emission of an *Acknowledge* message form agent A, which agent B does not recognize. Although, the experiment results show good evidence that the two agents are communicating efficiently even when their language definitions are quite different.

6 Conclusions

In this paper we have presented how an ontology approach can improve interoperability between heterogeneous negotiation agents. In particular we incorporated a translator solution for the problem of lack of understanding among seller and buyer agents during the exchange of messages at run time. We evaluated the ontology in the target application, and described the system architecture into which the negotiation processes are executed. We believe that semantic interoperability of ACL is an important issue that can be solved by incorporating a shared ontology. The experimental tests showed that the proposed architecture improves the continuity of the execution of negotiation processes, resulting in more agreements.

References

1. T. Finning, R. Fritzon, and R. McEntire: KQML as an agent communication language, in *Proceedings of the 3rd International Conference on Information and Knowledge Management*, November 1994.
2. FIPA – Foundation for Intelligent Physical Agents. FIPA Specifications, 2003; available at http://www.fipa.org/specifications/index.html.
3. Uschold, M. and King M., Towards a Methodology for Building Ontologies, *Workshop on Basic Ontological Issues in Knowledge Sharing*, 1995.
4. Grüninger, M. and Fox, M., The Role of Competency Questions in Enterprise Engineering, *IFIP WG 5.7 Workshop on Benchmarking*. Theory and Practice, Trondheim, Norway, 1994.
5. Fernández, M., Gómez-Pérez, A., and Juristo, N., METHONTOLOGY: From Onthological Art towards Ontological Engineering, *Proceedings of AAAI Spring Symposium Series*, AAAI Press, Menlo Park, Calif., pp. 33-40, 1997.

6. Müller, H. J., Negotiation Principles, *Foundations of Distributed Artificial Intelligence*, in G.M.P. O'Hare, and N.R. Jennings, New York: John Wiley & Sons.
7. Jin Baek Kim, Arie Segev, A Framework for Dynamic eBusiness Negotiation Processes, *Proceedings of IEEE Conference on E-Commerce*, New Port Beach, USA, 2003.
8. Stanley Y. W. Su, Chunbo Huang, Joachim Hammer, Yihua Huang, Haifei Li, Liu Wang, Youzhong Liu, Charnyote Pluempitiwiriyawej, Minsoo Lee and Herman Lam, An Internet-Based Negotiation Server For E-Commerce, *the VLDB Journal*, Vol. 10, No. 1, pp. 72-90, 2001.
9. Patrick C. K. Hung, WS-Negotiation: An Overview of Research Issues, *IEEE Thirty-Seventh Hawaii International Conference on System Sciences* (HICSS-37), Big Island, Hawaii, USA, January 5-8, 2004.
10. Anthony Chavez, Pattie Maes, Kasbah: An Agent Marketplace for Buying and Selling Goods, *Proceedings of the First International Conference on the Practical Application of Intelligent Agents and Multi-Agent Technology*, London, UK, April 1996.
11. Sonia V. Rueda, Alejandro J. García, Guillermo R. Simari, Argument-based Negotiation among BDI Agents, *Computer Science & Technology*, 2(7), 2002.
12. Haifei Li, Chunbo Huang and Stanley Y.W Su, Design and Implementation of Business Objects for Automated Business Negotiations, *Group Decision and Negotiation*, Vol. 11; Part 1, pp. 23-44, 2002.
13. Dignum, Jan Dietz, Communication Modeling – The language/Action Perspective, *Proceedings of the Second International Workshop on Communication Modeling*, Computer Science Reports, Eindhoven University of Technology, 1997.
14. J. Gennari, M. Musen, R. Fergerson, W. Grosso, M. Crubézy, H. Eriksson, N. Noy, and S. Tu: The evolution of Protégé-2000: An environment for knowledge-based systems development, *International Journal of Human-Computer Studies*, 58(1): 89-123, 2003.
15. H. Knublauch: An AI tool for the real world: Knowledge modeling with Protégé, *JavaWorld*, June 20, 2003.

Statistical Method of Context Evaluation for Biological Sequence Similarity

Alina Bogan-Marta[1,1], Ioannis Pitas[1], and Kleoniki Lyroudia[2]

1 Aristotle University of Thessaloniki, Department of Informatics,
Artificial Intelligence and Information Analysis Laboratory, Box 451,
54124 Thessaloniki, Greece, pitas@aiia.csd.auth.gr
2 Aristotle University of Thessaloniki, Department of Endodontology,
Dental School, Greece, lyroudia@aiia.csd.auth.gr

Abstract. Within this paper we are proposing and testing a new strategy for detection and measurement of similarity between sequences of proteins. Our approach has its roots in *computational linguistics* and the related techniques for quantifying and comparing content in strings of characters. The pairwise comparison of proteins relies on the content regularities expected to uniquely characterize each sequence. These regularities are captured by *n*-gram based modelling techniques and exploited by cross-entropy related measures. In this new attempt to incorporate theoretical ideas from computational linguistics into the field of bioinformatics, we experimented using two implementations having always as ultimate goal the development of practical, computationally efficient algorithms for expressing protein similarity. The experimental analysis reported herein provides evidence for the usefulness of the proposed approach and motivates the further development of linguistics-related tools as a means of analysing biological sequences.

1 Introduction

The practice of comparing gene or protein sequences with each other, in the hope of elucidating similarity conveying functional and evolutionary significance, is a subject of primary research interest in bioinformatics. The application of this type of analysis to complete genomes greatly expands its utility and implications. The rewards range from the purely technical, such as the identification of contaminated sequence phases, to the most fundamental ones, such as finding how many different domains define the tree of life. Proteins are large, complex molecules composed of

---

[1] Currently, she works at University of Oradea, Computer Science Department, Universitatii 1, Oradea, Romania.

Please use the following format when citing this chapter:

Bogan-Marta, A., Pitas, I., Lyroudia, K., 2006, in IFIP International Federation for Information Processing, Volume 217, Artificial Intelligence in Theory and Practice, ed. M. Bramer, (Boston: Springer), pp. 99–108.

amino acids and their comparison and clustering according to similarity, require dedicated algorithms.

The most frequently used methods for measuring protein similarities are based on tedious algorithmic procedures for sequence alignment. Smith-Waterman algorithm [1] remains the standard reference method for pairwise sequence similarity due to the accuracy of the obtained results. Other heuristic algorithms, like BLAST[1], FASTA[2] or CLUSTAL[3] provide higher computational efficiency at the expense of accuracy. Algorithms characterized by the computation of profiles for whole protein families are based on hidden Markov models [2], [3]. All the above mentioned methods are built over sequence alignment but a variety of new alternative methods has already become available for expressing similarity between biological sequences for use in different applications. In Sjolander's work [4] are used Dirichlet mixtures while the authors of [5] apply discriminative methods using the approach of support vector machines (SVMs). Latent semantic analysis (LSA) is another method used in the work of Ganapathiraju [6] and the universal similarity metric (USM) for structural similarity between pairs of proteins is proposed by Krasnogor and Pelta [7].

Despite the maturity of the developed methodologies working towards this direction, the derivation of protein similarity measures is still an active research area. The interest is actually renewed, due to the continuous growth in size of the widely available proteomic databases that call for alternative cost-efficient algorithmic procedures. They should reliably quantify protein similarity without resorting to any kind of alignment. Apart from efficiency, a second specification of equal importance for the establishment of similarity measures is the avoidance of parameters that need to be set by the user (a characteristic inherent in the majority of the above mentioned methodologies). It is often the case with the classical similarity approaches that the user faces a lot of difficulties in the choice of a suitable search algorithm, scoring matrix or function as well as set of optional parameters whose optimum values correspond to the most reliable similarity.

A new approach for measuring the similarity between two protein sequences is introduced in this paper. It is inspired by the successful use of the entropy concept for information retrieval in the field of statistical language modeling (Manning and Schütze [8], Jurafsky and Martin [9]). Although the n-gram concept has been used in earlier works, e.g. [10], [11], the presented work is following a first attempt to adopt this dual step for comparing biological sequences [12]. Therefore, some experiments were necessary in order to discover the most effective way in which these ideas could be applied in the specific domain. For a complete validation of the suggested similarity measure, we built an annotated database by selecting proteins from Astral SCOP genetic domain sequences (http://astral.berkeley.edu). Using standard procedures, well-known in the field of *exploratory data analysis* and *information retrieval*, we evaluated the performance of our measure and contrasted with the performance of a relevant similarity score obtained by applying the popular CLUSTAL W method to the same database. CLUSTAL W method performs multiple sequence alignment and generates pairwise similarity scores using the identification of conserved sequence regions. We show that our method provides an effective way for capturing the common characteristics of the compared sequences,

[1] http://www.ncbi.nlm.nih.gov/BLAST/

[2] http://www.ebi.ac.uk/fasta33/

[3] http://www.ebi.ac.uk/clustalw/

while avoiding the annoying task of choosing parameters, additional functions or evaluation methods. The high performance of the new method and the ready-to-plug-in character, taken together with its computational efficiency, make our approach a promising alternative to the well-known, sophisticated protein similarity measurements.

2 Methods

2.1 Theoretical background

There are various kinds of language models that can be used to capture different aspects of regularities in natural language [13]. Markov chains are generally considered among the more fundamental concepts for building language models. In this approach, the dependency of the conditional probability of observing a word w_k at a position k in a given text is assumed to depend only upon its immediate n predecessor words $w_{k-n} \ldots w_{k-1}$. The resulting stochastic models, usually referred as *n-grams*, constitute an heuristic approach for building language grammars and their linguistic justification has often been questioned in the past. However, in practice they have turned out to be extremely powerful theoretical tools. Nowadays n-gram language modeling stands out as superior to any formal linguistic approach [13] and has gained high popularity due to its simplicity.

Close related with the design of models for textual data are the algorithmic procedures used to validate them. Apart from the justification of a single model, they can facilitate the selection of the specific one (among competing alternatives) most faithfully representing the available data. *Entropy* is a key concept for this kind of procedures. In general, its estimation is considered to provide a quantification of the information in a text and has strong connections to probabilistic language modeling [14]. As described in [8] and [15], the entropy of a random variable X that ranges over a domain $\aleph$, and has a probability density function, $P(X)$ is defined as:

$$H(X) = -\sum_{X \in \aleph} P(X) \log P(X). \tag{1}$$

Recently, in Van Uytsel and Compernolle's work [16], the general idea of entropy has been adopted in the specific case that a written sequence W= $\{w_1, w_2, \ldots, w_{k-1}, w_k, w_{k+1}, \ldots\}$ is treated as a language model L based composition, having the following estimating formula:

$$\hat{H}_L(X) = -\frac{1}{N} \sum_{W*} Count\left(w_i^n\right) \log_2 p_L\left(w_{i+n} \middle| w_i^{n-1}\right) \tag{2}$$

where the variable X has the form of an n-gram $X = w_i^n \Leftrightarrow \{w_i, w_{i+1}, \ldots, w_{i+n-1}\}$ and $Count(w_i^n)$ is the number of occurrences of w_i^n. The summation runs over all the possible n-length combinations of consecutive w_i (i.e. W*=$\{\{w_1, w_2, \ldots, w_n\}, \{w_2, w_3, \ldots, w_{n+1}\}, \ldots\}$) and N is the total number of n-grams in the investigated sequence. The second term, $p(w_{i+n}|w_i^{n-1})$ in (2), is the conditional probability that relates the n-th element of an n-gram with the preceding n-1 elements. Following the principles of maximum likelihood estimation (MLE), it can be estimated by using the corresponding relative frequencies:

$$\hat{p}\left(w_{i+n}\middle|w_i^{n-1}\right) = \frac{Count\left(w_{i+n}\right)}{Count\left(w_i^{n-1}\right)}. \tag{3}$$

The *cross-entropy* between the actual probability distribution *P(X)* (over a random variable *X*) and the probability distribution *Q(X)* estimated from a model is defined as:

$$H\left(X,Q\right) = -\sum_{X \in \aleph} P\left(X\right)\log Q\left(X\right). \tag{4}$$

Two important remarks should be mentioned here. First, the cross entropy of a stochastic process, measured by using a model, is an upper bound on the entropy of the process (i.e. H(X)≤H(X,Q)) [8], [15]). Second, between two given models, the more accurate is the one with the lower cross-entropy [9].

The above entropic estimation together with the general form of (1) and (2), suggesting a direct way to pass from entropy to cross-entropy formulation, are the basis for building our protein similarity measure, described in the sequel.

2.2   The n-gram Based Protein Similarity Measure

Protein sequences from all different organisms can be treated as texts written in a universal language in which the alphabet consists of 20 distinct symbols, the amino-acids. The mapping of a protein sequence to its structure, functional dynamics and biological role then becomes analog to the mapping of words to their semantic meaning in natural languages. Recently, it was suggested that this analogy can be exploited by applying *statistical language modeling* and *text classification techniques* for the advancement of biological sequences understanding (topic on Biological Language Conference, 2003). Scientists within this hybrid research area believe that the identification of Grammar/Syntax rules could reveal entities/relations of high importance for biological and medical sciences.

In the presented approach, we adopted a Markov-chain grammar to build for our protein dataset 2-gram, 3-gram and 4-gram models. To clarify things we chose a hypothetical protein sequence WASQVSENR. In the 2-gram modeling the available tokens/words were {WA AS SQ QV VS SE EN NR}, while in the 3-gram representation they were {WAS ASQ SQV QVS VSE SEN ENR}. Based on the frequencies of these tokens/words (estimated by counting) and by forming the appropriate ratios of frequencies, the entropy of an *n*-gram model can be readily estimated using (2). This measure is indicative about how well a specific protein sequence is modeled by the corresponding *n*-gram model. While this measure could be applied to two distinct proteins (and help us to decide about which protein is better represented by the given model), the outcomes cannot be used for a direct comparison of them. Thus, the common information content between two proteins *X* and *Y* is expressed via the formula:

$$E\left(X,Y\right) = -\sum_{all\ w_i^n} P_X(w_i^n)\log P_Y\left(w_{i+n}\mid w_i^{n-1}\right) \tag{5}.$$

The first term $P_X\left(w_i^n\right)$ in (5) corresponds to the reference protein sequence X (i.e. it results from counting the words of that specific protein). The second term corresponds to the sequence Y based on which the model has to be estimated (i.e. it results from counting the tokens of that protein). Variable w_i^n ranges over all the words (that are represented by n-grams) of the reference protein sequence.

2.3 Database Searches with the New Similarity Measure

Having introduced the new similarity measure, we proceed here with the description of its use for performing searches within protein databases. The essential point of our approach is that the unknown query-protein (e.g. a newly discovered protein) as well as each protein in a given database (containing annotated proteins with known functionality, structure etc.) are represented via n-gram encoding and the above introduced similarity is utilized to compare their representations.

We considered two different ways in which the n-gram based similarity is engaged in efficient database searches. The most direct implementation is called hereafter as *direct method*. A second algorithm, the *alternating method*, was devised in order to cope with the fact that the proteins to be compared could be of very different length. It is easy to observe the need of having two methods if sequences of very different length are compared. The procedure of experimenting with both methods and contrasting their performances gave the opportunity to check the sensitivity of the proposed measure regarding the length of the sequences.

Direct method. Let S_q be the sequence of a query-protein and $\{S\}=\{S_1, S_2, \ldots S_N\}$ the given protein database. The first step is the computation of 'perfect' score (PS) or 'reference' score for the query-protein. This is done by computing $E(S_q,S_q)$ using the query-protein both as reference and model sequence (we call here "model" the sequence compared with the query) in equation (5). In the second step, each protein S_i, $i=1\ldots N$, from the database serves as the model sequence in the computation of a similarity score $E(S_q,S_i)$, with the query-protein serving as reference sequence. In this way, N similarities are computed $E(S_q,S_i)$, $i=1,\ldots,N$. Finally, these similarities are compared against the perfect score PS by computing the absolute differences $D(S_q,S_i)=|E(S_q,S_i)-PS|$. The 'discrepancies' in term of information content between the query-protein and the database-proteins are expressed. By ranking these N measurements, we can easily identify the most similar proteins to the query-protein as those which have been assigned the lowest distance $D(S_q,S_i)$.

Alternating method: The only difference with respect to the direct method is that when comparing the query-protein with those from the database, the role of reference and model protein can be interchanged based on the shortest (the shortest sequence plays the role of reference sequence in (5)). The other steps, perfect-score estimation, ranking and selection, follow as previously.

3   Experiments

3.1   Proteins database

The strategy proposed for measuring protein similarity was presented and validated using a set of 1460 proteins extracted from Astral SCOP 1.67 sequence resource database. From the available/original corpus of data, only those families containing at least 10 protein sequences were included in our new database (this restriction will be appreciated later, since it was dictated by the *Precision* measure adopted for evaluation). In this way, 31 different families unequally populated were finally included. We mention that the annotation of our database follows the original annotation, relaying on the biological meaning of similarity concept (and therefore can be considered as providing the 'ground-truth' for the protein classification and the attempted similarity measurements). As a consequence, we expected that all the proteins belonging to the same family would appear as a tight cluster of textual patterns and having a proper similarity measure we could differentiate the existent families.

Our database (of 1460 proteins) was organized in 3 different sets, since the experimental results obtained with the new methods had to be compared with the results obtained with CLUSTALW method that could accept as input, protein sets with up to 500 sequences. The complete protein database (organized in 3 data sets) is available up on request and/or it will be publicly available at the Biopattern website of our laboratory (see acknowledgment section).

3.2   Experimental Results

In order to illustrate the two methods of the proposed strategy, first we followed some classical steps of *Exploratory Data Analysis*. The matrix containing all possible dissimilarity measures $D(S_i, S_j)$, $i,j=1,2,...N$ for the sets 1-3 is depicted in Figures 1-3 respectively. The images are presenting in grey scale the two considered methods corresponding to three different n-gram models. In the adopted visualization scheme all the shown matrices (after proper normalization) share a common scale in which the 1/white corresponds to the maximum distance in each matrix. It is worth mentioning here that the 'ideal' spatial outlay is a white matrix with some black, square segments around the diagonal line. From these three figures, it is clearly evident that the 4-gram based modeling in by both versions of our algorithm has a very good performance when searching within the given database.

Second, in order to provide quantitative measures of performance for the new method, we adopted an index of search accuracy, which is derived from *Precision* measure [17]. This index is the ratio computed by dividing the correctly classified number of protein sequences (identified by the algorithm as the 10 most similar ones) with 10 representing the minimal number of sequences within a family. More specifically, each protein in turn was treated as query and we measured the accuracy of the first 10 sequences identified within the set as the most similar to the query-protein. In other words, by taking into consideration the class/family label of each protein, we counted the proteins sharing the same label as the query (i.e. a number from 1 to 10).

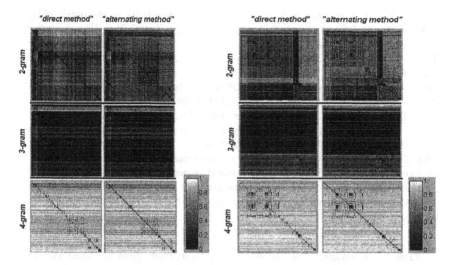

Fig. 1. Visualization of the matrices containing all the possible pairwise dissimilarities for the 497 proteins of Set1, for 2,3,4-gram models.

Fig. 2. Visualization of the matrices containing all the possible pairwise dissimilarities for the 497 proteins of Set2, for 2,3,4-gram models.

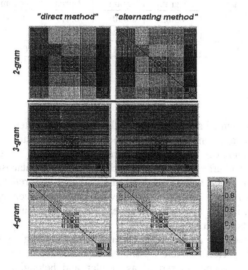

Fig. 1. Visualization of the matrices containing all the possible pairwise dissimilarities for the 466 proteins of Set3, for 2,3,4-gram models.

We repeated the procedure for all the proteins in the individual sets and finally were averaged the estimated parts in order to provide a total *Precision*-score for each set separately. To help the reader to appreciate the performance of our algorithms, we

repeated the same experimental procedure using the similarity scores obtained by
applying the CLUSTAL W method to the 3 different protein sets. The available
CLUSTAL W tool requires a set of input parameters, and we decided to use the
default values: Protein Gap Open Penalty = 10.0, Protein Gap Extension Penalty =
0.2, Protein matrix = Gonnet, provided at the European Molecular Biology
Laboratory and European Bioinformatics Institute (EMBL-EBI) web site
(http://www.ebi.ac.uk/). In Table 1 are included the precision scores provided by
CLUSTAL W and both of our approaches for different n-gram models. It is worth
mentioning that our algorithmic strategy almost reaches (in the case of 4-gram
modeling for the third set) the high performance of CLUSTAL W method. For the
sake of completeness, we repeated the *Precision* measurements with our method for
the overall set of 1460 proteins. The computed values were not significant different
from the values corresponding to the three different sets, providing some evidence
about the robustness of our method, indicating that its performance scales well with
the size of the database.

Table 1. The *precision* scores obtained from similarity results given by CLUSTAW tool
are in column 'CLUST.W', followed by those obtained using our similarity methods for
2,3,4-gram models for the three data sets.

Set	Clust.W	Direct Method			Alternating Method		
		2-gram	3-gram	4-gram	2-gram	3-gram	4-gram
1	0.872	0.439	0.662	0.830	0.471	0.646	0.823
2	0.921	0.446	0.650	0.874	0.439	0.605	0.860
3	0.932	0.534	0.865	0.931	0.574	0.828	0.919

4   Conclusions

The method we experimented and presented in this paper constitutes a step forward
in investigating the engagement of language modelling for characterizing, handling
and understanding biological data in the format of sequences. Specifically, we
studied the efficiency and effectiveness for searching in protein database of the new
measurement method. The experimental results indicate the reliability of our
algorithmic strategy for expressing similarity between proteins. Given the conceptual
simplicity of the introduced approach, it appears as an appealing alternative to
previous well-established techniques.

From the experimens, the *direct method* seems to perform slightly better. If the
second method would perform better, we should expect to have significant length
differences between sequences classified as similar and belonging to the same
family. In the exceptional case when all the compared sequences would have the
same length, the *direct method* is equivalent with the *alternating method* and
performs very well.

Regarding the order of the employed n-gram model, after testing with order of
2,3,4,5 we noticed, as can be seen in Table 1 and Fig.1-3 that the performance of the
method increases with the order of the model up to 4. After the order of 5 due to the
lack of data, the corresponding maximum likelihood estimates become unreasonable

uniform and very low. This sets an upper limit for our model order in the specific database (perhaps slightly higher order model could work in different protein databases).

If we pay more attention to the visual representation of our results (the emerging spots along the main diagonal in the 2D-displays correspond to well-formed groups of proteins, especially in the case of 4-gram modelling), we can consider that the structure revealed by using the new similarity measures bears a biological meaning. More explicitly, we assume that each defined group is indicative for the existence of a family/superfamily of proteins. Despite the fact that this aspect requires a deeper exploration, which is beyond the scope of this paper, it provides a hint that the new measures can be exploited within a proper clustering framework for mining extra information from given biological databases.

The comparison of our similarity scores with those provided by the CLUSTAL W method showed that in terms or performance in retrieval our method approaches the CLUSTAL W one. Considering the algorithmic simplicity and computational efficiency of the new approach, we are justified to suggest it as first choice when search in large databases are required. In terms of time complexity, in absence of a detailed analysis, we are motivated to consider this method as efficient especially when search procedure is running over large sequence databases with long strings of sequences. This motivates us to pursue further on how to achieve even higher performance. At this point, we have to remark that this is only a statistical in nature technique and it could be improved by incorporating biological knowledge such as working with functional groups of amino acids.

ACKNOWLEDGMENT

This work was supported by the EU project Biopattern: Computational Intelligence for biopattern analysis in Support of eHealthcare, Network of Excellence Project No. 508803.

References

1. T. Smith, and M. Watermann, Identification of common molecular subsequences, *J. Mol. Biol.* vol.147, pp.195-197 (1981).

2. A. Krogh, M. Brown, I. Mian, K. Sjolander, and D. Haussler, Hidden Markov models in computational biology: Application to protein modeling, *J. Mol. Biol.*, vol.235, pp.1501-1531 (1994).

3. P. Baldi, Y. Chauvin, T. Hunkapiller, and M.A. McClure, Hidden Markov models of biological primary sequence information, in *Proc. Natl. Acad. Sci. USA*, vol.91(3), pp.1059-1036 (1994).

4. K. Sjolander, K. Karplus, M. Brown, R. Hughey, A. Krogh, I.S. Mian, and D. Haussler, Dirichlet mixtures: a method for improved detection of weak but significant protein sequence homology, *J. Bioinformatics*, Vol 12, pp: 327-345 (1996).

5. H. Saigo, J-P. Vert, N. Ueda, and T. Akutsu, Protein homology detection using string alignment kernels, *J. Bioinformatics*, vol.20 no.11, pp.1682-1689 (2004).

6. M.K. Ganapathiraju, J. Klein-Seetharaman, N. Balakrishnan and R. Reddy, Characterization of protein secondary structure-application of latent semantic analysis using different vocabulary, *IEEE Signal Processing Magazine*, vol. 21, no.3, pp. 78-87 (2004).

7. N. Krasnogor, and D. A. Pelta, Measuring the similarity of protein structures by means of the universal similarity metric, *Bioinformatics Advance Access*, vol. 20, pp. 1015-1021 (2004).

8. C.D. Manning, and H. Schütze, 2000, Foundations of statistical natural language processing, Massachusetts Institute of Technology Press, Cambridge, Massachusetts London, England,pp.554 – 556;557 – 588.

9. D. Jurafsky, and J. Martin, 2000, *Speech and Language Processing*, Prentice Hall, pp. 223-231.

10. M. Ganapathiraju, V. Manoharan, and J. Klein-Seetharaman, Statistical sequence analysis using n-grams, *J. Appl. Bioinformatics*, vol.3 (2), pp.193-200 (2004).

11. S. Erhan, T.Marzolf, and L. Cohen, Amino-acid neighborhood relationships in proteins: breakdown of amino-acid sequences into overlapping doublets, triplets and quadruplets, Int. J. Biomed Comput, vol. 11(1), pp.67-75 (1980).

12. A.Bogan-Marta, N.Laskaris, M.A.Gavrielides, I.Pitas, and K. Lyroudia, A novel efficient protein similaritymeasure based on n-gram modeling, on electronical proceedings of CIMED2005, pp. 122-127.

13. S. Wang, D. Schuurmans, F. Pengun, and Y. Zhao, Semantic N-gram Language Modeling With The Latent Maximum Entropy Principle. In *IEEE International Conference on Acoustics, Speech, and Signal Processing (ICASSP-03)* available at : http://citeseer.nj.nec.com/575237.html

14. D. Van Compernolle, Spoken Language Science and Technology, 2003, http://www.esat.kuleuven.ac.be/~compi/pub/spoken_language/TOC.htm

15. P.F. Brown, A. S. Della Pietra, V.J. Della Pietra, L.R. Mercer Robert, and C.L. Jennifer, An estimation of an upper bound for the entropy of English, in *Association for Computational Linguistics*, Yorktown Heights, NY 10598, P.O. Box 704, 1992.

16. D.H. Van Uytsel, and D.Van Compernolle, Entropy-based context selection in variable-length n-gram language models, *IEEE Benelux Signal Proc. Symp.*, pp. 227-230 (1998).

17. R. Baeza-Yates and B. Ribeiro-Neto, in Retrieval Evaluation, *Modern Information Retrieval*, Ed. Addison Wesley, 1999, pp.75-81.

Biological inspired algorithm for Storage Area Networks (ACOSAN)

Anabel Fraga Vázquez[1]
1 Universidad Carlos III de Madrid
Av. Universidad, 30, Leganés, Madrid, SPAIN afraga@inf.uc3m.es

Abstract. The routing algorithms like Storage Area Networks (SAN) algorithms are actually deterministic algorithms, but they may become heuristics or probabilistic just because of applying biological inspired algorithms like Ant Colony Optimization (ACO) of Dorigo. A variant suggested by Navarro and Sinclair in the University of Essex in UK, it is called MACO and it may open new paths for adapting routing algorithms to changes in the environment of any network. A new algorithm is anticipated in this paper to be applied in routing algorithms for SAN Fibre Channel switches, it is called ACOSAN.

1 INTRODUCTION

This paper helps to create new paths for betters routing algorithms based in biological inspired algorithms like ACO (Ant Colony Optimization) of Dorigo [5,18,19]. The base of the paper is to apply these kind of algorithms and variants of that in Fibre Channel's switches (FC), for package routing in an adaptive way. In particular the Multiple Ant Colony Optimization of Navarro and Sinclair and ANTNET of Dorigo are very useful in that matter [11,13,18].

The reminder of this section establishes the history and introduction to the SAN networks, and benefits of this technology. Section 2 explains some key concepts and problems of Fibre Channel networks. Section 3 surveys some related previous work applying ACO to networking problems. Sections 4 describe basis for the algorithms proposed and the algorithm itself. And the final sections cover acknowledgments, future work and conclusions.

1.1. History and definitions

The increasing need year by year to connect disks to computers by SCSI connectors, which is a standard in the eighties in parallel connections, but not so fast as expected because of the problem that parallel connection have in front of serial connections.

Please use the following format when citing this chapter:

Vázquez, A.F., 2006, in IFIP International Federation for Information Processing, Volume 217, Artificial Intelligence in Theory and Practice, ed. M. Bramer, (Boston: Springer), pp. 109–118.

Day by day new faster connections are needed and technology does not stop and must not. The Fibre Channel technology is a prove of advance, it starts in the nineties and it has an appreciated speed which is over Gigabits, serial connection, and allows large distances over 10 kilometers.

The external storage is a new discovers, disks not connected anymore point-to-point to servers. Large storage arrays of disks now are the centre of the external storage, it may content five disks or even thousands of disks depending on the size of the company and the data to be storage, terabytes of information are connected by Fibre Channel to servers.

Brocade, an enterprise recognized in the area of Fibre Channel' s switches, is at the moment one of the factories for Fabric topologies in Storage Area Networks (SAN). This company defines SAN as a network for storage and system components, which are all communicated in a Fibre Channel net, used to consolidate and share information, offering high performance links, high availability links, higher speed backups, and support for clustering servers.

1.2. Providers

The main providers of SAN and Fibre Channel spares are placed in Table I. McData is the growing company in the area, followed by Brocade. McData works with IBM and Brocade works with Hewlett Packard (HP). These alliances are strategic for both companies in order to provide a whole package for the customers.

Table 1. Fibre Channel's switches providers

Rank	Provider	Growing rate (%)
1	McData (IBM)	17
2	Brocade (HP)	5
3	Cisco Systems	36
4	CNT/Inrange	8

Cisco is showed as one of the companies with the grater rate of growing but not only for SAN technology, the company is in a privileged position because of the large quantity of switches for any kind of network.

1.3. Structure and topology of SAN networks

There are different topologies for storage networks, the three basics are showed in Figures 1, 2 and 3. Figure 1 shows a point-to-point network with SCSI technology.

Figure 2 shows a Fibre Channel technology based network which covers over ten kilometres. And finally, Figure 3 shows a typical SAN network of Fabric typology.

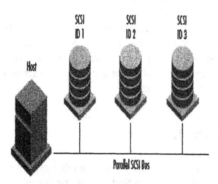

Fig. 1. Basic SCSI technology net between disks and server.

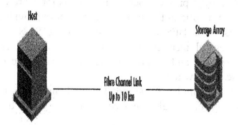

Fig. 2. Fibre Channel net for over 10 kilometres.

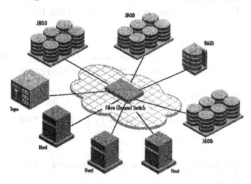

Fig. 3. Typical Fibre Channel network in multi-servers environment.

1.4. Benefits

Storage Area Networks (SAN) guarantee high availability in the nodes interconnected, allows consolidating information in disk arrays able to storage thousands of bits or bytes in a single point of storage. An additional advantage is to reduce network overload originated for automatic backups. Then again, allows to accelerate information access speed and makes certain fault tolerance. In case of a physical disaster, the availability that servers have because of been placed in different locations connected to the storage network makes possible to maintain unaffected the operation of a company.

2. FIBRE CHANNEL

Fibre Channel technology is a generic mechanism that allows high speed of transfers in long distances. It has physical definitions in the physical layer because of the transport protocol, like OSI for TCP/IP, the protocol tolerates TCP/IP and SCSI interfaces.

In general, it is easy to provide routing algorithms for Fibre Channel, but they are not specified or even public in the switches architecture provided. For example José Duato [12] published a BFS algorithm for routing SAN networks with Fibre Channel. But biological inspired algorithms are missing, and they could be an improvement for routing and adapting to networks exclusive of need for redefine algorithms or nodes in a switch.

Fredman, DataCore employee, defines Fibre Channel as a technology based on standards, innovative, functional to replace SCSI connections between disks, backup robots and servers.

Fibre Channel topologies are three:
1. Point-to-point: Based on simple links of connection between disks and servers.
2. Arbitrated Loop (FC-AL): Based on Hubs integrated to the net for routing packages.
3. Fabric: Based on switched network for routing packages.
Fibre Channel uses a communication protocol analogous to OSI with seven layers, similar to TCP/IP. The layers in the protocol are showed in Figure4.

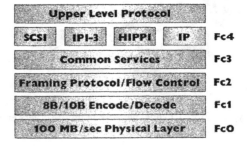

Fig. 4. Fibre Channel's protocol, similar to OSI model.

3. USES OF ANT COLONY OPTIMIZATION IN ROUTING ALGORITHMS

Marco Dorigo [6,18,19], the father of an special biological inspired algorithms based on studies of ants natural environments and behaviour: Ant Colony Optimization (ACO) and ANTNET. In general, ants leave pheromone trail in the way to the nest and the food location. So movements are based in quantities of pheromone in the paths to follow. As much pheromone located in one path then higher will be the probability to go in the course of that way. There are always of course ants that not follow the most probable path for obtaining new sources of provisions.

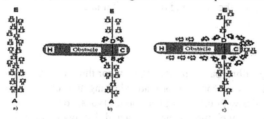

Fig. 5. Ants travelling from nest to food and suddenly an obstacle appears (Taken from Dorigo's paper explanation of ACO algorithms).

As a general rule, an heuristic function is involved in the movement of the ants in the natural environment where they are located. If in the way between nest and provisions suddenly appears an obstacle as showed in Figure 5 [13], then ants will generate a new trail and the shortest path will be used naturally because the pheromone trail is strongest in the short path for moving from nest to food and so on. This phenomenon occurs because more ants travel for the short path than for the long one. In case of two paths or more available and two shorts paths are accessible then a balance of ants traveling on them will be observed (Figure 6) [13].

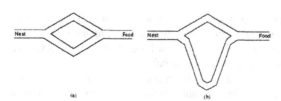

Fig. 6. More than one optimum path from nest to food.

The load balance of ants is showed in Figure 7 [13]. The first chart shows the case "a" of Figure 7 and the second chart shows the case "b" of that figure.
Dorigo [6] established an algorithm for pheromone evaporation, it occurs naturally, if not the search for new food would not be possible.

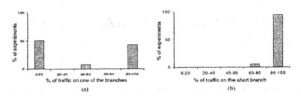

Fig. 7. Load balance of ants with more than one path possible [6,18,19].

4. ROUTING ALGORITHM

This section shows the basis and the algorithm itself.

4.1. Basis

MACO is an algorithm based in the ACO algorithm; it was originated in Essex University in UK. It was proposed for load balancing and routing in networks. It uses different ant colonies with different pheromones types, so ants of one colony will be repelled by others' pheromones and attracted by owns pheromones. It is an innovative approach and useful.

It has three kinds of algorithms. The first, it is based in local update of pheromone values. The second, it is based in update of pheromone values depending on distance. And the third, based in a global update of pheromone values depending on quantity of ants going on one path [13].

By this means, avoiding the problem of down nodes or faults in the network are interesting for adaptive environment algorithms.

4.2. Algorithm for storage area networks

Thanks to the MACO algorithm [13] and ANTNET [18] as a basic idea, is possible to postulate an algorithm called ACOSAN for Fibre Channel's switches as follows:

1. It is used more than one ant colony in order to produce different kinds of pheromones with the intention to find different optimal paths of routing for load balance purposes. A routing table will be filled with the information of routing between nodes of the net in the switch.
2. There must exist a first full filled routing table, it must be initialized using a deterministic algorithm, a manual default configuration or an existing table with default values of pheromone. It must be done in order to avoid the initial delay for generating the first version of that table.
3. Cycles of ant colonies will circumnavigate the network of switches and routing tables will be updated with new values of pheromones. It will allow maintaining distributed tables all the time.

4. The repelling mechanism will help ants to go over different routes, so load balancing routes could be generated.
5. In each cycle ants moves from every start and end possible at each point. The selection of links is stochastic, it depends of level of repelling and attraction of pheromones by ants, it is defined in the probabilistic function which is explained in the mathematical bases of the algorithm.
6. Once a loop is detected and no new version of the table is generated after a number finite of cycles, the ants are destroyed.
7. In the moment all ants are destroyed then a new cycle is placed after a variable of time defined in the algorithm in order to find better paths of routing in case of environmental changes in the links.
8. Ants must update pheromone trails in each cycle in local (on every switch). And trail must be updated as well after a cycle ends depending on global distances of paths and pheromone amounts in each path.
9. The pheromones are evaporated in each cycle as in the real life, if not new paths would not be found.
10. The best path in each cycle is stored for generate a final routing table of the cycle.

This algorithm can be applied in generic networks on top. But Fibre Channel is the primary target.

4.3. Mathematical bases for routing algorithm

The mathematical bases for the algorithm proposed are clearly established in Dorigo's papers [3,4,5,6] and Navarro and Sinclair's paper [13] and they are applied to this algorithm also, as shown in principle 1 to 7.

The algorithm will be able to control attraction of pheromones using formula (1), where is the weight of attraction for a link k by ant j, and will be the sum of pheromone over all links available, the ant must select one, where is the set of all links available for ant j depending on the position in the net.

$$\alpha_{kj} = \frac{p_{kj}}{\sum\limits_{i \in A_j} (P_{ij})} \tag{1}$$

The repelling formula for pheromones by each ant will be updated globally conditional on the amount of ants in each link (3), it is the best result as suggested by Navarro and Sinclair [13], where (2) represents the use of the link k, by total sum of ants of each types crossing the link k. But, is evaporated as pheromone at the end of each cycle represents the constant of evaporation.

$$u_k^{t+1} = \rho \bullet u_k^t \left(\forall k, t = \sum\limits_{i=1}^{T} S_i \right) \tag{2}$$

$$\beta_{kj} = \frac{u_k}{\sum_{i \in A_j}(u_i)}$$ (3)

The probability function for movement of an ant j for taking link k will be (4)
represented by where is an important constant defining the weight that repelling
will have for a different kind of pheromone found in the journey. Dividing by is
sure that probability will be improved as much as attraction is greater, and diminish
as much as repelling grows.

$$\gamma_{kj} = \frac{\alpha_{kj} / \beta_{kj}^c}{\sum_{i \in A_j}\left(\alpha_{ij} / \beta_{ij}^c\right)}$$ (4)

The pheromones' update rule is showed in equation (5) without evaporation, used
by Coloni [3,4,5] where Q is the amount of pheromone placed by an ant when
passing thought a link, and evaporation reduce in the amount of pheromone placed
for each link, it is denominated evaporation factor (6), where T represents each cycle
of the algorithm.

$$p_{kj}^{t+1} = p_{kj}^t + Q$$ (5)

$$p_{kj}^{t+1} = \rho \bullet p_{kj}^t \left(\forall j, \forall k, t = \sum_{i=1}^{T} S_i \right)$$ (6)

If global update is considered by distance and not by amount of ants in each link,
then equation for pheromone update will be (7) and factor would not be used,
where will be the distance of link k, in route followed by an ant j.

$$p_{kj}^{t+1} = p_{kj}^t + Q / L_j^T \left(\forall j, \forall k \in R_j^T, t = \sum_{i=1}^{T} S_i \right)$$ (7)

4.4. Probabilistic vs. Deterministic

Analyzing deterministic and probabilistic algorithms in references [13], as shown in
Figure 8, in general a heuristic algorithm will converge as a deterministic in similar
solutions, but a gap is in the beginning of the algorithms. That is the reason to use a
deterministic initial routing table for avoiding this gap at the beginning.

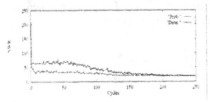

Fig. 8. Probabilistic/deterministic algorithms' general performance [13].

5. CONCLUSIONS AND FUTURE WORKS

An algorithm for routing in adaptive environments is shown in the paper using biological inspired algorithms like Ant Colony Optimization. It will help to detect changes in the network and overload in some nodes. In general, evolving algorithms are useful to solve these problems.

The need of an ACO algorithm for networks was touched by Dorigo [18,19] in the ANTNET seminal work in 1997, but applying those techniques to Fibre Channel networks for SAN are novel, it could be a preliminary approach for adapting such kind of algorithms into this technology.

ACO, MACO and new algorithms as shown in the paper are able to adapt to the environment without need of human interaction in case of failure.

Ants in the network are not a problem for high speed networks like Fibre Channel switches, if the problem of changing environments is solved by this kind of algorithms [9].

Mong's work refers to the use of ACO algorithm in routing switches instead of OSPF or RIP algorithms. Empirical results using ACO in routing and load balance are encouraging [11].

Formal studies like Gutjahr's studies [9] shown that convergence of ACO based algorithms tend to one, but this study was done for a typical NP problem: travelling salesman problem.

A future work to this paper is to apply the algorithm in a fabric switched network [16], but it is not an easy task. Some simulations were done by Navarro and Sinclair [13] in generic networks, but could be interested to apply this modified algorithm based in ACO and MACO in storage area networks.

The repelling factor is the key for disjunctive paths if it is settled properly. If the value of are higher then disjunctive paths will be obtain in the final routing tables.

6. ACKNOWLEDGMENTS

Thanks to anonymous people who reviewed this paper and helped with valuable comments to formulate it.

7. REFERENCES

1. C, Blum. *Beam-ACO hybridizing ant colony optimization with beam search: an application to open shop scheduling.* Computers & OR 32: 1565-1591 (Belgium, 2005).
2. *Brocade web page.* (October, 2005) http://www.brocade.com
3. A. Coloni, M.Y. Dorigo, V. Maniezzo. *An investigation of some properties of an ant algorithm.* (Proc. Parallel Problem Solving from Nature Conference PPSN`92, Brussels, Belgium, 1992) pp. 509-520.

4. A. Coloni, M. Dorigo, V. Maniezzo. *Distributed optimization by ant colonies.* (Proc. First European Conf. On Artificial Life (ECAL`91), París, France, 1991) pp. 134-142.
5. M. Dorigo, V. Maniezzo, A. Coloni. *The ant system: a cooperative learning approach to the travelling salesman problem.* IEEE Trans. Evolutionary Computation, 1(1):1-13, (1996).
6. M. Dorigo, V. Maniezzo, A. Colorni. *The Ant System: Optimization by a colony of cooperating agents.* IEEE Transactions on Systems, Man, and Cybernetics-Part B, 26(1):29-41. (1996).
7. *Fibre Channel Industry Association (FCIA)* (October, 2005) http://www.fibrechannel.org
8. M. Fredman. *An introduction to SAN Capacity Planning.* Datacore Software Company.
   http://www.demandtech.com/Resources/Papers/Intro%20to%20SAN%20cap acity%20planning.pdf (March, 2006)
9. W. Gutjahr. *A generalized convergence result for the Graph-Based Ant System Metaheuristic.* Future Generation Computer Systems. Vienna. (2000).
10. *McDATA page.* (October, 2005) http://www.mcdata.com
11. K. Mong, W. Hong. *Ant Colony Optimization for Routing and Load-balancing: Survey and New Directions.* IEEE Transactions on systems, man, and cybernetics – Part A: Systems and Humans, (33):5. (September, 2003).
12. X. Molero, F. Silla, V. Santonia, J. Duato. *Modeling and Evaluation of Fibre Channel Storage Area Networks.* http://csce.uark.edu/~aapon/courses/ ioparallel/presentations/31.ppt España. (2005).
13. G. Navarro, M. Sinclair. *Ant Colony Optimisation for Virtual-Wavelength-Path Routing and Wavelength Allocation. (MACO)* Univ. Of Essex. UK. (NASA). Proceedings of the Congress on Evolutionary Computation. (1999).
14. M. Reimann., M. Laumanns. *A hybrid ACO algorithm for the Capacitated Minimum Spanning Tree Problem.* ECAI2004. Workshop HYBRID METAHEURISTICS (HM 2004). (2004).
15. R. Schoonderwoerd, O. Holland, J. Bruten. *Ant-like agents for load balancing in telecommunication networks.* In: AGENTS '97: Proceedings of the first international conference on Autonomous agents, New York, NY, USA, ACM Press (1997). pp. 209-216.
16. *Storage Networking Industry Association web page (SNIA)* (October, 2005) http://www.snia.org
17. T. Skie, O. Lysne, J. Flich, P. López, A. Robles, J. Duato. *Lash-Tor: A generic transition-oriented routing algorithm.* ICPADS 2004. (2004) pp. 595-604.
18. G. Di Caro, M. Dorigo. *Two Ant Colony Algorithms for Best-Effort Routing in Datagram Networks.* Proceedings of PDCS'98 - 10th International Conference on Parallel and Distributed Computing and Systems. (Las Vegas, Nevada, October 28-31, 1998).
19. M. Dorigo, T. Stuetzle. *Ant Colony Optimization.* MIT Press. ISBN 0-262-04219-3. (2004).

Radial Basis Functions Versus Geostatistics in Spatial Interpolations

Cristian Rusu[1] and Virginia Rusu[2]

1   Pontificia Universidad Católica de Valparaíso, Escuela de
Ingeniería Informática, Av. Brasil No. 2241, Valparaíso, Chile,
cristian.rusu@ucv.cl, WWW home page: http://www.inf.ucv.cl
2   North University of Baia Mare, Faculty of Sciences,
Victoriei 76, Baia Mare, Romania,
crusu@vtr.net, WWW home page: http://www.ubm.ro

Abstract. A key problem in environmental monitoring is the spatial interpolation. The main current approach in spatial interpolation is geostatistical. Geostatistics is neither the only nor the best spatial interpolation method. Actually there is no "best" method, universally valid. Choosing a particular method implies to make assumptions. The understanding of initial assumption, of the methods used, and the correct interpretation of the interpolation results are key elements of the spatial interpolation process. A powerful alternative to geostatistics in spatial interpolation is the use of the soft computing methods. They offer the potential for a more flexible, less assumption dependent approach. Artificial Neural Networks are well suited for this kind of problems, due to their ability to handle non-linear, noisy, and inconsistent data. The present paper intends to prove the advantage of using Radial Basis Functions (RBF) instead of geostatistics in spatial interpolations, based on a detailed analyze and modeling of the SIC2004 (Spatial Interpolation Comparison) dataset.

1   Introduction

A key problem in many fields (including environmental monitoring) is spatial interpolation (sometimes referred as "surface modeling"). It consists of estimating the values of z variable at any location, based on set of (x_i, y_i, z_i) samples, which usually have a non-uniform distribution. Input data represent z values samples at given (x, y) locations, usually called control points. The problem occurs in geology, geophysics, meteorology, environmental sciences, agriculture, engineering, economy, medicine, social sciences, etc. [9], [19], [22], [23].

Two classes of methods are generally used in spatial interpolations: (1) triangulation, and (2) gridding. Triangulation requires a tessellation by an optimal network of

Please use the following format when citing this chapter:

Rusu, C., Rusu, V., 2006, in IFIP International Federation for Information Processing, Volume 217, Artificial Intelligence in Theory and Practice, ed. M. Bramer, (Boston: Springer), pp. 119–128.

triangles, with control points at all apices. The triangles set represents an approximation of the surface. A regular array of data is generated by gridding, z parameter being estimated on the grid nodes, based on a set of control points. Gridding offers at least two major advantages over triangulation: (1) it is not necessary to sample the extreme points of the surface to be estimated, and (2) subsequent operations on grid data are facilitated. Usually gridding is not an aim by itself; it is a preliminary step for further processing.

2   Geostatistics in Spatial Interpolations

The main current approach in spatial interpolation nowadays is geostatistical. Geostatistics was originated by the application of statistical methods to the study of geological phenomenon. A complex theory was later developed, being applied not only to earth sciences, but also to many other areas: natural, economic, social phenomenon, among others. Geostatistics use regionalized variables, which values are not random; neither are exactly describable by a function. A regionalized variable may consist of a drift component and residual. A third error component has to be considered.

Geostatistical interpolation estimates values by kriging. Kriging is an exact interpolator which uses geostatistical techniques to calculate the autocorrelation between data points, and produce a minimum variance unbiased estimate, taking in consideration the spatial configuration of the underlying phenomenon.

Geostatistics is neither the only nor the best spatial interpolation method. Actually there is no "best" method, universally valid [3], [12], [19], [24]. The choice of interpolation method may vary, mainly according to the type and nature of data, and the aim of modeling. Choosing of a particular method implies to make assumptions. The understanding of initial assumptions, of the used methods, and the correct interpretation of the interpolation results are key elements of the spatial interpolation process. Comparison between methods can be made based on criteria as goodness of representation (errors in honoring control points), dependency on data distribution, number of control points that can be handled, ease of implementation, speed of computation.

3   Soft Computing Methods in Spatial Interpolations

3.1 Soft Computing Methods

Soft computing methods offer the potential of a more flexible, less assumption dependent approach in spatial interpolations. Even if their validness as spatial interpolation methods was proved by many authors, their use in practice is still limited [2], [5], [8], [10], [20], [25]. Soft Computing differs from conventional (hard) computing in that, unlike hard computing, it is tolerant of imprecision, uncertainty, partial truth, and approximation [11].

3.2 Artificial Neural Networks in Spatial Interpolations

Artificial Neural Networks (ANNs) are information processors, trained to represent the implicit relationship and processes that are inherent within a data set [1], [6], [7], [15], [16]. Sometimes spatial relationship between inputs has to be found (like in geology, for instance). Other areas require the identification of both spatial and temporal relationships (meteorology, environmental sciences, etc.).

The original inspiration for ANN was biological; so much of the terminology of ANN reflects this biological heritage. The basic structure of an ANN consists of a number of simple processing units, also known as neurons (nodes). The basic role of each node is to take the weighted sum of the inputs and process this through an activation function. A connection joins the output of one node to the input of another. Each link has a weight, which represents the strength of the connection. The values of all the weights in a network represent the current state of learning of the network, in a distributed manner. These weights are altered during the training process to ensure that the inputs produce an output that is close to the desired value.

A learning function or algorithm is used to adjust the weights of the network during the training phase. Training can be supervised or unsupervised. Hybrid training techniques and reinforcement learning are also used. During the learning period both the input and output vector are supplied to the network. The network then generates an error signal based on the difference between the actual output and the target vector. The error is used to adjust the weights of the network adequately. Following training, input data are then passed through the trained network in its non-training (recall) mode, where they are transformed within the hidden layers to provide the modeling output values.

ANNs have emerged as an option for spatial data analysis approximately a decade ago. Training data are the observation samples used to derive the predictive model. The independent (predictor) variables are known as the input variables, and the dependent variables (response) are known as the output variables. In supervised learning, an ANN makes use of the input variables and their corresponding output variables to learn the relationship between them. Once found, the trained ANN is then used to predict values for the output variables given some new input data set. For unsupervised learning, an ANN will only make use of the input variables and attempts to arrange them based on their properties, hopefully in a way that is meaningful to the analyst.

3.3 Radial Basis Functions in Spatial Interpolations

Radial Basis Functions (RBF) have various applications in practice, due to their simplicity, generality and fast learning stage [11], [13], [14]. RBF are unidirectional ANNs, of hybrid learning (incorporating both supervised and unsupervised learning). Usually RBF have a three layers' architecture: (1) input layer – sends the input information to the hidden layer, (2) hidden layer – composed by non-linear neurons (usually gaussian), and (3) output layer – composed by linear neurons.

The hidden layer's neurons work based on the distance between the input vector and the synaptic vector of each neurons (centroid). Therefore they offer a localized response, which will have a significant intensity only if the input vector will be located near the centroid. Thus, a radial basis neuron acts as a detector that produces 1 whenever the input is identical to its weight vector, meaning that the input pattern was recognized. The output layer's neurons only compute the weighted sum of the output of the hidden layer.

The radial functions are usually symmetric, but asymmetric (ellipsoidal) functions may also be used. They will then have preferential search directions of the control points used in the interpolation, for a specific grid node. The gaussian functions are not the only type of radial functions that can be used. The type of the radial functions and their parameters are chosen based on the specific problem to solve and the characteristics of the input data.

Some of the reasons to use RBF in spatial interpolations are the following:

- depending on the radial functions type, the RBF model may offer a localized response (therefore is able to identify the local characteristics of the surface to be modeled), or a global response (identifying this way the global characteristics of the surface to be modeled),
- RBF are exact interpolators, honoring the control points when the point coincides with the grid node being interpolated,
- smoothing factors can be employed in order to reduces the effects of small-scale variability between neighboring data points.

4   RBF Versus Geostatistics

The progress made in spatial interpolation is usually presented only in journals or scientific meetings dedicated to statistics, mining, environmental etc. Users who have a different technical background often do not have in-depth knowledge of spatial interpolation methods. That is why the use of new techniques is often discouraging for newcomers. When spatial interpolation methods are integrated in software tools, they are often implemented in such a rigid way that users have no real choice in selecting the best possible method, according to the true nature of data to process, and the aim of modeling. Moreover, many required parameters are fixed, without any possible way to modify them.

The following is a comparison between RBF and geostatistics, at theoretical, correctness and efficiency levels, with special emphasis on method's usability.

4.1 Common Characteristics

The basis kernel of RBF is somehow analogous to variogram in geostatistics. The basis kernel functions define the optimal set of weights to apply to the data points when interpolating a grid node.

Both RBF and geostatistics (kriging) can be used as exact interpolators or smoothing interpolators. RBF will act like a smoothing interpolator when a smoothing factor will be incorporated to the basis function. Kriging will be a smoothing interpolator when an error nugget effect will be specified.

Both RBF and geostatistics are powerful and flexible methods, and are useful for gridding almost any type of data set. They generate quite similar results for most data sets. Computing time increases significantly when using large data sets. Precision of estimation is quite similar, excepting for small data sets, when a proper variographic study is difficult or impossible to perform, and therefore RBF give better results.

4.2 Problems with RBF

RBF architecture is actually imposed by the input data set itself. It is natural to use a number of RBF neurons equal to the number of the available control points, and to center the basis functions on the control point's locations. So a challenging problem when using ANN, the choose of the right architecture, is implicitly solved when using RBF in spatial interpolations.

Another problem to solve is the adequate choose of the type of the radial function to be used, as gaussian function is not always the best choice in spatial interpolation. Some alternative function may be multiquadric, multilog, inverse multiquadric, or natural cubic spline, among others. All these options where tested for real data sets (as the section 5 shows).

Once the radial function was chosen, setting the working parameters is by far less challenging then using geostatistics. Basically only smoothing factors have to be specified.

4.3 Problems with Geostatistics

Before actually performing the kriging, a variographic study has to be done. This may be quite a challenge, especially for inexperienced users. Based on the experimental variogram (obtained from the input data set), appropriate variogram model and adequate parameters have to be chosen. Moreover, many times different theoretical models have to be mixed in a complex all-in-one model.

The variogram is a measure of how quickly things change on the average. The underlying principle is that, on the average, two observations closer together are more similar than two observations farther apart. Because the underlying processes of the data often have preferred orientations, values may change more quickly in one direction than another. As such, the variogram is a function of direction. The variogram is a three dimensional function. There are two independent variables (the direction q, the separation distance h) and one dependent variable (the variogram value g(q,h)). The experimental variogram is a curve that displays the groups of variogram pairs on a plot of separation distance versus the estimated variogram.

Variogram modeling is not an easy or straightforward task. The development of an appropriate variogram model for a data set requires the understanding and application of advanced statistical concepts and tools. In addition, the development of an appropriate variogram model for a data set requires knowledge of the tricks, traps, pitfalls, and approximations inherent in fitting a theoretical model to real world data. An inappropriate variogram model can lead to completely false gridding results.

The development of an appropriate variogram model requires numerous decisions. These decisions can only be properly addressed with an intimate knowledge of the data at hand, and a competent understanding of the data genesis (i.e. the underlying processes from which the data are drawn).

The variogram model mathematically specifies the spatial variability of the data set and the resulting grid file. The interpolation weights, which are applied to data points during the grid node calculations, are direct functions of the variogram model. When the variogram is specified for kriging, the following parameters have to be set: sill, range, and nugget, but also the anisotropy information.

5   Study Case: SIC 2004

The Radioactivity Environmental Monitoring (REM) Group of the Institute for Environment and Sustainability at the Joint Research Center (JRC) of the European Commission has organized Spatial Interpolation Comparison Exercises (SIC97 and SIC2004). Participants were invited to estimate values of a variable observed at N locations with the help of a subset of n observed measurements. Once the participants have made their estimates, REM disclosed the true values observed at the N-n locations, so that the participants may assess the accuracy of their approach. The main objective of SIC97 and SIC2004 was to present the diversity of approaches taken by participants facing a problem that is identical for everyone, and to present the latest developments in the field of spatial statistics [3], [4], [17]. They offered an excellent occasion to test methods, compare results, and further orient research in the field of spatial interpolations.

The data used in SIC2004 were daily mean values of gamma dose rates measured in South West Germany, in an area of approximately 400 x 700 km, which includes 1008 monitoring stations. Participants were invited to estimate values of gamma dose rates variable at 808 locations, with the help of a subset of 200 observed measurements. Later on, the true 808 values where published. Additionally, 10 smaller data sets (of 200 observed measurements each one) where published, in order to allow the calibration of the methods and parameters [4]. The location of the 200 input data and the output 808 estimations are shown in fig. 1. All available SIC 2004 data sets where processed by the authors of the present paper, using various gridding methods [18], [21]. Only the results obtained by RBF and geostatistics will be shown and discussed here.

The interpolation results where compared with the real 808 values. The following statistics where used: Mean Error - ME, Mean Absolute Error - MAE, Percentage Mean Error - PMAE, Minimum Error - MIN, Maximum Error - MAX, Percentage Minimum Error - PMIN, Percentage Maximum Error - PMAX, Pearson's Coefficient of Correlation between the estimated and true values - PEAR.

The modeling results obtained by RBF are presented in a 3D view in fig. 1. The modeling results obtained by kriging are presented in a 3D view in fig. 2. Examining the two drawings, one could think that kriging brings more details, but the small differences are due, in fact, only to a different level of smoothness.

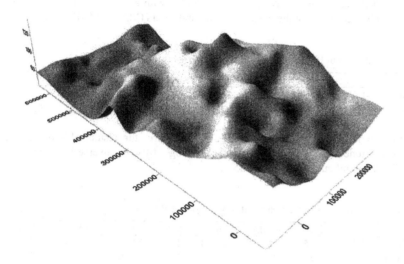

Fig. 1. Modeling results obtained by RBF

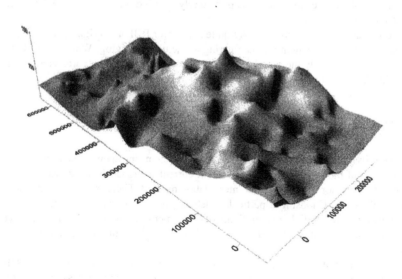

Fig. 2. Modeling results obtained by kriging

Table 1 shows the values of the above-mentioned indicators for RBF and kriging (KRG). RBF and kriging have got similar results, with a slight advantage for RBF over kriging, considering the most significant indicators (MAE, PMAE, PEAR).

Table 1. Statistics of RBF and kriging interpolation results

	ME	MAE	PMAE	MIN	MAX	PMIN	PMAX	PEAR
RBF	-1,41	9,15	9,20	-61,14	44,53	0,00	53,91	0,78
KRG	-1,31	9,28	9,34	-58,39	47,28	0,06	55,82	0,77

Various type of RBF where tested. Table 2 compares the results of applying the following functions: multiquadric - MQ, multilog - MLOG, inverse multiquadric - INVMQ, natural cubic spline - SPLINE.

Table 2. Statistics of interpolation results using various RBF types

	ME	MAE	PMAE	MIN	MAX	PMIN	PMAX	PEAR
MQ	-1,41	9,15	9,20	-61,14	44,53	0,00	53,91	0,78
MLOG	-1,19	9,82	9,94	-71,82	34,15	0,00	45,30	0,77
INVMQ	-12,18	199,40	190,78	-2017	1446	0,42	2004	-0,01
SPLINE	-2,94	53,23	54,59	-635,54	704,15	0,03	706,15	0,17

MQ and MLOG functions give the best results, but INVMQ and SPLINE should not be used in this particular case. The importance of choosing the right type of function is now obvious. Multiquadric-type radial functions offer a more global response than the gaussian-like type, so their use is particularly justified for rather sparse data, like SIC2004 data sets.

The results and the execution time are quite similar for RBF and kriging, but the easy of use of RBF is overwhelming, comparing to the use of kriging. When using RBF, user has to choose only the radial functions type and the smoothing parameter. When using kriging, a complex variogram modeling has to be done.

6 Conclusions

As we saw, spatial interpolation is a key problem in many fields, including environmental monitoring. Even if the main current approach is geostatistical, it is neither the only nor the best spatial interpolation method. There is no "best" method, universally valid. Choosing a particular method implies to make assumptions. The understanding of initial assumption, of the methods used, and the correct interpretation of the interpolation results are key elements of the spatial interpolation process.

A powerful alternative to geostatistics in spatial interpolation is the use of the soft computing methods. They offer the potential for a more flexible, less assumption dependent approach. ANNs are well suited for this kind of problems, due to their ability to handle non-linear, noisy, and inconsistent data. Particularly useful prove to be RBF.

Both RBF and geostatistics are powerful and flexible methods, and are useful for gridding almost any type of data set. They generate quite similar results for most data sets. Precision of estimation is quite similar, excepting for small data sets, when a proper variographic study is difficult or impossible to perform, and RBF give better results. RBF and geostatistics (kriging) can be used both as exact interpolators and smoothing interpolators.

Using RBF is easier than using geostatistics, even for inexperienced users. As section 4 shows, the geostatistics problems in spatial interpolations are far more complicated than the RBF problems. The development of an appropriate variogram model for a data set requires the understanding and application of advanced statistical concepts and tools. In addition, the development of an appropriate variogram model for a data set requires knowledge of the tricks, traps, pitfalls, and approximations inherent in fitting a theoretical model to real world data. An inappropriate variogram model can lead to completely false gridding results. Variogram modeling is especially difficult for relatively small data sets.

The above-mentioned conclusions where proved based on a detailed analyze and modeling of the SIC2004 (Spatial Interpolation Comparison) dataset, as the 6th section shows. That is way we strongly recommend the use of RBF in spatial interpolations.

7 References

[1] Aguilar M. and others: *Evaluación de diferentes técnicas de interpolación espacial para la generación de modelos digitales del terreno agrícola*, Mapping Interactivo, Electronic Journal, April, 2002.

[2] Demyanov V. and others: *Neural Network Residual Kriging Application For Climatic Data*, in Mapping radioactivity in the environment, edited by Dubois G, Malczewski J., and De Cort M., European Commission, Joint Research Center, Luxembourg, 2003, pp. 176-191.

[3] Dubois G.: *Spatial Interpolation Comparison 97: Foreword and Introduction*, Journal of Geographic Information and Decision Analysis, vol. 2, no. 2, 1998, pp. 1-10.

[4] Dubois G, Galmarini S.: *Introduction to the Spatial Interpolation Comparison (SIC) 2004 Exercise and Presentation of the Datasets*, Applied GIS, Vol. 1, No. 2, 2005, ISSN 1832-5505 (DOI: 10.2104/ag050009).

[5] Gilardi N., Bengio S.: *Local Machine Learning Models for Spatial Data*, Journal of Geographic Information and Decision Analysis, vol. 4, no. 1, 2000, pp. 11-28.

[6] Graubard S.: *El nuevo debate sobre la inteligencia artificial: sistemas simbólicos y redes neuronales*, Gedisa, Barcelona, España, 1999.

[7] Hilera J., Martínez V.: *Redes Neuronales Artificiales. Fundamentos, modelos y aplicaciones*, Alfaomega, Madrid, Spain, 2000.

[8] Huang Y., Wong P., Gedeon T.: *Spatial interpolation on overlapping partition surfaces using an optimized dynamic fuzzy-reasoning-based function estimator*, in

Mapping radioactivity in the environment, edited by Dubois G, Malczewski J., and De Cort M., European Commission, Joint Research Center, Luxembourg, 2003, pp. 201-210.

[9] Jones Th., Hamilton, D., Johnson C.: *Contouring Geological Surfaces with the Computer*, Van Nostrand Reinhold, New Zork, 1986.

[10] Lee S., Cho S., Wong P.: *Rainfall Prediction Using Artificial Neural Networks*, Journal of Geographic Information and Decision Analysis, vol. 2, no. 2, 1998, pp. 253-264.

[11] Mártin B., Sanz A.: *Redes Neuronales y Sistemas Difusos*, Alfaomega, Madrid, Spain, 2002.

[12] Nagy D. and others: *Comparison of various methods of interpolation and gridding*, XX General Assembly, IUGG, Vienna, Austria, 1991.

[13] Orr M.: *Introduction to Radial Basis Function Networks*, Center for Cognitive Science, University of Edinburgh, Scotland, 1996.

[14] Orr M.: *Recent Advances in Radial Basis Function Networks*, Institute for Adaptative and Neural Computation, Edinburgh University, Scotland, 1999.

[15] Pao Y.: *Adaptive Pattern Recognition and Neural Networks*, Addison-Wesley, Readings, USA, 1989.

[16] Peter A.: *Retele neuronale pentru aproximarea si predictia seriilor de timp*, Presa Universitară Clujeană, Cluj-Napoca, Romania, 2000.

[17] Rusu C.: *Interpolarea spatiala a datelor utilizand pachetul de programe ZAZA. Studiu de caz: modelarea cantitatilor de precipitatii dupa un accident nuclear*, Lucrările seminarului de creativitate matematică, vol. 9 (1999-2000), Universitatea de Nord Baia Mare, Romania, pp. 135-146.

[18] Rusu C.: *Modelado de superficies por métodos basados en redes neuronales artificiales*, Proyecto No. 209.736/2004, Pontificia Universidad Católica de Valparaíso, Chile, 2005.

[19] Rusu C.: *Modelarea suprafetelor asistata de calculator, cu aplicatii in geologie*, PhD Thesis, Universitatea Tehnică Cluj-Napoca, Romania, September 2001.

[20] Rusu C.: *Neural Network Methods in Surface Modeling. Preliminary Notes*, Creative Mathematics, Vol. 13 (2004), North University of Baia Mare, Romania, pp. 111-120.

[21] Rusu C., Rusu V.: *Uso de funciones de base radial en monitoreo ambiental*, Actas de la XXXI Conferencia Latinoamericana de Informática (CLEI 2005), Cali, Colombia, 10-14.10.2005.

[22] Swan A.R.H., Sandilands M.: *Introduction to Geological Data Analysis*, Blackwell Science, Oxford, 1995.

[23] Watson D.: *nngridr. An Implementation of Natural Neighbor Interpolation*, Vol. I of the Natural Neighbour Series, Claremont, Australia, 1994.

[24] Wingle W.: *Examining Common Problems Associated with Various Contouring Methods*, Particularly Inverce-Distance Methods, Using Shaded Relief Surfaces, Geotech '92 Conference Proceedings, Lakewood, Colorado, USA, September, 1992.

[25] Wong K.W. and others: *Rainfall Prediction Using Neural Fuzzy Technique*, in Mapping radioactivity in the environment, edited by Dubois G, Malczewski J., and De Cort M., European Commission, Joint Research Center, Luxembourg, 2003, pp. 213-221.

Neural Networks applied to wireless communications

Georgina Stegmayer[1] and Omar Chiotti[2]

[1] C.I.D.I.S.I., Universidad Tecnológica Nacional, Lavaise 610, 3000 Santa Fe, Argentina. e-mail: gstegmay@frsf.utn.edu.ar
[2] INGAR-CONICET, Avellaneda 3654, 3000 Santa Fe, Argentina. e-mail: chiotti@ceride.gov.ar

Abstract. This paper presents a time-delayed neural network (TDNN) model that has the capability of learning and predicting the dynamic behavior of nonlinear elements that compose a wireless communication system. This model could help speeding up system deployment by reducing modeling time. This paper presents results of effective application of the TDNN model to an amplifier, part of a wireless transmitter.

1 Introduction

In new generation wireless communications - i.e. third generation (3G) standards such as WCDMA (Wideband Code Multiple Division Access) and UMTS (Universal Mobile Telecommunications System) towards which most of the current cellular networks will migrate - system component modeling has become a critical task inside the system design cycle, due to modern digital modulation schemes [1].

New standards may introduce changes in the behavior of the devices that are part of the system (e.g. mobile phones and their internal components) mainly due to the modulation schemes they use, generating nonlinearities in the behavior and memory effects (when an output signal depends on past values of an input signal). Memory effects in the time-domain cause the output of an electronic device to deviate from a linear output when the signal changes, resulting in the deterioration of the whole system performance since the device begins behaving nonlinearly. In this work we are interested in modeling the nonlinear behavior that an amplifier can have inside a wireless transmission.

Amplifiers are a major building block of modern RF digital wireless transmitters (i.e. cellular phones). Figure 1 shows a simplified block diagram of what a cellular phone communication would be. The voice coming from the phone speaker (analog signal) has to be digitalized to be transmitted through the wireless network, and this is the task of an Analog/Digital converter. The digitalized voice then has to be compressed to reduce bit rate and bandwidth. It is also codified, to format the data so the receiver can detect and minimize errors by doing the reverse operation. After that, a modulator adds the carrier signal to

Please use the following format when citing this chapter:

Stegmayer, G., Chiotti, O., 2006, in IFIP International Federation for Information Processing, Volume 217, Artificial Intelligence in Theory and Practice, ed. M. Bramer, (Boston: Springer), pp. 129–138.

the data signal. The signal has to reach an antenna from the cellular phone with enough strength to guarantee the communication. But the signal suffers from attenuation and needs amplification before that. Therefore, the final element of the chain is a power amplifier (PA) which amplifies the signal before it travels to the nearer antenna and to the receiver side of the communications chain.

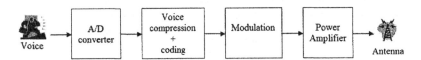

Fig. 1. Simplified block diagram of a digital wireless transmitter.

An amplifier works by increasing the magnitude of an applied signal. Amplifiers can be divided into two big groups: linear amplifiers, which produce an output signal directly proportional to the input signal, and power amplifiers which have the same function as the first ones, but their objective is to obtain maximum output power. A PA can work in different "classes": in Class A if it arrives at the limit of the linearity; and class B when it works in nonlinear regime. Moreover, in wireless communications, the transmitter itself introduces nonlinearities when operating near maximum output power [2].

Nonlinear behavior modeling has been object of increasing interest in the last years [3][4] since classical techniques that were traditionally applied for modeling are not suitable anymore. That is why new techniques and methodologies have been recently proposed, as for example neural network (NN) based modeling applied to PA modeling[5].

Neural networks, as a measurement-based technique, may provide a computationally efficient way to relate inputs and outputs, without the computational complexity of full circuit simulation or physics level knowledge [6], therefore significantly speeding up the analysis process. No knowledge of the internal structure is required and the modeling information is completely included in the device external response.

Although the NN approach has been largely exploited for static simulation, their application to dynamic systems modeling is a rather new research field. In this paper we present a new NN model for modeling nonlinear elements that belong ro a communications chain, using a network which takes into account device nonlinearity and memory effects. In particular, this paper presents the results of the proposed model to nonlinear PA modeling.

The organization of the paper is the following: in the next Section, NN-based modeling of electronic components is presented. Section 3 explains the neural network model presented in this paper and shows its architecture and parameters. In Section 4, measurements and validation results are shown. Finally, the conclusions are reported in Section 5.

2 Neural network-based modeling

Neural network-based models are nowadays seen as a potential alternative for modeling electronics elements having medium-to-strong memory effects along with high-order nonlinearity. NNs are preferred over traditional methods (i.e. equivalent-circuit, empirical models) because of their speed in implementation and accuracy. A NN model can be used during the stage of system design for a rapid evaluation of its performance and main characteristics. The model can be directly trained with measurements extracted from the real system, speeding up the design cycle. NN models can be more detailed and rapid than traditional equivalent-circuit models, more exact and flexible than empirical models, and easier to develop when a new technology is introduced. By profiting from their potential to learn a device behavior based on simulated or measured records of its input and output signals, they were used in nonlinear modeling and design of many microwave circuits and systems [7].

The increasing number of electronic devices models proposed using NNs that have appeared in the last years [8][13][10] shows their importance and interest. Many topologies of NNs are reported in the literature for modeling different types of circuits and systems, with different kinds of linear and nonlinear behavior [11]. However, until very recently, NNs for modeling were applied almost exclusively to instantaneous behavior of the input variables alone. Although this approach has been largely exploited for static simulation, their application to dynamic system is a rather new research field. Recently have appeared NN-based models taking into account the dynamic phenomena in RF microwave devices [12].

For representation of a system which has a nonlinear behavior and is dynamic, intending by dynamic not only that the device characteristic varies over time but also that it depends on past values of its controlling input variables, not any NN topology can be used. A neural model which includes time-dependence into the network architecture is the time-delayed neural network (TDNN), a special type of the well-known multilayer-perceptron (MLP). TDNNs have been successfully applied for solving the temporal processing problems in speech recognition, system identification, control and signal modeling and processing [13]. They are suited for dynamic systems representation because the continuous time system derivatives are approximated inside the model by discrete time-delays of the model variables.

A TDNN is based on the feedforward MLP neural network with the addition of tapped delay lines (Z^{-1}) which generate delayed samples of the input variables. They are used to add the history of the input signals to the model, needed for memory effects modeling. The TDNN entries include not only the current value of the input signal, but also its previous values, as illustrates figure 2. The memory depth M of the element or system analyzed is reflected on the length of the taps. The strategy followed to set the system memory is dictated by the bandwidth accuracy required.

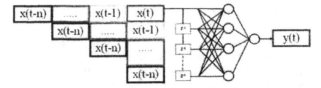

Fig. 2. Time-Delayed neural network (TDNN) model and its corresponding input data.

In this paper we propose the application of a TDNN model for modeling nonlinear and dynamic behavior of devices or elements, parts of a communication system. The model proposed is explained in detail in the next Section.

3 TDNN model

The proposed model has the classical three layers topology for universal approximation in a MLP: the input variable and its delayed samples, the nonlinear hidden layer and a linear combination of the hidden neurons outputs at the output neuron. The architecture of the TDNN is shown in figure 3.

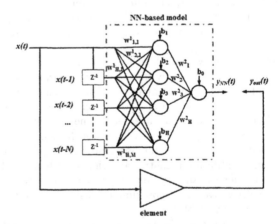

Fig. 3. Time-Delayed neural network (TDNN) to model a communications chain component.

The input layer has as inputs the samples of the independent variable, together with its time-delayed values. The model here presented shows a one-input variable dependence (x) of one output variable (y), but the model can be easily extended to more input/output variables. The variable can have a delay tap between 0 and N, then the total number of input neurons is M $(M = N + 1)$.

In the hidden layer, the number h of hidden neurons varies between 1 and H. The hidden units have a nonlinear activation function. In general, the hyperbolic tangent (tanh) will be used because this function is usually chosen in the electronics field for nonlinear behavior. In our model we have used H = 10, but if necessary, the number of neurons in the hidden layer can be changed to improve the network accuracy. The hidden neurons receive the sum of the weighted inputs plus a corresponding bias value for each neuron b_h. All the neurons have bias values. This fact gives more degrees of freedom to the learning algorithm and therefore more parameters can be optimized, apart from weights, to better represent a nonlinear system.

The weights between layers are described with the usual perceptron notation, where the sub-indexes indicate the origin and the destination of the connection weight, e.g. $w_{j,i}$ means that the weight w relates the destination neuron j with the origin neuron i. However, a modification in the notation was introduced, adding a super-index to the weights, to more easily identify to which layer they belong. Therefore, w^1 means that the weight w belongs to the connection between the inputs and the first hidden layer, and w^2 means that the weight w belongs to the connection between the first hidden layer and the second one (in our particular case, the second hidden layer happens to be the output layer). In this second group of connections weights, the sub-index which indicates the destination neuron has been eliminated because there is only one possible destination neuron (the output).

This unique output neuron has a linear activation function which acts as a normalization neuron (this is usual choice in MLP models). Therefore, the output of the proposed TDNN model is calculated as the sum of the weighted outputs of the hidden neurons plus the corresponding output neuron bias (b_0), yielding equation 1.

$$y_{NN}(t) = b_0 + \left[\sum_{h=1}^{H} w_h^2 \tanh \left(b_h + \sum_{i=0}^{N} w_{h,i+1}^1 x(t-i) \right) \right] \tag{1}$$

Network initialization is an important issue for training the TDNN with the back-propagation algorithm, in particular in what respects speed of execution. In this work the initial weights and biases of the model are calculated using the Nguyen-Widrow initial conditions [14] which allow reducing training time, instead of a purely random initialization.

Once the TDNN model has been defined, it is trained with time-domain measurements of the element output variable under study ($y_{out}(t)$), which is expressed in terms of its discrete samples. To improve network accuracy and speed up learning, the inputs are normalized to the domain of the hidden neurons nonlinear activation functions (i.e for the hyperbolic tangent tanh, the interval is $[-1; +1]$). The formula used for normalization is shown in equation 2.

$$x^{norm} = \frac{2 \left(x - min\{x\} \right)}{\left(max\{x\} - min\{x\} \right)} - 1 \tag{2}$$

During training, network parameters are optimized using a backpropagation algorithm such as the Levenberg-Marquardt [15], chosen due to its good performance and speed in execution. To evaluate the TDNN learning accuracy, the mean square error (mse) is calculated at each iteration k of the algorithm, using equation 3, where P is the number of input/output pairs in the training set, y_{out} is the output target and y_{NN} is the NN output.

$$mse = \frac{1}{P} \sum_{k=1}^{P} E(k)^2 = \frac{1}{P} \sum_{k=1}^{P} (y_{out}(k) - y_{NN}(k))^2 \tag{3}$$

The good generality property of a NN models says that it must perform well on a new dataset distinct from the one used for training. Even a excessive number of epochs or iterations on the learning phase could make performance to decrease, causing the over-fitting phenomena. That is why, to avoid it, the total amount of data available from measurements is divided into training and validation subsets, all equally spaced. We have used the "early-stopping" technique [16], where if there is a succession of training epoch in which accuracy improves only for the training data and not for the validation data, over-fitting has occurred and the learning is terminated. The obtained results are shown in the next section.

4 Measurements and validation results

For training the neural model, a dedicated test-set for accurate PA characterization has been used. It provides static and pulsed DC characterization, scattering parameter measurements, real-time load/source-pull at fundamental and harmonic frequencies, and gate and drain time-domain RF waveforms. The measurements are carried out with a Microwave Transition Analyzer and a large-signal Vector Network Analyzer.

Complete characterization was performed for different input power levels and different classes of operation at 1 GHz on a 2 ns window, as shows figure 4. Class A is biased at 50% IDSS, and class B with $IDS = 0$. A 1 mm total gate periphery GaN HEMT based on SiC with IDSS = 700 mA, has been measured at 1 GHz. The power sweep ranged from -21 to +27 dBm. Only the first 4 harmonics are taken into account.

The basic idea to characterize the nonlinear models for IDS is to collect input-output data with different tuned-load terminations, mapping the widest region in the I-V characteristic. Time-domain data have been collected only for load-pull characterization results in this case, that is three tuned-loads, 50 ohm, the best output power (Pout) and the best output efficiency (PAE). The dynamic load curves corresponding to the selected loads are rather close in class A operation, whereas they are fairly open in class B operation. This suggested to use the all three selected loads from class B characterization, and only 50 ohm load data from class A. The other characterization data will be

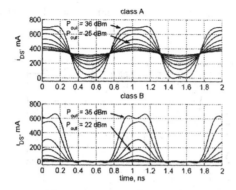

Fig. 4. Time-domain waveforms at 1 GHz at increasing power for class A (top), and B (bottom) at 50 Ohm load used for training.

used for model validation. In principle, however, this method does not need full load-pull characterization, but only to map gate and drain nonlinear models for different generic tuned-loads, in order to concern the widest region in the I-V characteristic. Input data vectors of VGS and VDS for each load and power level have been first copied and delayed as many times, to represent the network inputs, as necessary to account for memory, and then joined together to train the TDNN model with all the working classes, the selected load terminations and the power levels, simultaneously. This is shown in figure 5.

Class A   **Class B**
50 Ohm   **50 Ohm**   **opt Pout**   **opt PAE**

| Pin1, Pin2, ... | Pin1, Pin2, ... | Pin1, Pin2, ... | Pin1, Pin2, ... |

| Vds(t) |
| Vds(t-1) |
| Vds(t-2) |
| Vds(t-3) |
| Vds(t-4) |
| Vgs(t) |
| Vgs(t-1) |
| Vgs(t-2) |
| Vgs(t-3) |
| Vgs(t-4) |

...

| Vds(t) |
| Vds(t-1) |
| Vds(t-2) |
| Vds(t-3) |
| Vds(t-4) |
| Vgs(t) |
| Vgs(t-1) |
| Vgs(t-2) |
| Vgs(t-3) |
| Vgs(t-4) |

Training data

Fig. 5. TDNN model training data organization.

We report here some results for class A and B, at VDS=30V. The validation test includes the best Pout load, that has not been used for model training, and some intermediate points for input power levels not included in the training set. Results obtained show a rather good agreement between experimental and modelled data, in fact the relative mean square error is lower than 1e-04 (figure 6).

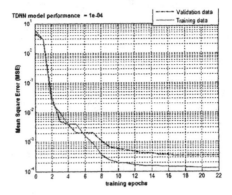

Fig. 6. TDNN model performance.

Figure 7 reports the output PA time-domain waveforms at increasing output power at 50 Ohm load: the upper plots are relative to a class A condition, while the bottom ones refer to class B operations. The left figures report the measurements, while the right ones show the TDNN simulation result. Figure 8 shows the comparison between the training (left) and validation (right) measurement data used for class A operation and the TDNN model response.

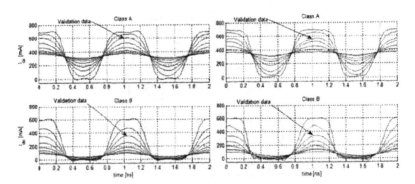

Fig. 7. Time-domain waveforms at 1 GHz at increasing power for class A (top), and B (bottom). Measurements (left), TDNN output (right). The pointed arrow waveform refers to a validation data subset.

From the comparison between measurements and model output, the waveforms good agreement in general. Also for the power levels excluded from the training data, used only for model validation. This is a key result to prove the model predictive capabilities. The model is also capable of recognizing the class in which the device is working and in consequence give a reasonable output response.

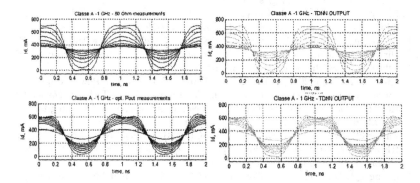

Fig. 8. Time domain waveforms at 1 GHz at increasing power for class A at 50 Ohm (used for training), and optimum Pout (used for validation). Measurements (left), TDNN output (right).

5 Conclusions

In this paper, a model that has the capability of learning and predicting the dynamic behavior of nonlinear PAs, based on a Time-Delayed Neural Network (TDNN), has been proposed. Validation and accuracy of the TDNN model in the time-domain showed good agreements between the TDNN model output data and measurements.

The TDNN model can be trained with input/output device measurements or simulations, and a very good accuracy can be obtained in the device characterization easily and rapidly. These properties make this kind of models specially suitable for new wireless communications components modeling, which are mostly nonlinear and require speed, accuracy and simplicity when designing and building the model.

6 Acknowledgement

The authors would like to thank Prof. Marco Pirola and Vittorio Camarchia, from Politecnico di Torino at Turin (IT), for providing the measurements used in this work. Also, we would like to thank Banco Ro and Red Universia for the financial support under project number INV-1334.

References

1. Evci C, Barth U, Sehier P, Sigle R. (2003) The path to beyond 3G systems: strategic and technological challenges. In: Proc. 4th Int. Conf. on 3G Mobile Communication Technologies, pp. 299-303

2. Elwan H, Alzaher H, Ismail M (2001) New generation of global wireless compatibility. IEEE Circuits and Devices Magazine 17: 7-19

3. Ahmed A, Abdalla MO, Mengistu ES, Kompa G. (2004) Power Amplifier Modeling Using Memory Polynomial with Non-uniform Delay Taps. In: Proc. IEEE 34th European Microwave Conf., pp. 1457-1460

4. Ku H, Kenney JS (2003) Behavioral Modeling of Nonlinear RF Power Ampli-fiers considering memory effects. IEEE Trans. Microwave Theory Tech. 51: 2495-2504

5. Root D, Wood J (2005) Fundamentals of Nonlinear Behavioral Modeling for RF and Microwave design. Artech House, Boston

6. Zhang QJ, Gupta KC, Devabhaktuni VK (2003) Artificial Neural Networks for RF and Microwave Design - From Theory to practice. IEEE Trans. Microwave Theory Tech. 51: 1339-1350

7. Zhang QJ, Gupta KC (2000) Neural Networks for RF and Microwave Design. Artech House, Boston

8. Schreurs D, Verspecht J, Vandamme E, Vellas N, Gaquiere C, Germain M, Borghs G (2003) ANN model for AlGaN/GaN HEMTs constructed from near-optimal-load large-signal measurements. IEEE Trans. Microwave Theory Tech. 51: 447-450

9. Liu T, Boumaiza S, Ghannouchi FM (2004) Dynamic Behavioral Modeling of 3G Power Amplifiers Using Real-Valued Time-Delay Neural Networks. IEEE Trans. Microwave Theory Tech. 52: 1025-1033

10. Ahmed A, Srinidhi ER, Kompa G (2005) Efficient PA modelling using Neural Network and Measurement setup for memory effect characterization in the power device. In: Proc. IEEE MTT-S International Microwave Symposium, pp. 1871-1874

11. Alabadelah A, Fernandez T, Mediavilla A, Nauwelaers B, Santarelli A, Schreurs D, Tazón A, Traverso PA (2004) Nonlinear Models of Microwave Power Devices and Circuits. In: Proc. 12th GAAS Symposium, pp. 191-194

12. Xu J, Yagoub MCE, Ding R, Zhang QJ (2002) Neural-based dynamic modeling of nonlinear microwave circuits. IEEE MTT-S Int. Microwave Symp. Dig. 1: 1101-1104

13. Liu T, Boumaiza S, Ghannouchi FM (2004) Dynamic Behavioral Modeling of 3G Power Amplifiers using real-valued Time-Delay Neural Networks. IEEE Trans. Microwave Theory Tech. 52: 1025-1033

14. Nguyen D, Widrow B (1990) Improving the learning speed of 2-layer neural networks by choosing initial values of the adaptive weights. In: Proc. IEEE Int. Joint Conf. Neural Networks, vol. 3, pp. 21-26

15. Marquardt DW (1963) An algorithm for least-squares estimation of non-linear parameters. Journal of the Society for Industrial and Applied Mathematics 11: 431-441

16. Sjoberg J, Ljung L (1995) Overtraining, regularization and searching for a minimum, with application to neural networks. Int. J. Control 62: 1391-1407

Anomaly Detection using prior knowledge: application to TCP/IP traffic

Alberto Carrascal[1], Jorge Couchet[2], Enrique Ferreira[3] and Daniel Manrique[4]

1: NEIKER: Instituto Vasco de Investigación y Desarrollo,
acarrascal@neiker.net

2: Shell Corporation, Uruguay, jorge.couchet@shell.com

3: Facultad de Ingeniería y Tecnologías, Universidad Católica del Uruguay,
enferrei@ucu.edu.uy

4: Dpto. Inteligencia Artificial. Facultad de Informática. Univ. Politécnica
de Madrid, dmanrique@fi.upm.es

Abstract. This article introduces an approach to anomaly intrusion detection based on a combination of supervised and unsupervised machine learning algorithms. The main objective of this work is an effective modeling of the TCP/IP network traffic of an organization that allows the detection of anomalies with an efficient percentage of false positives for a production environment. The architecture proposed uses a hierarchy of Self-Organizing Maps for traffic modeling combined with Learning Vector Quantization techniques to ultimately classify network packets. The architecture is developed using the known SNORT intrusion detection system to preprocess network traffic. In comparison to other techniques, results obtained in this work show that acceptable levels of compromise between attack detection and false positive rates can be achieved.

1 Introduction

Nowadays, Information Technology (IT) constitutes a necessity in most organizations. Actually, companies of all sizes have their vital infrastructure based on IT for all their activities. This strong dependence has its risks, e.g. an interruption of the IT services can cause severe problems, endangering the company's assets and image or even worse, its clients as well [1].

The stability of an IT platform may be affected in several ways. The main sources of instability are the following: problems related to hardware; application problems; inadequate personal training and Information Security [2].

In the last years we have seen a steep rise in the importance of the Information Security as a main issue for companies and consequently, the amount of resources invested in technological solutions to this problem has increased accordingly. Table

Please use the following format when citing this chapter:

Carrascal, A., Couchet, J., Ferreira, E., Manrique, D., 2006, in IFIP International Federation for Information Processing, Volume 217, Artificial Intelligence in Theory and Practice, ed. M. Bramer, (Boston: Springer), pp. 139–148.

1, taken from CERT [3], shows the increasing risks associated to Information Security since 1990.

Table 1. Number of security incidents reported to CERT annually.

Year	1990	1991	1992	1993	1994	1995	1996	1997	1998	1999
#Incidents	252	406	773	1,334	2,340	2,412	2,573	2,134	3,734	9,859

Year	2000	2001	2002	2003	2004
#Incidents	21,756	52,658	82,094	137,529	204,625

The growth showed in security incidents makes the development of efficient techniques for intrusion detection a necessity. Mainly, there are two ways to approach the development of an Intrusion Detection System (IDS): Misuse Detection (MD) and Anomaly Detection (AD) [4].

Techniques based on Misuse Detection work with patterns, usually called Signatures, which are configured to match attacks based on some known system vulnerability. Most IDS available today correspond to the MD type, since they are easier to implement. However, MD has some important drawbacks that affect its effectiveness: first, they are somewhat rigid, only able to detect those attacks for which a signature is available. Secondly, a signature database has to be available and maintained regularly and manually since signatures can only be created once a type of attack has been detected and therefore has compromised several systems already. Finally, an intruder with sufficient knowledge of signatures may modified the attacks slightly to avoid known signatures, cheating the IDS based on them.

The Anomaly Detection approach uses Machine Learning (ML) algorithms [5] to model normal activity in an organization. In this way it may detect deviations that can be considered abnormal or suspicious. Most of the drawbacks attributed to MD systems can be overcome by the use of an anomaly detection IDS, which may be able to adapt dynamically and automatically to the relevant characteristics of an organization's activities. In this way, it would not be necessary to know the attacks beforehand to detect them, improving the response time to a security attack. Consequently, the majority of the recent research in the Intrusion Detection area is focused in this direction as can be seen in [6,7,8].

One of the main issues with AD systems is a high percentage of false positive detections (*Normal* cases classified as *Attacks*). This is a very important issue to resolve for practical purposes. In a typical system the percentage of normal traffic is considerably larger than abnormal traffic, therefore, an IDS with a high percentage of false positives could potentially generate an alert file with most of its records due to false positives instead of real anomalies.

Several methods that use ML techniques such as Support Vector Machines (SVM) or K-Nearest Neighbor (KNN) to build an AD system. They have shown a high rate of detection but also a high percentage of false positives as well, making them very difficult to implement in a real system [8]. Recently, some other works have made use of Self Organizing Maps (SOM) [9] to address the issue of false positives. They show a comparable detection rate with a significant decrease in the number of false positive detections [10, 11]. In these works the SOMs are trained using information at packet and connection levels obtained with the IDS called Bro [12]. Although the results are positive, the percentage of false positives is still large to use such a detection system in a real situation. There may be a better way to exploit the information acquired by the SOMs to classify the incoming traffic.

In this work a new architecture aiming to solve the AD problem is presented. It is based on a hierarchy of SOMs combined with LVQ [9] to reduce the percentage of false positives. Only packet level information is used to analyze its contribution in the detection process. The system is implemented using the IDS Snort [13].

1.1   Self Organizing Maps

A SOM [9] is a type of neural network with a competitive unsupervised learning algorithm that performs a transformation of the input space. In general, it consists of a 2D dimensional map of neuron-like units. Each unit has an n-by-1 weight vector m_i associated, with n the dimension of the input space. That structure also determines a neighborhood relationship between the units. The basic SOM has a fix structure and number of units. The number of units determines the granularity of the transformation affecting the overall sensitivity and generalization ability of the map.

During the iterative training process, the unit weights will be adjusted to find common features, correlations and categories within the input data. Because of this, it is usually said that the neurons self organize themselves. Actually, the map tends to approximate the probability density of the input data. Weight vectors tend to zones where there is more input data and few units will cover zones of the input space where there is less information.

During a training step an input vector x is randomly chosen and the unit weight vector closer to x is found. That defines a winner unit c, such that

$$c = \arg \min_i \|x - m_i\| \qquad (1)$$

where the symbol $\|.\|$ refers to a norm, usually the Euclidean. The weight vectors of the unit c and its neighboring units are adjusted to get closer to the input data vector. A common update rule is given by

$$m_i(k+1) = m_i(k) + \alpha(k)(x - m_i(k)), \ i \in N_c(k) \qquad (2)$$

with k denoting the training step; $x(k)$ is the input vector chosen from the input data, $N_c(k)$ is the neighborhood set of unit c and $\alpha(k)$ is the learning rate at step k. The learning rate $\alpha(k)$ goes between 0 and 1 and decreases with k. Training evolves in two phases. During the first phase "big" values of α are used (from 0.3 to 0.99) while the second phase sees smaller values of α (below 0.1). $N_c(k)$ is usually fixed. Bigger neighborhoods are sometimes used in the first training phase.

1.2   Learning Vector Quantization

Learning Vector Quantization (LVQ) may also be considered a type of neural network like the SOM architecture [9]. An LVQ network has a set of units and weight vectors m_i associated to them. There are several training algorithms for LVQ. The algorithm used in this paper, LVQ1, is a supervised learning algorithm for classification, i.e. each input vector has a class assigned to them that the network would like to learn. Initially, each unit is assigned to a class. At step k, given a vector x randomly chosen from the input data, we find the weight vector closer to it m_c, with c given by (1). The vector m_c is updated in the following way:

$$m_c(k+1) = \begin{cases} m_c(k) + \alpha(k)(x - m_c(k)), \text{ if } x \text{ in same class as } m_c \\ m_c(k) - \alpha(k)(x - m_c(k)), \text{ else} \end{cases} \quad (3)$$

where $\alpha(k)$, the learning rate, is bound between 0 and 1 and can be constant or decrease monotonically with each time step.

1.3   Fundamentals of TCP/IP

Transmission Control Protocol (TCP) and Internet Protocol (IP) refers to the most widely used protocols to send and receive data through a network system. Because they work together at different levels of the system (transport and network layers respectively), they are usually named together as TCP/IP.

TCP/IP specifies how to establish and close a connection between processes in different parts of the network and how to send and receive messages between them. A TCP entity accepts messages from a process and breaks them up in pieces up to 64K bytes to send as *datagrams* by the corresponding IP entity. It is up to TCP to guarantee that all datagrams are received and the original message reassembled correctly. TCP datagrams have header and data sections. The minimum TCP header is 20 bytes long. It mainly contains source and destination addresses, packet sequence number for reassembly, several flags for connection purposes (URG, ACK, EOM, RST, SYN and FIN), a header checksum, some optional parameters and its own length.

An IP entity takes TCP datagrams, add its own IP header to generate what is called *network packets* and sends them to its destination. The IP header, which is also 20 bytes minimum, contains source and destination addresses, header and total length, protocol, type of service, flags, checksum and other attributes. In particular, type of service (1 byte) allows the user to select the quality of service it wants, from speed for voice connections to reliability for file transfer uses.

This is a very brief overview of TCP/IP, interested readers should refer to [14] for a complete explanation of computer networks and protocols. In this paper the information contained in the TCP and IP headers of the network packets is used to detect anomalies in network traffic.

2   Anomaly Detection based on SOM/LVQ

The three-layer architecture proposed is shown in Figure 1. The input to the classifier proposed is a vector comprising the main attributes of a window of predefined length of network packets. The output gives the class to which the input is classified: *Normal* or *Attack*.

The first layer examines the variation of each attribute over the time window separately. The second layer correlates the information from the first layer between attributes and makes a three-class decision: *Normal, Attack* or *Indefinite*. The class *Indefinite* introduced refers to the vectors that are *close* to the *Normal* class but have some *Attack* elements. The third layer decides whether the vectors in class *Indefinite* should be in *Normal* or *Attack* using a larger SOM network.

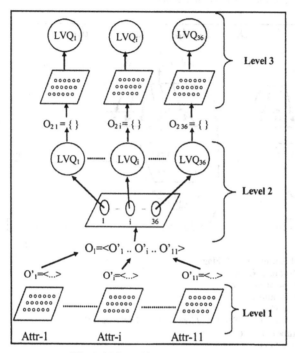

Fig. 1. Main architecture proposed.

2.1 First Level - Feature Clustering

The first level is composed of eleven SOMs, one per attribute selected to characterize TCP traffic. Each SOM takes an input vector of dimension twenty, given by a time window of length twenty of the selected attribute as shown in Figure 2. The goal at this level is to identify the main features of each attribute to obtain a model of the traffic analyzed. Once these SOMs are trained, six units per SOM are selected to reduce the dimensionality of the information to be passed to the second layer. The criteria used to select which units to select are two: the use of a *Potential Function* [10], or the selection of three units associated to normal traffic and three units associated to attack traffic.

2.2 Second Level - Aggregation and Classification

The second level of the architecture, shown in Figure 3, consists in a 6-by-6 SOM and a set of LVQs, one per SOM unit. The input vector to this SOM is composed of the distances of the input vector to the first layer, to all the units selected in the first level SOMs. Therefore, the dimension of the input vector to the second level is 6 times 11. The objective of this SOM is to capture the correlations between the features found by the SOMs of the first level, in order to make a better characterization of the traffic being studied.

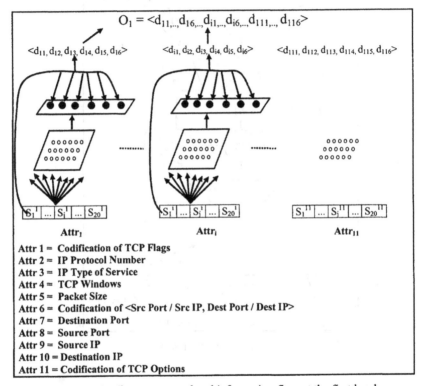

Attr 1 = Codification of TCP Flags
Attr 2 = IP Protocol Number
Attr 3 = IP Type of Service
Attr 4 = TCP Windows
Attr 5 = Packet Size
Attr 6 = Codification of <Src Port / Src IP, Dest Port / Dest IP>
Attr 7 = Destination Port
Attr 8 = Source Port
Attr 9 = Source IP
Attr 10 = Destination IP
Attr 11 = Codification of TCP Options

Fig. 2. Attributes extracted and information flow at the first level.

Once the SOM is trained, each LVQ associated to each unit is tuned in a supervised manner using the subset of inputs to the SOM that makes the unit associated to the LVQ the *winner* in the SOM sense. The label used to train the LVQs for each input is defined as:

$$MyLabel = \frac{\#\,attack\,packets}{\#\,packets} \tag{4}$$

where the number is computed over the time window of the input vector.

It is possible to train the LVQ network in two ways: using the values of *MyLabel* as defined or discretizing the values of *MyLabel* in *Normal*, *Attack* and *Indefinite*, where: $0 < MyLabel(Indefinite) < Attack\_threshold$. In tests, the value of *Attack_threshold* used was 30 %. In the last case, the system is making a 3-class decision at this level, leaving the final classification of the packets labeled in the *Indefinite* class to the next level.

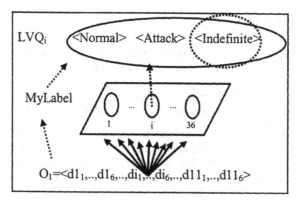

Fig 3. Second level processing.

2.3   Third Level - Indefinite Class Processing

At this level the architecture proposed analyses those input windows that have a relatively low percentage of attack packets, i.e. lower than *Attack_threshold*. Each LVQ from the second layer is associated to a 10-by-10 SOM that is trained with the packets linked to the windows classified as *Indefinite* by that particular LVQ. A LVQ network is assigned to each SOM to make the final classification using as input the distances of each packet to all the units in the associated SOM. The overall processing is shown in Figure 4.

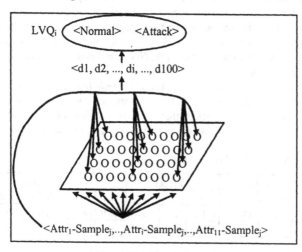

Fig. 4. Third level processing.

3 Experimental Results

The main objective in this work is to find an acceptable compromise between the Detection Rate (DR) and False Positive Rate (FPR) defined by:

$$DR = \frac{\#\,Attacks\,Detected}{Total\,Number\,of\,Attacks}, \quad FPR = \frac{\#\,of\,False\,Positives}{Total\,Number\,of\,Normals}$$

Data for experiments is taken from the DARPA 1998 Intrusion Detection Problem [15]. Two sets were built: the training set contains **1:514,848** records while the test set has **765,029** records. Results shown are computed over the test sets for networks trained using the training set. Training and test sets were generated from DARPA data using SNORT to extract the TCP/IP attributes selected. Only information at the packet level is used. The preprocessor developed works as a plugin to SNORT. It is also able to extract attributes at other levels (e.g. TCP connection) and protocols (e.g. UDP and ICMP). The implementation of SOM and LVQ is based on the package SOM_PAK [16]. Some modifications to this package were necessary to handle large data files as required for this application.

The packet attributes used, shown in Figure 2, were selected by its relevance in the TCP/IP protocol and hence its importance to model network traffic. The attributes that may have several values in the same packet, such as the TCP flags, were coded to reduce the dimensionality of the problem.

Tables 2, 3 and 4 summarize the results obtained with the most relevant experiments run on the architecture proposed. They use the following notation:

Classification: Refers to the amount of classifications performed by the system.

Correct: Represent the number of correct classifications per class made.

Deviations: Show the number of incorrect classifications of each type made.

The initials **N, I** and **A** are used for *Normal, Indefinite* and *Attack* respectively. In the case of deviations we use, for example, **N-I** to indicate the packets belonging to the *Normal* class but classified as *Indefinite*.

It should be noted that, at the third level the *Indefinite* class is sorted between *Normal* and *Attack*. At this level the SOM is not trained with a time window but with each of the twenty individual packets that composed each window. Due to this, each pattern at the second level is transformed into twenty patterns at the third level.

Table 2. Use of Potential function and *My Label* for training.

	Classification			Correct			Deviations					
	N	I	A	N	I	A	N-I	N-A	I-N	I-A	A-N	A-I
Level 2	396674	132355	236000	227250	7657	208396	41845	14382	28584	13222	140840	82853
Level 3	522269	0	71111	481170	0	50926	0	20185	0	0	41099	0

Table 3. Use of Potential function and *My Label* discretized for training.

	Classification			Correct			Deviations					
	N	I	A	N	I	A	N-I	N-A	I-N	I-A	A-N	A-I
Level 2	648290	66580	50159	239197	11238	33256	36754	7526	28848	9377	380245	18588
Level 3	859386	0	429934	701701	0	112103	0	317831	0	0	157685	0

Table 4. Use of 3 centers associated to *Normal* and 3 to *Attack*, and *My Label* discretized.

	Classification			Correct			Deviations					
	N	I	A	N	I	A	N-I	N-A	I-N	I-A	A-N	A-I
Level 2	413132	44929	306968	272431	3922	301335	6591	4455	44363	1178	96338	34416
Level 3	637367	0	261213	246029	0	233798	0	27415	0	0	391338	0

It can be observed that the best results are achieved when the selection of units to represent level one information is based on the classes to discriminate, in this case three for each class. The performance of this option is then:

$$DR = \frac{301335 + 233798/20}{301335 + 96338 + 34416} = 72\% \quad FPR = \frac{4455 + 27415/20}{272431 + 6591 + 4455} = 2\%$$

With respect to the results achieved in [10], the value of FPR is improved by 73% while DR decreased by only 19 %. In general, Table 5 resumes some results obtained in previous works where ML techniques were used for AD [8, 10].

Table 5. Results of other works using AD methods

Method	Detection Rate	False Positive Rate
Clustering	93%	10%
K-NN	91%	8%
SVM	98%	10%
SOM Hierarchy	89%	7.6%

It can be noted that the DR achieved here is below the ones obtained in the works presented in Table 5. A better inspection of the experiments also show that:

- An important percentage of the attacks presented in the data sets used corresponds to the *user to root* type. This type of attacks are quite difficult to model using TCP/IP protocol characteristics only.
- The prototype implemented is classifying TCP/IP packets up to now. Since a connection usually consists of hundreds of packets, it is expected that the **DR** may improve once the connection information is added to the system.

4 Conclusions

The AD method developed in this work introduces an efficient mechanism to reduce the false positives getting closer to generate sufficiently reliable alerts to be able to use an AD based IDS in a production environment.

It can also be observed that packet information is an important component in the detection of attacks. This work serves as a guide as to which packet information to use to model traffic for this purpose. However, the need to use connection level information is pointed out as well to reach an efficient DR with low FPR.

This investigation is based on a priori knowledge of traffic packets combined with ML techniques to set up the model and pattern recognition techniques for traffic classification. However, many steps are developed in an empirical manner which limits the conclusions that can be made. Therefore, there is the need to develop formal ways to obtain bounds on rates and efficiency of the AD methods.

From the results of this work we are following this research in two directions. First, we are exploring more efficient ML techniques for the intrusion detection problem. Besides, we are developing a theoretical framework to obtain a deeper understanding of the problem which may allow us to get robust models that are feasible to implement in the real world.

5 References

1. CSI, Computer Security Institute. *2004 CS//FBI Computer Crime and Security Survey.* (2004); http://www.gocsi.com/.

2. C. Kruegel, F. Valeur, and G. Vigna, *Intrusion Detection and Correlation - Challenges and Solutions* (Springer Verlag, New York, 2005).

3. CERT Coordination Center, CERT/CC Statistics (1988-2005); http://www.cert.org/stats/.

4. E. Carter. *Cisco Secure Intrusion Detection System* (Cisco Press, 2001).

5. T.M. Mitchell. *Machine Learning* (McGraw-Hill, 1997).

6. D.S. Kim, H.-N. Nguyen, and J.S. Park, Genetic algorithm to improve SVM based network intrusion detection system, 19th International Conference on Advanced Information Networking and Applications, Vol. 2, (2005), pp.155-158.

7. M. Markou, and S. Singh, Novelty Detection: A Review, Part II: Neural Network Based Approaches. Signal Processing, Vol. 83 (2003), pp. 2499-2521.

8. E. Eskin, A. Arnold, M. Prerau, L. Portnoy, and S Stolfo, A Geometric Framework for Unsupervised Anomaly Detection: Detecting intrusions in unlabeled data, In D. Barbara and S. Jajodia, editors, Applications of Data Mining in Computer Security (Kluwer, 2002).

9. T.Kohonen. *Self Organizing Maps*, Third Extended Edition (Springer, 2001).

10. H.G. Kayacik. *Hierarchical Self Organizing Map Based IDS on KDD Benchmark.* Master's thesis, Dalhousie University (2003).

11. P. Lichodzijewski, A.N. Zincir-Heywood, and M.I. Heywood, Host -based Intrusion Detection Using Self-Organizing Maps, IEEE World Congress on Computational Intelligence, International Joint Conference on Neural Networks, IJCNN (2002).

12. Bro. Intrusion detection system (2005); http://www.bro-ids.org/

13. Snort. open source network intrusion prevention and detection system (2005); http://www.snort.org.

14. A. S. Tanenbaum. *Computer Networks* (2nd Edition, Prentice-Hall, 1989).

15. MIT Lincoln Laboratory (1998); http://www.ll.mit.edu/IST/ideval/data/data index.html.

16. SOM_PAK, Helsinki University of Technology, Laboratory of Computer and Information Science (2005); http://www.cis.hut.fi/research/som_lvq_pak.shtml.

A study on the ability of Support Vector Regression and Neural Networks to Forecast Basic Time Series Patterns

Sven F. Crone[1], Jose Guajardo[2], and Richard Weber[2]

1 Lancaster University, Department of Management Science, Lancaster
LA1 4YX, Lancaster, UK s.crone@lancaster.ac.uk
2 University of Chile, Department of Industrial Engineering, Republica
701, Santiago, Chile {jguajard,rweber}@dii.uchile.cl

Abstract. Recently, novel learning algorithms such as Support Vector Regression (SVR) and Neural Networks (NN) have received increasing attention in forecasting and time series prediction, offering attractive theoretical properties and successful applications in several real world problem domains. Commonly, time series are composed of the combination of regular and irregular patterns such as trends and cycles, seasonal variations, level shifts, outliers or pulses and structural breaks, among others. Conventional parametric statistical methods are capable of forecasting a particular combination of patterns through ex ante selection of an adequate model form and specific data preprocessing. Thus, the capability of semi-parametric methods from computational intelligence to predict basic time series patterns without model selection and preprocessing is of particular relevance in evaluating their contribution to forecasting. This paper proposes an empirical comparison between NN and SVR models using radial basis function (RBF) and linear kernel functions, by analyzing their predictive power on five artificial time series: stationary, additive seasonality, linear trend, linear trend with additive seasonality, and linear trend with multiplicative seasonality. Results obtained show that RBF SVR models have problems in extrapolating trends, while NN and linear SVR models without data preprocessing provide robust accuracy across all patterns and clearly outperform the commonly used RBF SVR on trended time series.

1 Introduction

Support Vector Regression (SVR) and Artificial Neural Networks (NN) have found increasing consideration in forecasting theory, leading to successful applications in time series and explanatory forecasting in various domains, including business and management science [1, 2]. Methods form computational intelligence promise

Please use the following format when citing this chapter:

Crone, S., Guajardo, J., Weber, R., 2006, in IFIP International Federation for Information Processing, Volume 217, Artificial Intelligence in Theory and Practice, ed. M. Bramer, (Boston: Springer), pp. 149–158.

attractive features to business forecasting, being data driven, semi-parametric learning machines, permitting universal approximation of arbitrary linear or nonlinear functions from examples without a priori assumptions on the model structure, often outperforming conventional statistical approaches of ARIMA- or exponential smoothing- methods.

Despite their theoretical capabilities, NN as SVR are not established forecasting methods in business practice. Recently, substantial theoretical criticism of NN has raised skepticism regarding their ability to forecast even simple time series patterns of seasonality or trends without prior data preprocessing [3]. While all novel methods must ultimately be evaluated in an objective experiment using a number of empirical time series, adequate error measures and multiple origins of evaluation [4], the fundamental questions to their ability to approximate and generalize basic time series patterns must be evaluated beforehand. Time series can generally be characterized by the combination of basic regular patterns: level, trend, season and residual errors. For trend, a variety of linear, progressive, degressive and regressive patterns are feasible. For seasonality, an additive or multiplicative combination with level and trend further determines the shape of the final time series. Consequently, we evaluate SVR and NN on a set of artificially created time series derived from previous publications. We evaluate the comparative forecasting accuracy of each method to reflect their ability of learning and forecasting fundamental time series patterns relevant to empirical forecasting tasks.

This paper is organized as follows. First, we provide a brief introduction to SVR and NN in forecasting time series of observations. Section three presents the artificially generated time series and the experimental design. This is followed by the experimental results and their discussion. Conclusions are given in section 4.

2   Modelling SVR and NN for Time Series Prediction

2.1   Support Vector Regression

We apply the common Support Vector Regression (SVR) algorithm as proposed by Vapnik [5], which uses an ε-insensitive loss function for predictive regression problems. This function allows a tolerance degree to errors not greater than ε. The description is based on the terminology used in [6, 7]. Let $\{(x_1,y_1),....., (x_l,y_l)\}$, where $x_i \in R^n$ and $y_i \in R$, be the training data points available to build a regression model. The SVR algorithm applies a transformation function Φ to the original data points from the initial Input Space, to a higher-dimensional Feature Space F. In this new space, we construct a linear model, which corresponds to a non-linear model in the original space[1]:

---

[1] When Φ is the identity function, the Feature Space is equivalent to the Input Space, and the model constructed is linear in the original space.

$$\Phi : R^n \to F, w \in F$$
$$f(x) = \langle w, \Phi(x) \rangle + b$$

The goal when using the ε-insensitive loss function is to find a function that fits current training data with a deviation less or equal to ε, and at the same time is as flat as possible. This means that one seeks for a small weight vector w; one way to do that is e.g. by minimizing the quadratic norm of the vector w [6]. As this problem could be infeasible, slack variables ξ_i, ξ_i* are introduced to allow error levels greater than ε, arriving to the formulation proposed in [5]:

$$Min \frac{1}{2} \|w\|^2 + C \sum_{i=1}^{\ell} (\xi_i + \xi_i^*)$$
$$s.t. y_i - \langle w, \Phi(x_i) \rangle - b \le \varepsilon + \xi_i$$
$$\langle w, \Phi(x_i) \rangle + b - y_i \le \varepsilon + \xi_i^*$$
$$\xi_i, \xi_i^* \ge 0, i = 1, 2, ..., \ell$$

This is known as the primal problem of the SVR algorithm. The objective function takes into account generalization ability and accuracy in the training set, and embodies the structural risk minimization principle [8]. Parameter C measures the trade-off between generalization ability and accuracy in the training data, and parameter ε defines the degree of tolerance to errors. To solve the problem stated above, it is more convenient to represent the problem in its dual form. For this purpose, a Lagrange function is constructed, and once applying saddle point conditions, it can be shown that the following solution is obtained [8]:

$$w = \sum_{i=1}^{\ell} (\alpha_i - \alpha_i^*) \Phi(x_i)$$

$$f(x) = \sum_{i=1}^{\ell} (\alpha_i - \alpha_i^*) K(x_i, x) + b$$

Here, α_i and α_i^* are the dual variables, and the expression $K(x_i, x)$ represents the inner product between $\Phi(x_i)$ and $\Phi(x)$, which is known as the kernel function [8]. The existence of such a function allows us to obtain a solution for the original regression problem, without explicitly considering the transformation $\Phi(x)$ applied to the data. In our experiments we use radial basis functions (RBF) and linear kernel functions.

Limited research has been conducted to investigate the ability of SVR for predicting different time series patterns. Experiments performed by Hansen et. al [9] compare SVR performance with 3 statistical methods (e.g. ARIMA) on predicting 9 different patterns present in real world time series. Among other patterns, they tried trends, seasonality, cycles, and combinations of them. Their experiments show SVR models outperforming the other methods on 8 of the 9 patterns; particularly, they obtained very good results using SVR for extrapolating linear and non linear trends. Guajardo et al. [10] compared SVR with ARMAX models for predicting seasonal time series in a weekly sales forecasting domain for 5 different products. Their experiments show that SVR were slightly better than ARMAX models, succeeding in extrapolating seasonal patterns (without trends) with SVR.

2.2   Neural Networks

Forecasting with non-recurrent NN may encompass prediction of a dependent variable $\hat{y}$ from lagged realizations of the predictor variable y_{t-n}, 1 or i explanatory variables x_i of metric, ordinal or nominal scale as well as lagged realizations thereof, $x_{i,t-n}$. Therefore, NNs offer large degrees of freedom towards the forecasting design, permitting explanatory or causal forecasting through estimation of a functional relationship of the form $\hat{y} = f(x_1, x_2, ..., x_z)$, as well as general transfer function models and simple time series prediction. Following, we present a brief introduction to modelling NN for time series prediction; a general discussion is given in [11, 12].

Forecasting time series with NN is generally based on modelling the network in analogy to a non-linear autoregressive AR(p) model [2, 13]. At a point in time t, a one-step ahead forecast $\hat{y}_{t+1}$ is computed using $p=n$ observations $y_t, y_{t-1}, ..., y_{t-n+1}$ from n preceding points in time t, t-1, t-2, ..., t-n+1, with n denoting the number of input units of the NN. This models a time series prediction as of

$$\hat{y}_{t+1} = f(y_t, y_{t-1}, ..., y_{t-n+1}) .$$

The architecture of a feed-forward Multilayer Perceptron (MLP), a well researched NN paradigm, of arbitrary topology is displayed in figure 1.

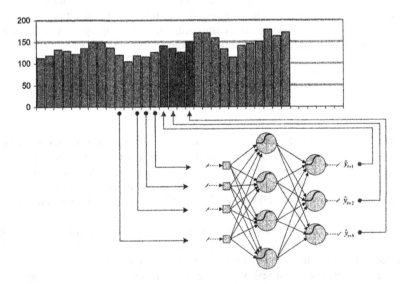

Fig. 1. Autoregressive MLP application to time series forecasting with a MLP of arbitrary topology, using n input neurons for observations in t, t-1, t-2, ..., t-n-1, m hidden units, h output units for time periods t+1, t+2, ..., t+h and a two layers of trainable weights. The bias is displayed within the units.

Data is presented to the MLP as a sliding window over the time series observations. The task of the MLP is to model the underlying generator of the data during training, so that a valid forecast is made when the trained NN is subsequently presented with a new input vector value.

The network paradigm of MLP offers extensive degrees of freedom in modelling for prediction tasks. Structuring the degrees of freedom, each expert must decide upon the selection and sampling of datasets, the degrees of data preprocessing, the static architectural properties, the signal processing within nodes and the learning algorithm in order to achieve the design goal, characterized through the objective function or error function. For a detailed discussion of these issues and the ability of NN to forecast univariate time series, the reader is referred to [2].

3 Experiments and Results

3.1 Description of the Artificial Time Series

We evaluate a set of five artificial time series of monthly retail sales motivated from Pegel's original classification, later extended by Gardner to incorporate degressive trends. Time series are composed of regular patterns of different forms of linear, progressive, degressive or regressive trends T, additively or multiplicatively combined with seasonality S, a constant level L and residual noise E. In addition, empirical time series are impacted by irregular patterns such as level shifts and pulses, which are disregarded. To evaluate the ability of different computational intelligence methods we create a set of benchmark time series for the most common regular time series patterns: linear trend and different forms of seasonality. Consequently, we create individual time series patterns and combine them accordingly, overlaying each with additive noise.

	No Seasonality (E)	Additive Seasonality (S_A)	Multiplicative Seasonality (S_M)
No Trend (L)			
Linear Trend (T_L)			

Fig. 2. Basic time series patterns of artificial time according to the Pegels- and Gardner-classification, combining Level, Trend and Seasonality with a medium additive noise level.

In contrast to Pegel's classification, a time series with multiplicative seasonality $L+S_M+E$ cannot display an increasing seasonality in the absence of level changes, it equals the pattern of additive seasonality and was consequently omitted from further analysis. Consequently, we create a set of five time series including a stationary time series L+E (E), seasonality without trend $L+S_A+E$ (S_A), linear trend $L+T_L+E$ (T_L), linear trend with additive seasonality $L+T_L+S_A+E$ (T_LS_A) and linear trend with multiplicative seasonality depending on the level of the time series $L+T_L*S_M+E$

(T_LS_M). The residual error term follows a Gaussian distribution $N(0, \sigma^2)$ applying a medium level of noise $\sigma^2 = 25$. The original time series data was taken from the experiments of [3] and represent monthly retail sales. All time series considered an additive noise term to allow an estimation of final forecasting accuracy in relationship to the original noise level. Each time series consists of 228 observations.

3.2   Experimental Design

This research investigates whether the five patterns described above can be accurately predicted with RBF SVR, Linear SVR and NN models. For each series, we defined a lag structure including the 13 previous observations as attributes for predicting the next series value (one period ahead prediction); thus, a total of 215 data points remain to build and parameterize models. Data was sequentially divided into training, validation and test sets using 119, 48 and 48 observations respectively; training data is used to build the model, validation data for parameter selection purposes, and test data to evaluate the accuracy on a hold-out data set. All models are parameterized using only training and validation data, withholding all information in the test set (also for scaling etc.) to assure valid ex ante testing. Data was transformed only by applying linear scaling into a [-0.5, 0.5] interval to avoid saturation effects, using minimum and maximum values only from the training and validation data. No other preprocessing procedures such as deseasonalization or detrending were carried out.

As mentioned in section 2.1., SVR models require setting of two parameters: C and ε. In addition, one needs to select an appropriate kernel function to carry out the transformation to a higher dimensional feature space. The RBF kernel function, which is the kernel function most widely utilized for regression (see e.g. [6, 14, 15]), requires the definition of an additional parameter σ. Our heuristic approach for RBF SVR parameter selection can be summarized as follows:

-    First, we determine starting values for the C and ε parameters on each time series by using the empirical rules proposed by Cherkassky and Ma [14], leading to   E {C=0.67538; ε=0.020373}, S_A {C=0.86224; ε=0.0056657}, T_L {C=0.70709; ε=0.0043011}, T_LS_A {C=0.74641; ε=0.0064901}   and T_LS_M {C=0.76968; ε=0.0064652}.
-    Second, we search for 'good' values of the RBF kernel parameter σ using the predetermined parameters C and ε, and evaluate 45 different alternatives for σ={0.001; 0.01; 0.03; 0.05; 0.08; 0.1; 0.3; 0.5; 0.8; 1; 1.3; 1.5; 1.8; 2; 2.3; 2.5; 2.8; 3; 3.3; 3.5; 3.8; 4; 4.3; 4.5; 4.8; 5; 5.3; 5.5; 5.8; 6; 7; 8; 9; 10; 15; 20; 25; 50; 80; 100; 200; 300; 400; 500; 1000}. The value of σ which generates the model with the lowest mean absolute error (MAE) in the validation set is defined as the base parameter for the kernel function. As result, we now have heuristic starting values for the three parameters of the SVR model, C', ε' and σ'.
-    Third, we define a grid around base parameters C', ε' and σ', and retain the best combination of parameters to be the final values used in the SVR model. In our experiments, we tried five different values for each parameter C, ε, σ (factors

0.5, 0.75, 1, 1.25 and 1.5 over the initial values), thus creating a grid of 125 possible parameter settings. The parameter candidate of the grid is selected by using the lowest MAE on the validation set as before.

The scheme for Linear SVR is very similar, but without considering parameter σ. Thus, second step for base parameter σ is not carried out, and the third step involves only 25 different combinations for C and ε. (for additional details see [10]).

For NN models, we used the backpropagation algorithm to train multiple candidates of multilayer perceptron (MLP) networks. The network topology was obtained using a grid search of different hidden nodes $\{0, 2, ..., 20\}$ and activation functions $\{\text{sigmoid; tanh}\}$ with fixed number of input and output nodes, selecting the architecture with the lowest MAE on the validation set. The final model was initialized 20 times using an (13-8-1) architecture comprised of 13 input nodes, 8 hidden nodes and a single output node for $t+1$ predictions, applying a sigmoid transfer function between the input and hidden layers, and a linear function between hidden and output layers. As for SVR models, we selected the network with the lowest validation mean absolute error (MAE) to calculate the test error results.

3.3 Experimental Results and Discussion

To evaluate our models we used the root mean squared error (RMSE), mean absolute error (MAE), and mean absolute percentage error (MAPE). Test set errors obtained using SVR and MLP models for each one of the five series analyzed in this paper are shown in Table 1. As can be seen from Table 1, RBF SVR has the best performance (denoted in bold) on a level time series superimposed with white noise (E) and additive seasonality (S_A) patterns across all error measures. Linear SVR is the best method for predicting linear trend (T_L) and linear trend with multiplicative seasonality patterns ($T_L S_M$), while MLPs provide best results for linear trends with additive seasonality ($T_L S_A$) pattern.

Table 1. Forecasting accuracy on the test set for RBF and linear SVR models and MLP

Series	RBF SVR			Linear SVR			MLP		
	RMSE	MAE	MAPE	RMSE	MAE	MAPE	RMSE	MAE	MAPE
Series E	**4.670**	**3.776**	1.387	5.036	4.108	1.496	4.851	3.946	**1.264**
Series S_A	**4.746**	**3.739**	**0.039**	6.961	5.637	0.058	5.787	4.766	0.048
Series T_L	11.501	10.408	0.046	**5.876**	**4.811**	**0.021**	6.058	4.966	0.022
Series $T_L S_A$	21.267	17.678	0.075	7.915	6.280	0.028	**7.083**	**5.878**	**0.027**
Series $T_L S_M$	14.758	10.842	0.043	7.927	**6.305**	**0.029**	7.673	6.454	0.030
Sum	56.942	46.443	1.590	33.715	27.141	1.632	**31.452**	**26.010**	**1.391**

Since we evaluated artificially constructed time series we can estimate the part of the forecasting errors caused by the artificially created noise, which due to its random nature cannot be forecasted. This permits an analysis to what extent each method was capable of separating noise from structure of varying complexity on the unbiased error measure of MAE. In applying the true mean of the Gaussian residuals as an optimal forecast, we estimate a MAE of 3.801 as a lower bound forecast error for all time series on the test set. It becomes apparent, that RBF SVR exceeds even a 'perfect' forecast for series E and S_A, which can be attributed to the randomness of the data inherent in all ex ante evaluations of forecasting experiments. In contrast, RBF SVR significantly underperform on trended time series patterns, indicating inadequacies of the chosen kernel function. On the contrary, linear SVR shows a more robust prediction of all time series patterns. As the forecasts deviates only slightly from the lower bound in comparison to the level of the time series, as would be reflected in the MAPE, SVR with linear kernel functions may be considered a robust method in forecasting arbitrary time series patterns without preprocessing. Similarly, MLPs forecast all time series patterns robustly and without preprocessing with a comparative high accuracy close to linear SVR and the lower bound.

In summarizing over all time series, applying an equal weight to each of the time series patterns, MLPs robustly outperform RBF SVR on all three error measures of MAE, MAPE and RMSE, whereas MLPs also moderately outperform linear SVR. This indicates that while particular kernel functions enable the SVR to outperform alternative parameterizations, MLPs or linear SVR may prove a more robust alternative in using a single method to forecast a set of time series of different patterns. In addition to these distance based error measures, we evaluate the relative performance by ranking each method by the individual error measure, provided in Table 2.

Table 2. Forecasting accuracy measured by ranks of methods for each error measure

	Rank by RMSE			Rank by MAE			Rank by MAPE		
	SVR RBF	SVR linear	MLP	SVR RBF	SVR linear	MLP	SVR RBF	SVR linear	MLP
Series E	1	3	2	1	3	2	2	3	1
Series S_A	1	3	2	1	3	2	1	3	2
Series T_L	3	1	2	3	1	2	3	1	2
Series $T_L S_A$	3	2	1	3	2	1	3	2	1
Series $T_L S_M$	3	2	1	3	1	2	3	1	2
Sum of Ranks	11	11	8	11	10	9	12	10	8

The findings by ranked error measures confirm little differences between linear SVR and MLPs, with MLPs providing the best results for the limited test design provided across all error measures. SVR with RBF kernel, the most frequently used implementation in time series prediction with SVR to date, performs significantly worse than the other methods.

As must be expected, different error measures identify different 'best' methods. In particular, RMSE and MAPE are considered to be biased error measures. To limit biases in the absence of a true objective function which could motivate the use of a particular error measure, we assume equal weight to each error and focus our conclusions on the MAE. To confirm the results of model accuracy from a statistical point of view, we performed a paired-samples t test on the absolute values of the residuals over the test set data points. Results obtained show that differences between model errors are statistically significant when comparing RBF SVR to Linear SVR ($t=7.337$; $df=239$; $p<0.001$), and RBF SVR to NN ($t=6.999$; $df=239$; $p<0.001$), although not when comparing NN to Linear SVR ($t=-0.989$; $df=239$; $p=0.324$). This indicates that no significant difference in forecasting accuracy between the methods of linear SVR and MLP may be derived from these experiments. Consequently, we need to extend this evaluation on additional time series and variations of MLPs. Results suggest that RBF SVR can predict seasonal patterns but no trends, while linear SVR and NN seem to be able to extrapolate trend as well as seasonal patterns accurately and without preprocessing. By examining the residuals of the models, it can be observed that RBF SVR systematically underestimate hold-out sample observations for trended series, which corresponds to saturation effects.

4 Conclusion

We have examined the ability of RBF SVR, linear SVR and MLP for predicting five basic artificial time series patterns: stationary, seasonality, linear trends, linear trend with additive seasonality, and linear trend with multiplicative seasonality. Results obtained using multiple error measures show that while RBF SVR outperform other methods on non-trended data, they do not provide robust results across all patterns. For time series with trend components, linear SVR and MLP significantly outperform RBF SVR models, which severely underestimate out-of-sample observations, consistently lagging behind upward trends. RBF SVR errors have shown to be statistically significantly higher than linear SVR and NN errors. MLP demonstrate robust performance, providing the highest overall forecasting accuracy in across time series and different statistical error measures and rank based metrics.

Our results confirm previous findings by Guajardo et. al [10], demonstrating accurate forecasts of seasonal time series without trends using RBF SVR, even outperforming established statistical methods such as ARIMAX. Also, they confirm results by Hansen et. al [9], who accurately predicted both linear and nonlinear trends using SVR, outperforming other methods such as ARIMA on several patterns. We assume that Hansen et al. also used linear kernels, as they did not fully document the kernel functions applied. A preliminary hypothesis for our poor results obtained with RBF SVR in extrapolating trend patterns lies in the linear nature of this trend. Previous publications report similar problems of closely related RBF-neural networks in predicting trends and instationary time series. While SVR with linear kernel functions and MLP with linear activation functions in the output units may be particularly suited to extrapolate linear trends, we did not conduct experiments as to their ability to extrapolate non-linear trends.

These issues will be evaluated in an extended set of experiments currently under investigation by the authors, increasing the number of time series patterns and considering additional kinds of trend patterns, also evaluating results against established statistical forecasting methods as benchmarks. Additionally, we will evaluate the influence of preprocessing procedures such as deseasonalization to evaluate alternative perspectives on the problem of extrapolating time series patterns.

Acknowledgement: This work has been supported in part by the Millennium Nucleus "Complex Engineering Systems" (www.sistemasdeingenieria.cl).

References

1. K. P. Liao and R. Fildes, The accuracy of a procedural approach to specifying feedforward neural networks for forecasting, Computers & Operations Research 32 (8) (2005) 2151-2169.
2. G.P. Zhang, B.E. Patuwo, and M.Y. Hu, Forecasting with artificial neural networks: The state of the art, *International Journal of Forecasting*, 1, **14**, 35-62 (1998)
3. G.P. Zhang and M. Qi, Neural network forecasting for seasonal and trend time series, *European Journal of Operational Research* **160**, 501-514 (2005).
4. L. J. Tashman, Out-of-sample tests of forecasting accuracy: an analysis and review, *International Journal of Forecasting* 16 (4) (2000) 437-450.
5. V.Vapnik, *The nature of statistical learning theory* (Springer, New York, 1995).
6. A.J. Smola and B. Schölkopf, A Tutorial on Support Vector Regression, NeuroCOLT Technical Report NC-TR-98-030, 1998 (Royal Holloway College, University of London, UK).
7. K. Müller, A. Smola, G. Rätsch, B. Schölkopf, J. Kohlmorgen, and V. Vapnik, in: Advances in Kernel Methods: Support Vector Learning/ Using Support Vector Machines for Time Series Prediction, edited by B. Schölkopf, J. Burges, and A. Smola (MIT Press, 1999) , pp. 243-254.
8. V.Vapnik, *Statistical Learning Theory* (John Wiley and Sons, New York, 1998).
9. J.V. Hansen, J.B. McDonald, and R.D. Nelson, Some evidence on forecasting time-series with Support Vector Machines, *Journal of the Operational Research Society*, 1, 1-11, 2005.
10. J. Guajardo, J. Miranda, and R. Weber, A Hybrid Forecasting Methodology using Feature Selection and Support Vector Regression, 5th International Conference on Hybrid Intelligent Systems HIS 2005 (Rio de Janeiro, Brazil, 2005), pp. 341-346.
11. C. M. Bishop, Neural networks for pattern recognition. Clarendon Press; Oxford University Press, Oxford, 1995.
12. S. Haykin, Neural networks: a comprehensive foundation, 2nd ed. Prentice Hall, Upper Saddle River, N.J., 1999.
13. A. Lapedes, R. Farber, and Los Alamos National Laboratory, Nonlinear signal processing using neural networks: prediction and system modelling, Los Alamos National Laboratory, Los Alamos, N.M. LA-UR-87-2662, 1987.
14. V. Cherkassky and Y. Ma, Practical selection of SVM parameters and noise estimation for SVM regression, *Neural Networks* **17**(1), 113-126 (2004).
15. D. Mattera and S. Haykin, in: Advances in Kernel Methods: Support Vector Learning/ Support Vector Machines for Dynamic Reconstruction of a Chaotic System, edited by B. Schölkopf, J. Burges and A. Smola (MIT Press, 1999), pp. 211-242.

Neural Plasma

Daniel Berrar and Werner Dubitzky
Systems Biology Research Group, School of Biomedical Sciences,
University of Ulster, Northern Ireland
{dp.berrar, w.dubitzky@ulster.ac.uk,
WWW home page: http://research.bioinformatics.ulster.ac.uk/~dberrar/

Abstract. This paper presents a novel type of artificial neural network, called *neural plasma*, which is tailored for classification tasks involving few observations with a large number of variables. Neural plasma learns to adapt its classification confidence by generating artificial training data as a function of its confidence in previous decisions. In contrast to multilayer perceptrons and similar techniques, which are inspired by topological and operational aspects of biological neural networks, neural plasma is motivated by aspects of high-level behavior and reasoning in the presence of uncertainty. The basic principles of the proposed model apply to other supervised learning algorithms that provide explicit classification confidence values. The empirical evaluation of this new technique is based on benchmarking experiments involving data sets from biotechnology that are characterized by the small-n-large-p problem. The presented study exposes a comprehensive methodology and is seen as a first step in exploring different aspects of this methodology.

1 Introduction

Recent experimentation techniques in biology are probing deeper and deeper into biological phenomena. These so-called high-throughput technologies (measuring thousands of systems parameters in a single experiment) are heralding a paradigm shift (a) from traditional hypothesis-driven to data-driven research in molecular biology and (b) to a systems or systemic, as opposed to reductionistic, approach, attempting to model entire systems in order to understand study their holistic properties and dynamic properties. However, the noisy and high-dimensional data sets generated by these methods present considerable analytical and computational challenges. This study addresses this problem by analyzing high-dimensional gene expression data obtained from DNA microarray experiments investigating cancer. DNA microarrays are a high-throughput technology facilitating the simultaneous measurement of activity and interaction of thousands of genes in a single experiment [1]. This technology has led to the discovery of new biomarkers for disease diagnosis and prognosis, promoted the development of novel drugs for cancer therapy, and has provided new insights into the genesis and progression of multiple types of cancer.

Please use the following format when citing this chapter:

Berrar, D., Dubitzky, W., 2006, in IFIP International Federation for Information Processing, Volume 217, Artificial Intelligence in Theory and Practice, ed. M. Bramer, (Boston: Springer), pp. 159–168.

Because of its importance to diagnostic and prognostic analysis, automated classification has attracted considerable interest in the context of microarray data analysis. For example, cancer types could be successfully classified based on the specific expression signatures [2,3,4]. However, microarray data classification presents substantially new challenges. First, microarray data exhibit high levels of noise due to various sources of systematic and random errors, including missing values. Second, microarray data are beset by a double 'curse' consisting of *high dimensionality* and *data set sparsity* [5]. Such data usually contain few (in the order of 10^2) observations (samples) and many (in the order of 10^4) parameters (genes). Many genes contain redundant or irrelevant information. Further, many data sets contain a relatively high number of classes but few cases per class. The curse of dimensionality in microarray data is commonly addressed by feature selection and dimension reduction techniques. However, the number of remaining genes that are significantly differently expressed in different classes can still be immense compared to the relatively small number of cases per class. This poses severe problems to an inductive learning of a classification function from such data. A desirable solution to the dimensionality problem would be to increase the number of cases. However, this is often not feasible because of (*i*) the limited number of available patients or specimens, and (*ii*) the relatively high costs of microarray experiments in terms of money and time.

Confidence values convey information about the class membership of the cases and are used in model fusion approaches such as bagging and boosting. Bagging involves a repeated random sampling (with replacement) of the original training set to generate m bootstrapped data sets. In noisy bagging, the bootstrapped data sets are disturbed by random noise and have shown to improve the generalization ability of ensembles of neural networks [6]. Adaptive boosting (Adaboost) creates several different models and combines their predictions using a weighted voting scheme (e.g., majority voting). Here, k different training set replicas are sampled adaptively (with non-uniform sampling probabilities and replacement) from the learning set. The predictions of the combined model are generated using a weighted voting scheme. The adaptive sampling procedures increase the probability of a hard-to-classify case to be sampled based on the performance of the classifier in the previous iteration. Cases that are most often misclassified are assigned an increased probability for being sampled in the next round.

The study presented in this paper is necessarily and intentionally comprehensive as it attempts to expose and discuss various elements of a full methodology rather than only a single method. As a consequence, not all parts of the presented methodology are discussed and evaluated in detail. It is our plan to explore and investigate different aspects of this comprehensive methodology in more detail in the future. This paper focuses on how the confidence values computed in the learning phase can be used for optimization of a single classifier in the context of the small-n-large-p problem. We present a model that calibrates its confidence in classification processes. In the learning phase, the model generates artificial training data as a function of its confidence in previous decisions and uses these data for calibrating its confidence in subsequent classifications. These artificial data play a pivotal role in determining the model's form or structure and performance, and have led to the model's name. (The Greek word *plasma* means 'to be formed' or 'molded'.)

2 Confidence in Classification

In practical applications without precise definition of costs for false positives and false negative classifications, exact characterization of the reward and penalty associated with a given prediction is not possible. Information-theoretic approaches typically translate a classifier's confidence into reward and penalty scores. This is based on the following rationale: *Misclassification with high confidence is more severe than misclassification with low confidence.* Let C be the real class associated with case $\mathbf{x}$ and $\hat{p}(C|\mathbf{x})$ be the model's confidence that the case belongs to C. Then, a *reward-penalty function* $R(\hat{p})$ can be defined as follows [7].

$$R(\hat{p}) = 1 + \log_2 \hat{p}(C \mid \mathbf{x}) \tag{1}$$

Key properties of this function are that it is not symmetrical with respect to rewards and penalties, and that the discrepancy becomes larger for higher confidence values. Extreme confidences that entail a misclassification, $\hat{p}(\neg C|\mathbf{x} \in C) = 1$, lead to a penalty of $-\infty$, whereas the maximum reward for a correct classification is only 1. To avoid extreme confidences, we force the minimum and maximum confidences towards $\hat{p}_{min} = 0.5/(N+1)$ and $\hat{p}_{max} = (N+0.5)/(N+1)$, where N is the number of cases in the learning set [8]. For example, if a training set contains $n = 100$ cases, then the maximum confidence for a single classification is $\hat{p}_{max} = 0.995$.

Korb *et al.* showed that if a model predicts a class with probability $\hat{p}$, and the real class will actually occur with frequency $f = \hat{p}$, then this model can be expected to obtain the highest reward [7]. Such a model is called *perfectly calibrated*. Miscalibration measures how much the probability estimates deviate from the *frequency of truth of events* [7]. Korb *et al.* proposed to measure a model's miscalibration by partitioning the range of a model's confidence values into cells, so that each cell contains at least ten confidence values and as few as possible above ten [7]. Then, the frequency of truth within the cells is compared with the confidence values that they contain. The miscalibration is defined as follows:

$$miscalibration = \sqrt{\sum_{i=1..n} \sum_{j=1..m} \frac{\left(\sum_k f_{ik} m^{-1} - \hat{p}_{ij}\right)^2}{m-1}} \tag{2}$$

where n is the number of partitions of the range of confidence values; m is the number of confidence values in the ith cell; k is the index of confidence values in the ith cell; f_{ik} is 1 if the kth prediction in the ith cell is correct, 0 otherwise; and $\hat{p}_{ij}$ is the jth confidence value in the ith cell. Korb's measure of miscalibration can be used to derive a measure to quantify the model's *timidity* by considering only those confidence values $\hat{p}_{ij}$ that lead to a correct classification.

3 Jittering

Jittered data (jitter) refers to data that is deliberately corrupted by artificial noise. Several studies have demonstrated that the generalization ability of neural networks can be significantly improved by injecting jitter into the data, particularly when the size of the training set is small [9,10]. The concept of jittering has been successfully applied to tasks that are characterized by the curse of dimensionality. Van Someren *et al.* followed this strategy to model robust genetic networks from time-course gene expression data [11]. Provided that the noise amplitude is small, jittering is equivalent to Tikhonov regularization [12]. Adding jitter can lead to an increased classification error in the training phase, but to a decreased error in the test phase. Chawla *et al.* investigated classification problems that involve imbalanced classes, i.e., data sets with classification categories that are not (approximately) equally balanced [13]. They presented the method of SMOTE, an approach for over-sampling the minority class using synthetic training cases. The generation of these synthetic cases is effectively a jittering approach that improves the classification performance in the context of skewed class distributions [13]. Empirical results have shown that SMOTE performs better than over-sampling with replacement of the minority class; it also performs better than under-sampling of the majority class [13].

Consider the classification problem that involves the learning of the mapping from a vector $\mathbf{x}$ to a class label y, where $\mathbf{x}$ is a p-dimensional vector of gene expression data and y is a discrete variable (e.g., a cancer class). The jittered version of this vector is $\tilde{\mathbf{x}} = \mathbf{x} + \varepsilon$, and $\tilde{\mathbf{x}}$ has class label y. The noise vector $\varepsilon = (\varepsilon_1, \varepsilon_2, ..., \varepsilon_p)$ has a distribution of mean m_ε and standard deviation s_ε.

For cancer microarray data sets, we often observe that genes exhibit a similar expression profile in samples of the same cancer type. We propose that the magnitude of the noise level takes into account the magnitude of the actual expression levels; otherwise, the class-discriminatory effect of low-level expressed genes might vanish.

Let the ith original expression profile be $\mathbf{x}_i = (x_{i1}, x_{i2}, ..., x_{ip})$. The jittered version of this vector, $\tilde{\mathbf{x}}_i$, is given by Equation 3 as follows:

$$\tilde{\mathbf{x}}_i = (\tilde{x}_{i1}, \tilde{x}_{i2}, ..., \tilde{x}_{ip}), \text{ with } \tilde{x}_{ik} = (\beta_{ik}\alpha_{ik}\rho_{ik} + 1)x_{ik} \qquad (3)$$

where β_{ik}, α_{ik}, and ρ_{ik} are random variables, and $\beta_{ik} \in \{1, 0\}$, $\alpha_{ik} \in \{-1, 1\}$, and $\rho_{ik} \in [\rho_{min}, \rho_{max}]$, with $\rho_{min}, \rho_{max} \in]0, 1[$. The values 1 and 0 are equally likely for β_{ik}, so that β_{ik} controls the number of variables (i.e., genes) to be jittered. If $\beta_{ik} = 0$, then the kth component of the ith jittered expression profile is identical to the kth component of the ith original profile. If $\beta_{ik} = 1$, then the kth component of the ith jittered expression profile is a jittered version of the kth component of the ith original profile. This noise is determined by both α_{ik} and ρ_{ik}.

4   Calibration Using Jittering

Equation 3 provides a general means for generating a jittered expression profile. When adding jittered duplicates to a data set, three questions need to be answered: (1) How many jittered cases should be added?, (2) Which cases are candidates for jittering?, and (3) Which distribution (type and parameters) of distortion noise should be chosen?

We can distinguish two situations: (*i*) all confidence values within a cell lead to a correct classification, and (*ii*) at least one confidence value leads to a misclassification. Consider the latter case first. If a cell contains a value that leads to a misclassification, then we decide that the respective training case should be jittered. If all confidence values in a cell lead to a correct classification, and if all cases were classified with confidence 1, then the contribution to the timidity component of the miscalibration would be zero, but such extreme confidences are not allowed (see above). Suppose that each probability in a cell is relatively high, for instance, each confidence is $\hat{p} = 0.95$. Then this cell's contribution to (the square root of) the timidity is $10\times(1 - 0.95)^2/9 = 0.003$, which may be deemed sufficiently small. If the confidence values are all relatively small, e.g., 0.70, then the cell's contribution to (the square root of) the timidity is 0.10, which can be considered rather large. The confidence values might be too small to be judged valuable. Therefore, if the contribution to timidity in a cell is greater than a small positive threshold δ, then *all* respective training cases within this cell should be jittered.

Neural plasma is based on the probabilistic neural network (PNN) [14]. Figure 1 depicts the topology of neural plasma, illustrated for two classes of three cases each and two test cases.

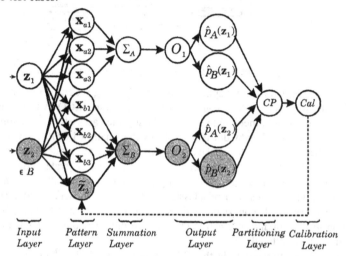

| Input Layer | Pattern Layer | Summation Layer | Output Layer | Partitioning Layer | Calibration Layer |

Fig 1. The topology of neural plasma.

The first part of neural plasma – input, pattern, summation, and output layer – is identical to the basic PNN. The difference consists in the *partitioning layer* and the *calibration layer*. The cell partitioning neuron *CP* receives the computed class posteriors and partitions them into cells of approximately equal size in such a way that each cell is guaranteed to contain at least ten elements and as few as possible above that number. The calibration neuron *Cal* determines the model's calibration with respect to boldness and timidity and determines which cases are candidates for jittering. Then, the calibration neuron generates jittered cases according to Equation 3 and feeds these cases back to the pattern layer. Consider the shaded parts in Figure 1. The case z_2 is a member of class B. This case is assigned to one of the classes A or B, depending on which estimated class posterior is the highest. The neuron O_2 outputs these posteriors for z_2. Suppose that $\hat{p}(B\,|\,z_2)$ is the highest, i.e., leading to a correct classification, but $\hat{p}(B\,|\,z_2)$ is still too small with respect to the calibration criterion. Or suppose that $\hat{p}(B\,|\,z_2)$ is *not* the highest, leading to a misclassification of z_2. In both cases, the calibration layer will generate a jittered duplicate of this case, $\check{z}_2$, and add it to the pattern layer. We propose a k-fold sampling procedure with the sampling methodology as shown in Figure 2.

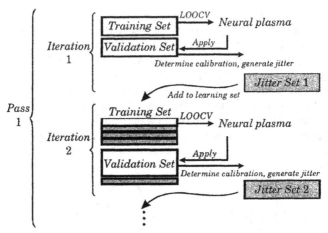

Fig. 2. One pass in the cross-validation procedure.

The learning set is randomly split in half into a training set and a validation set. Using the training set in leave-one-out cross-validation (LOOCV), the model determines the optimal kernel bandwidth. To classify the cases of the validation set, neural plasma uses that bandwidth that produces the smallest LOOCV error in the training set. Based on the performance on the validation set, the model determines its miscalibration. Based on the miscalibration, neural plasma generates jittered data. For each cell, the candidate cases for jittering are determined as follows. If at least one confidence value leads to a misclassification, then the misclassified cases are jittered. Otherwise, if all confidence values entail a correct classification, but the contribution to the timidity in a cell is greater than the threshold $\delta = 0.01$, then *all* cases in this cell are jittered.

The amount of jittered data in the ith iteration represents the ith *jitter set* that is added to the learning set in the $(i+1)^{th}$ iteration. Here, the learning cases are randomly mixed with the jittered cases of the previous iteration. The learning set for iteration #2 comprises now the original learning cases from iteration #1 plus the jittered cases.

In iteration #2, the model constructs the training and the validation set in such a way that they both comprise roughly the same number of cases. The jittered cases have a three times higher chance of being sampled for the training set than for the validation set. Using the training set again in LOOCV, the model optimizes the bandwidth and classifies the cases of the validation set. Again, depending on miscalibration, the model generates jittered data. The jitter set resulting from iteration #2 is mixed with the learning set and split into a training and a validation set for the next iteration. As before, jittered cases have a three times higher chance of being sampled for the training set than for the validation set. With an increasing number of iterations, both the training set and the validation set grow in size. The unequal sampling probability for jittered and original cases to be selected for the sets guarantees that the model is trained, relatively, on more artificial data and validated on more original data.

Consider Figure 2 and suppose that the depicted iterations are repeated, with the test set being the same. One *pass* encompasses n iterations with an *identical* test set. The performance – both on the test and the validation set – can vary in the iterations, because both the generation and the sampling of the jittered data are stochastic. After multiple passes have been performed, one model emerges with the smallest miscalibration. Let the number of passes be m. For example, if the model's miscalibration in the 7th iteration in the 10th pass is smaller than the miscalibration of the remaining $(m \times n - 1)$ models, then this model is selected. The training and the validation set – including the jittered data – of this model are merged to one set, the *best jitter-inflated set*. The entire procedure involving m passes of n iterations represents one fold in a k-fold cross-validation. Neural plasma uses the best jitter-inflated set to classify the cases of the test set of the kth fold. For the present study, neural plasma uses $m = 20$ passes with $n = 10$ iterations each.

There exists a trade-off between too little and too much noise. In general, too few jittered cases will not have the desired regularization effect, whereas too many will increase the computational time and, more importantly, result in a 'blurring' of the data set, i.e., previously separated classes may become overlapping. The effect of the jittered cases will also depend on the characteristics of the data set at hand, for example, on the amount of measurement noise that the data set already contains. It has been suggested to determine the type of the noise distribution and the respective parameters using cross-validation procedures [9]. For example, ten-fold cross-validation can be repeated with different choices for these settings (e.g., uniform sampling of ρ_{ik} from (0, 0.05], (0.05, 15.0], etc.), and those parameters that provide for smallest mean classification error are considered optimal for the data set at hand. In the present study, we found that a uniform sampling of ρ_{ik} from (0.15, 0.25] provides for an acceptable trade-off between too little and too much noise for the three data sets investigated.

5 Materials and Methods

The experiments in this study comprise three well-studied, publicly available microarray data sets: (*i*) the NCI60 data set comprising gene expression profiles of 60 human cancer cell lines of various origins [2]. The data set contains 60 cases from nine cancer classes and 1,405 genes. The NCI60 data set is further pre-processed using principal component analysis and the first 23 'eigengenes' explaining over 75% of the total variance are selected. (*ii*) The ALL data set represents the expression profiles of 327 acute lymphoblastic leukemia samples [4]. This data comprises ten classes and the expression profiles of a total of 12,600 genes. (*iii*) The GCM data set contains 16,063 gene expression profiles of 198 specimens (190 primary tumors and eight metastatic samples) of predominantly solid tumors of 14 cancer types [15].

For the ALL and the GCM data set, feature selection was performed as follows. Based on the learning set L_i only, we determined the signal-to-noise (S2N) weight for each gene with respect to each class [16]. Then, we performed a permutation test involving a random permutation of the class labels and the re-computation of the S2N weights. This procedure was repeated 1,000 times to assess the significance of the signal-to-noise weights for the unpermuted class labels [17]. Based on the S2N weights and associated p-values, we selected the top-ranking genes per class; all other genes were discarded from further analysis. This approach was repeated ten times to generate ten pairs, each consisting of a filtered learning set L_i and a test set T_i with the corresponding genes. Information contained in the test sets was not used in any way for feature selection.

Neural plasma and boosting are related approaches, but there exist two fundamental differences: (*i*) Neural plasma is trained on jittered duplicates, and (*ii*) boosting is a multi-model approach for generating an ensemble of classifiers. Less robust or 'brittle' classifiers such as decision trees often benefit from boosting [18]. We compare neural plasma with PNN and boosted decision trees C5.0.

The performance of the models is assessed in a 10-fold repeated random sampling procedure. In short, the procedure produces $i = 1..10$ pairs of learning sets L_i and test sets T_i with original data. L_i comprises ~70% and T_i comprises ~30% of the original cases. Notice that the learning and test cases are identical for all models, and the test sets are never used for model selection or feature selection to avoid feature selection bias [19].

6   Results

Table 1 shows the 95%-confidence intervals for the prediction accuracy of the models, averaged over the ten test sets.

Table 1. 95%-confidence intervals for the true average prediction accuracy (in %).

	NCI60	ALL	GCM
Neural plasma	79.3 ± 6.4	77.9 ± 2.4	78.9 ± 3.6
PNN	76.7 ± 6.7	77.4 ± 2.4	79.6 ± 3.6
2-fold boosted C5.0	64.3 ± 7.6	68.6 ± 2.7	64.5 ± 4.3
3-fold boosted C5.0	58.5 ± 7.8	71.0 ± 2.7	63.0 ± 4.3
4-fold boosted C5.0	62.4 ± 7.6	72.6 ± 2.6	66.5 ± 4.2
5-fold boosted C5.0	62.4 ± 7.6	72.5 ± 2.6	68.0 ± 4.2

There exist only relatively small differences between neural plasma and PNN for the ALL and GCM data sets. However, on the data set comprising the smallest number of cases, NCI60, neural plasma achieved a remarkably higher accuracy than PNN. Next, we assess whether the differences in performance between neural plasma and the best-boosted trees are statistically significant. Let p_{Ai} be the observed proportion of test cases misclassified by model A and let p_{Bi} be the observed proportion of misclassified test cases by model B during the ith cross-validation fold. Assume that in each fold N cases are used for learning and M cases are used for testing. The statistic for the *variance-corrected resampled paired t-test* is then given by Equation 4 as follows [20].

$$T_c = \frac{\overline{p}}{\sqrt{(k^{-1} + M / N)s^2}} \sim t_{k-1} \qquad (4)$$

Empirical results show that this corrected statistic drastically improves on the standard resampled t-test with respect to Type I error [20].

The difference in performance on NCI60 between neural plasma and 2-fold boosted C5.0 is significant ($P = 0.03$). The difference in performance on GCM between neural plasma and 5-fold boosted C5.0 is significant ($P = 0.003$). However, the difference in accuracy on the ALL data set ($77.9 \pm 2.4\%$ for neural plasma vs. $72.6 \pm 2.6\%$ for 4-fold boosted C5.0) is not significant ($P = 0.06$).

7 Discussion and Conclusions

Neural plasma methodology presented in this study involves several elements. Given the space limitations, not all aspects of this methodology are discussed in exhaustive detail. The neural plasma approach distinguishes itself from other neural networks with respect to two critical aspects. First, in contrast to multilayer perceptron and similar techniques, neural plasma does not attempt to mimic the topology (neurons, synapses, activation potentials, etc.) of biological neural networks. Instead, it focuses on characteristics related to intelligent behavior and reasoning, such as *timidity* (and its opposite: *boldness*). Thus, neural plasma is potentially useful for classification problems that require explicit representation of these notions in the decision process. Future work on neural plasma will concentrate on further evaluating and interpreting these concepts in the context of decision and reasoning theory.

Second, neural plasma generates artificial training cases as a function of its performance and thereby increases the learning set artificially. Within the context of high-throughput applications on biology and biotechnology, this is a novel approach to tackling the dimensionality problem in classification problems. In contrast to our approach, the SMOTE algorithm by Chawla *et al.* generates synthetic training cases only for the minority class [13].

How could the model's calibration be computed more effectively and efficiently? Neural plasma determines the miscalibration as a function of the frequency of truth in the cells. However, the partitioning into cells, each containing approximately ten elements, is based only on the empirical results by Korb *et al.* [7]. Which cross-validation procedure should be chosen, and which sampling procedure for the original and jittered cases should be adopted? The jittered data were sampled for the training set with a three times higher probability than the original cases, so that the model is trained on more artificial data and validated on more original data; however, other sampling ratios need to be investigated. What is considered a 'timid' classification is clearly context-dependent and can be controlled by the threshold δ, which was set to 0.01 in the present study. Future work will focus on the model's sensitivity to overfitting and on how these empirically determined parameters could be optimized.

In summary, we believe that the neural plasma methodology represents an interesting framework for exploring classification tasks in the context of faculties such as timidity and boldness, which are inherent factors of human reasoning. The evaluation presented in this study focuses on a limited set of criteria of a more comprehensive framework. As such, this study is seen as a first step in presenting and exploring this framework. Future work will explore different aspects in more detail.

8   References

[1] Brown, P.O. and Botstein, D. (1999) Exploring the new world of the genome with DNA microarrays. *Nat. Gen.* **21**(1): 33–37.

[2] Ross, D.T., Scherf, U., Eisen, M.B., *et al.* (2000) Systematic variation in gene expression patterns in human cancer cell lines. *Nat. Gen.* **24**(3):227–235.

[3] Alizadeh, A.A., Eisen, M.B., Davis, R.E., *et al.* (2000) Distinct types of diffuse large B-cell lymphoma identified by gene expression profiling. *Nature* **403**:503–511.

[4] Yeoh, E.J., Ross, M.E., Shurtleff, S.A., *et al.* (2002) Classification, subtype discovery, and prediction of outcome in pediatric acute lymphoblastic leukemia by gene expression profiling. *Cancer Cell* **1**:133–143.

[5] Somorjai, R.L., Dolenko, B., and Baumgartner, R. (2003) Class prediction and discovery using gene microarray and proteomics mass spectroscopy data: curses, caveats, cautions. *Bioinformatics* **19**(12):1484–1491.

[6] Raviv, Y., and Intrator, N. (1996) Boostrapping with noise: An effective regularization technique. *Connection Science* **8**(3–4):355–372.

[7] Korb, K.B., Hope, L.R., Hughes, M.J. (2001) The evaluation of predictive learners: some theoretical and empirical results. *Proc. 12th Europ. Conf. Machine Learning*, 276–287.

[8] Dowe, D.L., Farr, G.E., Hurst, A.J., Lentin, K.L. (1996) Information-theoretic football tipping. *Proc. 3rd Austr. Conf. Math. & Computers in Sport*, Australia, 233–241.

[9] Koistinen, P., and Holmström, L. (1992) Kernel regression and backpropagation training with noise. *Advances in Neural Inf. Proc. Sys.* **4**:1033–1039.

[10] Reed, R., Oh., S., Marks, R.J. (1992) Regularization using jittered training data. *Proc. Int. J. Conf. Neural Networks*, Baltimore MD, III147–III152.

[11] van Someren, E.P., Wessels, L.F.A., Reinders M.J.T, Backer, E. (2001) Robust genetic network modeling by adding noisy data. *Proc. IEEE Workshop on Nonlinear Signal and Image Processing*, Baltimore, Maryland.

[12] Bishop, C.M. (1994) Training with noise is equivalent to Tikhonov regularization. *Neural Computation* **7**:108–116.

[13] Chawla, N.V., Bowyer, K.W., Hall, L.O., Kegelmeyer, W.P. (2002) SMOTE: Synthetic Minority Over-sampling Technique. *J. Art. Int. Res.* **16**:321–357.

[14] Specht, D.F. (1990) Probabilistic neural networks. *Neural Networks* **3**:109–118.

[15] Ramaswamy, S., Tamayo, P., Rifkin, R., *et al.* (2001) Multiclass cancer diagnosis using tumor gene expression signatures. *Proc. Natl. Acad. Sci. USA.* **98**(26), 15149–15154.

[16] Slonim, D., Tamayo, P., Mesirov, J., *et al.* (2000) Class prediction and discovery using gene expression data. *Proc. 4th Ann. Int. Conf. Comp. Mol. Biol.*, Tokyo, Japan, 263–272.

[17] Radmacher, M.D., McShane, L.M., Simon, R. (2002) A paradigm for class prediction using gene expression profiles. *J. Comp. Bio.* **9**(3):505–511.

[18] Duda R.O., Hart P.E., Stork D.G. (2001) *Pattern Classification.* 2nd ed., John Wiley & Sons, New York, p. 461.

[19] Ambroise, C. and McLachlan, G.J. (2002) Selection bias in gene extraction on the basis of microarray gene expression data. *Proc. Natl. Acad. Sci. USA* **98**:6562–6566.

[20] Nadeau, C., and Bengio, Y. (2003) Inference for generalization error. *Machine Learning* **52**:239–281.

Comparison of SVM
and Some Older Classification Algorithms
in Text Classification Tasks

Fabrice COLAS[1] and Pavel BRAZDIL[2]

[1] LIACS, Leiden University, THE NETHERLANDS, fcolas@liacs.nl
[2] LIACC-NIAAD, University of Porto, PORTUGAL, pbrazdil@liacc.up.pt

Summary. Document classification has already been widely studied. In fact, some studies compared feature selection techniques or feature space transformation whereas some others compared the performance of different algorithms. Recently, following the rising interest towards the Support Vector Machine, various studies showed that SVM outperforms other classification algorithms. So should we just not bother about other classification algorithms and opt always for SVM ?

We have decided to investigate this issue and compared SVM to kNN and naive Bayes on binary classification tasks. An important issue is to compare optimized versions of these algorithms, which is what we have done. Our results show all the classifiers achieved comparable performance on most problems. One surprising result is that SVM was not a clear winner, despite quite good overall performance. If a suitable preprocessing is used with kNN, this algorithm continues to achieve very good results and scales up well with the number of documents, which is not the case for SVM. As for naive Bayes, it also achieved good performance.

1 Introduction

The aim of using artificial intelligence techniques in text categorization is to build systems which are able to automatically classify documents into categories. But as the feature space, based on the set of unique words in the documents, is typically of very high dimension, document classification is not trivial. Various feature space reduction techniques were suggested and compared in [13, 9]. A large number of adaptive learning techniques have also been applied to text categorization. Among them, the k nearest neighbors and the naive Bayes are two examples of commonly used algorithms (see for instance [7] for details). JOACHIMS applied the Support Vector Machine to document classification [4]. Numerous classifier comparisons were done in the past [12, 14, 4, 2].

Some algorithms like the SVM are by default binary classifiers. Therefore, if we have a problem with more than two classes, we need to construct as

Please use the following format when citing this chapter:

Colas, F., Brazdil, P., 2006, in IFIP International Federation for Information Processing, Volume 217, Artificial Intelligence in Theory and Practice, ed. M. Bramer, (Boston: Springer), pp. 169–178.

many classifiers as there are classes (*one versus all* strategy). However, it is not fair to compare a single multi-class naive Bayes (or *k*NN) classifier to *n* SVM classifiers (for *n* classes). This is why we have decided to focus on *one against one* classification tasks. Moreover, FÜRNKRANZ [3] showed that a *round robin* approach using the set of *one against one* classifiers, performs at least as well as a *one versus all* approach. These binary problems involve also smaller amounts of data, which means that the classifiers are faster to train. The properties of the train set have much influence on the classifier learning abilities. Therefore, focusing on binary classification tasks allows one to carefully control the nature of train sets. Finally, directly studying multi-class classification tasks tends to obscure the particular behaviors of the classifiers on some classes which may be of interest.

We seek answers to the following questions. *Should we still consider old classification algorithms in text categorization or opt systematically for SVM classifiers ? What are the strength and weaknesses of the SVM, naive Bayes and kNN algorithms in text categorization on a set of simple binary problems ? Are there some parameter optimization results transferable from one problem to another ?* Before giving the answers, our experimental settings and evaluation methodology are described. Then, our results regarding the parameter optimization are presented. The optimized versions are then used in further comparative studies, which are used to answer the above questions.

2 Document Collection, Algorithms and Evaluation Methodology

2.1 Document Collection

For our experiments we used the well known 20newsgroups dataset composed of 20000 newsgroup emails (removed email headers and no stemming). We chose to study the set of *one against one* binary classification tasks of this dataset. Thus, $\frac{20(20-1)}{2} = 190$ classification tasks were examined. Given the large dimensions of the problem, sub sampling techniques were applied to observe the classifier learning abilities for an increasing train set size. We also used the *Information Gain* to impose an ordering on a set of attributes. We chose this heuristic for its simplicity and its good performance [13, 9].

2.2 Algorithms

In this paper, two well known classifiers are compared to the Support Vector Machine namely the *k*NN and the naive Bayes. These two classifiers were chosen because of their simplicity and their generally good performance reported in document classification. With respect to the SVM, the SMO implementation of PLATT, available in the libbow [6] library, has been used.

Let us consider the classification function Φ of the data points x_i $(i = 1...l)$ into a class $y_i \in C = \{+1, -1\}$. Let d be the dimension of the feature space. The three classification algorithms are presented in the following subsections.

Support Vector Machine.

The SVM problem (*primal*) is to find the decision surface that maximizes the margin between the data points of the two classes. Following our results and previously published studies in document classification [12, 14], we limit our discussion to *linear* SVM. The *dual* form of the *linear* SVM optimisation problem is to maximize :

$$\alpha^* = \text{maximise}_\alpha \sum_{i=1}^{l} \alpha_i - \frac{1}{2} \sum_{i=1}^{l} \sum_{j=1}^{l} y_i y_j \alpha_i \alpha_j \langle x_i, x_j \rangle,$$

$$\text{subject to } \sum_{i=1}^{l} y_i \alpha_i = 0 \tag{1}$$

$$0 \leq \alpha_i \leq C, i = 1...l$$

with α_i the weight of the examples and C the relative importance of the complexity of the model and the error. The class prediction $\hat{\Phi}(x')$ of the point x' is given by :

$$\hat{\Phi}(x') = sign(\sum_{i=1}^{l} \alpha_i y_i \langle x_i, x' \rangle + b) = sign(\langle w^*, x' \rangle + b) \tag{2}$$

where $w^* = \sum_{i=1}^{l} \alpha_i y_i x_i$.

k Nearest Neighbors.

Given a test point, a predefined similarity metric is used to find the k most similar points from the train set. For each class y_i, we sum the similarity of the neighbors of the same class. Then, the class y_i with the highest score is assigned to the data point x' by the k nearest neighbors algorithm.

$$\hat{\Phi}(x') = argmax_{y_j \in C} \sum_{i=1}^{k} \delta(y_j, \Phi(x_i)) sim(x_i, x') \tag{3}$$

Naive Bayes

Let $P(y_i)$ be the prior probability of the class y_i and $P(a'_j | y_i)$ be the conditional probability to observe attribute value a'_j given the class y_i. Then, a naive Bayes classifier assign to a data point x' with attributes $(a'_1...a'_d)$ the class $\hat{\Phi}(x')$ maximizing :

$$\hat{\Phi}(x') = argmax_{y_i \in C} P(y_i) \prod_{j=1}^{d} P(a'_j | y_i) \qquad (4)$$

2.3 Evaluation Methodology

A classical 10-fold cross validation was used to estimate classifier performance. We chose the macro averaged F_1 measure $MF_1 = \frac{2 \times MPrecision \times MRecall}{MPecision + MRecall}$ [10], where the *MPrecision* and the *MRecall* measures are the averages of the precision and the recall computed on the basis of the two confusion matrices (in one, a class is considered positive and the other negative ; in the other the assignment is interchanged). Finally, we recorded the global processing time in seconds (the sum of the training and the testing time). As the size of the test set is nearly the same for each experiment, this processing time reflects mostly the train time of the classifiers.

3 Experimental Results

3.1 Parameter Optimization Results

We ran some preliminary experiments on 20newsgroups to find the best parameter values. These experiments were restricted to three binary classification tasks[3]. Our results are presented in the following sections for SVM and kNN.

Support Vector Machines.

Various parameters of SVM were considered in the attempt to optimize the performance of this algorithm. The parameter C was varied and various kernel functions were tried as well. None of those lead to interesting improvements in terms of performance (MF_1) or processing time. So, the default value $C = 200$ and a *linear* kernel are used.

We have also varied the ϵ parameter controlling the accepted error. We have found that ϵ had no influence on MF_1 as long as its value was smaller or equal to 0.1. However, ϵ did affect the training time. Indeed the time could be reduced by a factor of 4 in the best case (see Fig. 1 (A) with 500 features), when the largest value of ϵ (0.1) was used. Our hypothesis is that the precision of the optimisation problem is simplified when an acceptable optimal hyper plane is bounded by a larger error ϵ. Therefore, it seems that no high precision is needed to train SVM on these binary classification tasks. Fig. 1 (A) and (B) portray the training time of SVM for various values of ϵ when the size of the feature space is varied and when the number of documents in the train set is increased.

---

[3] alt.atheism vs. talk.religion.misc, comp.sys.ibm.pc.hardware vs. comp.-sys.mac.hardware, talk.politics.guns vs. talk.politics.misc

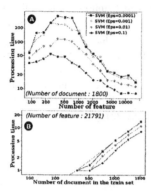

Fig. 1. *Processing time of the SVM classifier on* alt.atheism *vs.* talk.-religion.misc, *for several values of* ϵ, *given an increasing number of features (A) and an increasing number of documents in the train set (B).*

k Nearest Neighbors.

Two parameters were considered to optimize the performance of the kNN, the *number k of nearest neighbor* and the *feature space transformation*. Indeed, to achieve good performance with kNN, the feature space should be transformed to a new one. Common transformation in text mining are based on the number of occurences of the ith term tf_i, the inverse document frequency which is defined as the ratio between the total number of documents N and the number of documents containing the term df_i, a normalization constant κ.

$$\Phi_{\text{atc}}(x_i) = \frac{(\frac{1}{2} + \frac{tf_i}{2tf_{max}}) \, log(\frac{N}{df_i})}{\kappa}$$

$$\Phi_{\text{ntn}}(x_i) = tf_i \, log(\frac{N}{df_i}) \tag{5}$$

$$\Phi_{\text{lnc}}(x_i) = \frac{log(tf_i)}{\kappa}$$

Thirty measures (3 problems, 10-fold cross validation) caracterized the experimental results for each parameter setting. To compare these results, a simple heuristic based on a pairwise t-test (95% confidence interval) was used. When a significative difference was observed regards the results of one parameter setting to one other, a victory point was attributed to the best setting. In case of tie, no point was given. Train sets with the maximum number of document[4] were used whereas the feature space was composed of *all* the possible attributes.

Number of Nearest Neighbors.

We observed that large k values lead to relatively good performance. Indeed, the contribution towards the class score of the neighbors is weighted by their

---

[4] A binary task involves 2×1000 documents. Considering that 10-fold cross validation is used, each training set includes 1800 documents and the test set 200.

similarity to the test point. Therefore, the farthest neighbors have little effect on the class score. However, the best number of nearest neighbors is $k = 49$. This optimal k value (49) is interestingly quite close to the one of YANG (45) in [12] with completely different experimental settings (Reuters-21570, classification task seen as a single multi-class problem). As a result, it seems that k values between 45 and 50 are well suited for text classification tasks.

We first ran all our experiments with $k = 5$. Therefore the kNN results could be slightly improved in the following comparative study if we used the optimized value for k.

Feature Space Transformation.

About 400 transformations were evaluated. Our observation is that any term frequency is suitable, but not the binary transformation (value 1 or 0), depending whether a particular word is (or is not) present. This is coherent to the previous study of McCALLUM et al. [5]. In the same way, the inverse document frequency should be systematically applied because, as it is well known, it decreases the importance of common words occurring in numerous documents. The normalization did not affect the performance. In the coming comparative study, the transformations[5] presented in formulas 5 are used.

3.2 Some Classifier Comparisons

The aim of our experiments was to examine the classifier learning abilities for an increasing number of documents in the train set (learning curves), and also, how the performance is affected by the number of attributes of the feature space. In the study involving learning curves, *all the features* were selected. Similarly, when the behaviors for an increasing number of features were studied, the train set was composed of its *maximum size*, containing as many documents of both classes.

First of all, we have observed that architectural variables (sample selection, algorithm parameters, feature subset selection, working feature space) had often a *larger* impact on the performance than the choice of individual classifiers. In fact, if suitable architectural variables are chosen and if the parameter settings of the classifiers get correctly optimized, then the differences between the algorithms are not very large.

Moreover, the behaviors of the classifiers are very similar across the classification tasks. This is illustrated in Fig. 2 (A) and (B) which shows the performance of the three algorithms on two *typical* binary classification tasks among the 190. The figure shows how the performance depends on the number of documents in the train set. Fig. 2 (A) shows that naive Bayes is slightly

---

[5] A weighting scheme is composed of two parts, for example ntn.lnc or atc.atc (SMART Information Retrieval System notations). The first group of three letters word describes the feature space transformation for the documents in the train set, whereas the second group describes the feature space for the test documents.

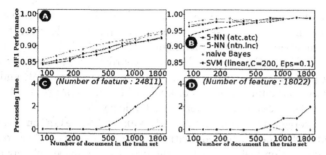

Fig. 2. *Performance (A), (B) and processing time (C), (D) of kNN, SVM and naive Bayes for two problems : comp.graphics vs.comp.sys.ibm.pc.hardware (A), (C) and comp.os.ms-windows.misc vs. talk.politics.misc (B), (D) for an increasing number of documents in the train set.*

better than the other algorithms for all train sizes. However, the difference from the worst performer is not very large (about 2 or 3%).

Fig. 2 (B) shows that naive Bayes starts with an advantage when a small number of documents are used in the train set, but then as the number of documents increases, the difference diminishes. When 1800 documents are used, the performance is virtually identical to the other classifiers. SVM is however in a disadvantage, when we consider the processing times. These are not only much higher than for the other algorithms, but also, the processing time tends to grow quadratically with the number of documents in the train set (see Fig. 2 (C), (D) and Fig. 4 (D)).

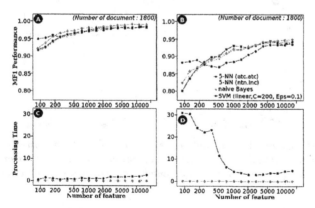

Fig. 3. *Performance (A), (B) and processing time (C), (D) of kNN, SVM and naive Bayes for two problems : rec.motorcycles vs. sci.med (A), (C) and comp.-sys.ibm.pc.hardware vs.sci.electronics (B), (D) for an increasing number of attribute in the feature space.*

Regards the number of features, all three classifiers tend to achieve better performance on large feature set (see Fig. 3 (A) and (B)). However, the SVM processing time can be particularly high if the number of features is small (see Fig. 3 (D) and Fig. 4 (C)). Besides, regards performance of SVM an interesting pattern can be observed on some tasks (see Fig. 3 (B) and Fig. 4 (A)). First, a maximum is reached for a relatively small feature set. Then, the performance decreases until it reverses its tendency again.

On the problem involving `alt.atheism` and `talk.religion.misc` (Fig. 4), both three classifiers achieved relatively poor performance when compared to other classification tasks. In fact, as the two newsgroups are closely related, it is difficult to determine to which category the documents belong. In this task, SVM outperforms naive Bayes and kNN for small feature spaces (see Fig. 4 (A), 100-200) whereas it performs poorly on large feature spaces (500-20000). Although this behavior is specific to this task, it is still a surprising result. Indeed, it is often said that SVM deals well with large number of features. It appears that naive Bayes and kNN do this better here. However, it could be taken into consideration when constructing the learning curves. For instance, the learning curve of SVM shown in Fig. 4 (B) which uses *all* the possible features (21791), could be pushed up if a smaller feature set was used (200).

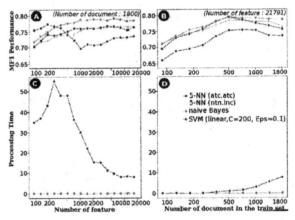

Fig. 4. *Performance (A), (B) and processing time (C), (D) of naive Bayes, kNN and SVM on* `alt.atheism` *versus* `talk.religion.misc`, *given an increasing number of features (A), (C) and an increasing number of documents in the train set (B), (D). right.*

On most of the classification tasks, the training time of SVM increases linearly with the number of features (see Fig. 3 (C)). However, the search for the optimal hyper plane of SVM may require very large training time. For example, the largest training times among the 190 classification tasks occur on the problem presented in Fig. 4. Indeed, correlating the above-mentioned pattern, SVM training time is higher for small feature spaces than for large ones (Fig. 4 (C) and Fig. 3 (D)). Therefore, training SVM on a extended feature space tends to be faster on these particular tasks.

Discussion.

As explained earlier, comparing a single multi-class naive Bayes (or kNN) to n SVM classifiers (n the number of categories) is definitively not fair for naive Bayes (or kNN). However, this is the approach followed in some published comparative studies [2, 12, 14].

In [2], the SVM SMO version of PLATT was claimed to outperform naive Bayes and other learning methods. However, the optimal number of features was not investigated for each classifier. Indeed, 300 features were selected for SVM which may not be far from the optimal setting. But only 50 were used for naive Bayes. According to our results naive Bayes performs much better with large number of features. Also, the Mutual Information (MI) was used to select features which may not be the best option according to [13]. Finally, they studied the set of *one-against-all* classifiers for each type of algorithm. However, this approach tends to obscur the particular behavior of the classifiers on the various classification tasks.

Recently, a study [1] showed that the architectural parameters often have a more significant impact on performance than the choice of individual learning technique. The work presented here also confirms this. This is why we have decided not to do simple classifier comparisons and present tables with performance results. We preferred to compare the general tendencies of different classifiers when certain parameters are varied.

4 Conclusion

Firstly, we showed that kNN and naive Bayes are still worth considering. Both classifiers achieved good overall performance and are much faster than SVM to use. Indeed, the cost to train SVM for large train set is a clear drawback.

Secondly, compared to SVM, both kNN and naive Bayes are very simple and well understood. SVM is however, more appealing theoretically and in practice, its strength is its power to adress non-linear classification taskw. Unfortunately, most of the tasks examined here were not like that. The simplest SVM based on a *linear* kernel and a large error ϵ were found to be sufficient.

We also observed that results highly depend of the adopted methodology. We have focused here on simple binary classification tasks. Regards kNN, the optimal number k of nearest neighbors is interestingly close to the ones used in other comparative studies carried out on different problems.

As our primary objective is to arrive at general conclusions, transferable from one domain to another, we need to validate our results on other document classification tasks. For this purpose, new experiments are actually being carried out. Moreover, if we are interested to recommend a classifier with suitable parameter settings, we should have a good way of characterizing the given documents and develop a good meta-learning strategy.

Acknowledgements. The first author wishes to thank P. BRAZDIL of the LIACC-NIAAD, and also A.-M. KEMPF and F. POULET of the ESIEA Recherche Institute, for having him introduced to his research. We wish to express our gratitude to K. R. PATIL and C. SOARES for their relecture and to all colleagues from LIACC-NIAAD, University of Porto for their encouragement and help. Finally, the Portuguese Pluri-annual support provided by FCT is gratefully acknowledged.

References

1. W. Daelemans, V. Hoste, F. D. Meulder, and B. Naudts. Combined optimization of feature selection and algorithm parameters in machine learning of language. In *Proceedings of the European Conference of Machine Learning*, pages 84–95, 2003.
2. S. Dumais, J. Platt, D. Heckerman, and M. Sahami. Inductive learning algorithms and representations for text categorization. In *Proceedings of the 7th International Conference on Information and Knowledge Management*, pages 148–155, 1998.
3. J. Fürnkranz. Pairwise classification as an ensemble technique. In *Proceedings of the 13th European Conference on Machine Learning*, pages 97–110, 2002.
4. T. Joachims. Making large-scale support vector machine learning practical. In *Advances in Kernel Methods: Support Vector Machines*. 1998.
5. A. McCallum and K. Nigam. A comparison of event models for naive bayes text classification. *AAAI-98 Workshop on Learning for Text Categorization*, 1998.
6. A. K. McCallum. Bow: A toolkit for statistical language modeling, text retrieval, classification and clustering. http://www.cs.cmu.edu/~mccallum/bow, 1996.
7. T. M. Mitchell. *Machine Learning*. McGraw-Hill, 1997.
8. J. Platt. Sequential minimal optimization: A fast algorithm for training support vector machines. Technical Report 98-14, Microsoft Research, 1998.
9. M. Rogati and Y. Yang. High-performing feature selection for text classification. In *Proceedings of the 11th International Conference on Information and Knowledge Management*, pages 659–661, 2002.
10. Y. Yang. An evaluation of statistical approaches to text categorization. *Information Retrieval*, pages 69–90, 1999.
11. Y. Yang. A scalability analysis of classifiers in text categorization. In *Proceedings 26th ACM International Conference on Research and Development in Information Retrieval*, 2003.
12. Y. Yang and X. Liu. A re-examination of text categorization methods. In *Proceedings of the 22nd Annual International ACM SIGIR Conference on Research and Development in Information Retrieval*, pages 42–49, 1999.
13. Y. Yang and J. O. Pedersen. A comparative study on feature selection in text categorization. In *Proceedings of the 14th International Conference on Machine Learning*, pages 412–420, 1997.
14. T. Zhang and F. J. Oles. Text categorization based on regularized linear classification methods. *Information Retrieval*, pages 5–31, 2001.

An automatic graph layout procedure to visualize correlated data

Mario Inostroza-Ponta, Regina Berretta,
Alexandre Mendes, and Pablo Moscato

Newcastle Bioinformatics Initiative
School of Electrical Engineering and Computer Science
Faculty of Engineering and Built Environment
The University of Newcastle, Callaghan, NSW, 2308, Australia

and
ARC Centre in Bioinformatics
Contact email:Pablo.Moscato@newcastle.edu.au

Abstract. This paper introduces an automatic procedure to assist on the interpretation of a large dataset when a similarity metric is available. We propose a visualization approach based on a graph layout methodology that uses a Quadratic Assignment Problem (QAP) formulation. The methodology is presented using as testbed a time series dataset of the Standard & Poor's 100, one the leading stock market indicators in the United States. A weighted graph is created with the stocks represented by the nodes and the edges' weights are related to the correlation between the stocks' time series. A heuristic for clustering is then proposed; it is based on the graph partition into disconnected subgraphs allowing the identification of clusters of highly-correlated stocks. The final layout corresponds well with the perceived market notion of the different *industrial sectors*. We compare the output of this procedure with a traditional dendogram approach of hierarchical clustering.

1 Introduction

The Standard & Poor's 100 index is one the leading stock market indicators in the United States. It measures the performance of the 100 largest U.S. companies, corresponding to over US$ 6 trillion in terms of market capitalization[1] and it is composed of stocks from different sectors.In the stock market, the changes of the value of a given company are highly correlated with the time series of its stock price. Two contributions to the study of market dynamics ([1];[2]) reported on the application of *Self-Organizing Maps* and *Chaotic Map Synchronization* to two different datasets composed of the price variation of the stocks in the Dow Jones index. A graph-based approach using 6,546 *financial instruments* (stocks, indexes, etc.) traded in the US markets has also been recently introduced [3].

---

[1] http://www2.standardandpoors.com/spf/pdf/index/factsheet_sp100.pdf

---

Please use the following format when citing this chapter:

Inostroza-Ponta, M., Berretta, R., Mendes, A., Moscato, P., 2006, in IFIP International Federation for Information Processing, Volume 217, Artificial Intelligence in Theory and Practice, ed. M. Bramer, (Boston: Springer), pp. 179–188.

In this paper we propose a new graph layout visualization method and use it to uncover interesting relationships between the stocks of the S&P100 index used as a case study. We will consider that each stock corresponds to a node of a graph; the edges' weights will be related to the correlation between stocks. The method recursively divides the graph in disconnected subgraphs. Once the subgraphs (clusters) are defined, we solve a sequence of Quadratic Assignment Problems (QAP) using a memetic algorithm (MA) which will determine their relative position in the layout. Finally, another instance of the QAP is solved to find how the clusters are distributed, now considering each cluster as a single element.

The Quadratic Assignment Problem (QAP) belongs to the *NP-hard* [4] class and is a well-studied combinatorial optimization problem [5, 6, 7]. Informally, we are given a set of n facilities and m locations ($m \geq n$), and the task is to assign each facility to a location taking into account the flow between each facility and the distance between the locations. The objective is to minimize the overall transportation cost between all the facilities. For our case study, we will use the correlation between stocks to determine the flow between facilities. The locations will be points in a grid, with the distances between them given by the Euclidean metric. We have as input a flow matrix between the stocks, and from this matrix we create a weighted graph. We can understand this graph as a proximity graph; its edges will also have a strong influence in the layout process as will be described later. The result is a graph layout where clusters of stocks with similar dynamical behavior are promptly identified, and no user-intervention is required during the process.

The use of MAs to address the QAP can be dated back to Carrizo et al.(1992) [8] and Merz and Freisleben (1999) [9]. In this paper, we employ a similar MA to those successfully used before for other combinatorial optimization problems, including Number Partitioning [10] and the Asymmetric Travelling Salesman [11] problems among others. Two local search methods are used; one of them has an embedded Tabu Search [12].

This paper is organized as follows. In Sec. 2 we describe the graph layout procedure. Section 3 describes the memetic algorithm for the QAP. The result of applying this method on the S&P100 dataset is presented in Sec. 4, followed by the conclusions in Sec. 5.

2 Graph Layout Procedure

The graph layout procedure proposed in this paper is composed of 3 steps: *creation of a distance matrix, proximity graph clustering algorithm* and *creation of QAP instances that will be solved using the MA*. We explain each step using the S&P100 dataset.

2.1 Distance Matrix

To create the distance matrix D of the S&P100 dataset, we took the second derivative of the weekly closing price variation of the stocks that compose the index, between the years 1999 and 2004. The work of Ausloos and Ivanova (2002) [13] advocates the use of the second derivative (which represents the acceleration of the stock price), arguing in their studies of *"pressure, acceleration and force indicators"* that it contains more information than the first derivative. The expression of the three-point rule for the second derivative of the stock price at time t is given by

$$y_i(t) = \frac{P_i(t-h) - 2.P_i(t) + P_i(t+h)}{h^2}, \tag{1}$$

where $P_i(t)$ represents the closing price of the stock i in the week t and h represents the interval used to calculate the derivative; in this case, $h = 1$ week. At the end, we normalize the result by dividing it by $P_i(t-h)$, so to eliminate any bias introduced by the actual price of the stock. The distance matrix $D = \{d_{ij}\}$ is defined as $d_{ij} = 1 - \rho_{ij}$, where ρ_{ij} is the Pearson correlation between stocks i and j using the values calculated with function 1. The two most correlated stocks ($\rho = 0.802$) are Schlumberger Ltd. and Baker Hughes Inc., while the two most anti-correlated ($\rho = -0.38$) are Alcoa Inc. and Anheuser-Busch Co. There are only 459 pairs of stocks with $\rho < 0$.

2.2 Proximity graph clustering algorithm

We use the matrix D to build our *ad-hoc* proximity graph using the *minimum spanning tree* and the *k-nearest neighbors* graphs, which we will refer to as G_{MST} and G_{kNN} respectively, as follows: Initially, we create a complete undirected weighted graph $G(V, E, w)$, using the matrix D, where the weight $w_{ij} = d_{ij}$. The minimum spanning tree $G_{MST}(V, E_{MST})$ is defined as a connected, acyclic subgraph containing all the nodes of G and whose edges sum has minimum total weight. The graph G_{kNN} is represented by $G_{kNN}(V, E_{kNN})$, where $e_{ij} \in E_{kNN}$ iff j is one of the k nearest neighbors of i. Our proximity graph, namely $G_{cluster}(V, E_{cluster})$, is constructed such that $E_{cluster} = E_{MST} \cap E_{kNN}$. This type of proximity graphs was used also in González-Barrios and Quiroz (2003) [14]. In this work we decided to set k as the minimal value such that G_{kNN} is still connected while in Ref. [14] they have a different approach.

2.3 Creating and solving QAP instances

We consider the QAP with n elements and $m > n$ positions. The QAP has as input a matrix $F = \{f_{ij}\}$ of flows between the n elements and a matrix $L = \{l_{ij}\}$ of distances between m grid locations. The objective is to assign the n elements to the m locations such that the function $Cost(S) = \sum_{i=1}^{n} \sum_{j=1}^{n} f_{ij} l_{S(i)S(j)}$ is minimized, where the notation $S(i)$ represents the assigned location of element i in solution S. The flow matrix F is created using distance matrix D according to:

$$f_{ij} = \begin{cases} \frac{1000}{d_{ij}} & \text{if } e_{ij} \in E_{cluster}; \\ \frac{1}{d_{ij}} & \text{otherwise.} \end{cases} \qquad (2)$$

Clearly, higher (respectively lower) flows will correspond to elements that are similar (respectively dissimilar). A good solution for the QAP will thus put the elements with a high flow closer in the layout, which is exactly our goal. Additionally, two elements with an edge in $G_{cluster}$ have their flow multiplied by a factor of 1,000, thus enforcing their proximity in the final layout. The matrix L is generated from the distances of points in a square grid of $m = g^2$ positions, with $m \gg n$. In this work, we set $\lceil g = 2\sqrt{n} \rceil$ and l_{qp} is the Euclidean distance between each locations p and q for all $1 \leq q, p \leq m$).

Assume that the graph $G_{cluster}$ contains c disconnected subgraphs ($G_{cluster}^1$, $G_{cluster}^2$, ..., $G_{cluster}^c$). Then each subgraph $G_{cluster}^i$ becomes a QAP instance and is solved separately. Finally, we solve one last QAP, where each element is a subgraph $G_{cluster}^i$. The instance for this problem is created by building a fully connected graph $G_C(V_C, E_C, w_C)$ where $|V_C| = c$ and the weight $w_{C_{ij}}$ corresponds to the flow between subgraphs $G_{cluster}^i$ and $G_{cluster}^j$, calculated as:

$$w_{C_{ij}} = \frac{\sum_{p \in G_i} \sum_{q \in G_j} f_{pq}}{|V_{cluster}^i| * |V_{cluster}^j|}. \qquad (3)$$

In the next section, we will describe the main characteristics of the memetic algorithm used to tackle the QAP problem.

3 Memetic Algorithm

Memetic Algorithms (MAs) is a name that designates a class of powerful population-based metaheuristics with many successful practical applications ([15, 16, 17]). In our MA implementation (see the pseudo-code in Figure 1), we have a population of *agents* composed of two solutions (namely *pocket* and *current*). The idea behind this is that while the *current* solutions are constantly being modified by recombination and mutation, the *pockets* maintain a memory of the best solutions found. The population is organized with a hierarchical ternary tree structure, divided in four overlapped subpopulations of four agents each (one *leader* and three *supporters*). The *supporters* of the first subpopulation are the *leaders* of the others. This population structure has been used before [10] and in Ref. [11] this was the best structure in a comprehensive test of alternative topologies. The method **updatePop()** is responsible for making the best solutions climb the tree towards the upper agents. The method initially verifies the *pocket* solution of each agent, checking whether it is worse than the *current* one. Whenever that happens, the *pocket* is replaced by the

memeticAlgorithm()
    pop = **initializePop()**; **updatePop(***pop***)**
    repeat
        for *i*=0 to 12
            offspring =**recombination(selectSol(***parentA,parentB***))**
            localSearchTS(*offspring***)**
        updatePop(*pop***)**; **8-neighborLS(***agent$^0_{pocket}$***)**
    until *max_number_of_generations*

Fig. 1. Pseudo-code of the memetic algorithm implemented for the QAP.

current. Then, for each subpopulation, the method replaces the leader's *pocket* solution with the best supporter's *pocket* whenever the latter has better cost. A solution is represented as an integer array S of size n, where $S(i) = k$ means that the element i is assigned to location k. The agents are initialized with random solutions, where the elements are spread uniformly at random across all the available locations. Also during the initialization step, we optimize the *pocket* solutions by applying a local search that incorporate a Tabu Search (see Section 3.2).

3.1 Recombination

Concerning the selection of the parent solutions, the method **selectSol()** uses two strategies, depending on whether the population has lost diversity or not. We consider that a population is diverse if its *pocket* solutions differ at least in one value from a set of 20% of randomly chosen positions. If *diversity has not been lost*, one of the parents is the *pocket* solution of a leader agent. The second parent is the *pocket* solution from a supporter agent *within the same subpopulation.* The new solution created replaces the *current* solution of the supporter agent selected. On the contrary, if *diversity has been lost*, both parents are *pocket* solutions from supporter agents. However, in this case *the agents belong to different subpopulations.* The offspring replaces the *current* solution in one of the supporter agent. Once the parents were selected, a recombination algorithm is used to create a new solution. Our memetic algorithm uses a similar recombination to that introduced by Merz [9] and it is explained with the help of a step-by-step example described in Figure 2. Initially, all the elements assigned to the same location in both parents are copied to the offspring (elements A and E). Afterwards, we select at random an unassigned element from the offspring, say D, and look at its location in one of the parents, say parent 2. Thus, the method assigns location #3 to element D. Next, we look at the location of D in parent 1 (i.e. location #1) and check which element is in location #1 in parent 2 (i.e. element G), assigning its location to the offspring (i.e. element G goes to location #1). The process is repeated, now checking the location of element G in parent 1 (location #4). However, as location #4 is not present in parent 2, the process stops. We repeat the process starting with element H in parent

1. After processing all the elements in the offspring, element B still does not have a location because both locations #3 and #12 have already been taken. This does not happen when $n = m$. In Ref. [9] the authors do not envision this possibility because they considered only the case $n = m$. In this case, we consider a straight path between those locations and choose a random location over it, in this case location #6. If all the locations along the line have already been taken, a random one from any of the parents is chosen. Complementary to

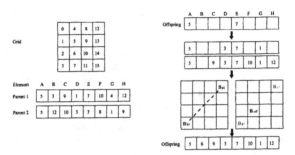

Fig. 2. A step-by-step description of the crossover procedure for the QAP problem.

the recombination operator, the mutation swaps the locations of three randomly selected elements in the solution. We use a 3-element swap scheme because in the **localSearchTS()** method (explained next in Section 3.2) all the 2-element swap movements are already considered. Mutation is always applied over the offspring after recombination.

3.2 Local Search algorithms

We implemented two local search methods (see Figure 1). (**localSearchTS()**) includes a Tabu Search implementation [12] and it is described next. The neighborhood of a solution S is defined by the swap of all pairs of elements of S. The algorithm chooses the swap that causes the best improvement in the QAP objective function. If such swap does not exist, we perform the swap that least worsens the solution. After a swap is done, any swap that brings the elements back to their previous positions become *tabu* for a number of iterations. However, a *tabu* swap shall be accepted if the objective function value of the new solution is better than the incumbent – i.e. an *aspiration criterion*. This local search is applied on each *pocket* solution of the population at the beginning of the MA and on each *current* solution after the recombination phase.

The second local search method (**8-neighborLS()**) iteratively selects an element at random and tries to move it to the eight surrounding locations in the grid, using a best-improvement strategy. Every time an element is moved to a new position, we test again its eight adjacent locations, until no improvement is possible anymore. The process iterates for all elements of the solution. As this algorithm performs just a fine-tuning of the solution, it is applied only to the *pocket* solution of the leader agent of the population.

4 Computational Results

The memetic algorithm was coded using Java SDK 1.5.1 and generated the graph layout for the S&P100 dataset in less than 20 seconds of CPU time in a 3.0 GHz Pentium IV machine with 512Mb of RAM. The resulting graph contains 10 clusters and is shown in Figure 3. In this instance all the elements are labelled according to the industrial sector that they belong to; this allows us to better analyze the quality of the layout. Initially, this analysis takes into consideration each cluster defined by the proximity graph, as we expect those clusters to reflect the classification by industrial sector. Then, within each cluster, we will analyze any relevant structure uncovered by the QAP. Because of the space restrictions, we only give the analysis of one cluster.

Cluster #8 could be easily classified as a *services* cluster because 10 of its 17 elements belong to that sector. However, a better classification of the elements in this cluster could be obtained using the information from the layout produced by our method. In the left side of the layout there are four companies related with the packaging industry (**Alcoa, Du Pont, Allegheny Technologies** and **3M**) and two related with paper products (**OfficeMax** and **Weyerhaeuser**). These companies have been joined together with **International Paper**, which has a participation in both industries. Next to them, we can find the two railroad companies, **Norfolk Southern** and **Burlington Northern Santa Fe**. Finally there is a group of seven companies (**Black & Decker, Limited Brands, May Department Stores, Wal-Mart, Radioshack, Home Depot** and **Sears**) mainly related with the stores industry. The last company of this cluster is **Rockwell Automation**. It has no clear relation with the other companies, but as a *conglomerate* we cannot consider it an outlier. To compare our layout we use the classical dendogram (Figure 4) obtained with a hierarchical cluster-ing method provided by the European Bioinformatics Institute (EBI)[2], using average linkage (UPGMA) clustering based on "correlation measure based dis-tance" (uncentered). Even though the clustering methods developed at EBI are aimed to analyze biological datasets, their hierarchical clustering is a general approach which can be used in datasets from any source. The input is also the second derivatives of the weekly stock prices. While some technological sec-tors seems present, the dendogram analysis has its problems. Clusters are only defined when we "cut" the tree. Our methodology managed to automatically separate most of the sectors into distinct natural clusters uncovering similari-ties in the dynamics of groups of stocks. In addition, for the clusters without a sound sector majority, the QAP created a layout where the elements from dif-ferent sectors were organized into smaller groups (e.g. clusters #7 and #8). The

---

[2] http://ep.ebi.ac.uk/EP/EPCLUST/

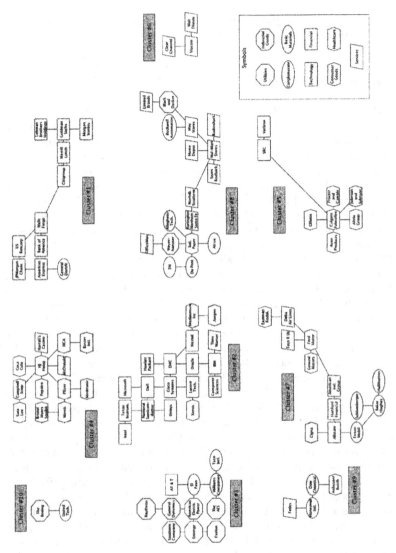

Fig. 3. Graph layout for the S&P100 dataset. The memetic algorithm solved one QAP for each cluster and an extra QAP considering each cluster as a single element, obtaining the final layout. Each shape indicates a different industrial sector represented in the dataset.

quality of the results for the S&P100 dataset supports the use of this method as a new clustering/visualization tool for other time-series data analysis problems. Our visualization methodology is not restricted to the clustering method used

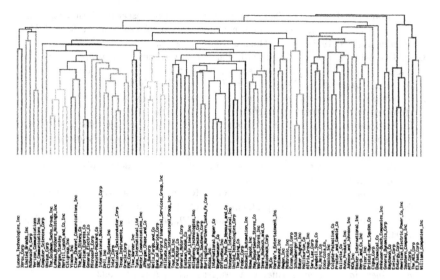

Fig. 4. Dendogram representing the average linkage hierarchical clustering from EBI.

here and the use of the QAP model and a memetic algorithm can be a good alternative for another approach to the automatic layout of weighted graphs.

5 Conclusions

A methodology for correlated data visualization based on the Quadratic Assignment Problem (QAP) was introduced in this paper. It uses a recursive partition approach that divides the dataset into small clusters. A memetic algorithm solves a separate QAP for each subgraph. The final solution obtained by our methodology correctly identifies the majority of the sectors present in a stock market dataset. In some cases, elements from distinct sectors but similar dynamical behaviors are located within the same component of the proximity graph. The success in obtaining a high-quality layout for a financial market instance – which is a challenge due to their inherent near-chaotic behaviour – makes us believe that this technique can be very useful for other problem domains.

References

1. V.V. Gafiychuk, B. Yo. Datsko, and J. Izmaylova. Analysis of data clusters obtained by self-organizing methods. *Physica A: Statistical Mechanics and its Applications*, 341:547–555, 2004.

2. N. Basalto, R. Bellotti, F. De Carlo, P. Facchi, and S. Pascazio. Clustering stock market companies via chaotic map synchronization. *Physica A: Statistical Mechanics and its Applications*, 345(1-2):196–206, 2005.

3. V. Boginski, S. Butenko, and P.M. Pardalos. On structural properties of the market graph. In A. Nagurney, editor, *Innovations in Financial and Economic Networks*, pages 28–45. Edward Elgar Publishing Inc, 2003.

4. S. Sahni and T. González. P-complete approximation problems. *Journal of the Association for Computing Machinery*, 23(3):555–565, 1976.

5. R. Burkard, E. Çela, P. Pardalos, and L. Pitsoulis. The quadratic assignment problem. In P. Pardalos and D. Du, editors, *Handbook of Combinatorial Optimization*, pages 241–338. Kluwer Academic Publishers, 1998.

6. E. Taillard. Robust taboo search for the quadratic assignment problem. *Parallel Computing*, 17(4-5):443–455, 1991.

7. C.A. Oliveira, P.M. Pardalos, and M.G.C. Resende. Grasp with path-relinking for the quadratic assignment problem. In C.C. Ribeiro and S.L. Martins, editors, *Lecture Notes in Computer Science*, volume 3059, pages 356–368. Springer-Verlag, 2004.

8. J. Carrizo, F.G. Tinetti, and P. Moscato. A computational ecology for the quadratic assignment problem. In *Proceedings of the 21st Meeting on Informatics and Operations Research*, Buenos Aires, Argentina, August, 1992.

9. P. Merz and B. Freisleben. A comparison of memetic algorithms, tabu search and ant colonies for the quadratic assigment problem. In *Proceedings of the 1999 International Congress of Evolutionary Computation (CEC'99)*, Washington DC, USA, 6-9 July, 1999.

10. R. Berretta and P. Moscato. The number partitioning problem: An open challenge for evolutionary computation? In D. Corne and M. Dorigo, editors, *New Ideas in Optimization*, pages 261–278. McGraw-Hill, 1999.

11. L.S. Buriol, P.M. Franca, and P. Moscato. A new memetic algorithm for the asymmetric traveling salesman problem. *Journal of Heuristics*, 10(3):483–506, 2004.

12. F. Glover and M. Laguna. *Tabu Search*. Kluwer Academic Publishers, Norwell, Massachusetts, 1997.

13. M. Ausloos and K. Ivanova. Mechanistic approach to generalized technical analysis of share prices and stock market indices. *The European Physical Journal B*, 27:177–187, 2002.

14. J.M. González-Barrios and A.J. Quiroz. A clustering procedure based on the comparison between the k nearest neighbors graph and the minimal spanning tree. *Statistics & Probability Letters*, 62(1):23–34, 2003.

15. P. Moscato, C. Cotta, and A. Mendes. Memetic algorithms. In G. Onwubolu and B. Babu, editors, *New Optimization Techniques in Engineering*, pages 53–86. Springer-Verlag, 2004.

16. P. Moscato. Memetic algorithms. In P. Pardalos and M. Resende, editors, *Handbook of Applied Optimization*. Oxford University Press, New York, NY, USA, 2002.

17. P. Moscato and C. Cotta. Memetic algorithms. In T.F. Gonzalez, editor, *Handbook of Approximation Algorithms and Metaheuristics*. Chapman & Hall/CRC, 2006. to appear.

Knowledge Perspectives in Data Grids

Luis Eliécer Cadenas, Emilio Hernández

Universidad Simón Bolívar, Departamento de Computación y T. I.,
Apartado 89000, Caracas 1080-A, Venezuela

Abstract. In this paper a methodology for accesing scientific data repositories on data grids is proposed. This methodology is based on ontology specification and knowledge representation. The concept of *Knowledge Perspective* is introduced, as the action of applying particular scientific conjectures or theories to the interpretation of experimental data and information. Data grid environments provide high levels of security and virtualization, which allow the users to create new data services on the data server side. These new services are based on the user's knowledge perspective. An implementation of this concept is presented, on a Globus-enabled Java execution platform.

1 Introduction

Computationally intensive technologies are very important in many areas of scientific research. These technologies are currently used to process, either locally or in distributed environments, considerable amounts of data and information. A new term has been coined to reference scientific research strongly dependent on computational and net-based collaboration: e-science [1]. Distributed platforms for data processing, increasingly known as grids, provide basic technologies for integrating multi-institutional sets of computational resources to support data processing. However, available tools are far from offering the levels of flexibility and capability required to transit the long way between data processing and knowledge generation. In this paper we propose and evaluate the concept of *knowledge perspective*, a tool for managing scientific data and experimental information in Data Grids environments. We define a knowledge perspective, or simply a *perspective*, as the consequence of applying a formalization of a theory to scientific data in order to help in the interpretation of experimental data and information.

In principle, scientific theories can be formalized as sets of universal quantified sentences, using First Order Logic (FOL). By selecting a set of such sentences we can define a theoretical framework (i.e an interpretation or viewpoint) for a specific experimental dataset. This selection may define relevant facts for the contrastation process of a particular theory. We can define, using FOL, concepts, properties, relations and sentences (i.e. closed formulas) that represent subsets of a particular scientific theory. In the context of processing a data source (or a combination of several data sources) for knowledge generation, there could be a first processing level in which the "raw" data is processed in

Please use the following format when citing this chapter:

Cadenas, L.E., Hernández, E., 2006, in IFIP International Federation for Information Processing, Volume 217, Artificial Intelligence in Theory and Practice, ed. M. Bramer, (Boston: Springer), pp. 189–198.

order to generate annotations and/or indexes. These indexes and annotations could highlight the relevant facts of the data according to the theory. In further processing levels the annotations can be semantically correlated in order to corroborate theories or conjectures.

The main contribution of this work is a computational model that allows the users to process data, in the context of Data Grids, which is epistemologically consistent with the nature of the scientific research activity. The users can safely create their own knowledge perpectives on the server or grid side, without the intervention of grid or system administrators. The operational base helps us manipulate and process efficiently very big distributed data sources in Data Grids. We implemented this model using SUMA/G [2], a distributed architecture for execution of Java programs which is implemented on top of Globus.

The rest of this paper is organized as follows. Section 2 formalizes the knowledge perspective concept and its relationship with the scientific and research activity. Section 3 introduces a general architecture to implement a knowledge perspective service in grids environments. Section 4 shows a practical example of the usage of this system to a bibliographic data source. Section 5 revises related work and section 6 offers our conclusions and future work.

2 Knowledge Perspectives

We define the concept of Knowledge Perspective from the definition of three sets. Lets Γ be the set that represents the objects x_i in the data source:

$$\Gamma = \{x_1, x_2, x_3, \ldots x_{n_2}\}$$

Given a set of predicates $P = \{p_1, p_2, p_3, \ldots p_{n_1}\}$, where each p_i represent attributes or relationships among elements of Γ, we can define Ω, which is a set of sets Φ_i:

$$\Omega = \{\Phi_1, \Phi_2, \Phi_3, \ldots \Phi_{n_1}\}$$

where the elements in each set Φ_i are tuples with elements in Γ satisfying the predicate p_i. Each p_i stands for a property or relationship in the ontology used to process the data source and could be organized in a taxonomical hierarchy. This hierarchy is described using description logic formalisms. This process is a first step to produce the knowledge perspective. Normally, elements of Ω (i.e sets Φ_i) are the product of annotating the data source using the concepts or properties p_i.

Λ is a possibly empty set of closed formulas (i.e. sentences) of predicate logic $A_i = W_i(x_1, x_2 \ldots x_{h_i})$. Each A_i represents conjectures or definitions about objects, properties and relationships in the data source, based on atoms p_i in P.

A Knowledge Perspective is then defined as an ordered tuple of sets:

$$\Pi = (\Gamma, \Omega, \Lambda)$$

In order to process a Knowledge Perspective we define at least two steps.

First, the annotation process over the data source, which consists in checking which objects are related through the predicate p_i. In order to do so, the user should provide the methods to verify each predicate over the data source. These methods are used to annotate the data source, probably producing indexes to objects having the property or standing in the relationship represented by p_i.

We define then the second stage of a knowledge perspective computation as the process of producing a set Ω' using Ω and Λ. We can say that tuples $(\Gamma, \Omega, \Lambda)$ and $(\Gamma, \Omega', \Lambda)$ represent the same Knowledge Perspective. However, the validation of the conjectures A_i can be considered as the production of new knowledge, restricted to the data sources analyzed and using the vocabulary contained in P.

As an example to illustrate the previous definitions we can think of Γ as a data repository with astronomical images, Ω as a collection of sets of stars where each set has all the stars with the same apparent magnitude. Λ could be a set of predicate logic formulas (i.e. sentences or assertions in the theory) explaining the formation of supernovas, as a consequence of changes in the apparent magnitude within particular time frames. The computation of the apparent magnitude (i.e. the process to produce Ω) is done through an ontological annotation of the elements in Γ, and could be the product of processing the images or the result of using some existing catalogue.

3 Knowledge Perspectives implementation in Data Grids

We implement perspectives as new services, installed directly on the data source by the users. This is possible in data grids because of the security levels they provide. This approach has several advantages. Firstly, the user could send a short specification in a high level language (i.e. FOL) and the process is done at the data source. In this way it is possible to reduce the cost of data transfers. Secondly, it would facilitate data processing in places with legal restrictions for data transfers. In third place, it permits multiple views about the same data set. In this way different researchers or members of a comunity can share different points of view for the same data. Finally, new data services can evolve with the data source through updating mechanisms of the defined knowledge perspectives. Any data provider should offer, in addition to a normal data access service, a mechanism to process data *in-situ* and hosting services associated with data models installed by authorized users.

3.1 Architecture

The proposed architecture provides services to install new data queries and access services. These new services are built by processing the original data sets, providing in this way an additional perspective.

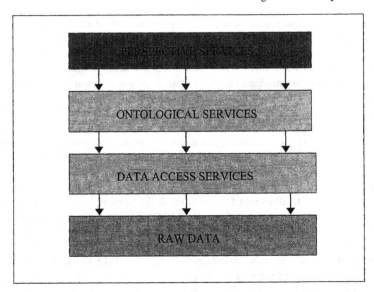

Fig. 1. Service Levels

Figure 1 shows the proposed architecture from the point of view of the services required in the Grid to offer perspective services. We defined the interfaces (API) required at each level and the related operational semantic. Through these interfaces we can virtualize the knowledge perspective service and integrate the same concept across many architectures, facilitating the deployment of distributed perspectives.

We propose a three layer architecture:

- The *Data Access Services* layer defines basic interfaces and the required services to access data sources. This service level would be typically installed by the data provider and offers abstractions to manipulate data sources, regardless the data format.
- The *Ontological Services* layer defines the interfaces and services required to create, store, manipulate and reason over ontologies. (i.e. UploadOntology, CheckOntology, etc). Using services at this level, the users can design an ontology which is adequate to their perspectives, with the required description of objects, properties and relationships. The users must then develop methods to produce the first level annotations. After this process the users obtain what we call the (*perspective 0*) level. Finally, the users develop the set of assertions (conjectures set and logical inferences) to be applied to *perspective 0* data in order to produce the *perspective 1* output.
- Finally, the *Perspective Manipulation Service* layer defines basic interfaces required to create, store and manipulate perspectives as objects, at both *perspective 0* and *perspective 1* levels (i.e. MakePerspective, QueryPerspective).

The execution of these services materialize both perspective levels by creating indexes using the data source and the user-provided ontology and theory. The first processing level establishes a match among objects in the data source and the satisfied predicates. The second one uses logical assertions in the Λ set to produce new satisfied inferences.

Currently, perspective, data and ontology services are defined and installed in SUMA/G[3], a grid infrastructure to execute Java bytecode in distributed environments, based on Globus services. In this software architecture we implemented a metaservice to install new services (SIMG). A *service* in this context is defined using a *service name*, a list containing all the services required to execute the new service (*requirements*), an *API*, a *documentation* and the set of packages that implements the service. The infrastructure offers great flexibility to install new services represented by java objects. This java object could have a constructor to annotate the data source and offers methods to access the annotated data source. For a future version we are defining a specialized *proxy* to query distributed databases processed using the perspective service. We provide facilities to query the data source, through the perspective service, using an option called *submit*. This option executes the queries asynchronously, and the results are stored temporarily in the execution agent. The user can ask at any time for these results using a mediator.

The service for installing new services directly by the users (SIMG) is crucial for the developing and installation of knowledge perspectives as defined in this work. The main reason is flexibility, because the users can process remote data transparently, i.e. in the same way they would process local data, in a secure way.

4 An example using Wordnet

As a proof of concept we implemented an example that allows us to improve data recovery from a Mysql database that contains information about scientific papers. We used Wordnet, a lexicographic reference system, available online [4]. The database was installed in an execution agent of SUMA/G, together with database access services, ontologies and perspectives as described in section 3.1. We used a Prolog version of Wordnet and developed a metainterpreter. The metainterpreter receives as input an english word and produces recursively as output an RDF file representing a taxonomical subtree with all the hiponyms of the word. This ontology is computed automatically by the metainterpreter and can be manipulated using primitives and methods provided through perspective and ontologies services. Using our perspective service we produce an index that points to papers which mention in the title any of the words contained in the hyponim tree.

In this example the data source is a relational database that contains information about scientific papers. Each table in this database represents a type of object in the universe. We use an ontology (*science* [5]) to describe the objects represented in the data source. We defined an RDF Schema to describe in a generic way any relational database. This schema is shown in figure 2.

```
<rdf_:Tabla rdf:about="&rdf_;kb_db_00055"
 rdf_:Nombre_de_tabla="Profesores"
 rdf_:Representa="Science:Academic-Staff"
 rdf_:tamano="7912"
 rdfs:label="kb_db_00055">
<rdf_:tiene_atributos rdf:resource="&rdf_;kb_db_00056"/>
<rdf_:tiene_atributos rdf:resource="&rdf_;kb_db_00058"/>
<rdf_:tiene_atributos rdf:resource="&rdf_;kb_db_00059"/>
<rdf_:tiene_atributos rdf:resource="&rdf_;kb_db_00060"/>
</rdf_:Tabla>
<rdf_:Atributo rdf:about="&rdf_;kb_db_00056"
 rdf_:Longitud_atributo="50"
 rdf_:Nombre_Atributo="Science:First-Name"
```

Fig. 2. RDF description of the database

Through this schema we describe the objects in our data source and the meanings they stand for, using an ontology as reference (*science*). For example, the relation *Talkabout* could be defined in such a way that express the user's perspective. *Talkabout(paper, biology)* would mean that *paper* is a scientific paper about biology. In the predicate *Talkabout* the second argument is taken from a controlled vocabulary (i.e. the subtree of hyponim relationships produced through the metainterpreter). We want to process the data source to identify all the objects in the relationship *Talkabout*.

In this example, when we process a perspective, an index over the data source is generated. This index is an interpretation in the framework of a particular theory. Each sentence in the theory used to produce the perspective (each sentente A_i in Λ) generates a table with as many columns as the arity of A_i plus one column identifying the predicate. In our example, the only relation is hyponymy. The following sentences show a part of the subtree produced by the word *biology*:

$$\forall(X)Embriology(X) \to Biology(X)$$
$$\forall(X)Botany(X) \to Biology(X)$$
$$\forall(X)Phytology(X) \to Biology(X)$$

For this example our perspective $\Pi = (\Gamma, \Omega, \Lambda)$ is defined as follows:

- Γ has scientific papers. In order to identify properties, predicates and relevant objects in the table we have used a description based on a RDF Schema and the *Science* Ontology.

- Ω are all the papers X_i satisfying the predicate TalkAbout(X_i,Biology).
- Ω' has all the papers X_i added beacuse it satisfies the sentences in Λ.
- Λ has the transitive clausure of the hyponim relation in the Biology subtree.

In this way we produce an index for each word in the subtree using an RDF Schema and the science ontology to clarify the meaning of table names in the original database. This is the annotation process at the *perspective 0* level. Then we use the hyponym relations to add relations between words in the index, corresponding to our second level of annotation *perspective 1*.

Once the perspective is represented by an index (or by any other data structure implemented by the user) later queries take a considerably shorter time. In other words, from the point of view of performance, the *perspective 0* creation could take a long time, depending on the size of the database and the kind of processing performed on the raw data. However, once created, the annotations and indexes will speed up further processing, such as *perspective 1* creation and later queries and conjecture validations. In our example, such queries to the paper database take a time in the order of a few milliseconds, when executed from a remote computer located in the same local area network.

5 Related Work

Semantic techniques on grid environments can be roughly classified into two groups: those that provide knowledge about the grid resources and those that provide knowledge about the data grid contents [6]. The first one is used to describe, discover, manipulate and compose services while the second one is used to produce more knowledge through ontological resources in order to describe and discover new data relationships. In [7] a general architecture is proposed, in which there is a clear separation between the semantic grid level and the knowledge grid level. The semantic grid level uses ontologies to describe services in the grid while the knowledge grid level uses semantic techniques to process data and produce knowledge. Some of these proposals are based on computer agents [8] which can offer autonomy and negotiation capabilities to grid environments [9]

The Semantic Grid research community is mainly working on developing techniques using ontologies in order to improve knowledge access and recovery in the grid [10][11][12][13][14]. Ontology languages and reasoning techniques are fundamental to describe resources and services in this framework [15][16]. Most of the languages being considered use description logic to provide an automatic classification of resources and services with a model theoretic semantic. Recently, some proposals account for the lack of nonmonotonic reasoning techniques and rule languages usage in order to implement some of the requirements of the semantic web and semantic grid communities (for example negotiation of services) [17]. A main concern is to provide the adequate level of expressivity without loosing decidibility or tractability. The capability to describe resources and services in a declarative language helps us to create automatic discovering and composition techniques which could improve the current capability of the grid to produce new knowledge.

The Virtual Data System [18] is an architecture for data virtualization. Using the virtual data language *VDL* users can describe workflows over datasets. Data transformation processes could be discovered and composed. Metadata about transformations, derivations, and datasets are registred in the distributed virtual data catalog. The *Knowledge Grid* [19] is an architecture for distributed data mining. The system uses ontologies [20] to describe data mining services and help users to elaborate data mining workflows. Comb-e-chem [21] is creating the infrastructure to analyze correlations and predict properties in chemical structures using techniques known as publication at source. Comb-e-chem provides services to create workflows, aggregate experimental data, select datasets and also annotate and edit data sources. Using the concept of *publication at source* all these data can be reused many times. MyGrid [22] offers an infrastructure to support research in bioinformatic. MyGrid provides data and resource integration services using semantic technologies to improve service discovery, data flow and distributed processing. Comparatively our proposal offers:

- A technique to link logical theories, described using FOL and Description Logics with data sources. This link explicitly shows relations among theories and data subsets producing indexes. These indexes improve data access in large datasets.
- Facilities to use a high level language (FOL) to describe data processing in data grids. Our data modeling process is completely defined with reference to FOL sentences. Annotation methods required to make *Perspective 0* annotations could be provided as libraries. In this way a researcher needs only to define the process by using FOL.
- A processing technique which leaves the data source unchanged.
- A flexible way to create views over data. Each user could have her own perspective over each data set.
- A process to identify objects, properties and relations in the framework of an arbitrary, user defined, theory. In this way the researcher could identify data objects confirming the theory used to process it.
- A technique for processing data at the source, avoiding issues related to the transfer of large amounts of data.
- An architecture of ontology services to implement the knowledge perspective concept.
- A technique to provide many points of view over data, increasing opportunities of knowledge discovery and scientific advance.

This is achieved through the combination of (1) a methodology based on ontology specification and knowledge representation and (2) appropriate data grid services that allow users to define their own ontological services.

6 Conclusions and Future Work

In this work we propose a methodology that establishes a bridge between data manipulation techniques based on ontological criteria and secure data access in grids. We base this methodology in a concept we call *Knowledge Perspective* which allows researchers to manipulate scientific data according to a theoretical framework.

From the viewpoint of knowledge representation and management, we propose the use of a high level language (First Order Logic) and a specification about how to compute a knowledge perspective. Using the grid environment each user could have the authorization level and enough computational and data resources to create indexes in the data source. We present a Globus-enabled Java platform that allows the users to define their own data services based on ontological description of the data. Both contributions allow the grid users to define new services and data access interfaces, consistent with their own knowledge perspectives.

Our initial results, reported in this paper, show the feasibility of using this concept when applied to frameworks where the information has low complexity levels. We need further research and tests for larger and more complex datasets. We describe distributed data sources using ontologies, facilitating data mediation and integrated access to heterogeneus data sources. We plan to implement further mediation techniques in the future. Ongoing research is oriented to applying and evaluating this technology in databases where the data objects are more complex, such as images. In this case the predicates associated to the objects can be satisfied using image processing algorithms.

References

1. Hey, T., Trefethen, A.: "e-science and its implications". Philosophical Transactions of the Royal Society **361**(1809) (2003) 1809–1825
2. Blanco, E., Cardinale, Y., Figueira, C., Hernndez, E., Rivas, R., Rukoz, M.: Remote data service installation on a grid-enabled java platform. In: 17th International Symposium on Computer Architecture and High Performance Computing SBAC-2005. (2005) 85–91
3. Cardinale, Y., Hernández, E.: Parallel Checkpointing on a Grid-enabled Java Platform. Lecture Notes in Computer Science (European Grid Conference EGC2005) (2005) To appear.
4. Fellbaum, C.: Wordnet: An Electronic Lexical Database. MIT Press (1999)
5. Freitas, F.: Ontology of science. Technical report, Universidade Federal de Santa Catarina (2001)
6. Goble, C., De Roure, D., Shadbolt, N., Fernandes, A.: Enhancing services and applications with knowledge and semantics. In Foster, I., Kesselman, C., eds.: The Grid 2: Blueprint for a New Computing Infrastructure. Morgan-Kaufmann (2004)

7. Goble, C., De Roure, D.: The semantic grid: Myth busting and bridge building. In: 16th European Conference on Artificial Intelligence (ECAI-2004), Valencia, Spain (2004) 1129–1135

8. Rana, O.F., Pouchard, L.: Agent based semantic grids: Research issues and challenges. Journal of Parallel and Distributed Computing Practices (2003)

9. Roure, D.D., Shadbolt, N., Jennings, N.: The semantic grid: Past, present and futur. In: Proceedings of The IEEE. (2005)

10. Goble, C., De Roure, D.: The semantic web and grid computing. In Kashyap, V., Shklar, L., eds.: Real World Semantic Web Applications. Volume 92 of Frontiers in Artificial Intelligence and Applications. IOS Press (2002)

11. Cannataro, M., Talia, D.: Semantics and knowledge grids: Building the next-generation grid. IEEE Intelligent Systems 19(1) (2004) 56–63

12. Chen, L., Shadbolt, N., Tao, F., Puleston, C., Goble, C., Cox, S.: Exploiting semantics for e-science on the semantic grid. In: Web Intelligence (WI2003) workshop on Knowledge Grid and Grid Intelligence. (2003) 122–132

13. De Roure, D., Hendler, J.: E-science: the grid and the semantic web. IEEE Intelligent Systems 19(1) (2004) 65–71

14. Newhouse, S., Mayer, S., Furmento, S., McGough, S., Stanton, J., Darlington, J.: Laying the foundations for the semantic grid. In: AISB Workshop on AI and Grid Computing. (2002)

15. Horrocks, I.: Daml-oil: A reason-able web ontology language. In: Proceedings of EDBT. Number 2287 in Lecture Notes in Computer Science, Springer (2002) 2–13

16. et al, M.D.: Owl: Web ontology language 1.0 reference. Technical report, World Wide Web Consortium (2002)

17. Kifer, M., Bruijn, J.d., Boley, H., Fensel, D.: A realistic architecture for the semantic web. In: International Conference on Rules and Rule Markup Languages for the Semantic Web. (2005)

18. Foster, I., Voeckler, J., Wilde, M., Zhao, Y.: The virtual data grid: A new model and architecture for data-intensive collaboration. In: CIDR 2003 Conference on Innovative Data System Research. (2003)

19. Cannataro, M., Talia, D.: The knowledge grid. CACM 46(1) (2003) 89–93

20. Cannataro, M., Comito, C.: A data mining ontology for grid programming. In: 1st International Workshop on Semantics in Peer-to-Peer and Grid Computing (SemPGrid2003). (2003)

21. Frey, J.G., Bradley, M., Essex, J., Hursthouse, M., Lewis, S., Luck, M., Moreau, L., De Roure, D., Surridge, M., Welsh, A.: Combinatorial chemistry and the grid. In Berman, F., Hey, A.J., Fox, G.C., eds.: Grid computing: making the global infrastructure a reality. Wiley Series in Communications Networking and Distributed Systems. John Wiley & Sons Ltd., Chichester, UK (2003) 945–962

22. Goble, C., Pettifer, S., Stevens, R., Greenhalgh, C.: Knowledge integration: In silico experiments in bioinformatics. In Foster, I., Kesselman, C., eds.: The Grid: Blueprint for a New Computing Infrastructure Second Edition. Morgan Kaufman (2004)

On the Class Distribution Labelling Step
Sensitivity of CO-TRAINING

Edson T. Matsubara, Maria C. Monard, and Ronaldo C. Prati

Department of Computer Science
ICMC/USP - São Carlos
Laboratory of Computational Intelligence - LABIC
P.O. Box 668
13560-970 São Carlos,SP, Brazil.
{edsontm,mcmonard,prati}@icmc.usp.br

Abstract. CO-TRAINING can learn from datasets having a small number of labelled examples and a large number of unlabelled ones. It is an iterative algorithm where examples labelled in previous iterations are used to improve the classification of examples from the unlabelled set. However, as the number of initial labelled examples is often small we do not have reliable estimates regarding the underlying population which generated the data. In this work we make the claim that the proportion in which examples are labelled is a key parameter to CO-TRAINING. Furthermore, we have done a series of experiments to investigate how the proportion in which we label examples in each step influences CO-TRAINING performance. Results show that CO-TRAINING should be used with care in challenging domains.

1 Introduction

Semi-supervised learning uses a set of examples where only a few examples are labelled, and the goal is to predict the labels of the remaining unlabelled examples. The main idea of semi-supervised learning is to investigate ways whereby using the unlabelled data it is possible to effectively improve classification performance, compared with a classifier build only using the labelled data, *i.e.* without considering the unlabelled data. For these reasons, semi-supervised learning is considered as the middle road between supervised and unsupervised learning.

Methods that have been proposed under this paradigm include the multi-view semi-supervised CO-TRAINING method (1), dealt with in this work. CO-TRAINING applies to datasets that have a natural separation of their attributes into at least two disjoint sets, so that there is a partitioned description of each example into each distinct view. For each view, the set of few labelled examples is given to learning algorithms to induce independent classifiers. Each classifier is used to classify the unlabelled data in its respective view. Afterwards, examples which have been classified with a higher degree of confidence for all views are included in the set of labelled examples and the process is repeated

Please use the following format when citing this chapter:

Matsubara, E.T., Monard, M.C., Prati, R.C., 2006, in IFIP International Federation for Information Processing, Volume 217, Artificial Intelligence in Theory and Practice, ed. M. Bramer, (Boston: Springer), pp. 199–208.

using the augmented labelled set until a stop criterion is met. However, due to the limited number of initial training examples available in semi-supervised learning, it is not possible to estimate the class distribution of the dataset in advance. Furthermore, when examples are labelled, as there is no information concerning class distribution, we do not know in which class proportion the higher confidence labelled examples should be included in the set of labelled examples in each iteration. This is a question of practical importance, and in this work we analyse the effect of class distribution in CO-TRAINING. Experimental results of CO-TRAINING performance with respect to accuracy, number of incorrectly labelled examples and AUC show that, although the best results are obtained if the true class distribution of the examples is known, for some domains where there is a great separability among classes the performance of CO-TRAINING can also be competitive when this information is not available. However, CO-TRAINING should be used with caution in challenging domains.

The rest of this work is organised as follows: Section 2 presents related work on semi-supervised learning. Section 3 describes CO-TRAINING. Section 4 discusses the class distribution sensitivity problem. Section 5 reports the experimental results, and Section 6 concludes the work.

2 Related Work

Semi-supervised learning algorithms can be divided into single-view and multi-view (2; 3). In a single-view scenario the algorithms have access to the entire set of domain attributes. Single-view algorithms can be split up into transductives (4), Expectation Maximization (EM) variations (5), background knowledge based algorithms (6) and graph-based methods (3). In a multi-view setting, the attributes are presented in subsets (views) which are sufficient to learn the target concept. Multi-view algorithms are based on the assumption that the views are both *compatible* (all examples are labelled identically by the target concepts in each view), and *uncorrelated* (given the label of any example, its descriptions in each view are independent)

The CO-TRAINING algorithm provides the basis for multi-view learning. Following CO-TRAINING some multi-view learning algorithms have been proposed, such as: CO-EM (7) which combines EM and CO-TRAINING; CO-TESTING (2) which combines active and semi-supervised learning, and CO-EMT (2) an extension of CO-TESTING with CO-EM. The use of Support Vector Machines (SVM) instead of *Naive Bayes* (NB) as the base-learning learner is proposed in (8). An improved version of CO-EM using SVM is proposed in (9) showing experimental results that outperform other algorithms. CO-TRAINING requires the instance space to be described with sufficient and redundant views. On the other hand, the TRI-TRAINING algorithm (10) neither requires this nor imposes any constraints on the supervised learning algorithm; its applicability is broader than previous CO-TRAINING style algorithms. The majority of these applications and related work barely consider the class distribution.

3 The CO-TRAINING Algorithm

Given a set of N examples $E = \{E_1, ..., E_N\}$ defined by a set of M attributes $\mathbf{X} = \{X_1, X_2, ..., X_M\}$ and the class attribute Y, where we only know the class attribute for a few examples, CO-TRAINING needs at least two disjoint and compatible views D_1 and D_2 of the set of examples E to work with. In other words, for each example $j = 1, 2...N$ in D_1 we should have its j-th counterpart (compatible example) in D_2. We shall refer to these two views as $\mathbf{X}_{D_1}$ and $\mathbf{X}_{D_2}$ such that $\mathbf{X} = \mathbf{X}_{D_1} \cup \mathbf{X}_{D_2}$ and $\mathbf{X}_{D_1} \cap \mathbf{X}_{D_2} = \emptyset$. Furthermore, the set of labelled examples in each view should be adequate for learning.

Set E can be divided into two disjoint subsets L (Labeled) and U (Unlabelled) of examples. Both subsets L and U are further divided into two disjoint views respectively called, L_{D_1}, L_{D_2} and U_{D_1}, U_{D_2}. These four subsets L_{D_1}, L_{D_2}, U_{D_1} and U_{D_2}, illustrated in Figure 1, as well as the maximum number of iterations k, constitute the input of CO-TRAINING described by Algorithm 1.

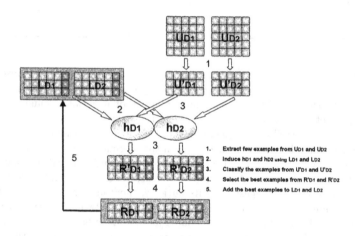

Fig. 1. CO-TRAINING

Initially, two small pools U'_{D_1} and U'_{D_2} of compatible unlabelled examples, withdrawn from U_{D_1} and U_{D_2} respectively, are created, and the main loop of Algorithm 1 starts. First, the sets of training examples L_{D_1} and L_{D_2} are used to induce two classifiers h_{D_1} and h_{D_2}, respectively. Next, the set of examples U'_{D_1} is labelled using h_{D_1} and inserted in R'_{D_1}, and the set of examples from U'_{D_2} is labelled using h_{D_2} and inserted in R'_{D_2}. Both sets of labelled examples are given to the function $bestExamples$ which is responsible for ranking compatible examples from R'_{D_1} and R'_{D_2} that have the same class label prediction, and

---

Algorithm 1: CO-TRAINING

Input: $L_{D_1}, L_{D_2}, U_{D_2}, k$
Output: L_{D_1}, L_{D_2}
Build U'_{D_1} and U'_{D_2} as described;
$U_{D_1} = U_{D_1} - U'_{D_1}$;
$U_{D_2} = U_{D_2} - U'_{D_2}$;
for $i = 0$ *to* k **do**
 Induce h_{D_1} from L_{D_1};
 Induce h_{D_2} from L_{D_2};
 $R'_{D_1} = h_{D_1}(U'_{D_1})$ set of classified examples from U'_{D_1};
 $R'_{D_2} = h_{D_2}(U'_{D_2})$ set of classified examples from U'_{D_2};
 $(R_{D_1}, R_{D_2}) = bestExamples(R'_{D_1}, R'_{D_2})$;
 $L_{D_1} = L_{D_1} \cup R_{D_1}$;
 $L_{D_2} = L_{D_2} \cup R_{D_2}$;
 if $U_{D_1} = \emptyset$ **then return**(L_{D_1}, L_{D_2}) **else**
  Randomly select compatible examples from U_{D_1} and U_{D_2} to replenish
  U'_{D_1} and U'_{D_2} respectively;
 end
end
return(L_{D_1}, L_{D_2});

---

selecting from them the "best" pairs of compatible examples to be inserted in L_{D_1} and L_{D_2} respectively. After that the process is repeated until a stop criterion is met — either the maximum number of iterations defined by the user or the set U_{D_1} (or its counterpart U_{D_2}) is empty.

Algorithm 1 describes the general idea of CO-TRAINING using the same base-learning learning algorithm (*Naive Bayes* in the original proposal) which makes it possible to construct a third classifier from h_{D_1} and h_{D_2} called combined classifier (1). Furthermore, Algorithm 1 only uses two visions and binary class datasets. However, as suggested by its authors, there are several features that can be included in the original version. Our implementation of CO-TRAINING includes several such features which enable us to test its behavior under different situations. These features include: more than two visions; more than two classes; variable number of examples and proportion of examples by class in the initial labelled sets L_{D_i} as well as sets U'_{D_i}; different base-learning algorithms; maximum number of "best" classified examples in each class that can be inserted in L_{D_i} during each iteration, and others.

4 Class proportion labelling sensitivity of CO-TRAINING

A common assumption in the design of standard learning algorithms is that training examples are drawn from the same underlying distributions the model is expected to make predictions. In CO-TRAINING, though, this assumption does not hold because the training set of examples is growth while the algorithm is running, and the amount of labelled examples, as well as the proportion in which examples are labelled, is generally a parameter of the algorithm set by the user.

For example, suppose we are using CO-TRAINING to label data for web page classification. In a typical application, we construct a robot crawler that visits some web sites and downloads all pages of interest. We then ask a human expert to hand label some web pages with the classes we are interested in. As we generally do not know how many examples should be labelled for each class, a fair option is to ask the expert to label an even number of examples for each class. Another option is to draw a small sample of examples and ask the expert to label this sample. Although one may argue that the latter option would produce a more reliable estimate of the class distribution than the former, this is not necessarily true as the crawler might have some bias when retrieving web pages. Thus, in both cases we do not have a good estimate of which proportion we should label examples in each CO-TRAINING iteration.

As CO-TRAINING is an iterative process, where examples labelled in previous iterations are used to build models to label new data, in this work we argue that the proportion in which examples are labelled is a key parameter of the CO-TRAINING algorithm. The main point is that we may not know beforehand the true underlying distribution we should use as a parameter for CO-TRAINING beforehand. As the base-classifier might be sensitive to class skews, feeding the algorithm with a class distribution different from the true one would bias the base-classifier used by CO-TRAINING towards an inaccurate classifier. As a consequence, the number of examples incorrectly labelled would increase, degrading the performance of CO-TRAINING.

Although it is very difficult to characterize the effect that changing class distribution would have in learning algorithms, several studies evaluate its behaviour for a number of well-known algorithms. (11) conducts an extensive experimentation using the decision tree algorithm C4.5 with datasets sampled under several different class distributions. The authors conclude that, on average, the natural class distribution produces the most accurate classifiers. (12) claims that when the independence assumption of attributes is violated, the Naive Bayes algorithm is affected by changing class distributions. The author shows that this sensitivity also holds for other algorithms, such as logistic regression and hard margin SVMs. (13) further extends these results claiming that the sensitivity could not only be attributed to the learning system but also to the dataset at hand. As CO-TRAINING uses learning algorithms as base-classifiers, this sensitivity is automatically inherited from the learning system. The next section shows how this sensitivity affects the results for the datasets used in our experiments.

5 Experimental Evaluation

We carried out an experimental evaluation using three different text datasets:
a subset of the UseNet news articles (20-NewsGroups) (14); abstracts of academic papers, titles and references collected from *Lecture Notes in Artificial
Intelligence* (LNAI) (15) and links and web pages from the COURSE dataset (1).

For the first dataset we created a subset of the 20-newsgroups selecting 100
texts from `sci.crypt`, `sci.electronics`, `sci.med`, `sci.space`,
`talk.politics.guns`, `talk.politics.mideast`, `talk.politics.misc` and
`talk.religion.misc`. All texts from the first 4 newsgroups were labelled as `sci`
(400 - %50) and texts from the remaining newsgroups were labelled as `talk` (400
- %50). The LNAI dataset contains 396 papers from *Case Based Reason* (277
- 70%) and *Inductive Logic Programming* (119 - 30%). The COURSE dataset[1]
consists of 1051 web pages collected from various Computer Science department
web sites, and divided into several categories. This dataset already provides the
two views for each web page example. One view consists of words appearing
on the page, and the other view consists of the underlined words from other
pages which point to the web page. However, analysing the examples in the
original dataset, we found 13 examples which are either empty (no text) or
its compatible example in the counterpart view is missing. Thus, the original
dataset was reduced to 1038 examples. Similar to (1), web pages were labelled
as course (221 - 20%), and the remaining categories as non-course (817 - 80%).

Using PRETEXT [2], a text pre-processing tool we have implemented (16), all
text datasets were decomposed into the attribute value representation using the
bag-of-words approach. Stemming and Luhn cut-offs were also carried out. For
datasets NEWS and LNAI the two views were constructed following the approach
we proposed in (17), using *1-gram* representation as one view and *2-gram* as
the second view of the datasets. For the *2-gram* view in the NEWS dataset, the
minimum Luhn cut-off was set to 3. For the remaining views, the minimum
Luhn cut-off was set to 2. The maximum Luhn cut-offs were left unbounded.
For dataset COURSE *1-gram* was used in both views, named TEXT and LINKS.
Table 1 summarises the datasets used in this work. It shows the dataset name
(Dataset); number of documents in the dataset (#Doc); number of generated
stems (#Stem); number of stems left after performing Luhn cut-offs in each
view (#Attributes), and class distribution (%Class).

As all datasets are completely labelled, we can compare the labels assigned
by CO-TRAINING in each iteration with the true labels of the datasets. In other
words, we use CO-TRAINING in a simulated mode, in which the true labels are
hidden from the algorithm and are only used to measure the number of examples
wrongly labelled by CO-TRAINING. In our experiments we used *Naive Bayes*
(NB) as a CO-TRAINING base-classifier. In order to obtain a lower bound of the
error that CO-TRAINING can reach on these datasets, we measured the error

---

[1] http://www.cs.cmu.edu/afs/cs.cmu.edu/project/theo-51/www/co-training/
data/

[2] http://www.icmc.usp.br/~edsontm/pretext/pretext.html

rate of NB using all labelled examples using 10-fold cross-validation. Results (mean error and respective standard deviation) are shown in the last column (NB Error) of Table 1.

Dataset	#Doc	View	#Stem	#Attr.	Class	%Class	NB Error	Overall Error
NEWS	800	1-gram	15711	8668	sci	50%	2.5 (1.7)	
					talk	50%	0.8 (1.2)	1.6 (1.0)
		2-gram	71039	4521	sci	50%	2.0 (2.0)	
					talk	50%	0.5 (1.1)	1.3 (1.2)
LNAI	396	1-gram	5627	2914	ILP	30%	1.7 (3.7)	
					CBR	70%	1.4 (1.9)	1.5 (1.8)
		2-gram	21969	3245	ILP	30%	1.8 (1.7)	
					CBR	70%	1.5 (1.9)	1.8 (1.7)
COURSE	1038	TEXT	13198	6870	course	20%	16.3 (5.4)	
					non-course	80%	3.8 (2.0)	6.5 (2.3)
		LINKS	1604	1067	course	20%	9.6 (7.6)	
					non-course	80%	16.0 (4.7)	14.6 (3.5)

Table 1. Datasets description and *Naive Bayes* error

To assess the behaviour of CO-TRAINING using cross-validation, we adapted the sampling method as follows: first, the examples in both views are paired and marked with an ID. Then, we sample the folds so that both training and test samples are compatible, *i.e.*, an example marked with a given ID appears only in the training or test sample in both views.

All experiments were carried out using the same number of initial labelled examples (30 examples) evenly distributed by class (50% - 50%). In each iteration, up to 10 "best" examples were allowed to be labelled. Furthermore, to analyse the impact of the class distribution we varied the number of examples in each class. We used 0.6 as a threshold to select the best examples, *i.e.* compatible candidates must have been labelled by NB with a probability greater than 0.6.

Table 2 shows the mean value and standard deviation of results obtained using 10-fold cross validation. The first line indicates the maximum number of examples by class that can be labelled in each iteration: sci/talk for NEWS, ILP/CBR for LNAI and course/non-course for COURSE dataset. For each dataset the first four lines show the number of examples in each class that have been wrongly (W) or rightly (R) labelled; LSize is the number of examples labelled by CO-TRAINING, including the 30 initial examples; USize is the number of unlabelled examples left; Error and AUC are respectively the error rate and the area under the ROC curve of the combined classifier, and Wrong is the total number of examples wrongly labelled. The best mean results for these last three measures are in bold.

For all datasets CO-TRAINING ended due to reaching the condition of an empty set of unlabelled examples in iterations 64, 28 and 86 for datasets NEWS, LNAI and COURSE respectively. As can be observed, best results for NEWS and

COURSE datasets are obtained whenever examples are labelled considering the dataset distribution (5/5 for NEWS and 2/8 for COURSE). For LNAI dataset, although the best result is not obtained for its exact proportion 3/7, it is obtained by its similar proportion 2/8. For this dataset, labelling examples using a slight biased proportion towards the minority and most error-prone class (see Table 1) seems to improve classification. In both cases the total number of labelled examples is the same (LSize $\simeq$ 300). The main difference is in the error of each class: while 3/7 proportion labels all CBR examples correctly, 2/8 proportion labels all ILP examples correctly.

Moreover, for the best results the mean error rate of the combined classifiers are compatible with the once obtained using the labelled examples (Table 1), although the COURSE dataset presents a far greater variance.

	2/8	3/7	5/5	7/3	8/2
NEWS dataset					
sci(W)	18.00 (26.45)	10.60 (15.47)	1.10 (1.85)	0.40 (0.52)	0.80 (0.42)
sci(R)	344.50 (2.72)	339.40 (2.50)	325.70 (11.51)	203.60 (0.52)	139.50 (1.51)
talk(W)	1.60 (1.17)	2.20 (0.63)	5.70 (10.03)	42.50 (30.34)	131.00 (18.89)
talk(R)	139.40 (1.17)	201.80 (0.63)	324.30 (10.03)	345.70 (1.89)	347.80 (3.08)
LSize	503.50 (26.53)	554.00 (15.30)	656.80 (9.77)	592.20 (30.07)	619.10 (17.00)
U'Size	206.50 (26.53)	156.00 (15.30)	53.20 (9.77)	117.80 (30.07)	90.90 (17.00)
Error	3.00 (3.24)	2.38 (3.70)	**1.88 (2.14)**	6.25 (5.14)	19.00 (3.53)
AUC	0.98 (0.02)	0.98 (0.03)	**0.99 (0.02)**	0.97 (0.04)	0.92 (0.05)
Wrong	19.80 (26.96)	12.80 (15.80)	**6.80 (11.77)**	43.70 (30.29)	133.50 (19.31)
LNAI dataset					
ilp(W)	0.00 (0.00)	1.30 (1.25)	5.40 (1.71)	9.30 (3.23)	12.30 (5.10)
ilp(R)	69.00 (0.00)	94.20 (2.20)	101.00 (1.49)	100.80 (1.14)	101.70 (1.57)
cbr(W)	0.70 (0.95)	0.00 (0.00)	0.00 (0.00)	0.00 (0.00)	0.00 (0.00)
cbr(R)	230.30 (0.95)	204.00 (0.00)	150.00 (0.00)	96.00 (0.00)	69.00 (0.00)
LSize	300.00 (0.00)	299.50 (1.08)	256.40 (2.41)	206.10 (3.54)	183.00 (5.10)
U'Size	50.00 (0.00)	50.50 (1.08)	93.60 (2.41)	143.90 (3.54)	167.00 (5.10)
Error	**1.26 (1.33)**	2.02 (2.00)	2.03 (1.07)	3.28 (1.69)	4.80 (3.03)
AUC	**1.00 (0.00)**	1.00 (0.01)	0.99 (0.01)	0.99 (0.01)	0.99 (0.01)
Wrong	**0.70 (0.95)**	1.30 (1.25)	5.60 (1.90)	9.30 (3.23)	12.50 (5.04)
COURSE dataset					
course(W)	34.40 (29.73)	103.90 (66.05)	252.30 (72.89)	423.40 (27.35)	434.80 (112.58)
course(R)	146.00 (26.82)	132.80 (27.26)	155.50 (13.34)	175.40 (6.00)	179.30 (10.89)
ncourse(W)	5.30 (3.13)	7.20 (8.00)	4.20 (4.59)	1.50 (2.92)	2.40 (3.34)
ncourse(R)	505.20 (154.07)	307.10 (227.37)	146.80 (110.20)	81.60 (31.65)	81.30 (56.98)
LSize	690.90 (150.92)	551.00 (186.16)	558.80 (49.82)	681.90 (23.39)	697.80 (66.62)
U'Size	239.10 (150.92)	379.00 (186.16)	371.20 (49.82)	248.10 (23.39)	232.20 (66.62)
Error	**14.11 (13.26)**	32.65 (20.15)	49.43 (15.95)	61.91 (8.07)	60.29 (17.28)
AUC	**0.92 (0.08)**	0.82 (0.11)	0.71 (0.09)	0.68 (0.07)	0.67 (0.07)
Wrong	**40.20 (31.71)**	112.80 (67.28)	258.70 (72.08)	429.80 (25.59)	442.60 (111.98)

Table 2. CO-TRAINING results for NEWS, LNAI and COURSE datasets

Analysing the behaviour of CO-TRAINING when changing the class distribution of labelled examples shows an interesting pattern. For the balanced dataset NEWS, skewing the proportion of labelled examples towards the talk class (*i.e*, labelling more examples from the talk class: 7/2 and 8/2) does not diminish the performance significantly. The other way dramatically increases the error rate (from 1.88 in 5/5 labelling to 19.00 in 8/2 labelling) as well as in the number of examples incorrectly labelled (6.8% to 133.50%). For the imbalanced datasets the picture is clearer. Both the error rate and the number of incorrectly labelled examples increase as we go towards the opposite direction in terms of proportion of labelled examples.

Another interesting result is related to the AUC. For the datasets with high AUC values — NEWS and LNAI —(near 1), the degradation in performance is weaker than for the COURSE dataset. This is because AUC values near 1 are a strong indication of a domain with a great separability, *i.e.*, domains in which the classes could be more easily separated from the others, and it is easy for the algorithm to construct accurate classifiers even if the proportion of examples in the training set is different from the natural one.

6 Conclusions and Future Work

In this work we analyse, for a fixed set of few labelled examples, the relationship between the unknown class distribution of domains and CO-TRAINING performance with respect to which proportion we should label examples in each iteration. Experimental results evaluated using the labelling accuracy, combined classifier error rate and AUC show that the best performance is achieved whenever we label examples in a proportion equal or close to the natural class distribution present in the datasets. Furthermore, labelling examples in proportions very different from the natural class distribution seems to decrease CO-TRAINING performance, especially in challenging domains. These results should be interpreted as a warning to anyone who is using CO-TRAINING for data labelling.

As future work, we are investigating ways to neutralise or overcome the class proportion labelling dependency of CO-TRAINING. (12) presents some methods aimed at correcting the class proportion when this proportion is not known in a classification context. It would be interesting to adapt this method to CO-TRAINING learning. A possible adaptation would be to label examples in the same proportion as the best examples appear in the L' set. This approach leads to labelling a flexible proportion of examples in each iteration and could bias the class distribution in the L set towards the natural one. However, experimental research should be carried out to analyse the feasibility of this approach.

Acknowledgements: The authors would like to thank FAPESP (Process 2005/03792-9) and CAPES, Brazil, for financial support.

References

[1] Blum, A., Mitchell, T.: Combining labeled and unlabeled data with co-training. In: Proc. 11th Annu. Conf. on Comput. Learning Theory, ACM Press, New York, NY (1998) 92–100

[2] Muslea, I.: Active Learning with Multiple Views (2002) PhD Thesis, University Southern California.

[3] Zhu, X.: Semi-supervised learning literature survey. Technical Report 1530, Computer Sciences, University of Wisconsin-Madison (2005) http://www.cs.wisc.edu/~jerryzhu/pub/ssl_survey.pdf.

[4] Vapnik, V.: Statistical learning theory. John Wiley & Sons (1998)

[5] Nigam, K., Ghani, R.: Analyzing the effectiveness and applicability of co-training. In: Conference on Information and Knowledge Management. (2000) 86–93

[6] Wagstaff, K., Cardie, C., Rogers, S., Schroedl, S.: Constrained k-means clustering with background knowledge. In: Proc. of the 18th Int. Conf. on Machine Learning. (2001) 577–584

[7] Nigam, K., McCallum, A.K., Thrun, S., Mitchell, T.M.: Text classification from labeled and unlabeled documents using EM. Machine Learning **39** (2000) 103–134

[8] Kiritchenko, S., Matwin, S.: Email classification with co-training. Technical report, University of Otawa (2002)

[9] Brefeld, U., Scheffer, T.: Co-EM Support Vector Learning. In: Proc. of the Int. Conf. on Machine Learning, Morgan Kaufmann (2004) 16

[10] Zhou, Z.H., Li, M.: Tri-training: Exploiting unlabeled data using three classifiers. In: IEEE Transactions on Knowledge and Data Engineering. Volume 17. (2005) 1529–1541

[11] Weiss, G.M., Provost, F.J.: Learning when training data are costly: The effect of class distribution on tree induction. J. Artif. Intell. Res. (JAIR) **19** (2003) 315–354

[12] Zadrozny, B.: Learning and evaluating classifiers under sample selection bias. In Brodley, C.E., ed.: Proc of the 21st Int. Conf. on Machine Learning (ICML 2004), ACM (2004) 114–121

[13] Fan, W., Davidson, I., Zadrozny, B., Yu, P.S.: An improved categorization of classifier's sensitivity on sample selection bias. In: Proc of the 5th IEEE Int. Conf. on Data Mining (ICDM 2005), IEEE Computer Society (2005) 605–608

[14] Blake, C., Merz, C.: UCI Repository of Machine Learning Databases (1998) http://www.ics.uci.edu/~mlearn/MLRepository.html.

[15] Melo, V., Secato, M., Lopes, A.A.: Automatic extraction and identification of bibliographical information from scientific articles (in Portuguese). In: IV Workshop on Advances and Trend in AI, Chile (2003) 1–10

[16] Matsubara, E.T., Martins, C.A., Monard, M.C.: Pretext: A preprocessing text tool using the bag-of-words approach. Technical Report 209, ICMC-USP (2003) (in portuguese) ftp://ftp.icmc.sc.usp.br/pub/BIBLIOTECA/rel_tec/RT_209.zip.

[17] Matsubara, E.T., Monard, M.C., Batista, G.E.A.P.A.: Multi-view semi-supervised learning: An approach to obtain different views from text datasets. In: Advances in Logic Based Intelligent Systems. Volume 132., IOS Press (2005) 97–104

Two new feature selection algorithms with Rough Sets Theory

Yailé Caballero[1], Rafael Bello[2], Delia Alvarez[1], Maria M. Garcia[2]

[1]Department of Computer Science, University of Camagüey, Cuba.

{yaile, dalvarez}@inf.reduc.edu.cu

[2]Department of Computer Science, Universidad Central de Las Villas, Cuba.

{rbellop, mmgarcia}@uclv.edu.cu

Abstract: Rough Sets Theory has opened new trends for the development of the Incomplete Information Theory. Inside this one, the notion of reduct is a very significant one, but to obtain a reduct in a decision system is an expensive computing process although very important in data analysis and knowledge discovery. Because of this, it has been necessary the development of different variants to calculate reducts. The present work look into the utility that offers Rough Sets Model and Information Theory in feature selection and a new method is presented with the purpose of calculate a good reduct. This new method consists of a greedy algorithm that uses heuristics to work out a good reduct in acceptable times. In this paper we propose other method to find good reducts, this method combines elements of Genetic Algorithm with Estimation of Distribution Algorithms. The new methods are compared with others which are implemented inside Pattern Recognition and Ant Colony Optimization Algorithms and the results of the statistical tests are shown.

1. Introduction

Feature selection is an important task inside Machine Learning. It consists of focusing on the most relevant features for use in representing data in order to delete those features considered as irrelevant and that make more difficult a knowledge discovery process inside a database. Feature subset selection represents the problem of finding an optimal subset of features (attributes) of a database according to some criterion, so that a classifier with the highest possible accuracy can be generated by an inductive learning algorithm that is run on data containing only the subset of features [Zho01].

Rough Sets Theory was proposed by Z. Pawlak in 1982 [Paw82] and had received many extensions from his author that can be reviewed in [Paw91], [Paw94] and [Paw95]. The Rough Set philosophy is founded on the assumption that some information is associated with every object of the universe of discourse [Kom99a] and [Pol02]. Rough Set Model has several advantages to data analysis. It is based only on the original data and does not need any external information; no assumptions about data are necessary; it is suitable for analyzing both quantitative and qualitative features, and results of Rough Set Model are easy to understand [Tay02]. Several toolkits based on rough sets to data analysis have been implemented, such as Rosetta [Ohr97], and ROSE [Pre98]. An important issue in the RST is about feature selection.

An important issue in the RST is about feature reduction based on reduct concept. A reduct is a minimal set of attributes $B \subseteq A$ such that $IND(B)=IND(A)$, where $IND(X)$ is called the X-indiscernibility relation. In other words, a reduct is a minimal set of attributes from A that preserves the partitioning of universe (and hence the ability to perform classifications) [Kom99b].

The employment of reducts in the selection and reduction of attributes has been studied by various authors, among them are [Koh94], [Car98], [Pal99], [Kom99b], [Ahn00] and [Zho01].

However, this beneficial alternative is limited because of the computational complexity of calculating reducts. [Bel98] shows that the computational cost of finding a reduct in the information system that is limited by $l^2 m^2$, where l is the length of the attributes and m is the amount of objects in the universe of the information system; while the complexity in time of finding all the reducts of information system is $O(2^l J)$, where l is the amount of attributes and J is the computational cost required to find a reduct. However, good methods of calculating reducts have been developed, among them are those based on genetic algorithms, which allow you to calculate reducts with an acceptable

Please use the following format when citing this chapter:

Caballero, Y., Bello, R., Alvarez, D., Garcia, M.M., 2006, in IFIP International Federation for Information Processing, Volume 217, Artificial Intelligence in Theory and Practice, ed. M. Bramer, (Boston: Springer), pp. 209–216.

cost [Wro95], [Wro96], and [Wro98]; and others based on heuristic methods [Deo95], [Cho96], [Bel98], and [Deo98].

In this paper, two new methods for feature selection and its experimental results are presented: one of them using an evolutionary approach (epigraph 2) and the other by a greedy algorithm with heuristic functions (epigraph 3), which uses Rough Sets Theory.

2. Feature selection by using an evolutionary approach

The evolutionary approach had been used to develop methods for calculating reducts. Genetic Algorithms (GA) are search methods based on populations: Firstly, a population of random individuals is generated, the best individuals are selected, and lastly, the new individuals that make up the population will be generated using the mutation and crossover operators. In [Wro95], three methods for finding short reducts are presented. These use genetic algorithms and a greedy method and have defined the adaptability functions $f1, f2$ and $f3$.

An adaptation of the Genetic Algorithm plan is the Estimation of Distribution Algorithms (EDA) [Muh99] but most of them don't use crossover or mutation because the new population is generated from the distribution of the probability estimated from the selected set. The principal problem of the EDA is the estimation of $ps(x, t)$ and the generation of new points according to this distribution in a way that the computational effort is reasonable. For this reason, different approaches have been introduced to obtain the estimation of $ps(x, t)$.

One of the members of this family is the Univariate Marginal Distribution Algorithm (UMDA) for discrete domain [Muh98], which shows taking into account only univariate probabilities. This algorithm is capable of optimizing non-lineal functions, always and when the additive variance (lineal) of the problem has a reasonable weight in the total variance. The UMDA for continuous domain was introduced in 1999. In every generation and for every variable, the UMDA carries out statistic tests to find the density function that best adjusts to the variable. UMDA for continuous domain is an algorithm of structure identification in the sense that the density components are identified through hypothesis tests.

We have defined a method for calculating reducts starting from the integration of the adaptability functions $(f1, f2, y f3)$ of the methods reported by Wróblewski in [Wro95] and the UMDA method, obtaining satisfactory results which are shown in Table 1. The values of the parameters that were used were: $N = 100$; $g = 3000$; $e = 50$; $T = 0.5$; where N is the number of individuals, g is the maximum number of evaluations that will be done, e is elitism, which means that the best 50 pass directly to the next generation; T is the percentage of the best that were selected to do all the calculations.

Table 1. Results obtained with the proposed Estimation Distribution Algorithms (EDA)

Name of data base	Algorithms with the different functions of Wróblewskii								
	f1			f2			f3		
(CaseCount, FeatureCount)	AT	LR	NR	AT	LR	NR	AT	LR	NR
Ballons-a (20,4)	0.167	2	1	1.860	2	1	0.260	2	1
Iris (150,4)	82.390	3	4	3.540	3	4	17.250	3	4
Hayes-Roth (133,4)	40.830	4	1	30.100	4	1	22.450	4	1
Bupa (345,6)	436	3	6.85	995.300	3	8	466	3	8
E-Coli (336,7)	64.150	3	6.85	1514	3	7	169.200	3	7
Heart (270,13)	337	3	8	2782	3	18	1109	3	17
Pima (768,8)	2686	3	17	6460	3	18.4	4387	3	18.6
Breast- Cancer (683,9)	1568	4	6.55	8250	4	7.83	2586	4	8
Yeast (1484,8)	1772	4	2	12964	4	2	2709	4	2
Dermatology (358,34)	1017	6.05	10.15	15553	6	14.90	30658	6	47
Lung-Cancer (27,56)	7.780	4.2	9.55	0.0956	4	15.95	264.200	4	38.6

AT: Average time required to calculate reducts (in seconds)   *LR*: Average length of reducts found

NR: Average number of reducts found

The use of functions described by Wróbleskii [Wro95] in the Estimation of Distribution Algorithms resulted successful. EDA did the calculation of short reducts in little time when the set of examples was not very large (<600 cases), even when the number of attributes that describe the problem was large. The best combination resulted with Wróblewskii's function f1 with respect to the execution time; however f3 found a larger number of reducts in acceptable times.

3 Feature selection using Rough Sets Theory

Rough Sets Theory is a mathematical tool that had been used successfully to discover data dependencies and reduce the number of attributes contained in a dataset by purely structural methods [Jen03].

Reducts that are obtained by using Rough Sets are very informative and all the other attributes can be removed with a minimal information loss due to the use of the degree of dependency measure suggested by Ziarko in [Zia01] and very used by many others authors [Mod93], [Zho01], [Jen03].

Algorithms that calculate reducts are usually designed by using heuristics or random search strategies in order to reduce complexity. Heuristic search is very fast because this is not necessary to wait until the search ends but it doesn't' guarantee the best solution although a better one is known when it is founded in the process.

Now we are able to present RSReduct, a new method for finding reducts with Rough Sets. This is a greedy algorithm that starts with an empty set of attributes and builds good reducts in acceptable times by means of heuristic searches and it works adding the best measurement features by the heuristic function.

The idea of this algorithm is based on criteria of the ID3 method with respect to the normalized entropy and the gain of the attributes [Mit97] and dependency between attributes by means of Rough Sets.

In this algorithm we use the terms $R(A)$ and $H(A)$ proposed in [Piñ03].

The expression for R(A) which is a relevant measure of the attributes ($0 \le R(A) \le 1$) is:

$$R(A) = \sum_{i=1}^{k} \frac{|S_i|}{|S|} e^{(1-c_i)}$$

(1)

Where k is the number of different values of feature A. C_i is the number of different classes present in the objects that have the value i for the feature A. $|S_i|$ the amount of objects with the value i in the feature A, and $|S|$ is the amount of objects of the training set. This measure maximizes the heterogeneity among objects of different classes and minimizes the homogeneity among objects of the same one.

$H(A)$ is obtained by the following algorithm:

1. For all the attributes of the problem, calculate their $R(A)$ and form a vector. Determine the n best attributes for the calculations of the previous step. The value of n can be selected by the user. As a result of this step the vector $RM=(R(Ai), R(Aj),..)$ with $n = |RM|$ is obtained.
2. Determine the combinations of n in p (the value selected by the user) from the selected attributes in step II. The combination vector is obtained.

$$Comb = (\{Ai, Aj, Ak\},...\{Ai, At, Ap\}$$ (2)

3. Calculate the dependency grade of the classes with respect to each one of the combinations obtained in the previous step. As a result of this step, the dependency vectors are obtained.

$$DEP(d) = (k(Comb1, d), k(Comb2, d),...k(Combr, d))$$ (3)

$$k = \frac{|POS_B(D)|}{|U|}$$

where (4) and

$$POS_B(D) = \cup_{B.(x)}$$ (5)

If $k=1$ then d totally depends on B, while if $k<1$ then d partially depends on B.

4. For each attribute "A" the value of $H(A)$ is calculated by the following formula :

$$H(A) = \sum_{\forall i / A \in Combi} k(Combi, d) \quad (6)$$

Another alternative measure that has been used successfully is the gain ratio [Mit97]:

$$SplitInformation(S, A) = -\sum_{i=1}^{c} \frac{|S_i|}{|S|} \log_2 \frac{|S_i|}{|S|} \quad (7)$$

where C are the values of attribute A. This measure is the entropy of S with respect to attribute A.

The Gain Ratio measure ($G(A)$) is defined in terms of the earlier Gain measure [Mit97] and it means how much information gain produce attribute A or how important is this one to the database, as well a this SplitInformation, as follows:

$$G(A) = \frac{Gain(S, A)}{SplitInformation(S, A)} \quad (8)$$

$$Gain\ (S, A) = Entropy\ (S) - \sum_{v \in values\ (A)} \frac{|S_v|}{|S|} Entropy\ (S_v) \quad (9)$$

where, $values\ (A)$ is the set of possible values by attribute A and S_v is the subset of S for which A has the value v, that is, $S_v = \{s \in S | A(S) = v\}$.

$$Entropy\ (S) = \sum_{i=1}^{c} -P_i \log_2 P_i \quad (10)$$

where, P_i is the proportion of S belonging to class i.

Schlimmer and Tan in 1993 demonstrate that more efficient recognition strategies are learned, without sacrificing classification accuracy, by replacing the information gain attribute selection measure by the following measure [Mit97]:

$$C(A) = \frac{Gain^2(S, A)}{Cost(A)} \quad (11)$$

where $Cost(A)$ is a parameter entered by the user which represents the cost of attribute A, a value between 0 and 1.

Nuñez in 1988 describes other measure [Mit97]:

$$C(A) = \frac{2^{Gain(S,A)} - 1}{(Cost(A) + 1)^w} \quad (12)$$

where $Cost(A)$ is a parameter entered by the user which represents the cost of attribute A, a value between 0 and 1 and W is a constant value between 0 and 1 that determines the relative importance of the cost versus information gain.

Considering the measures $R(A)$, $H(A)$, $G(A)$ and $C(A)$ the new algorithm RSReduct, was written as follows:

Step1. Form the distinction table with a binary matrix B $(m^2-m)/2 \times (N+1)$. Each row corresponds to a pair of different objects. Each column of this matrix corresponds to an attribute; the last column corresponds to the decision (treated as an attribute).

Let $b((k,n), i)$ an element of B corresponding to the pair (Ok, On) and the attribute i, for i that belongs to $\{1, ..., N\}$

$$b((k,n), i) = \begin{cases} 1, if a_i(O_k) \neg \Re a_i(O_n) \\ 0, if a_i(O_k) \Re a_i(O_n) \end{cases} i \in \{1, ...N\} \quad (13)$$

$$b((k,n), N+1) = \begin{cases} 0, if d_i(O_k) \neq d_i(O_n) \\ 1, if d_i(O_k) = d_i(O_n) \end{cases} \quad (14)$$

where $\Re$ is similarity relation depending on the type of attribute a_i.

Step2. For each attribute "A", calculate the value of $RG(A)$ for any of the following three heuristics and then form an ordered list of attributes starting from the most relevant attribute (which maximizes $RG(A)$).

Heuristic1: $RG(A)=R(A)+H(A)$ (15)

Heuristic2: $RG(A)=H(A)+G(A)$ (16)

Heuristic3: $RG(A)=H(A)+C(A)$ (17)

Step3. With $i=1$, R = an empty set and $(A1, A2,...An)$ an ordered list of attributes according to step 2, consider if $i<=n$ then $R=R \cup Ai$, $i=i+1$.

Step4. If R satisfies the Condition I then Reduct = minimal subset $R' \subseteq R$ does meet Condition I, stop (which means end).

$$\forall k,n \quad \forall a_i \in R \quad a_i(o_k)\Re a_i(o_n) \Rightarrow d(o_k) = d(o_n)$$ (Condition I)

Step5. In other case, repeat from step 3.

The Condition I, in step P4, uses the following relation between the objects x and q for the feature a:

$$q_a \Re x_a \Leftrightarrow sim(x_a,q_a) \geq \varepsilon$$, where $0 \leq \varepsilon \leq 1$

RSReduct algorithm was tested with several datasets from the UCI machine learning repository that is available in the ftp site of the University of California. Some of the databases belong to real world data such as Vote, Iris, Breast Cancer, Iris, Heart and Credit, the other ones represent results obtained in labs such as Balloons-a, Hayes-Roth, LED, M-of-N, Lung Cancer and Mushroom.

The following results were obtained after using RSReduct with the three heuristic functions defined, also the execution time of the algorithm is compiled in each case:

Table 2. Results obtained with the proposed Algorithm according to the different heuristics.

Name of Data Base (CaseCount, FeatureCount)	Heuristic 1		Heuristic 2		Heuristic 3	
	Time (second)	Length of reduct	Time (second)	Length of reduct	Time (second)	Length of reduct
Ballons-a (20,4)	5.31	2	3.12	2	16.34	2
Iris (150,4)	40.15	3	30.79	3	34.73	3
Hayes-Roth (133,4)	36.00	3	32.30	3	39.00	3
Bupa (345,6)	74.20	6	89.00	6	89.00	6
E-Coli (336,7)	57.00	5	41.15	5	46.60	5
Heart (270,13)	30.89	9	16.75	9	54.78	10
Pima (768,8)	110.00	8	110.00	8	110.00	8
Breast- Cancer (683,9)	39.62	4	31.15	4	32.56	5
Yeast (1484,8)	82.00	6	78.00	6	85.70	6
Dermatology (358,34)	148.70	8	125.9	8	190.00	9
Lung-Cancer (27,56)	25.46	7	18.59	7	31.5	8
LED (226,25)	78.10	9	185.00	8	185	9
M-of-N (1000,14)	230.26	6	162.50	6	79.4	6
Exactly (780,13)	230.00	11	215.00	11	230	11
Mushroom (3954,22)	86.20	8	64.10	8	67.2	8
Credit (876,20)	91.20	14	86.01	14	90.2	15
Vote (435,16)	37.93	12	21.25	11	26.9	12

$C(A) \rightarrow$ Nuñez's measure, $Cost (A) \rightarrow$ aleatories values, $W=0.1$

To illustrate how much was the reduction, the following graphic illustrates the initial length (colored with dark blue) of each dataset and the size of the reduct obtained with the three heuristic functions (colored with red, yellow and light blue respectively):

Figure 1 Reduction of the dataset length by RSReduct

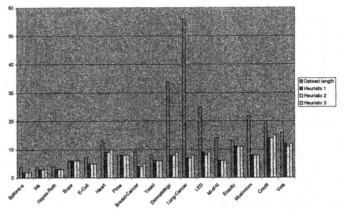

Attending to the size of the reduct obtained, we can conclude that the algorithm is very efficiently. To support this affirmation, experimental results obtained with RSReduct were compared statistically with other feature selection methods implemented with Pattern Recognition (PR) [Alv05], Estimation of Distribution Algorithms (EDA) (epigraph 2) and Ant Colony Optimization Algorithms (ACO) [Cab05]. The tables of the results of the comparison among these methods are omitted, only we will give the results of the statistical tests. In this chance, we used Kruskal-Wallis test, this is a non parametrical test based on rank sums that compares more than two related groups at time in order to discover differences among them. Table 2 shows the P Values obtained for Kruskal-Wallis test with respect to execution time of the algorithms, as can be seen; for all the cases the results were lower than 0.05 with a 95% of statistical significance, in other words, there are significant difference among those methods.

Table 3. P *Values* for Kruskal-Wallis test among the three heuristic functions of RSReduct and other feature selection methods.

Representative datasets	P Value Heuristic 1 vs PR, EDA and ACO	P Value Heuristic 2 vs PR, EDA and ACO	P Value Heuristic 3 vs PR, EDA and ACO
Breast Cancer	0.0039	0.0039	0.0039
Lung Cancer	0.002	0.002	0.002
Mushroom	0.0034	0.0034	0.0034
Heart	0.0039	0.0039	0.0039
Dermatology	0.0265	0.0265	0.0265

The conclusion for this analysis is that if a sufficiently good reduct related to length and class differentiation can be obtained in a lower time, then the new method RSReduct decreases the computational cost in classification problems.

3. Conclusions

In this paper, the problem of selecting features by using the reduct concept was studied by presenting two new methods for the selection of attributes one of them combines EDA algorithms with Wroblewski functions and experimental results show that they are very efficiently taking into account that they calculate exhaustively all the reduct for the dataset. The other method is based on heuristics that don't guarantee to find better solution but an optimal one, a good reduct in this case. It was tested on several examples of training sets and experimental results show that this algorithm can build shorter reducts than others and also the computational time is decreased.

References

[Alv05] Álvarez, D. Feature selection for data analysis using Rough Sets Theory. Thesis of Computer Science Engineering. Thesis Director: Yailé Caballero, M.Sc. University of Camagüey, Cuba. 2005.

[Ahn00] Ahn, B.S. et al.. The integrated methodology of rough set theory and artificial neural networks for business failure predictions. Expert Systems with Applications 18, 65-74. 2000.

[Bel98] Bell, D. and Guan, J. Computational methods for rough classification and discovery. Journal of ASIS 49, 5, pp. 403-414. 1998.

[Cab05] Caballero, Y. Using Rough Sets Theory to treatment of the data. Thesis of Master in Computer Science. Thesis Director: Rafael Bello, PhD. Universidad Central de Las Villas, Cuba. 2005.

[Car98] Carlin, U.S. et al.. Rough set analysis of medical datasets and A case of patient with suspected acute appendicitis. In ECAI 98 Workshop on Intelligent data analysis in medicine and pharmacology.

[Cho96] Choubey, S.K. et al. A comparison of feature selection algorithms in the context of rough classifiers. In Proceedings of Fifth IEEE International Conference on Fuzzy Systems, vol. 2, pp. 1122-1128. 1996.

[Cho99] Chouchoulas, A. and Shen, Q. A rough set-based approach to text classification. Lectures Notes in Artificial Intelligence no. 1711, pp. 118-127. 1999.

[Deo95] Deogun, J.S. et al. Exploiting upper approximations in the rough set methodology. In Proceedings of First International Conference on Knowledge Discovery and Data Mining, Fayyad, U. Y Uthurusamy, (Eds.), Canada, pp. 69-74. 1995.

[Deo98] Deogun, J.S. et al. Feature selection and effective classifiers. Journal of ASIS 49, 5, pp. 423-434. 1998.

[Dim66] Dimitriev, A. N.; Zhuravlev, J. I.; Krendeleiev, F. P. . About mathematical principles of objects and phenomenon classification. Diskretnyi Analiz No. 7, pp. 3-15, 1966.

[Gre01] Greco, S. Et al. Rough sets theory for multicriteria decision analysis. European Journal of Operational Research 129, pp. 1-47, 2001.

[Jen03] Jensen R. and Qiang, S. "Finding rough sets reducts with Ant colony optimization". http://www.inf.ed.ac.uk/publications/online/0201.pdf 2003.

[Koc98] Koczkodaj, W.W. et al.. Myths about Rough Set Theory. Comm. of the ACM, vol. 41, no. 11, nov. 1998.

[Koh94] Kohavi, R. and Frasca, B. Useful feature subsets and Rough set Reducts. Proceedings of the Third International Workshop on Rough Sets and Soft Computing. 1994.

[Kom99a] Komorowski, J. Pawlak, Z. et al.. Rough Sets: A tutorial. In Pal, S.K. and Skowron, A. (Eds) Rough Fuzzy Hybridization: A new trend in decision-making. Springer, pp. 3-98. 1999.

[Kom99b] Komorowski, J. et al.. A Rough set perspective on Data and Knowledge. In The Handbook of Data mining and Knowledge discovery, Klosgen, W. and Zytkow, J. (Eds). Oxford University Press, 1999.

[Mau96] Maudal, O. Preprocessing data for neural network based classifiers: Rough sets vs Principal Component Analysis. Project report, Dept. of Artificial Intelligence, University of Edinburgh. 1996.

[Muh98] Mühlenbein H. The equation for the response to selection and its use for prediction. Evolutionary Computation 5(3), pp. 303-346, 1998.

[Muh99] Mühlenbein, H; Mahnig, T.; Ochoa, A. Schemata, distributions and graphical models on evolutionary optimization. Journal of Heuristics, 5(2), pp. 215-247. 1999.

[Ohr97] Ohrn, A. and Komorowski, J.. Rosetta: A rough set toolkit for analysis of data. In Proc. Third Int. Join Conference on Information Science, Durham, NC, USA, march 1-5, vol. 3, pp. 403-407. 1997.

[Pal99] Pal, S.K. and Skowron, A. (Eds).. Rough Fuzzy Hybridization: a new trend in decision-making. Springer-Verlag, 1999.

[Pal02] Pal, S.K. et al. Web mining in Soft Computing framework: Relevance, State of the art and Future Directions. IEEE Transactions on Neural Networks, 2002.

[Paw82] Pawlak, Z. Rough sets. International Journal of Information & Computer Sciences 11, 341-356, 1982.

[Paw91] Pawlak, Z. Rough SetsTheoretical Aspects of Reasoning About Data. Kluwer Academic Publishing, Dordrecht, 1991. En: http://citeseer.ist.psu.edu/context/36378.html

[Paw94] Pawlak, Z. and Skowron, A. "Rough sets rudiments". Bulletin of International Rough Set Society. Volume 3, Number 3. http://www.kuenstliche-intelligenz.de/archiv/2001_3/pawlak.pdf

[Paw95] Pawlak, Z. "Rough Sets, Rough Relations and Rough functions". R. Yager, M.Fedrizzi, J. Keprzyk (eds.): Advances in the Dempster – Shafer Theory of Evidence, Wiley, New Cork, pp 251 – 271. 1995 http://citeseer.ist.psu.edu/105864.html

[Piñ03] Piñero, P; Arco, L; García, M. and Caballero, Y. Two New Metrics for Feature Selection in Pattern Recognition. Lectures Notes in computer Science (LNCS 2905), pp. 488-497. Springer, Verlag, Berlin Heidelberg. New York. ISSN 0302-9743. ISBN 3-540-20590-X.

[Pol02] Polkowski, L.. Rough sets: Mathematical foundations. Physica-Verlag, p. 574. Berlin, Germany. 2002.

[Pre98] Predki, B. et al.. ROSE- Software implementation of the Rough Set Theory. In Polkowski, L. and Skowron, A. (Eds) Rough Sets and Current Trends in Computing, Proceedings of the RSCTC98 Conference. Lectures Notes in Artificial Intelligence vol. 1424, Berlin pp. 605-608.

[Tay02] Tay, F.E. and Shen, L.. Economic and financial prediction using rough set model. European Journal of Operational Research 141, pp. 641-659. 2002.

[Wil98] Wilson, Randall. Martinez, Tony R. Reduction Techniques for Exemplar-Based Learning Algorithms. Machine Learning. Computer Science Department, Brigham Young University. USA 1998.

[Wro95] Wroblewski, J. Finding minimal reducts using genetic algorithms. In Wang, P.P. (Ed). Proceedings of the International Workshop on Rough Sets Soft Computing at Second Annual Joint Conference on Information Sciences, North Carolina, USA, p. 679, pp. 186-189. 1995.

[Wro96] Wroblewski, J. Theoretical foundations of order-based genetic algorithms. Fundamenta Informaticae, vol. 28 (3,4), pp. 423-430. IOS Press. 1996.

[Wro98] Wroblewski, J. Genetic algorithms in decomposition and classification problems. In Polkowski, L. and Skowron, A. (Eds.). Rough sets in Knowledge Discovery 1: Applications, Case Studies and Software Systems. Physica-Verlag, pp. 472-492. 1998.

[Zho01] Zhong, N. et al.. Using Rough sets with heuristics for feature selection. Journal of Intelligent Information Systems, 16, 199-214. 2001.

Global Convexity in the Bi-Criteria Traveling Salesman Problem

Marcos Villagra[1,2], Benjamín Barán[1,2], and Osvaldo Gómez[1,2]

[1] National University of Asuncion
[2] Catholic University of Asuncion
{mvillagra, bbaran}@cnc.una.py, ogomez@illigal.ge.uiuc.edu

Abstract. This work studies the solution space topology of the Traveling Salesman Problem or TSP, as a bi-objective optimization problem. The concepts of category and range of a solution are introduced for the first time in this analysis. These concepts relate each solution of a population to a Pareto set, presenting a more rigorous theoretical framework than previous works studying global convexity for the multi-objective TSP. The conjecture of a globally convex structure for the solution space of the bi-criteria TSP is confirmed with the results presented in this work. This may support successful applications using state of the art metaheuristics based on Ant Colony or Evolutionary Computation.

Key words: Traveling Salesman Problem, Multi-Objective Optimization, Global Convexity.

1 Introduction

Metaheuristics are a class of optimization algorithms that today constitute one of the best options to solve very complex problems. These algorithms try to combine basic heuristic methods in higher level frameworks aimed at efficiently and effectively exploring a search space [1].

The research in the field of metaheuristics has evolved on the basis of trial and error [2], often motivated by the competition for improving the best known solutions for given problems, and not by identifying the reasons for the success and failure of these algorithms.

The Traveling Salesman Problem or TSP has been used as a benchmark problem for the study of many metaheuristics. The topology of the single-objective TSP has been study in [3–6], and the three-objective TSP in [2], for specific instances. In general, all these results suggest that the solution space has a globally convex structure.

Global Convexity is not convexity in the strict sense [2], but may be used to denote the empirical observation that the best local optima are gathered in a small part of the solution space, which hopefully includes the global optimum. Metaheuristics exploit this by concentrating their search in that part of the solution space [2].

Please use the following format when citing this chapter:

Villagra, M., Barán, B., Gómez, O., 2006, in IFIP International Federation for Information Processing, Volume 217, Artificial Intelligence in Theory and Practice, ed. M. Bramer, (Boston: Springer), pp. 217–226.

This work studies the solution space topology of the bi-objective TSP in a more practical way than the studies carried out in [2], by means of two new metrics, *category* and *range* of a solution. The former, relates a solution with the number of solutions that dominate it; the latter, establishes a hierarchy in the solution space. The whole solution space was studied for random instances with 7, 8, 9 and 10 cities. Then, subsets of the solution space ware analyzed for larger problems with 100 and 150 cities. It is interesting to mention that when global convexity exists, it may be exploited in metaheuristics for multi-objective combinatorial optimization [2]. Global convexity can be used to design good algorithms or to explain the reason of success of well known metaheuristics that make good use of this property, like Ant Colony Optimization (ACO) and Evolutionary Algorithms (EA) [7].

The remainder of this work is organized as follows. Section 2 presents a general definition of a multiple objective problem. The multi-objective TSP is presented in section 3. Global convexity is described in section 4. The theoretical framework and experimental results are explained in section 5. Finally, conclusions and future work are left for section 6.

2 Multi-Objective Optimization Problems

A general Multi-Objective Optimization Problem (MOP) includes a set of n decision variables, k objective functions, and m restrictions. Objective functions and restrictions are functions of decision variables. This can be expressed as:

$$\begin{aligned}
&\text{Optimize} \quad \mathbf{y} = f(\mathbf{x}) = (f_1(\mathbf{x}), f_2(\mathbf{x}), \dots, f_k(\mathbf{x})) \\
&\text{Subject to } \gamma(\mathbf{x}) = (\gamma_1(\mathbf{x}), \dots, \gamma_m(\mathbf{x})) \geq 0 \\
&\text{where} \quad \mathbf{x} = (x_1, x_2, \dots, x_n) \in \mathbf{X} \quad \text{is the decision vector, and} \\
&\qquad\qquad \mathbf{y} = (y_1, y_2, \dots, y_k) \in \mathbf{Y} \quad \text{is the objective vector}
\end{aligned}$$

$\mathbf{X}$ denotes the decision space while $\mathbf{Y}$ is the objective space. Depending on the problem, "optimize" could mean minimize or maximize. The set of restrictions $\gamma(\mathbf{x}) \geq 0$ determines the set of feasible solutions $\mathbf{X}_f \subseteq \mathbf{X}$ and its corresponding set of objective vectors $\mathbf{Y}_f \subseteq \mathbf{Y}$. A multi-objective problem consists in finding $\mathbf{x}$ that optimizes $f(\mathbf{x})$. In general, there is no unique "best" solution but a set of solutions, none of which can be considered better than the others when all objectives are considered at the same time. This comes from the fact that there can be conflicting objectives. Thus, a new concept of optimality should be established for MOPs. Given two decision vectors $\mathbf{u}, \mathbf{v} \in X$:

$$\begin{aligned}
f(\mathbf{u}) = f(\mathbf{v}) \quad &\text{iff} \quad \forall i \in 1, 2, \dots, k : \quad f_i(\mathbf{u}) = f_i(\mathbf{v}) \\
f(\mathbf{u}) \leq f(\mathbf{v}) \quad &\text{iff} \quad \forall i \in 1, 2, \dots, k : \quad f_i(\mathbf{u}) \leq f_i(\mathbf{v}) \\
f(\mathbf{u}) < f(\mathbf{v}) \quad &\text{iff} \quad f(\mathbf{u}) \leq f(\mathbf{v}) \wedge f(\mathbf{u}) \neq f(\mathbf{v})
\end{aligned}$$

Then, in a minimization context, they comply with one of three conditions:

$$\mathbf{u} \succ \mathbf{v} \quad (\mathbf{u} \quad \text{dominates} \quad \mathbf{v}), \quad \text{iff} \quad f(\mathbf{u}) < f(\mathbf{v})$$
$$\mathbf{v} \succ \mathbf{u} \quad (\mathbf{v} \quad \text{dominates} \quad \mathbf{u}), \quad \text{iff} \quad f(\mathbf{v}) < f(\mathbf{u})$$
$$\mathbf{u} \sim \mathbf{v} \quad (\mathbf{u} \quad \text{and} \quad \mathbf{v} \quad \text{are non-comparable}), \quad \text{iff} \quad \mathbf{u} \nsucc \mathbf{v} \wedge \mathbf{v} \nsucc \mathbf{u}$$

Alternatively, $\mathbf{u} \rhd \mathbf{v}$ will denote that $\mathbf{u} \succ \mathbf{v}$ or $\mathbf{u} \sim \mathbf{v}$. A decision vector $\mathbf{x} \in \mathbf{X}_f$ is non-dominated with respect to a set $V \subseteq \mathbf{X}_f$ iff: $\mathbf{x} \rhd \mathbf{v}$, $\forall \mathbf{v} \in V$. When $\mathbf{x}$ is non-dominated with respect to the whole set $\mathbf{X}_f$, it is called an optimal Pareto solution; therefore, the Pareto optimal set $\mathbf{X}_{true}$ may be formally defined as: $\mathbf{X}_{true} = \{\mathbf{x} \in \mathbf{X}_f : \mathbf{x} \quad \text{is non-dominated with respect to} \quad \mathbf{X}_f\}$. The corresponding set of objective vectors $\mathbf{Y}_{true} = f(\mathbf{X}_{true})$ constitutes the Optimal Pareto Front.

A solution $\mathbf{z}$ is attainable if there exists a solution $\mathbf{x} \in \mathbf{X}_f$ such that $\mathbf{z} = f(\mathbf{x})$. The set of all attainable solutions is denoted as $\mathbf{Z}$. The ideal solution $\mathbf{z}^*$, is defined as $\mathbf{z}^* = (\min f_1(\mathbf{x}), \ldots, \min f_k(\mathbf{x}))$.

3 The Multi-Objective TSP

Given a complete, weighted graph $G = (N, E, d)$ with N being the set of nodes, E being the set of edges fully connecting the nodes, and d being a function that assigns to each edge $\langle i, j \rangle \in E$ a vector d_{ij}, where each element corresponds to a certain measure (e.g. distance, cost) between i and j, then the multi-objective TSP (MOTSP) [8] is the problem of finding a "minimal" Hamiltonian circuit of the graph, i.e., a closed tour visiting each of the $n = |N|$ nodes of G exactly once, where "minimal" refers to the notion of Pareto optimality [8]. In this study, we consider symmetric problems, i.e. $d_{ij} = d_{ji}$ for all pairs of nodes i, j.

We will consider the bi-objective TSP:

Minimize $\mathbf{y} = f(\mathbf{x}) = (y_1 = f_1(\mathbf{x}), y_2 = f_2(\mathbf{x}))$
subject to $f(\mathbf{x}) > 0$
where $\mathbf{x} = (\langle 1, 2 \rangle, \langle 2, 3 \rangle, \ldots, \langle n-1, n \rangle, \langle n, 1 \rangle) \in \mathbf{X}$
and $\mathbf{y} = (y_1, y_2) = (f_1(\mathbf{x}), f_2(\mathbf{x})) \in \mathbf{Y}$

where f_1 and f_2 could be considered as the length of the tour, and the time required to traverse it respectively.

We will measure similarity of two solutions $\mathbf{x}, \mathbf{x}'$ by the number of common edges $\langle i, j \rangle \in \mathbf{x}, \mathbf{x}'$. On the contrary, the distance $\delta(\mathbf{x}, \mathbf{x}')$ is defined as the number of non-common edges, i.e. n minus the similarity.

4 Global Convexity

The structure of the single-objective TSP has been studied by Boese et al. [3,4]. Their results indicate that the cost surface exhibits a globally convex structure, where good solutions are together in a small region of the search space, and the best solutions are located centrally with respect to the others.

In a minimization context, Boese suggested an analogy with a big valley structure, in which the set of local minima appears convex with one central global minimum [4]. Even though there is no standard definition of global convexity, figure 1 gives an intuitive picture of a globally convex structure.

Fig. 1. Intuitive picture of the big valley or globally convex solution space structure

The global convexity idea is based on two assumptions [2]:

- *Convexity*: Local optima are gathered in a relatively small region of the solution space.
- *Centrality*: The best local optima are located centrally with respect to the population of local optima.

If both assumptions are valid, we should also expect that local optima are gathered in a small region close to the best local optimum [2]. Besides, any assessment of global convexity only makes sense once a topology has been established in the solution space [2].

Global Convexity has also been studied by Borges and Hansen in [2] for the three-objective TSP, by means of scalarization functions. These results were based on observed behavior rather than on theoretical analysis, and they are not very practical. In fact, Borges and Hansen reduced the multi-objective problem to a single-objective one [2], loosing several characteristics of a truly multi-objective problem, whose theoretical solution is a whole Pareto set and not an ideal solution which is not attainable in practice. Therefore, this work introduces truly multi-objective concepts as *category* and *range*, trying to achieve a more general multi-objective framework. This generalization allows a more rigorous analysis of a MOP for any number of objective functions or measurement units.

5 Topological Analysis of the Solution Space

Boese used the length of a tour to study the quality of a solution [4], what is completely valid in a single-objective context. For a MOP, Borges and Hansen proposed the use of scalarization functions that reduce the multi-objective problem to a single-objective one [2].

In what follows, the concepts of *category* and *range* of a solution are presented for the first time as quality metrics, to allow a further topological analysis of the bi-objective TSP.

A population $P = \{x_1, x_2, \ldots, x_{|P|}\}$ is defined as a set of valid solutions $x_i \in X_f$ of the bi-objective TSP, with cardinality $|P|$.

Definition 1. *Let $P \subset X_f$ be a population, and $x \in P$ a solution. The category of a solution x in a population P is defined as:*

$$cat(x, P) = |\{u \in P : u \succ x\}|$$

Then, the *category* of the solution x is the number of solutions in P that dominates x. Therefore, a solution of the Pareto front will always have a 0 *category*, i.e. if $u \in X_{true}$ then $cat(u, X_f) = 0$.

Definition 2. *Let $P \subset X_f$ be a population. The non-dominated frontier of P is defined as:*

$$\mathbf{NF}(P) = \{u \in P : cat(u, P) = 0\}$$

If $P = X_f$ then $\mathbf{NF}(P) = X_{true}$.

Definition 3. *Let $P \subset X_f$ be a population, and $x \in P$ a solution. The range of a solution x in a population P, denoted as $rng(x, P)$, is defined according to the following algorithm:*

if $\quad x \in \mathbf{NF}(P) \quad$ **then** $rng(x, P) = 0$
else $\qquad\qquad\qquad rng(x, P) = 1 + rng(x, P') \quad$ *where* $\quad P' = P - \mathbf{NF}(P)$

From now on, the use of the parameter P will be omitted from the *range* and *category* notation. Therefore, they will be denoted as $rng(x)$ and $cat(x)$ respectively. The parameter P is left only for ambiguous cases.

A definition of distance is now presented for the study of global convexity in the bi-objective TSP.

Definition 4. *Let $P \subset X_f$ be a population, and $x \in P$ a solution. The mean distance of a solution x to a population P is defined as:*

$$\delta(x, P) = \frac{1}{|P| - 1} \sum_{i=1}^{|P|} \delta(u, x) \quad \forall u \in P.$$

This paper is inspired in Boese's approach [4], where different solutions of an n city problem are saved in a set P; consequently, each solution x has:

- A *category* $cat(x)$.
- A *range* $rng(x)$.
- A mean distance to the other solutions of P denoted as $\delta(x, P)$.
- A distance to the non-dominated frontier denoted as $\delta(x, \mathbf{NF}(P))$ (defined in the next section).

This work is divided in two parts. For the first part, small random instances were thoroughly analyzed, and for the second part, analyses based on larger instances from TSPLIB[1] were made.

5.1 Exhaustive Study of the Solution Space

The study is based on random generated instances with 7, 8, 9 and 10 cities, named litAB7, omiAB8, encAB9 and asuAB10. These problems are described in [9].

Due to the presence of multiple optimal solutions, a definition of distance to the non-dominated frontier is needed.

Definition 5. *Let $P \subset \mathbf{X}_f$ be a population, and $\mathbf{x} \in P$ a solution. The distance of a solution $\mathbf{x}$ to the non-dominated frontier of P is defined as:*

$$\delta(\mathbf{x}, \mathbf{NF}(P)) = min\{\delta(\mathbf{x}, \mathbf{x}_i^*) : \mathbf{x}_i^* \in \mathbf{NF}(P)\} \tag{1}$$

The e best solutions of P will be denoted as $P_{(e)}$; e.g. $P_{(100)}$ denotes the set of the best 100 solutions of P, i.e., the 100 solutions with the smallest *category*.

For the calculations, an exhaustive search was made. The obtained population is the whole solution space for an n city problem, i.e. $P = \mathbf{X}_f$, therefore, $|\mathbf{X}_f| = |P| = \frac{(n-1)!}{2}$, and, $\mathbf{NF}(P) = \mathbf{X}_{true}$.

For each solution $\mathbf{x} \in P$, correlations between the following variables were calculated:

- the distance to the non-dominated frontier $\delta(\mathbf{x}, \mathbf{NF}(P))$ and the *category* of a solution $cat(\mathbf{x})$, denoted as $\rho(cat(\mathbf{x}), \delta(\mathbf{x}, \mathbf{NF}(P)))$;
- the mean distance to the population $\delta(\mathbf{x}, P)$ and the *category* of a solution $cat(\mathbf{x})$ denoted as $\rho(cat(\mathbf{x}), \delta(\mathbf{x}, P))$;
- the distance to the non-dominated frontier $\delta(\mathbf{x}, \mathbf{NF}(P))$ and the mean distance to the population $\delta(\mathbf{x}, P)$ denoted as $\rho(\delta(\mathbf{x}, P), \delta(\mathbf{x}, \mathbf{NF}(P)))$;
- the mean distance to the population $\delta(\mathbf{x}, P)$ and the *range* of a solution $rng(\mathbf{x})$ denoted as $\rho(rng(\mathbf{x}), \delta(\mathbf{x}, P))$;
- the distance to the non-dominated frontier $\delta(\mathbf{x}, \mathbf{NF}(P))$ and the *range* of a solution $rng(\mathbf{x})$ denoted as $\rho(rng(\mathbf{x}), \delta(\mathbf{x}, \mathbf{NF}(P)))$;
- the *range* and *category* of a solution denoted as $\rho(rng(\mathbf{x}), cat(\mathbf{x}))$.

A summary for these values is shown in tables 1 to 4, and the figures for these correlations can be found in [9].

These results suggest that *range* and *category* are very similar quality metrics, with correlations between them larger than 0.9.

High values can be observed for the correlations $\rho(cat(\mathbf{x}), \delta(\mathbf{x}, P))$ and $\rho(rng(\mathbf{x}), \delta(\mathbf{x}, P))$, which suggests a concentration of very good solutions in the center of the solution space, satisfying the centrality assumption of a globally convex structure. Also, the correlations $\rho(cat(\mathbf{x}), \delta(\mathbf{x}, \mathbf{NF}(P)))$ and

---

[1] http://www.iwr.uni-heidelberg.de/groups/comopt/software/TSPLIB95/

Table 1. Correlations for the problem litAB7

	P	$P_{(\lvert P\rvert-1)}$	$P_{(\frac{\lvert P\rvert}{2})}$	$P_{(\frac{\lvert P\rvert}{4})}$
$\rho(cat(\mathbf{x}),\delta(\mathbf{x},P))$	0	0.602793	0.761135	0.659006
$\rho(cat(\mathbf{x}),\delta(\mathbf{x},\mathbf{NF}(P)))$	0.767441	0.763554	0.548112	0.585267
$\rho(\delta(\mathbf{x},P),\delta(\mathbf{x},\mathbf{NF}(P)))$	0	0.582333	0.633253	0.706702
$\rho(rng(\mathbf{x}),\delta(\mathbf{x},P))$	0	0.628991	0.752562	0.661246
$\rho(rng(\mathbf{x}),\delta(\mathbf{x},\mathbf{NF}(P)))$	0.786593	0.783295	0.567543	0.633579
$\rho(rng(\mathbf{x}),cat(\mathbf{x}))$	0.960048	0.960550	0.937163	0.933828

Table 2. Correlations for the problem omiAB8

	P	$P_{(\lvert P\rvert-1)}$	$P_{(\frac{\lvert P\rvert}{2})}$	$P_{(\frac{\lvert P\rvert}{4})}$
$\rho(cat(\mathbf{x}),\delta(\mathbf{x},P))$	0	0.645277	0.868166	0.782142
$\rho(cat(\mathbf{x}),\delta(\mathbf{x},\mathbf{NF}(P)))$	0.774954	0.774225	0.627201	0.524996
$\rho(\delta(\mathbf{x},P),\delta(\mathbf{x},\mathbf{NF}(P)))$	0	0.549804	0.686872	0.555586
$\rho(rng(\mathbf{x}),\delta(\mathbf{x},P))$	0	0.644026	0.929499	0.853578
$\rho(rng(\mathbf{x}),\delta(\mathbf{x},\mathbf{NF}(P)))$	0.810660	0.810222	0.678969	0.594514
$\rho(rng(\mathbf{x}),cat(\mathbf{x}))$	0.976814	0.976843	0.973864	0.959215

Table 3. Correlations for the problem encAB9

	P	$P_{(\lvert P\rvert-1)}$	$P_{(\frac{\lvert P\rvert}{2})}$	$P_{(\frac{\lvert P\rvert}{4})}$
$\rho(cat(\mathbf{x}),\delta(\mathbf{x},P))$	0	0.572255	0.825523	0.697679
$\rho(cat(\mathbf{x}),\delta(\mathbf{x},\mathbf{NF}(P)))$	0.641862	0.641802	0.435708	0.409532
$\rho(\delta(\mathbf{x},P),\delta(\mathbf{x},\mathbf{NF}(P)))$	0	0.329447	0.478431	0.371982
$\rho(rng(\mathbf{x}),\delta(\mathbf{x},P))$	0	0.564819	0.894474	0.759983
$\rho(rng(\mathbf{x}),\delta(\mathbf{x},\mathbf{NF}(P)))$	0.672059	0.671998	0.483163	0.492397
$\rho(rng(\mathbf{x}),cat(\mathbf{x}))$	0.971607	0.971621	0.974710	0.971266

Table 4. Correlations for the problem asuAB10

	P	$P_{(\lvert P\rvert-1)}$	$P_{(\frac{\lvert P\rvert}{2})}$	$P_{(\frac{\lvert P\rvert}{4})}$
$\rho(cat(\mathbf{x}),\delta(\mathbf{x},P))$	0	0.508309	0.830280	0.734061
$\rho(cat(\mathbf{x}),\delta(\mathbf{x},\mathbf{NF}(P)))$	0.712957	0.712944	0.536178	0.488927
$\rho(\delta(\mathbf{x},P),\delta(\mathbf{x},\mathbf{NF}(P)))$	0	0.392366	0.577878	0.442818
$\rho(rng(\mathbf{x}),\delta(\mathbf{x},P))$	0	0.493534	0.899061	0.803484
$\rho(rng(\mathbf{x}),\delta(\mathbf{x},\mathbf{NF}(P)))$	0.750817	0.750809	0.583105	0.533937
$\rho(rng(\mathbf{x}),cat(\mathbf{x}))$	0.970935	0.970937	0.976167	0.975501

$\rho(rng(\mathbf{x}),\delta(\mathbf{x},\mathbf{NF}(P)))$, indicate that these solutions are gathered in a relatively small region of the solution space, satisfying the convexity assumption.

As both assumptions are fulfilled, it is expected that these solutions are close to the Pareto front, which is consistent with a globally convex structure conjecture.

The correlations for the bi-objective TSP do not present the high values obtained by Boese for the single-objective case [4]. The reason for this fact is due to the existence of a whole set of Pareto solutions. As a consequence, non-

Pareto solutions could be more central in the solution space than other Pareto solutions.

Larger problems are analyzed in the next section using the same metrics with subsets of the solution space.

5.2 Study of a Subset of Solutions

This analysis was based on the TSPLIB instances kroAB100, kroCD100, kroAD100, kroBC100 and kroAB150. From each of these bi-objective TSPs, n^2 random samples were taken. The local search algorithm 2-Opt was used for the optimization of each sample set, achieving populations containing local optima solutions. This search strategy was chosen because it presents a simple neighborhood structure, and allows the study of local optima distribution in the solution space.

The methodology of the analysis remains the same, using subsets of the solution space instead of considering the whole solution space. The correlations obtained are shown in table 5.

Table 5. Correlations for the instances kroAB100, kroCD100, kroAD100, kroBC100, kroAB150

	kroAB100	kroCD100	kroAD100	kroBC100	kroAB150
$\rho(cat(\mathbf{x}), \delta(\mathbf{x}, P))$	0.616596	0.596558	0.603098	0.589122	0.571318
$\rho(cat(\mathbf{x}), \delta(\mathbf{x}, \mathbf{NF}(P)))$	0.396173	0.401700	0.391263	0.396632	0.384648
$\rho(\delta(\mathbf{x}, P), \delta(\mathbf{x}, \mathbf{NF}(P)))$	0.613169	0.626019	0.611728	0.653360	0.633580
$\rho(rng(\mathbf{x}), \delta(\mathbf{x}, P))$	0.639641	0.628951	0.645090	0.617764	0.606404
$\rho(rng(\mathbf{x}), \delta(\mathbf{x}, \mathbf{NF}(P)))$	0.432760	0.441982	0.449073	0.437721	0.423266
$\rho(rng(\mathbf{x}), cat(\mathbf{x}))$	0.945914	0.941865	0.937078	0.941890	0.938438

The results for the problem kroAB100 are shown in figure 2. The figures for the other problems can be found in [9]. Correlations between *range* and *category*, still maintain a value larger than 0.9, which confirms their similarity, although *range* presents better results in the whole study.

A concentration of the best solutions centrally with respect to the population is observed in figures 2.a and 2.d. Despite low correlations in the previous figures (around 0.6), figure 2.c shows that solutions located centrally are closer to the non-dominated frontier, and suggests the existence of a globally convex structure. The same results were obtained for the rest of the studied instances.

6 Conclusions and Future Work

The concepts of *category* and *range* proved to be very effective quality metrics for the bi-objective TSP, and the generalization of these concepts can be easily made for any instance of the MOTSP. Besides, they can be used in any MOP

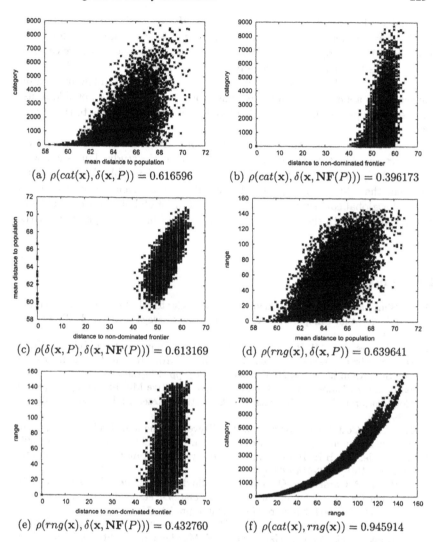

(a) $\rho(cat(\mathbf{x}), \delta(\mathbf{x}, P)) = 0.616596$

(b) $\rho(cat(\mathbf{x}), \delta(\mathbf{x}, \mathbf{NF}(P))) = 0.396173$

(c) $\rho(\delta(\mathbf{x}, P), \delta(\mathbf{x}, \mathbf{NF}(P))) = 0.613169$

(d) $\rho(rng(\mathbf{x}), \delta(\mathbf{x}, P)) = 0.639641$

(e) $\rho(rng(\mathbf{x}), \delta(\mathbf{x}, \mathbf{NF}(P))) = 0.432760$

(f) $\rho(cat(\mathbf{x}), rng(\mathbf{x})) = 0.945914$

Fig. 2. Population of 10,000 optimized solutions for the instance kroAB100

without definition changes. Although these concepts seem to be very similar, *range* showed better results.

Category, range, mean distance to the population and distance to the non-dominated frontier experimentally demonstrated to be correlated, showing the topological characteristic of global convexity. These metrics could be used for the study of global convexity in other MOPs, where metaheuristics, as ACO or EA, have shown to be very efficient, and for the creation of new metaheuristics that could exploit this type of structure. However, since the results were obtained experimentally, it is not certain that this structure holds for every instance of the bi-objective TSP. Nevertheless, for the single-objective case, no instance was found without a globally convex structure [6].

A problem with a known global convexity structure will allow us to limit the search to a smaller solution area, and from there, it will be possible to use another appropriate algorithms to achieve better approximations to the Pareto set.

There is a lot to do in the study of global convexity, like the creation of meta-heuristics based on the exploitation of this structure, the study of instances with correlated objectives, and the use of another kind of neighborhood structure (different than 2-Opt). Also, it can be considered the development of a formal theory for global convexity, and the identification of globally convex problems. Just [3, 4, 6] refers to the subject of global convexity in the TSP, and [2] for the MOTSP.

References

1. C. Blum, and A. Roli, Metaheuristics in Combinatorial Optimization: Overview and Conceptual Comparison, ACM Computing Surveys (CSUR), 35(3), 268-308 (2003).
2. P.C. Borges, and P.H. Hansen, A Study of Global Convexity for a Multiple Objective Traveling Salesman Problem, edited by C.C. Ribeiro and P. Hansen, (Essays and Surveys in Metaheuristics, Kluwer, 2000), pp. 129-150.
3. K. Boese, A. Kahng, and S. Muddu, A new Adaptive Multi-Start Technique for Combinatorial Global Optimization, Operations Research Letters, 16, 101-113 (1994).
4. K. Boese, Cost versus Distance in the Traveling Salesman Problem, Computer Science Department, University of California, Technical Report No. 950018, 1995.
5. T. Stützle, and H.H. Hoos, Max-Min Ant System, Future Generation Computer Systems, 16(8), 889-914 (2000).
6. B. Barán, P. Gardel, and O. Gómez, Estudio del Espacio de Soluciones del Problema del Cajero Viajante, edited by M. Solar, D. Fernández and E. Cuadros-Vargas, (CLEI 2004, Arequipa, Perú, 2004), pp. 745-756.
7. O. Gómez, and B. Barán, Reasons of ACO's Success in TSP, edited by M. Dorigo, M. Birattari, C. Blum, L. Gambardella, F. Mondada and T. Stüzle, (Ant Colony Optimization and Swarm Intelligence, 4th International Workshop, ANTS 2004), pp. 226-237.
8. L. Paquete, M. Chiarandini, and T. Stützle, A Study of Local Optima in the Biobjective Travelling Salesman Problem, Computer Science Department, Darmstadt University of Technology, Technical Report No. AIDA-02-07, 2002 (Presented at the Multi-Objective Metaheuristics Workshop, MOMH 2002).
9. M. Villagra, B. Barán, and O. Gómez, Convexidad Global en el Problema del Cajero Viajante Bi-Objetivo, Centro Nacional de Computación, Universidad Nacional de Asunción, Technical Report No. 001/05, 2005 (unpublished); http://www.cnc.una.py.

Evolutionary Algorithm for State Encoding

Valery Sklyarov, Iouliia Skliarova
University of Aveiro, Department of Electronics and
Telecommunications/IEETA, 3810-193 Aveiro, Portugal
skl@det.ua.pt, iouliia@det.ua.pt
WWW home page: http://www.ieeta.pt/~skl/
http://www.ieeta.pt/~iouliia/

Abstract. This paper presents an encoding technique that is common for many different logic synthesis problems. It enables us to construct a system of Boolean functions, and then to decompose this system into sub-systems in such a way that a dependency of functions, included into each sub-system, on the respective arguments is reduced. For complex applications such type of encoding has a high computational complexity and the paper proposes a novel evolutionary algorithm for the solution of this problem.

1 Introduction

There are many combinatorial tasks that involve encoding algorithms. These tasks appear in particular at various steps in the logic synthesis of digital circuits. One of these tasks is based on such encoding technique that enables us to construct a system of Boolean functions, and then to decompose this system into sub-systems for which we are able to reduce dependency of the functions, included into each sub-system, on the respective arguments [1,2]. Commonly the logic scheme of a finite state machine (FSM) is composed of a combinational circuit and a memory (a set of flip-flops). The combinational circuit implements a system of Boolean functions $D_1,...,D_R$ that depend on variables $x_1,...,x_L,\tau_1,...,\tau_R$. The $x_1,...,x_L$ are external input variables and $\tau_1,...,\tau_R$ bring the code of the state a_{from} from which we have to carry out transition(s). The functions $D_1,...,D_R$ enable the FSM to calculate the code of the next state a_{to}. The lines $\tau_1,...,\tau_R$ are the outputs from the FSM memory and the lines $D_1,...,D_R$ are the inputs to the FSM memory. For example, the FSM can be described as shown in Table 1 (at the beginning let us ignore all symbols enclosed in parenthesis). Here, a_{from} - is an initial state, $K(a_{from})$ and $K(a_{to})$ - are the codes of the states a_{from} and a_{to}, respectively, a_{to} - is the next state, $X(a_{from},a_{to})$ - is a product of inputs that forces a corresponding transition. We assume that FSM memory is built from D flip-flops. Let us consider various transitions from the same state. We can see that for all

Please use the following format when citing this chapter:

Sklyarov, V., Skliarova, I., 2006, in IFIP International Federation for Information Processing, Volume 217, Artificial Intelligence in Theory and Practice, ed. M. Bramer, (Boston: Springer), pp. 227–236.

conditional transitions (i.e. for all transitions except from the state a_6), all the sub-functions of $D_1,...,D_3$ that must be activated on transitions from a state, depend on both the state and inputs. We will say that a sub-function is active if it has to be assigned to 1. Since all the sub-functions depend on states and inputs, the relevant Boolean expressions, that are used to calculate the values $D_1,...,D_3$, contain variables from the full set $\{x_1,...,x_L,\tau_1,...,\tau_R\}$, where L - is the number of external inputs (in our example L=5) and R - is the size of the FSM memory (in our example R=3).

Table 1. An example of FSM

a_{from}	$K(a_{from})$	$X(a_{from},a_{to})$	a_{to}	$K(a_{to})$	$D(a_{from},a_{to})$
a_1	000 (000)	x_1x_2	a_1	000 (000)	- (-)
		$not\_x_1\ not\_x_2$	a_2	001 (011)	$D_3 (D_2,D_3)$
		$not\_x_1x_2$	a_3	010 (001)	$D_2 (D_3)$
		$x_1\ not\_x_2$	a_6	101 (010)	$D_1,D_3 (D_2)$
a_2	001 (011)	x_3	a_3	010 (001)	$D_2 (D_3)$
		not_x_3	a_5	100 (101)	$D_1 (D_1, D_3)$
a_3	010 (001)	not_x_1	a_4	011 (100)	$D_2,D_3 (D_1)$
		x_1x_2	a_5	100 (101)	$D_1 (D_1, D_3)$
		$x_1\ not\_x_2$	a_7	110 (111)	$D_1,D_2 (D_1, D_2, D_3)$
a_4	011 (100)	not_x_4	a_1	000 (000)	- (-)
		x_4	a_4	011 (100)	$D_2,D_3 (D_1)$
a_5	100 (101)	x_1	a_1	000 (000)	- (-)
		not_x_1	a_6	101 (010)	$D_1,D_3 (D_2)$
a_6	101 (010)	1	a_7	111	D_1,D_2,D_3
a_7	110 (111)	x_5	a_2	001 (011)	$D_3 (D_2, D_3)$
		not_x_5	a_7	110 (111)	$D_1,D_2 (D_1, D_2, D_3)$

Consider all sub-functions of $D_1,...,D_3$ that are generated for proper transitions from a state. For example, sub-functions $D_1^3,...,D_3^3$, that have to be activated in transitions from the state a_3 (later we will also mark such sub-functions with a corresponding superscript) are the following: $D_1^3 = a_3x_1$; $D_2^3 = a_3$ $(not\_x_1 \vee not\_x_2)$; $D_3^3 = a_3not\_x_1$ (these expressions can easily be obtained from Table 1). Note that since there exist 3 transitions from a_3, they can be distinguished with the aid of just two Boolean variables, such as $D_1^3,...,D_3^3$. As a result, inputs such as x_1 and x_2 can affect (and change) just two variables from the set $\{D_1^3,...,D_3^3\}$ and the remaining variables (in our example one variable from the set $\{D_1^3,...,D_3^3\}$) can be independent of external inputs from the set $X = \{x_1,...,x_L\}$, i.e. they will only depend on the current state (in our example on the state a_3). If the number of different (non coinciding) next states in state transitions from a_m is equal to q_m, then $(R-intlog_2q_m)$ variables from the subset $D_1^m,...,D_R^m$ can be independent of the input variables from the set X.

Let us suppose now that the states for our example have been coded as shown in parenthesis in Table 1. The values of the sub-functions $D_1^r,...,D_3^r$ (r=1,2,...,M, M - is the number of FSM states and for our example M=7) that do not depend on input variables, are marked with bold and italic bold fonts. Note that the bold font has been used for passive values, and italic bold font for active values of the sub-functions.

Now the combinational circuit S of the FSM can be decomposed into two sub-circuits in such a way that the first sub-circuit S_{ax} implements all active values of $D_1^1, ..., D_3^M$ that are not bold. The functions of S_{ax} depend on both FSM inputs and states. The second sub-circuit S_a implements all active values of $D_1^1, ..., D_3^M$ that are bold. The functions of S_a depend only on the states and for our example they are:

$$D_1 = a_3 \vee a_6; D_2 = a_6 \vee a_7; D_3 = a_2 \vee a_6 \vee a_7;$$

Such functions are well suited for minimization and are usually very simple. For instance, S_a can be constructed from just four 2-input logic elements of types XOR, AND and OR, which convert values of τ_1, τ_2, τ_3 to values of D_1, D_2, D_3. On the other hand, such kind of decomposition enables us to essentially simplify the sub-functions of S_{ax}, i.e. the active sub-functions that are not bold in Table 1. Finally, even for our very simple example, the proposed state encoding permits the number of logic elements to be reduced by approximately 20%.

Similar problems appear in a large number of practical applications and we will point out just some of them:

- One-level control circuits based on blocks, such as programmable logic arrays (see [3, p. 182]. It allows reducing essentially the total number of interconnections by eliminating the repeated outputs for different blocks;
- RAM-based implementation of FSMs [2], etc.

The paper presents an evolutionary algorithm that allows the encoding considered above to be achieved. It should be noted that the technique of artificial evolution has been widely used for hardware design [4]. Evolutionary algorithms (EA) are based on a process of "generate-and-test" [5] and this strategy can be applied at different levels. For example, in [6] a genetic algorithm is employed to search for circuits that represent the desired state transition function. Many examples demonstrating EAs that have been successfully employed for hardware design are presented in [7-9]. For some circuits they produced unforeseen results of very high quality (for example, [10]), which have never been obtained by human designers.

The remainder of this paper is organized in four sections. Section 2 presents the detailed description of the proposed evolutionary algorithm. Section 3 discusses feasible variations of the algorithm. Section 4 presents the results of experiments, which clearly demonstrate the advantages of the proposed encoding technique. The conclusion is in section 5.

2 Evolutionary Algorithm

The basic idea of EA was used for the considered problem in the traditional simple way [11]. The algorithm includes the following steps:

1. Production of an initial population composed of individuals that represent a set of randomly generated codes for a given number of variables (FSM states).

2. Evaluation of the population and measuring its fitness.

3. Variation of the population by applying such operations as reproduction, mutation and crossover. A reproduction operator makes a copy of the individual (with a probability based on its fitness) for inclusion in the next generation of the population. A mutation operator creates new individuals by performing some changes in a single individual, while the crossover operator creates new individuals (offspring) by combining parts of two or more other individuals (parents) [9].

4. Performing a selection process, where the most fit individuals survive and form the next generation.

Points 2-4 are repeated until a predefined termination condition is satisfied.

Let us assume that a population π including v individuals $\pi_1,...,\pi_v$ has been randomly generated. In order to evaluate each individual π_ι, $\iota=1,...,v$, it is necessary to specify a fitness function. For our problem it is very easy. Let $A=\{a_1,...,a_M\}$ be a set of variables that have to be encoded, M is the number of variables in the set A. The variables in each individual subset $A(a_{from})$ (where $A(a_{from})$ is a set of states to which there exist direct conditional transitions from the state a_{from}, $k_m=|A(a_{from})|>1$, $m=1,...,M$) have to be encoded in such a way that the number w_m ($w_m=R-intlog_2k_m$) of their bits with the same indices have equal values. Here $R=intlog_2M$ is the minimum number of bits in the codes of states assuming binary encoding. Thus, any solution for which the fitness function W is equal to Σw_m ($k_m>1$, $m=1,...,M$) gives an optimal result (we assume that such result exists, which, in fact, is not true for a general case). Actually we can discover several optimal results and for each of them the function W has the same maximum possible value. Any of these results provides the best solution to the problem so we just have to find out the first of them.

Now the fitness can be estimated very easily. For randomly generated codes π_ι we have to calculate the function W_i and compare the result with the value W. The less the difference $W-W_i$ the better the fitness for the individual π_ι.

The next step produces a variation of the population and can be carried out by applying such operations as reproduction, mutation and crossover. Two kinds of reproduction have been examined and compared. The first one is based on elitist rule [11] where the best solutions in the population are certain to survive to the next generation. This rule has been implemented as follows. For reproduction purposes 10% of individuals with the best fitness have been copied to the next generation of the population. The second kind of reproduction uses the same percentage of individuals, but it is based on proportional selection [11].

The mutation operation runs on one parental individual selected with a probability based on fitness and creates one new offspring individual to be inserted into the new population at the next generation. In order to choose which parents will produce offspring, a fitness proportional selection is employed. Each parent π_i is assigned a weight W_i, calculated at the previous step. The probability of selection for each parent is proportional to its weight. The main idea of the mutation operation will be illustrated by an example of state encoding for FSM with specification presented in [12]. The FSM has 10 states and the following transitions $a_{from}\Rightarrow A(a_{from})$: $a_1\Rightarrow\{a_2,a_3,a_4\}$, $a_2\Rightarrow\{a_2,a_4,a_5\}$, $a_3\Rightarrow\{a_6,a_7,a_8,a_9\}$, $a_4\Rightarrow\{a_5\}$, $a_5\Rightarrow\{a_3\}$, $a_6\Rightarrow\{a_5,a_7\}$, $a_7\Rightarrow\{a_3,a_9\}$, $a_8\Rightarrow\{a_2,a_{10}\}$, $a_9\Rightarrow\{a_{10}\}$, $a_{10}\Rightarrow\{a_1\}$. Since M=10 and R=4 for each individual we can chose any 10 from $2^4=16$ possible codes. Suppose that at some step of EA we found the codes for an individual I shown in Table 2 and this individual has to be mutated.

Table 2. An individual I that has been selected for mutation operation

Codes	0000	0001	0010	0011	0100	0101	0110	0111
I	0	0	**4**	8	0	0	0	3
Codes	1000	1001	1010	1011	1100	1101	1110	1111
I	**5**	6	**2**	9	**7**	0	**10**	1

For the individual I all the state codes have to be examined and all the weights $w^I_1,...,w^I_M$ that exceed the value 1 have to be calculated. Some (or all for the best result) of these weights correspond to an optimal result. For all weights w^I_m that have an optimal value the respective states a_m have to be selected (see in Table 2 **bold underlined** numbers m of states a_m). For example, we have the following state transitions $a_1 \rightarrow$ {K(a_2)=1010, K(a_3)=0111, K(a_4)=0010}, $a_2 \rightarrow$ {K(a_2)=**1010**, K(a_4)=**0010**, K(a_5)=**1000**}$_{opt}$, $a_3 \rightarrow$ {K(a_6)=1001, K(a_7)=1100, K(a_8)=0011, K(a_9)=1011}, $a_6 \rightarrow$ {K(a_5)=**1000**, K(a_7)=**1100**}$_{opt}$, etc. Optimal solutions are indicated by subscript "opt" and the respective bits (i.e. bits with coincident indices that have equal values) of the codes are marked with bold font. The mutation operation permits a new child individual to be created and includes the following steps.

Step 1. All the elements that correspond to an optimal solution (see **bold underlined** numbers in Table 2) are included in the new individual (offspring).

Step 2. The codes for the remaining elements will be randomly regenerated in such a way that just free codes (i.e. such codes that have not been already chosen at step 1) can be selected.

Crossover is the most complicated operation of the considered EA. The main idea of this operation will also be illustrated by the same example of FSM. Suppose that at some step of EA we have found the codes for two individuals I1 and I2 shown in Table 3 and these individuals were chosen to be parents for creating a new individual that is a child. For all weights $w^{I1}_m(w^{I2}_s)$ that have an optimal value the respective states a_m (a_s) have to be selected (see **bold** underlined numbers m of states a_m for the first individual I1 and *italic* underlined numbers s of states a_s for the second individual I2). The parents are chosen on the base of proportional selection [11].

Table 3. The results of encoding for two individuals

Codes	0000	0001	0010	0011	0100	0101	0110	0111
I1	0	0	**4**	8	0	0	0	3
I2	8	0	*5*	*4*	10	1	0	*2*
Codes	1000	1001	1010	1011	1100	1101	1110	1111
I1	**5**	6	**2**	9	**7**	0	**10**	1
I2	7	0	*9*	*3*	0	0	0	6

The crossover operation permits a new child individual to be created and includes the following steps.

Step 1. The first solution (see Table 4) is formed from the selected elements of the first individual I1 (see **bold** underlined numbers in Table 3).

Step 2. Permitted selected elements from the second individual I2 (see *italic underlined* numbers in Table 3) are added to the first solution (i.e. to the child). An element is allowed for step 2 if:

a) It was not included into the child during the first step; and

b) It does not have a code that has already been used during the first step.

Table 5 shows the result of step 2 for our example.

Step 3. All the remaining permitted elements from the first and the second individuals are added to the child. An element is allowed for step 3 if it has not yet been included in the child and:

a) It has the same code for both individuals I1 and I2; or

b) It is included in the second individual I2 and the respective code of the first individual I1 was not used for the states; or

c) It is included in the first individual I1 and the respective code of the second individual I2 was not used for the states;

Table 6 shows the result of step 3 for our example.

Table 4. The result of step 1

Codes	0000	0001	0010	0011	0100	0101	0110	0111
Child			4					
Codes	1000	1001	1010	1011	1100	1101	1110	1111
Child	5		2		7		10	

Table 5. The result of step 2

Codes	0000	0001	0010	0011	0100	0101	0110	0111
Child			4					
Codes	1000	1001	1010	1011	1100	1101	1110	1111
Child	5		2	3	7		10	

Table 6. The result of step 3

Codes	0000	0001	0010	0011	0100	0101	0110	0111
Child	8		4			1		
Codes	1000	1001	1010	1011	1100	1101	1110	1111
Child	5	6	2	3	7		10	

Step 4. All the remaining states that have not been assigned yet are recorded in free boxes for codes from left to right.

Table 7 presents the final result of the crossover operation.

Individuals I1, I2 and the child can be evaluated as follows: $W_{I1} = W_{I2} = 11$, $W_{child} = 13$ (i.e. the child is better than any of the parents I1 and I2) and the optimal weight $W = 15$.

There are two termination conditions for the considered EA: obtaining an optimal solution or exceeding a specified time limit.

Table 7. The result of step 4 that gives the final result of the crossover operation

Codes	0000	0001	0010	0011	0100	0101	0110	0111
Child	8	9	4			1		
Codes	1000	1001	1010	1011	1100	1101	1110	1111
Child	5	6	2	3	7		10	

3 Variations of the Evolutionary Algorithm

Note that for many practical applications it is allowed that a state has more than one code. If the FSM circuit is constructed from RAM blocks then using multiple codes does not make the circuit more complicated [2]. Moreover applying this technique enables us to improve the results of encoding. It should be noted that for some practical problems an optimal solution, that only permits each state to be assigned a single unique code, cannot be obtained. For example, such solution cannot be found for the following set of state transitions: $a_1 \Rightarrow \{a_1, a_2\}$, $a_2 \Rightarrow \{a_2, a_3\}$, $a_3 \Rightarrow \{a_4, a_5\}$, $a_4 \Rightarrow \{a_1, a_3\}$, $a_5 \Rightarrow \{a_1\}$. However, if more than one code is permitted for the states we can find an optimal solution, which is: $K(a_1)=000$, $K(a_2)=001$, $K(a_3)=100$ and 101, $K(a_4)=011$, $K(a_5)=111$. The EA can be modified slightly in order to produce the proper solution. Indeed if an optimal result cannot be found within a predefined time interval we can allow using more than one code for states. Thus, the algorithm is relatively flexible when it comes to future improvements and modifications.

4 Experimental Results

The results of the proposed EA were estimated for more than 100 digital circuits that required the considered above encoding technique within the respective process of synthesis. Fig. 1 shows these results for 25 FSMs. We considered block-based decomposition of FSMs [3], where $R=\text{int}\log_2 M$ and R_{av} is an average number of outputs for the blocks. So the considered technique makes possible the number of outputs required for each block to be decreased on average by 1.8.

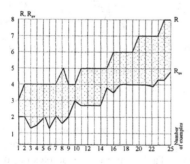

Fig. 1. The results of experiments.

The EA has been analyzed in several contexts. Firstly, we evaluated primary genetic operations that are reproduction (based on elitist rule and proportional selection criteria), mutation and crossover. The considered options A, B, C and D are listed below:

A: the crossover operation was carried out in order to form 90% of population for the next generation and 10% of population for the next generation was chosen with a probability based on fitness (i.e. based on proportional selection);

B: firstly the crossover operation was carried out in order to form 100% of population, secondly the mutation operation based on proportional selection was performed for 10% of individuals of the new generation and finally 10% of individuals in the next generation were replaced with 10% of randomly generated individuals;

C: the mutation operation based on proportional selection was carried out in order to form 100% of population for the next generation and 10% of individuals in the next generation were replaced with 10% of randomly generated individuals;

D: the crossover operation was carried out in order to form 90% of population for the next generation and 10% of population for the next generation was chosen based on elitist rule.

Fig. 2 shows how the execution time for all four options depends on the number of individuals in population. This dependency was considered for an FSM with 15 states (M=15) and with at maximum 4 transitions from each state. The experiments were performed on PentiumIII/800MHz/256MB. Fig. 3 shows how the number of required generations for all four options depends on the number of individuals in population.

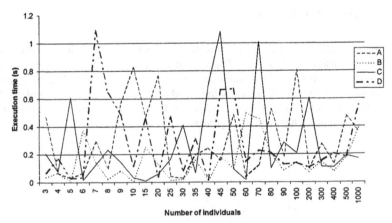

Fig. 2. Dependency of execution time on the number of individuals in population

Secondly, we examined practical applications that could benefit from the considered encoding technique. This enabled us to estimate some parameters, such as the expectable size of codes. Table 8 presents examples of control circuits used in assembly lines for manufacturing purposes. The number of individuals in population was chosen to be 15. Here NG is the number of generations, W is the optimal weight, W_e is the obtained weight, ET is the execution time, $G_{min} = \max \ (intlog_2|A(a_m)|)$, $m=1,...,M$.

Thirdly, we performed a set of experiments for randomly generated examples with different initial data (such as the number of individuals in populations) and variable requirements (such as using one code for each state of FSM or employing more than one code for some states). Table 9 shows the best results for options A, B, C, D obtained for arbitrary selected examples (the option that gave the best result is indicated in the first column in parentheses). For the examples aex7 and aex8 just the option D was used and we received $W_e<W$ because the value W cannot be obtained when using just one code for each state. If we allow to employ more than one code for some states then the result with $W_e=W$ can be easily found (ET = 41.12 s for aex7 and ET = 9.38 s for aex8).

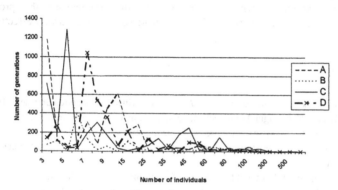

Fig. 3. Dependency of the number of generations on the number of individuals in population

Table 8. The results of experiments for practical examples

Example	NG	W	W_e	ET (s)	M	G_{min}
Ex1	134	32	32	0.424	20	2
Ex2	63	36	36	0.261	29	2
Ex3	99	7	7	0.202	12	4
Ex4	111	30	30	0.255	15	2

Table 9. Experiments with arbitrary selected FSMs

Example	NG	W	W_e	ET (s)	M	G_{min}
aex1 (B)	15	21	21	0.052	21	2
aex2 (B,D)	4	25	25	0.017	28	2
aex3 (D)	146	15	15	0.216	10	2
aex4 (B)	23682	34	34	61.767	15	3
aex5 (B)	490	31	31	3.897	47	2
aex6 (B)	12854	42	42	49.201	16	3
aex7	5534	88	87	1000	52	2
aex8	1024	38	37	1000	49	3

5   Conclusion

In the previous discussion we have presented the evolutionary algorithm for state encoding that allows Boolean functions to be decomposed in such a way that the dependency of sub-functions obtained as a result of the decomposition on the arguments can be reduced. The algorithm has been analyzed in several contexts. Firstly, we evaluated the primary genetic operations that are reproduction, mutation and crossover. Secondly, we examined practical applications that require the considered encoding technique. This enabled us to estimate some parameters, such as the expectable size of codes. Thirdly, we performed a set of experiments with different initial data (such as the number of individuals in populations) and variable requirements (such as using one code for each state of finite state machine or employing more than one code for some states). The examples in the paper and the results of experiments with a C++ program that implements the proposed evolutionary algorithm have shown that the considered approach is very effective.

References

1. S. Baranov, *Logic Synthesis for Control Automata* (Kluwer Academic Publishers, 1994).

2. V. Sklyarov, Reconfigurable models of finite state machines and their implementation in FPGAs, Journal of Systems Architecture, 47, 2002, pp. 1043-1064.

3. V. Sklyarov, *Synthesis of Finite State Machines Based on Matrix LSI* (Minsk, Science and Technique, 1984).

4. J. Torresen, Possibilities and Limitations of Applying Evolvable Hardware to Real-World Applications, Proceedings of FPL, Villach, Austria, August, 2000, pp. 230-239.

5. A. Thompson, P. Layzell, and R.S. Zebulum, Exploration in Design Space: Unconventional Electronics Design Through Artificial Evolution, *IEEE Transactions on Evolutionary Computations*, vol. 3, No. 3, September, 1999, pp. 167-176.

6. C. Manovit, C. Aporntewan, and P. Chongstitvatana, Synthesis of Synchronous Sequential Logic Circuits from Partial Input/Output Sequences, Proceedings of ICES'98, Evolvable Systems: From Biology to Hardware, Springer, N 1478, 1998, pp. 98-105.

7. H. Hemmi, J. Mizoguchi, and K. Shimohara, Development and Evolution of Hardware Behaviors, Toward Evolvable Hardware, Springer, N 1062, 1996, pp. 250-265.

8. J. Mizoguchi, H. Hemmi, and K. Shimohara, Production genetic algorithms for automated hardware design through an evolutionary process, IEEE Conference on Evolutionary Computations, 1994, pp. 250-265.

9. J.R. Koza, F.H. Bennet III, D. Andre, and M.A. Keane, *Genetic Programming III* (Morgan Kaufmann Publishers, 1999).

10. J.F. Miller, P. Thomson, and T. Fogarty, Designing Electronic Circuits Using Evolutionary Algorithms. Arithmetic Circuits: A Case Study, Genetic Algorithms and Evolution Strategies in Engineering and Computer Science (John Wiley&Sons, 1998), pp. 105-131.

11. Z. Michalewicz and D.B. Fogel, *How to Solve It: Modern Heuristics* (Springer, 2000).

12. V. Sklyarov, Synthesis of Control Circuits with Dynamically Modifiable Behavior on the Basis of Statically Reconfigurable FPGAs, Proceeding of 13th Symposium on Integrated Circuits and Systems Design: SBCCI, Manaus, Brazil, 18-24 September 2000, pp. 353-358.

Hypercube FrameWork for ACO applied to timetabling

Franklin Johnson[1], Broderick Crawford[1], and Wenceslao Palma[1]

1   Pontificia Universidad Católica de Valparaíso, Escuela de
Ingenieria Informática, Valparaiso, Chile
franklin.johnson.p@mail.ucv.cl
{broderick.crawford,wenceslao.palma}@ucv.cl

Abstract. We present a resolution technique of the University course Timetabling problem (UCTP), this technique is based in the implementation of Hypercube framework using the Max-Min Ant System. We presented the structure of the problem and the design of resolution using this framework.

A simplification of the UCTP problem is used, involving three types of hard restrictions and three types of soft restrictions. We solve experimental instances and competition instances the results are presented of comparative form to other techniques. We presented an appropriate construction graph and pheromone matrix representation. A representative instance is solved in addition to the schedules of the school of Computer science engineering of the Catholic University of Valparaiso. The results obtained for this instance appear. Finally the conclusions are given.

1   Introduction

The Timetabling problems are faced periodically by each school, college and university in the world. In a basic problem, a set of events (particular classes, conferences, classes, etc) must be assigned to a set of hours of a way that all the students can attend all of their respective events. With the reservation of which restrictions of hard type which necessarily they must be satisfied and soft restrictions exist that deteriorate the quality of the generated schedule. Of course, the difficulty of any particular case of the UCTP [1] [2] depends on many factors and in addition the assignment of rooms perceivably makes the problem more difficult in general.

Many techniques have been used in the resolution of this problematic one, between these we can find evolutionary algorithms, simulated annealing, and tabu-search. Other technique has presented good results is the genetic algorithms [3]. But we looked for here specifically to represent the resolution through the ant colony optimization (ACO) and through the implementation of Hypercube framework for Max-Min Ant System (abbreviation in Spanish MTH-SHMM). We give a representation for the problem, generating an appropriate construction graph and the respective pheromone matrix associated.

Please use the following format when citing this chapter:

Johnson, F., Crawford, B., Palma, W., 2006, in IFIP International Federation for Information Processing, Volume 217, Artificial Intelligence in Theory and Practice, ed. M. Bramer, (Boston: Springer), pp. 237–246.

In the following sections we present the UCTP problem, the problem design for Hypercube framework. The instances of the problem used and the results of the experimentation. Finally the conclusions of the work appear.

2   University Course Timetabling Problem (UCTP)

2.1   Problem description

The problem timetabling considered to make this study similar to one is presented initially by Paechter in [4]. Timetabling of university courses is a simplification of a typical problem [5]. It consists of a set of events E and must to be scheduled in a set of timeslots $T = \{t_1, ..., t_k\}$ ($k = 45$, they correspond to 5 days of 9 hours each), a set of rooms R in which the events will have effect, a set of students S who attend the events, and a set of features F required by the events and satisfied by the rooms. Each student attends a number of events and each room has a maximum capacity. A feasible timetable is one in which all the events have bee assigned a timeslot and a room so that the following hard constraints are satisfied:

- No student attends more than one event at the same time;
- The rooms must be sufficiently great for all students who attend a class and to satisfy all the features required by the event;
- Only one event is in each room at any timeslot.

In addition, All possible timetable generated is penalized for each occurrence according to the number of violations that exists of the soft constraint of problem. Some of these restrictions appear next:

- A student has a class in the last slot of the day;
- A student has more than two classes in a row;
- A student has exactly one class on a day.

Feasible solutions are always considered to be superior to infeasible solutions, independently of the numbers of soft constraint violations. In fact, in any comparison, all infeasible solutions are to be considered equally worthless. The objective is to minimize the number of soft constraint violations in a feasible solution.

3   Design of Hypercube Framework SHMM for Timetabling (MTH-SHMM)

3.1   Resolution Structure

Given restrictions presented in the previous section and the characteristics of problem, we can now consider the option to design an effective MTH-SHMM for the UCTP. We have to decide how to transform the assignment problem (to assign events to *timeslots*) into an optimal path problem which the ants can solve [12]. To do this we must create an appropriate construction graph for the ants to follow. We must then decide on an appropriate pheromone matrix and heuristic information to influence the paths the ants will take through the graph.

We present the principal elements used to generate the UCTP solutions, presenting in a figure 1 these three elements.

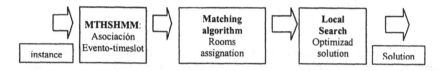

Figure 1. An instance of the problem is received like input, this it happens through an association process *event-timeslot*, assigns events to a *timeslot*, later a matching algorithm [8] is used for makes the assignation from rooms to each one of events associated to *timeslot*. In this point a solution is complete, but is low quality. Then a local search algorithm [16] is applied that improves the quality of the solution and gives like final result one optimal solution to the UCTP.

3.2   Construction graph

One of the main elements of the ACO metaheurístic is the power to model to the problem on construction graph [6] [7], that way a trajectory through the graph represents a problem solution. In this formulation of the UCTP it is required to assign each one of $|E|$ events to $|T|$ *timeslots*. Where direct representation of the construction graph this dice by $E \times T$; east dice graph we can then establish that the ants walk throughout a list of events, choosing *timeslot* for each event. The ants follow one list of events, and for each event *and*, the ants decide *timeslot t*. each event a this single time in *timeslot*, thus in each step an ant chooses any possible transition as it is in the figure 2.

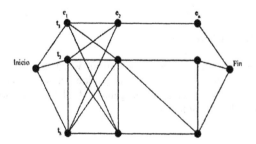

Figure 2. Each ant follows a list of events, and for each event $e \in E$, an ant chooses a *timeslot* $t \in T$.

The ants travel through the construction graph selecting ways of probabilistically way. Using the following function:

$$p_{(e,t_i)} = \frac{\left(\tau_{(e,t_i)}\right)^\alpha}{\sum_{\theta \in T}\left(\tau_{(e,t_\theta)}\right)^\alpha} \tag{1}$$

This probability function is come off the used in [6]. This function of probability directly depends on the pheromone information τ, they have the possible ways to follow. The parameter α is like appendix of the original function in [6], for this case its value is 1.

3.3 The Pheromone matrix

In search of a pheromone matrix we represented that pheromones indicates the absolute position where the events must be placed. With this representation the pheromone matrix is given by $\tau(A_i) = \tau$, $i=1,...,|E|$, the pheromone does not depend on the partial assignments A_i. It can to observe that in this case the pheromone will be associated with nodes in the construction graph rather than edges between the nodes.

A disadvantage of this directs pheromone representation is that the absolute position of events in the *timeslots* it does not matter very much in producing a good timetable. The relative placement of events is more important. For example, given a perfect timetable, it is usually possible to permute many groups of *timeslots* without affecting the quality of the timetable.

By another side we defined that for the use of the heuristic information η it must use a function that calculates a weighted sum of several or all of the soft and hard constrains in each assignation, which is to incur very high a computational cost stops this class of problem [8]. For this we will not use east type of information to orient the route of the ants.

3.4 Algorithm Description

We show the general structure of the algorithm, in which some modifications are made of presented in [9] [11]. A new assignation values to τ_{max}, τ_{min} ,a new pheromone update rules. We define the assignment A_i like the *timeslot* selected for the event i. The algorithm is the following:

```
1 Input: Problem instance I
2 τ_max ← 1
3 τ_(e, t) ← τ_max ∀ (e, t) ∈ E×T
4 calculate c(e, e') ∀ (e, e') ∈ E²
5 calculate d(e)
6 sort E according «, resulting in e₁ « e₂ « ... « e_n
7 while time limit not reached do
8    for a = 1 to m do
9        {construction process of ant a}
10       A₀← ∅
11       for i = 1 to |E| do
12           chooser timeslots t according to probabilities p_(e,t) for event e_i
13               A_i ← A_{i-1} ∪ {(e_i, t)}
14           end for
15           C←matching_algorithm (A_n)
16           C_best_iteration ← best of C and C_best_iteration
17       end for
18   C_best_iteration ← applying local search to C_best_iteration
19   C_global_best ← best of C_best_iteration y C_global_best
20   global pheromone update for τ using C_global_best. implicated to MTH
21 end while
22 Output: An optimized candidate solution C_global_best for I
```

Only the solution that causes the fewest number of hard constraint violations is selected for improvement by the Local Search. The pheromone matrix is updated only once by each iteration, and the global best solution is used for the update. Then A_{global_best} be the assignment of the best candidate solution C_{global_best} found since the beginning. The following update rule is used:

$$\tau(e,t) = \begin{cases} \rho \cdot \tau_{(e,t)} + (1-\rho) \cdot \Delta\tau_{(e,t)}^{upd} & \text{if } A_{major\_global}(e) = t, \\ \rho \cdot \tau_{(e,t)} & \text{otherwise} \end{cases}$$

(2)

In the right part of the equation is reduced to $\Delta\tau_{(e,t)}^{upd} = 1$ if $A_{global\_best}(e) = t$ and 0 in otherwise. Where A_{global_best} is the solution used for pheromone update. With this update rule to makes sure that the pheromone values of the graph, are going to be always between values [0,1]. The rate of evaporation $\rho \in [0.1]$.

4   Experimentation

4.1   Tests

The algorithm was implemented in C++ programming language, under Linux system using GNU G++ compiler GCC 2.96. The behavior of Hypercube framework Max-Min Ant System (MTH-MMAS) was observed in the resolution of the UCTP. The used instances appear to continuation.

Instances 1: Instances of the UCTP are structured using a generator described in [10]. This generator allows generating classes of instances *small, medium*, which reflect varied problems of timetabling of several sizes.

Instances 2: In addition it was used a series of 20 instances created for International Timetabling Competition, these instances is made with the same generator used in instances 1.

The parameters study is made initially, to evaluate the best values than they must to assume these parameters. The small (small1) instances was used for using the MTH-MMAS without local search making evaluations with different ants numbers m and with different evaporations factors ρ, the parameters of $\alpha = 1$, number on attempts = 10 and a maximum time by attempt = 90 seconds for all the tests. The results are in the following table.

Table 1. It presents the best results obtained when proving the instance small1.tim varying ants number m and evaporation factor ρ.

Best solutions MTH-SHMM					
m	Evaluation	T° seg.	ρ	Evaluation	T° seg.
5	17	6,79	0,2	15	7,11
10	16	7,46	0,5	13	8,1
20	16	6,06	0,8	17	6,79

In the table to be observed the best results are obtained using the parameter m=20 obtaining a evaluation of 16 in 6.06 seconds. And for the case of evaporation factor the best value is =0,5 in 8.1 seconds.

The values shown in the tables previously presented they belong to a series of executions that allow of experimental form to determine as are more advisable parameters to use in the execution of the algorithm of MTH-MMAS. This way we compared the algorithm of the Max-Min Ant System with and without Hypercube framework, in addition the local search is included to increment the quality of the solutions in different instances.

4.2   Distribution results

We show a graphic in which they are a series of boxplot which they represent relative distribution of the number of constrained violations for hypercube framework Max-Min Ant System (MTH-SHMM) and the Max-Min Ant System (MMAS) pure for all the instances of type small and medium with which they were proven.

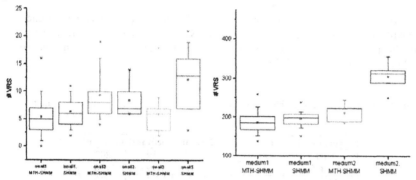

Figure 3. Like it is possible to be observed in most of the results for the different instance types, the obtained results using hypercube framework they are of better quality (smaller violation of soft constrain VRS) since 50% of the data represented by a horizontal line always are under the level of the same instance for the Max-Min Ant System (SHMM) pure.

4.3   Comparison with other techniques

Here it present a comparative picture between the solutions obtained for different instances for the UCTP doing use of different techniques like Simulated annealing, advanced search and simulated annealing with local search [13][14][16]. The results obtained for the competition instances appear.

Table 2. It present the best results obtained when proving the instances of the International Timetabling Competition compared with other techniques.

Technique	1	2	3	4	5	6	7	8	9	10
SA	45	25	65	115	102	13	44	29	17	61
AS	257	112	266	441	299	209	99	194	175	308
SA-LS	211	128	213	408	312	169	281	214	164	222
MTH-MMAS	270	193	294	586	406	221	305	244	201	358

Technique	11	12	13	14	15	16	17	18	19	20
SA	44	107	78	52	24	22	86	31	44	7
AS	273	242	364	156	95	171	148	117	414	113
SA-LS	196	282	315	345	185	185	409	153	281	106
MTH-MMAS	268	312	341	403	222	234	371	184	345	201

For these instances and compared with the other solutions the MTH-MMAS it present two characteristics a to evaluate; first it has the capacity to generate feasible solutions for these instances. These instances are of great you make difficult since they are for Timetabling competitions. Second the quality of the generated solutions is of very low category compared with the technique based on Simulated Annealing, which has the best found historical results for these instances, but in comparison with the other instances do not present great difference. These evaluations are not feasible in order to decide if a technique is better than other, since the differences in variable results can be for different external variables.

To continuation it presents the comparison for the small and medium instances. We will compare the algorithm of MTH-MMAS and the MMAS pure with respect to Ant Colony System algorithm of Krzysztof Socha (ACS) and to algorithm based on random restart local search (RRLS).

Tabla 3. It present best results obtained when proving the test instances small and medium.

Technique	Small1	small2	small3	medium1	medium2
RRLS	11	8	11	199	202
ACS	1	3	1	195	184
MMAS	3	6	3	152	250
MTH-MMAS	0	4	1	138	186

As it is possible to be observed for these instances in the MTH-MMAS present a superiority in the quality of the generated solutions (smaller VRS). Always by on the quality the solutions generated with the MMAS. We can to say that the hypercube framework it improves the quality of the ant algorithm applied.

5   In the Practices

5.1   UCV Instance

As a form to approach investigation of the project to a practice plane we implemented a resolution for the UCTP using the Hypercube framework Max-Min Ant System. This problematic is common and it is present in all type of institution of study. It is by that one has been implemented resolution to this problematic creating an instance of the problem for the Catholic University of Valparaiso and specifically for the school of Informatics Engineering.

A tool in C language was implemented, to which him the courses enter indicating the semester, assistants, if it has assistantship, times to the week that are dictated and his characteristics. In addition the rooms are entered to him, certain their capacity and characteristics. The system generates an instance introducing a factor of correlation between the events, generating therefore an instance with the same format that those of competition, small, medium. Stored this information in file ucv.tim. Ready pair to use by the MTH-MMAS algorithm

Instance characteristic: Total number of rooms and laboratories: 9. total number of event: 194, total Attending: 600. Number of characteristics: 5, maximum of events by student: 8, maximum of students by event: variable according to the event.

Before using the instance it was necessary to correct some parameters of MTH-MMAS algorithm implemented, since for the instance of UCV the number of *timeslot* that they are used are 40 and not 45 like for other problems of the UCTP. in addition to an adaptation for the evaluation of soft constraint.

The instance was executed using a number of ants = 20, evaporation factor = 0.5. Time local search 100 seconds, total time by reboots = 900 seconds, number of reboots = 10. The best solution was obtained approximately to the 600 seconds with an evaluation of (# VRS) = 0. Which implies that the algorithm generated a complete timetable feasible and with the best possible quality.

Had to the quality of the solution it can be inferred that the generated instance previously that simulated the hour load of a semester of the school of computer science engineering had a low degree of correlation between courses of different semesters, thus a high performance in the resolution was obtained of the problem.

Table 4. Show the first 20 assigned events a its respective timeslot and rooms as a form to represent the solutions.

Event	1	2	3	4	5	6	7	8	9	10	11	12	13	14	15	16	17	18	19	20
Timeslot	2	36	36	43	41	13	31	32	18	16	19	30	27	20	0	19	19	18	7	29
Room	0	0	1	3	0	4	3	4	2	1	3	3	2	3	4	0	4	4	4	3

In addition a file is had which has associate the classes with its respective ones events, since a class can have to correspond to several events in one week. This is a form to make a more visible and usable timetable.

6 Conclusion

A formal model was given to apply Hypercube framework to solve the University course timetabling problem (UCTP) making use of Max-Min Ant System, was generated an efficient model that solves instances of this problem creating good construction graph of and expressing a good pheromone matrix.

We presented the test result made for the Max-Min Ant System doing use of Hypercube framework. We was observed traverse of the given results that this propose framework is good means of resolution of combinatorial problems and for the case of the UCTP it presented good results for instances of small and medium type. Although the results were of low quality for the instances of the Competition. it emphasizes the fact that always it generates solutions feasible and for instances of normal difficulty of good evaluation. not obtain the best results for this problem, but if it improves in contrast with the Max-Min Ant System without work frame. It was managed to present a applied instance to the school of Computer science of the UCV, for which created a solution feasible thus it clarifies the fact to a technique useful in real applications.

References

1. T. B. Cooper and J. H. Kingston. The complexity of timetable construction problems. In Proceedings of the 1st International Conference on Practice and Theory of Automated Timetabling (PATAT 1995). 1996.
2. H. M. M. ten Eikelder and R. J. Willemen. Some complexity aspects of secondary school timetabling problems. In Proceedings of the 3rd International Conference on Practice and Theory of Automated Timetabling (PATAT 2000), 2001.
3. E. K. Burke, J. P. Newall, and R. F. Weare. A memetic algorithm for university exam timetabling. In Proceedings of the 1st International Conference on Practice and Theory of Automated Timetabling (PATAT 1995), 1996.
4. B. Paechter. Course timetabling. Evonet Summer School, 2001.
5. B. Paechter, R. C. Rankin, A. Cumming, and T. C. Fogarty. Timetabling the classes of an entire university with an evolutionary algorithm. (1998).
6. M. Dorigo and G. Di Caro. The Ant Colony Optimization meta-heuristic. New Ideas in Optimization, 1999.
7. Christian Blum, Marco Dorigo, Andrea Roli, HC-ACO: The Hyper-Cube Framework for Ant Colony Optimization IEEE Transactions on Systems, Man and Cybernetics B, 34(2), 1161 - 1172, 2001.
8. Krzysztof Socha, Max-Min Ant System for International Timetabling Competition. (2003)
9. Krzysztof Socha, J. Knowles, y M. Sampels. Max-Min Ant System for the University Course Timetabling Problem.(2003)
10. http://www.dcs.napier.ac.uk/~benp
11. Thomas Stützle y H.H. Hoos, MAX-MIN Ant System. Future Genetic Computing System. 2000.
12. Christian Blum, Marco Dorigo, The Hyper-Cube Framework for Ant Colony Optimization IEEE Transactions on Systems, Man and Cybernetics B, 2004. HCF 2004.
13. http://www.or.ms.unimelb.edu.au/timetabling/ttframe.html?ttucp1.html
14. http://www.idsia.ch/Files/ttcomp2002/results.htm
15. http://www.idsia.ch/Files/ttcomp2002/IC_Problem/node3.html
16. Rossi-Doria, Blue, Knowles, Sampels, A local search for timetabling problem.(2002)

Multitree-Multiobjective Multicast Routing for Traffic Engineering

Joel Prieto[1], Benjamín Barán[1,2], Jorge Crichigno[1]

[1] Catholic University of Asunción. Tte. Cantaluppi y Villalón. PO Box 1638,
Asunción, Paraguay
jprieto@telesurf.com.py, jcrichigno@ece.unm.edu
[2] National Computer Centre, National University of Asunción. PO Box 1439.
San Lorenzo, Paraguay
bbaran@cnc.una.py

Abstract. This paper presents a new traffic engineering multitree-multiobjective multicast routing algorithm (M-MMA) that solves for the first time the GMM model for Dynamic Multicast Groups. Multitree traffic engineering uses several trees to transmit a multicast demand from a source to a set of destinations in order to balance traffic load, improving network resource utilization. Experimental results obtained by simulations using eight real network topologies show that this new approach gets trade off solutions while simultaneously considering five objective functions. As expected, when M-MMA is compared to an equivalent singletree alternative, it accommodates more traffic demand in a high traffic saturated network.

1 Introduction

Multicast consists of concurrently data transmission from a source to a subset of all possible destinations in a computer network [1]. In recent years, multicast routing algorithms have become more important due to the increased use of new point to multipoint applications, like radio and TV, on-demand video and e-learning. Such applications generally have some quality-of-service (QoS) requirements as maximum end-to-end delay and minimum bandwidth resources.

When a dynamic multicast problem considers various traffic requests, not only QoS parameters must be considered, but also load balancing and network resource utilization [2]. These objectives cannot be met by traditional *Best Effort* Internet routing approaches.

In order to solve this problem, Traffic Engineering proposes the optimization of network resources using load-balancing techniques. The main idea behind a load balancing technique for multicast transmission is to partition a data flow into several

Please use the following format when citing this chapter:

Prieto, J., Barán, B., Crichigno, J., 2006, in IFIP International Federation for Information Processing, Volume 217, Artificial Intelligence in Theory and Practice, ed. M. Bramer, (Boston: Springer), pp. 247–256.

sub flows –or trees– between a source and all destination nodes. This objective is usually accomplished by minimizing the utilization (α) of the most heavily used network resource, as a link (what is known as *maximum link utilization*). Load balancing technique not only reduces hot spots over the network, but also provides the possibility of supporting connections of high bandwidth requirements through several links of low capacity.

Multicast Traffic Engineering problems (MTE) simultaneously consider several objectives to be optimized; therefore, it has been recognized as a Multiobjective Optimization Problem (MOP) [3]. A lot of multiobjective algorithms for multicast routing were proposed in the literature [3-6, 8-13, 15-18]. They are generalized in the *GMM model for Dynamic Multicast Groups* [11, 18]. GMM model considers a multitree multicast load-balancing problem with splitting in a multiobjective context.

This work presents a multitree routing algorithm that solves for the first time the dynamic problem of multicast routing considering not only static routing, but also dynamic routing, where multicast groups arrive one after another into a network.

The remainder of the document is organized as follows: Section 2 presents the mathematical formulation of the problem. A brief introduction to multiobjective optimization problems appears in Section 3. A complete explanation of the proposed algorithm is presented in Section 4. Testing scenarios are shown in Section 5. The experimental results are discussed in Section 6, while the final conclusions and future works are left for Section 7.

2   Problem Formulation

A network is modelled as a direct graph $G(V,E)$, where V is the set of nodes and E is the set of links. Let $(i,j) \in E$ be the link from node i to node j. For each link (i,j) let z_{ij}, d_{ij} and $t_{ij} \in \Re^+$ be its capacity, delay and current traffic respectively. Let $s \in V$ denotes the source node, $N \subseteq V - \{s\}$ denote the set of destination nodes, and $\phi \in \Re^+$ the traffic demand (in kbps) of a multicast request, which is treated as a flow f. Let consider that f can be split into a number of sub flows f_k ($k=1,2,..,|K|$), where $|K|$ denotes the cardinality of set K. For each f_k, a multicast tree $T_k(s,N)$ must be constructed to transport a traffic ϕ_k, which is part of the total flow demand ϕ, as shown in (9).

Let $p_{Tk}(s, n) \subseteq T_k(s, N)$ denote the path that connects the source node s with a destination node $n \in N$ using tree T_k. Finally, let $d(p_{Tk}(s, n))$ and $h(p_{Tk}(s, n))$ represent the delay and the hop count of $p_{Tk}(s, n)$, i.e.,

$$d\big(p_{Tk}(s,n)\big) = \sum_{(i,j) \in p_{Tk}(s,n)} d_{ij} \qquad (1) \qquad h\big(p_{Tk}(s,n)\big) = \sum_{(i,j) \in p_{Tk}(s,n)} 1 \qquad (2)$$

Using the above definitions, the multicast routing problem for traffic engineering treated in this paper is formulated as a MOP that tries to find a set of $|K|$ multicast trees $T_k(s,N)$ that minimizes the following five objective functions:

a-   Maximal link utilization:

$$\alpha = \underset{\substack{(i,j) \in T_k \\ k \in K}}{Max} \left\{ (t_{ij} + \sum_{k=1}^{|K|} \phi_k)/z_{ij} \right\} \qquad (3)$$

b-   Average delay:

$$D_A = \frac{1}{|N||K|} \sum_{k \in K} \sum_{n \in N} d\big(p_{Tk}(s,n)\big) \qquad (4)$$

c- Maximal delay:

$$D_M = \underset{\substack{n \in N \\ k \in K}}{Max} \{d(p_{Tk}(s,n))\} \quad (5)$$

d- Hop count average:

$$H_A = \frac{1}{|N||K|} \sum_{k \in K} \sum_{n \in N} h(p_{Tk}(s,n)) \quad (6)$$

e- Total bandwidth consumption:

$$BW = \sum_{k \in K} \phi_k \cdot |T_k| \quad (7)$$

subject to:

f- Link capacity constraint:

$$t_{ij} + \sum_{k \in K} \sum_{(i,j) \in Tk} \phi_k \leq z_{ij} \quad (8)$$

g- Total information constraint:

$$\sum_{k=1}^{|K|} \phi_k = \phi \quad (9)$$

It should be mentioned that not all $|K|$ sub flows are necessary used. Therefore, if any $\phi_k = 0$ ($k = 1,2,..,|K|$), Eq. (4), (5) and (6) do not consider the corresponding $p_{Tk}(s,n)$ for calculation given that the tree is not used to transmit any information. Of course, the value of $|K|$ should be properly adjusted.

3 Multiobjective Optimization Problems

A general Multiobjective Optimization Problem (MOP) includes a set of l decision variables, r objective functions, and c restrictions. Objective functions and restrictions are functions of decision variables. This can be expressed as:

Optimize $\quad y = g(x) = (g_1(x), g_2(x), \dots, g_r(x))$.
Subject to $\quad e(x) = (e_1(x), e_2(x), \dots, e_c(x)) \geq 0$,
Where $x = (x_1, x_2, \dots, x_l) \in X$ is the decision vector, and
$\quad\quad\quad y = (y_1, y_2, \dots, y_r) \in Y$ is the objective vector.

X denotes the decision space while the objective space is denoted by Y. Depending on the problem at hand, *"optimize"* could mean minimize or maximize. The set of restrictions $e(x) \geq 0$ determines the set of feasible solutions X_f and its corresponding set of objective vectors Y_f. A multiobjective problem consists in finding x that optimizes $g(x)$. In general, there is no unique "best" solution but a set of solutions, none of which can be considered better than the others when all objectives are considered at the same time. This derives from the fact that there can be conflicting objectives. Thus, a new concept of optimality should be established for MOPs. Given two decision vectors $p, q \in X_f$:

$\quad\quad g(p) = g(q)$ iff $\forall i \in \{1, 2,..., r\}$: $g_i(p) = g_i(q)$
$\quad\quad g(p) \leq g(q)$ iff $\forall i \in \{1,2,..., r\}$: $g_i(p) \leq g_i(q)$
$\quad\quad g(p) < g(q)$ iff $g(p) \leq g(q)$ and $g(p) \neq g(q)$

Then, in a minimization context, two solutions $p, q \in X_f$ satisfy one and only one of the following three conditions:

$\quad\quad p \succ q$ (p dominates q), iff $g(p) < g(q)$
$\quad\quad q \succ p$ (q dominates p), iff $g(q) < g(p)$
$\quad\quad p \sim q$ (p and q are non-comparable), iff $p \not\succ q$ and $q \not\succ p$.

A decision vector $x \in X_f$ is non-dominated with respect to a set $Q \subseteq X_f$ iff: $x \succ q$ or $x \sim q$, $\forall q \in Q$. When x is non-dominated with respect to the whole set X_f, it is called an optimal Pareto solution; therefore, the *Pareto optimal set* X_{true} may be formally defined as: $X_{true} = \{x \in X_f \mid x$ is non-dominated with respect to $X_f\}$. The corresponding set of objective vectors $Y_{true} = f(X_{true})$ constitutes the *Optimal Pareto Front*.

4 Proposed Algorithm

Inspired in the SPEA scheme [14] the proposed M-MMA algorithm holds an evolutionary population P and an external Pareto solution set P_{nd}. The algorithm begins with a set of random configurations called initial population. Each individual in the population represents a potential solution to the problem.

At each generation, the individuals are evaluated using an adaptability function, also known as *fitness*, proposed by SPEA, which is based on the dominance criterion presented in section 3. Based on this value, some individuals called parents are selected. The probability of selection of an individual is related to its *fitness*. Then, genetic probabilistic operators are applied to the parent to construct new individuals that will be part of a new population. The process continues until a stop criterion (as a maximum number of generations) is satisfied. M-MMA is summarized in Fig. 1.

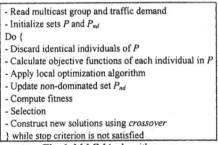

- Read multicast group and traffic demand
- Initialize sets P and P_{nd}
Do {
- Discard identical individuals of P
- Calculate objective functions of each individual in P
- Apply local optimization algorithm
- Update non-dominated set P_{nd}
- Compute fitness
- Selection
- Construct new solutions using *crossover*
} while stop criterion is not satisfied

Fig. 1. M-MMA algorithm

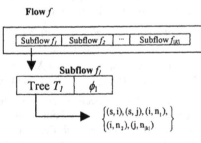

Fig. 2. Chromosome representation

4.1. Encoding

Each chromosome or individual is a candidate solution for the problem. Inspired in the GMM-model [11], an individual is represented by a set of trees transporting a flow f (Fig. 2). Each flow is split in $|K|$ sub flows, as shown in (9), with a tree T_k transmitting sub flow f_k. A tree is represented by the set of links belonging to it [6]. The field ϕ_k associated to each sub flow is the total information transmitted through T_k. This encoding scheme was selected motivated by the promising results obtained by Crichigno *et al.* [6], who conclude that better solutions are found when the trees are represented as a set of links instead of different paths.

4.2. Initial population

The procedure proposed in M-MMA to generate each initial solution of P is shown in Fig. 3. The initialization procedure, called PrimRST (Prim Random Steiner

Tree), was proposed in [6]. Starting with a source node s, at each iteration, the algorithm expands the tree T_k by choosing a new link from a set A, which contains all possible new links for the tree. A set V_c contains the nodes already in the tree. The procedure continues until all destination nodes N are included in V_c. The value of ϕ_k is initialized as $\phi/|K|$. The value of $|K|$ should be previously decided by the traffic engineer. For the experimental results that follows, $|K| = 2$ was chosen. We have considered this small value because the problem is very complex. Moreover, in GMM model [11] the quantity of sub flows is considered as an objective function, because this algorithm is thought for MPLS networks [2], where the quantity of labels is limited. The PrimRST algorithm is iteratively used to construct each tree T_k of the $|K|$ trees that constitute a chromosome, as shown in Fig. 2.

```
PrimRST(G(V,E), s, N)
- T_k = {};
- V_c = {s};
- A = {(s,j) | (s,j) ∈ E, j ∈ V};
do{
      - Choose a link (i, j) ∈ A at random.
      - A = A - {(i,j)}.
      If j ∉ V_c Then
           - T_k = T_k ∪ {(i,j)}.
           - V_c = V_c ∪ {j}.
           - A = A ∪ {(j, w) | (j, w) ∈ E , w ∉ V_c};
      End if
} while (N ∪ {s} ⊄ V_c)
- Prune useless links of T_k
- Return T_k
```

Fig. 3. Procedure PrimRST used to build random multicast Trees

```
Local Optimization (P, Δ_0, ε )
For i=1 until |P|
      Δ=Δ_0
      While Δ > ε
           If φ_1^i + Δ·φ^i ≤ φ^i then
                φ_1* = φ_1^i + Δ·φ^i
                φ_2* = φ^i - φ_1^i
                Evaluate individual f*
                If f* > f^i then
                     φ_1^i = φ_1*
                     φ_2^i = φ_2*
                else
                     Δ = Δ / 2
                End if
           else
                Δ = Δ / 2
           End if
      End while
End for
```

Fig. 4. Local Optimization Procedure

4.3. Local optimization

This procedure tries to optimize the amount of information ϕ_k to be transmitted through each sub flow, satisfying (8) and (9). In order to differentiate between two individuals of P, let f^i be the i-th flow or individual of P ($i=0,1,\ldots,|P|$), ϕ^i the total flow demand for that individual, and ϕ_k^i the k-information amount transmitted through sub flow f_k^i. Local Optimization procedure is presented in Figure 4. The process modifies the values of ϕ_k^i in the following way:

a) ϕ_1^i is increased and ϕ_2^i is decreased in a percentage Δ of ϕ^i. In fact, ϕ_2^i is calculated as $(\phi^i - \phi_1^i)$. Initial value for Δ (known as Δ_0) and its minimum value ε are parameters of the procedure.

b) If total information constraint (9) is fulfilled, new temporal values ϕ_1^* and ϕ_2^* are calculated and objective vector $f *$ is evaluated; otherwise, Δ is reduced to $\Delta/2$ and the process goes back to step a).

c) If the new solution $f *$ dominates f^i, new values ϕ_1^* and ϕ_2^* are accepted as current best value and the process continues; otherwise, Δ is reduced to $\Delta/2$ and the procedure goes back to step a).

d) Iteration continues while $\Delta > \varepsilon$.

Once the iteration is completed, a new iteration begins, but instead of incrementing ϕ_l^i, it is decreased.

4.4. Crossover

The crossover algorithm is based on the one originally presented by Zhengying *et al.* [16]. It was also used in several other publications [6, 7, 15]. The algorithm has four stages:

1. choose one tree from each parent;
2. identify common links of the selected pair. These links will be part of the child tree that will be in the next generation of P. Given that common links of the parents could lead to a child composed of disjoined sub-trees, new links may be added [16];
3. connect the disjoined sub-trees until a multicast tree is constructed. At this step, the sub-trees are connected at random. Each sub-tree has a root node. At each iteration, an interconnection algorithm adds a new link, which has a source-node already in a sub-tree. Two sub-trees are connected when the root of one sub-tree (T_1) is the destination node of the selected link, and the source node of the link belongs to the other sub-tree (T_2); the root of the new sub-tree is the root of T_2;
4. calculate $\phi_j = \left(\phi_j^p + \phi_j^q\right)/2$, for both sub flows j=1, 2, where ϕ_j^p and ϕ_j^q are the j-information amount (ϕ_j) from the two parent trees p and q.

In order to fulfil the flow constraint given by (9), a normalized process computing ϕ_k is used. For a new individual, the new ϕ_k is given by the following equation:

$$\phi_k^{new} = \phi\left(\phi_k / \sum_{k=1}^{|K|} \phi_k\right) \tag{10}$$

5 Testing Scenario

Eight network topologies were used for testing purpose. They were: NTT (Nippon Telephone and Telegraph Co., Japan) [5], NSF (National Science Foundation, United States-US) [5], Telstra (Australia) [19], Sprintlink (US) [19], Ebone (Europe) [19], Tiscali (Europe) [19], Exodus (US) [19] and Abovenet (US) [19].

In order to compare M-MMA behaviour under several traffic loads over the network, three scenarios were defined for every topology: (a) low load, (b) high load and (c) saturation. For every scenario, Ψ traffic requests were generated, simulating a dynamic situation in which they arrive one after another. Each traffic request was created using a *groupGenerator* algorithm [7], summarized in Fig. 5.

The *groupGenerator* algorithm generates a multicast group with a destination size between $|N|_{min}$ and $|N|_{max}$; then, *random*(unif, 0, 2000) gives the arrival time of the group, with a uniform distribution between 0 and 2000 seconds. The duration of each group was exponentially distributed, with an average of 60 seconds. Finally,

```
groupGenerator
group(i)  =   groupGenerator(|N|_{min}, |N|_{max});
T_{beg}(i)  =   random(unif, 0,2000);
T_{end}(i)  =   T_{beg}(i) + random(exp, 0,2000);
φ (i)   =   random(unif, φ_{min}, φ_{max});
End  groupGenerator
```

Fig. 5. GroupGenerator algorithm

the traffic demand is set to a value between ϕ_{min} and ϕ_{max}. The parameters used to generate each scenario are given in Table 1.

Talavera *et al.* [7] showed that most MOEAs may suit for the task of routing multicast demand, but the main factor to define performance in a dynamical environment is the policy used to choose a specific solution from a Pareto front. They proposed different policies to perform this task, proving that the policy of choosing the closest solution to the origin provides excellent trade-off values, outperforming the traditional policy of choosing the solution with better α. Consequently, we use that approach to select a solution from a Pareto front in our experiments. It is useful to mention that [7] concluded that average number of rejected groups might be considered an important metric to compare different algorithms and policies.

Table 1. Parameters used to generate testing scenarios

Network topology			Scenarios load	Parameters				
Name (Location)	Nodes	Links		Ψ	$|N|_{min}$	$|N|_{max}$	ϕ_{min}	ϕ_{max}
Telstra (Australia)	57	118	Low	200	4	10	25	50
			High	300	10	25	50	200
			Saturation	400	10	35	75	300
Sprintlink (US)	44	166	Low	200	3	6	25	50
			High	300	9	12	50	200
			Saturation	400	9	20	75	300
Ebone (Europe)	23	76	Low	200	3	6	25	50
			High	300	5	10	50	200
			Saturation	400	8	15	75	300
Tiscali (Europe)	49	172	Low	200	4	6	25	50
			High	300	9	12	50	200
			Saturation	400	10	20	75	300
Exodus (US)	22	74	Low	200	3	6	25	50
			High	300	5	10	50	200
			Saturation	400	8	15	75	300
Abovenet (US)	33	84	Low	200	3	6	25	50
			High	300	5	10	50	200
			Saturation	400	8	15	75	300
NTT (Japan)	55	144	Low	200	4	10	100	200
			High	300	10	25	200	800
			Saturation	400	10	35	200	800
NSF (US)	14	42	Low	200	2	5	25	50
			High	300	3	7	50	200
			Saturation	400	6	9	75	300

For this problem, M-MMA was compared against MMA2 algorithm [6]. MMA2 is a multiobjective multicast algorithm that routes a request demand through only one tree. We have chosen this algorithm because of its promising results when compared to other alternatives as MMA1 [4, 5] and SK [17]. The following dominance metrics were taken into account:

D_{MMA2}: Percentage of solutions selected using MMA2 that dominates the corresponding M-MMA solutions.

$D_{M\text{-}MMA}$: Percentage of solutions selected using M-MMA that dominates the corresponding MMA2 solutions.

I: Percentage of indifference relationships. This occurs when solutions found by MMA2 and M-MMA are non-comparables.

Eq: Percentage of solutions found by both algorithms that have equal values for objective functions.

We also have compared the amount of solutions selected by M-MMA that uses only one tree to transmit the traffic demand. Finally, percentages of rejected groups for lack of link capacity are given for each scenario.

6 Experimental results

Results for the simulations performed on eight network topologies are shown in tables 2, 3 and 4.

Table 2 summarizes the amount of solutions for each scenario according to the dominance metrics defined in section 5. There is not a clear dominant algorithm, given that many solutions are indifferent (in a multiobjective context) or they have identical values for the objective vectors. Shadowed cells in table 2 highlight this fact. This result is not a surprise, given that we are considering several conflicting objective functions.

Table 2. Classification of solutions according to dominance metrics

Network	Scenario	D_{MMA2}	$D_{M\text{-}MMA}$	I	Eq	Network	Scenario	D_{MMA2}	$D_{M\text{-}MMA}$	I	Eq
Telstra	Low	32.50	5.50	60.50	11.50	Exodus	Low	8.50	2.50	4.00	85.00
	High	11.33	17.67	57.33	13.67		High	9.33	7.67	1.00	82.00
	Saturation	26.00	8.75	48.00	17.25		Saturation	6.50	12.00	10.25	71.25
Sprintlink	Low	3.00	11.50	2.50	83.00	Abovenet	Low	11.50	4.50	5.50	78.50
	High	3.67	16.33	0.67	79.33		High	2.67	10.33	1.00	86.00
	Saturation	21.50	11.75	14.25	52.50		Saturation	11.75	12.50	22.50	53.25
Ebone	Low	7.50	13.00	3.00	76.50	NTT	Low	0.50	34.50	0.50	64.50
	High	21.00	12.67	3.33	63.00		High	2.33	27.67	0.33	69.67
	Saturation	7.50	10.75	29.25	52.50		Saturation	5.50	22.50	2.75	69.25
Tiscali	Low	7.00	13.50	3.00	76.50	NSF	Low	4.50	9.50	6.50	79.50
	High	2.33	0.00	3.67	94.00		High	0.67	10.33	0.00	89.00
	Saturation	9.25	0.75	28.50	61.50		Saturation	8.00	15.50	2.75	73.75

The percentage of multicast groups routed by a single tree is given in Table 3. We should clarify that M-MMA solutions not always use multitree, given that one tree may transport the whole information ϕ. In many cases, both algorithms found the same unitree solution. Multitree solution is used only when it is clearly better than unitree. This is the main reason why M-MMA could find better global solutions.

Actually, a mean of 63.2% of the best solutions had only one tree, and M-MMA is able to find those solutions, just as MMA2. However, in several opportunities the best solution for a given situation is multitree and therefore, only M-MMA is able to find it, making clear why M-MMA outperforms MMA2.

Finally, table 4 gives an idea about multitree performance considering the percentage of rejected groups for lack of link capacity. This result illustrates that M-MMA solutions fulfil the Traffic Engineering purpose, using load-balancing techniques in order to optimize network resources, and therefore, accommodating more traffic than a purely unitree approach like MMA2.

Table 3. Percentage of multicast groups routed by a single tree

Network	Scenario	%
Telstra	Low	93.50
	High	91.67
	Saturation	58.25
Sprintlink	Low	53.00
	High	85.00
	Saturation	83.75
Ebone	Low	46.00
	High	68.33
	Saturation	57.25
Tiscali	Low	82.50
	High	82.00
	Saturation	83.00
Exodus	Low	41.50
	High	53.00
	Saturation	60.25
Abovenet	Low	50.50
	High	77.33
	Saturation	74.50
NTT	Low	25.00
	High	28.33
	Saturation	46.50
NSF	Low	62.00
	High	50.00
	Saturation	42.00

Table 4. Percentage of groups rejected for lack of link capacity for both algorithms

Network	Scenario	% Rejected by	
		MMA2	M-MMA
Telstra	Low	0.00	0.00
	High	5.67	5.67
	Saturation	37.75	35.75
Sprintlink	Low	0.00	0.00
	High	0.33	0.00
	Saturation	14.00	9.00
Ebone	Low	0.00	0.00
	High	2.00	2.00
	Saturation	27.00	27.00
Tiscali	Low	0.00	0.00
	High	3.00	0.00
	Saturation	28.50	7.75
Exodus	Low	0.00	0.00
	High	0.00	0.00
	Saturation	10.25	10.00
Abovenet	Low	0.00	0.00
	High	0.00	0.00
	Saturation	22.00	19.50
NTT	Low	0.00	0.00
	High	0.33	0.00
	Saturation	2.50	1.50
NSF	Low	0.00	0.00
	High	0.00	0.00
	Saturation	1.75	1.25

7 Conclusion and future work

This paper presents the M-MMA algorithm, which is able to solve for the first time the GMM-model in a dynamical environment, considering multitree. The proposed algorithm treats the multiobjective problem of multicast routing in a network, splitting traffic demand into several trees (multitree context) to optimize network resource utilization. To better accomplish the optimization goal, M-MMA proposes a local optimization procedure that finds better solutions improving the relative amount of information to be transmitted through each tree.

Results obtained by simulations on dynamical environments where traffic demands come one after another show that no studied algorithm is clearly dominant. In fact, many times the best solution under the given policy had only one tree; however, the best solution for a given situation is sometimes a multitree and therefore, only

M-MMA is able to find it. As a consequence, M-MMA is able to accommodate more traffic demand under a saturated scenario. For further study, we plan to consider simultaneous routing of several multicast requests in optical networks.

References

1. A. Tanenbaum: *Computer Networks*, Prentice Hall, 2003.
2. D. Awdueche, J. Malcolm, J. Agogbua, M. O'Dell, and J. McManus: *Requirements For Traffic Engineering Over MPLS*. RFC 2702. 1999.
3. J. Crichigno, and B. Barán: *Multiobjective Multicast Routing Algorithm*. IEEE ICT'2004, Ceará, Brazil, 2004.
4. B. Barán, and J. Crichigno: *A Multicast Routing Algorithm Using Multiobjective Optimization*. IEEE ICT'2004, Ceará, Brazil, 2004.
5. J. Crichigno, and B Barán: *Multiobjective multicast routing algorithm for traffic engineering*. IEEE ICCCN 2004, Chicago USA.
6. J. Crichigno, F. Talavera, J. Prieto, and B. Barán: *Enrutamiento Multicast utilizando Optimización Multiobjetivo*. CACIC'2004, Buenos Aires, Argentina, 2004. pp. 147-158.
7. F. Talavera, J. Crichigno, and B. Barán: *Policies for Dynamical MultiObjective Environment of Multicast Traffic Engineering*. IEEE ICT 2005, South Africa.
8. Y. Donoso, R. Fabregat, and J. Marzo: *Multi-Objective Optimization Algorithm for Multicast Routing with Traffic Engineering*. IEEE ICN 2004.
9. R. Fabregat, Y. Donoso, J.L. Marzo, and A. Ariza: *A Multi-Objective Multipath Routing Algorithm for Multicast Flows*. SPECTS 2004.
10. R. Fabregat, Y. Donoso, F. Solano, and J.L. Marzo: *Multitree Routing for Multicast Flows: A Genetic Algorithm Approach*. CCIA 2004.
11. Y. Donoso, R. Fabregat, F. Solano, J. L. Marzo, and B. Barán: *Generalized Multiobjective Multitree model for Dynamic Multicast Groups*. IEEE ICC 2005, Seul Corea.
12. A. Roy, N. Banerjee, and S. Das: *An efficient Multi-Objective QoS-Routing Algorithm for Wireless Multicasting*. INFOCOM 2002.
13. X. Cui, C. Lin, and Y. Wei: *A Multiobjective Model for QoS Multicast Routing Based on Genetic Algorithm*. ICCNMC 2003.
14. E. Zitzler, and L. Thiele: *Multiobjective Evolutionary Algorithms: A comparative Case Study and the Strength Pareto Approach*. IEEE Trans. Evolutionary Computation, Vol. 3, No. 4, 1999, pp. 257-271.
15. P. Texeira de Araújo, and G. Barbosa Oliveira: *Algoritmos Genéticos Aplicados al Ruteamiento Multicast en Internet, Contemplando Requisitos de Calidad de Servicio e Ingenieria de Tráfico*. VII Brazilian Symposium on Neural Networks (SBRN'02), 2002.
16. W. Zhengying, S. Bingxin, and Z. Erdun: *Bandwidth-delay-constraint least cost multicast routing based on heuristic genetic algorithm*. Computer Communications. 2001. Vol. 24. pp. 685-692.
17. Y. Seok, Y. Lee, Y Choi, and C. Kim: *Explicit Multicast Routing Algorithm for Constrained Traffic Engineering*. IEEE ISCC'02. Italia, 2002.
18. R. Fabregat, Y. Donoso, B. Barán, F. Solano, and J.L. Marzo: *Multi-objective Optimization Scheme for Multicast Flows: a Survey, a Model and a MOEA Solution*. IFIP/ LANC 2005.
19. Spring, R Mahajan, and D. Wetheral: *Measuring ISP topologies with Rocketfuel*. Proceedings of the ACM SIGCOMM'02 Conference, 2002.

Road Segment Identification in Natural Language Text

Ahmed Y. Tawfik and Lawrence Barsanti

School of Computer Science, University of Windsor
Windsor, Ontario, Canada
Email atawfik@uwindsor.ca, barsant@uwindsor.ca

Abstract. This paper describes a technique to extract geographic location information from a natural language description of a location. The technique relies on a set of domain specific tags and a set of keywords. The tags are used to identify roads, intersections, and landmarks. Tag combinations are used to discover road segments. The technique is applied to understanding highway construction reports for the Canadian Province of Ontario.

1. Introduction

Location information has traditionally been expressed in two main forms: natural languages and maps. Maps represent a rich visual representation that captures a host of spatial relationships among collocated elements. Natural languages provide a set of focused abstractions of the spatial relationships represented in a map. In natural languages, the choice of the relevant abstraction is generally task dependent. Maps and natural language interfaces to geographic information systems continue to be complementary. For example, systems that generate driving directions like Yahoo! Maps, MapPoint and MapQuest [6] provide a linguistic description of a map. Coral [1] applies natural language generation techniques to make the linguistic description more natural. Understanding and visualizing textual geographic references on a map has attracted less attention as a research focus. By grounding named entities to spatial locations, a system can answer spatial queries [3]. A geo-parser combines data from multilingual gazetteer with natural language text and a geographic information system to produce a map highlighting the locations mentioned in the text [4].

The focus here is on defining a set of special purpose tags that are designed to understand urban location descriptions like driving directions that can be used in translating location information expressed in natural language to a segment or region on a map. The application that has motivated this work is building a system that determines the location of highway construction based on construction report summaries. These summaries include some structured fields (e.g. affected highway, closest city, length of construction) and a natural language description of the traffic impact. The traffic impact typically includes detailed location information. Figure 1 shows an example of highway construction summary for highway 401 in Ontario[1], Canada.

---

[1] From the Ontario highway construction reports available at http://www.mto.gov.on.ca/english/index.html

Please use the following format when citing this chapter:

Tawfik, A.Y., Barsanti, L., 2006, in IFIP International Federation for Information Processing, Volume 217, Artificial Intelligence in Theory and Practice, ed. M. Bramer, (Boston: Springer), pp. 257–266.

Start of Construction:	June 01, 2004
Estimated End of Construction:	November 25, 2005
Highway:	401
Length of Construction:	10.6 kilometers
Close To:	Tilbury
Type of Contract:	Road Construction
Traffic Impact: Highway 401, from Highway 77 easterly To Essex County Road 42. Highway 401 will be reduced to a single lane of traffic in each direction separated by temporary concrete barrier wall. The speed limit is reduced to 80 kilometers per hour.	
Region of Ontario:	Southwestern

Figure 1. Sample Construction Report Summary

Section 2 presents the knowledge representation that serves as a foundation to the work. Section 3 introduces the two level parsing technique used in the interpretation of some natural language location descriptions. Section 4 presents the results of analysing construction reports and Section 5 presents a brief conclusion.

2. Elements of the Knowledge Representation

Topological and metric spatial relationship expressed in natural language has to be interpreted before the location can be correctly determined. In general, we consider that we have linear entities and regions. A road is represented as a linear entity. Linear entities include highways, creeks, rivers, and boundary lines. Towns, cities, counties, and mountains are considered as regions. The intersections of two lines define a point. The intersection of a line and a region defines a line segment. Specifying a location relies on the identification of the relationship that holds between lines or between a line and region. Interpreting the natural language terms describing these relationships relies on the two-level part-of-speech-tagging described in the next section.

The knowledge representation is based the 9-intersection model [5]. According to this model, each spatial object divides the space into three components: the boundary of the object, the space internal to the object, and every thing else is external to the object. Therefore, a simple line (that has no self loops) has two boundary points, and a continuous sequence of internal points joining the two boundary points. Similarly, a region has a closed boundary, an internal area and an external area. For simplicity, we assume that the map is a 2D space.

Line-line Relations

Shariff et al. [5] identify 33 topological relationships that may hold between two lines. To simplify the representation, we omit self-similar (symmetric) relationships. A relationship is self-similar if its inverse has the same 9-intersection matrix as the original relationship The 33 relations include 11 self-similar relationships in addition to 11 relationships with 11 respective inverses. . For example, *equal* (LL22) and *intersect* (LL2) are self-similar relationships. However, *contains* (LL5) has an inverse (LL5^{-1}).

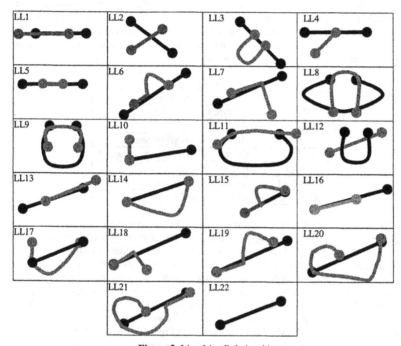

Figure 2. Line-Line Relationships

Figure 2 illustrates the topological relationships that may hold between two lines. It is possible to divide these topological relationships into relationships involving overlapping segments (LL5, LL6, LL7, LL11, LL12, LL15, LL16, LL18, LL19, LL21, and LL22) and others involving 0, 1 or 2 boundary points (LL1, LL2, LL3, LL4, LL8, LL9, LL10, LL13, LL14, LL17, and LL20).

3. Parsing Location Information

In order to understand location text, it is important to extract references to locations in the text. In general, this a difficult problem as special attention should be given to the use of prepositions (at, from, to, …etc.) and a great deal of disambiguation may be involved in distinguishing references to places from other proper nouns. A gazetteer is useful in distinguishing references to cities and towns from other proper nouns in the text. However, some commonsense knowledge is necessary to correctly parse "Mr.

England flew to India" and figure out that England refers to a person while India is a place. Fortunately, in our application, location information was easily identifiable and a rather limited amount of effort went into disambiguation. The tagging technique introduced here assigns special tags to spatial words and phrases indicating direction as in northerly, left, southbound, and Windsor-bound.   Special tags are also assigned to words and phrases denoting proximity or distance like near, close, next to, or distance (like a mile). As some numbered highways also have a name (e.g. County Road 19 is also Manning road), a special tag (ALT_ROAD) is necessary. Table 1 lists the set of domain specific tags used here.

Table 1. Domain Specific Tags

Tag	Represents
INT_ID	Intersection Identifier
ROAD	Road / Highway
OFF	Offset/Proximity/Distance
DIR	Direction of Traffic (set of lanes)
NLM	Natural Landmark
MLM	Manmade Landmark
ALT_ROAD	Alternate Road Name

The assignment of these domain-specific tags is performed as a second level tagging after the text has been tagged using a standard part-of-speech tagger. Here, we use CLAWS [2] for first level tagging. CLAWS tag set includes locative tags NNL, NNL1 and NNL2. However, we found that the names of most roads and landmarks consist of a sequence of singular common nouns (NN1), singular proper nouns (NP1), numbers (MC), and in some cases title nouns (NNSB). Phrases that contain these tag sequences are of interest, we identify these phrases as potential name phrase (PNP). A PNP is defined as a sequence of one or more words whose tags are any combination of the NN1, NP1, and NNB tags; see Figure 3. Locative tags still play an important role in identifying locations.   For example, both roads and natural landmarks can be found by searching for the sequence of tags PNP NNL1. It is the word represented by the NNL1 tag that distinguishes between them. That is why some of the tag sequences presented in Table 3 have keywords associated with them. Table 2 lists the keywords used in assigning spatial tags. Adjectives (JJ), prepositions (II), nouns of direction (ND), units of measurements (NNU), the preposition "for" (IF), and participle (or past) form of verbs (VVN/VVD) all proved useful in identifying road segments.

Text	Highway	77	,	From	Highway	77	Easterly	To	Essex	County	Road	42	.
Tags	NN1	MC	,	II	NN1	MC	JJ	II	NP1	NN1	NN1	MC	.
	PNP				PNP				PNP				

Figure 3. Example of Potential Name Phrase Tags

Notice that in Table 3 some of the patterns contain domain specific tags. For this reason the order in which tags are found is important; the following order is used: INT_ID, PNP, ROAD, ALT_ROAD, OFF, DIR, NLM, MLM.

Table 2. Keyword Lists

Feature	Keywords
Road Indicator	avenue, boulevard, parkway, way, expressway, drive, road
Numbered Roads	Highway, route, road
Natural landmark	river, creek, brook, lake, island, isle, islet, narrows, mountain, forest
Manmade landmark	bridge, span, overpass, underpass, tunnel, structure, culvert, skyway
Direction	Northbound, northward, southbound, southward, eastbound, eastward, westbound, westward
Destination	Bound
Intersection	Intersection, junction, crossroad, crossway, crossing, corner, interchange
Road type	regional, municipal, county
Directional Adjective	Northerly, southerly, easterly, westerly

Table 3. Patterns for detecting domain specific tags

Special Tag	Sequence	Keywords From Table 2	Example
INT_ID		Intersection	
ROAD	PNP MC	PNP ends with Numbered Rd	County Road 42
	PNP NNL1	NNL1 not a landmark	Queen Street
	PNP NNL1 MC	NNL1 not a landmark	County Road 121
	JJ PNP MC	JJ Road Type	Regional Road 3
	PNP	Starts with a numbered road or ends with a road indicator	Highway QEW Van Horne Ave.
OFF	ND1 IO		East of
	MC NNU1 ND1 IO		1 kilometer East of
	MC NNU2 ND1 IO		2 kms East of
	JJ MC NNU1	JJ directional adjective	Northerly 1.0 km
	JJ MC NNU2	JJ directional adjective	northerly 2.3 kms
	JJ IF MC NNU1	JJ directional adjective	Northerly for 1 km
	JJ IF MC NNU2	JJ directional adjective	Northerly for 2 kms
DIR	ROAD ANY	ANY is direction	Highway 401 westbound
	ANY ROAD	ANY is direction	Eastbound Highway QEW
	PNP VVD	VVD is destination	Toronto Bound
	ND1 VVN	VVN is destination	west bound
	ANY	ANY is direction	Westbound
	ROAD ND1		Highway 8 East
NLM	PNP	Last word natural landmark	Pike Creek
	PNP NNL1	NNL1 in natural landmark	
MLM	NLM ANY	Any in manmade landmark	Pike Creek Bridge
	PNP	Last word in manmade landmark	Thorold Tunnel
ALT_ROAD	(ROAD)		(Manning Road)

However, using only patterns does not provide good enough results. For instance some people may use short forms like "Take Highway 401 to Walker Road. Get off the 401 and go south on Walker." In this sentence both "the 401" and "Walker" refer to roads, but would not be matched by any of the listed patterns. To handle this type of situation every time a road is found the rules in Table 4 are used to generate potential short form for the road. After all the patterns have been searched a second pass can find and tag these short forms.

Lastly, in some cases CLAWS tags a word like road as a noun (NN1) when it should be a locative noun (NNL1). That is why there are redundant rules like "proper noun followed by a number" (PNP MC) and "proper noun followed by a common noun and a number" (PNP NNL1 MC).

Identifying Road Segments

Usually, road segments are defined as either the stretch of road between two points (Figure 4a), or as a stretch of a given length starting at a given point (Figure 4b). For example, construction may affect a highway segment between two intersections or it may affect the area around a bridge or intersection. According to the 9 intersection model, a point is the intersection of two lines (LL2) or a segment and a line (LL4). A segment can also be defined in terms of the portion of a line intersecting a region. In this case, the points defining the ends of the segment are defined by the intersections of the region boundaries with the line.

Table 4. Rules for creating short forms

Pattern	Short Form
PNP MC	"the MC" and "the highway" (if PNP is the word highway)
PNP NNL1	PNP (i.e. road name without street, road, etc...)
PNP NNL1 MC	"the MC"
JJ PNP MC	"the MC"
PNP	"the PNP" without first word or PNP without last word

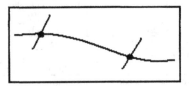   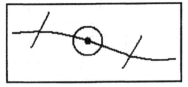

Figure 4a. Segment delimited by two points   **Figure 4b.** Segment around a point

Table 5. Segment Identification Rewriting Rules

Type	Pattern	Rewrite As
Segment with two points	$ROAD^1$ $ROAD^2$ to $ROAD^3$	$ROAD^1$ & $ROAD^2$ to $ROAD^1$ & $ROAD^3$
	$ROAD^1$ $ROAD^2$ to NLM	$ROAD^1$ & $ROAD^2$ to $ROAD^1$ & NLM
	$ROAD^1$ NLM to $ROAD^3$	$ROAD^1$ & NLM to $ROAD^1$ & $ROAD^2$
	$ROAD^1$ NLM^1 to NLM^2	$ROAD^1$ & $ROAD^2$ to $ROAD^1$ & MLM
	$ROAD^1$ $ROAD^2$ to $ROAD^3$	$ROAD^1$ & MLM to $ROAD^1$ & $ROAD^2$
	$ROAD^1$ between $ROAD^2$ and $ROAD^3$	$ROAD^1$ & $ROAD^2$ to $ROAD^1$ & $ROAD^3$
	Note: if DIR was found using either the 1st or 2nd pattern in Table 3 it could substitute for one of the ROAD tags. i.e. ROAD westbound ROAD to MLM	
Segment with a single point	$ROAD^1$ at $ROAD^2$	$ROAD^1$ at $ROAD^2$ (no interjecting words)
	ROAD at NLM	ROAD at NLM (no interjecting words)
	ROAD at MLM	ROAD at MLM (no interjecting words)
	$ROAD^1$ OFF^1 $ROAD^2$ OFF^2	$ROAD^1$ at $ROAD^2$
	$ROAD^1$ $ROAD^2$	$ROAD^1$ at $ROAD^2$
	ROAD NLM	ROAD at NLM
	ROAD MLM	ROAD at MLM

Table 5 shows how the domain specific tags and CLAWS part-of-speech tags are used to identify road segments. The sequences used to identify road segments consist of tags and keywords. The tags and keywords in a pattern have to appear in the order laid out by the pattern; but they do not have to be consecutive. For example, the sentence in figure 5 matches the first pattern in Table 5 and produces the phrase "Highway 58 & Regional Road 3 to Highway 58 & Forks Road". The rewriting rules in Table 5 try to deal with implicit references to points and intersections. For example, in the phrase "Construction on Highway 22 from Howard Ave to Walker Rd." implicitly means that the construction starts at the intersection of Howard Ave. and Highway 22 and ends at the intersection of Walker Road and Highway 22.

Text	Highway 58	,	Regional Road 3	To	South	Of	Forks Road	.
Tags	ROAD	,	ROAD	II		OFF	ROAD	.

Figure 5. Example of Road Segment Identification

4. Implementation and Performance Results

The algorithm described in this paper has been implemented in Java. The implementation consists of two main components: a special purpose tagger and a road segment identification module. It uses a separate file for the keywords and patterns shown in Tables 2, 3, 4, and 5 to maintain modularity and make it easy to add new patterns or keywords. An input text is first submitted to CLAWS to get a part-of-speech (POS) tagged text. In the POS tagged sequence, keywords are identified and the sequence is matched to the patterns given in the keywords/patterns file to get a text tagged with our application-specific tags in addition the part-of-speech tags. If a word could have more than one POS tag, the tags are considered in the order of their likelihood until a matching pattern is found. If a word sequence matches multiple patterns, (e.g. PNP NNL1 and PNP NNL1 MC), the longest sequence, that overlaps the shorter one, is used. The road segment identification module applies the rewriting rules in Table 5 and generates a list of road segments. The algorithm looks for road segments delimited by two points first before trying to identify road segments that are near a point. The following example illustrates the outputs from the tagger and the segment identifier.

Input	Hwy 401 , 10 Kms east of Interchange Number 661 At the Donovan Creek Bridge											
POS	NN1	MC	, MC	NNU2	ND1	IO	NN1	NN1	MC	II	AT	NP1	NN1	NN1
Domain Tag	ROAD			OFF			INT_ID					MLM		
Segment	(ROAD AT MLM) OFF: Hwy 401 at Donovan Creek Bridge, 10 Kms East											

To test the performance of the tagger, we used 25 construction reports from Ontario road construction web site. Each construction report was manually tagged using the domain specific tag set, and then the reports were tagged by the tagger. The tags found by the domain tagger were then checked for incorrect tagging. The results are summarized in Table 6.

From the results it clear that the patterns for both natural and manmade landmarks contributed a large number of errors. There are too many false positives for natural landmarks. A more semantic approach to finding natural landmarks should reduce the number of false positives because the false positives all occurred when the tagger failed to find either a manmade landmark (i.e. the rule NLM ANY failed because of the keyword list) or road. As for manmade landmarks, a wider range of patterns and better generalization would probably improve their results as the test set simply contained keywords that were not identified in the initial analysis.

To evaluate the performance of the road segment identification, twenty-three of the twenty-five construction reports used for domain tagging were read by a person who looked for occurrences of road segments as explained in Figure 4. The tagged reports were processed by the system and the strings it produced were reviewed for correctness and counted. Additionally, all of the misses and partially correct (e.g. near A instead of between A & B) results were examined to determine if the problem was a consequence of the domain tagging. Table 7 presents a summary of the results.

We found that inaccuracies in the tagging seriously degraded the quality of the information extracted. A second look at the tagging results revealed that even though the domain tagger has an average accuracy of 76.7% only 12 of the 25 reports (48%) were tagged flawlessly. In fact, every other report had at least one error, which could easily throw off the segment identification.

Table 6. Tagging Results

Tag	Actual	Total Found	False Positives	Percent Correct
INT_ID	12	12	0	100
ROAD	63	50	2	76.2
OFF	28	26	1	89.3
DIR	17	13	0	76.5
NLM	1	4	4	0
MLM	14	7	1	42.9
ALT_ROAD	2	1	0	50
Weighted Average				76.7

Table 7. Road segment identification results

Type	Actual	Correctly Identified with automatic tagging	Correctly Identified with manual tagging
Two Points	10	3	9
Single Point	19	12	16
Other	1	0	0
Overall	30	15	25

We then added a CITY tag that matches the city name from the structured information associated with the construction report. The CITY tag is useful to avoid interpreting a phrase like "Riverside Drive, Windsor" as an intersection.

Surprisingly, in our tests of the road segment identification algorithm, no false positives were produced; however in some cases weaker, but correct information was found (e.g. near A instead of between A & B). This is surprising because the last three patterns in Table 5 are rather lenient. Also, note that information such as direction and offset could also be leveraged in order to improve the extracted information. For instance, the pattern ROAD1 OFF1 ROAD2 OFF2, occurred in four reports and was defined as a region around an intersection, but it would have been better defined as a road segment delimited by two points.

5. Discussion and Conclusions

Determining the location of the highway construction described in Figure 1 requires parsing the text to extract the starting landmark or intersection (Highway 401 and Highway 77) and the ending landmark or intersection (Highway 401 and Essex County Road 42). Using a gazetteer as a dictionary to look up road names, landmarks, and populated places should improve the performance [4]. However, in many cases the construction zone is bound by harder to define landmarks. Consider the following examples:

- "Highway 35, Victoria/Haliburton Boundary Northerly for 8.1 kilometres to 0.3 kilometres north of Miners Bay."

- "Highway 21, from the north limits of Goderich northerly for 2.0 kilometres and Straughn's Creek Culvert 8 kilometres south of the town of Goderich."

- "Highway 401, from 2.55 kilometres west of Boundary Road, easterly to 0.75 kilometres east of Boundary Road and westbound lanes 0.5 kilometres east of Brookdale Avenue, easterly for 0.5 kilometres."

In the first example, the construction zone is defined in terms of the highway intersection with the boundary between two regions. In the second example, the construction zone is apparently discontinuous as it spans two kilometres from the north limits of a town and 8 kilometres from a small creek to the south of the same town. In the third example, the word "Boundary" is the name of a road not a region boundary as in the first example.

This work has provided a technique to identify road segments that are of interest for some reason (in our case, they were affected by construction). The technique can be useful in other applications like understanding driving directions. The results reported here are for a relatively small test corpus obtained from a single source and may not be statistically significant. However, these results highlight some of the strengths and limitations of the proposed approach.

Acknowledgements

This work is supported by a Discovery Grant from the Natural Sciences and Engineering Research Council (NSERC), Canada.

References

1. Dale, R., Geldof, S., and Prost, J.-P.: CORAL: Using Natural Language Generation for Navigational Assistance", Twenty-sixth Australasian Computer Science Conference (ACSC2003), Adelaide, South Australia, (2003).
2. Garside, R., and Smith, N. : A Hybrid Grammatical Tagger: CLAWS4, in Garside, R., Leech, G., and McEnery, A. (eds.) Corpus Annotation: Linguistic Information from Computer Text Corpora. Longman, London, (1997) 102-121.
3. Leinder, J., Sinclair, G., Webber, B.: Grounding Spatial Named Entities for Information Extraction and Question Answering. Workshop on the Analysis of Geographic References at NAACL-HLT 2003 Conference, Edmonton, Alberta, Canada, (2003).
4. Poluiquen, B., Steinberger, R., Ignat, C. and De Groeve, T.: Geographical Information Recognition and Visualization in Texts Written in Various Languages. The 2004 ACM Symposium on Applied Computing (SAC'04), Nicosia, Cyprus, (2004) 1051-1058.
5. Shariff, R.B.M., Egenhofer, M.J., Mark, D.M.: Natural-Language Spatial Relations between Linear and Areal Objects: The Topology and Metric of English-Language Terms. International Journal of Geographical Information Science, Vol. 12 No. 3, (1998) 215-246.
6. Forth, S.: Online Mapping Services Guide the Way. Plugged In, 16 :11 (2005) 48-50.

Learning Discourse-new References in Portuguese Texts

Sandra Collovini and Renata Vieira

Universidade do Vale do Rio dos Sinos
CP 275, CEP 93022-000, São Leopoldo, RS, Brazil
sandrac@exatas.unisinos.br, renatav@unisinos.br

Abstract. This work presents the evaluation of a discourse status classifier for the Portuguese language. It considers two distinguished classes of discourse novelty: *Brand-new* and *New* references. An evaluation of the relevant features according to different linguistic levels are presented in detail.

1 Introduction

The identification of discourse status has been recognized as a relevant task in natural language understanding. Many systems have been proposed to classify referring expressions [2, 14, 12, 5, 13, 8] in order to recognize if they are new or old information. This comes along with the problem of anaphora resolution, it is usually useful establish the relations of old expressions with their antecedents. It is important, for instance, to identify antecedents for pronouns (it, he, she) to interpret the meaning of the discourse. Our work focuses on definite descriptions (DDs), those referring to expressions with a definite article (such as *the boy, the girl*) , because they are numerous in texts and are the main source of ambiguity regarding novelty, as opposed to other expressions. Pronouns, for instance are mainly old and indefinite descriptions are mainly new.

Whereas most of the literature in this area refers to the English language, we built and evaluated a system to classify discourse status in Portuguese texts. Besides proposing and evaluating such a system for a new language, this work is original by considering two different classes of discourse-new DDs. At first, we classified *Brand-new* definite descriptions. However, as the distinction between *Brand-new* and *Anchored-new* DDs is remarkably difficult [9], a second study was made considering the more general class *New*, which includes both *Brand-new* and *Anchored-new*. Also original in this study is that the relevance of the features used for learning the classifier is analyzed considering different levels of linguistic knowledge.

This paper is organized as follows. In Section 2 we discuss the related work. Classes of discourse status are defined and exemplified in Section 3. In Section 4, a corpus study and the features used to build our classifier are presented. In Section 5 we discuss the resulting decision trees and the relevance of the features is discussed in Section 6. In Section 7, this work also shows an evaluation of the resulting system on completely unseen data. In Section 8 we present our final remarks.

Please use the following format when citing this chapter:

Collovini, S., Vieira, R., 2006, in IFIP International Federation for Information Processing, Volume 217, Artificial Intelligence in Theory and Practice, ed. M. Bramer, (Boston: Springer), pp. 267–276.

2 Related Work

There are in the literature several proposals of referring expressions classifiers. In [2] a classifier for DDs was developed. The authors define new DDs as independent existential expressions, understood by the readers isolately, without needing a context. This system conjugates 9 syntactic heuristics (restrictive pre-modifiers and post-modifiers, relative clauses, adjective constructions etc.) and other heuristics like DDs that occur in the first sentence of a text. As a result, they achieved 78% of recall, 87% of precision and 82% of F-measure for the classification of independent existing DDs. In [14] a heuristic based discourse-new DD classification system was developed, reaching 69% of recall, 72% of precision and 70% of F-measure, on the basis of 9 such features.

In [13] a classifier for discourse-new DDs and unique expressions was presented, where discourse new DDs were defined as the first mention of an entity in the discourse and unique expressions were said to specify their referent totally, and for this reason are understood without any context. The author took into consideration 32 features (syntactic, contextual and definite probability) including data from the web. The reported result was 82.3% of recall, 84.8% of precision and 83.5% of F-measure in discourse-new DDs classification and 68.8% of recall, 85.2% of precision and 76.1% of F-measure were reported for unique expressions classification. In [8] a group of common features in these previous work for another discourse-new DDs classifier (9 features) was reviewed and applied. The classifier resulted in 95.1% of recall, 85.8% of precision and 90.2% of F-measure.

All works cited above refer to the English language. Some other languages are also studied but not so extensively [1, 4, 5]. There are some corpora studies about coreference for the Portuguese language [11], but to the best of our knowledge there is no implemented DD resolution or classification system for Portuguese, so far. In addition to that, another difference of our work is that we give a detailed analysis of the features that were actually relevant to the classification, whereas in these previous work there is usually none. An exception is [7], which examines anaphoricity information to improve a learning-based coreference system and presents a list of the most informative features.

This work is the first one to present a classifier for DDs in Portuguese language. Based on a corpus study, DDs were analyzed and a set of features was organized in 3 groups considering three distinct linguistic levels. Features specifically related to the noun phrase structure constitute the first group, features which consider the sentence structure are in the second one, and the third group is based on information about the previous sentences. In the next section, we present the classes in detail.

3 Classes Description

The classes of DDs considered in this work are mainly based on [10], but they are also related to many of the studies discussed in Section 2. In the examples below, DDs are presented in boldface and their antecedents are underlined.

New DDs: these are definite referring expressions that introduce new entities into the discourse. In this work we consider two types of New DDs, *Brand-new* and *Anchored-new*.

- **Brand-New DDs** (discourse-new or non-anaphoric): introduce entities which are new in the discourse:

  A Folha de São Paulo apresentou as listas apreendidas na operação contra o crime organizado. [The Folha de São Paulo presented the lists arrested in the operation against the organized crime.]

- **Anchored-new DDs** (associative anaphors or bridging): refer to entities that have a semantic connection with an antecedent expression, which is necessary to their interpretation:

  *A Folha de São Paulo apresentou as listas apreendidas na operação contra o crime organizado. O jornal tentou ouvir **o delegado encarregado**. [The Folha de São Paulo presented the lists arrested in the operation against the organized crime. The newspaper tried to listen to **the police chief in charge**.]*

Old DDs: refer to entities mentioned in the previous discourse. Old DDs can be *Plain-old* and *Related-old*.

- **Plain-old DDs** (direct anaphors): have an identity relation with their antecedents and share with them the same head-noun:

  *... as listas apreendidas na operação contra o crime organizado. Alguns delegados também são citados **nas listas**. ... [the lists arrested in the operation against the organized crime. Some police chiefs are also mentioned in **the lists**.]*

- **Related-old DDs** (indirect anaphors): have an identity relation with their antecedents however they present a distinguished head-noun:

  *A Folha de São Paulo apresentou as listas apreendidas ... **O jornal** tentou ouvir .... [The Folha de São Paulo presented the lists arrested ... **The newspaper** tried ...]*

4 Corpus study

Our work was based on two corpora. Corpus 1 was formed by 24 newspaper articles from Folha de São Paulo, written in Brazilian Portuguese, corresponding to part of the NILC[1] corpus. Out of 2319 noun phrases (NPs) we identified 1331 DDs. Corpus 1 was used for the learning phase. Corpus 2 was composed by 4 texts from the Public newspaper, written in European Portuguese from CETEMPublico[2] corpus. Out of 770 noun phrases we identified 482 DDs. Corpus 2 was used for the final evaluation.

The corpora were automatically annotated with syntactic information using the parser PALAVRAS[3] [3] to Portuguese. They were also manually annotated with coreference using MMAX [6]. The first annotation task was to distinguish *New* and *Old* DDs. The second task was pointing to the antecedent for the old cases. Corpus 1 was

---

[1] http://www.nilc.icmc.usp.br
[2] http://www.linguateca.pt/CETEMPublico
[3] http://visl.sdu.dk/visl/pt/parsing/automatic

annotated by three annotators. The agreement for the first task was close to 90.0%. Corpus 2 was annotated by four annotators. For the first task, the agreement resulted in 94.7% among the four annotators, for all other cases there was agreement among three annotators. This two-fold distinction is much easier than for the four classes, which explains why agreement was high whereas other work usually report much less than that. For the second task, antecedents annotation for those classified as old, four annotators agreed in 73.9% of the cases, in other 6.3% of the cases there was agreement among three annotators, in 0.84% only two annotators agreed, and complete disagreement was verified for the remaining 18.9%. The results are shown in Table 1.

Table 1: Manual Annotation

Corpus	New DDs (%)	Old DDs (%)	Total (%)
1	816 (61.3%)	515 (38.7%)	1331 (100%)
2	308 (63.9%)	174 (36.1%)	482 (100%)

The corpus was further analyzed, dividing *New* and *Old* DDs in their subclasses as presented in Section 1 (see Table 2). The usual large quantity of *Brand-new* DDs was confirmed. In Corpus 1, 52.3% were *Brand-new* and in Corpus 2 this number was even higher, 59.5%. DDs of Corpus 1 were studied against the features described in previous work, as presented in Section 3. A total of 16 features were identified in three groups of features according to different levels of linguistic knowledge. Group G1 considers information about the noun phrase alone, G2 considers information about the sentence in which the DD appears, G3 takes into account information about the previous text detailed in Table 3. Examples from the corpus illustrating each of the features are presented.

- PP: *Os membros da classe jurídica. [The members of the juridical class.]*
- APP: *O Prefeito de Gravataí, Daniel Luiz Bordignom. [The Gravataí major, Daniel Luiz Bordignom.]*
- PN_APP: *O delegado Elson Campelo. [The Police Chief Elson Campelo.]*
- REL_CL: *O texto que deve ser assinado pelos jornalistas. [The text that must be signed by jornalists.]*
- CPN_HEAD: *O Othon Palace Hotel. [The Othon Palace Hotel.]*
- AP: *As conversas mais antigas. [The older conversations.]*
- ADJ_PRE: *O primeiro grau. [The first degree.]*
- NUM_PRE: *Os 65 anos. [The 65 years.]*
- NUM: *Os anos 60. [The sixties (decade).]*
- PRON_DET: *Os nossos arqueólogos. [The (our) archaeologists.]*
- SUP_PRE: *Os melhores alunos. [The best students.]*
- SUP: *O Christofle líquido é o melhor. [The Liquid Christofle is the best.]*
- SIZE: *O quilômetro 430 da rodovia Assis Chateau Briand. [The 430 Km from Assis Chateau Briand road.]*
- COP: *O coreano seria a língua dos anjos. [(The) Koren would be the angels tongue.]*

These features were used for decision trees learning on the basis of examples from Corpus 1. After the learning process, the best resulting trees were implemented and further tested on unseen data (Corpus 2).

Table 2: New and Old subclasses

Corpus	New DDs		Old DDs	
	B-new (%)	A-new (%)	P-old (%)	R-old (%)
1	696 (52.3%)	120 (9.0%)	364 (27.35%)	151 (11.3%)
2	287 (59.5%)	21 (4.4%)	159 (33.0%)	15 (3.1%)

Table 3: Groups of Features

Groups	Feature	Description
G1	PP	Prepositional phrase.
	APP	Apposition.
	PN_APP	Appositive proper name with no explicit mark.
	REL_CL	Relative clause.
	CPN_H	When the head is a compound proper name.
	AP	Adjectival phrases.
	ADJ_PRE	Adjective preceding the head.
	NUM_PRE	Number before the head.
	NUM	Number after the head.
	PRON_DET	Other determinant besides the definite article.
	SUP_PRE	Superlative premodifier.
	SUP	Superlative alone.
	SIZE	Containing five terms or more.
G2	COP	DDs in a copular construction.
	S1	DDs that occur in the first sentence of the text.
G3	NO_ANT	DDs head is a word that does not occur previously in the text.

In [8] a set of 9 features from 6 groups (anaphora, predicative NPs, proper names, functionality, establishing relative, text position) was proposed. Our study takes 3 groups of features which are different from those presented in [8], but the features themselves are similar. They consider proper name, apposition, prepositional phrase, relative clause, superlative, copular construction, position in text, and anaphora. Our choice of 3 groups was motivated by the analysis of the NP alone, the NP plus sentence structure and position, and the NP, sentence plus previous text.

5 Decision Trees Learning

The learning algorithm used was Weka[4] *j48*, with 10 fold cross-validation. We tested different combinations of the 3 group of features for the decision trees generation: G1, G12 (=G1+G2) and G123 (=G1+G2+G3). Group G1 considers the noun phrase alone, G12 considers the noun phrase features and also information about the sentence, G123 will take into account noun phrase and sentence information but also the existence of a noun phrase with the same head as the DD in the previous text.

The first classification experiment considered the classes *Brand-new* (expressions that do not have an antecedent) and *Other* (expressions that have an antecedent). The results are presented in Table 4 and the features considered for the resulting trees in Table 5, in order of appearance in the trees. G123 presented the best results of precision, recall and F-measure for the *Brand-new* class, and the higher number of correctly classified occurrences in general. G1 alone, however, results in precision as high as other groups. It is in recall that G123 shows improvements when compared to the others. The number of features went down to 4 in G123.

Table 4: Brand-new classification
Correct(C); Precision (P); Recall (R); F-measure (F)

Classes	G1				G12				G123			
	C	P	R	F	C	P	R	F	C	P	R	F
B-new	63%	65%	55%	60%	64%	66%	57%	61%	70%	65%	88%	75%
Other		61%	70%	65%		62%	71%	60%		82%	53%	64%

Table 5: Features for classifying Brand-new DDs

	Relevant features
G1	SIZE, AP, CPN_H, ADJ_PRE,NUM_PRE, PN_APP
G12	S1, SIZE, AP, ADJ_PRE,CPN_H, PN_APP
G123	S1, NO_ANT, SUP_PRE, NUM

Table 6: New classification
Correct(C); Precision (P); Recall (R); F-measure (F)

Classes	G1				G12				G123			
	C	P	R	F	C	P	R	F	C	P	R	F
New	61%	71%	58%	64%	61%	71%	61%	66%	77%	76%	89%	82%
Other		53%	66%	59%		55%	66%	60%		81%	60%	69%

---

[4] http://www.cs.waikato.ac.nz/ml/weka

Table 7: Features for classifying New DDs

	Relevant features
G1	SIZE, NUM, PN_APP, AP, CPN_H,ADJ_PRE, PP, NUM_PRE
G12	S1, SIZE, PN_APP, NUM, AP, CPN_H,ADJ_PRE, PP, COP
G123	NO_ANT, NUM, S1, SUP_PRE

The second classification considered the classes *New* (including both *Brand-new* and *Anchored-new*) and *Other*, corresponding to *Old*. The results are presented in Table 6. Results were all higher than for *Brand-new*. G123 shows higher precision and a much higher recall than the other groups. The number of resulting attributes was again 4 in G123 (see Table 7).

6 Feature Analysis

Tables 5 and 7, in the previous section, show the features included in the generated decision trees. The larger number of attributes in a tree was 8 and 9, for G1 and G12. When NO_ANT was considered, this number went down to 4. Features APP, REL_CL, PRON_DET, SUP were never included in the resulting trees. The attributes were evaluated separately to verify which of them contributed individually and strongly for the classification.

The prominent features for *Brand-new* DD classification of each group are displayed in Table 8. In G1, SIZE was a feature that, alone, was able to reach 44% F-measure, with 67% precision. S1 in G2, although has shown 100% precision, is of limited recall, since it only applies to the first sentence of each text. In G3, NO_ANT had 73% F-measure and 64% precision. The SIZE feature is an original attribute that is simple to be verified and has presented a significant precision result if compared to the entire group G1 and also with higher precision than NO_ANT of G3. For these reasons, we analyzed decision trees generated on the basis of G1 but without the SIZE feature (G1 without SIZE), in Table 9. We noticed that the feature SIZE replaces other features commonly present in related work (prepositional phrases, relative clauses) in a satisfactory way and presents increases in the number of correctly classified descriptions and in precision in the classification of *Brand-new* DDs. When SIZE is not considered, the resulting tree includes PP, ADJ_PRE, REL_CL, which didn't appear before.

Table 8: Feature analysis
Precision (P); Recall (R); F-measure (F)

Feature Alone	P	R	F
SIZE (G1)	67%	33%	44%
S1 (G2)	100%	6%	11%
NO_ANT (G3)	64%	86%	73%

Table 9: Feature SIZE
Correct C); Precision (P); Recall (R); F-measure (F)

Features	C	P	R	F
G1	63%	65%	55%	60%
G1 without SIZE	62%	63%	58%	61%

In the *New* DD classification, the only feature that presented a distinction when applied alone was NO_ANT with 76% of correct classification, precision of 76% and recall of 86%. Other features alone were not able to distinguish the examples. When the previous text is considered as a feature, the features related to the noun phrase structure seem to loose their importance for the task.

7 Evaluation on unseen data

The decision trees learned in the experiments shown in the last section were applied to completely unseen data - Corpus 2. So we could also check the adequacy of the learned trees for this variant of Portuguese. The results are presented below.

The results of the *Brand-new* classifier applied to Corpus 2 can be seen in Table 10. We adopted as baseline (B) an algorithm that classifies all definite descriptions as *Brand-new*. As before, group G123 showed the best results. The difference from G123 to G1 and G12 was significant (99.5%). We verified significant gains in precision (from 60% to 86%) and F-measure (from 75% to 80%) considering the given baseline. Note that for the *Other* class, F-measure was never lower than 66%. G1 alone shows improvements in precision compared to the baseline (from 60% to 80%).

Table 10: Brand-new Classification
Correct(C); Precision (P); Recall (R); F-measure (F)

Classes	B				G1				G12				G123			
	C	P	R	F	C	P	R	F	C	P	R	F	C	P	R	F
B-new	59%	60%	100%	75%	68%	80%	62%	70%	69%	80%	64%	71%	78%	86%	76%	80%
Other		0	0	0		58%	77%	66%		59%	76%	66%		70%	82%	75%

For the class *New*, the results of Group G123 are significantly higher than the others (99.5%), 83% of precision and 85% of F-measure, against a baseline of 64%, and 78% (see Table 11). Again, group G1 presents improvements in comparison to the baseline (from 64% to 80%).

The results reported are even better than the ones shown for the learning phase, this is probably related to the higher number of *Brand-new* and *New* DDs in the European Portuguese Corpus (Table 2). Features related to the noun phrase structure have been used in many of the previous work, and we can see here that they alone can indicate, with considerable precision, the novelty level of DDs.

Table 11: New Classification
Correct (C); Precision (P); Recall (R); F-measure (F)

Classes	B				G1				G12				G123			
	C	P	R	F	C	P	R	F	C	P	R	F	C	P	R	F
New	64%	64%	100%	78%	65%	80%	61%	70%	67%	79%	66%	72%	81%	83%	88%	85%
Other		0	0	0		52%	73%	61%		54%	70%	61%		76%	69%	72%

8 Final Remarks

This work presented the evaluation of a classification system of *Brand-new* and *New* DDs for Portuguese. The evaluation was carried out on completely unseen data. The results were stable. Classifying *New* DDs seems to be easier than classifying *Brand-new* DDs, as we can see higher F-measure values for this class (although this was clearer in the first experiments with corpus 1). In the classification of *Brand-new* DDs, Group G123 has shown a F-measure of 80%. Group G1 has shown a precision of 80%. Group G12 doesn't show much improvement due to the limited number of cases in copular constructions and in first sentences. In the classification of *New* DDs, the attributes in G123 showed a F-measure of 85%. In G1, the precision is 80%, near to 83% seen in G123.

We were interested in the contribution of the noun phrase alone for the classification (G1), and we found that it was indeed enough for achieving high precision. These findings might have interesting consequences for other tasks, such as summarization. In an extracted summary, for instance, DDs can be analyzed solely according to their intrinsic structure, to verify if they are new in the discourse. In these cases they would not bring problems of coherence to the summary due to the lack of an antecedent.

A detailed evaluation of the features was made. We found that the feature SIZE alone presented a better precision than other features in Group 1 altogether (67%). This feature seems to replace well several complex syntactic features often used in other systems, such as relative clauses and prepositional phrases. It is a simple feature that has not been mentioned in previous work so far. The feature NO_ANT (G3) was rather relevant in both classifications, confirming the findings of [7] for English. In fact, when classifying *New* DDs it is the only salient feature. Also, this feature minimizes the importance of other features. Indeed, looking for the presence of an identical antecedent seems to do alone most of the job.

We acknowledge that related work deal with different kinds of NPs, different features, languages and data. This of course makes the comparison difficult. However, we can see that, in general, the results of the proposed system are not far from the state of the art in the area as reported by previous work (Table 12). From a initial set of 16 features our classifier achieved best measures on the basis of 4 of them. As future work, we intend to carry out an investigation into other romance languages and other classes (*Plain-old, Related-old, Anchored-new*).

Table 12: Related work

Related Work	P	R	F	#Features
[2] - Independent existential DDs	87%	78%	82%	10
[14] - Discourse new DDs	72%	69%	70%	9
[13] - Discourse new DDs	85%	82%	83%	32
[8] - Discourse new DDs	95%	86%	90%	9
We - Brand-new DDs	86%	76%	80%	16/4
We - New DDs	83%	88%	85%	16/4

References

1. C. Aone and S. Bennett. Evaluating automated and manual acquisition of anaphora resolution strategies. In *Proceedings of the 33rd Annual Meeting of the ACL*, pages 122–129, Cambridge, Massachusetts, USA, 1995.

2. D. L. Bean and E. Riloff. Corpus-based indentification of non-anaphoric noun phrases. In *Proceedings of the 37th Annual Meeting of the Association for Computational Linguistics*, pages 373–380, College Park, Maryland, USA, 1999.

3. E. Bick. *The Parsing System PALAVRAS: Automatic Grammatical Analysis of Protuguese in a Constraint Grammar Framework*. PhD thesis, Arhus University, Arhus, 2000.

4. R. M. Guillena, M. Palomar, and A. Ferrández. Processing of spanish definite descriptions. In *Proceedings of the Mexican International Conference on Artificial Intelligence*, pages 526–537. Springer-Verlag, 2000.

5. C. Müller, S. Rapp, and M. Strube. Applying co-training to reference resolution. In *Proceedings of the 40th Annual Meeting of the ACL*, pages 352–359, Philadelphia, PA, 2002.

6. C. Müller and M. Strube. Mmax: A tool for the annotation of multi-modal corpora. In *Proceedings of the 2nd IJCAI Workshop on Knowledge and Reasoning in Practical Dialogue Systems*, pages 45–50, Seattle, Washington, 2001.

7. V. Ng. Learning noun phrase anaphoricity to improve coreference resolution: Issues in representation and optimization. In *Proceedings of the 42th Annual Meeting of the Association for Computational Linguistics (ACL)*, pages 151–158, Barcelona, Spain, 2004.

8. M. Poesio, M. Alexandrov-Ksbadjov, R. Vieira, R. Goulart, and O. Uryupina. Does discourse-new detection help definite description resolution? In *Proceedings of the 6th International Workshop on Computational Semantics*, pages 236–246, Tiburg, 2005.

9. M. Poesio and R. Vieira. A corpus-based investigation of definite description use. *Computational Linguistics*, 24(2):183–216, 1998.

10. E. F. Prince. Toaward taxonomy of given-new information. In *P. Cole, editor Radical Gramatics*, pages 223–256, New York, 1981. Academic Press.

11. S. Salmon-Alt and R. Viera. Nominal expressions in multilingual corpora: Definites and demonstratives. In *Proceedings of the LREC*, pages 1627–1634, Las Palmas, 2002.

12. W. M. Soon, H. T. Ng, and D. C. Y. Lim. A machine learning approach to coreference resolution of noun phrases. In *Computational Linguistics*, volume 27, pages 521–544, 2001.

13. O. Uryupina. High-precision identification of discourse new and unique noun phrases. In *Proceedings of the 41st Annual Meeting on ACL*, pages 80–86, Sapporo, Japan, 2003.

14. R. Vieira and M. Poesio. An empirically-based system for processing definite descriptions. *Computational Linguistics*, 26(4):525–579, 2000.

Analysing Definition Questions by Two Machine Learning Approaches

Carmen Martínez and A. López López

Instituto Nacional de Astrofísica, Óptica y Electrónica
Luis Enrique Erro # 1
Santa María Tonanzintla, Puebla, 72840, México
carmen@inaoep.mx, allopez@inaoep.mx

Abstract

In automatic question answering, the identification of the correct target term (i.e. the term to define) in a definition question is critical since if the target term is not correctly identified, then all subsequent modules have no chance of providing relevant nuggets. In this paper, we present a method to tag a question sentence experimenting with two learning approaches: QTag and Hidden Markov Model. We tested the methods in five collections of questions, PILOT, TREC 2003, TREC 2004, CLEF 2004 and CLEF 2005. We performed ten-fold cross validation for each collection and we also tested with all questions together. The best accuracy rates for each collection were obtained using QTag, but with all questions together the best accuracy rate is obtained using HMM.

1. Introduction

Question Answering (QA) is a computer-based activity that tries to improve the output generated by Information Retrieval (IR) systems, and involves searching large quantities of text and "understanding" both questions and textual passages, to the degree necessary to recommend a text fragment as an answer to a question.

Regarding the input of QA systems, according to [1] there are five sorts of questions:

1. Factual questions. The answer is a number, short phrase or sentence fragment obtained from one document (e.g. When was the telegraph invented?).

2. List questions. The answer is a list of an exact number of short phrases or sentence fragments from different documents (e.g. Name 20 countries that produce coffee).

3. Definition questions. The answer is a list of complementary short phrases or sentence fragments from different documents (e.g. What are nanoparticles?, Who was Christopher Reeve?).

4. Complex questions. The question is separated in sub-questions so, to answer the complex question, the sub-questions have to be answered first (e.g. How have thefts impacted on the safety of Russia's nuclear navy, and has the theft problem been increased or decreased over time? a) What specific instances of theft do we know about? . . . e) What is meant by nuclear navy?).

5. Speculative questions. To answer this kind of question, it is necessary some kind of reasoning (e.g. Is the airline industry in trouble?).

There are seven interrogative adverbs (*who, why, how, which, what, where, when*), from these only *what* and *who* can be interrogative adverbs for definition questions since they express a request for *a concise explanation of the meaning of a word, phrase, symbol or explanation of the nature of a person or thing.*

Please use the following format when citing this chapter:

Martínez, C., López, A.L., 2006, in IFIP International Federation for Information Processing, Volume 217, Artificial Intelligence in Theory and Practice, ed. M. Bramer, (Boston: Springer), pp. 277–284.

Who can be used to formulate both factual and definition questions. So, if a question is *who is the president of Mexico?*, this is not a definition question since just requires a name, but *who is Vicente Fox?*, demands an explanation about a specific person.

Usually, when we talk about a definition we mean a sentence or a paragraph. For instance, a definition of *nugget* would be *a solid lump of a precious metal (especially gold) as found in the earth*. But according to the current state of the art in definition question answering [2], the reply is a set of only sentence fragments (precisely called nuggets). So, for the example "nugget", the answer can be the following fragments: *a solid lump, precious metal, gold, earth*.

When evaluating systems answering definition questions, a set of terms are given by assessors, who developed the questions. Also, these topics are given already classified as *vital* (important) and *ok* or non vital (less important).

Nowadays, definition questions have drawn much attention [2]. Answering definition questions is different to answering factual questions, as we described above, since in definition questions, there are several vital and non vital nuggets. In contrast, in factual questions the answer is a unique number, short phrase, or sentence fragment. Two representative works to definition questions answering are: Hildebrandt et. al. [3] presented a multi-strategy approach using a database constructed offline with surface patterns, a Web-based dictionary, and an off-the-shelf document retriever. They employed a simple pattern-based parser using regular expressions to analyze the questions. On the other hand, Tsur [4] used text categorization and a biography learner to improve the task, i.e. definition question answering. Questions analysis is rather naive based on keywords, articles, determiners, capitalization, and name recognition.

For all definition question systems, the first module is target extraction, i.e. the term to define. However, some authors [5, 6] that present an analysis of their errors, found that they obtained poor efficacy because many errors can be traced back to problems with target extraction. If the target term is not correctly identified, then all subsequent modules have no chance of providing relevant nuggets. So, given the question, a key problem to resolve is to obtain the target term since this will be the term to define. For instance, in the following questions:

What are nanoparticles?
Who is Niels Bohr?
What is Friends of the Earth?
Who was Abraham in the Old Testament?

Nanoparticles, Niels Bohr, Friends of the Earth and Abraham are target terms. We can identify three different structures of questions: when the target is a single term, e.g. a noun, when the target is a named entity, and when the target term comes with some other words that are possibly its context.

The main idea to analyze the definition question and obtain the target term and additional information (context terms) is: the interrogative adverb and the verbal form are removed from each question. Then, we apply a named entity tagger, if the result is only one word or one named entity, then there is no choice, that is the target term. For the rest of the questions, we apply a Part-Of-Speech (POS) tagger. From this, the idea is to check if the question follows a previously found pattern that can immediately reveal the target and context terms. To achieve this, we have to tag previously the known sentences to obtain a training set and make a special purpose tagger, i.e. a *question sentence tagger*. The principal tags that we used are V, for terms that can be ignored, T for the target term, and C for context terms.

The paper is organized as follows: next section describes briefly the learning algorithms: Hidden Markov Model (HMM) and QTag; Section 3 presents the method to tag question sentences; Section 4 reports experimental results; finally, some conclusions and directions for future work are presented in Section 5.

2. Learning Algorithms

In this section, we describe the two Machine Learning approaches, Hidden Markov Model and QTag, that we applied to solve the problem.

2.1. Hidden Markov Model

A Hidden Markov Model (HMM), as Rabiner describes in [7], is a Markov chain, where each state generates an observation. An HMM is specified by a five-tuple (S,K,Π,A,B), where S is the set of states, K the output alphabet and Π, A, B are the probabilities for the initial state, state transitions, and symbol emission, respectively.

Given appropriate values of S,K,A,B, and Π, the HMM can be used as a generator to return an observation sequence

$$O = O_1 O_2 \cdots O_T$$

where each observation O_t is one of the symbols from B, and T is the number of observations in the sequence.

There are three basic questions that we want to know about an HMM:

1. Given the observation sequence $O = O_1O_2 \cdots O_T$ and a model $\lambda = (A, B, \Pi)$, how do we efficiently compute $P(O|\lambda)$, the probability of the observation sequence, given the model?.

2. Given the observation sequences O, and the model λ, how do we choose a corresponding state sequence $Q = q_1q_2 \cdots q_t$ which is optimal in some meaningful sense (i.e., best "explains" the observations)?

3. How do we adjust the model parameters λ to maximize $P(O|\lambda)$?

In question 1, given a model and a sequence of observations, how do we compute the probability that the observed sequence was produced by the model. Question 2 is intended to uncover the hidden part of the model, i.e., to find the "correct" state sequence. Question 3 points to the process to optimize the model parameters to best describe how a given observation sequence is generated.

2.2. Applying HMMs to POS tagging

HMMs can be used to POS tagging but for this task, parameters can not be randomly initialized, since this would leave the tagging task too unconstrained. The symbol emission probabilities is initialized using the method of Jelinek [8]:

$$b_{j.l} = \frac{b_{j.l}^* C(w^l)}{\sum_{w^m} b_{j.m}^* C(w^m)}$$

where the sum is over all words w^m in the dictionary, and

$$b_{j.l}^* = \begin{cases} 0 & \text{if } t^j \text{ is not a part of speech allowed for } w^l \\ \frac{1}{T(w^l)} & \text{otherwise} \end{cases}$$

where $T(w^j)$ is the number of tags allowed for w^j.

2.3. QTag

QTag [9] is a robust probabilistic parts-of-speech tagger. This is a program that reads text and, for each token in the text, returns the part-of-speech (e.g. noun, verb, punctuation, etc). QTag was advantageous for our needs because we can create our own resource files for a different language or tagset, we simply supply a pre-tagged training corpus. The size of the training data is obviously important for the accuracy of the tagging procedure.

3. The Method to Tag Question Sentences

The process to obtain the target term is the following:

We remove the interrogative adverb (*who* or *what*) and the verbal form (*is, are* or *was*) from each question. For example, from the questions given above, we get:

> nanoparticles?
> Niels Bohr?
> Friends of the Earth?
> Abraham in the Old Testament?

Then, we apply a named entity tagger (LingPipe) [10]. For the same questions, we obtain the following:

> nanoparticles?
> < type="PERSON" Niels Bohr > ?
> Friends of the < type="LOCATION" Earth > ?
> Abraham in the Old < type="PERSON" Testament > ?

CC	Coordinating Conjunction
CD	Cardinal number
DT	Determiner
IN	Preposition or Subordinating conjunction
JJ	Adjective
NN	Noun, singular or mass
NNS	Noun, plural
NNP	Proper noun, singular
NNPS	Proper noun, plural
'	'
,	,
''	''
''	''
(	(
)	)
?	end

Table 1. Subset of tags produced by MBT.

V	void
T	target
C	context
,	,
,	,
''	''
''	''
(	(
)	)
?	end

Table 2. Tags used by the Question Sentence Tagger.

If the result is a single word or a named entity (as the first and second examples), then that is the target term. For the rest of the questions, we apply a Part-Of-Speech (POS) tagger, in our case Memory Based Tagging (MBT) [11] that, by the way, has a better performance tagging English questions than QTag. Table 1 details the subset of tags obtained so far. For the examples that we are using to illustrate and two additional examples, we obtain:

> Friends/NNPS of/IN the/DT Earth/NNP ?/.
> Abraham/NNP in/IN the/DT Old/NNP Testament/NNP ?/.
> Treasury/NNP Secretary/NNP
> Robert/NNP Rubin/NNP ?/.
> the/DT International/NNP Committee/NNP
> of/IN the/DT Red/NNP Cross/NNP ?/.

By tagging the sentence with part-of-speech, we generalize and work thereafter with patterns of questions, rather than raw text. Named entities within a context are also processed in this way (as noun phrases) in order to identify simultaneously target (named entity) and context. For the examples, we keep the following sequences of tags:

> NNPS IN DT NNP ?
> NNP IN DT NNP NNP ?
> NNP NNP NNP NNP ?
> DT NNP NNP IN DT NNP NNP ?

Then we tagged these sequences of part-of-speech labels according to our needs to obtain a training set and reach a special purpose tagger, i.e. a *question sentence tagger*. This is done in two ways, using QTag and HMM. Table 2 shows tags used by the *question sentence tagger*.

For the previous examples, we have

NNPS/T IN/V DT/V NNP/C ?/?
NNP/T IN/V DT/V NNP/C NNP/C ?/?
NNP/C NNP/C NNP/T NNP/T ?/?
DT/V NNP/T NNP/T IN/V
DT/V NNP/C NNP/C ?/?

These examples are part of the training set. Now if we have a new question, Who is Akbar the Great?, we apply the previous process:

Who is Akbar the Great?
Akbar the Great?
Akbar the < type="ORGANIZATION" Great > ?
Akbar/NNP the/DT Great/NNP ?/.
NNP DT NNP ?

The last sequence (NNP DT NNP ?) is tagged by the *question sentence tagger* using QTag or HMM. The correct tags are: NNP/T DT/V NNP/C ?/?, since "Great" serves as a context helpful to focus the search for a definition of the target term "Akbar".

4. Experimental Setting

We used definition questions from five collections:

COLLECTION	Simple	Complex	Total
PILOT	17	8	25
TREC 2003	31	19	50
TREC 2004	36	29	65
CLEF 2004	65	25	90
CLEF 2005	26	24	50
Total	175	105	280

In this table, by "simple" we refer to the questions where the target term is a single word or named entity and "complex" when the target term comes with some other words that are possibly its context. The collection PILOT [2] contains questions used in the pilot evaluation of definition questions performed by NIST and AQUAINT program contractors. TREC 2003 and TREC 2004 are sets of definition questions used to evaluate Questions Answering systems in the Text REtrieval Conference [12] in 2003 and 2004 respectively. The collections CLEF 2004 and CLEF 2005 are questions obtained from the Cross Language Evaluation Forum [13] in 2004 and 2005.

As mentioned above, we developed also a *question sentence tagger* using Hidden Markov Models (HMM) and QTag. An HMM is specified by a five-tuple (S, K, Π, A, B), where S is the set of states (each state is a tag), K the output alphabet, Π the initial state probabilities, A the state transition probabilities and B the symbol emission probabilities. The values used when the collection is ALL, are:

$$S = \{ \text{BEGIN}, V, T, C, ', ', '', '', (,), ? \}$$
$$K = \{ \text{BEGIN}, DT, NNP, NN, NNPS, NNS, JJ,$$
$$IN, CC, CD, ', ', '', '', (,), ? \}$$
$$\Pi = \{ 1\ 0\ 0\ 0\ 0\ 0\ 0\ 0\ 0\ 0\ 0 \}$$

The transition probabilities (A) are generated randomly and improved with the training examples and B is initialized using the method of Jelinek described in the section 2.2. In order to form the training set used by QTag, we tagged the sequences of part-of-speech labels with the tags shown in Table 2, those tags are the same of the set S in the HMM.

	Complex	Global
PILOT	62.50	88
TREC 2003	33.33	76
TREC 2004	31.03	69.23
CLEF 2004	84	95.56
CLEF 2005	91.66	96
Average	60.50	84.96

Table 3. Comparison of the accuracy rates of the Question Sentence Tagger using QTag

	Complex	Global
PILOT	50	84
TREC 2003	27.78	74
TREC 2004	24.14	66.15
CLEF 2004	80	94.44
CLEF 2005	83.33	92
Average	53.05	82.12

Table 4. Comparison of the accuracy rates of the Question Sentence Tagger using HMM

5. Results

We performed two different experiments. In the first experiment, we tested separately each collection of questions, Table 3 shows the accuracy rates using QTag and the Table 4 shows the accuracy rates using HMM. In all tests, we made a ten-fold cross validation and the results are the average of five runs.

From the first experiment, we can observe that QTag performs better than HMM on the questions of interest, possibly because that is the kind of processing it was designed for. On the other hand, HMM performs poorly, caused by the small size of the training sets.

In the second experiment, we joined four collections of questions, PILOT, TREC 2003, TREC 2004, CLEF 2004 to form the collection that we called ALL. The collection ALL_1 contains the questions from the five collections. The collection ALL can be used as baseline since we can test if our method improves its performance when the training set increases. Table 5 shows the accuracy rates using QTag and the Table 6 displays the accuracy rates using HMM. Also we performed a ten-fold cross validation for each test.

The results of the second experiments show that HMM behaves better than QTag, from the beginning, with an increased training set. However, QTag is more sensitive to the increment in size of the training set, reflected in a higher percentage of improvement.

As one can observe, the results show that the method is feasible and delivers an acceptable level of accuracy for both approaches. As we increase the training set of question patterns, we expect to increase also the accuracy identifying target and context terms.

Our questions sentence tagger, in either version, had trouble tagging sentences with patterns under-represented. From very few examples, the pattern can not be learnt properly during training. Two instances of this kind of patterns are:

what is Micro Compact Car (MCC)?
NNP NN NN ?
what is the Order of the Solar Temple?
DT NNP IN DT NNP NNP ?

This problem will be overcome as the size of the training set increases.

	Complex	Global
ALL	38.75	78.70
ALL_1	51.43	81.80
% of Improvement	32.72	3.94

Table 5. Comparison of the accuracy rates of the Question Sentence Tagger using QTag

	Complex	Global
ALL	51.25	83.04
ALL_1	60	85
% of Improvement	17.07	2.36

Table 6. Comparison of the accuracy rates of the Question Sentence Tagger using HMM

6. Conclusions and Future Work

We have presented a method to identify the target term in an automatic, fast and flexible way. The method can be extended easily for new complex questions. As far as we know, definition question analysis has not been approached as a special tagging task, and given the results, seems very promising since questions are usually short and following certain patterns.

Moreover, with this method, we have additional information for the search of passages or documents for the answer, since the method identifies the target term along some other terms that are the context and valuable to refine the search for the definition.

Another advantage of our approach with a special purpose tagger is that we do not depend completely on a named entity tagger, specially in complex questions. For instance, the tagger can miss a named entity within a context, but the question tagger can identify target and context adequately.

Future work includes extending the corpus to train, and explore ensemble methods to improve the special purpose tagging. And finally, we have to integrate this method to the complete process of definition questions answering.

7. Acknowledgements

This work was partially supported by a CONACyT research grant U39957 and the scholarship 157233 for the first author.

References

[1] Dan Modolvan, Marius Pasca, Sanda Harabagiu, and Mihai Surdeanu. Performance Issues and Error Analysis in an Open-Domain Question Answering System. In *Proceedings of the 40th Annual Meeting of the Association for Computational Linguistics (ACL)*, pages 33–40, Philadelphia, July 2002.

[2] Ellen M. Voorhees. Evaluating Answers to Definition Questions. *NIST*, pages 1–3, 2003.

[3] Wesley Hildebrandt, Boris Katz, and Jimmy Lin. Answering Definition Question Using Multiple Knowledge Sources. In *Proceedings of HLT/NAACL*, pages 49–56, Boston, 2004.

[4] Oren Tsur. Definitional Question-Anwering Using Trainable Text Classifiers. Master's thesis, Institute of Logic Language and Computation, University of Amsterdam, 2003.

[5] S. Harabagiu and F. Lacatusu. Strategies for Advanced Question Answering. In *Proceedings of the Workshop on Pragmatics of Question Answering at HLT-NAACL*, pages 1–9, 2004.

[6] Jinxi Xu, Ana Licuanan, and Ralph Weischedel. TREC 2003 QA at BBN: Answering Definitional Questions. In *The Twelfth Text Retrieval Conference (TREC 2003)*, pages 28–35, 2003.

[7] Lawrence Rabiner. A Tutorial on Hidden Markov Models and Selected Applications in Speech Recognition. In *Proc. IEEE*, volume 77, pages 257–286, 1989.

[8] Christopher D. Manning and Hinrich Schutze. *Foundations of Statistical Natural Languaje Processing*. The MIT Press Cambridge, Massachusetts, London, England, 1999.

[9] Oliver Manson. Qtag-A portable probabilistic tagger. *Corpus Research, The University of Birmingham, U.K.*, 1997.

[10] http://www.alias-i.com/lingpipe/index.html.

[11] Walter Daelemans, Jakub Zavrel, Peter Berck, and Steven Gillis. MBT: A Memory-Based Part of Speech Tagger-Generator. In *Proceedings of the Fourth Workshop on Very Large Corpora, Copenhagen, Denmark,*, pages 14–27, 1996.

[12] http://trec.nist.gov/.

[13] http://www.clef-campaign.org/.

Fuzzy Rule-Based Hand Gesture Recognition*

Benjamín C. Bedregal[1], Antônio C. R. Costa[2] and Graçaliz P. Dimuro[2]

[1] Department of Informatics and Applied Mathematics
Federal University of Rio Grande do Norte, Brazil
[2] Informatics School, Graduate Programme in Computer Science
Catholic University of Pelotas, Brazil
bedregal@dimap.ufrn.br, {rocha,liz}@ucpel.tche.br

Abstract. This paper introduces a fuzzy rule-based method for the recognition of hand gestures acquired from a data glove, with an application to the recognition of some sample hand gestures of LIBRAS, the Brazilian Sign Language. The method uses the set of angles of finger joints for the classification of hand configurations, and classifications of segments of hand gestures for recognizing gestures. The segmentation of gestures is based on the concept of monotonic gesture segment, sequences of hand configurations in which the variations of the angles of the finger joints have the same sign (non-increasing or non-decreasing). Each gesture is characterized by its list of monotonic segments. The set of all lists of segments of a given set of gestures determine a set of finite automata, which are able to recognize every such gesture.

1 Introduction

Fuzzy set theory [1] is the oldest and most widely reported component of present-day soft computing (or computational intelligence), which deals with the design of flexible information processing systems [2], with applications in control systems [3], decision making [4], expert systems [5] etc. The significance of fuzzy set theory in the realm of pattern recognition was justified in [2].

A fuzzy system encompasses the implementation of a (usually nonlinear) function, defined by a linguistic description of the relationship between its input variables. Standard fuzzy systems presents an architecture such as the one depitecd in Fig. 1. The *fuzzificator* is the component that computes the membership degrees of the crisp input values to the linguistic terms (fuzzy sets) associated to each input linguistic variable. The *rule base* is composed by inference rules associating linguistic terms of input linguistic variables to linguistic terms of output linguistic values. The *information manager* is the component for searching in the rule base the adequate rules to be applied for the current input. The *inference machine* gives the membership degrees of the output values in the output sets, by the application of the rules selected in the rule base.

---

* This work is partially supported by FAPERGS and CNPq (Proc. 470871/2004-0, Proc. 470556/2004-8).

Please use the following format when citing this chapter:

Bedregal, B.C., da Rocha Costa, A.C., Dimuro, G.P., 2006, in IFIP International Federation for Information Processing, Volume 217, Artificial Intelligence in Theory and Practice, ed. M. Bramer, (Boston: Springer), pp. 285–294.

Finally, the *defuzzificator* determines a single output value as a function of the output values and their membership degrees to the output sets.

We remark, however, that there are many approximate methods (e.g., classification or pattern recognition procedures) that do not produce a single final result. On the contrary, they may give several alternative solutions to a single problem (e.g., the different classes to which a given input may belong). Examples of such methods are several fuzzy methods for pattern recognition [2], such as fuzzy relations, fuzzy clustering, fuzzy neural systems etc. [6], with applications to signature verification [7], and face recognition [8], for example. Thus, for some specific applications, it is reasonable to consider a fuzzy rule based method, which determines a system architecture as shown in Fig. 2.

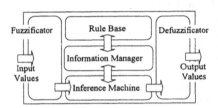

Fig. 1. Architecture of standard fuzzy systems.

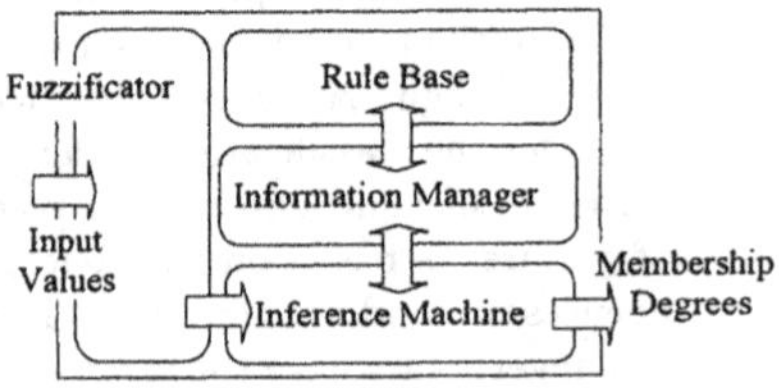

Fig. 2. Architecture of a fuzzy rule based system.

It is possible to find an extensive literature about methods and systems for gesture recognition in general, and hand gesture recognition in particular. There are systems for the recognition of 3-D and 2-D gestures captured by different devices (data gloves, cameras etc.) [9], systems for the graphical recognition of traces left on tablet devices [10] etc. Among several methods for gesture recognition, there are methods based on fuzzy logic and fuzzy sets, methods based on neural networks, hybrid neuro-fuzzy methods [11], fuzzy rule [12] and finite state machine [13] based methods, methods based on hidden Markov models [14] etc. In particular, considering methods for sign language recognition, some literature can be found related to fuzzy methods, such as, for example, fuzzy decision trees [15] and neuro-fuzzy systems [16].

In this paper, we propose a fuzzy rule-based method for the recognition of hand configurations and hand gestures acquired from a data glove, with an application to the recognition of some sample hand gestures of LIBRAS, the Brazilian Sign Language [17]. The method uses the set of angles of finger joints for the classification of hand configurations, and classifications of sequences of hand configurations for recognizing gestures. The segmentation of gestures is based on the concept of *monotonic gesture segment*, sequences of gestures in which the variations of the angles of the finger joints have the same sign (non-increasing or non-decreasing).

Any monotonic gesture segment is characterized by an initial hand configuration, a terminal hand configuration and a list of relevant intermediate configurations. Each gesture is characterized by a list of monotonic segments. That set of lists of segments determine a set of finite automata, which are able to recognize the gestures being considered.

The paper is organized as follows. In Sect. 2, we introduce our fuzzy rule-based method for hand gesture recognition. A case study is discussed in Sect. 3, with the recognition of LIBRAS hand gestures. Section 4 is the Conclusion.

2 The Fuzzy Rule Based for Hand Gesture Recognition

The objective is to recognize some hand gestures with data obtained from a data glove. Consider a hypothetical data glove with 15 sensors, as shown in Fig. 3. The fingers are labelled as: F1 (little finger), F2 (ring finger), F3 (middle finger), F4 (index finger) and F5 (thumb). The joints in the fingers are labelled as J1 (the knuckle), J2 and J3, for each finger. A separation between two fingers is labelled as Sij to indicate that it is a separation between the fingers Fi and Fj.

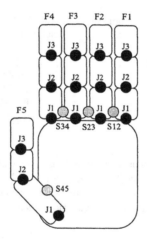

Fig. 3. Localization of sensors in the data glove.

Since any movement can be represented as a sequence of frames, a hand movement using a data glove is represented as a sequence of hand configurations, one for each discrete time instant. That is, at each time instant, the data glove sensors should provide the set of angles of joints and finger separation that characterizes a hand configuration.

In order to simulate this data transfer, a random generator of hand configurations was implemented, generating at each instant one hand configuration represented by a tuple of angles corresponding to each sensor shown in Fig. 3:

((F1J1,F1J2,F1J3), S12, (F2J1,F2J2,F2J3), S23, (F3J1,F3J2,F3J3), S34, (F4J1,F4J2,F4J3), S45, (F5J1,F5J2,F5J3))

Given a hand configuration c and a sensor s, denote the value of each sensor angle by $s(c)$, e.g., F1J1(c), S45(c) etc.

2.1 Fuzzification

To each sensor corresponds a linguistic variable, whose values are linguistic terms representing typical angles of joints and separations. For the joints in the fingers (linguistic variables F1J1, F1J2, F1J3 etc.) the linguistic terms are: STRAIGHT, CURVED and BENT. For the separations between fingers F1 and F2, F2 and F3, F4 and F5 (linguistic variable S12, S23, S45), the linguistic terms are: CLOSED, SEMI-OPEN and OPEN. For the separations between fingers F3 and F4 (linguistic variable S34), the linguistic terms are: CROSSED, CLOSED, SEMI-OPEN and OPEN. Tables 1 and 2 present the notations used for linguistic terms of linguistic variables representing joints and separations, respectively. Figures 4, 5, 6, 7 and 8 show the fuzzification adopted for those variables.

Table 1. Linguistic terms of linguistic variables representing finger joints.

Linguistic Term	Notation
STRAIGHT	St
CURVED	Cv
BENT	Bt

Table 2. Linguistic terms of linguistic variables representing finger separations.

Linguistic Term	Notation
CROSSED	Cr
CLOSED	Cd
SEMI-OPEN	SOp
OPEN	Op

The hand configuration is the main linguistic variable of the system, denoted by HC, whose linguistic terms are names of hand configurations, which names are application dependent. For instance, in Sect. 3, names of Brazilian Sign Language (LIBRAS) hand configurations (see Fig. 10) were used for such linguistic terms.

2.2 The Recognition Process

The hand gesture recognition process is divided into four steps: (1) recognition of finger configurations, (2) recognition of hand configurations, (3) segmentation of the gesture in monotonic hand segments and (4) recognition of the sequence of monotonic hand segments.

For the step 1 (*recognition of finger configurations*), 27 possible finger configurations are considered. These configurations are codified in the following format: XYZ, where X is the value of the linguistic variable corresponding to the first joint J1, Y is the value of the linguistic variable corresponding to the second joint J2 and Z is the value of the linguistic variable corresponding to the third joint J3. For example, StStSt is used to indicate that the three joints are

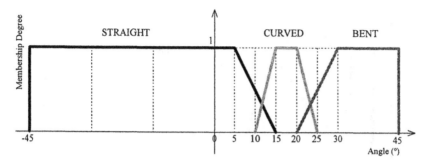

Fig. 4. Fuzzification of the linguistic variable of the joint F5J2 in the thumb finger F5.

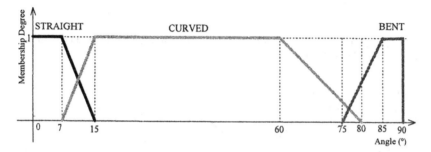

Fig. 5. Fuzzification of the linguistic variables of remaining finger joints.

STRAIGHT, StCdCd indicates that the first joint is STRAIGHT whereas the others are CURVED etc.

The 27 possible finger configurations determine 27 inference rules that calculate membership degree of each finger to each configuration. For example:

```
If F4J1 is STRAIGHT and F4J2 is CURVED and F4J3 is CURVED
Then F4 is StCdCd
```

The next step is 2 (*recognition of hand configurations*), where the hand configuration is determined, considering each finger configuration and each separation between fingers. For example, the rule for the hand configuration [G] of LIBRAS (see Fig. 10) is described below:

```
If F1 is BtBtSt and S12 is Cd and F2 is BtBtSt and S23 is Cd and
F3 is BtBtSt and S34 is Cd and F4 is StStSt and S45 is Cd and
F5 is StStSt
Then HC is [G]
```

In 3 (*segmentation of the gesture in monotonic hand segments*), we divide each gesture in a sequence of k limit hand configurations $l_1, \ldots, l_k$, where l_1 is the initial gesture configuration and l_k is the terminal gesture configuration.

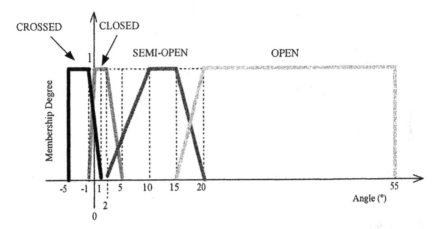

Fig. 6. Fuzzification of the linguistic variable of the separation S34 between the middle finger F3 and the index finger F4.

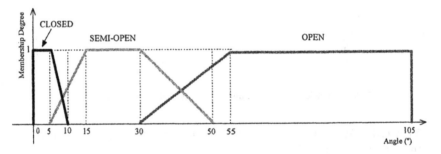

Fig. 7. Fuzzification of the linguistic variable of the separation S45 between the index finger F4 and the thumb finger F5.

The limit configurations are such that, for each c between l_i and l_{i+1}, and for each sensor s, $s(c) - s(l_i)$ has the same sign of $s(l_{i+1}) - s(l_i)$, for $i = 1, \ldots, k-1$ (a difference equal to 0 is compatible with both negative and positive signs).

The limit hand configurations are the points that divide the gesture into monotonic segments, that is, segments in which each sensor produces angle variations with constant (or null) sign. For each monotonic segment $l_i l_{i+1}$, l_i and l_{i+1} are its initial and terminal hand configurations, respectively.

The procedure for step 3 is the following. To find any monotonic segment $l_i l_{i+1}$, the next n configurations sent by the data glove after l_i are discarded, until a configuration c_{n+1}, such that the signs of $s(c_{n+1}) - s(c_n)$ and $s(c_n) - s(l_1)$ are not the same (or, c_{n+1} is the last configuration of the gesture). Then, c_n (resp., c_{n+1}) is the terminal hand configuration l_{i+1} of the considered monotonic segment, and also coincides with the initial configuration of the next segment

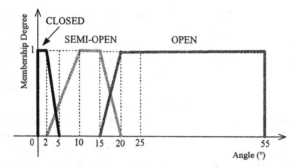

Fig. 8. Fuzzification of the linguistic variables of the separations between remaining fingers.

$l_{i+1}l_{i+2}$ (if there is one). The process starts with $l_i = l_1$, which is the initial gesture configuration, and is repeated until the end of the gesture, generating the list of k limit hand configurations.

In 4 (*recognition of the sequence of monotonic hand segments*), the recognition of each monotonic segment l_il_{i+1} is performed using a list of reference hand configurations $r_1, r_2, \ldots, r_m$ that characterizes the segment, where r_1 and r_m are the initial and terminal hand configurations of the segment, respectively. A monotonic segment is recognized by checking that it contains its list of reference hand configurations. The process is equivalent to a recognition based on a linear finite automaton (shown in Fig. 9), where $l_i = r_1$ and $l_{i+1} = r_m$.

Fig. 9. Automaton for the recognition of monotonic segments.

3 Case Study: Hand Gestures of LIBRAS

As any other sign language (e.g., ASL – American Sign Language, used in the USA), LIBRAS (Língua Brasileira de Sinais – Brazilian Sign Language) is a natural language endowed with all the complexity normally found in the oral-auditive languages. Thus, it can be analyzed at all the various linguistic levels encountered in such languages, such as the "phonetic-phonological" level (also called "cheremic" level, for its relationship with the movement of the hands), the syntactic level, and the semantic and pragmatic levels [17].

As a language of the specific modality called visual-gestural, however, the elements that constitute many of those linguistic levels are of a specific nature.

For instance, the main parameters that characterize the "phonological" units of sign languages are: the configurations of the hands used in the gestures, the main spatial location (relative to the persons who is signing) where the movements of the gestures are performed, the different movements (of the fingers in the hand, of the hands and arms in the space, of the whole body) that constitute the gesture, the facial expressions that express different syntactic, semantic and pragmatic marks during the production of the signs etc.

In the various works on automatic recognition of sign languages that have been developed along the years (see Sect. 1) the recognition of hand gestures has occupied a prominent place. Using capture devices like data gloves and cameras, hand gestures have been analyzed and recognized in order to allow the computer understanding of such basic component of sign languages.

To support that recognition process, a reference set of hand configurations is usually adopted, driven either from the linguistic literature on sign languages, or dynamically developed by the experimenters with an ad hoc purpose. For our purposes, we have chosen a standard set of hand configurations (some of them shown in Fig. 10), taken from the linguistic literature on LIBRAS [17].

Since we take the set of hand configurations from the literature, our method requires that each sign be thoroughly characterized in terms of its monotonic segments and the sequences of hand configurations that constitute such segments, and that the identification of the monotonic segments and hand configurations be manually provided to the system. Of course, a capture device such as a data glove can be used to help to identify the typical values of the angles of the finger joints, but the final decision about the form of the membership functions that characterize the linguistic terms used in the system has to be explicitly taken and manually transferred to the system.

We illustrate here the application of the method by the definition of the necessary parameters for the recognition of the hand gestures that constitute the sign CURIOUS, in LIBRAS. CURIOUS is a sign performed with a single hand placed right in front of the dominant eye of the signer, with the palm up and hand pointing forward. The initial hand configuration is the one named [G1] in Fig. 10. The gesture consists of the monotonic movement necessary to perform the transition from [G1] to [X] and back to [G1] again, such movements been repeated a few times (usually two or three). Thus, a possible analysis of the hand gestures that constitute the sign CURIOUS in LIBRAS is:

Initial configuration: [G1]
Monotonic segment S1: [G1]-[G1X]-[X]
Monotonic segment S2: [X]-[G1X]-[G1]
State transition function for the recognition automaton: see Fig. 11.

To support the recognition of the monotonic segments of CURIOUS, we have chosen to use one single intermediate hand configuration, [G1X]. It is an intermediate configuration that does not belong to the reference set (Fig. 10) and whose characterization in terms of the set of membership functions for linguistic terms was defined in an ad hoc fashion, for the purpose of the recognition of CURIOUS. Together with [G1] and [X], it should be added to the list of hand configurations used by the recognition system.

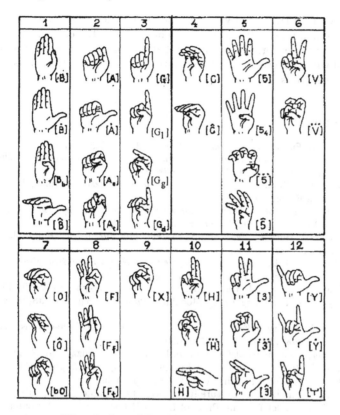

Fig. 10. Some LIBRAS hand configurations.

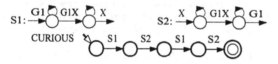

Fig. 11. Automaton for the recognition of hand gestures of the sign CURIOUS.

4 Conclusion and Final Remarks

We presented a fuzzy rule-based for the recognition of hand gestures. The method is highly dependent on a detailed previous analysis of the features of the gestures to be recognized, and on the manual transfer of the results of that analysis to the recognition system. This makes it suitable for the application to the recognition of hand gestures of sign languages, because of the extensive analysis that linguists that have already done of those languages. Prototypes of a random gesture generator and of the gesture recognizer were implemented in the programming language Python. In the fuzzification process, we considered only trapezoidal fuzzy sets and the minimum (or Gödel) t-norm, motivated by simplicity. Initial experimentation indicated promising results. Future work is concerned with the recognition of arm gestures, by including the analysis of the angles of arm joints.

References

1. L.A. Zadeh, Fuzzt Sets, *Information Control* **8**, 338–353 (1965).
2. S. Mitra, S.K. Pal, Fuzzy Sets in Pattern Recognition and Machine Intelligence, *Fuzzy Sets and Systems* **156**, 381–386 (2005).
3. G. Chen, T.T. Pham, *Fuzzy Sets, Fuzzy Logic, and Fuzzy Control Systems* (CRC Press, Boca Raton, 2001).
4. C. Carlsson, R. Fuller, *Fuzzy Reasoning in Decision Making and Optimization* (Physiva-Verlag Springer, Heidelberg, 2002).
5. W. Siler, J.J. Buckley, *Fuzzy Expert Systems and Fuzzy Reasoning* (John Wiley & Sons, Inc., New York, 2004).
6. C.T. Lin, C.S.G. Lee, *Neural Fuzzy Systems: A Neuro-fuzzy Synergism to Intelligent Systems* (Prentice Hall, Upper Saddle River, 1996).
7. M. Hanmandlu, M.H.M. Yusof, V.K. Madasu, Off-line Signature Verification and Forgery Detection Using Fuzzy Modeling, *Pattern Recognition* **38**(3), 341–356 (2005).
8. K. Kwak, W. Pedrycz, Face Recognition Using a Fuzzy Fisherface Classifier, *Pattern Recognition* **38**(10), 1717–1732 (2005).
9. O. Bimber, Continuous 6DOF Gesture Recognition: a Fuzzy-logic Approach, in: Proc. of VII Intl. Conf. in Central Europe on Computer Graphics, Visualization and Interactive Digital Media, V. 1. (1999), pp. 24–30
10. J. Ou, X. Chen, J. Yang, Gesture Recognition for Remote Collaborative Physical Tasks Using Tablet PCs, in: Proc. of IX IEEE Intl. Conf. on Computer Vision, Work. on Multimedia Technologies in E-Learning and Collaboration (Nice, 2003).
11. N.D. Binh, T. Ejima, Hand Gesture Recognition Using Fuzzy Neural Network, in: Proc. ICGST Conf. Graphics, Vision and Image Proces (Cairo, 2005), pp. 1–6.
12. M. Su, A Fuzzy Rule-based Approach to Spatio-temporal Hand Gesture Recognition, *IEEE Transactions on Systems, Man and Cybernetics, Part C* **30**(2). 276–281 (2000).
13. P. Hong, M. Turk, T.S. Huang, Gesture Modeling and Recognition Using FSM, in: Proc. of IEEE Conf. Face and Gesture Recognition (Grenoble, 2000), pp. 410–415.
14. G. Rigoll, A. Kosmala, S. Eickeler, High Perfomance Real-time Gesture Recognition Using Hidden Markov Models, in: Gesture and Sign Language in Human-Computer Interaction, Proc. of International Gesture Workshop, Bielefeld, 1997, edited by I. Wachsmuth, M. Frölich (n. 1371 in LNAI, Springer, 1998), pp. 69–80.
15. G. Fang, W. Gao, D. Zhao, Large Vocabulary Sign Language Recognition Based on Fuzzy Decision Trees, *IEEE Transactions on Systems, Man and Cybernertics* **34**(3), 305–314 (2004).
16. O. Al-Jarrah, A. Halawani, Recognition of Gestures in Arabic Sign Language Using Neuro-fuzzy Systems, *Artificial Intelligence* **133**(1–2), 117–138 (2001).
17. L.F. Brito, *Por uma Gramática de Línguas de Sinais* (Tempo Brasileiro, Rio de Janeiro, 1995) (in Portuguese).

Comparison of distance measures for historical spelling variants

S. Kempken, W. Luther, and T.Pilz

Institute of Computer Science and Interactive Systems
Universität Duisburg-Essen
D-47048 Duisburg, Lotharstr. 65, Germany
{kempken, luther, pilz}@informatik.uni-duisburg.de

Abstract. This paper describes the comparison of selected distance measures in their applicability for supporting retrieval of historical spelling variants (hsv). The interdisciplinary project Rule-based search in text databases with nonstandard orthography develops a fuzzy full-text search engine for historical text documents. This engine should provide easier text access for experts as well as interested amateurs. The FlexMetric framework enhances the distance measure algorithm found to be most efficient according to the results of the evaluation. This measure can be used for multiple applications, including searching, post-ranking, transformation and even reflection about one's own language.

1 Introduction

In recent years, many countries have started retro-digitization projects of precious originals. Events like the disastrous fire in the German Herzogin Anna Amalia Library, a World Heritage Site, in September 2004 show plainly the importance of such preservation, at least of the intellectual contents. Furthermore, these projects make accessible historical texts by building digital libraries that are of interest to scholars of all text-focused disciplines (philologists, historians, linguists, etc.) as well as interested amateurs. Right now, more than one hundred scientific initiatives are involved in the digitization of text collections, electronic editions, rare manuscripts, dictionaries, charters and illustrated books. Most of these initiatives provide digitized facsimiles, some offer additional full text. Hockey [11] provides a survey of important international projects.

The amount of time required to build a digital archive is not to be underestimated. Therefore, many retro-digitization projects focus on the constructional steps of the digitization process, which involve digitizing as well as tagging and aligning the text. Subsequent steps, like manual post processing or elaborate search functions, often need to be put at the bottom of the list. Compact Memory, a project for the digitization of historical Jewish periodicals, for example, combines a comely interface with a respectable archive and is well used. But, as it is a publicly funded project, the operator cannot devote his resources to manually revising optical character recognition (OCR) errors in the digitized texts

Please use the following format when citing this chapter:

Kempken, S., Luther, W., Pilz, T., 2006, in IFIP International Federation for Information Processing, Volume 217, Artificial Intelligence in Theory and Practice, ed. M. Bramer, (Boston: Springer), pp. 295–304.

or to offering advanced search capabilities. A reliable search engine, however, is the means that makes the data fully accessible.

Particularly historical but also regional texts often involve another important problem, apart from OCR errors: they contain spelling variants. German texts prior to 1901, when a major reform of German orthography took place, are not standardized. The result is a reduced recall ratio in those texts, due to queries that do not cover all possible spellings. The frequency of variant spelling increases significantly with the age of the text documents. Figure 1 shows the amount in percent of nonstandard tokens in 35 historical German texts from 1463 to 1876.

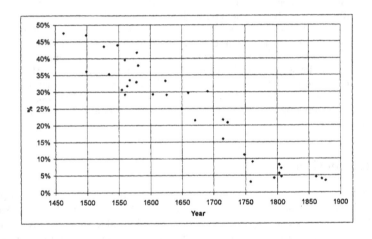

Fig. 1. Frequency of variant spellings in historical text documents

Historical spellings are by no means solely a German problem. Spelling variation is known to occur in English historical corpora also. An initiative by the University Centre for Computer Research on Language (UCREL) of Lancaster University and the University of Central Lancashire (UCLan) has developed a VARiant Detector (VARD) trained on 16th to 19th century data [18].

The interdisciplinary project Rule-based Search in Text Databases with Nonstandard Orthography (RSNSR) supported by the Deutsche Forschungsgemeinschaft (DFG [German Research Foundation]) is currently developing a fuzzy trainable full-text search engine for historical text documents [17]. Since our main focus is the time period from 1700 - 1900, regarding the results shown in Figure 1, 2 - 25% variant spellings are estimated for those texts. In the worst case, up to one quarter of a text will consist of nonstandard spellings.

In contrast to capacious glossary projects like the *Deutsches Rechtswörterbuch (DRW)* of the *Heidelberger Akademie der Wissenschaften* or *Das Deutsche Wörterbuch von Jacob und Wilhelm Grimm auf CD-ROM und im Internet (DBW)* of the Universität Trier, RSNSR uses linguistic as well as statistical rules to represent highly varied spellings. These rules can be automatically derived from evidence data with the possibility of further expert adjustment. This allows a search engine to proceed successfully even for rare spellings without the need of extensive manual operation. A Java-based search engine with a phonetic rule set has already been built [16]. Future versions will be easily integrable into other projects. We are already cooperating with Deutsch Diachron Digital (DDD) [5], which contains texts from Old High German to Modern German. In 2006, after a prototyped solution has been achieved, we plan to integrate the fully functional search engine into the retro-digitization project Nietzsche-CD. In cooperation with UCREL and UCLan we are currently researching the possibilities for a rule-based search engine for Indo-European languages [1].

2 Requirements for hsv-distance measures

One of the main operational points in building a search engine for historical spelling variants is a reliable distance measure. Such a measure can be used in different stages of a query and therefore in more than one module of the engine:

- *Search.* Text retrieval on text in non-standard orthography is obviously more difficult than usual text retrieval. Most standard information retrieval systems build up an index of occurring terms, allowing the user to quickly find all documents containing the words he queried for. As mentioned above, an exact search may not yield good results for historical texts. An adequate distance measure operating on spelling variants provides arbitrary degrees of search fuzziness within a reasonable retrieval time. Standard fuzzy search, though, is of limited use as it does not take linguistic features into account. For example, if the user queries for the German term `urteil` (=judgment), the well known Levenshtein algorithm [14] does not differentiate between the existing variant `urtheil` and, for instance, `ubrteil` with respect to the string distance. A measure that takes heed of linguistic connections will be able to determine the actual variant from a list of candidates.
- *Ranking of Boolean results.* Retrieval in historical text documents is also possible starting from a given query term, using automatically or manually built rules that generate spelling variants. The variants produced are used for Boolean retrieval returning unclassified results. Afterwards, an hsv-distance measure is required to rank the results according to their distance to the term queried.

- *Transformation.* Historical spelling variants should be automatically transformed into their modern counterparts. The hsv-distance measure is used to identify the correct spelling in a dictionary.
- *Reflection.* The differences between a historical or regional spelling variant and its modern equivalent are often hard to evaluate, even for native speakers. An hsv-distance measure is a means of mapping linguistic distinctions on a single number. The visualization of word distances supports the reflection about language as being in a state of constant change.

The amount of support a distance measure can provide depends on its practicability in the particular context of historical spelling variants. Given the abundance of different distance measures and edit-distances available, a thorough evaluation is needed.

3 Comparative study of distance measures

In this section, we briefly describe the measures we compared regarding their retrieval effectiveness: the string edit distance, distances based on an evaluation of n-grams and the Editex algorithm by Zobel and Dart [21], a stochastic distance measure and the new hvs-distance measure computed with our FlexMetric algorithm.

The string edit distance is defined as the minimum number of edit operations needed to transform the one string into the other. These operations consist of character replacements, insertions and deletions. Levenshtein [14] presented a recursive algorithm for calculating the edit distance: Let the function $d(i,j)$ denote the costs needed to transform the first i characters of the string s into the first j characters of the string t. Then the following equations hold obviously:

$$d(0,0) = 0, d(i,0) = i, d(0,j) = j.$$

The complete edit distance for the two strings can then be calculated using the following recursive equation:

$$d(i+1,j+1) = min \begin{pmatrix} d(i+1,j) + 1, \\ d(i,j+1) + 1, \\ d(i,j) + cost(s_i, t_j) \end{pmatrix}, cost(a,b) = \begin{cases} 0 & \text{if a=b} \\ 1 & \text{otherwise} \end{cases}$$

A more efficient way is to use a dynamic programming approach, as described by Wagner and Fischer [20]. The string edit distance is widely used in a variety of applications as it can be determined efficiently and delivers good results.

Another type of string distance measure relies on the comparison of the n-grams derived from each of the strings. The term n-gram denotes a continuing sequence of n characters. Using padding tokens, $(l + n - 1)$ subsequences can be extracted from a particular string, where l denotes the length of the actual string. For instance, the string 'HISTORICAL' yields the following bigrams:

.H HI IS ST TO OR RI IC CA AL L.

Usually, sets of bigrams or trigrams are compared. There are several possible ways of deriving a non-negative number that represents a distance [6] derived from comparison of the n-gram sets. In our experiments, we used formula 1. In contrast to the other algorithms, it does not denote a distance but a similarity measure for the two strings x and y, where B_x denotes the set of bigrams derived from string x and B_y of string y, respectively:

$$sim(x, y) = 2\frac{|B_x \cap B_y|}{|B_x| + |B_y|} \tag{1}$$

Zobel and Dart [21] presented the Editex algorithm as a new phonetic matching technique. It combines the properties of string edit distances with letter-grouping strategies used in well-known phonetic indexing algorithms like Soundex [13] or Phonix [9]. By doing so, they achieved superior results for tasks of phonetic matching. Basically, it defines an enhancement to the simple string edit distance by introducing a more complex cost function that takes the actual characters being modified into account. Additionally, a double occurrence of characters is implicitly reduced to a single one.

Ristad and Yianilos [19] suggest a stochastic interpretation of string distances. They model them according to the probability of individual operations needed to transform one string into the other. These operations are equivalent to the character replacements, insertions and deletions used to define the string edit distance. Additionally, the probability of identity operations (e.g. a to a) is taken into account. The actual probabilities are learned from a training set of string pairs using an expectation-maximization algorithm. The authors suggest two different distance measures: the so-called Viterbi distance, which takes into account only the most likely path when transforming the start into the end string, and the stochastic edit distance, which considers all possible paths and also was the one used in our experiments.

The FlexMetric framework developed by one of the authors [12] combines the simplicity of a dynamic programming algorithm with the flexibility of defining arbitrary costs for each possible character transformation.

The basic idea is very similar to the concept behind the string edit distance. The only difference is that, rather than the number of transformations, the costs for the individual operations are taken into account. The costs for the least expensive sequence of operations required to transform the one string into the other define the distance between the two strings. The cheapest sequence can be calculated using a dynamic programming algorithm resembling the one used for evaluating the string edit distance.

As the edit operations correspond with the transformations regarded in the stochastic evaluation previously described, it is possible to derive the actual costs from the probability distribution learned using the expectation-maximization algorithm according to the following principle: The more likely a particular transformation is, the lower the costs that should be assigned to it. This way, character deviations between modern and historical spellings that occur frequently in the training set lead to cheaper corresponding transformations. Thus, the resulting distance value will also be smaller. The best results are achieved using a logarithmic transformation, as shown in [12].

4 Evaluation methodology

As there are several use cases for a hsv-distance measure and therefore several methods of evaluation, we first describe the assumptions and constraints that lead to solid quality criteria for the particular algorithms. As we concentrate on the effectiveness and not the efficiency of the algorithms, aspects like memory consumption and time needed are not taken into account.

The main problem in judging the quality of string distance measures lies in comparing their applicability for different tasks. It is obvious that a distance measure that has been specifically trained to detect certain linguistic deviations can no longer yield objective results when used to quantify a relation between spellings as it necessarily valuates the trained deviation with lower costs, leading to a shorter distance. Thus, if, for instance, the measure is used to build up a genealogical tree of spelling variants of the same term, it inherently prefers relations it was specifically trained for. This effect leads to unusable results.

In order to avoid this conflict, we have to concentrate on evaluating the potential of the various algorithms for the following text retrieval task: the user queries for the modern spelling, and all documents containing the query term or a historical variant should be returned as results.

Hence, a synthetic information retrieval system (IRS) has to be constructed consisting of a document collection, a retrieval function, and a set of queries along with relevance judgments. This allows the evaluation of the effectiveness of the algorithms with standard methods in Information Retrievalrecall and precision [2].

As we want to concentrate on the algorithms' ability to cognize connections between a query term and its historical spellings, we do not regard a collection of complete texts, but rather a list of words. This way, further factors influencing retrieval results (such as term frequency in the documents) are ignored.

We assembled a list of 3,156 unique pairs of strings, each consisting of a historical deviant spelling and the modern standard spelling. These were manually compiled from 40 historical German documents written from 1350 to 1876. Thus, a number of queries (modern spellings) and relevant answers (historical spellings) for the IRS are found.

The string edit, Editex and FlexMetric distances, can be turned into a normalized similarity function for two strings a, b according to equation 2. The stochastic distance is normalized according to equation 3. These functions yield values between 0 (no similarity / maximum distance) and 1 (identity / no distance). Thus, they can be used to classify the term collection according to the computed similarity to the query in the IRS.

$$sim(a, b) = 1 - \frac{dist(a, b)}{\max\{|a|, |b|\}} \qquad (2)$$

$$sim(a, b) = \frac{\min_{c \in Testset} dist(c, b)}{dist(a, b)} \qquad (3)$$

To build a collection of searchable terms and spelling variants, we use a manually maintained dictionary of 217,000 contemporary German words derived from the free spelling-correction tool Excalibur. The historical word forms found by the IRS are added to the dictionary, whereas the corresponding modern terms are removed. In this way, it is ensured that no other relevant documents (spelling variants) are in the collection. Hence, we are able to exactly determine the medium recall level after retrieving the first one to five most similar terms and the medium precision level at 100% recall as quality indicators.

If two or more terms are equidistant to the term queried, but just one of them is considered relevant, the worst case is assumed: the sequence of answers is arranged in such a way that the relevant term comes last.

A special problem arises in the case of the stochastic distance measure and the FlexMetric approach as these algorithms require a decent training set of string pairs. In order to maximize the utilization of the manually compiled list, we used cross-validation. The list is randomly split into ten parts of preferably equal length. Nine of them are used to train the distance measures. The newly trained measure is evaluated on the remaining records. This is done ten times, once for each part. The individual results are averaged afterwards.

5 Results and interpretation

Measure	Pr.	R 1	R 2	R 3	R 4	R 5
Bigram evaluation	37.9 %	24.5 %	35.6 %	42.6 %	48.2 %	54.4 %
Editex	56.1 %	43.3 %	55.2 %	63.4 %	69.2 %	72.6 %
Levenshtein	38.9 %	22.9 %	36.6 %	47.1 %	53.4 %	58.9 %
FlexMetric	55.0 %	38.6 %	58.2 %	65.7 %	70.8 %	75.0 %
Stochastic measure	62.4 %	46.7 %	65.3 %	74.7 %	79.6 %	83.1 %

Table 1. Evaluation results

The actual experimental results shown in table 1 can be summarized as follows:

- The string edit distance and n-gram algorithms yield comparable results. This was to be expected as both of them evaluate a deviation regardless of its context or the affected characters respectively.

- The Editex algorithm delivers superior results. It takes into account linguistic aspects due to its letter-grouping strategy. For example, the replacement of a vowel sound with another is in terms of a cost measure cheaper than the replacement of a vowel with a consonant sound. Also, phonetically similar letters are grouped. As our results clearly show, this strategy better reflects linguistic developments than the algorithms that process simple character transformations.
- The results yielded by the stochastic distance and the FlexMetric approach are also above those produced by the basic string edit distance and n-gram algorithms. As they both rely on the same learned probability distribution, this is not surprising. The main difference lies in their conceptual complexity: whereas the stochastic distance measure needs an extensive evaluation of the probability distribution for each term pair, the FlexMetric uses a derived cost measure in a simple dynamic programming algorithm. Hence, it allows intuitive optimizations like re-using previously calculated values for $1 : n$ comparisons. Furthermore, and most important to our field of application, the derived cost measure is more likely to be understood and optimized by a human user, for example, for linguistic analysis.
- In [12], the stochastic and FlexMetric distance delivered precision values of 73.7% and 69.0% respectively. We explain this gain in performance with the nature of the tested set. The evidences evaluated in [12] were compiled from a set of documents originating in a smaller time interval. The advantage of the trainable measures is their ability to adapt to specific features of the training set. Hence, this advantage is lost if the set of documents used for evaluation is compiled from a too broad range of origins and thus contains too many different spelling variants (cf. figure 1).

6 Conclusion

From the results shown above, we draw the following conclusions:

- The better adapted an algorithm is to specific phenomena in the domain of historical spellings, the better the retrieval results that can be expected from it.
- The paramount results of a trained distance measure can be transferred to a simpler evaluation algorithm without significant loss in quality.

In this sense, we have created a simple, easy to handle string distance measure by using a decent training set of string pairs. As an result of our evaluation, this distance measure is capable of correctly identifying unknown historical spelling variants of a given query term with an accuracy of more than 50% and is thus superior to common fuzzy search algorithms like Levenshtein string edit distance or n-gram-based comparisons. We expect a further improvement of the retrieval quality from the usage of a set of trained distance measures: By evaluating a document's metadata, that measure that has been trained on spelling variants from about the same time interval and location can be used for retrieval. The verification of this assumption is part of our current research.

7 Further work and outlook

The FlexMetric distance measure reflects properties of the spellings it was trained on. Thus, it may be used to detect the occurrence of certain deviations. The fact of their occurrence is, in turn, an indicator of the place and date of the origin of the text. Hence, the FlexMetric can be used to classify texts of unknown origin. Several measures can be trained on text evidence from different times and places. The measure that yields the best results on an unclassified text is assumedly trained on spellings occurring in a text from the same period and location.

Currently, we are developing a collection of trained measures for three time periods between 1350 and 1900 and three German language areas. The evaluation of this approach is part of our research.

The RSNSR project will provide an online search engine that can be used for literature studies by both experts and amateurs. Following the cognitions of a developed prototype, a simplistic interface will be set up. Among its functions is already a visualization of the rules used. An automatic text categorization that estimates the time and location of origin will follow soon.

This engine will then be integrated into different projects in the context of digitizing historical texts. One of these projects will be DDD. The development of our search engine is accompanied by other projects that also provide modules for successful retro-digitization and literature research. Two of these are also held at the Universität Duisburg-Essen: the development of partial text recognition software for German Fraktur fonts [15] and a web-based system for assisted literature research [3]. With these and RSNSR, a framework for the retro-digitization of historical documents is taking shape.

8 Acknowledgements

The presented research was carried out in a recent project Rule-based search in text databases with nonstandard orthography and funded by the German Research Council.

References

1. D. Archer, A. Ernst-Gerlach, S. Kempken S, T. Pilz, and P. Rayson, *The identification of spelling variants in English and German historical texts: manual or automatic?*, proposed for Digital Humanities 2006, July 4 - 9, Paris, France.
2. R. Baeza-Yates, B. Ribeiro-Neto, *Modern Information Retrieval*, Addison-Wesley, 2000.

3. D. Biella, W. Luther, T. Pilz, *A web-based system for assisted literature research*, Proceedings of the 3rd European Conference on e-Learning 2004, Nov. 25 - 26, Paris, France.

4. Bibliotheca Augustana, FH Augsburg; http://www.fh-augsburg.de/~harsch/augustana.html (accessed 05 Jan. 2006)

5. Deutsch Diachron Digital; http://www.deutschdiachrondigital.designato.de (accessed 05 Jan. 2006)

6. K. Erikson, *Approximate Swedish Name Matching - Survey and Test of Different Algorithms*, Nada report TRITA-NA-E9721, 1997.

7. Excalibur; http://www.eg.bucknell.edu/~excalibr/excalibur.html (accessed 05 Jan. 2006)

8. documentArchiv.de; http://www.documentarchiv.de (accessed 05 Jan. 2006)

9. T. Gadd, PHONIX: The Algorithm, *Program: Automated Library and Information Systems* **24**(4): pp. 363 - 366 (1990).

10. Hessisches Staatsarchiv Darmstadt; http://www.stad.hessen.de/DigitalesArchiv/anfang.html (accessed 05 Jan. 2005)

11. S. Hockey, Living with Google: Perspectives on Humanities Computing and Digital Libraries, *Literary and Linguistic Computing*, **20**: pp. 7 - 24 (2004).

12. S. Kempken, *Bewertung von historischen und regionalen Schreibvarianten mit Hilfe von Abstandsmaßen*, Thesis, Universität Duisburg-Essen (2005).

13. D. Knuth, *The Art of Computer Programming, Vol. 3: Searching and Sorting*, Addison-Wesley, pp. 391 - 392 (1973).

14. V. Levenshtein, Binary codes capable of correcting deletions, insertions and reversals, *Soviet Physics Doklady*, **10** (8): pp. 707 - 710 (1966).

15. L. Mischke, W. Luther, *Document Image De-Warping Based on Detection of Distorted Text Lines*, in: Fabio Roli, Sergio Vitulano (eds.), *Image Analysis and Processing - ICIAP 2005 proceedings*, Cagliari, Italy, September 2005, LNCS 3617, Springer, pp. 1068 - 1075.

16. T. Pilz, *Unscharfe Suche in Textdatenbanken mit nichtstandardisierter Rechtschreibung am Beispiel von Frakturtexten zur Nietzsche-Rezeption*, Thesis (civil service examination), Universität Duisburg-Essen (2003).

17. T. Pilz, W. Luther, N. Fuhr, U. Ammon, *Rule-based search in text databases with nonstandard orthography*, Proceedings ACH/ALLC 2005, June 15 - 18 Victoria, Canada.

18. P. Rayson, D. Archer, N. Smith, *VARD versus Word: A comparison of the UCREL variant detector and modern spell checkers on English historical corpora*, Proceedings of the Corpus Linguistics 2005 conference, July 14 - 17, Birmingham, UK.

19. E. Ristad, P. Yianilos, Learning String Edit Distance, *IEEE Transactions on Pattern Recognition and Machine Intelligence* **20** (5), pp. 522 - 532 (1998).

20. R. Wagner, J. Fischer, The String-to-String Correction Problem, *Journal of the ACM* **21** (1), pp. 168 - 173 (1974).

21. J. Zobel, P. Dart, *Phonetic String Matching: Lessons from Information Retrieval*, Proceedings of the 19th Annual International ACM SIGIR Conference on Research and Development in Information Retrieval, pp. 166 - 172 (1996).

Patterns in Temporal Series of Meteorological Variables Using SOM & TDIDT

Marisa Cogliati, Paola Britos and Ramón García-Martínez

Geography Department. School of Human Sciences. National University of Comahue
cogliati@uncoma.edu.ar
Software & Knowledge Engineering Center. Graduate School. Buenos Aires Institute of
Technology
Intelligent Systems Laboratory. School of Engineering. University of Buenos Aires
{pbritos,rgm}@itba.edu.ar

Abstract. The purpose of the present article is to investigate if there exist any such set of temporal stable patterns in temporal series of meteorological variables studying series of air temperature, wind speed and direction an atmospheric pressure in a period with meteorological conditions involving nocturnal inversion of air temperature in Allen, Río Negro, Argentina. Our conjecture is that there exist independent stable temporal activities, the mixture of which give rise to the weather variables; and these stable activities could be extracted by Self Organized Maps plus Top Down Induction Decision Trees analysis of the data arising from the weather patterns, viewing them as temporal signals.

1. Introduction

Classical laws of fluid motion govern the states of the atmosphere. Atmospheric states exhibit a great deal of correlations at various spatial and temporal scale. Diagnostic of such states attempt to capture the dynamics of various atmospheric variables (like temperature and pressure) and how physical processes influence the behaviour. Thus weather system can be thought as a complex system whose components interact in various spatial and temporal scales. It is also known that the atmospheric system is chaotic and there are limits to the predictability of its future state [Lorenz, 1963, 1965]. Nevertheless, even though daily weather may, under certain conditions, exhibit symptoms of chaos, long-term climatic trends are still meaningful and their study can provide significant information about climate changes. Statistical approaches to weather and climate prediction have a long and distinguished history that predates modelling based on physics and dynamics [Wilks, 1995; Santhanam and Patra, 2001]. Intelligent systems are appearing as useful alternatives to traditional statistical modelling techniques in many scientific disciplines [Hertz *et al.*, 1991; Rich & Knight, 1991; Setiono & Liu, 1996; Yao & Liu, 1998; Dow & Sietsma, 1991; Gallant, 1993; Back *et al.*, 1998; García Martínez & Borrajo, 2000; Grosser *et al.*, 2005]. In their overview of applications of neural networks (as example of intelligent system) in the atmospheric sciences, Gardner and Dorling [1998] concluded that neural networks

Please use the following format when citing this chapter:

Cogliati, M., Britos, P., Garcia-Martinez, R., 2006, in IFIP International Federation for Information Processing, Volume 217, Artificial Intelligence in Theory and Practice, ed. M. Bramer, (Boston: Springer), pp. 305–314.

generally give as good or better results than linear methods. So far, little attention has been paid to combining linear methods with neural networks or other types of intelligent systems in order to enhance the power of the later. A general rule in this sort of applications says that the phenomenon to be learned by the intelligent system should be as simple as possible and all advance information should be utilized by pre-processing [Haykin, 1994]. This trend continues today with newer approaches based on machine learning algorithms [Hsieh and Tang, 1998; Monahan, 2000].

The term intelligent data mining [Evangelos & Han, 1996; Michalski et al., 1998], is the application of automatic learning methods [Michalski et al., 1983; Holsheimer & Siebes, 1991] to the non-trivial process of extract and present/display implicit knowledge, previously unknown, potentially useful and humanly comprehensible, from large data sets, with object to predict of automated form tendencies and behaviours; and to describe of automated form models previously unknown, [Chen et al., 1996; Mannila, 1997; Piatetski-Shapiro et al., 1991; 1996; Perichinsky & García-Martínez, 2000; Perichinsky et al., 2003] involve the use of machine learning techniques and tools.

2. Problem.

The central problem in weather and climate modelling is to predict the future states of the atmospheric system. Since the weather data are generally voluminous, they can be mined for occurrence of particular patterns that distinguish specific weather phenomena. It is therefore possible to view the weather variables as sources of spatio-temporal signals. The information from these spatio-temporal signals can be extracted using data mining techniques. The variation in the weather variables can be viewed as a mixture of several independently occurring spatio-temporal signals with different strengths. Independent component analysis (ICA) has been widely studied in the domain of signal and image processing where each signal is viewed as a mixture of several independently occurring source signals. Under the assumption of non-Gaussian mixtures, it is possible to extract the independently occurring signals from the mixtures under certain well known constraints. Therefore, if the assumption of independent stable activity in the weather variables holds true then it is also possible to extract them using the same technique of ICA. One basic assumption of this approach is viewing the weather phenomenon as a mixture of a certain number of signals with independent stable activity. By 'stable activity', meaning spatiotemporal stability, i.e., the activities that do not change over time and are spatially independent. The observed weather phenomenon is only a mixture of these stable activities. The weather changes due to the changes in the mixing patterns of these stable activities over time. For linear mixtures, the change in the mixing coefficients gives rise to the changing nature of the global weather [Stone, Porrill, Buchel, and Friston, 1999; Hyvarinen, 2001].

The purpose of the present article is to investigate if there exist any such set of temporal stable patterns related to the observed weather phenomena. Our conjecture is that there exist independent stable temporal activities, the mixture of which give rise to the weather variables; and these stable activities could be extracted by neural networks analysis of the data arising from the weather and climate patterns, viewing them as temporal signals.

3. Proposed Solution

The variables as presented in the paper could not be considered random ones because of presence of temporal cycles. In addition, a linear behaviour as result of mixture of latent variables could not be assumed [Hyvarinen *et al.*, 2001]. In order to establish if there exist any such set of temporal stable patterns related to observed weather or climate phenomena we select weather station data described in [Flores *et al*, 1996]. The records of the observed weather temporal series [Ambroise *et al.*,2000; Malmgren and Winter, 1999 ; Tian *et al.*, 1999] are clustered with SOM [Kohonen, 2001; Kasi, *et al.*, 2000; Tirri, 1991; Duller, 1998] and rules describing each obtained cluster were built applying TDIDT [Quinlan, 1993] to each cluster records. The described process is shown in figure 1.

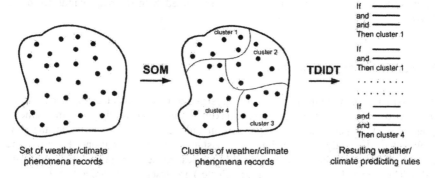

Fig. 1. Process for establishing temporal stable patterns related to observed weather/ climate phenomena

4. Data for experiments

The original data was a set of temperature, wind speed, wind direction and atmospheric pressure observations, taken every fifteen minutes from 13/10/94 to 17/10/94 in Allen, Río Negro province, Argentina. The weather station was located in the agricultural region called Upper Río Negro Valley (URNV) encompassing the lower valleys of the Limay and Neuquén rivers and the upper valley of the Negro river. The arable lands of best quality are located on the river terraces extending from the side pediments up to the floodplain. The terraces are limited by cliffs and the side pediments of the Patagonian plateau that surrounds the valleys. The valley is broad and shallow with steplike edges. The Negro river valley has a WNW-to-ESE orientation in the study area. The mean height differences with the North Patagonian Plateau is 120m for the Río Negro valley. The weather station data was obtained during MECIN (stands in spanish for: MEdiciones de la Capa de Inversión Nocturna:

Nocturnal Inversion Layer Measurements] field experience carried out in the URNV [Flores *et al*, 1996] from September through October of the years 1992 to 1997. The data was complete, without using any replacement technique. The so called Upper Río Negro Valley in Argentina is one of the most important fruit and vegetable production regions of the country. It comprises the lower valleys of the Limay and Neuquén rivers and the upper Negro river valley. Out of the 41,671 cultivated hectares, 84.6% are cultivated with fruit trees, especially apple, pear and stone fruit trees [Cogliati, 2001]. Late frosts occurring when trees are sensitive to low temperatures have a significant impact on the regional production. This study presents an analysis of meteorological variables in one weather station in the Upper Río Negro Valley. To such effect, observations made when synoptic-scale weather patterns were favourable for radiative frosts (light wind and clear sky) or nocturnal temperature inversion in the lower layer were used. Calm winds were more frequent within the valleys. In Allen, air flow behaviour might be associated with forced channelling with wind direction following valley direction. In the night time, some cases of very light NNE wind occurred, which may be associated with drainage winds from the *barda*.

5. Results of experiments

The first analysis implementing SOM analysis determined nine clusters, that could be associated to different wind directions, maximum and mean wind speed, atmospheric pressure and temperature. Air temperature includes periodic daily variation, that was included in the analysis to explore relationship with wind variations. Four of nine groups identified, included the 94 percent of cases and several statistically significant rules. The detected rules for each group (cluster) are described in tables 1 to 9.

Groups A and B describe strongest wind cases with maximum wind speed greater than 5.8 m/s and mean wind speed greater than 1.3 m/s. Group C describe cases considering greater temperatures and wind speed with wind direction from south. Group D describes cases of wind speed up to 5 m/s from north to south directions and wind speed up to 5 m/s. In groups F and G and H cases present non obvious characteristics. Group J discriminates calm wind and groups Z_1 and Z_2 describes undetermined cases. The required frost analysis involve nocturnal and diurnal processes identification, so, the time of observation is a variable that might be included. The inclusion of date and time of observation produced a diminution of the quantity of groups involved, but an important increment in the number of rules (38 rules). This inclusion of new characteristics in the TDIDT analysis produced too much behaviour rules that produces confusion and detect obvious patterns as well as useful ones. This item would need further additional analysis. A confidence limit was pointed in order to study the rules.

Considering confidence level above 0.6 and rules involving more than 25 cases results in 11 rules. This rules pointed some groups characteristics. Group A includes 135 cases with relative higher air pressure mainly in the morning. The 324 cases in Group B present lower air pressure and wind speed. Prevailing wind direction was western sector. Group C discriminated weaker mean wind speed (less than 0.2 m/s) during the morning and relative higher air pressure (371 cases) and cooler air temperature mainly from northern to southern direction. Group D presented westerly wind but cooler air temperature (96 cases) and F includes early afternoon and afternoon cases (154 cases).

RULES	SUPORT DATA	CONFI-DENCE
IF C5294P >= 992.84 AND C5294VVE < 0.20 AND HOUR < 10.33 THEN GROUP = A	26	0.85
IF C5294P >= 990.64 AND C5294P < 991.68 AND C5294VMX >= 0.65 AND HOUR >= 10.33 AND HOUR < 16.48 AND C5294TOU >= 16.75 THEN GROUP = A	12	0.92
IF C5294P >= 991.68 AND C5294VMX >= 0.65 AND HOUR >= 10:33 AND (1) (1) HOUR < 16:48 THEN GROUP = A	51	1
IF C5294P >= 989.61 AND C5294VVE >= 0.20 AND HOUR >= 6:57 AND HOUR < 10.33 THEN GROUP = A	26	1

Table 1. Rules from Group A (Cluster A)

RULES	SUPORT DATA	CONFI-DENCE
IF C5294P < 986.54 AND C5294VVE >= 0.20 AND HOUR < 10:33 THEN GROUP = B	44	0.91
IF C5294P < 989.24 AND C5294VMX >= 0.65 AND HOUR >= 10:33 AND C5294TOU >= 15.15 THEN GROUP = B	265	0.9
IF C5294P < 985.14 AND C5294VMX >= 0.65 AND C5294VMX < 1.55 AND HOUR >= 10:33 AND C5294TOU < 15.15 THEN GROUP = B	6	0.67
IF C5294P < 986.14 AND C5294VMX >= 1.55 AND HOUR >= 10:33 AND C5294TOU < 15.15 THEN GROUP = B	18	1
IF C5294P >= 986.14 AND C5294P < 989.24 AND C5294VMX >= 1.55 AND C5294VVE >= 1.10 AND HOUR >= 10:33 AND C5294TOU < 15.15 THEN GROUP = B	7	1
IF C5294P < 979.48 AND C5294VMX >= 0.65 AND C5294VVE < 0.20 AND HOUR < 8:09 AND C5294TOU < 10.35 THEN GROUP = B	2	1

Table 2. Rules from Group B (Cluster B)

RULES	SUPORT DATA	CONFI-DENCE
IF C5294P < 992.84 AND C5294VMX < 0.65 AND C5294VVE < 0.20 AND HOUR < 8.09 THEN GROUP = C	225	0.99
IF C5294P < 992.84 AND C5294VMX < 0.65 AND C5294VVE < 0.20 AND HOUR >= 8.09 AND HOUR < 10.33 AND C5294TOU < 5.40 THEN (1.00) (1) GROUP = C	5	1
IF C5294P >= 987.15 AND C5294P < 992.84 AND C5294VMX < 0.65 AND C5294VVE < 0.20 AND HOUR >= 8.09 AND HOUR < 10.33 AND C5294TOU >= 5.40 THEN GROUP = C	6	1
IF C5294P >= 984.49 AND C5294P < 987.15 AND C5294VMX < 0.65 AND C5294VVE < 0.20 AND HOUR >= 8.09 AND HOUR < 8.34 AND C5294TOU >= 5.40 THEN GROUP = C	4	0.75
IF C5294P >= 988.14 AND C5294P < 992.84 AND C5294VMX >= 0.65 AND C5294VVE < 0.20 AND (1) (1) HOUR >= 8.09 AND (1) (1) HOUR < 10.33 THEN GROUP = C	29	0.83
IF C5294P < 992.84 AND C5294VMX >= 0.65 AND C5294VVE < 0.20 AND HOUR < 8.09 AND C5294TOU >= 10.35 THEN GROUP = C	50	0.74
IF C5294P >= 989.61 AND C5294VVE >= 0.20 AND HOUR >= 6.57 THEN GROUP = C	35	0.60
IF C5294P >= 989.05 AND C5294P < 992.84 AND C5294VMX >= 0.65 AND C5294VVE < 0.20 AND HOUR < 8.09 AND C5294TOU < 10.35 THEN GROUP = C	15	1
IF C5294P >= 989.24 AND C5294P < 990.64 AND C5294VMX >= 0.65 AND C5294VVE < 0.20 AND HOUR >= 10.33 AND HOUR < 16.48 THEN GROUP = C	12	0.92

Table 3. Rules from Group C (Cluster C)

RULES	SUPORT DATA	CONFI-DENCE
IF C5294P >= 979.48 AND C5294P < 989.05 AND C5294VMX >= 0.65 AND C5294VVE < 0.20 AND HOUR < 8:09 AND C5294TOU < 10.35 THEN GROUP = D	25	0.68
IF C5294P >= 986.54 AND C5294P < 989.61 AND C5294VVE >= 0.20 AND HOUR < 10:33 THEN GROUP = D	8	0.63
IF C5294P >= 989.24 AND C5294VMX >= 2.00 AND HOUR >= 16:48 THEN GROUP = D	24	0.67
IF C5294P >= 989.24 AND C5294P < 990.64 AND C5294VMX >= 0.65 AND C5294VVE >= 0.20 AND HOUR >= 10:33 AND HOUR < 16:48 THEN GROUP = D	6	0.67
IF C5294P >= 990.64 AND C5294P < 991.68 AND C5294VMX >= 0.65 AND HOUR >= 10:33 AND HOUR < 16:48 AND C5294TOU < 16.75 THEN GROUP = D	8	0.63
IF C5294P >= 986.14 AND C5294P < 989.24 AND C5294VMX >= 1.55 AND C5294VVE < 1.10 AND HOUR >= 10:33 AND C5294TOU < 15.15 THEN GROUP = D	26	0.81
IF C5294P >= 984.92 AND C5294P < 988.14 AND C5294VMX >= 0.65 AND C5294VVE < 0.20 AND HOUR >= 8:09 AND HOUR < 10:33 THEN GROUP = D	7	1

Table 4. Rules from Group D (Cluster D)

RULES	SUPORT DATA	CONFI-DENCE
IF C5294P >= 981.17 AND C5294VMX < 0.65 AND HOUR >= 12:45 THEN GROUP = F	159	1
IF C5294P >= 985.14 AND C5294P < 989.24 AND C5294VMX >= 0.65 AND C5294VMX < 1.55 AND HOUR >= 20:24 AND C5294TOU >= 13.20 AND C5294TOU < 15.15 THEN GROUP = F	2	1

Table 5. Rules from Group F (Cluster F)

RULES	SUPORT DATA	CONFI-DENCE
IF C5294P < 981.17 AND C5294VMX < 0.65 AND HOUR >= 10:33 THEN GROUP = G	15	0.93
IF C5294P >= 985.14 AND C5294P < 989.24 AND C5294VMX >= 0.65 AND C5294VMX < 1.55 AND HOUR >= 20:24 AND C5294TOU < 13.20 THEN GROUP = G	12	0.92
IF C5294P >= 989.24 AND C5294VMX >= 0.65 AND C5294VMX < 2.00 AND HOUR >= 16:48 THEN GROUP = G	20	0.4

Table 6. Rules from Group G (Cluster G)

RULES	SUPORT DATA	CONFI-DENCE
IF C5294P >= 981.17 AND C5294VMX < 0.20 AND HOUR >= 10:33 AND HOUR < 12:43 THEN GROUP = H	10	0.9
IF C5294P < 984.49 AND C5294VMX < 0.65 AND C5294VVE < 0.20 AND HOUR >= 8.09 AND HOUR < 10:33 AND >= 5.40 THEN GROUP = H	11	1
IF C5294P >= 984.49 AND C5294P < 992.84 AND C5294VMX < 0.65 AND C5294VVE < 0.20 AND HOUR >= 9:36 AND HOUR < 10:33 AND C5294TOU >= 5.40 THEN GROUP = H	7	1
IF C5294P >= 984.49 AND C5294P < 987.15 AND C5294VMX < 0.65 AND C5294VVE < 0.20 AND HOUR >= 8:38 AND HOUR < 9:36 AND C5294TOU >= 5.40 THEN GROUP = H	5	1

Table 7. Rules from Group H (Cluster H)

RULES	SUPORT DATA	CONFI-DENCE
IF C5294P >= 985.14 AND C5294P < 989.24 AND C5294VMX >= 0.65 AND C5294VMX < 1.55 AND HOUR >= 10:33 AND HOUR < 20:24 AND C5294TOU < 15.15 THEN GROUP = J	4	0.5

Table 8. Rules from Group J (Cluster J)

RULES	SUPORT DATA	CONFI-DENCE	RULES	SUPORT DATA	CONFI-DENCE
IF C5294P >= 981.17 AND C5294VMX >= 0.20 AND C5294VMX < 0.65 AND HOUR >= 10:33 AND HOUR < 12:43 THEN GROUP = UNDETERMINATE	6	0.33	IF C5294P < 984.92 AND C5294VMX >= 0.65 AND C5294VVE < 0.20 AND HOUR >= 8:09 AND HOUR < 10:33 THEN GROUP = UNDETERMINATE	10	0.4

Table 9. Rules from Group Z_1 and Z_2 (indeterminated cluster)

In "C5294...", "C52" is the meteorological station code and "94" is the year (1994). In "C5294vdd", "vdd" is the wind orientation. In "C5294vve", "vve" is average wind intensity. In "C5294tou", "tou" is air temperature (C°). In "C5294P", "P" is pressure (hPa).

The figure 2 presents the maximum wind speed versus local time for the different groups selected. The discrimination of different meteorological situations could differentiate physical relationships in the analyzed cases, further analysis considering atmospheric temporal variations could improve the selection, discarding the obvious deterministic patterns.

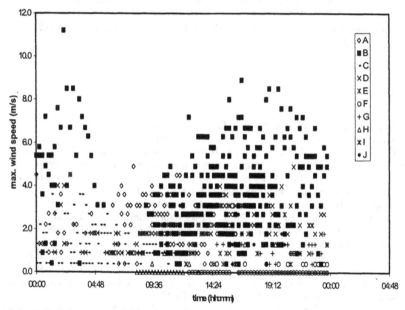

Fig. 2. Scatter plot of different groups data of maximum wind speed versus time in Allen (Río Negro Argentina) from 13/10/94 to 17/10/94.

6. Conclusions

The so called Upper Río Negro Valley in Argentina is one of the most important fruit and vegetable production regions of the country. It comprises the lower valleys of the

Limay and Neuquén rivers and the upper Negro river valley. Late frosts occurring when trees are sensitive to low temperatures have a significant impact on the regional production. Time series analysis of air temperature, atmospheric pressure, wind speed and direction involves a large amount of data and data mining could be an alternative to statistical traditional methods to find clusters with stable signals.

This study presents an analysis of meteorological variables in one weather station in the Upper Río Negro Valley by means of SOM analysis and applying TDIDT to build rules. To such effect, observations made when synoptic-scale weather patterns were favourable for radiative frosts (light wind and clear sky) or nocturnal temperature inversion in the lower layer were used. The obtained rules represent wind, temperature and pressure characteristics, the groups separate calm, and nocturnal and diurnal main characteristics according to prior traditional methods analysis (Cogliati, 2001), newer found relationships might be studied in advance.

The inclusion of a larger number of variables such time and date produces a large number of rules without defining precise intervals that produces confusion and detect obvious patterns as well as useful ones. This item would need further extensive study.

The variation in the weather variables can be viewed as a mixture of several independently occurring spatio-temporal signals with different strengths.

Acknowledgements: The authors would like to thank Jorge Lässig for providing the meteorological data obtained in MECIN field experiment.

7. References

Ambroise, C., Seze, G., Badran, F., and Thiria, S. 2000. *Hierarchical clustering of self-organizing maps for cloud classification.* Neurocomputing, 30(1):47–52

Back, B., Sere, K., & Vanharanta, H. 1998. *Managing complexity in large data bases using self-organizing maps.* Accounting Management & Information Technologies 8, 191-210.

Chen, M., Han, J., Yu, P. 1996. *Data mining: An overview from database perspective.* IEEE Transactions on Knowledge and Data Engineering 8(6): 866-883.

Cogliati, M.G. 2001. *Estudio térmico y del flujo del aire en septiembre y octubre en los valles de los ríos Limay, Neuquén y Negro.* Doctoral Dissertation. University of Buenos Aires.

Dow R. J. y Sietsma J. 1991. *Creating Artificial Neural Networks that Generalize.* Neural Networks . 4(1): 198-209.

Duller, A. W. G. 1998. *Self-organizing neural networks: their application to "real-world" problems.* Australian Journal of Intelligent Information Processing Systems, 5:175–80

Evangelos, S., Han, J. 1996. *Proceedings of the Second International Conference on Knowledge Discovery and Data Mining.* Portland, EE.UU.

Flores, A. ; Lässig, J. ; Cogliati, M. ; Palese, C., Bastanski, M. 1996. *Mediciones de la Capa de Inversión Nocturna en los valles de los ríos Limay, Neuquén y Negro.* Proceedings VII Argentine Congress on Meteorology. VII Latinamerican and Iberic Congress on Meteorology. Buenos Aires.

Gallant, S. 1993. *Neural Network Learning & Experts Systems.* MIT Press, Cambridge, MA.

García Martínez, R. y Borrajo, D. 2000. *An Integrated Approach of Learning, Planning & Executing.* Journal of Intelligent & Robotic Systems. 29(1): 47-78.

Gardner, M., Dorling, S. 1998. *Artificial neural networks (the multilayer perceptron) – a review of applications in the atmospheric sciences.* Atmospheric Environment 32: 2627-2636

Grosser, H., Britos, P. y García-Martínez, R. 2005. *Detecting Fraud in Mobile Telephony Using Neural Networks*. Lecture Notes in Artificial Intelligence 3533: 613-615.

Haykin, S., 1994. *Neural networks: A comprehensive foundation*. Prentice-Hall, Englewood Cliffs, NJ.

Hertz J., A. Krogh y R. Palmer 1991. *Introduction to the Theory of Neural Computation*. Reading, MA: Addison-Wesley.

Holsheimer, M., Siebes, A. 1991. *Data Mining: The Search for Knowledge in Databases*. Report CS-R9406, ISSN 0169-118X, Amersterdam, The Netherlands.

Hsieh, W. , and Tang, B. 1998. *Applying neural network models to prediction and data analysis in meteorology and oceanography*. Bulletin of American Meteorological Society 79: 1855-1870.

Hyvarinen, A. 2001. *Complexity pursuit: Separating interesting components from time-series*. Neural Computation 13: 883-898.

Hyvarinen, A., Karhunen, J. and Oja, E. 2001. *Independent Component Analysis*. John Wiley & Sons.

Kaski, S., Venna, J., and Kohonen, T. 2000. *Coloring that reveals cluster structures in multivariate data*. Australian Journal of Intelligent Information Processing Systems, 6:82–8.

Kohonen, T. 2001. *Self-Organizing Maps*. Springer Series in Information Sciences, Vol. 30, Springer, Berlin.

Lorenz, E. 1963. *Deterministic non-periodic flow*. Journal of Atmospheric Sciences 20: 130-141.

Malmgren, B. A. and Winter, A. 1999. *Climate zonation in Puerto Rico based on principal components analysis and an artificial neural network*. Journal of Climate, 12:977–85

Mannila, H. 1997. *Methods and problems in data mining*. In Proc. of International Conference on Database Theory, Delphi, Greece.

Michalski, R., Carbonell, J., Mitchell, T. 1983. *Machine learning I: An AI Approach*. Morgan Kaufmann, Los Altos, CA.

Michalski, R.S., Bratko, I., Kubat, M. 1998. *Machine Learning and Data Mining, Methods and Applications*. John Wiley & Sons Ltd, West Sussex, England.

Monahan, A. 2000. *Nonlinear principal component analysis by neural networks: Theory and applications to the Lorenz system*. Journal of Climate 13: 821-835.

Perichinsky, G., García-Martínez, R. 2000. *A Data Mining Approach to Computational Taxonomy*. Proceedings Argentine Computer Science Researchers Worksop: 107-110.

Perichinsky, G., Servetto, A., García-Martínez, R., Orellana, R., Plastino, A. 2003. *Taxomic Evidence Applying Algorithms of Intelligent Data Minning Asteroid Families*. Proceedings de la International Conference on Computer Science, Software Engineering, Information Technology, e-Bussines & Applications 308-315.

Piatetski-Shapiro, G., Frawley, W., Matheus, C. 1991. *Knowledge discovery in databases: an overview*. AAAI-MIT Press, Menlo Park, California.

Piatetsky-Shapiro, G., Fayyad, U.M., Smyth, P. 1996. *From data mining to knowledge discovery*. AAAI Press/MIT Press, CA.

Quinlan, R. 1993. *C4.5: Programs for Machine Learning*. Morgan Kaufmann Publishers. San Mateo California.

Rich E. y Knight, K. 1991. *Introduction to Artificial Networks*. Mac Graw-Hill. Publications.

Santhanam M., and Patra, P. 2001. *Statistics of atmospheric correlations*. Physical Review E 64: 016102-1-1-7.

Setiono R. & Liu. H. 1996. *Symbolic representation of neural networks*. IEEE Computer Magazine 29(3): 71-77.

Stone, J., Porrill, J., Buchel, C., and Friston, K. 1999. *Spatial, temporal and spatiotemporal independent component analysis of fMRI data*. In 18th Leed Statistical Research Workshop on Spatiotemporal Mdeling and its Applications. University of Leeds.

Tian, B., Shaikh, M. A., Azimi Sadjadi, M. R., Vonder Haar, T. H., and Reinke, D. L. 1999. *Study of cloud classification with neural networks using spectral and textural features.* IEEE Transactions on Neural Networks, 10(1):138–151

Tirri, H. 1991. *Implementing Expert System Rule Conditions by Neural Networks.* New Generation Computing. 10(1): 55-71.

Wilks, D. 1995. *Statistical methods in Atmospheric Sciences.* Academic Press, London.

Yao X. y Liu Y. 1998. *Toward Designing Artificial Neural Networks by Evolution.* Applied Mathematics & Computation 91(1): 83-90.

Applying Genetic Algorithms to Convoy Scheduling

Edward M. Robinson[1] and Ernst L. Leiss[2]

1 Binary Consulting, Inc. 4405 East-West Highway, Suit 109,
Bethesda, MD 20814 USA, erobinson@binary-consulting.com
2 Ernst L. Leiss, Dept. of Computer Science, University of Houston,
coscel@cs.uh.edu

Abstract. We present the results of our work on applying genetic algorithms combined with a discrete event simulation to the problem of convoy scheduling. We show that this approach can automatically remove conflicts from a convoy schedule thereby providing to the human operator the ability to search for better solutions after an initial conflict free schedule is obtained. We demonstrate that it is feasible to find a conflict free schedule for realistic problems in a few minutes on a common workstation or laptop. The system is currently being integrated into a larger Transportation Information System that regulates highway movement for the military.

1 Introduction

The objective of this work is to automatically remove conflicts from a convoy schedule. The technique applied was to use a genetic algorithm approach combined with a simulation engine and real world data.

1.1 Convoys

Convoys are used to move equipment and people from one point to another [1], with equipment being trucks and vehicles that can perform the movement. A large military container ship can carry 800 containers and 1200 vehicles, which must be unloaded and moved quickly from the port to their final destination. This movement is managed by a Movement Control Team (MCT) that must organize and schedule the convoys and, at the same time, must integrate the convoy movement with the ongoing transportation of services within their area of responsibility. Data obtained from experienced transporters (human operators) report that 100 convoys per day are not uncommon. The challenge facing the MCT is to schedule the convoys and daily movements so that roads are uniformly used and, more importantly, that two or more

Please use the following format when citing this chapter:

Robinson, E.M., Leiss, E.L., 2006, in IFIP International Federation for Information Processing, Volume 217, Artificial Intelligence in Theory and Practice, ed. M. Bramer, (Boston: Springer), pp. 315–323.

convoys do not run into conflict for a given resource. The term used by transporters for removing conflicts from a schedule is "deconfliction".

An example of a conflict occurs when two convoys attempt to exit the same gate (assuming that only a single convoy at a time will use the gate) at the same time. Other conflicts include two convoys trying to cross (at right angles) through a single intersection, one convoy passing another on a single route leg, and two convoys merging onto the same highway segment. While these conflicts are most common, other issues can arise based on local rules and regulations so the system must be able to be extended to support these cases. Our system currently detects convoys attempting to merge or cross at a single node and one convoy overtaking another. Military doctrine restricts convoys to one at a time on a given road segment in most cases and further requires a 20-30 minute gap between convoys. This aspect is being added to the automatic conflict removal module as it is being integrated into the target system.

The workflow for convoy scheduling starts when a convoy commander submits a request for a convoy clearance to the MCT. This request includes a list of trucks and other vehicles, a route or strip map, the origin and destination, and a requested time of departure. The MCT will either grant the request without changes or change the departure time or route if the situation requires it.

1.2 Convoy Scheduling

To determine if convoys will run into conflicts, information is supplied regarding the speed of the convoys, the maximum speed on each road segment, the number of vehicles and their dimensions, the required gaps between vehicles, and the routes in a common format. The length of the convoy and speed along a given segment (the lesser of the convoy speed and segment speed) can be used along with the convoy length to calculate the pass time of the convoy (the time elapsed between lead vehicle and trail vehicle crossing the same point). Figure 1 illustrates convoy structure and length.

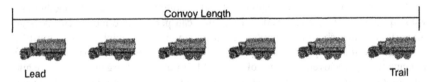

Fig. 1. Example of convoy organization.

Using the speed of the convoy and the pass time each convoy can be stepped forward in time along its given route tracking the times that the lead and the trail pass a given node. A conflict occurs when the lead from another vehicle reaches a node between the crossings of the lead and trail of the original convoy. Another conflict will occur if one convoy passes another on a single segment. This can be observed if the convoys reach the node at the end of the segment in a different order than they passed the node at the beginning of a segment. We coin the term "inversion" for this kind of conflict.

1.3 Goals

Our primary goal for this project was to create a module for a Transportation Information System (TIS) that automatically adjusts an initial schedule to remove conflicts. Allowable changes include adjusting the departure time or selecting an alternate route (with the same origin and destination). The suitability of new schedules is ranked according to removal of all conflicts followed by a weighted evaluation of the changes to the schedule including closeness to requested departure time, convoy priority, and number of route changes.

Additional goals include support for incremental rescheduling based on changes in the field and extensibility to take into account local rules, guidelines, and opportunities (such as using roadside rest areas to allow one convoy to pass another). A final, but operationally vital constraint for all modules in the TIS is that the system must be field portable, i.e., it must be able to operate on a laptop without Internet access. Implied by this is a relative speedy operation; execution times of several hours are not conducive to responsiveness to developments and changes in the field. Execution times within 10 minutes are considered acceptable as conveyed by experienced transportation personnel.

2   Related Work

Convoy deconfliction is unique enough that there is limited amount of research on the subject. However, there do exist systems that automatically remove conflict from schedules as well as papers describing work on building conflict free convoy schedules while minimizing total time.

2.1 MOBCON

MOBCON [1,2] is a mature system used for scheduling convoys within the continental United States (CONUS). There are no publications that discuss the algorithm used to remove conflicts from convoy schedules. However, it is a reasonable assumption that MOBCON performs this function. MOBCON is tightly integrated with the rules and regulations for executing convoys and obtaining permission from each state to allow the convoy to use its highways; this would make it difficult to extract an extensible core algorithm. Also, MOBCON is a mainframe application, which clearly violates the requirement to be field portable.

2.2 Convoy Movement Problem (CMP)

The Convoy Movement Problem (CMP) attempts to find the minimum overall time for routing multiple convoys from the origins to destinations. [3] showed that the problem is NP-complete in simple cases, and more complicated in more realistic situations. The fundamental culprit is the aimed-for optimality of a solution. Optimality is not required – at present, convoys are scheduled manually, with very limited computational support; therefore, the presently applied scheduling algorithms are obviously not optimal. Consequently, it is far more useful to apply heuristics in some form, which will improve solutions, but do not necessarily guarantee optimality. The approach taken in [4] recognized this and combined genetic algorithms with a branch and bound approach; however, the results, especially the time requirements of the programs rendered it rather impractical.

3 Our Approach

Our approach to meeting the objectives described in section 1.3 combines genetic algorithms with a simulation engine. The decision to use genetic algorithms (GA) was based on discussions with domain experts in convoys and interaction in the past with researchers in the GA area that emphasized the speed of recalculation in the face of changing conditions. The work done in [3, 4] supports our decision. Also, the notion of modifying a DNA string closely aligns with modifying a string of offset times. The results of the genetic algorithm directly communicated to the domain expert in the field with no translation other than appending the unit of time and name of convoy to the result.

There exist many conflict free schedules for a given set of convoys (a trivial approach would be to start each convoy on a different day). An optimal schedule was believed to be too expensive to calculate (since at best it is NP-complete) but discussions with domain experts determined that an optimal schedule was *not* the goal. The goal was to find a conflict free schedule that favored the priorities and original request times. Such a goal is ideal for a heuristic approach.

Further discussion with domain experts showed that the conditions for conflict and techniques for working around conflict change from location to location. The ideal system would support easy extension and the ability to adapt local business rules into the solver. Experience recommended the use of a discrete event simulation as the method for evaluating a schedule for conflicts. The simulation approach has the benefit of being easy to explain and validate with the domain experts as changes were made. The ability to refine the fitness function with data collected from probes inserted into the simulation to monitor key events and the ability to extend the simulation to handle new constraints and restrictions has been a major win over the more simplified closed forms of convoy interaction.

3.1 Genetic Algorithm Structure

The DNA string in our genetic algorithm consists of offset times to be applied to the requested departure time to determine the actual departure time for the convoy. This offset is taken from a set of offsets, which is a configuration parameter. A nice benefit of this approach is that the resulting DNA string when combined with the convoy names is straightforward to read (ex: convoy 1 starts 15 minutes earlier, convoy 2 starts on time, convoy 3 starts 20 minutes later). In practice, the offsets are generally in multiples of 5, 10, or 15 minutes.

Mutation was applied by randomly selecting a given offset entry and selecting a randomly different offset time. For crossover, two "parents" are selected at random from the top half of the population and crossing the parent DNA strings at a randomly selected crossover point creates two new "children". Each single string represented an alternate schedule and individual offsets (convoys) were treated independently.

Randomly selected offsets were used to create the initial population strings along with a single zeroed out string to represent the schedule "as-is" to ease tracking performance. The following steps were applied to each generation:

- Mutate
- Breed
- Evaluate
- Sort

The evaluation step was used to determine the fitness of each string (schedule), which combined a simple evaluation of weights with the simulation of the schedule to determine the number and type of conflicts.

The initial fitness function was determined through interviews with experienced transportation personnel to closely support transportation mission objectives. Inversions were considered worse than contention for a given node and the presence of any conflict was considered worse than other considerations such as closeness of actual departure time to requested departure time, closeness of predicted arrival time to requested arrival time, and favoring a higher priority to selected convoys that might carry fuel or ammunition. Several weights and formulas were tested for convergence on sample data with the final technique to calculate fitness being

$$\sum \frac{100}{inversions} + \frac{10}{conflicts} + \frac{1}{\sum offsets}$$

3.2 Simulation

A discrete event simulation (see Fig. 2) was used to step each convoy through its route starting at the time determined by adding the offset to its requested departure time. Active agents were used to model the lead and trail vehicles; route nodes and legs (edges) were modeled as resources, which were used to track which convoy was utilizing the node at a given time. A global simulation clock was used to determine which event occurs next and to issue an event trigger to the agent that had scheduled the event. Node resources allow locking by the head of a convoy and unlocking by the trail of a convoy. If the node is already locked (indicating that this resource is already being used by another convoy), the node resource will flag the conflict with a monitor that keeps count of all conflicts encountered.

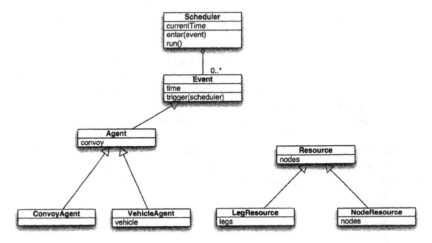

Fig. 2. Class model used to execute the simulation.

Simple queues located with leg resources are used to detect inversions. A convoy is added to the queue when it enters a leg of a route; it is removed from the queue when it exits it. A convoy that overtakes the first convoy would attempt to remove itself out of order and the leg resource would register that with a monitor that keeps a count of inversions.

3.3 Convoy Data

Convoy data were taken from the database used to test the TIS as well as generated from templates. Also, data collected from a simulation of a single convoy were vetted against documented training examples. These data were stored in an object model serving the simulation. The object model's class diagram is illustrated in Figure 3.

The convoy schedule holds all of the convoys and their information. Routes are shared amongst the convoys since that is the case in the field. Additionally, military doctrine allows for convoys to be hierarchically structured into march-units, serials, and columns. This is modeled with a tree structure in the object model to simplify logic. Vehicle information is used to provide the length of the vehicle, which is used in turn to calculate convoy length and pass time. Additionally, the height and weight of a vehicle is needed to determine the validity of switching routes. If an alternate route has a low or weak bridge the convoy may not be able to traverse that route. Also, cargo contents may impact the ability of a convoy to cross a given leg. For example, fuel trucks are not allowed to pass near water in some European countries.

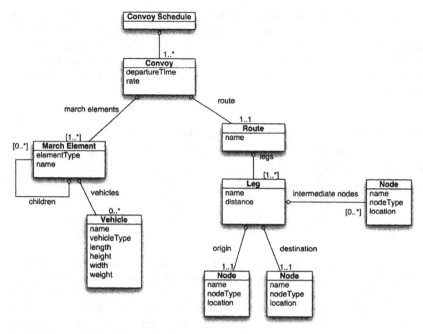

Fig. 3. Object model used for representing convoy in simulation.

4   Results

We tested our system using convoy sizes of 10, 25, and 50 each with 30 vehicles. We were able to reach conflict free schedule within 50 generations for each test case by varying the size of the time window. The results of these runs are given in Table 1. Each convoy requests departure between 9AM and 8PM on a single day. In each case, a conflict free schedule is found within a minute on a reasonably powerful workstation (a 2.7 GHz dual processor PowerPC). The code is written in Java 1.4.2 with no performance tuning or the use of the HotSpot server runtime. Tests were run on Pentium 4 laptops used in the field with comparable performance (within 2 minutes maximum processing time).

Table 1. Window sizes were adjusted to find a conflict free solution in fewer than 50 steps.

Number of convoys – Size	Steps to first conflict free	Time window in minutes	Average offset in minutes	Elapsed time in seconds
10 – 30	23	150	79	8.3
25 – 30	40	480	288	33.8
50 – 30	36	2160	1131	57.7

The time window, which is the maximum amount of time that a convoy schedule entry can be delayed or advanced, has a significant impact on the performance of the search algorithm. We constructed a test to compare the impact of window size on performance on the 25-convoy test data. The results in Table 2 show this performance. Each test run took approximately 2 minutes of user time to complete 150 steps.

Table 2. Test case showing the effect of changing window size on 25convoys.

Time window in minutes	Steps to first conflict free	Average offset at step 50	Average offset at step 100	Average offset at step 150
360	62	141.3	109.6	110.0
390	36	170.2	121.7	92.9
420	31	178.2	135.6	98.0
450	44	233.1	154.6	117.1
480	46	173.0	150.0	125.7

Clearly the system is sensitive to the time window size with an apparent minimum average offset. This demonstrates the utility of having a human operator in the loop. The operator can guide the solution according to the tactical situation. If speed is the preeminent condition, the operator will stop the simulation as soon as a conflict free schedule is achieved. However, if more time is available, the operator can adjust the time window as well as allow the simulation to run longer in order to achieve a better solution.

5   Conclusion and Future Work

We have shown that a field portable system can be implemented to automatically find a conflict free schedule given an initial convoy schedule. The system is able to find a solution within a minute for up to 50 convoys and can continue searching according to the needs of and as directed by the human operator. This system is currently being integrated into an existing Transportation Information System in order to be fielded in the 2006 to 2007 timeframe.

In the future, we will address improving the performance of the code through standard tuning techniques and developing a larger set of test scenarios to analyze common situations (such as unloading large container ships or return trip deployment). We will also investigate different techniques to manage the sensitivity of the time window to finding better solutions. Finally, the transportation community is interested in utilizing the same techniques for non-convoy transportation uses such as supply chain management and backhaul optimization.

6 References

1. Army Field Manuals: FM 55-1, FM 55-30, and FM 55-65. GlobalSecurity.org http://www.globalsecurity.org/military/library/policy/army/fm/index.html

2. R.J. Shun, Army Logistics Management College (ALMC). Automating Convoy Operations. http://www.almc.army.mil/alog/issues/NovDec97/MS214.htm

3. P. Chardaire, G.P. McKeown, S.A. Verity-Harrison, and S.B. Richardson, "Solving a Time-Space Formulation for the Convoy Movement Problem", Operations Research, vol. 53, no. 2, pp. 219-230, 2004.

4. Y.N. Lee, G.P. McKeown, and V.J. Rayward-Smith, The Convoy Movement Problem with Initial Delays, *Modern Heuristic Search Methods* (John Wiley & Sons, 1996).

A GRASP algorithm to solve the problem of dependent tasks scheduling in different machines

Manuel Tupia Anticona

Pontificia Universidad Católica del Perú
Facultad de Ciencias e Ingeniería, Departamento de Ingeniería, Sección
Ingeniería Informática
Av. Universitaria cuadra 18 S/N
Lima, Perú, Lima 32
tupia.mf@pucp.edu.pe

Abstract. Industrial planning has experienced notable advancements since its beginning by the middle of the 20th century. The importance of its application within the several industries where it is used has been demonstrated, regardless of the difficulty of the design of the exact algorithms that solve the variants. Heuristic methods have been applied for planning problems due to their high complexity; especially Artificial Intelligence when developing new strategies to solve one of the most important variants called task scheduling. It is possible to define task scheduling as: .a set of N production line tasks and M machines, which can execute those tasks, where the goal is to find an execution order that minimizes the accumulated execution time, known as makespan. This paper presents a GRASP meta heuristic strategy for the problem of scheduling dependent tasks in different machines

1 Introduction

The task-scheduling problem has its background in industrial planning [1] and in task-scheduling in the processors of the beginning of microelectronics [2]. That kind of problem can be defined, from the point of view of combinatory optimization [3], as follows:

Considering M machines (considered processors) and N tasks with Tij time units of duration for each i-esim task executed in the j-esim machine, we wish to program the N tasks in the M machines, trying to obtain the most appropriate execution order,

Please use the following format when citing this chapter:

Anticona, M.T., 2006, in IFIP International Federation for Information Processing, Volume 217, Artificial Intelligence in Theory and Practice, ed. M. Bramer, (Boston: Springer), pp. 325–334.

fulfilling certain conditions that satisfy the optimality of the required solution for the problem.

The scheduling problem presents a series of variants depending on the nature and the behavior of both, tasks and machines. One of the most difficult to present variants, due to its high computational complexity is that in which the tasks are dependent and the machines are different.

In this variant each task has a list of predecessors and to be executed it must wait until such is completely processed. We must add to this situation the characteristic of heterogeneity of the machines: each task lasts different execution times in each machine. The objective will be to minimize the accumulated execution time of the machines, known as *makespan* [3]

Observing the state of the art of the problem we see that both its practical direct application on industry and its academic importance, being a NP-difficult problem, justifies the design of a heuristic algorithm that search for an optimal solution for the problem, since there are no exact methods to solve the problem. In many industries such as assembling, bottling, manufacture, etc., we see production lines where wait periods by task of the machines involved and saving the resource time are very important topics and require convenient planning.

From the previous definition we can present a mathematical model for the problem as in the following illustration and where it is true that:
- X_0 represents makespan
- X_{ij} will be 0 if the j-esim machine does not execute the i-esim task and 1 on the contrary.

Minimize X_0

$$\text{s.a} \qquad X_0 \geq \sum_{i=1}^{N} T_{ij} * X_{ij} \quad \forall j \in 1..M$$

$$X_0 \geq \sum_{j=1}^{M} X_{ij} = 1 \quad \forall i \in 1..N$$

Fig. 1. A mathematical model for the task-scheduling problem.

1.1   Existing methods to solve the task-scheduling problem and its variants

The existing solutions that pretend to solve the problem, can be divided in two groups: exact methods and approximate methods.

Exact methods [6, 7, 8, 9] try to find a sole hierarchic plan by analyzing all possible task orders or processes involved in the production line (exhaustive exploration). Nevertheless, a search and scheduling strategy that analyzes every possible combination is computationally expensive and it only works for some kinds (sizes) of instances.

Approximate methods [3, 4 and 5] on the other hand, do try to solve the most complex variants in which task and machine behavior intervenes as we previously mentioned. These methods do not analyze exhaustively every possible pattern combinations of the problem, but rather choose those that fulfill certain criteria. In the end, we obtain sufficiently good solutions for the instances to be solved, what justifies its use.

1.2 Heuristic Methods to Solve the Task-scheduling variant

According to the nature of the machines and tasks, the following subdivision previously presented may be done:
- Identical machines and independent tasks
- Identical machines and dependent tasks
- Different machines and independent tasks
- Different machines and dependent tasks: the most complex model to be studied in this document.

Some of the algorithms proposed are:
A Greedy algorithm for identical machines propose by Campello and Maculan [3]: the proposal of the authors is to define the problem as a discreet programming one (what is possible since it is of the NP-difficult class), as we saw before.

Using also, Greedy algorithms for different machines and independent tasks, like in the case of Tupia [10] The author presents the case of the different machines and independent tasks. Campello and Maculan's model was adapted, taking into consideration that there were different execution times for each machine: this is, the matrix concept that it is the time that the i-esim task takes to be executed by the j-esim machine appears.

A GRASP algorithm, as Tupia [11]. The author presents here, the case of the different machines and independent tasks. In this job the author extended the Greedy criteria of the previous algorithm applying the conventional phases of GRASP technique and improving in about 10% the results of the Greedy algorithm for instances of up to 12500 variables (250 tasks for 50 machines).

1.3   GRASP Algorithms

- GRASP algorithms (for *Greedy Randomized Adaptive Search Procedure*) are meta heuristic techniques. T. Feo and M. Resende developed such technique by the end of the 80's [5] While the Greedy criteria let us select only the best value of the objective function, GRASP algorithms *relax or increase* this criteria in such a way that, instead of selecting a sole element, it forms a group of elements, that candidate to be part of the solution group and fulfill certain conditions, it is about this group that a random selection of some of its elements.

This is the general scheme for GRASP technique:

```
GRASP Procedure (Instance of the problem)
    1.   While <stop-condition is not true> do
        1.1  Construction Phase (Sk)
        1.2  Improvement Phase (Sk)
    2.   Return (Best Sk)
End GRASP
```

Fig. 2. General structure of GRASP algorithm

About this algorithm we can affirm:

Line 1: the GRASP procedure will continue while the stop condition is not fulfilled. The stop condition can be of several kinds: optimality (the result obtained presents a certain degree of approximation to the exact solution or it is optimal enough); number of executions carried out (number of interactions); processing time (the algorithm will be executed during a determined period of time).

Lines 1.1 and 1.2: the two main phases of a GRASP algorithm are executed, later: construction stage of the adapted random Greedy solution; and the stage of improvement of the previously constructed solution (combinatorial analyses of most cases).

2 Proposed GRASP Algorithm

We must start from the presumption that there is a complete job instance that includes what follows: a quantity of task and machines (N and M respectively); an execution time matrix T and the lists of predecessors for each task in case there were any.

2.1   Data structures used by the algorithm

Let us think that there is at least one task with predecessors that will become the initial one within the batch, as well as there are no circular references among predecessor tasks that impede their correct execution:

> **Processing Time Matrix T:** (T_{ij}) MxN, where each entry represents the time it takes the j-esim machine to execute the i-esim task.

Accumulated Processing Times Vector A: (A^i), where each entry Ai is the accumulated working time of Mi machine.

P_k: Set of predecessor tasks of J_k task.

Vector U: (U_k) with the finalization time of each J_k task.

Vector V: (V_k) with the finalization time of each predecessor task of J_k, where it is true that $V_k = = \max\{U_r\}, J_r \in P_k$

S_i: Set of tasks assigned to M_i machine.

E: Set of scheduled tasks

C: Set of candidate tasks to be scheduled

Fig. 3. Data structures used by the algorithm

We are going to propose to selection criteria during the development of the GRASP algorithm, what is going to lead us to generate two relaxation constants instead of only one:

- Random GRASP selection criteria for the best task to be programmed, using relaxation constant α.
- Random selection criteria for the best machine that will execute the task selected before, using an additional θ parameter.

2.2 Selection criteria for the *best task*

These criteria bases on the same principles as the Greedy algorithm presented before:

Identifying the tasks able to be programmed: this is, those that have not been programmed yet and its predecessors that have already been executed (or do not present predecessors).

For each one of the tasks able, we have to generate the same list as in the Greedy algorithm: accumulated execution times shall be established starting from the end of the last predecessor task executed.

The smallest element from each list must be found and stored in another list of local minimums. We shall select the maximum and minimum values of the variables out of this new list of local minimums: *worst and best* respectively.

We will form a list of candidate tasks RCL analyzing each entry of the list of local minimums: if the corresponding entry is within the interval [best, best+ α*(worst-best)] then it becomes part of the RCL. A task is chosen by chance out of those that form the RCL.

2. 3 Selection criteria for the *best machine*

Once a task has been selected out of RCL, we look for the best machine that can execute it. This is the main novelty of the algorithm proposed. The steps to be followed are the next ones:

The accumulated time vector is formed once again from the operation of the predecessors of the j-esim task, which is being object of analyses. Maximum and minimum values of the variables are established: worst and best respectively.

Then we form the list of candidate machines MCL: each machine that executes the j-esim task in a time that is in the interval (best, best+ θ*(worst-best)) is part of the MCL. Likewise, we will select one of them by chance, which will be the executioner of the j-esim task.

2. 4 Presentation of the algorithm

GRASP Algorithm_Construction (M, N, T, A, S, U, V, α, θ)
1. **Read and initialize N, M, α, θ, J_1, J_2,...,J_N, T, A, S, U, V**
2. **E = ø**
3. **While |E| $\neq$ N do**
    3.1 C = ø
    3.2 best = + ∞
    3.3 worst = 0
    3.4 For t: 1 to N do
       If ($P_t \subseteq$ E) ^ ($J_t \in$ E) => C = C $\cup$ {J_t}
    3.5 Bmin = ø
    3.6 For each $J_t \in$ C do
       3.6.1 $V_L = \max_{J_j \in P_k} \{U_l\}$
       3.6.2 $B_{min} = B_{min} \cup Min_{p \in [1,M]} \{T_{pl} + \max\{A_p, V_l\}\}$
    End for 3.6
    3.7 best = *Min* {B_{min}} {Selection of the best task. Formation of RCL}
    3.8 worst = *Max* {B_{min}}
    3.9 RCL = ø
    3.10 For each $J_t \in$ C do
       If $Min_{p \in [1,M]} \{T_{pl} + \max\{A_p, V_l\}\} \in$ **[best, best + a* (worst-best)] =>**
       RCL = RCL $\cup$ {J_t}
    3.11 k = ArgRandom$_{JL\bullet RCL}${RCL}
    3.12 MCL = ø {Selection of the best machine}
    3.13 best = $Min_{p \in [1,M]} \{T_{pk} + \max\{A_p, V_k\}\}$
    3.14 worst = $Max_{p \in [1,M]} \{T_{pk} + \max\{A_p, V_k\}\}$
    3.15 For i: 1 to M do

If $T_{ik} + \max\{A_i, V_k\} \in$ **[best, best + 0* (worst-best)] => MCL = MCL** $\cup$ **{M$_i$}**

3.16 i = $ArgAleatorio_{M_i \in MCL}\{MCL\}$

3.17 $S_i = S_i \cup \{J_k\}$

3.18 $E = E \cup \{J_k\}$

3.19 $A_i = T_{ik} + \max\{A_i, V_k\}$

3.20 U$_k$ = A$_i$

End While 3

4. makespan = $\max_{k \to 1..M} A_k$

5. Return S_i, $\forall i \in [1, M]$

End GRASP Algorithm_construction

Comments on the GRASP Algorithm proposed:

- Line 1: entry of the variables e initialization of the data structures needed for the working instance as N, M, T, A, U, V, E, Si for each machine, α, θ etc.
- Line 2: the process ends when all the programmed tasks of the batch are in group E.
- Line 3.1: the list of apt tasks C is initialized empty.
- Line 3.2: best and worst variables that will be used to work the intervals of the relaxation criteria are initialized.
- Line 3.4: the list of apt tasks C is formed
- Line 3.5: the list of local minimums Bmin is initialized.
- Line 3.6 – 3.6.2: entries corresponding to list V are actualized; list Bmin is formed adding each minor element of the accumulated time list of each task.
- Lines 3.7 – 3.8: maximum and minimum values of Bmin are assigned to worst and best variables respectively.
- Line 3.9: RCL list is initialized empty
- Lines 3.10 – 3.11: RCL list is formed when the condition $Min_{p \in [1,M]}\{T_{pl} + \max\{A_p, V_l\}\} \in$ [best, best + α* (worst-best)] is true, then an element from this list (k) is chosen by chance.
- Lines 3.12 – 3.16: minimum and maximum execution times for the task selected in 3.11 are chosen. MCL will form from the machines that execute such task fulfilling the condition: $T_{ik} + \max\{A_i, V_k\} \in$ [best, best + θ* (worst-best)]. In the end a machine is also chosen in an aleatoric way (variable i).
- Lines 3.17 – 3.20: structures E, A, U and S$_i$ are actualized where it corresponds.
- Line 3: makespan is determined as the major entry of A.
- Line 4: assigned results found are given back.

3. Numeric Experiences

The instances with which the algorithm was tested are formed by an M quantity of machines, N of task and a T matrix of execution times. The values used for M and N, respectively, were:

- Number of tasks N: within the interval of 100 to 250, taking 100, 150, 200 and 250 values as points of reference.
- Number of machines M: a maximum of 50 machines taking 12, 25, 37 and 50 values as point of reference.
- Processing time matrix: it will be generated in a random way with values from 1 to 100 time units[1].

We have a total of 16 combinations for the machine-tasks combinations. Likewise, for each combination 10 different instances will be generated, which gives a total of 160 test problems solved.

3.1 Quality of the GRASP solution compared to a simply Greedy solution

As there is no literature on pre-determined test instances for such problem, we decided to confront the results with those of a Greedy algorithm[2]. In the first summary table average results of Greedy and GRASP algorithms execution (in that order) over the respective instances are shown; CPU times consumed by both algorithms, the quantity of executed iterations in the GRASP Construction phase and the values assigned to constants α and θ; finally the efficiency of the GRASP result over the Greedy result calculated as follows is also shown: 1-(GRASP Result/Greedy Result)

Machine \ Task	Makespan Greedy	CPU Used Time	GRASP			Iterations (Average)	CPU Used Time	Efficient
			Makespan	$\cup$	$\cup$			
100 \ 12	213.3	0.56	193.7	0.26	0.04	3750	102.53	9.189%
100 \ 25	113.7	0.59	108.6	0.24	0.01	3750	115.8	4.485%
100 \ 37	76.5	0.56	74.3	0.155	0.01	3750	127.6	2.876%
100 \ 50	59.1	0.52	57.8	0.145	0.01	3750	140.91	2.200%
150 \ 12	283.1	0.58	258.2	0.25	0.01	3000	151.18	8.795%
150 \ 25	125.2	0.52	114	0.21	0.01	3000	170.49	8.946%
150 \ 37	86.1	0.55	84.1	0.155	0.01	3000	201.7	2.323%
150 \ 50	68.6	0.53	67.4	0.115	0.01	3000	224.35	1.749%
200 \ 12	325.9	0.54	307	0.07	0.01	2500	216.83	5.799%
200 \ 25	127	0.57	117	0.247	0.01	2500	229.2	7.874%
200 \ 37	109.8	0.57	105.2	0.112	0.01	2500	248.75	4.189%
200 \ 50	76.4	0.47	74.6	0.155	0.01	2500	274.58	2.356%
250 \ 12	411.8	0.46	377.1	0.15	0.01	2500	249.2	8.426%
250 \ 25	183.5	0.58	168.2	0.28	0.01	2500	282.34	8.338%
250 \ 37	125.3	0.57	119.6	0.26	0.01	2500	309.03	4.549%
250 \ 50	96.5	0.55	91.1	0.123	0.01	2500	343.32	5.596%
Efficient								5.481%

Table 1. Summary table of GRASP vs. Greedy numeric experiments

[1] : We shall notice that a very high execution time (+ oo) may be interpreted as if the machine does not execute a determined task. In this case an execution time equal to 0 may be confuse as the machine executes the task so fast that it does it instantaneously, without taking time

[2] : In order to have a Greedy behavior it is enough to make constant a equal to 0 without regardless of selection of the best machine; that is why the algorithm is not added.

3.2 Real quality of the GRASP solution confronted with mathematical model's solutions

In order to determine the real quality of the solutions we decided to apply the mathematical model of the problem to linear programming problem solver packages as LINDO tool in its student version, in order to obtain exact solutions and confront them with those of the proposed GRASP algorithm.

The two tables that follow summarize the exact results obtained confronted with the heuristic (voracious solution) and meta heuristic (GRASP solution) results. In addition to this we will present the values of the relaxation constants used for the GRASP construction phase where nearly 7000 iterations for all the cases were carried out.

Table 2. Experimental results for M = 3

Matrix	N	M	Lindo Model	Greedy Algorithm	GRASP Algorithm	% Lindo/Greedy	% Lindo/GRASP
6x3_0	6	3	28	35	35	25.00%	0.00%
6x3_1	6	3	67	67	67	0.00%	0.00%
6x3_2	6	3	75	87	85	16.00%	2.30%
8x3_0	8	3	40	45	44	12.50%	2.22%
8x3_1	8	3	88	102	102	15.91%	0.00%
8x3_2	8	3	64	82	64	28.13%	21.95%
12x3_0	12	3	130	162	162	24.62%	0.00%
12x3_1	12	3	121	134	121	10.74%	9.70%
12x3_2	12	3	80	108	89	35.00%	17.59%
15x3_0	15	3	162	201	168	24.07%	16.42%
15x3_1	15	3	125	137	125	9.60%	8.76%
15x3_2	15	3	164	190	176	15.85%	7.37%
Efficient mean						18.12%	7.19%

Table 3. Experimental results for M = 5

Matrix	N	M	Lindo Model	Greedy Algorithm	GRASP Algorithm	% Lindo/Greedy	% Lindo/GRASP
10x5_0	10	5	45	61	46	35.56%	24.59%
10x5_1	10	5	40	52	40	30.00%	23.08%
10x5_2	10	5	61	74	61	21.31%	17.57%
15x5_0	15	5	59	60	59	1.69%	1.67%
15x5_1	15	5	64	77	64	20.31%	16.88%
15x5_2	15	5	41	65	41	58.54%	36.92%
20x5_0	20	5	88	121	106	37.50%	12.40%
20x5_1	20	5	66	74	66	12.12%	10.81%
20x5_2	20	5	82	115	87	40.24%	24.35%
25x5_0	25	5	96	121	113	26.04%	6.61%
25x5_1	25	5	109	147	129	34.86%	12.24%
25x5_2	25	5	86	96	96	11.63%	0.00%
Efficient mean						27.48%	15.59%

4. Conclusions

Both criteria adapted to the kind of algorithm presented: the criteria were voracious in the case of the voracious algorithm (un-modifiable selection); or adaptable and random as in the case of the GRASP algorithm. In the literature there are not any GRASP algorithm that considers a double relaxation criteria at the moment of making the correspondent selections: conventional GRASP ones, were just part of a RCL list of candidates for the tasks to be executed. In 100% of the cases the result of the GRASP algorithm is better than that of voracious algorithm for high enough test instances (proportion 4 to 1, 5 to 1). In small instances it is at least equal to the voracious solution or it does not reach the same level by a very little percentage. The percentage of advantage of the GRASP algorithm confronted to the voracious algorithm is in average 5%.

GRASP algorithm get much closer to the exact solution for analyzed instances, within an average range of 5% to 9% of those solutions. In multiple cases it equals the solution, behavior that has been seen as we reduce the task-machine proportions, this is, when the number of available machine increases.

REFERENCES

[1] G. Miller, E. Galanter. Plans and the Structure of Behavior. Holt Editorial, 1960.

[2] M. Drozdowski. Scheduling multiprocessor tasks: An overview. *European Journal Operation Research*, 1996, pp. 215 - 230.

[3] R. Campello, N. Maculan. Algorithms e Heurísticas: desenvolvimiento e avaliaçao de performance. Apolo Nacional Editores. Brasil, 1992.

[4] M. Pinedo. Scheduling: Theory, Algorithms and Systems, Prentice Hall, 2002.

[5] T. Feo, M. Resende, Greedy Randomized Adaptive Search Procedure. *In Journal of Global Optimization*, No. 6, 1995, pp. 109-133.

[6] W. Rauch, Aplicaciones de la inteligencia Artificial en la actividad empresarial, la ciencia y la industria - tomo II. Editorial Díaz de Santos. España, 1989.

[7] P. Kumara Artificial Intelligence: Manufacturing theory and practice. NorthCross - Institute of Industrial Engineers, 1988.

[8] A. Blum, M. Furst. Fast Planning through Plan-graph Analysis. *In 14th International Joint Conference on Artificial Intelligence*. Morgan- Kaufmann Editions, 1995, pp. 1636 -1642.

[9] R. Conway. Theory of Scheduling, Addison–Wesley Publishing Company, 1967

[10] M. Tupia. Algoritmo voraz para resolver el problema de la programación de tareas dependientes en máquinas diferentes. *In International Conference of Industrial Logistics (7, 2005, Uruguay)* ICIIL. Editors. H. Cancela, Montevideo – Uruguay, 2005, p. 345.

[11] M. Tupia., D. Mauricio. Un algoritmo GRASP para resolver el problema de la programación de tareas dependientes en máquinas diferentes. In *CLEI (30, 2004, Perú)* Editors. M. Solar, D. Fernández-Baca, E. Cuadros-Vargas, Arequipa – Perú, 2004, pp. 129—139.

A support vector machine as an estimator of mountain papaya ripeness using resonant frequency or frequency centroid

P.B. Bro[1], C. Rosenberger[2], H. Laurent[2], C. Gaete-Eastman[3], M. Fernández[1], and M.A. Moya-León[3]

[1] Department of Engineering Science
Universidad de Talca
Curicó, Chile
pbro@utalca.cl
[2] Laboratoire de Vision et Robotique - UPRES EA 2078
ENSI de Bourges - Université d'Orléans
10 Boulevard Lahitolle, 18020 Bourges cedex, France
christophe.rosenberger@ensi-bourges.fr
[3] Institute of Plant Biology and Biotechnology
Universidad de Talca
Talca, Chile

Summary. Mountain papaya fruits (*Vasconcella pubescens*) were tested for firmness with a nondestructive acoustic method for 14 days after harvest. The response of each fruit was analyzed with the Fourier transform to obtain a firmness index (FI) based on the second resonant frequency and with the Short Time Fourier Transform (STFT) to obtain a spectrogram frequency centroid (FC) index. The indexes were processed with a support vector machine (SVM) learning procedure in which days since harvest was taken as the basic truth of ripeness which the measured indexes attempt to estimate. The analysis of the results demonstrate that different groupings of the days into classes to be estimated give widely varying recognition rates and that the best rates are obtained when the classes are delimited using prior knowledge.

1.1 Introduction

The objective of the research reported in the paper was to use a support vector machine to evaluate quantitatively estimations of ripeness for mountain papaya (*Vasconcella pubescens*) using different measurement techniques. The basic test involved is to estimate how many days each fruit had been stored at room temperature since harvest on the basis of each method and to compare the accuracy of each method. The fundamental goal is to predict

Please use the following format when citing this chapter:

Bro, P.B., Rosenberger, C., Laurent, H., Gaete-Eastman, C., Fernández, M., Moya-León, M.A., 2006, in IFIP International Federation for Information Processing, Volume 217, Artificial Intelligence in Theory and Practice, ed. M. Bramer, (Boston: Springer), pp. 335–344.

the future evolution of the fruit from the knowledge of an easily measured, non-destructive quality parameter.

The firmness measurement methods used in this research are based on acoustic measurements of vibrational response of the fruit to impulsive mechanical excitation. This is quite similar to the fine art of testing watermelons by thwacking them with the palm of the hand, or evaluating the quality of a used car by kicking the tires. Despite almost three decades of academic research and development, the determination of the firmness index through acoustic testing has not been widely accepted in industry. Many factors must contribute to this lag; one may be that the acoustic test is overly sensitive to variations in fruit form. One purpose of the overall research of which this report forms a part, is to investigate methods of reducing the variability of the estimation procedure using machine learning.

1.1.1 Fruit firmness

The current industry standard method for measuring the firmness of fruit is a pressure tester based on work by Magness and Taylor [12] originally developed for apples. The basic procedure is to push a cylindrical probe (typically 11mm diameter) into the pared flesh of fruit (to typical depth of 7.9mm). Tests have shown average firmness values obtained with different brands of tests that are statistically significantly different from each other, and show significant dependence of the pressure on the operator [11]. Despite its variability, the pressure test is still the technique of choice for industrial operators.

As an alternative procedure to replace the pressure test, a firmness index has been developed ([8, 1, 5]). The firmness index method is based on exciting vibration in the fruit and determining its resonant frequencies. The firmness index is defined as:

$$FI = (f_{n=2})^2 m^{(2/3)} \qquad (1.1)$$

where

$$m - mass$$

$$f_{n=2} - second\ resonant\ frequency$$

Cooke and Rand [6] suggest that the first resonant frequency corresponds to a spheroid mode and that the second resonant frequency corresponds to a torsional mode and developed equation (1.1) based on torsional spherical models. Terasaki *et al.* [16] observed the vibration modes of apples using speckle pattern interferometry and concluded that the second resonant frequency mode in fact of an oblate-prolate mode of spherical vibration. This result invalidates the theoretical foundation for equation (1.1) however the authors conclude that the firmness index is of practical value as stated and does not merit alteration.

The vibration induced in a fruit in response to an impulsive excitation has a character which depends highly on the time and consequently one must assume that the standard FT is not fundamentally appropriate for analyzing the acoustic response of fruit to impulsive excitation. The short time Fourier transform (STFT) can be used [13] to determine the time varying properties of a signal. With the STFT the data is screened by a sliding window such that only a short duration of the signal is transformed before moving the window to the next portion of the signal. More formally, the FT of each portion of the signal is convolved with the FT of the window. As a result a spectrogram is obtained, a set of spectra as a function of time, also equivalent to the magnitude of the STFT.

As background to this current report, [2] analyzed mountain papaya with the acoustic method and found that the centroid of a portion of the time-frequency spectrogram gives a more robust index of fruit ripeness than does the second resonant frequency. A hypothesis of this research is that the time-frequency analysis shows the response of the fruit in a fashion which is more productive than the static resonant analysis.

1.1.2 Machine learning

The framework for machine learning in the current context is to start with a set of pairs of parameters describing fruit ripeness: $\{x_i, y_i\}_{i=1,\cdot\ell}$ where x_i describes the fruit ripeness and y_i is a quality index of the fruit In our case y_i is the number days since harvest, the basic truth which is known, and x_i is the resonant or centroid frequency, which is measured. Our objective is to learn, on the basis of a training set $\{x_i, y_i\}$, a function f that will be able to estimate accurately the index quality on the basis of the measured parameter. The procedure is to divide a data set of parameter pairs into a learning set and a validation set. One would assume that if the learning set approaches 100% of the total data base, then the validation will also be relatively high.

We use a supervised learning framework to define the estimation functional. This is a multi-class learning problem in which the number of classes depends on the cardinality of index quality. For instance, the fruit firmness can be discretized on a period of 10 days yielding thus into a 10-class problem in a d dimension space. The multi-class problem is addressed through a polychotomy based on a *one-against-one* approach [9]. In the present case, the classes into which the fruit are to be classified are groups of days since harvest. Note that during the first few days after harvest, the change in frequencies is significant, but after about a week, the fruit is already quite mature, and the frequencies do not change thereafter. Therefore, the class grouping might not necessarily be uniformly distributed across the days.

Our machine learning algorithm for each binary problem is a 2-norm support vector machine (SVM) [7], which has already demonstrated its efficiency in other applications [10, 3, 14, 17].

In this method we look for a hyperplane in $\mathcal{H}$ space defined as:

$$f(x) = \sum_{i=1}^{\ell} \alpha_i^* y_i K(x_i, x) + b \qquad (1.2)$$

that maximizes the separation, or margin, between the hyperplane and the data points x_i projected onto $\mathcal{H}$. Here α_i^* are the solutions to the following optimization problem:

$$\begin{cases} \max_{\alpha_i} \sum_i \alpha_i - \frac{1}{2} \sum_{i,j} \alpha_i \alpha_j y_i y_j (K(x_i, x_j) + \frac{1}{C}\delta_{i,j}) \\ \text{with} \sum_i \alpha_i y_i = 0 \quad 0 \le \alpha_i \end{cases} \qquad (1.3)$$

where K is the kernel associated with $\mathcal{H}$, $\delta_{i,j}$ is the Kronecker delta function and C is a trade-off parameter between the margin width and the number of training examples located outside the margin.

1.2 Materials and methods

1.2.1 Plant Material

Mature mountain papaya (*Vasconcellea pubescens*) fruits were collected during summer season of 2004 from commercial orchards located at Lipimavida (34°51'S; 72°08'W; 5 m ASL), on the coastal area of VII Region, Chile. Fruits that were below 5% of yellow color and free from any injuries were harvested using a random sampling method. Then fruits were randomly separated in two groups: one group was treated with 1-MCP ($0.3 \; \mu l.l^{-1}$) during 16 hours at 20°C in the same day of harvest (1-MCP group), while the other group was left untreated (control group). The fruit was allowed to ripen in a room at 20°C. In this paper we deal only with the control group, not the 1-MCP treated fruit.

Four fruits were randomly chosen from each group, and pressure (destructive method) and ethylene production were followed during ripening at 20°C every two days (February 2004 set). The experiment was repeated on March 2004, in which pressure was followed on each fruit in a daily base by using the non-destructive acoustic method. In order to obtain a more complete data set, the results of both trials were combined by normalizing the measurement date to be number of days since harvest.

1.2.2 Pressure and firmness measurements

Acoustic response for firmness measurement was obtained submitting each fruit to impulsive excitation, using a light hammer and piezoelectric sensor similar to the configuration of [15]. The piezoelectric film sensor (Imageco Corp., New York, USA), measuring 80mm long by 15mm wide, was glued to a 10mm think foam pad in a plastic apple processing line cup, measuring 160mm wide by 140mm long and 40mm deep. The hammer, made of an 8mm diameter wooden dowel, 300mm long, was given a 50g lead counter weight and balanced so as to rebound after contacting the fruit and not return to touch the fruit a second time. The experimental setup is illustrated in Figure 1.1.

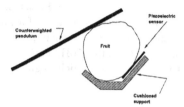

Fig. 1.1. Experimental equipment for firmness measurement.

The signal was captured to a PC running Fedora Linux, through the audio card (Creative Sound Blaster, Audigy Plus) at a 44100Hz sampling rate for 4096 samples. The signal capture software was written in C language using the Open Sound System (http://www.opensound.com) application program interface. The signal was captured to a file for off-line analysis, programmed using Octave (http://www.octave.org), an open source language and library of routines for numerical analysis and MatLab®.

First the FT was taken of each signal to determine the second resonant peak. A search procedure was programmed to pick out the frequency of the highest peak after 100Hz. This threshold was chosen so as to skip the first resonant peak which in many cases is of higher amplitude than the second resonance. The second analysis of the response signal was to perform the STFT. Since the highest frequencies were less than 2KHz, the signal was decimated by a factor of 8. A Hamming window of 71 sample width was used to obtain the spectrograms.

The SVM was applied using the libSVM library published by [4] and available on-line. The initial steps were to process the data using MatLab® to calculate the spectra, and the time frequency responses. The resonant and centroid frequencies were recorded in the format expected by the libSVM sequence of programs along with the day since harvest, on which the SVM was trained and then used for prediction. The learning set was repeatedly altered so that each part of the data was used to predict the other part of the data set. The data set was grouped into subsets, with varying sizes and numbers of members, to investigate whether size of subset affects the prediction results. Different percentages of the data were used as the learning data set to establish the improvement of recognition as a function of percentage of the data used for learning, and the grouping of days since harvest was varied.

1.3 Results

The results of the initial tests are represented by the graph in Figure 1.2. The daily spectra obtained from one fruit (Control fruit 1, February tests) are plotted with the value of the ordinate offset to distinguish between each day. The first day is at the top of the graph and later days follow sequentially below. A first resonance at about 40Hz is common for all the days, and higher resonances between 150 and 350Hz change their position and form with the day. Note that the resonance at about 150Hz can be regarded as increasing in importance relative to the resonance which begins at 300Hz and ends near 250Hz.

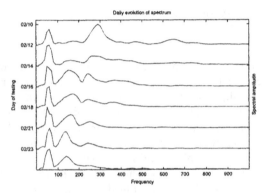

Fig. 1.2. Evolution of spectrum, fruit 1.

The FI described in the previous section is based on the second resonant frequency. In Figure 1.2 the daily evolution of the this frequency is illustrated for one fruit. In order to calculate the FI, one must decide which resonant peak is to be taken as the second resonance. We have used an automated procedure which simply takes the highest peak above 100Hz as the second resonance. With this value one can visualize the daily evolution of the second resonance of the various fruit being tested.

The results of the time-frequency analysis are illustrated in Figure 1.3 where spectrograms are given for the same fruit as illustrated in Figure 1.4. The centroid used in this paper refers to the average frequency of a small portion of the spectrogram at the initial part of the signal. Figure 1.4 illustrates the evolution over time of the resonant and centroid frequencies, the two basic measurements which this paper seeks to compare.

The recognition rate for the SVM is illustrated in Figure 1.5, which includes rates for both centroid frequency and resonant frequency as the independant parameter, x_i, from which the quality index, y_i is estimated. The variation of number of sample sets and size of each set had very little effect on

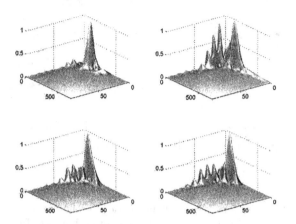

Fig. 1.3. Spectrograms control fruit 01, February data.

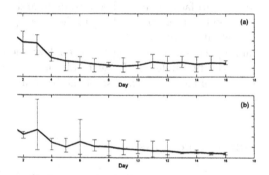

Fig. 1.4. Resonant (a) and centroid (b) frequencies, control fruit.

the recognition rate; the results presented here are for 17 sets of 5 elements each.

Several groupings for days since harvest are used:

1. Each individual day forms one class
2. Each day up to day 6 form individual classes and all days thereafter form an additional class
3. Each day up to day 6 form individual classes and all days thereafter are discarded
4. Days are grouped 1+2, 3+4, 5+6, >6
5. Days are grouped 1+2, 3+4, 5+6, all days greater than 6 are discarded

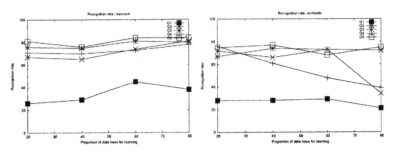

Fig. 1.5. Recognition rate for resonant (a) and centroid (b) frequencies, control fruit .

These groupings were chosen from inspection of the curves relating centroid frequency or resonant frequency to day after harvest. In both cases, after about 6 days, the frequencies no longer vary with day. This is because the fruits have reached a state of ripeness where they no longer become softer with each passing day. In fact the fruits begin to mold and the outer peel begins to form a new slightly stiffer material where the fungal growth contributes to the structural stability of the fruit.

In the concluding section of this paper we analyze the evolution of the recognition rate of the two indexes. These results are somewhat surprising and lead to careful thinking about the use of the SVM and the value of the firmness indexes.

1.4 Discussion and conclusions

The original objective of this research was to compare the FI with the FC methods of ripeness estimation, using the SVM to obtain a quantitative measure of the accurate of each measurement method. The hypothesis was that the centroid method would give a more robust and dependable prediction than the resonance method, due to the clearer functional dependance of centroid frequency on day, with respect to the dependance of resonant frequency on day, as per the conclusion reported by [2] and reflected in Figure 1.4.

This quantitative measure has been achieved in the results of this research, as the recognition rate obtained by the SVM, however it is most decidedly not the expected result, but higher for the resonant than for the centroid frequency. This was not expected since the dependance of centroid frequency on day after harvest is clearer than for the resonant frequency. However the mature fruit resonance peaks are more centralized than are the centroid frequencies of these same fruit.

An initial conclusion to be drawn from the results is that the grouping of the parameter pairs, $\{x_i, y_i\}_{i=1,\cdot\ell}$ into classes by individual days (G1) results in a much lower recognition rate than by more general groupings. Using the knowledge that the fruit after day 6 is overripe and grouping all this fruit into one class, or by directly discarding these parameter pairs, results in significantly higher recognition rates.

A second result that was unexpected is that the recognition does not increase notably as the size of the learning data base increases. In particular for the centroid based recognition, the groupings of all the days greater than 6 into one class (G2 and G4) drop rather sadly when 80% of the data base is used for learning and only 20% is used for validation. This can be termed counterintuitive, since one would expect a priori that use of a higher percentage of the data base for learning would ensure a high validation rate. The resonance estimations are not significantly affected by the size of the learning data base, not improving much, but at least not getting worse. We do not have a convincing explanation for this result.

The resonant frequencies of the overripe fruit also show less variability than the centroids of the same fruit at that stage. This homogeneity may be an artifact of the technique for calculating the resonant frequency, and indeed may be the reason that the SVM predicts the day after harvest more successfully with resonant frequency than with the centroid frequency.

This research is part of an overall effort to assist the fruit processing industry produce uniform, high quality food. Future directions must include extensive, large scale testing to determine if one or another of these nondestructive indexes is most suited for classifying fruit into commercially relevant categories. One such activity will be to test a large number of fruit, as opposed to the very limited sample used in this research. As was mentioned in the materials and methods section, the initial data set in each of the trial runs consists of only four fruits, due to the equipment available for capturing ethylene gas. This represents a clear limitation of the present study; future research will concentrate on the physical, acoustic tests, and so a larger test sample may be used.

Another important goal of future activities is to associate the significance of the secondary peaks with precise physiological events in the ripening process. We have seen that these peaks rise and fall over the ripening period, confounding the second resonant technique. However the information contained in the relative importance of the peaks reflects the internal state of the fruit, which is precisely what the phytophysiologist needs to understand. In this research we have not reaped all the information made available through the time-frequency analysis, and intend to continue exploring the use the Fourier and wavelet transforms for fruit response analysis. Finally, we would like to explore other machine learning techniques which might be useful for assessing fruit characteristics with non-destructive, on-line testing.

References

1. J.A. Abbott, N.F. Childers, G.S. Bachman, J.V. Fitzgerald, and F.J. Matusk. Acoustic vibration for detecting textural quality of apples. *Am. Soc. for Hortic. Sci.*, 93:725–737, 1968.

2. P.B. Bro, C. Rosenberger, H. Laurent, C. Gaete-Eastman, M.A. Moya-León, and M. Fernández. Application of a support vector machine to spectrograms for determinatino of papaya ripeness. In *Proc. Workshop on Artificial Intelligence*, Valdivia, Chile, November 2005. Sociedad Chilena de las Ciencias de la Computación.

3. Doina Caragea, Dianne Cook, and Vasant Honavar. Towards simple, easy-to-understand, yet accurate classifiers. *IEEE Conf. on Data Mining*, page 497, 2003.

4. Chih-Chung Chang and Chih-Jen Lin. *LIBSVM: a library for support vector machines*, 2001. Software available at http://www.csie.ntu.edu.tw/~cjlin/libsvm.

5. J.R. Cooke. An interpretation of the resonant behavior of intact fruit and vegetables. *Transactions ASAE*, 15(6):1075–1080, 1972.

6. J.R. Cooke and R.H. Rand. A mathematical study of resonance in intact fruits and vegetables using a three media elastic sphere model. *J. of Agric. Eng. Research*, 18:141–157, 1973.

7. Cristianini and J. Shawe-Taylor. *Introduction to Support Vector Machines*. Cambridge University Press, 2000.

8. E.E. Finney. Dynamic elastic properties of some fruits during growth and development. *J. of Agric. Eng. Research*, 12(4):249–256, 1967.

9. C.-W. Hsu and C.-J. Lin. A comparison of methods for multi-class support vector machines. *IEEE Transactions on Neural Networks*, 13:415–425, 2002.

10. Anil K. Jain, Robert P.W. Duin, and Jianchang Mao. Statistical pattern recognition: A review. *IEEE Transactions on Pattern Analysis and Machine Intelligence*, 22(1), January 2000.

11. Eugene Kupferman and Nairanjana Dasgupta. Comparison of pome fruit firmness testing instruments. *Postharvest Information Network*, 2001.

12. J.R. Magness and G.R. Taylor. An improved type of pressure tester for the determination of fruit maturity. *USDA Circular*, 350, 1925.

13. Alan V. Oppenheim and Ronald W. Schafer. *Discrete-time signal processing*. Prentice-Hall, 2 edition, 1998.

14. C. Rosenberger, A. Rakotomamonjy, and B. Emile. Generic target recognition. In *EUROSIP Journal on Applied Signal Processing*, pages 1613–1616, 2004.

15. I. Shmulevich, N. Galili, and D. Rosenfeld. Detection of fruit firmness by frequency analysis. *Transactions ASAE*, 39(3):1047–1055, 1996.

16. S. Terasaki, N. Sakurai, N. Wada, T. Yamamishi, R. Yamamoto, and Nevins D.J. Analysis of the vibration mode of apple tissue using electronic speckle pattern interferometry. *Transactions ASAE*, 44(6):1697–1705, 2001.

17. P. G. Wetzlr, R. Honda, B. Enke, W. J. Merline, C. R. Chapman, and M. C. Burl. Learning to detect small impact craters. *IEEE Workshop on Applications of Computer Vision*, 1(1):178–184, 2005.

FieldPlan: Tactical Field Force Planning in BT

Mathias Kern, George Anim-Ansah, Gilbert Owusu, and Chris Voudouris

Intelligent Systems Research Centre
BT Group CTO Office
Adastral Park, Martlesham Heath
Ipswich IP5 3RE, UK
{mathias.kern,george.anim-ansah,gilbert.owusu,chris.voudouris}@bt.com

Abstract. In a highly competitive market, BT[1] faces tough challenges as a service provider for telecommunication solutions. A proactive approach to the management of its resources is absolutely mandatory for its success. In this paper, an AI-based planning system for the management of parts of BT's field force is presented. FieldPlan provides resource managers with full visibility of supply and demand, offers extensive what-if analysis capabilities and thus supports an effective decision making process.

1 Introduction

BT is a leading provider of telecommunication solutions servicing customers in the UK and throughout the world. Like any other service organisation, BT is faced with the stern challenge of delivering services optimally to its customers. The effective management of resources is a fundamental and critical part of this challenge. A proactive resource management approach, i.e. an approach that provides full visibility of the service chain, that offers extensive analysis capabilities, that is automated and user-friendly, is required. [1, 2] are examples of the considerable research and development effort put into the automation of resource management.

BT's Intelligent Systems Research Center has developed a fully integrated suite of applications for the management of field force resources [3, 4]. Among other components, this suite includes:

- *FieldForecast* allows the forecasting of expected demand volumes.
- *FieldPlan* is an application for resource planning.
- *FieldSchedule* is a resource scheduling system.
- *FieldExchange* facilitates the redistribution and exchange of resources.
- *FieldPeople* is a tool for gathering and managing all people-related information such as availability and working patterns.
- *FieldReserve* is a reservation system for incoming work requests.

---

[1] British Telecommunications plc

Please use the following format when citing this chapter:

Kern, M., Anim-Ansah, G., Owusu, G., Voudouris, C., 2006, in IFIP International Federation for Information Processing, Volume 217, Artificial Intelligence in Theory and Practice, ed. M. Bramer, (Boston: Springer), pp. 345–354.

The main focus of this paper is FieldPlan. FieldPlan is a planning system for the management of field force resources such as engineers and technicians. It incorporates a planning algorithm based on heuristic search that efficiently and effectively aligns the expected demand for services with the available field force supply. While doing so, resource managers can actively engage in scenario modeling and thus can analyse the problem from different perspectives in order to reach better informed decisions.

The paper is structured as follows. In section 2, the scenario for field force planning in BT is described. Section 3 is a detailed account of the FieldPlan planning approach. Initial results are presented in section 4, followed by concluding remarks in section 5.

2 The BT Field Force Planning Scenario

With regard to resource planning, one has to distinguish between three main types: scheduling, tactical planning and strategic planning. Scheduling is resource management very close to the actual time of service provision, and may look a few hours up to one or two days ahead. Tactical resource planning is short to mid-term planning as it deals with time windows of a few days up to several weeks. If planning is performed for longer time phases, i.e. up to several years, this is then viewed as a strategic planning task.

The resource planning scenario to address here is a tactical one. A workforce of field engineers, the resources, have to be optimally deployed to serve expected demand in form of jobs. This means that plans have to be generated for the field force, on a per day or per week basis, for up to 12 weeks. FieldPlan has to deploy up to 300 engineers to fulfil up to 20,000 job requests in a single planning run. The main planning objective is to optimally utilise the field engineers to complete jobs while reducing operational costs. Jobs and engineers are characterised by the attributes listed below:

Job	Engineer
geographical location	list of geographical locations, with preferences
skill	list of skills, with preferences
product	list of products, with preferences
time window	availability over time
type (actual or forecasted)	type (standard, loan-in, contractor, etc.)

Each job is either an actual job, i.e. a real customer demand, or is forecasted by the FieldForecast system. A job involves the provision, repair or cease of a product at a particular location and requires a specific skill. This should be accomplished within a given time frame. The importance of a job indicates the value of the respective work to the business.

Engineers, on the other hand, possess sets of skills, can provide various products and are flexible in their choice of working area. Preferences for particular areas, skills and products[2] are possible. Different types of engineers can be deployed, e.g. standard BT engineers or contractors. The engineers show varying daily availabilities, in terms of working hours, during the planning time window.

General importance and productivity rates of skills and products are also known.

In contrast to scheduling systems [5] which assign engineers to particular jobs, the goal here is to determine the best arrangement of engineers in terms of areas, skills and products. For every time period within the planning horizon, each engineer has to be assigned to an area or a set of areas, a skill or a set of skills, and a product or a set of products. Furthermore, the respective numbers of engineer working hours have to be established. The decision about what jobs engineers will actually work on is left to a scheduler at a later point.

Results of the planning process are presented in two forms: capacity and deployment plans. A capacity plan is a coarse-grained summary of the service situation purely in volumes: how many jobs are expected to be cleared/uncleared per area, skill and product; how many engineers are available and utilised per area, skill and product; in short, can the demand be met with the available supply. The deployment plan refines this information by giving explicit area, skill and product deployment recommendations together with expected utilisation percentages for each engineer.

3 The FieldPlan System

In this section, the planning algorithm and its main components are described and important issues are discussed. A schematic outline of the planning approach is given in figure 1.

FieldPlan Algorithm
  FOR all planning time periods:
      1. Aggregate jobs
      2. Generate baseline plan
      3. Optimise baseline plan
      4. Decompose job aggregates
      5. Generate output
  Return all outputs

Fig. 1. The FieldPlan planning algorithm

---

[2] In the current version of FieldPlan in BT, engineers are deployed by default to all products.

Planning Time Window and Periods The process of resource planning is performed for a given time frame. This time window is usually further divided into shorter intervals, and plans have to be generated for all individual stages. A typical tactical example is the planning for two weeks on a per day basis.

The FieldPlan system captures this notion by introducing planning time periods. A planning time period is defined by a start and end time and thus represents a time interval. The overall planning time window is, consequently, a sequence of non-overlapping time periods. By basing the core planning mechanism in FieldPlan purely on the generic concept of time periods, we are able to express the algorithm without any reference to actual time intervals like days or weeks.

A central characteristic of our planning algorithm is the iterative construction of the overall plan out of partial plans. For each individual time period, a partial solution is constructed. Rather than constructing a single plan for the whole time window in one step, a number of steps yields a number of partial solutions which are finally combined to form the complete plan.

Initial Planning Time Period The first planning time period represents the current time period, i.e. it contains the current time at the point of planning. It differs therefore from all subsequent time intervals in two aspects:

- At the point of planning, engineers might already be working. Consequently, they are already assigned to specific areas, skills and products for the first time period. These restricted choices have to be considered when evaluating the future course of the first period.
- Furthermore, parts of the initial time period might have already past at the point of planning. This must be reflected by reduced working hours of the engineers. If, for instance, 50% of time period 1 have already past then the available engineer capacities must be reduced by half.

Job Aggregation and Decomposition In contrast to scheduling systems, FieldPlan does not assign engineers to work on particular jobs. The aim of tactical planning is of a more general nature, namely to decide what kind of engineers have to be deployed to which location to fulfil what kind of jobs. This generalisation allows the planning process to work with job categories rather than single jobs. Hence our planning system merges single jobs into more general objects referred to as job aggregates and bases all planning decisions purely on these aggregations. The advantage of this approach is clear: reduced complexity while maintaining a sufficient level of granularity. Planning becomes easier, faster and more scalable.

In our scenario, a job aggregate is described by the following information:

Job Aggregate
geographical location
skill
product
state
volume

This means that jobs that match in area, skill, product and state are aggregated. Instead of a time window, job aggregates possess a state: backlog, current or future. Backlog job aggregates should have been finished before the current planning time period, current aggregates should be completed within the current time period, and future job aggregates have a later target completion. The volume indicates the number of aggregated jobs.

In the main planning algorithm, all jobs are initially aggregated during each time period. After generating the baseline plan and optimising it, the cleared and uncleared job aggregates are decomposed back into cleared and uncleared jobs.

Objective Function The objective function is the central instrument of evaluating the quality of a particular resource deployment. By assigning a numeric value to each such deployment, comparing candidate solutions and thus selecting the better one is made possible. The compositions of the FieldPlan objective is illustrated below.

For a given job aggregate $A = (area, skill, product, state, volume)$, the *job aggregate clearance score* $jacs(A)$ is defined as

$$jacs(A) = importance(A) \cdot \frac{volume}{productivity(skill, product)}. \tag{1}$$

It is a measure for the value of clearing the job aggregate. The formula normalises the volume with regard to the productivity: the longer work takes, the higher is the score. The score is also better if the job aggregate is more important. In our current implementation, $importance(A)$ is calculated as $importance(skill) + importance(state)$, but more complex measures that consider area and skill as well are possible.

For an engineer $\mathcal{E}$ with assigned job aggregates $A_1^{\mathcal{E}}, \ldots, A_n^{\mathcal{E}}$, the *engineer clearance score* $ecs(\mathcal{E})$ is given as

$$ecs(\mathcal{E}) = \sum_{i=1}^{n} jacs(A_i^{\mathcal{E}}). \tag{2}$$

While the engineer clearance score only evaluates the (quality of) service delivered by an engineer, the *engineer score* $es(\mathcal{E})$ takes also service costs into account as it considers the actual deployment of the engineer:

$$es(\mathcal{E}) = ecs(\mathcal{E}) \cdot$$
$$area\_penalty(\mathcal{E}) \cdot skill\_penalty(\mathcal{E}) \cdot product\_penalty(\mathcal{E}) \cdot$$
$$utilisation\_penalty(\mathcal{E}) \cdot technician\_type\_penalty(\mathcal{E}). \tag{3}$$

Above penalty functions return values between 0 and 1. The original engineer clearance score is reduced by this formula if the engineer is not assigned to the preferred area, skill or product. Further penalties might be applied in case of poor utilisation or if the engineer has to be brought in as additional workforce like contractors or on overtime.

The overall *objective score obj* of a deployment of the engineers $\mathcal{E}_1, \ldots, \mathcal{E}_n$ can be calculated as

$$obj(\mathcal{E}_1, \ldots, \mathcal{E}_n) = \sum_{i=1}^{n} es(\mathcal{E}_i). \tag{4}$$

This objective is a balanced measure of the quality of service delivered by all engineers and the incurred service costs.

Baseline Plan Generation The initial baseline plan is generated by assigning all engineers to their default choices, i.e. to their preferred areas, skills and products. The least flexible engineers in terms of available ares, skills and products are deployed first to ensure that even highly constrained engineers are able to pick up work. Assigning engineers to such choices involves the assignment of matching uncleared job aggregates according to their capacities.

Plan Optimisation The strategy employed in FieldPlan to optimise an initial baseline plan is a hill-climbing algorithm. The current plan is iteratively modified in small steps which are referred to as moves. Each new modification of the solution is characterised by an improved, i.e. higher, objective function evaluation. Three types of moves are considered by FieldPlan:

- *Move-to moves:* Deployments of single engineers are altered by assigning them to new areas, skills and/or products.
- *Swap moves:* The deployments of two engineers are exchanged.
- *Replacement moves:* This move type involves a chain of two or more engineers. The first engineer replaces the second engineer, the second engineer replaces the third, and so on. The final engineer is thus freed and can be moved elsewhere. Currently, only chains of length two and three are considered.

The optimisation routine repeatedly applies the three types of moves to the engineers. As long as improvements are found, the process continues. Only when none of the considered moves offer any improvements anymore, the optimisation is halted as a local maximum is reached.

Heuristic search algorithms such as Simulated Annealing [6], Tabu Search [7], Genetic Algorithms [8] or Guided Local Search[9] employ strategies to escape such local extrema and to improve the generated solution even further. Although these advanced search methods can be easily incorporated in FieldPlan using the defined objective function and move operators, we use the more basic hill-climber due to computation time restrictions. As interactivity is application critical, fast computation and response times are of uttermost importance. The less time intensive hill-climbing approach can meet these requirements and is thus an appropriate choice.

Output At the end of each optimisation cycle, the compiled planning solution is analysed by FieldPlan to provide resource managers with vital information on the state of the supply chain. In addition, FieldPlan computes data that can be utilised as inputs by further systems. The following list gives an overview of the different categories of analysis:

- *Capacity plan:* On the one hand, this plan analysis provides data about the available capacity in the form of engineers. On the other hand, it lists required capacity in form of jobs. Resource managers are able to see how well both match, how many cleared and uncleared jobs can be expected and how well the engineers will be utilised.
- *Deployment plan:* This output makes explicit area, skill and product recommendations for each engineer for all time periods. This deployment information can consequently be used as direct input to a scheduling system.
- *Under-utilisation:* FieldPlan identifies engineers who are not fully utilised. If the utilisation level fall below a certain threshold, reasons for the poor efficiency are compiled and recommendations for improving the utilisation are given.
- *Training:* By analysing the demand for each skill, bottlenecks can be identified and according training recommendations can be given.
- *Resource redistribution:* A resource redistribution system like FieldExchange aims to balance resources across a wider geographical area. Resource shortages and surpluses indicated by FieldPlan can be used as a data feed.
- *Appointment booking:* The analysis of available engineer capacity can be used by appointment booking systems.

Plan Types and Planning Options FieldPlan distinguishes three levels of plan optimisation: baseline plans, optimised plans and user-specified plans. The main differentiator is the level of flexibility the planning mechanism is given in deploying the resources. On one side of the scale, baseline plans do not offer any flexibility at all. All technicians are restricted to their default areas, skills and products, and no overtime is available. On the other side of the scale, optimised plans do not restrict technician deployments in any way, e.g. technicians can be moved to any of their areas, skills and products, and allow the full utilisation of all available overtime. User-specified plans enable resource managers to vary the level of flexibility between the two extrema via a set of planning controls. The most important parameters for such what-if analysis in FieldPlan are:

- The amount to penalise engineers, in terms of the engineer score, for not being deployed to their default areas, skills and products can be varied.
- Productivity rates can be set by the user.
- The importance of skills can be varied.

– The importance of job aggregate states can be varied.
– The usage of overtime can be switched on or off.
– A minimum target utilisation can be specified.
– Jobs can be excluded from the planning by area, skill, product and type.
– Resource managers can choose to not deploy engineers to backlog, current or
  future work.

All these options are calendarisable, i.e. can be set independently for each
planning time period. They provide resource managers with rich scenario modeling capabilities and thus support the decision making process.

4 Results

We present planning results for four real-life scenarios for a single planning time
period and compare the performance of FieldPlan's baseline plans (BL), plans
produced by FieldPlan's hill-climbing method (HC) and plans generated by
standard Tabu Search[3] (TS) and Simulated Annealing[4] (SA) implementations
which are based on the same neighbourhood structure and objective function
as the hill-climber.

For each of the test cases, the following table shows the objective score for
each plan type, together with the number of area/skill moves[5], total number of
cleared jobs and number of cleared backlog/current/future jobs. Backlog jobs
had the highest importance in all four scenarios, followed by current jobs and
future jobs. The number of deployed engineers ranged from 35 to 150.

We can observe that the baseline plans have the lowest objectives in each
of the scenarios. The hill-climber produces improved objective scores, but the
best results are always achieved by Tabu Search and by Simulated Annealing.
The improvements from baseline plans to hill-climber plans are much more dra-
matic than the improvements from hill-climber plans to Tabu Search/Simulated
Annealing plans.

While the baseline plans disallow any kind of area/skill moves, the other
algorithms redeploy engineers in terms of area or skill. This increased flexibility
results in better plans. The hill-climber, Tabu Search and Simulated Annealing
produce plans which show higher total job clearance rates in all scenarios except
case two. However, notedly more high importance jobs (backlog) are cleared by
those algorithms in that particular scenario.

Overall we can state that plan optimisation through hill-climbing, Tabu
Search and Simulated Annealing leads to the clearance of more and more important jobs in our experimental study with the latter two approaches consistently

---

[3] The Tabu Search algorithm employs aspiration, marks technicians who are involved
  in a move as taboo for $\frac{\text{number of engineers}}{5} \pm 2$ cycles and runs for 500 iterations.
[4] The Simulated Annealing method uses an exponential cooling scheme and runs for
  $40,000$ moves (accepted and refused).
[5] Engineer deployments away from default choices.

Plan Type	Objective	# Moves	#Cleared Jobs	#Backlog	#Current	#Future
BL	27.91	0	227	88	139	0
HC	30.44	3	236	100	136	0
TS	31.07	4	245	101	144	0
SA	31.09	3	246	100	146	0
BL	112.40	0	776	405	222	149
HC	124.41	17	746	489	233	24
TS	125.65	23	746	525	204	17
SA	126.11	24	751	517	227	7
BL	98.85	0	781	351	244	186
HC	116.44	22	822	442	271	109
TS	117.57	28	815	464	266	85
SA	117.56	27	803	459	268	76
BL	107.55	0	793	354	323	116
HC	119.91	24	822	516	235	71
TS	122.02	33	841	568	194	79
SA	122.85	36	834	571	189	74

performing best. But these two algorithms come with higher computational costs. Both Tabu Search and Simulated Annealing take about 50 times longer than the hill-climbing method. In real-life scenarios, the improvements achieved by Tabu Search and Simulated Annealing are not significant enough to justify their much slower response times. Computation times of more than 5 minutes on typical server hardware for seven day plans are not acceptable for an interactive planning system. FieldPlan therefore employs the hill-climbing algorithm for plan optimisation to balance between performance and computation time.

After a successful trial period, the FieldPlan system is currently used nationwide (UK) for the deployment of 4,000 engineers of a BT sub-division. Reports indicate improvements in all their key performance measures, examples of which include:

– 8%-14% more engineers are assigned a job first thing in the morning, i.e. do not have to wait. The respective travel time has been reduced from 95min to 85min due to the better initial placement of engineers.
– Because of automation gains with FieldPlan, manual intervention by controllers has been limited to 18% (down from 31%).
– Quality of service has been improved, e.g. 1.1% more business provision jobs are completed on time.

The application of FieldPlan to a wider field force of 25,000 BT engineers is currently in preparation. Deployments are expected to start in February/March 2006.

5 Conclusions

The Aberdeen Group [10, 11] argues that service organisations have to optimise and automate the operations of their field services in order to improve efficiency, profitability and customer satisfaction. Without the constant drive for such improvements, survival in the highly competitive market places of the 21st century seems impossible. BT, as a provider of telecommunication services, faces these challenges every day.

In this paper, we have introduced FieldPlan, a tactical resource planning solution for the optimisation of parts of BT's field force. We have outlined the resource management scenario, have described the core planning mechanism and have discussed the extensive scenario modelling options. Initial results of the application of FieldPlan to the management of $4,000$ field engineers are promising.

The current development work focuses on the large-scale application of FieldPlan to $25,000$ BT field engineers. Future research will include the development of a generic planning framework and its extension to strategic planning scenarios.

References

1. Azarmi N. and Smith R. (1995) Intelligent Scheduling and Planning Systems for Telecommunications Resource Management. In BT Technology Journal, 13(1):7–15.
2. Laithwaite R. (1995) Work Allocation Challenges and Solutions in a Large-Scale Work Management Environment. In BT Technology Journal, 13(1): 46–54.
3. Voudouris C. et.al. (2005) ARMS: An Automated Resource Management System for British Telecommunications plc., In European Journal of Operational Research.
4. Owusu G. et. al. (2003) ARMS: Application of AI and OR Methods to Resource Management, In BT Technology Journal, 21(4):27–32.
5. Lesaint D., Voudouris C. and Azarmi, N. (2000) Dynamic Workforce Scheduling for British Telecommunications plc., In Interfaces, 30(1):55–66.
6. Kirkpatrick S., Gelatt C. D. and Vecchi M. P. (1983) Optimization by Simulated Annealing, In Science, 220(4598):671–680.
7. Glover F. (1989) Tabu search: Part I. In OSRA Journal on Computing, 1(3):190-206.
8. Holland J. H. (1975) Adaptation in Natural and Artificial Systems, University of Michigan Press, Ann Arbor, Michigan.
9. Voudouris C. and Tsang E. (1999) Guided Local Search and its application to the Travelling Salesman Problem. In European Journal of Operational Research, 113(2):469–499.
10. Aberdeen Group Report (2004) The Field Service Optimization Benchmark Report - Tapping the Service Supply Chain for Profit and Competitive Advantage.
11. Aberdeen Group Report (2005) Optimising Field Service to Achieve Profitability Goals.

An Agent Solution to Flexible Planning and Scheduling of Passenger Trips

Claudio Cubillos[1] and Franco Guidi-Polanco[2]

1 Escuela de Ingeniería Informática, Pontificia Universidad Católica de
Valparaíso, Av. Brazil 2241, Valparaíso, Chile
claudio.cubillos@ucv.cl
2 Escuela de Ingeniería Industrial, Pontificia Universidad Católica de
Valparaíso, Av. Brasil 2241, Valparaíso, Chile
fguidi@ucv.cl

Abstract. This work presents the MADARP agent architecture, devoted to the planning and scheduling of trip requests under a dynamic scenario within the context of passenger transportation systems. The architecture provides a set of base agents that perform the basic interface, planning and support services for managing different types of transportation requests by using a heterogeneous fleet of transport vehicles. The architecture was used to implement three planning models by extending base agents' behaviours. The results obtained for a set of 20 scenarios is analyzed.

1 Introduction

The field of passenger transport systems has received an increasing attention as citizens require more flexible transportation alternatives in their cities. As response, new alternatives to satisfy the transport demands of citizens are being conceived [1].

Changes in transport requirements in European citizens have brought the opportunity to create new services aimed to fulfill special transportation demand in addition to regular population mobility services. Their objective is to satisfy personal transportation requests at relatively low costs, thanks to an integrated planning with the use of the different available resources on transport networks.

From a technological perspective, the recent advances in network systems together with the low cost of the processing power have move us to the era of distributed systems and ubiquity. In this trend, the integration, transparency and interoperation among heterogeneous systems are a must. Hence, the multiagent paradigm [16] appears as a promising technology, capable of tackling these newer requirements in an efficient and sustainable way.

Please use the following format when citing this chapter:

Cubillos, C., Guidi-Polanco, F., 2006, in IFIP International Federation for Information Processing, Volume 217, Artificial Intelligence in Theory and Practice, ed. M. Bramer, (Boston: Springer), pp. 355–364.

This work presents the MADARP architecture, devoted to the implementation of flexible passenger transportation systems. It provides agents which implement the basic planning and scheduling functionality for processing transport requests coming from different kinds of users and by considering a heterogeneous fleet of transport vehicles.

2 Transportation Requirements

From a mathematical point of view the transportation problem involved corresponds to the dynamic version of the Dial-a-ride Problem (D-DARP) known to be NP-hard. For this reason all of the commercial solutions and most of the research are focused in heuristic solutions.

Clients commonly specify transport requests with a pick-up and delivery place. They also indicate time windows, that is, time intervals within which the client has to be picked-up at the origin node and delivered at the destination node. Moreover, the requests can include further descriptions of the desired service like type and number of places, shared or exclusive use of the vehicle, wheelchair place use and any other complementary services.

Besides, the passenger transportation system we are tackling considers heterogeneous fleets of vehicles, composed by busses, minivans, vehicles for disabled people, taxis, among others. These vehicles may have diverse characteristics such as: limited passenger's capacity and availability time-periods along the day, an specific area to cover, types of seats, low floor, wide access, no stairs or complementary services like Bar, WC, air conditioning and bicycle transport among others. These properties usually affect the client's comfort and consequently their perception of the received transport service.

In addition, a dynamic scenario is considered, in which the vehicle progress is monitored; clients can modify or cancel their trip requests, vehicle delays can occur, clients may not show up at the pickup place and vehicles can breakdown, all of them involving the re-scheduling of the trips and their management.

2.1 Related work

A software system for D-DARP was proposed by Horn [7]. The optimization capabilities of the system are based on least-cost insertions of new requests and periodic re-optimization of the planned routes. Finally, Coslovich et al. [4] have addressed a dynamic dial-a-ride where people might unexpectedly ask a driver for a trip at a given stop by using a two-phase method and a neighborhood of solutions generated off-line.

Newer research tackling the dynamic problem tends to use a distributed market-based philosophy based in the Contract-Net Protocol (CNP) (see [3], [5], [6] and [11]). The MARS System [6] and the TeleTruck [3] approach use the Extended Contract-Net Protocol (ECNP) with Simulated Trading improvement for dealing with dynamics and uncertainty in a transportation scheduling problem.

Soft computing has also been applied to the transport domain with the use of genetic algorithms (GA) for the optimization of the assignment (see [8] and [15]) and systems based on an ant-colony as reported in [12]. Teodorovic and Radivojevic [14] have later studied a generic version of the dynamic DARP using fuzzy logic for the travel times, as well as Kikuchi and Donnelly [9].

Finally, agent-based systems are presented in [5], [10] and [13]. All of them make use of the CNP for the assignment of client's rides. In addition, [10] uses a stochastic post-optimization phase to improve the result initially obtained. It works in a similar way to the simulated trading. In [13] is presented the Provisional Agreement Protocol (PAP), based on the ECNP and de-commitment. Its improvement is to allow biddings for partial routes and overcomes the Eager Bidder Problem of the CNP, that is, the contractor commits to the bid even though the bid has not been granted and hence cannot make the same bid to another.

3 The Agent Architecture

The agent architecture is built-up over the Jade agent platform [2], which provides a distributed environment organized in containers where agents can work, communicate and migrate within them. Figure 1 shows the MADARP agent architecture [5] which shows four layers that group the agents and structures according to the functionality provided. The Interface layer connects the system with the real world; the Planning layer performs the trips processing; and the Service layer provides different complementary functionalities. At the bottom the Service Ontology provides a means to integrate and make interacting the different agents and actors from the upper layers in a transparent and coherent way.

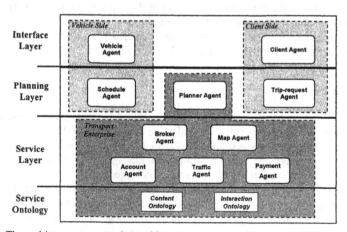

Fig. 1. The multiagent transportation architecture.

Figure 1 shows also the three main actors involved in the transportation chain: vehicles, clients and the transportation enterprise; each of them modeled in terms of agents. Consequently, each vehicle actor is represented by a Vehicle agent and a Schedule agent. In a similar way, each client is characterized by a Client agent and a Trip-request agent. In both cases, the pair of agents is tightly coupled as they are modeling different aspects of the same real entity. The third actor is the transport enterprise, which is built up by a series of agents and structures that provide support to diverse services related with the planning and control of the passenger transportation service provided.

The routing and scheduling functionality provided by the architecture is based on the contract-net protocol (CNP) plus a possible negotiation phase. The interaction among the planning agents is as follows (see Figure 1): First, each transportation request coming from a Client is received by the corresponding Trip-request agent of the couple, which asks the Planner to process it. Next, the Planner processes the request first by obtaining from the Broker agent the vehicles that match the required profile, and then by making a call for trip-proposals to all the corresponding Schedule agents (call for bids in contract-net) that represent the different vehicles of the considered fleet. They send back their proposals and the Planner selects the most suitable alternatives among the received trip proposals by applying filters and starts a negotiation process with the client (through its Trip-request agent). After arriving to agreement the Planner tells the Schedule agent that won the proposal to add the trip to its actual schedule and tells the others their proposal rejection.

Upon differences in the planning (due to breakdowns, traffic jam, etc) the Schedule agent re-plans. In the case of having an infeasible trip request (mainly due to the time-window restrictions), it informs the Planner agent about the situation. The Planner makes a call for trip-proposals to try reallocating the request in other available vehicle. In any case, the result is informed to the corresponding Trip-request agent, which depending on its degree of autonomy will process the alternatives and take a decision or will inform the client about the change. This change may imply a different vehicle processing the trip only or also a delay or an anticipation of the pickup and delivery times defined previously. This default planning implementation can be modified or extended by overwriting the set of behaviours of the different base agents, which are detailed in the following.

3.1   Client Side

Individual clients and their requirements are captured by Client and Trip-request agents. Together they provide full communication and interoperability of the real end user with the transportation system. The Client agent is in charge of providing a personalized user interface while the Trip-request manages the process of requesting the service, its characteristics and the decision making required.

The interface provided by Client agents should be adaptable to the different devices (cell phones, PDAs or PCs). In addition, the Client agent is responsible for capturing all the client's requirements not only concerning the desired type of transport service but also his preferences upon contingency situations (e.g. delays, traffic jams, deviations, etc). The Trip-request takes these requirements and preferences to act on behalf of the real client during the whole process. Depending on the degree of autonomy provided by the client, the Trip-request can act as a personal trip assistant or simply as a mere proxy of the client decisions.

This agent contains three base behaviours. The Schedule_me_Behaviour is a one-shot behaviour which in its default implementation is in charge of receiving the desired transport service from the real client through the client agent that acts as interface. The message contains the request profile that is then forwarded to the planner inside a trip request message.

The Negotiate_Behaviour processes the subsequent messages coming from the planner in order to arrive to an agreement. This depends on the underlying negotiation protocol implemented by both, the Trip-request and the planner agents. The default implementation for this behaviour receives a list with filtered proposals which are evaluated by using the client's utility function.

The Send_status_Behaviour is a cyclic behaviour performing a utility service. It turns back to the sender the status of the request being treated.

3.2   Vehicle Side

Each real vehicle is represented by an agent couple, the Vehicle and the Schedule agents. They provide interoperability between the vehicle they represent and the transportation system to which they belong to. The Vehicle agent plays an interface role, providing the vehicle and its driver with a communication channel with the rest of the transportation system. Through it, the driver is able to communicate along the journey about any contingency that could arise. The Schedule agent is in charge of managing the vehicle's route and processing any new request for client transportation.

The Vehicle agent contains two behaviours. The Register_Behaviour performs the registration of the vehicle with the broker agent. Therefore, it sends a subscribe message to the broker containing a Service Profile.

The Inform_event_Behaviour is the core behavior as it enables the agent to inform about the status of the vehicle and its route advancement. It sends an inform message to its corresponding Schedule agent containing an event description, such as the vehicle arrival to a pickup/delivery place, the presentation or no presentation of the client at the predefined stop, a vehicle malfunction, an emergency, the vehicle deviation due to an accident, traffic jam, etc.

Base Schedule agents implement two cyclic behaviours. The Evaluate_trip_Behaviour evaluates the insertion of a trip (client) in its current schedule. The default implementation listens to the calls-for-proposals coming from the Planner. In case of not being committed by that time with other call (not already finished) it will prepare a proposal, otherwise it will answer back with a refusal message. When preparing the proposal (profile), the behaviour decodes the client's Request Profile description attached in the call's content and evaluates the trip inclusion in the vehicle route.

The Wait_proposal_answer_Behaviour is much coupled to the previous one, as it process the planner's answer with respect to the formulated proposal. For this, the default behaviour checks the planner's message to see if the proposal has been accepted or rejected. In case of an accepted proposal, the behaviour uses the generic interface to insert the trip in the vehicle's route.

3.3   Transportation Enterprise Side

The transportation service role is mainly carried out by the Planner agent acting as a front face to Trip-requests and Schedule agents. The Planner has seven behaviours.

As it name says, the Process_request_Behaviour processes the incoming Schedule-me messages of Trip-request agents. The agent creates a registry of the new request to add to its list. It also decodes the Request Profile contained in the incoming message, and sends a query message to the broker asking for the vehicles that match the requirements contained in the Request Profile.

The CallForProposals_Behaviour receives the broker's answer containing the list of agents that match the desired service described in the Request Profile. The behaviour decodes the list and sends a call-for-proposal message to all the corresponding ScheduleAgents contained in the list. In case of a failure message from the broker, the behaviour will forward it to the corresponding Trip-request agent.

The Process_proposal_Behaviour receives the answer messages from the ScheduleAgents. These messages carry in their content the trip proposals (Proposal Profiles). The behaviour checks if all ScheduleAgents have answered back to the call. If that is the case, then a StartNegotiation_Behaviour is instantiated and activated in the agent.

The StartNegotiation_Behaviour is a one shoot behaviour that can start in two ways; by a Process_proposal_Behaviour that received the last pending answer to the call or by a Request_timeout_Behaviour triggered by the call deadline. The behaviour gets all the proposals received for a given trip request and applies them the filters (if any) contained in its policies list. This will result in discarding some of the proposals. After the filter process, the behaviour starts the negotiation procedure with the Trip-request agent by sending a message to it.

The Process_client_choose_Behaviour also depends on the implemented negotiation protocol. The behaviour receives the Trip-request answers and sends counter proposals until a deal is obtained or the protocol finishes. In any case, the result is forwarded to the involved ScheduleAgents by sending an accept proposal message to the winner and a reject proposal message to the rest.

Finally, the Process_schedule_confirm_Behaviour ensures that the winning ScheduleAgent has committed to the transport request. The default behaviour receives the winner's answer and forwards it to the corresponding Trip-request agent.

Besides the Planner Agent, there is a whole set of service agents collaborating to give support to the different required functions, such as the matching of request to vehicles, the geographical data access, the accountability of the transactions and the service payment among others. From them, the most critical ones from the planning and control point of view are the Broker and the Map agents.

The Broker is the one in charge of carrying out the matching of transport requests with available vehicles. For that is able to manage service descriptions coming from both sides, understand their semantics and perform the search.

The Map agent represents the geographic area being considered where it can be a zone, a city or a part of it. The Map provides the enterprise with a series of information regarding the actual zone being covered such as localization of addresses and stops, street names and distances between localizations, among others.

4 Concrete Planning Systems

Three models of transport planning system were implemented in order to test the agent-based architecture. These were: a centralized, a market-based (decentralized) and a mediated one. For each model, the architecture's base agents were extended and modified. These are explained in the following.

The *Centralized Model* (C) considers the optimization of the global utility for the system. It pursues the minimization of a disutility function of the fleet operator (number of vehicles required, fixed and variable travelling costs) and the served users (effective waiting time, effective ride time). For this to happen, the behaviour of Schedule agents is overwritten in order to consider the vehicle utility function plus the client's one.

The implemented *Decentralized Model* (D) is an approach based in the contract-net (CNP) under self-interested agents. Therefore, Vehicle agents pursued the optimization of the travelling costs (utility function with total slack time and total travel time) and Client agents were oriented towards the maximization of the perceived service quality (utility function with excess travel time and waiting time).

The *Mediated Model* (M) takes advantage of the mediation role of the Planner by filtering the received proposals. The mediated model involves a two-phase planning: First, a Call-For-Proposals (CFP) started by the Planner and answered by the Schedule agents and then a negotiation process that pursues an agreement between the Planner and the client. This two-phased model offers a major difference; the Planner with its filtering and negotiation policies performs a mediation role. It implements the partial centralization of this mixed approach, getting solutions closer to the global optimum when compared with complete decentralized models.

In practical terms the steps are implemented as in the previous approach (the decentralized one). It only changes the Planner role. In this implementation the Planner does apply a filtering policy to the list of received proposals.

4.1 Results

Here are presented some of the results obtained with the 3 concrete models. All the tests considered the same geographical net and 20 demand scenarios with 50 trip requests each, distributed uniformly in a two-hour horizon. For each demand scenario 25 runs were done.

The tests on the three models (see Figure 2) have shown that on average the Mediated model is able to provide results in the gap between the Centralized and Decentralized models.

In general terms, the decentralized model will provide better results for the clients, in terms of both, Waiting Time and Excess Ride Time as these are variables that measure the solution quality from the clients' perspective. In fact, when looking at Figure 2 the Decentralized values are the lowest almost for all the scenarios, while the Centralized values correspond to the highest ones. This is explained because this model provides solutions that are better for vehicle operators and worse for clients.

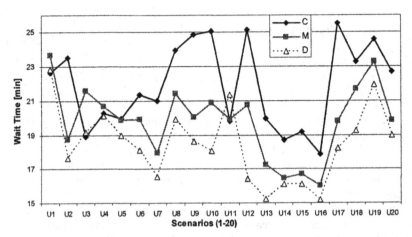

Fig. 2. Graph showing the wait time obtained for the 20 scenarios under the three planning models.

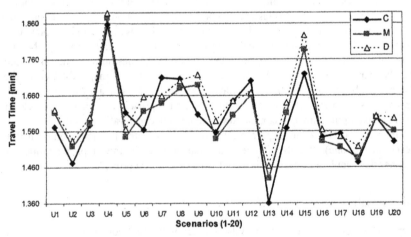

Fig. 3. Graph showing the travel time obtained for the 20 scenarios under the three planning models.

In the same Figure 2 we can appreciate that the Mediated model is just in between, providing almost in all scenarios a middle value for the wait time measure. A similar thing happens with the other client measure considered in the tests, the excess ride time.

As already mentioned, the Centralized approach tends to provide results that in terms of preference, tend to benefit more the vehicle operators rather than clients, which is just the opposite way for the decentralized model. Therefore, when comparing the results of values regarding performance measures of the vehicles' operators, the situation is inverted. For example, in the case of the travel time, the values corresponding to the Centralized model are the lowest for almost all cases as Figure 3 shows. In fact, within the 20 considered scenarios in only five occasions the centralized was the highest among the three alternatives.

In a similar way, the Decentralized approach behaves providing the highest values for the travel time. Again in most scenarios (16 out of 20) the travel time from the decentralized model was the highest among the three alternatives. The interesting thing is that the Mediated model provides results just in between or even below the others in all 20 scenarios. Analogous results are obtained for the other operators' performance measure considered in the test, the slack time.

Finally by looking at Figure 4 that shows the average total cost of the three models on the 20 scenarios, it is possible to see that the Mediated model provides in-between or lower costs in all the 20 scenarios.

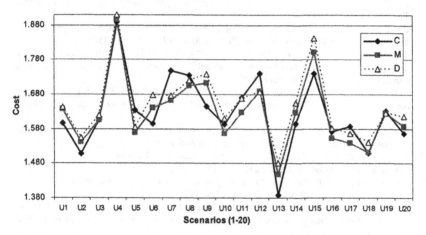

Fig. 4. Graph showing the cost obtained for the 20 scenarios under the three planning models.

To sum up, the analysis shows that the Mediated model gives better results for the clients, in terms of both, Waiting Time and Excess Ride Time when compared with the Centralized model. On the other hand, when compared with de Decentralized model, it gives better results from the vehicle's (or operator's) viewpoint, this in terms of Travel Time and Slack Time.

5 Conclusions

The MADARP architecture for implementing agent-based passenger transportation systems was described. The layered model enforces the system reutilization and maintainability, as more low level and general services (provided by JADE) are decoupled from the domain specific ones (base agents plus ontology). By extending the base agents is possible to obtain an ad-hoc concrete planning system. MADARP provides a transparent and flexible way to integrate users, vehicles, and support-service providers into a single architecture. The agent use ensures the system maintainability, its ability to cope with newer requirements and the possibility to integrate other actors and systems.

The architecture has been tested by implementing three transport planning models and results show that comparable results are obtained. The idea is to continue testing the architecture with diverse scheduling algorithms and negotiation schemes and with a distributed test bed.

References

1. Ambrosino, G. et al, EBusiness Applications to Flexible Transport and Mobility Services. 2001. Available online at: http://citeseer.nj.nec.com/ ambrosino01ebusiness.html.
2. Bellifemine, F. et al, JADE - A FIPA Compliant Agent Framework. C SELT Internal Technical Report, 1999.
3. Bürckert, H; Fischer, K.; et al.. "TeleTruck: A Holonic Fleet Management System", 14th European Meeting on Cybernetics and Systems Research, 1998, pp 695-700.
4. Coslovich, L.; Pesenti, R.; Ukovich, W. "A Two-Phase Insertion Technique of Unexpected Customers for a Dynamic Dial-a-Ride Problem". Technical Report Working paper, Universita di Trieste, Italy, 2003.
5. Cubillos, C. et al. Multi-Agent Infrastructure for Distributed Planning of Demand-Responsive Passenger Transportation Service. IEEE Int. Conf. on SMC, 2004, pp. 2013 – 2017.
6. Fischer, K.; Müller, J.P.; Pischel, M. Cooperative Transportation Scheduling: An application Domain for DAI. Journal of Applied Artificial Intelligence, Vol. 10, 1996.
7. Horn, M.E.T. "Fleet Scheduling and Dispatching for Demand-Responsive Passenger Services". Transportation Research C, Vol. 10C, 2002, pp. 35-63.
8. Jih, W; Hsu, J. Dynamic Vehicle Routing using Hybrid Genetic Algorithms. IEEE Int. Conf. on robotics & Automation. Detroit, May, 1999.
9. Kikuchi, S.; Donnelly, R.A. "Scheduling Demand-Responsive Transportation Vehicles using Fuzzy-Set Theory". Journal of Transportation Engineering, Vol. 118, No. 3, 1992, pp. 391-409.
10. Kohout, R; Erol, K. Robert C. In-Time Agent-Based Vehicle Routing with a Stochastic Improvement Heuristic. AAAI/IAAI Int. Conf. Orlando, Florida, 1999, pp. 864-869.
11. Miyamoto T.; Nakatyou, K.; Kumagai, S. Route planning method for a dial -a-ride problem, IEEE Int. Conf. on SMC, Vol. 4, 2003, pp. 4002 – 4007.
12. Montemanni, R.; Gambardella, et al. A new algorithm for a dynamic vehicle routing problem based on ant colony system, 2nd Int. Workshop on Freight Transportation and Logistics, 2003.
13. Perugini, D.; Lambert, D.; et al. "A distributed agent approach to global transportation scheduling". IEEE/ WIC Int. Conf. on Intelligent Agent Technology, 2003, pp 18-24.
14. Teodorovic, D.; Radivojevic, G. "A Fuzzy Logic Approach to Dynamic Dial-A-Ride Problem". Fuzzy Sets and Systems, Vol. 116, 2000, pp. 23-33.
15. Uchimura, K. et al. "Demand responsive services in hierarchical public transportation system". IEEE Trans. on Vehicular Technology, Vol. 51, Issue 4, 2002, pp. 760 – 766.
16. Weiss, G., Multiagent Systems: A Modern Approach to Distributed Artificial Intelligence, MIT Press, Massachusetts, USA. 1999.

Facial expression recognition using shape and texture information

I. Kotsia[1] and I. Pitas[1]

Aristotle University of Thessaloniki
pitas@aiia.csd.auth.gr
Department of Informatics
Box 451 54124
Thessaloniki, Greece

Summary. A novel method based on shape and texture information is proposed in this paper for facial expression recognition from video sequences. The Discriminant Non-negative Matrix Factorization (DNMF) algorithm is applied at the image corresponding to the greatest intensity of the facial expression (last frame of the video sequence), extracting that way the texture information. A Support Vector Machines (SVMs) system is used for the classification of the shape information derived from tracking the Candide grid over the video sequence. The shape information consists of the differences of the node coordinates between the first (neutral) and last (fully expressed facial expression) video frame. Subsequently, fusion of texture and shape information obtained is performed using Radial Basis Function (RBF) Neural Networks (NNs). The accuracy achieved is equal to 98,2% when recognizing the six basic facial expressions.

1.1 Introduction

During the past two decades, many studies regarding facial expression recognition, which plays a vital role in human centered interfaces, have been conducted. Psychologists have defined the following basic facial expressions: anger, disgust, fear, happiness, sadness and surprise [?]. A set of muscle movements, known as Action Units, was created. These movements form the so called *Facial Action Coding System (FACS)* [?]. A survey on automatic facial expression recognition can be found in [?].

In the current paper, a novel method for video based facial expression recognition by fusing texture and shape information is proposed. The texture information is obtained by applying the DNMF algorithm [?] on the last frame of the video sequence, i.e. the one that corresponds to the greatest intensity of the facial expression depicted. The shape information is calculated as the difference of Candide facial model grid node coordinates between the first and the last frame of a video sequence [?]. The decision made regarding

Please use the following format when citing this chapter:

Kotsia, I., Pitas, I., 2006, in IFIP International Federation for Information Processing, Volume 217, Artificial Intelligence in Theory and Practice, ed. M. Bramer, (Boston: Springer), pp. 365–374.

the class the sample belongs to, is obtained using a SVM system. Both the DNMF and SVM algorithms have as an output the distances of the sample under examination from each of the six classes (facial expressions). Fusion of the distances obtained from DNMF and SVMs applications is attempted using a RBF NN system. The experiments performed using the Cohn-Kanade database indicate a recognition accuracy of 98,2% when recognizing the six basic facial expressions. The novelty of this method lies in the combination of both texture and geometrical information for facial expression recognition.

1.2 System description

The diagram of the proposed system is shown in Figure ??.

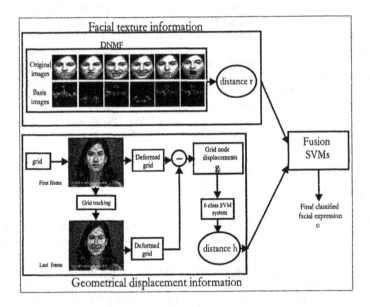

Fig. 1.1. System architecture for facial expression recognition in facial videos

The system is composed of three subsystems: two responsible for texture and shape information extraction and a third one responsible for the fusion of their results. Figure ?? shows the two sources of information (texture and shape) used by the system.

1.3 Texture information extraction

Let $\mathcal{U}$ be a database of facial videos. The facial expression depicted in each video sequence is dynamic, evolving through time as the video progresses. We

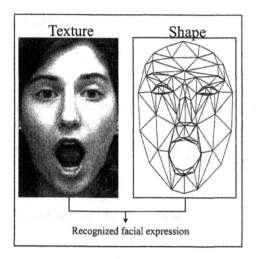

Fig. 1.2. Fusion of texture and shape.

take under consideration the frame that depicts the facial expression in its greatest intensity, i.e. the last frame, to create a facial image database Y. Thus, $\mathcal{Y}$ consists of images where the depicted facial expression obtains its greatest intensity . Each image $\mathbf{y} \in \mathcal{Y}$ belongs to one of the 6 basic facial expression classes $\{\mathcal{Y}_1, \mathcal{Y}_2, \ldots, \mathcal{Y}_6\}$ with $\mathcal{Y} = \bigcup_{r=1}^{6} \mathcal{Y}_r$. Each image $\mathbf{y} \in \Re_+^{K \times G}$ of dimension $F = K \times G$ forms a vector $\mathbf{x} \in \Re_+^F$. The vectors $\mathbf{x} \in \Re_+^F$ will be used in our algorithm.

The algorithm used was the DNMF algorithm, which is a extension of the Non-negative Matrix Factorization (NMF) algorithm. The NMF algorithm algorithm is an object decomposition algorithm that allows only additive combinations of non negative components. DNMF was the result of an attempt to introduce discriminant information to the NMF decomposition. Both NMF and DNMF algorithms will be presented analytically below.

1.3.1 The Non-negative Matrix Factorization Algorithm

A facial image $\mathbf{x}_j$ after the NMF decomposition can be written as $\mathbf{x}_j \approx \mathbf{Zh}_j$, where $\mathbf{h}_j$ is the j-th column of $\mathbf{H}$. Thus, the columns of the matrix $\mathbf{Z}$ can be considered as basis images and the vector $\mathbf{h}_j$ as the corresponding weight vectors. Vectors $\mathbf{h}_j$ can also be considered as the projections vectors of the original facial vectors $\mathbf{x}_j$ on a lower dimensional feature space .

In order to apply NMF in the database $\mathcal{Y}$, the matrix $\mathbf{X} \in \Re_+^{F \times G} = [x_{i,j}]$ should be constructed, where $x_{i,j}$ is the i-th element of the j-th image, F is the number of pixels and G is the number of images in the database. In other words the j-th column of $\mathbf{X}$ is the $\mathbf{x}_j$ facial image in vector form (i.e. $\mathbf{x}_j \in \Re_+^F$).

NMF aims at finding two matrices $\mathbf{Z} \in \Re_+^{F \times M} = [z_{i,k}]$ and $\mathbf{H} \in \Re_+^{M \times L} = [h_{k,j}]$ such that :

$$\mathbf{X} \approx \mathbf{ZH}. \tag{1.1}$$

where M is the number of dimensions taken under consideration (usually $M \ll F$).

The NMF factorization is the outcome of the following optimization problem :

$$\min_{\mathbf{Z},\mathbf{H}} D_N(\mathbf{X}||\mathbf{ZH}) \text{ subject to} \tag{1.2}$$

$$z_{i,k} \geq 0, \ h_{k,j} \geq 0, \ \sum_i z_{i,j} = 1, \ \forall j.$$

The update rules for the weight matrix $\mathbf{H}$ and the bases matrix $\mathbf{Z}$ can be found in [?].

1.3.2 The Discriminant Non-negative Matrix Factorization Algorithm

In order to incorporate discriminants constraints inside the NMF cost function (??), we should use the information regarding the separation of the vectors $\mathbf{h}_j$ into different classes. Let us assume that the vector $\mathbf{h}_j$ that corresponds to the jth column of the matrix $\mathbf{H}$, is the coefficient vector for the ρth facial image of the rth class and will be denoted as $\boldsymbol{\eta}_\rho^{(r)} = [\eta_{\rho,1}^{(r)} \ldots \eta_{\rho,M}^{(r)}]^T$. The mean vector of the vectors $\boldsymbol{\eta}_\rho^{(r)}$ for the class r is denoted as $\boldsymbol{\mu}^{(r)} = [\mu_1^{(r)} \ldots \mu_M^{(r)}]^T$ and the mean of all classes as $\boldsymbol{\mu} = [\mu_1 \ldots \mu_M]^T$. The cardinality of a facial class $\mathcal{Y}_r$ is denoted by N_r. Then, the within scatter matrix for the coefficient vectors $\mathbf{h}_j$ is defined as:

$$\mathbf{S}_w = \sum_{r=1}^{6} \sum_{\rho=1}^{N_r} (\boldsymbol{\eta}_\rho^{(r)} - \boldsymbol{\mu}^{(r)})(\boldsymbol{\eta}_\rho^{(r)} - \boldsymbol{\mu}^{(r)})^T \tag{1.3}$$

whereas the between scatter matrix is defined as:

$$\mathbf{S}_b = \sum_{r=1}^{6} N_r(\boldsymbol{\mu}^{(r)} - \boldsymbol{\mu})(\boldsymbol{\mu}^{(r)} - \boldsymbol{\mu})^T. \tag{1.4}$$

The discriminant constraints are incorporated by requiring $\text{tr}[\mathbf{S}_w]$ to be as small as possible while $\text{tr}[\mathbf{S}_b]$ is required to be as large as possible.

$$D_d(\mathbf{X}||\mathbf{Z}_D\mathbf{H}) = D_N(\mathbf{X}||\mathbf{Z}_D\mathbf{H}) + \gamma\text{tr}[\mathbf{S}_w] - \delta\text{tr}[\mathbf{S}_b]. \tag{1.5}$$

where γ and δ are constants and D is the measure of the cost for factoring $\mathbf{X}$ into $\mathbf{ZH}$ [?].

Following the same Expectation Maximization (EM) approach used by NMF techniques [?], the following update rules for the weight coefficients $h_{k,j}$ that belong to the r-th facial class become:

$$h_{k,j}^{(t)} = \frac{T_1 + \sqrt{T_1^2 + 4(2\gamma - (2\gamma + 2\delta)\frac{1}{N_r})h_{k,j}^{(t-1)}}}{2(2\gamma - (2\gamma + 2\delta)\frac{1}{N_r})}$$

$$\frac{\sum_i z_{i,k}^{(t-1)} \frac{x_{i,j}}{\sum_l z_{i,l}^{(t-1)} h_{l,j}^{(t-1)}}}{2(2\gamma - (2\gamma + 2\delta)\frac{1}{N_r})}. \tag{1.6}$$

where T_1 is given by:

$$T_1 = (2\gamma + 2\delta)(\frac{1}{N_r} \sum_{\lambda, \lambda \neq l} h_{k,\lambda}) - 2\delta\mu_k - 1. \tag{1.7}$$

The update rules for the bases $\mathbf{Z}_D$, are given by:

$$z_{i,k}^{(t)} = z_{i,k}^{(t-1)} \frac{\sum_j h_{k,j}^{(t)} \frac{x_{i,j}}{\sum_l z_{i,l}^{(t-1)} h_{l,j}^{(t)}}}{\sum_j h_{k,j}^{(t)}} \tag{1.8}$$

and

$$z_{i,k}^{(t)} = \frac{\acute{z}_{i,k}^{(t)}}{\sum_l \acute{z}_{l,k}^{(t)}}. \tag{1.9}$$

The above decomposition is a supervised non-negative matrix factorization method that decomposes the facial images into parts while, enhancing the class separability. The matrix $\mathbf{Z}_D^\dagger = (\mathbf{Z}_D^T \mathbf{Z}_D)^{-1} \mathbf{Z}_D^T$, which is the pseudo-inverse of $\mathbf{Z}_D$, is then used for extracting the discriminant features as $\acute{x} = \mathbf{Z}_D^\dagger x$. The most interesting property of DNMF algorithm is that it decomposes the image to facial areas, i.e. mouth, eyebrows, eyes, and focuses on extracting the information hiding in them. Thus, the new representation of the image is a better one compared to the one acquired when the whole image was taken under consideration.

For testing, the facial image $\mathbf{x}_j$ is projected on the low dimensional feature space produced by the application of the DNMF algorithm:

$$\acute{\mathbf{x}}_j = \mathbf{Z}_D^\dagger \mathbf{x}_j \tag{1.10}$$

For the projection of the facial image $\acute{\mathbf{x}}_j$, one distance from each center class is calculated. The smallest distance defined as:

$$r_j = \min_{k=1,\dots,6} \|\acute{\mathbf{x}}_j - \boldsymbol{\mu}^{(r)}\| \tag{1.11}$$

is the one that is taken as the output of the DNMF system.

1.4 Shape information extraction

The geometrical information extraction is done by a grid tracking system, based on deformable models [?]. The tracking is performed using a pyramidal implementation of the well-known Kanade-Lucas-Tomasi (KLT) algorithm. The user has to place manually a number of Candide grid nodes on the corresponding positions of the face depicted at the first frame of the image sequence. The algorithm automatically adjusts the grid to the face and then tracks it through the image sequence, as it evolves through time. At the end, the grid tracking algorithm produces the deformed Candide grid that corresponds to the last frame i.e. the one that depicts the greatest intensity of the facial expression.

The shape information used from the j video sequence is the displacements $\mathbf{d}_j^i$ of the nodes of the Candide grid, defined as the difference between coordinates of this node in the first and last frame [?]:

$$\mathbf{d}_j^i = [\Delta x_j^i \Delta y_j^i]^T \quad i \in \{1, \dots, K\} \quad \text{and} \quad j \in \{1, \dots, N\} \qquad (1.12)$$

where i is an index that refers to the node under consideration. In our case $K = 104$ nodes were used.

For every facial video in the training set, a feature vector $\mathbf{g}_j$ of $F = 2 \cdot 104 = 208$ dimensions, containing the geometrical displacements of all grid nodes is created:

$$\mathbf{g}_j = [\mathbf{d}_j^1 \quad \mathbf{d}_j^2 \quad \dots \quad \mathbf{d}_j^K]^T. \qquad (1.13)$$

Let $\mathcal{U}$ be the video database that contains the facial videos, that are clustered into 6 different classes $\mathcal{U}_k$, $k = 1, \dots, 6$, each one representing one of 6 basic facial expressions. The feature vectors $\mathbf{g}_j \in \Re^F$ labelled properly with the true corresponding facial expression are used as an input to a multi class SVM and will be described in the following section.

1.4.1 Support Vector Machines

Consider the training data:

$$(\mathbf{g}_1, l_1), \dots, (\mathbf{g}_N, l_N) \qquad (1.14)$$

where $\mathbf{g}_j \in \Re^F$ $j = 1, \dots, N$ are the deformation feature vectors and $l_j \in \{1, \dots, 6\}$ $j = 1, \dots, N$ are the facial expression labels of the feature vector. The approach implemented for multiclass problems used for direct facial expression recognition is the one described in [?] that solves only one optimization problem for each class (facial expression). This approach constructs 6 two-class rules where the k-th function $\mathbf{w}_k^T \phi(\mathbf{g}_j) + b_k$ separates training vectors of the class k from the rest of the vectors. Here ϕ is the function that maps the deformation vectors to a higher dimensional space (where the data are supposed to be linearly or near linearly separable) and $\mathbf{b} = [b_1 \dots b_6]^T$ is the bias vector. Hence, there are 6 decision functions, all obtained by solving a different SVM problem for each class. The formulation is as follows:

$$\min_{\mathbf{w}, b, \boldsymbol{\xi}} \quad \frac{1}{2} \sum_{k=1}^{6} \mathbf{w}_k^T \mathbf{w}_k + C \sum_{j=1}^{N} \sum_{k \neq l_j} \xi_j^k \qquad (1.15)$$

subject to the constraints:

$$\mathbf{w}_{l_j}^T \phi(\mathbf{g}_j) + b_{l_j} \geq \mathbf{w}_k^T \phi(\mathbf{g}_j) + b_k + 2 - \xi_j^k \qquad (1.16)$$

$$\xi_j^k \geq 0, \quad j = 1, \ldots, N, \quad k \in \{1, \ldots, 6\} \backslash l_j.$$

where C is the penalty parameter for non linear separability and
$\boldsymbol{\xi} = [\ldots, \xi_i^m, \ldots]^T$ is the slack variable vector. Then, the function used to
calculate the distance of a sample from each center class is defined as:

$$s(\mathbf{g}) = \max_{k=1,\ldots,6} (\mathbf{w}_k^T \phi(\mathbf{g}) + b_k). \qquad (1.17)$$

That distance was considered as the output of the SVM based shape extraction
procedure. A linear kernel was used for the SVM system in order to avoid
search for appropriate kernels.

1.5 Fusion of texture and shape information

The application of the DNMF algorithm on the images of the database resulted in the extraction of the texture information of the facial expressions
depicted. Similarly, the classification procedure performed using the SVM system on the grid following the facial expression through time resulted in the
extraction of the shape information .

More specifically, the image $\mathbf{x}_j$ and the corresponding vector of geometrical displacements $\mathbf{g}_j$ were taken into consideration. The DNMF algorithm,
applied to the $\mathbf{x}_j$ image, produces the distance r_j as a result, while SVMs
applied to the vector of geometrical displacements $\mathbf{g}_j$, produces the distance
s_j as the equivalent result. The distances r_j and s_j were normalized in $[0,1]$
using Gaussian normalization. Thus, a new feature vector $\mathbf{c}_j$, defined as:

$$\mathbf{c}_j = [r_j \quad s_j]^T. \qquad (1.18)$$

containing information from both sources was created.

1.5.1 Radial Basis Function (RBF) Neural Networks (NNs)

A RBF NN was used for the fusion of texture and shape results. The RBF
function is approximated as a linear combination of a set of basis functions
[?]:

$$p_k(\mathbf{c}_j) = \sum_{n=1}^{M} w_{k,n} \phi_n(\mathbf{c}_j) \qquad (1.19)$$

where M is the number of kernel functions and $w_{k,n}$ are the weights of the
hidden unit to output connection. Each hidden unit implements a Gaussian
function:

$$\phi_n(\mathbf{c}_j) = exp[-(\mathbf{m}_n - \mathbf{c}_j)^T \Sigma_n^{-1}(\mathbf{m}_n - \mathbf{c}_j)] \qquad (1.20)$$

where $j = 1, \ldots M$, $\mathbf{m}_n$ is the mean vector and Σ_n is the covariance matrix [?].

Each pattern $\mathbf{c}_j$ is considered assigned only to one class l_j. The decision regarding the class l_j of $\mathbf{c}_j$ is taken as:

$$l_j = \underset{k=1,\ldots,6}{\operatorname{argmax}} p_k(\mathbf{c}_j) \qquad (1.21)$$

The feature vector $\mathbf{c}_j$ was used as an input to the RBF NN that was created. The output of that system was the label l_j that classified the sample under examination (pair of texture and shape information) to one of the 6 classes (facial expressions).

1.6 Experimental results

In order to create the training set, the last frames of the video sequences used were extracted. By doing so, two databases were created, one for texture extraction using DNMF and another one for shape extraction using SVMs. The texture database consisted of images that corresponded to the last frame of every video sequence studied, while the shape database consisted of the grid displacements that were noticed between the first and the last frame of every video sequence.

The databases were created using a subset of the Cohn-Kanade database that consists of 222 image sequences, 37 samples per facial expression. The leave-one-out method was used for the experiments [?]. For the implementation of the RBF NN, 25 neurons were used for the output layer and 35 for the hidden layer.

The accuracy achieved when only DNMF was applied was equal to 86,5%, while the equivalent one when SVMs along with shape information were used was 93,5%. The obtained accuracy after performing fusion of the two information sources was equal to 98,2%. By fusing texture information into the shape results certain confusions are resolved. For example, some facial expressions involve subtle facial movements. That results in confusion with other facial expressions when only shape information is used. By introducing texture information, those confusions are eliminated. For example, in the case of anger, a subtle eyebrow movement is involved which cannot probably be identified as movement, but would most probably be noticed if texture is available. Therefore, the fusion of shape and texture information results in correctly classifying most of the confused cases, thus increasing the accuracy rate.

The confusion matrix [?] has been also computed. It is a $n \times n$ matrix containing information about the actual class label l_j, $j = 1, .., n$ (in its columns) and the label obtained through classification o_j, $j = 1, .., n$ (in its rows). The diagonal entries of the confusion matrix are the numbers of facial expressions that are correctly classified, while the off-diagonal entries correspond to mis-classification. The confusions matrices obtained when using DNMF on texture information, SVM on shape information and when the proposed fusion is applied are presented in Table ??.

Table 1.1. Confusion matrices for DNMF results, SVMs results and fusion results, respectively.

$lab_{cl}\backslash^{lab_{ac}}$	anger	disgust	fear	happiness	sadness	surprise
anger	13	0	0	0	0	0
disgust	10	37	0	0	0	0
fear	4	0	37	0	0	1
happiness	2	0	0	37	0	0
sadness	7	0	0	0	37	5
surprise	1	0	0	0	0	31

$lab_{cl}\backslash^{lab_{ac}}$	anger	disgust	fear	happiness	sadness	surprise
anger	24	0	0	0	0	0
disgust	5	37	0	0	0	0
fear	0	0	37	0	0	1
happiness	0	0	0	37	0	0
sadness	8	0	0	0	37	0
surprise	0	0	0	0	0	36

$lab_{cl}\backslash^{lab_{ac}}$	anger	disgust	fear	happiness	sadness	surprise
anger	33	0	0	0	0	0
disgust	2	37	0	0	0	0
fear	0	0	37	0	0	0
happiness	0	0	0	37	0	0
sadness	2	0	0	0	37	0
surprise	0	0	0	0	0	37

1.7 Conclusions

A novel method for facial expression recognition is proposed in this paper. The recognition is performed by fusing the texture and the shape information extracted from a video sequence. The DNMF algorithm is applied at the last frames of every video sequence corresponding to the greatest intensity of the facial expression, extracting that way the texture information. Simultaneously, a SVM system classifies the shape information obtained by tracking the Candide grid between the first (neutral) and last (fully expressed facial expression) video frame. The results obtained from the above mentioned methods are then fused using RNF NNs. The system achieves an accuracy of 98,2% when recognizing the six basic facial expressions.

1.8 Acknowledgment

This work has been conducted in conjunction with the "SIMILAR" European Network of Excellence on Multimodal Interfaces of the IST Programme of the European Union (www.similar.cc).

References

1. P. Ekman, and W.V. Friesen, "Emotion in the Human Face," *Prentice Hall*, 1975.
2. T. Kanade, J. Cohn, and Y. Tian, "Comprehensive Database for Facial Expression Analysis," *Proceedings of IEEE International Conference on Face and Gesture Recognition*, 2000.
3. B. Fasel, and J. Luettin, "Automatic Facial Expression Analysis: A Survey," *Pattern Recognition*, 2003.
4. S. Zafeiriou, A. Tefas, I. Buciu and I. Pitas, "Exploiting Discriminant Information in Non-negative Matrix Factorization with application to Frontal Face Verification," *IEEE Transactions on Neural Networks*, accepted for publication, 2005.
5. D. D. Lee and H. S. Seung, "Algorithms for non-negative matrix factorization," *Advances in Neural Information Processing Systems*, vol. 13pp. 556–562, 2001.
6. I. Kotsia, and I. Pitas, "Real time facial expression recognition from image sequences using Support Vector Machines," *IEEE International Conference on Image Processing (ICIP 2005)*, 11-14 September, 2005.
7. V. Vapnik, "Statistical learning theory," 1998.
8. A. G. Bors and I. Pitas, "Median Radial Basis Function Neural Network," *IEEE Transactions on Neural Networks*, vol. 7, pp. 1351-1364, November 1996.

Limited Receptive Area neural classifier for texture recognition of metal surfaces

Oleksandr Makeyev[1], Tatiana Baidyk[2] and Anabel Martín[2]
1 National Taras Shevchenko University of Kyiv,
64, Volodymyrska Str., 01033, Kiev, Ukraine
mckehev@hotmail.com
2 Center of Applied Sciences and Technological Development, National
Autonomous University of Mexico, Cd. Universitaria, Circuito Exterior s/n,
Coyoacán, 04510, México, D.F., Mexico
tbaidyk@aleph.cinstrum.unam.mx; anabelmartin@lycos.com

Abstract. The Limited Receptive Area (LIRA) neural classifier is proposed for texture recognition of mechanically treated metal surfaces. It can be used in systems that have to recognize position and orientation of complex work pieces in the task of assembly of micromechanical devices. The performance of the proposed classifier was tested on specially created image database in recognition of four texture types that correspond to metal surfaces after: milling, polishing with sandpaper, turning with lathe and polishing with file. The promising recognition rate of 99.7% was obtained.

1 Introduction

The main approaches to microdevice production are the technology of micro electromechanical systems (MEMS) [1, 2] and microequipment technology (MET) [3-6]. To get the best of these technologies it is important to have advanced image recognition systems.

Texture recognition systems are widely used in industrial inspection, for example, in textile industry for detection of fabric defects [7], in electronic industry for inspection of the surfaces of magnetic disks [8], in decorative and construction industry for inspection of polished granite and ceramic titles [9], etc.

Numerous approaches were developed to solve the texture recognition problem. Many statistical texture descriptors are based on a generation of co-occurrence matrices. In [8] the texture co-occurrence of n-th rank was proposed. The matrix contains statistics of the pixel under investigation and its surrounding. Another approach was proposed in [9]. The authors proposed the coordinated cluster representation (CCR) as a technique of texture feature extraction. The underlying principle of the CCR is to extract a spatial correlation between pixel intensities using

Please use the following format when citing this chapter:

Makeyev, O., Baidyk, T., Martín, A., 2006, in IFIP International Federation for Information Processing, Volume 217, Artificial Intelligence in Theory and Practice, ed. M. Bramer, (Boston: Springer), pp. 375–384.

the distribution function of the occurrence of texture units. Experiments with one-layer texture classifier in the CCR feature space prove this approach to be very promising. Leung et al. [10] proposed textons (representative texture elements) for texture description and recognition. The vocabulary of textons corresponds to the characteristic features of the image. There are many works on applying neural networks in texture recognition problem [11, 12].

In this paper we propose the LIRA neural classifier [4] for metal surface texture recognition. Four types of metal surfaces after mechanical treatment were used to test the proposed texture recognition system.

Different lighting conditions and viewing angles affect the grayscale properties of an image due to such effects as shading, shadowing, local occlusions, etc. The real metal surface images that it is necessary to recognize in industry have all these problems and what is more there are some problems specific for industrial environment, for example, metal surface can have dust on it.

The reason to choose a system based on neural network architecture for the current task was that such systems have already proved their efficacy in texture recognition due to significant properties of adaptability and robustness to texture variety [13].

We have chosen the LIRA neural classifier because we have already applied it in the flat image recognition problem in microdevice assembly and the results were very promising [4]. We have also tested it in handwritten digit recognition task and its recognition rate on the MNIST database was 0.55% [4] that is among the best results obtained on this database.

2   Metal surface texture recognition

The task of metal surface texture recognition is important to automate the assembly processes in micromechanics [3]. To assembly a device it is necessary to recognize the position and orientation of the work pieces to be assembled [4]. It is useful to identify the surface of a work piece to recognize its position and orientation. For example, let the shaft have two polished cylinder surfaces for bearings, one of them milled with grooves for dowel joint, and the other one turned with the lathe. It will be easier to obtain the orientation of the shaft if we can recognize both types of the surface textures.

There are works on fast detection and classification of defects on treated metal surfaces using a back propagation neural network [14], but we do not know any on texture recognition of metal surfaces after mechanical treatment.

To test our texture recognition system we created our own image database of metal surface images. Four texture classes correspond to metal surfaces after: milling, polishing with sandpaper, turning with lathe and polishing with file (Fig. 1). It can be seen that different lighting conditions affect greatly the grayscale properties of the images. The textures may also be arbitrarily oriented and not centered perfectly. Metal surfaces may have minor defects and dust on it. All this image properties correspond to the conditions of the real industrial environment and make the texture recognition task more complicated. Two out of four texture classes that correspond to polishing with sandpaper and to polishing with file sometimes can be hardly distinguished with the naked eye (Fig. 1, columns *b* and *d*).

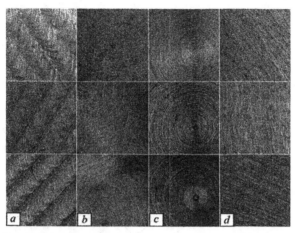

Fig. 1. Examples of metal surfaces after (columns): a) milling, b) polishing with sandpaper, c) turning with lathe, d) polishing with file

3   The LIRA neural classifier

The LIRA neural classifier [4] was developed on the basis of the Rosenblatt perceptron [15]. The three-layer Rosenblatt perceptron consists of the sensor *S*-layer, associative *A*-layer and the reaction *R*-layer. The first *S*-layer corresponds to the retina. In technical terms it corresponds to the input image. The second *A*-layer corresponds to the feature extraction subsystem. The third *R*-layer represents the system's output. Each neuron of this layer corresponds to one of the output classes.

The associative layer *A* is connected to the sensor layer *S* with the randomly selected, non-trainable connections. The weights of these connections can be equal either to 1 (positive connection) or to -1 (negative connection). The set of these connections can be considered as a feature extractor.

A-layer consists of 2-state neurons; their outputs can be equal either to 1 (active state) or to 0 (non-active state). Each neuron of the *A*-layer is connected to all the neurons of the *R*-layer. The weights of these connections are modified during the perceptron training.

We have made four major modifications in the original perceptron structure. These modifications concern random procedure of arrangement of the *S*-layer connections, the adaptation of the classifier to grayscale image recognition, the training procedure and the rule of winner selection.

We propose two variants of the LIRA neural classifier: LIRA_binary and LIRA_grayscale. The first one is meant for the recognition of binary (black and white) images and the second one for the recognition of grayscale images. The structure of the LIRA_grayscale neural classifier is presented in Fig. 2.

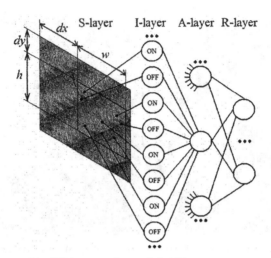

Fig. 2. The structure of the LIRA_grayscale neural classifier

The one-layer perceptron has very good convergence but it demands the linear separability of the classes in the parametric space. To obtain linear separability it is necessary to transform the initial parametric space represented by pixel brightness to the parametric space of larger dimension. In our case the connections between the S-layer and the A-layer transform initial ($W_S \cdot H_S$)-D space (W_S and H_S stand for width and height of the S-layer) into N-dimension space represented by binary code vector. In our experiments $W_S = H_S = 220$ and N varied from 64,000 to 512,000. Such transformation improves the linear separability. The coding procedure used in the LIRA classifier is the following.

3.1   Image coding

Each input image defines the activities of the A-layer neurons in one-to-one correspondence. The binary vector that corresponds to the associative neuron activities is termed the image binary code $A = (a_1, ..., a_N)$, where N is the number of the A-layer neurons. The procedure that transforms the input image into the binary vector A is termed the image coding.

We connect each A-layer neuron to S-layer neurons randomly selected not from the entire S-layer, but from the window $h \cdot w$ that is located in the S-layer (Fig. 2).

The distances dx and dy are random numbers selected from the ranges: dx from $[0, W_S - w)$ and dy from $[0, H_S - h)$. We create the associative neuron masks that represent the positions of connections of each A-layer neuron with neurons of the window $h \cdot w$. The procedure of random selection of connections is used to design the mask of A-layer neuron. This procedure starts with the selection of the upper left corner of the window $h \cdot w$ in which all connections of the associative neuron are located.

The following formulas are used:

$dx_i = random_i (W_S - w)$,

$dy_i = random_i (H_S - h)$,

where i is the position of a neuron in associative layer A, $random_i (z)$ is a random number that is uniformly distributed in the range $[0, z]$. After that position of each connection within the window $h \cdot w$ is defined by the pair of numbers:

$x_{ij} = random_{ij} (w)$,

$y_{ij} = random_{ij} (h)$,

where j is the number of the connection with the retina.

Absolute coordinates of the connection on the retina are defined by the pair of the numbers:

$X_{ij} = x_{ij} + dx_i$,

$Y_{ij} = y_{ij} + dy_i$.

To adapt the LIRA neural classifier for grayscale image recognition we have added the additional 2-state neuron layer between the S-layer and the A-layer. We term it the I-layer (intermediate layer, see Fig. 2).

The input of each I-layer neuron is connected to one neuron of the S-layer and the output is connected to the input of one neuron of the A-layer. All the I-layer neurons connected to one A-layer neuron form the group of this A-layer neuron. There are two types of I-layer neurons: ON-neurons and OFF-neurons. The output of the ON-neuron i is equal to 1 when its input value is larger than the threshold θ_i and it is equal to 0 in opposite case. The output of the OFF-neuron j is equal to 1 when its input value is smaller than the threshold θ_j and it is equal to 0 in opposite case. For example, in Fig. 2, the group of eight I-layer neurons, four ON-neurons and four OFF-neurons, corresponds to one A-layer neuron. The thresholds θ_i and θ_j are selected randomly from the range $[0, \eta \cdot b_{max}]$, where b_{max} is maximal brightness of the image pixels, η is the parameter selected experimentally from the range $[0, 1]$. The i-th neuron of the A-layer is active ($a_i = 1$) only if outputs of all the neurons of its I-layer group are equal to 1 and is non-active ($a_i = 0$) in opposite case.

Taking into account the small number of active neurons it is convenient to represent the binary code vector not explicitly but as a list of numbers of active neurons. Let, for example, the vector A be:

$A = 000100001000000010000$.

The corresponding list of the numbers of active neurons will be 4, 9, and 16. Such compact representation of code vector permits faster calculations in training procedure. Thus, after execution of the coding procedure every image has a corresponding list of numbers of active neurons.

3.2   Training procedure

Before starting the training procedure the weights of all connections between neurons of the A-layer and the R-layer are set to 0. As distinct from the Rosenblatt perceptron our LIRA neural classifier has only non-negative connections between the A-layer and the R-layer.

The first stage. The training procedure starts with the presentation of the first image to the LIRA neural classifier. The image is coded and the R-layer neuron excitations E_i are computed. E_i is defined as:

$$E_i = \sum_{j=1}^{N} a_j \cdot w_{ji},$$

where E_i is the excitation of the i-th neuron of the R-layer, a_j is the output signal (0 or 1) of the j-th neuron of the A-layer, w_{ji} is the weight of the connection between the j-th neuron of the A-layer and the i-th neuron of the R-layer.

The second stage. Robustness of the recognition is one of the important requirements the classifier must satisfy. After calculation of the neuron excitations of the R-layer, the correct class c of the image under recognition is read. The excitation E_c of the corresponding neuron of the R-layer is recalculated according to the formula:

$$E_c^* = E_c \cdot (1 - T_E),$$

where $0 \le T_E \le 1$ determines the reserve of excitation the neuron that corresponds to the correct class must have. In our experiments the value T_E varied from 0.1 to 0.5.

After that we select the neuron with the largest excitation. This winner neuron represents the recognized class.

The third stage. Let us denote the winner neuron number as j keeping the number of the neuron that corresponds to the correct class denoted as c. If $j = c$ then nothing is to be done. If $j \ne c$ then following modification of weights is to be done:

$$w_{ic}(t+1) = w_{ic}(t) + a_i,$$

$$w_{ij}(t+1) = w_{ij}(t) - a_i, \text{ if } (w_{ij}(t+1) < 0) \text{ then } w_{ij}(t+1) = 0,$$

where $w_{ij}(t)$ and $w_{ij}(t+1)$ are the weights of the connection between the i-th neuron of the A-layer and the j-th neuron of the R-layer before and after modification, a_i is the output signal (0 or 1) of the i-th neuron of the A-layer.

The training process is carried out iteratively. After all the images from the training set have been presented the total number of training errors is calculated. If this number is larger than one percent of the total number of images then the next training cycle is performed, otherwise training process is stopped. The training process is also stopped if the number of performed training cycles is more than a predetermined value.

It is obvious that in every new training cycle the image coding procedure is repeated and gives the same results as in previous cycles. Therefore in our experiments we performed the coding procedure only once and saved the lists of active neuron numbers for each image on the hard drive. Later, during the training procedure, we used not the images, but the corresponding lists of active neurons. Due to this approach, the training process was accelerated approximately by an order of magnitude.

It is known [16] that the performance of the recognition systems can be improved with implementation of distortions of the input image during the training process. In our experiments we used different combinations of horizontal, vertical and bias image shifts, skewing and rotation.

3.3   Recognition procedure

In our LIRA neural classifier we use image distortions not only in training but also in recognition process. There is an essential difference between implementation of distortions for training and recognition. In the training process each distortion of the initial image is considered as an independent new image. In the recognition process it is necessary to introduce a rule of decision-making in order to be able to make a decision about a class of the image under recognition based on the mutual information about this image and all its distortions. The rule of decision-making that we have used consists in calculation of the R-layer neuron excitations for all the distortions sequentially:

$$E_i = \sum_{k=0}^{d} \sum_{j=1}^{N} a_{kj} \cdot w_{ji},$$

where E_i is the excitation of the i-th neuron of the R-layer, a_{kj} is the output signal (0 or 1) of the j-th neuron of the A-layer for the k-th distortion of the initial image, w_{ji} is the weight of the connection between the j-th neuron of the A-layer and the i-th neuron of the R-layer, d is the number of applied distortions (case $k = 0$ corresponds to the initial image).

After that we select the neuron with the largest excitation. This winner neuron represents the recognized class.

4   Results

To test our texture recognition system we created our own image database of mechanically treated metal surfaces (see Section 2 for details). We work with four texture classes that correspond to metal surfaces after: milling, polishing with sandpaper, turning with lathe and polishing with file. 20 grayscale images of 220x220 pixels were taken for each class. We randomly divide these 20 images into the training and test sets for the LIRA_grayscale neural classifier. The number of images in training set varied from 2 to 10 images for each class.

All experiments were performed on a Pentium 4, 3.06 GHz computer with 1.00 GB RAM.

We carried out a large amount of preliminary experiments first to estimate the performance of our classifier and to tune the parameter values. On the basis of these preliminary experiments we selected the best set of parameter values and carried out final experiments to obtain the maximal recognition rate. In preliminary experiments the following parameter values were set: window $h \cdot w$ width $w = 10$, height $h = 10$, parameter that determines the reserve of excitation the neuron that corresponds to the correct class must have $T_E = 0.3$. The following distortions were chosen for the final experiments: 8 distortions for training including 1 pixel horizontal, vertical and bias image shifts and 4 distortions for recognition including 1 pixel horizontal and vertical image shifts. The number of training cycles was equal to 30.

The numbers of ON-neurons and OFF-neurons in the I-layer neuron group that corresponded to one A-layer neuron were chosen in order to keep the ratio between the number of active neurons K and the total number of associative neurons N within the limits of $K = c \cdot \sqrt{N}$, where c is the constant selected experimentally from the range [1, 5]. This ratio corresponds to neurophysiological data. The number of active neurons in the cerebral cortex is hundreds times less than the total number of neurons. For example, for the total number of associative neurons N = 512,000 we selected three ON-neurons and five OFF-neurons.

In each experiment we performed 50 runs to obtain statistically reliable results. That is, the total number of recognized images was calculated as number of images in test set for one run multiplied by 50. New mask of connections between the S-layer and the A-layer and new division into the training and test sets were created for the each run.

In the first stage of final experiments we changed the total number of associative neurons N from 64,000 to 512,000. The results are presented in Table 1. Taking into account that the amount of time needed for 50 runs of coding and classifier's training and recognition with N = 512,000 is approximately 3 h and 20 min we can conclude that such computational time is justified by the increase in the recognition rate. That is why we used N = 512,000 in all the posterior experiments.

Table 1. Dependency of the recognition rate on the total number of associative neurons

Total number of associative neurons	Number of errors / Total number of recognized images	% of correct recognition
64,000	20 / 2000	99
128,000	13 / 2000	99.35
256,000	8 / 2000	99.6
512,000	6 / 2000	99.7

In the second stage of final experiments we performed experiments with different combinations of distortions for training and recognition. The results are presented in Table 2. It can be seen that distortions used in training process have great impact on the recognition rate that is no wonder if to take into account that the use of 8 distortions for training allows to increase the size of training set 9 times. Distortions used in recognition process also have significant positive impact on the recognition rate.

Table 2. Dependency of the recognition rate on the distortions

Distortions		Number of errors / Total number of recognized images	% of correct recognition
Training	Recognition		
-	-	1299 / 2000	35.05
-	+	1273 / 2000	36.35
+	-	14 / 2000	99.3
+	+	6 / 2000	99.7

In the third stage of final experiments we performed experiments with different numbers of images in the training and test sets. The results are presented in Table 3. The note tr./t. reflects how many images were used for training (tr.) and how many for testing (t.). It can be seen that even in case of using only 2 images for training and 18 for recognition the LIRA_grayscale neural classifier gives a good recognition rate of 83.39%.

Table 3. Dependency of the recognition rate on the number of images in training set

tr./t.	Number of errors / Total number of recognized images	% of correct recognition
2/18	598 / 3600	83.39
4/16	174 / 3200	94.56
6/14	34 / 2800	98.78
8/12	8 / 2400	99.67
10/10	6 / 2000	99.7

5   Discussion

The LIRA neural classifier was tested in the task of texture recognition of mechanically treated metal surfaces. This classifier does not use floating point or multiplication operations. This property combined with the classifier's parallel structure allows its implementation in low cost, high speed electronic devices. Sufficiently fast convergence of the training process and very promising recognition rate of 99.7% were obtained on the specially created image database (see Section 2 for details). There are quite a few methods that perform well when the features used for the recognition are obtained from a training set image that has the same orientation, position and lighting conditions as the test image; but as soon as orientation or position or lighting conditions of the test image is changed with respect to the one in the training set the same methods will perform poorly. The usefulness of methods that are not robust to such changes is very limited and that is the reason for developing of our texture classification system that works well independently of the particular orientation, position and lighting conditions. In this regard the results obtained in experiments are very promising.

6   Conclusion

This paper continues the series of works on automation of micro assembly processes [3, 4].

The LIRA neural classifier is proposed for texture recognition of mechanically treated metal surfaces. It can be used in systems that have to recognize position and orientation of complex work pieces in the task of assembly of micromechanical devices as well as in surface quality inspection systems. The performance of the proposed classifier was tested on specially created image database in recognition of four texture types that correspond to metal surfaces after: milling, polishing with sandpaper, turning with lathe and polishing with file. The promising recognition rate of 99.7% was obtained.

Acknowledgment

The authors gratefully acknowledge Dr. Ernst Kussul, National Autonomous University of Mexico, for constructive discussions and helpful comments.

This work was supported by projects PAPIIT 1112102, PAPIIT IN116306-3, PAPIIT IN108606-3, NSF-CONACYT 39395-A.

References

1. W.S. Trimmer (ed.), Micromechanics and MEMS. Classical and Seminal Papers to 1990 (IEEE Press, New York, 1997).
2. A.M. Madni, L.A. Wan, Micro Electro Mechanical Systems (MEMS): an Overview of Current State-of-the Art, Aerospace Conference 1, 421-427 (1998).
3. E. Kussul, T. Baidyk, L. Ruiz-Huerta, A. Caballero, G. Velasco, L. Kasatkina, Development of Micromachine Tool Prototypes for Microfactories, J. Micromech. Microeng. 12, 795-813 (2002).
4. T. Baidyk, E. Kussul, O. Makeyev, A. Caballero, L. Ruiz, G. Carrera, G. Velasco, Flat Image Recognition in the Process of Microdevice Assembly, Pattern Recogn. Lett. 25(1), 107-118 (2004).
5. C.R. Friedrich, M.J. Vasile, Development of the Micromilling Process for High- aspect-ratio Micro Structures, J. Microelectromech. S. 5, 33-38 (1996).
6. Naotake Ooyama, Shigeru Kokaji, Makoto Tanaka, et al, Desktop Machining Microfactory, Proc. of the 2-nd International Workshop on Microfactories, 14-17 (2000).
7. Chi-ho Chan, Grantham K.H, Pang, Fabric Defect Detection by Fourier Analysis, IEEE T. Ind. Appl. 36(5), 1267-1276 (2000).
8. L. Hepplewhite, T.J. Stonham, Surface Inspection Using Texture Recognition, Proc. of the 12th IAPR International Conference on Pattern Recognition 1, 589-591 (1994).
9. R. Sanchez-Yanez, E. Kurmyshev, A. Fernandez, One-class Texture Classifier in the CCR Feature Space, Pattern Recogn. Lett. 24, 1503-1511 (2003).
10. T. Leung, J. Malik, Representing and Recognizing the Visual Appearance of Materials Using Three-dimensional Textons, Int. J. Comput. Vision 43(1), 29-44 (2001).
11. M.A. Mayorga, L.C. Ludeman, Shift and Rotation Invariant Texture Recognition with Neural Nets, Proc. of the IEEE International Conference on Neural Networks 6, 4078-4083 (1994).
12. Woobeom Lee, Wookhyun Kim, Self-organization Neural Networks for Multiple Texture Image Segmentation, Proc. of the IEEE Region 10 Conference TENCON 99 1, 730-733 (1999).
13. M.A. Kraaijveld, An Experimental Comparison of Nonparametric Classifiers for Time-constrained Classification Tasks, Proc. of the Fourteenth International Conference on Pattern Recognition 1, 428-435 (1998).
14. C. Neubauer, Fast Detection and Classification of Defects on Treated Metal Surfaces Using a Back Propagation Neural Network, Proc. of the IEEE International Joint Conference on Neural Networks 2, 1148-1153 (1991).
15. F. Rosenblatt, Principles of Neurodynamics (Spartan books, New York, 1962).
16. Y. LeCun, L. Bottou, Y. Bengio, P. Haffner, Gradient-based Learning Applied to Document Recognition, P. IEEE 86(11), 2278-2344 (1998).

A Tracking Framework for Accurate Face Localization

Ines Cherif, Vassilios Solachidis and Ioannis Pitas

Department of Informatics, Aristotle University of Thessaloniki
Thessaloniki 54124, Greece.
Tel: +30-2310996304
{ines,vasilis,pitas}@aiia.csd.auth.gr

Abstract. This paper proposes a complete framework for accurate face localization on video frames. Detection and forward tracking are first combined according to predefined rules to get a first set of face candidates. Backward tracking is then applied to provide another set of possible localizations. Finally a dynamic programming algorithm is used to select the candidates that minimize a specific cost function. This method was designed to handle different scale, pose and lighting conditions. The experiments show that it improves the face detection rate compared to a frame-based detector and provides a higher precision than a forward information-based tracker.

1 Introduction

Achieving a good localization of faces on video frames is of high importance for an application such as video indexing and thus, multiple approaches were proposed to increase the face detection rate. In this paper, we introduce a new method making full use of the information provided by a backward tracking process and merging the latter with the detection and forward tracking results using a Dynamic Programming (DP) algorithm. Detection and forward tracking were associated in several research works to improve the detection rate [1]. Combining forward and backward tracking, on the other hand is a rather new idea. It is suitable for analyzing movie or prerecorded content, since in such cases, we have access to the entire video. An extension to particle filtering is described in [2]. In this probabilistic framework, the preliminary detected faces are propagated by sequential forward tracking. A backward propagation is then performed to refine the previous results. As for Dynamic Programming techniques, they are widely used to tackle various issues, among them motion estimation [3], feature extraction and object segmentation [4]. They were also used to perform the face detection and tracking, searching for the best matching region for a given face template [5]. In [6], a multiple object tracking is presented, where the Viterbi Algorithm is used to find the best path between candidates selected according to skin color criteria.

In this paper, a new deterministic approach is presented. It applies face detection, forward tracking and backward tracking, using some predefined rules.

Please use the following format when citing this chapter:

Cherif, I., Solachidis, V., Pitas, I., 2006, in IFIP International Federation for Information Processing, Volume 217, Artificial Intelligence in Theory and Practice, ed. M. Bramer, (Boston: Springer), pp. 385–393.

From all the possible extracted candidates, a Dynamic Programming algorithm selects those that minimize a cost function.

The paper is organized as follows: Section 2 presents the new framework for the extraction and labelling of the candidates for the face localizations. Section 3 describes how the trellis structure is applied to select the trajectory with the lowest cost. Section 4 provides the results obtained on several video sequences and section 5 concludes the paper.

2 Tracking Framework

In order to achieve a high detection rate on each frame of a video sequence, detection and tracking algorithms were combined and some rules were defined to form a complete tracking framework.

2.1 Detection

The implemented face detector is based on Haar-like features [7]. The algorithm provides good detection results in case the orientation of the face is almost frontal. But it also produces some false alarms. Therefore, a postprocessing step is added for rejecting detected faces, if the number of skin-like pixels present in the detected bounding box is below a threshold. The region of the image containing the detected face is converted into the HSV color space and two morphological operations, erosion and dilation are performed, in order to remove the sparse pixels. The detection bounding box is then replaced by the smallest bounding box containing all the skin-like pixels. This operation helps removing a part of the background and thus better defining the tracked region. The skin-like pixels are identified as those that fulfill the three following conditions:

$$0 < h < 0.1 \tag{1}$$

$$0.23 < s < 0.68 \tag{2}$$

$$0.27 < v \tag{3}$$

where h, s and v are the coordinates of the HSV color space. This approach is similar to the one used in [8].

The detection process is applied on the first and last frame of a shot and every five frames within the shot. This detection frequency appears to provide satisfactory results. Ideally, if a person is once correctly located in each shot, then the forthcoming processes will provide the missing localizations in the other frames.

2.2 Forward Tracking

To be able to localize faces on every video frame, a forward tracking process is performed on each frame, starting from frames where faces have been detected. The tracking algorithm used is the one described in [9], based on the so-called morphological elastic graph matching (EGM) algorithm. It is initialized by the output of the face detection algorithm and the faces can then be tracked until the next detection of the same face or until the end of the shot, if the faces are not detected again.

In fact, one face can be detected several times in a shot, this can lead to multiple tracking of a same actor, which is time consuming. To overcome this problem, a tracking rule is used in order to identify if newly detected faces correspond to previously tracked faces. This rule is based on the percentage of overlap P_{over} between the detected bounding boxes (D_i) and the ones resulting from the forward tracking (F) in the same frame. We define P_{over} as follows:

$$P_{over}(F) = \max_i \frac{A_{(F \bigcap D_i)}}{\min(A_{D_i}, A_F)} \tag{4}$$

where A_{D_i} is the area of the ith detection bounding box and A_F is the area of the forward tracking bounding box. As for $A_{(F \bigcap D_i)}$, it corresponds to the area recovered by both bounding boxes. If P_{over} is higher than 70%, the two bounding boxes correspond to the same actor and the new detection is used to re-initialize the tracker.

This rule is illustrated on Fig 1. On the first frame of the shot, D_1 represents a detected face and is associated to a first actor. The forward tracking of the detected face is performed until the next detection frame and the bounding boxes are assigned the same label (Actor 1). On the next detection frame, D_2 and D_3 are compared to the tracking bounding box on the same frame. The face that fulfills the overlap condition (D_3) is assigned the same label (Actor 1) while the other (D_2) is associated to a new actor (Actor 2). This rule is applied to the other detections D_4 and D_5 as well.

2.3 Backward Tracking

In order to provide a new set of face candidates, a backward tracking process is performed on each frame. The tracker is initialized by the face detection results as shown in Fig 1. This backward process is very useful in case a face is not detected at the beginning but in the middle of a shot. The forward tracking provides the bounding box localizations from the detection frame to the end of the shot. As for the backward tracking, it will provide the missing results from the first frame of the shot to the frame where the last face detection has been performed.

A more interesting contribution of the backward tracking is obtained when the forward tracking or the detection process fails to accurately locate the face of

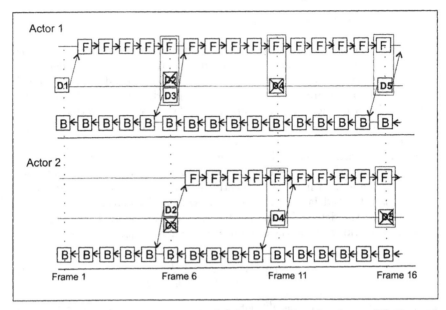

Fig. 1. Illustration of the tracking rule. (D): Detection bounding boxes, (F): Forward tracking bounding boxes and (B): Backward tracking bounding boxes

an actor on a frame i, due for instance to an occlusion, bad illumination or if the tracker sticks to the background. If the next detection of this same actor on the frame $(i + 5n,\ n \in N^*)$ is more precise, then this information will be propagated back and might generate, on i, a new face candidate with a higher accuracy.

Proceeding this way, we will get one, two or three candidates per frame for the face localization, corresponding to respectively the face detection, forward tracking and backward tracking results.

3 A trellis structure for optimal face detection

Now in order to improve face localization, Dynamic Programming is used as a postprocessing. In Section 2, each bounding box was assigned a label. Therefore a trellis can be defined for each actor as represented in Fig 2. The labels D, F and B define the states of the trellis diagram. The frames, where face detection took place can have states D, F and B, while the other frames can have states F and B only.

The complexity of the trellis is considerably reduced in comparison with other approaches that draw the trellis using all the bounding boxes provided by the detector or the tracker [6]. In fact, the number of possible paths in the trellis grows exponentially with the number of nodes. Therefore, limiting the number of candidates to three is a major advantage of this method.

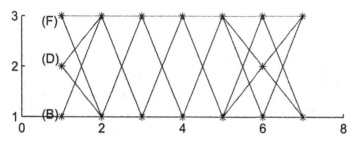

Fig. 2. Model of trellis with 7 frames ($N = 7$). (D): Detection results,(F): Forward tracking results and (B): Backward tracking results

3.1 Cost

Finding the optimal face detection/tracking is equivalent to a best path extraction from a trellis. For each frame of the video sequence we have one, two or three states representing the face candidates provided by the face detection/tracking framework. The cost of a path until the frame l can be expressed as follows:

$$C(l) = -\sum_{i=1}^{l} C(s_i) - \sum_{i=2}^{l} C(s_{i-1}, s_i) \qquad (5)$$

For each edge connecting a state s_{i-1}(corresponding to a bounding box B_{i-1} in the previous frame) to another state s_i(corresponding to a bounding box B_i in the current frame) we define the transition cost $C(s_{i-1}, s_i)$ as a combination of two metrics $C_1(s_{i-1}, s_i)$ and $C_2(s_{i-1}, s_i)$:

1. The first cost C_1 takes into account the overlap between the bounding boxes referenced B_i and B_{i-1}.

$$\mathcal{O}(B_{i-1}, B_i) = \frac{A_{(B_{i-1} \cap B_i)}}{\min(A_{B_{i-1}}, A_{B_i})} \qquad (6)$$

where A_{B_i} is the area of the bounding box B_i. $A_{(B_{i-1} \cap B_i)}$ represents the area of the intersection of the bounding boxes B_i and B_{i-1}. We will assume that the bounding boxes of two consecutive frames must have a non-zero overlap. C_1 will take a $-\infty$ value in order to forbid the transition between non-overlapping bounding boxes.

$$C_1(s_{i-1}, s_i) = \begin{cases} \mathcal{O}(B_i, B_{i+1}), \text{ if } \mathcal{O}(B_i, B_{i+1}) > 0 \\ -\infty, \text{ otherwise} \end{cases} \qquad (7)$$

Practically, a very small negative value will suffice.

2. The cost C_2 is equal to the ratio between the areas of the bounding boxes as specified by Eq.8. This metric penalizes big changes of the bounding box area during tracking.

$$C_2(s_{i-1}, s_i) = \frac{min(A_{B_{i-1}}, A_{B_i})}{max(A_{B_{i-1}}, A_{B_i})} \tag{8}$$

The transition cost $C(s_{i-1}, s_i)$ is then deduced from $C_1(s_{i-1}, s_i)$ and $C_2(s_{i-1}, s_i)$ e.g. by simple multiplication.

To obtain now the node cost $C(s_i)$, we compute the distance between the center of the bounding box (x_{c_i}, y_{c_i}) and the centroid $(\bar{x}, \bar{y})$ of the skin-like pixels.

$$C(s_i) = \exp\left(-\frac{\sqrt{(\bar{x} - x_{c_i})^2 + (\bar{y} - y_{c_i})^2}}{\sqrt{H^2 + W^2}}\right) \tag{9}$$

with H and W being the height and width of the frame.

The position of the centroid is defined as follows:

$$\bar{x} = \frac{1}{nm} \sum_{i=1}^{n} \sum_{j=1}^{m} j A(i,j) \tag{10}$$

$$\bar{y} = \frac{1}{nm} \sum_{i=1}^{n} \sum_{j=1}^{m} i A(i,j) \tag{11}$$

where A is an $n \times m$ matrix, whose elements take the value 1 when the corresponding pixel in the bounding box B_i is skin-like and 0 otherwise.

Once both node and transition costs are defined, the optimal path will be extracted as follows. For each node on the frame l, the accumulate cost $C(l)$ from the first frame to l is calculated using the accumulate cost $C(l-1)$ to the different states in the frame $l-1$. The lowest cost provides the shortest path to the current node and the sequence of nodes leading to this cost are memorized. This process is iterated until the last frame. The shortest path is then retrieved by backtracking the path to the first frame. An example of optimal path is presented on Fig 3 for 30 video frames.

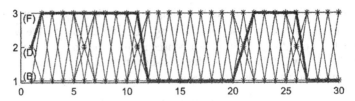

Fig. 3. Shortest path extracted from a 30-frame trellis.

4 Experiments and results

4.1 Metrics for performance evaluation

Three metrics are used to evaluate the performance of the algorithm described above:

- Detection Rate (DR)

$$DR = \frac{N_{GD}}{N_{GT}} \tag{12}$$

where N_{GD} is the number of good detections within the set of detected bounding boxes. N_{GT} is the number of ground-truth bounding boxes. A detected bounding box is considered as good detection if $\frac{A_{(GT \bigcap D)}}{A_{GT}} > 0.3$, where $A_{(GT \bigcap D_i)}$ is the overlapping area between the ground-truth bounding box and the detected bounding box associated to it.
- False Alarm rate (FA)

$$FA = \frac{N_{FA}}{N_D} \tag{13}$$

where N_{FA} refers to the number of false alarms within the set of detected bounding boxes. N_D is the number of bounding boxes detected. A bounding box is counted as false alarm if $\frac{A_{(GT \bigcap D)}}{A_{GT}} < 0.3$.
- Overlap precision measure (P)

$$P = \frac{1}{N_{GD}} \sum_{i=1}^{N_{GD}} \frac{A_{(GT \bigcap D_i)}}{\sqrt{A_{GT} A_{D_i}}} \tag{14}$$

This metric evaluates the overlap between the ground-truth and the correctly detected bounding boxes [10]. This measure not only favors the bounding boxes presenting a high overlap with the ground-truth bounding boxes, but also penalizes those that contain a lot of non-ground-truth pixels

4.2 Results

Ground-truth has been generated manually for a series of video sequences in order to evaluate the performance of the algorithm.
The metrics were calculated for three sets of results. The first set (A) corresponds to the detections performed on each frame, the second set (B) contains the results of the detection (with a five-frame period) combined with a forward tracking process, while the third set (C) represents the detection, forward and backward results merged by the proposed algorithm as shown in the previous sections. The results obtained on three video sequences are presented in Table1.

In the three cases, we notice that the Detection Rate (DR) increases when forward tracking is used. In fact, the face detector fails to determine the position

	Sequence 1			Sequence 2			Sequence 3		
	setA	setB	setC	setA	setB	setC	setA	setB	setC
Detection Rate(DR)	0.6923	1	1	0.7345	1	1	0.6281	0.9587	1
False Alarm (FA)	0	0	0	0	0	0	0.4685	0.5105	0.5105
Precision (P)	0.7911	0.7183	0.7595	0.7971	0.7985	0.8044	0.8262	0.8242	0.8515

Table 1. Performance results.

of some faces due to the pose or the poor illumination. The missed faces can be recovered by the forward tracking process. The Detection Rate (DR) also further increases when both forward and backward tracking have been used, since the face was not detected at the beginning of the shot but after several frames. For each of these frames, the trellis contained only one candidate resulting from backward tracking.

Once candidates were provided by the detector, forward and backward trackers, the trellis performed a selection that always improved the overlap precision (P), i.e. the face localization on the video frame.

We can also notice that one drawback of the tracking approach is that when a face is erroneously detected, then it is tracked on the whole shot thus increasing the False Alarm rate (FA), as can be seen in the case of the sequence 3.

5 Conclusion

In this paper, we proposed a forward/backward tracking process providing an accurate face localization in digital videos. It can also be applied for tracking any object for which we process an object detector. The described process combines detection, forward and backward tracking algorithms in order to extract possible faces. These candidates are used as nodes in a trellis diagram. The extraction of the optimal path from this trellis provided us the optimal choice of the facial bounding boxes. Our approach was mainly oriented towards face localization improvement and we noticed in fact that the precision rate was increased, while realizing a good detection rate. In our future work we will go further into exploiting the trellis structure and work towards decreasing the false alarm rate by merging distinctive trajectories.

6 Acknowledgement

The work presented was developed within NM2 (New Media for a New Millenium), a European Integrated Project (http://www.ist-nm2.org), funded under the European Commission IST FP6 programme.

References

1. R.C. Verma, C. Schmid, and K. Mikolajczyk, "Face detection and tracking in a video by propagating detection probabilities," *IEEE Transactions PAMI*, vol. 25, no. 10, pp. 1215–1228, Oct. 2003.
2. Ji Tao and Yap-Peng Tan, "Accurate face localization in videos using effective information propagation," in *Proc. of the IEEE International Conference on Image Processing (ICIP 2005)*, Genoa, September 2005.
3. M. Gong, "Motion estimation using dynamic programming with selective path search," in *International Conference on Pattern Recognition*, Cambridge, United Kingdom, august 2004, vol. 4, pp. 203–206.
4. Changming Sun and Ben Appleton, "Multiple paths extraction in images using a constrained expanded trellis," *IEEE Trans. Pattern Anal. Mach. Intell.*, vol. 27, no. 12, pp. 1923–1933, 2005.
5. Z. Liu and Y. Wang, "Face detection and tracking in video using dynamic programming," in *Proc. of the IEEE Int. Conf. on Image Processing (ICIP 2000)*, 2000, pp. 53–56.
6. F. Pitié, S-A. Berrani, R. Dahyot, and A. Kokaram, "Off-line multiple object tracking using candidate selection and the viterbi algorithm," in *Proc. of the IEEE Int. Conf. on Image Processing (ICIP 2005)*, Genoa, September 2005.
7. Paul Viola and Michael J. Jones, "Robust real-time face detection," in *IEEE ICCV Workshop on Statistical and Computational Theories of Vision*, Vancouver, Canada, 2001.
8. N. Nikolaidis G. Stamou, M. Krinidis and I. Pitas, "A monocular system for automatic face detection and tracking," in *Proc. of Visual Communications and Image Processing (VCIP 2005)*, Beijing, China, July 2005.
9. N. Nikolaidis G. Stamou and I. Pitas, "Object tracking based on morphological elastic graph matching," in *Proc. of the IEEE Int. Conf. on Image Processing (ICIP 2005)*, Genova, Italy, September 2005.
10. S. Huovinen B. Martinkauppi, M. Soriano and M. Laaksonen, "Face video database," in *Proc. First European Conference on Color in Graphics, Imaging and Vision (CGIV 2002)*, Poitiers, France, April 2002.

A Combination of Spatiotemporal ICA and Euclidean Features for Face Recognition

Jiajin Lei, Tim Lay, Chris Weiland and Chao Lu

Department of Computer and Information Sciences, Towson University
8000 York Road Towson, MD 21252, USA
Email: clu@towson.edu

Abstract

ICA decomposes a set of features into a basis whose components are statistically independent. It minimizes the statistical dependence between basis functions and searches for a linear transformation to express a set of features as a linear combination of statistically independent basis functions. Though ICA has found its application in face recognition, mostly spatial ICA was employed. Recently, we studied a joint spatial and temporal ICA method, and compared the performance of different ICA approaches by using our special face database collected by AcSys FRS Discovery system. In our study, we have found that spatiotemporal ICA apparently outperforms spatial ICA, and it can be much more robust with better performance than spatial ICA. These findings justify the promise of spatiotemporal ICA for face recognition. In this paper we report our progress and explore the possible combination of the Euclidean distance features and the ICA features to maximize the success rate of face recognition.

Keywords: Machine vision, Face recognition, Spatiotemporal ICA.

1. INTRUDUCTION

Face recognition is one of the most successful applications of image processing and analysis, and it has become one of the major topics in the research areas of machine vision and pattern recognition in the recent years. The applications can be seen in, but not limited to, the following areas: access control, advanced human-computer interaction, video surveillance, automatic indexing of images, video database and etc. In reality the process of face recognition is performed in two steps: (1) feature extraction and selection; and (2) classification of objects. These two steps are mutually related. Although the performance of classifier is crucial, a successful face recognition methodology may also depend heavily on the particular choice of features used by the classifier. So as far as face recognition is concerned, much effort has been put on how to extract and select the representative features [1]. Feature extraction and selection involve the derivation of salient features from the raw input data for classification and provide enhanced discriminatory power. Various kinds of methods have been proposed in the literatures [1]. Among them statistical techniques, such as principle component analysis (PCA), independent component analysis (ICA), have been widely used for face recognition. These techniques represent a face as a linear combination of low rank basis images. They employ feature vectors consisting of coefficients that are obtained by simply projecting facial images onto a set of basis images [2]. The practice proved that statistical method offers much more robustness and flexibility in terms of handling variations in image intensity and feature shapes. PCA uses eigenvectors with the largest eigenvalues to obtain a set of basis functions such that the original function can be represented by a linear combination of these basis functions [3]. The basis functions found by the PCA are uncorrelated, i.e. they cannot be linearly predicted from each other. However, higher order dependencies still exist in the PCA and, therefore, the basis functions are not properly separated [4]. ICA is a method that is sensitive to high-order relationship [5, 6]. By using ICA we can explore the important information hidden in high-order relationship among the basis functions. On the other hand Euclidean features are extracted from distances between certain important points on the face. This technique takes the advantage of the fact that different people have different face shape. But how to precisely locate the face organs is a big challenge.

Recently, Chen [7] proposed a spatiotemporal ICA algorithm to identify dynamic micro-Doppler motions. Continuing his work, we have applied spatiotemporal idea to face recognition. All experiments were performed on our special face database collected by AcSys FRS Discovery system. Two face datasets have been set up. One face dataset has less variation, while the other encompasses much more changes in terms of face expression and head side

Please use the following format when citing this chapter:

Lei, J., Lay, T., Weiland, C., Lu, C., 2006, in IFIP International Federation for Information Processing, Volume 217, Artificial Intelligence in Theory and Practice, ed. M. Bramer, (Boston: Springer), pp. 395–403.

movements. In this study a comparison of performances among different face recognition approaches has been made. And we also explore the possible combination of the Euclidean distance features and the spatiotemporal ICA features to maximize the success rate of face recognition.

2.   THE FACE ORGAN LOCALIZATION AND EUCLIDEAN FEATURE COMPUTATION

Feature based face recognition seeks to extract, from a face image, a set of numerical characteristics that can uniquely identify that face. Our proposed feature set is based upon the physical distances between common points of the face. In our study two features were chosen. The first feature was calculated by obtaining the distance between the centers of the eyes and the distance from the center of the left eye to the center of the mouth. These two values were then used to form a ratio in order to normalize for variance in the scaling of each image. The second feature was determined symmetrically with the center of the right eye. The third feature was extracted by making a ratio of the distance between two eyes and distance from the mouth to the middle point of two eyes.

To obtain the centers of the eyes and the mouth, a number of image processing methods were employed. In order to find the eyes, pattern matching was used to locally identify possible eyes. Specifically, the light to dark to light contrast of the pupils and eyelashes was looked for in the original grayscale image. All areas exuding this appearance were highlighted for closer scrutiny in a more global pattern-matching scheme after all potential eyes within a certain area were highlighted.

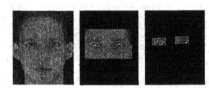

Figure 1. Identify eyes on a face

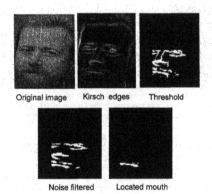

Original image   Kirsch edges   Threshold

Noise filtered   Located mouth

Figure 2. Finding the month on a face

After all areas of interest were highlighted, a simple symmetry detection scheme was implemented to identify possible pairs of eyes. The two pairs closest in size and shape to a predefined notion of an eye were chosen. More specifically, for each pixel, the number of highlighted pixels within a short distance of that pixel was stored at that pixel's location in a two dimensional array. Then two local maxima were searched for which were on approximately the same level. These two points were chosen as the approximate center of the eye, and everything not within a short distance of these areas was erased from the image. The procedures can be seen from Figure 1.

To find the mouth, a kirsch edge detection [8] filter was applied to the preprocessed grayscale image. The image had its edges removed and was then threshed based on the distribution of its histogram. The threshold value was set at the 80th percentile of the gray distribution. The mouth is one of the most contrasting features of the face, and thus with kirsch edge detection, it is featured more brightly than most parts of the face. The image was divided into small blocks in order to search for thin vertical lines and remove them as noise. The next step was to search through the binary image and obtain the characteristics of each cohesive group of remaining pixels. Objects were matched to a predefined notion of what a mouth could be, based on height verse width and area. The best matching group of pixels was taken as the mouth. The procedures of finding the mouth on a face are illustrated in Figure 2.

Obviously the above algorithms have their own problems and weaknesses. These revolve around alterations to the face and large variances in lighting. Dark framed glasses or glasses with any significant glare resulted in erroneous measurements. Asymmetrical facial expressions also resulted in off measurements, especially when the center of the mouth was shifted. Mustaches extending over the mouth also resulted in errors finding and reading the whole of the mouth. When part of the face was cast in a heavy shadow, unsatisfactory features were obtained. Because of these problems it is hard to use these features exclusively for classification. Combination with other features is necessary.

3.   SPATIAL ICA AND SPATIOTEMPORAL ICA FOR FACE RECOGNITION

ICA is a statistical data processing technique to de-correlate the high order relationship of input. It was originally used for blind source separation (BSS). The basic ideal behind is to represent a set of random variables using basic functions, where the components (basic functions) are statistically as independent as possible. The observed random data (signal) $X = (x_1, x_2, ..., x_m)^T$ can be linear combination of independent components (signals) $S = (s_1, s_2, ..., s_n)^T$. We may express the model as

$$X = AS, \tag{1}$$

where A is an unknown constant matrix, called the mixing matrix. In feature extraction the columns of A represent features, and s_i is the coefficient of the ith feature in the data vector X. Several methods for estimation of this model have been proposed [9, 10]. Here we used fixed-point fast ICA algorithm for independent components (ICs) estimation [11].

3.1 Spatial ICA

If we concatenate a 2-D face image column-wisely, it can be represented as a 1-D signal (space-varying signal) as shown in Figure 3. Thus, a single face image becomes one entry in matrix X of (1). In face recognition, the first step is to find the ICs as well as A or its inverse W as in (2) from X by using an ICA algorithm. Each IC component can also be represented by an image. Figure 4 illustrates the procedure, and Figure 5 shows some samples of ICs.

$$\tilde{IC} = W * X, \tag{2}$$

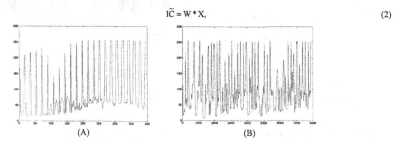

(A)   (B)

Figure 3. Face image signals created by concatenating rows of the image: (A) One face image; (B) A sequence of images

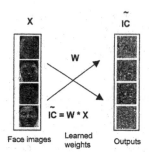

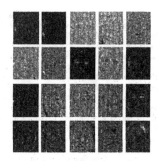

Figure 4. Estimate a set of ICs using ICA algorithm   Figure 5. Some examples of spatial ICs

After ICs have been obtained, any observed new face image can be represented by linear combination of these ICs with a coefficient vector **A** as illustrated in Figure 6, and expressed in (3):

$$X_k(x, y) = \sum_{n=1}^{N} A_n IC_n(x, y), \qquad (3)$$

where $(A_1, A_2, ..., A_n) = $ **A**. The vector **A** is the desirable feature set of the observed image and will be used for classification.

3.2 Spatiotemporal ICA

Basically, spatiotemporal ICA shares the similar ideal with spatial ICA, but using an image sequence instead of a single image as operating unit. The face image sequence contains the features in both the space-domain and the time-domain. The goal of the spatiotemporal approach is to add time-domain feature into spatial 2-D feature set. So an entry in the **X** contains multiple images. A typical temporal image sequence is presented in Figure 7.

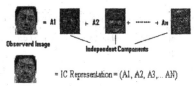

Figure 6. Representation of observed image with ICs

Figure 7. A sample of a face image sequence

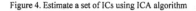

Figure 8. An examples of spatiotemporal ICs

Figure 9. Representation of observed image sequence with spatiotemporal ICs

Similar to the spatial ICA, spatiotemporal ICs can be obtained by using joint spatial and temporal algorithm. That is the entries of **X** in (1) are image sequences. Spatiotemporal ICs are also sequences. Figure 8 illustrates an example of spatiotemporal ICs, where each sequence consists of 12 images.

Observed face image sequences can be represented by the spatiotemporal ICs as illustrated in Figure 9 and expressed with

$$X_k(x,y,t) = \sum_{n=1}^{N} A_n IC_n(x,y,t), \tag{4}$$

where $(A_1, A_2, ..., A_n) = \mathbf{A}$. Notice in (4) that the time feature has been included, which means more information is added in this model with respect to spatial ICA.

4. LOCALIED ICA

With respect to PCA, ICA is spatially more localized [2, 6]. But it does not display perfectly the local characteristics and still uses the whole face information for operation if the input is with entire face images. Actually to recognize a person, ICA only bases on the important and valuable part of face information, such as eyes, mouth, and nose. If the whole face information is used, it may not add any more help. On the other hand, it may "dilute" the essential ones and makes performance deteriorated. So additional localization constraints should be imposed on ICA for better performance. For this purpose we take the advantage of the fact that eyes and mouth can be localized by the algorithm established in section 2. After positions of eyes and mouth have been found, a certain size of patches around eyes and mouth are respectively dug out. These two patches are concatenated together into a vector as the operation unit for matrix **X** of (1).

5. AcSys FRS DISCOVERY SYSTEM AND FACIAL DATABASE PREPARATION

Face database used in this work was produced by AcSys FRS Discovery System, which is powered by HNet technology and developed by AcSys Biometrics Corp., Canada. The System, which is not just a video camera, can track precisely the human face and store a sequence of face images in real time. The purpose of our study is to consider complicated situations, such as different face expressions, face side movements, and other variations (such as with glasses) in the image sequences. The AcSys FRS system can help us to achieve this goal, while other commercially available database cannot. Figure 10 shows the main display screen of the system. Using the functions provided by the system, we can customize and take the sequential face images for different purposes. In this study, two facial datasets have been collected, one with less variation (dataset 1), and the other one with more changes in terms of face expressions and head side movements (dataset 2). For each person 200 face images were sequentially recorded for each dataset. Every face image was manually cropped to 112-by-92 pixel size.

Figure 10. FRS main screen

6. THE EXPERIMENTS

Face recognition experiments respectively using spatial ICA, spatiotemporal ICA, localized ICA, and Euclidean feature were conducted. Instead of one single image used for input data unit as with spatial ICA and localized ICA, spatiotemporal ICA employs a sequence of images (12 images used in our experiments). As a result the dimension of image signal vector can become 12x112x92=123648, which is impracticable in terms of computational speed. To reduce the dimension we resized all the face images to 31-by-21 pixels. For each person 12 image sequences were produced in the following way. In the 200 image long sequence, we randomly choose a starting point, and took the following 12 images as an image sequence like given in Figure 7. For experiments of spatial ICA, localized ICA, and Euclidean features, 20 facial images were randomly picked from 200 images for each individual. In localized ICA, the patch sizes are 20-by-40 for eyes and 20-by-20 for month. For each experiment, we used half of the dataset (6 sequences for spatiotemporal ICA, 10 images for the others) for training and the remaining half for testing.

As mentioned earlier, in order to apply ICA algorithms to 2-D images, we concatenate rows of a 2-D image into a vector. The concatenated face image (space-varying) shares the same syntactic characteristics to regular time-varying signal (see Figure 3). This ensures that ICA can be applied to face image data [12]. After matrix X has been constructed with multi-image vectors, we also apply data normalization to eliminate the variation of images. Independent components (ICs) were estimated using training dataset. With the estimated ICs each observed new face image (sequence) can be represented by variant linear combination of ICs as building blocks. The variation is reflected in the amplitudes of coefficients of ICs (that is rows of matrix A), which can be found by

$$A = X * ICs^{-1} \; , \tag{5}$$

where X is the new image (sequence) matrix (multi-images or image sequences). This matrix A contains representing features of the images (or image sequence). We used it as input data set for classification. For the purpose of performance evaluation, the numbers of ICs (features) from 2 to 200 with 10 as steps were respectively estimated. Classification was done on all of these numbers of features respectively. We calculated 3 Euclidean features for each image. Classification was conducted only once for this experiment.

We also explored performance of feature set combined from ICA features and Euclidean features. For this purpose we just appended Euclidean features to ICA feature space and repeated the above procedures. It must be noted all the experiments were conducted on both dataset1 and dataset2 parallelly.

In our experiments, linear Bayes normal classifier (LDC) and k-nearest neighbor (KNN) classifier [13] were used.

7.   RESULTS AND DISCUSSION

The face recognition rates with respect to different numbers of features for different approaches are shown in Figure 11. The highest values are listed in the Table 1. The results show that spatiotemporal ICA outperforms any other approaches. This gracefully conforms to our expectation. In addition, all approaches perform better using dataset 1 than using dataset 2. This is not surprising since dataset 1 represents more stable condition. What worth noticing at this point are the disparities of performances between using different datasets within the same approach. Even though in Figure 11 (D) we see two performance curves apart in the middle part of the figure, they tend to converge at the end. Especially in Figure 11 (A) two curves get very close. For the other methods the two performance curves are consistently separated. This observation proofs that spatiotemporal ICA is less affected by variations of face expression and other factors. That is spatiotemporal ICA should be more robust than other methods. These findings justify the promise of spatiotemporal ICA for face recognition.

Table 1   The highest recognition rate for each experiment

	Classifier	Spatial ICA		Spatiotemporal ICA		Localized ICA		Euclidean	
		Dataset 1	Dataset 2	Dataset 1	Dataset 2	Dataset 1	Dataset 2	Dataset 1	Dataset 2
Highest Correct Rate	LDC	0.6823	0.6212	0.9724	0.9615	0.7616	0.7043	0.4016	0.3143
	K-NN	0.7002	0.6389	0.8954	0.7979	0.7530	0.7028	0.4021	0.3087

The recognition rate of spatial ICA itself is not good. But after the features were localized the performance was apparently improved (see Figure 11 (B), (C), (E) and (F)). So localization of face images before conducting ICA is a choice for improvement. It is worth for further investigation.

Though Euclidean features can be used in face recognition, it shows very poor performance with 40% recognition rate. In the hope that Euclidean distance features may give help for other approaches, we explored the combination of the Euclidean distance features with ICA features. Figure 12 displays the changes of recognition rates after Euclidean distance features have been added to ICA feature spaces. It seems that when the size of ICA feature space is small, Euclidean distance features put great weight for the performance improvement. But when the number of ICA features gets large the weight of Euclidean features in the total feature space dies away dramatically. This means Euclidean features only helps when the ICA performance is not good enough.

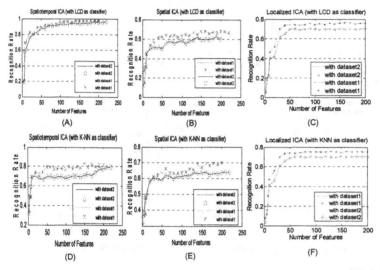

Figure 11. Face recognition rate against different feature numbers

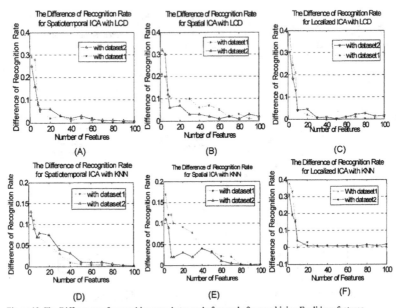

Figure 12. The Differences of recognition rates between before and after combining Euclidean features

Acknowledgements

We would like to thank Dr. Victor C. Chen of NRL, who has made many suggestions and provided support and advice.

References

[1] W. Zhao, R. Chellappa, P. J. Phillips, and A. Rosenfeld, Face Recognition: A Literature Survey, ACM Computing Surveys, Vol.35, No. 4, 399-458, December, 2003.

[2] Jongsun Kim, Jongmoo Choi, Juneho Yi, and Matthew Turk, Effective Representation Using ICA for Face Recognition Robust to Local Distortion and partial Occlusion, IEEE Transactions on Pattern Analysis and Machine Intelligence, Vol. 27, No. 12, 2005, 1977-1981.

[3] M. Turk, A. Pentland, Eigenfaces for Recognition, Journal of Cognitive Neuroscience 3(1), 71-86, 1991.

[4] R. Brunell and T. Poggio, Face Recognition: Features vs. Templates, IEEE Trans. Pattern Analysis and Machine Intelligence, 15(10):1042-1053, 1993.

[5] Chengjun Liu and Harry Wechsler, Comparative Assessment of Independent Component Analysis (ICA) for Face Recognition, In: the 2nd International Conference on Audio- and Video-Based Biometric Person Authentication, AVBPA'99, Washington D.C. USA, March 22-24,1999.

[6] M. Stewart Bartlett, J. R. Movellan, and T. J. Sejnowski, Face Recognition by Independent Component Analysis, IEEE Transactions on Neural Network, Vol.13, Nov., 1450-1464, 2002.

[7] Victor C. Chen, "Spatial and Temporal Independent Component Analysis of Micro-Doppler Features" In: 2005 IEEE International Radar Conference Record, 348 – 353, 9 – 12 May 2005, Arlington, VA, USA.

[8] Umbaugh, Scott E. Computer Imaging: Digital Image Analysis and Processing. New York, Taylor & Francis,2005.

[9] Bruce A. Draper, Kyungim Baek, Marian S. Bartlett, and J. Ross Beveridge, Recognizing Faces with PCA and ICA, http://www.face-rec.org/algorithms/Comparisons/draper_cviu.pdf

[10] Andreas Jung, An Introduction to a New Data Analysis Tool: Independent Component Analysis, http://andreas.welcomes-you.com/research/paper/Jung_Intro_ICA_2002.pdf.

[11] FastICA MATLAB package: http://www.cis.hut.fi/projects/ica/fastica

[12] James V. Stone, *Independent Component Analysis: A Tutorial Introduction*, Bradford Book, 2004.

[13] *R.P.W. Duin, P. Juszczak, P. Paclik,E. Pekalska, D. de Ridder, D.M.J. Tax, Prtools, http://www.prtools.org/.*

Three Technologies for Automated Trading

John Debenham and Simeon Simoff

University of Technology, Sydney, Australia {debenham, simeon}@it.uts.edu.au

Three core technologies are needed for automated trading: data mining, intelligent trading agents and virtual institutions in which informed trading agents can trade securely both with each other and with human agents in a natural way. This paper describes a demonstrable prototype that integrates these three technologies and is available on the World Wide Web. This is part of a larger project that aims to make informed automated trading a reality.

1 Introduction

Three core technologies are needed to fully automate the trading process:

- data mining — real-time data mining technology to tap information flows from the marketplace and the World Wide Web, and to deliver timely information at the right granularity.
- trading agents — intelligent agents that are designed to operate in tandem with the real-time information flows received from the data mining systems.
- virtual institutions — virtual places on the World Wide Web in which informed trading agents can trade securely both with each other and with human agents in a natural way.

This paper describes an e-trading system that integrates these three technologies. The e-Market Framework is available on the World Wide Web[1]. This project aims to make informed automated trading a reality, and develops further the "Curious Negotiator" framework [1]. The data mining systems that have been developed for mining information both from the virtual institution and from general sources from the World Wide Web are described in Sec. 2. Intelligent agent that are built on an architecture designed specifically to handle real-time information flows are described in Sec. 3. Sec. 4 describes the work on virtual institutions — this work has been carried out in collaboration with "Institut d'Investigacio en Intel.ligencia Artificial[2]", Spanish Scientific Research Council, UAB, Barcelona, Spain. Sec. 5 concludes.

2 Data Mining

We have designed information discovery and delivery agents that utilise text and network data mining for supporting real-time negotiation. This work has addressed the

---

[1] http://e-markets.org.au
[2] http://www.iiia.csic.es/

Please use the following format when citing this chapter:

Debenham, J., Simoff, S., 2006, in IFIP International Federation for Information Processing, Volume 217, Artificial Intelligence in Theory and Practice, ed. M. Bramer, (Boston: Springer), pp. 405–414.

central issues of extracting relevant information from different on-line repositories with different formats, with possible duplicative and erroneous data. That is, we have addressed the central issues in extracting information from the World Wide Web. Our mining agents understand the influence that extracted information has on the subject of negotiation and takes that in account.

Real-time embedded data mining is an essential component of the proposed framework. In this framework the trading agents make their informed decisions, based on utilising two types of information (as illustrated in Figure 1): first, information extracted from the negotiation process (i.e. from the exchange of offers), and, second, information from external sources, extracted and provided in condensed form.

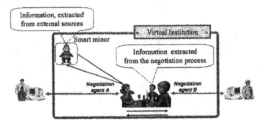

Fig. 1. The information that impacts trading negotiation

The embedded data mining system provides the information extracted from the external sources. The system complements and services the information-based architecture developed in [2] and [3]. The information request and the information delivery format is defined by the interaction ontology. As these agents operate with negotiation parameters with a discrete set of feasible values, the information request is formulated in terms of these values. As agents proceed with negotiation they have a topic of negotiation and a shared ontology that describes that topic. As the information-based architecture assumes that negotiation parameters are discrete, the information request can be formulated as a subset of the range of values for a negotiation parameter. The collection of parameter sets of the negotiation topic constitutes the input to the data mining system. Continuous numerical values are replaced by finite number of ranges of interest.

The data mining system initially constructs data sets that are "focused" on requested information, as illustrated in Figure 2. From the vast amount of information available in electronic form, we need to filter the information that is relevant to the information request. In our example, this will be the news, opinions, comments, white papers related to the five models of digital cameras. Technically, the automatic retrieval of the information pieces utilises the universal news bot architecture presented in [4]. Developed originally for news sites only, the approach is currently being extended to discussion boards and company white papers.

The "focused" data set is dynamically constructed in an iterative process. The data mining agent constructs the news data set according to the concepts in the query. Each concept is represented as a cluster of key terms (a term can include one or more words), defined by the proximity position of the frequent key terms. On each iteration the most frequent (terms) from the retrieved data set are extracted and considered to be related to the same concept. The extracted keywords are resubmitted to the search engine. The process of query submission, data retrieval and keyword extraction is repeated until the search results start to derail from the given topic.

The set of topics in the original request is used as a set of class labels. In our example we are interested in the evidence in support of each particular model camera model. A simple solution is for each model to introduce two labels — positive opinion and negative opinion, ending with ten labels. In the constructed focused data set, each news article is labelled with one of the values from this set of labels. An automated approach reported in [4] extends the tree-based approach proposed in [5].

Once the set is constructed, building the "advising model" is reduced to a classification data mining problem. As the model is communicated back to the information-based agent architecture, the classifier output should include all the possible class labels with an attached probability estimates for each class. Hence, we use probabilistic classifiers (e.g. Naïve Bayes, Bayesian Network classifiers [6] without the min-max selection of the class output [e.g., in a classifier based on Naïve Bayes algorithm, we calculate the posterior probability $\mathbb{P}_p(i)$ of each class $c(i)$ with respect to combinations of key terms and then return the tuples $< c(i), \mathbb{P}_p(i) >$ for all classes, not just the one with maximum $\mathbb{P}_p(i)$. In the case when we deal with range variables the data mining system returns the range within which is the estimated value. For example, the response to a request for an estimate of the rate of change between two currencies over specified period of time will be done in three steps: (i) the relative focused news data set will be updated for the specified period; (ii) the model that takes these news in account is updated, and; (iii) the output of the model is compared with requested ranges and the matching one is returned. The details of this part of the data mining system are presented in [7]. The currently used model is a modified linear model with an additional term that incorporates a news index Inews, which reflects the news effect on exchange rate. The current architecture of the data mining system in the e-market environment is shown in Figure 3. The $\{\theta_1, \ldots, \theta_t\}$ denote the output of the system to the information-based agent architecture.

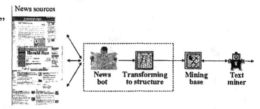

Fig. 2. The pipeline of constructing "focused" data sets

3 Trading Agents

We have designed a new agent architecture founded on information theory. These "information-based" agents operate in real-time in response to market information flows. We have addressed the central issues of trust in the execution of contracts, and the reliability of information [3]. Our agents understand the value of building business relationships as a foundation for reliable trade. An inherent difficulty in automated trading — including e-procurement — is that it is generally multi-issue. Even a simple trade, such as a quantity of steel, may involve: delivery date, settlement terms, as well as price and the quality of the steel. The "information-based" agent's reasoning is

Fig. 3. The architecture of the agent-based data mining system

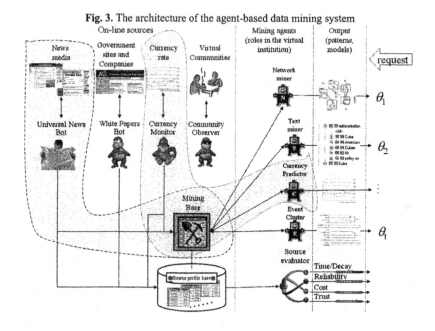

based on a first-order logic world model that manages multi-issue negotiation as easily as single-issue.

Most of the work on multi-issue negotiation has focussed on one-to-one bargaining — for example [8]. There has been rather less interest in one-to-many, multi-issue auctions — [9] analyzes some possibilities — despite the size of the e-procurement market which typically attempts to extend single-issue, reverse auctions to the multi-issue case by post-auction haggling. There has been even less interest in many-to-many, multi-issue exchanges.

The generic architecture of our "information-based" agents is presented in Sec. 3.1. The agent's reasoning employs entropy-based inference and is described in [2]. The integrity of the agent's information is in a permanent state of decay, [3] describes the agent's machinery for managing this decay leading to a characterization of the "value" of information. Sec. 3.2 describes metrics that bring order and structure to the agent's information with the aim of supporting its management.

3.1 Information-Based Agent Architecture

The essence of "information-based agency" is described as follows. An agent observes events in its environment including what other agents actually do. It chooses to represent some of those observations in its world model as beliefs. As time passes, an agent may not be prepared to accept such beliefs as being "true", and qualifies those representations with epistemic probabilities. Those qualified representations of prior observations are the agent's *information*. This information is primitive — it is the agent's representation of its beliefs about prior events in the environment and about the other agents prior actions. It is independent of what the agent is trying to achieve, or what the agent believes the other agents are trying to achieve. Given this information, an agent may then choose to adopt goals and strategies. Those strategies may be based on game theory, for example. To enable the agent's strategies to make good use of its information, tools from information theory are applied to summarize and process that information. Such an agent is called *information-based*.

An agent called Π is the subject of this discussion. Π engages in multi-issue negotiation with a set of other agents: $\{\Omega_1, \cdots, \Omega_o\}$. The foundation for Π's operation is the information that is generated both by and because of its negotiation exchanges. Any message from one agent to another reveals information about the sender. Π also acquires information from the environment — including general information sources —to support its actions. Π uses ideas from information theory to process and summarize its information. Π's aim may not be "utility optimization" — it may not be aware of a

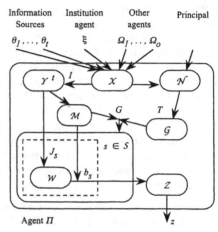

Fig. 4. Basic architecture of agent Π

utility function. If Π *does* know its utility function *and* if it aims to optimize its utility *then* Π may apply the principles of game theory to achieve its aim. The information-based approach does not to reject utility optimization — in general, the selection of a goal and strategy is secondary to the processing and summarizing of the information.

In addition to the information derived from its opponents, Π has access to a set of information sources $\{\Theta_1, \cdots, \Theta_t\}$ that may include the marketplace in which trading takes place, and general information sources such as news-feeds accessed via the Internet. Together, Π, $\{\Omega_1, \cdots, \Omega_o\}$ and $\{\Theta_1, \cdots, \Theta_t\}$ make up a multiagent system. The integrity of Π's information, including information extracted from the Internet, will decay in time. The way in which this decay occurs will depend on the type of information, and on the source from which it was drawn. Little appears to be known about how the integrity of real information, such as news-feeds, decays, although its validity can often be checked — "Is company X taking over company Y?" — by proactive action given a cooperative information source Θ_j. So Π has to consider how and when to refresh its decaying information.

Π has two languages: C and $\mathcal{L}$. C is an illocutionary-based language for communication. $\mathcal{L}$ is a first-order language for internal representation — precisely it is a first-order language with sentence probabilities optionally attached to each sentence representing Π's epistemic belief in the truth of that sentence. Fig. 4 shows a high-level view of how Π operates. Messages expressed in C from $\{\Theta_i\}$ and $\{\Omega_i\}$ are received, time-stamped, source-stamped and placed in an *in-box* $\mathcal{X}$. The messages in $\mathcal{X}$ are then translated using an *import function* I into sentences expressed in $\mathcal{L}$ that have integrity decay functions (usually of time) attached to each sentence, they are stored in a *repository* $\mathcal{Y}^t$. And that is all that happens until Π triggers a goal.

Π triggers a goal, $g \in \mathcal{G}$, in two ways: first in response to a message received from an opponent $\{\Omega_i\}$ "I offer you €1 in exchange for an apple", and second in response to some need, $\nu \in \mathcal{N}$, "goodness, we've run out of coffee". In either case, Π is motivated by a need — either a need to strike a deal with a particular feature (such as acquiring coffee) or a general need to trade. Π's goals could be short-term such as obtaining some information "what is the time?", medium-term such as striking a deal with one of its opponents, or, rather longer-term such as building a (business) relationship with one of its opponents. So Π has a trigger mechanism T where: $T : \{\mathcal{X} \cup \mathcal{N}\} \rightarrow G$.

For each goal that Π commits to, it has a mechanism, G, for selecting a strategy to achieve it where $G : \mathcal{G} \times \mathcal{M} \rightarrow \mathcal{S}$ where $\mathcal{S}$ is the strategy library. A *strategy* s maps an information base into an action, $s(\mathcal{Y}^t) = z \in \mathcal{Z}$. Given a goal, g, and the current state of the social model m^t, a strategy: $s = G(g, m^t)$. Each strategy, s, consists of a *plan*, b_s and a *world model* (construction and revision) *function*, J_s, that constructs, and maintains the currency of, the strategy's *world model* W_s^t that consists of a set of probability distributions. A *plan* derives the agent's next action, z, on the basis of the agent's world model for that strategy and the current state of the social model: $z = b_s(W_s^t, m^t)$, and $z = s(\mathcal{Y}^t)$. J_s employs two forms of entropy-based inference:

- Maximum entropy inference, J_s^+, first constructs an *information base* $\mathcal{I}_s^t$ as a set of sentences expressed in $\mathcal{L}$ derived from $\mathcal{Y}^t$, and then from $\mathcal{I}_s^t$ constructs the world model, W_s^t, as a set of complete probability distributions using maximum entropy inference.
- Given a prior world model, W_s^u, where $u < t$, minimum relative entropy inference, J_s^-, first constructs the incremental information base $\mathcal{I}_s^{(u,t)}$ of sentences derived from those in $\mathcal{Y}^t$ that were received between time u and time t, and then from W_s^u and $\mathcal{I}_s^{(u,t)}$ constructs a new world model, W_s^t using minimum relative entropy inference.

3.2 Valuing Information

A chunk of information is valued first by the way that it enables Π to do something. So information is valued in relation to the strategies that Π is executing. A strategy, s, is chosen for a particular goal g in the context of a particular representation, or environment, e. One way in which a chunk of information assists Π is by altering s's world model W_s^t — see Fig. 4. A model W_s^t consists of a set of probability distributions: $W_s^t = \{D_{s,i}^t\}_{i=1}^n$. As a chunk of information could be "good" for one distribution and "bad" for another, we first value information by its effect on each distribution. For a model W_s^t, the *value* to W_s^t of a message received at time t is the resulting decrease in entropy in the distributions $\{D_{s,i}^t\}$. In general, suppose that a set of stamped messages $X = \{x_i\}$ is received in $\mathcal{X}$. The *information* in X at time t with respect to a particular distribution $D_{s,i}^t \in W_s^t$, strategy s, goal g and environment e is:

$$\mathbb{I}(X \mid D_{s,i}^t, s, g, e) \triangleq \mathbb{H}(D_{s,i}^t(\mathcal{Y}^t)) - \mathbb{H}(D_{s,i}^t(\mathcal{Y}^t \cup I(X)))$$

for $i = 1, \cdots, n$, where the argument of the $D_{s,i}^t(\cdot)$ is the state of $\varPi$'s repository from which $D_{s,i}^t$ was derived. The environment e could be determined by a need ν (if the evaluation is made in the context of a particular negotiation) or a relationship ρ (in a broader context). It is reasonable to aggregate the information in X over the distributions used by s. That is, the information in X at time t with respect to strategy s, goal g and environment e is:

$$\mathbb{I}(X \mid s, g, e) \triangleq \sum_i \mathbb{I}(X \mid D_{s,i}^t, s, g, e)$$

and to aggregate again over all strategies to obtain the value of the information in a statement. That is, the *value of the information* in X with respect to goal g and environment e is:

$$\mathbb{I}(X \mid g, e) \triangleq \sum_{s \in S(g)} \mathbb{P}(s) \cdot \mathbb{I}(X \mid s, g, e)$$

where $\mathbb{P}(s)$ is a distribution over the set of strategies for goal g, $S(g)$, denoting the probability that strategy s will be chosen for goal g based on historic frequency data. and to aggregate again over all goals to obtain the (potential) information in a statement. That is, the *potential information* in X with respect to environment e is:

$$\mathbb{I}(X \mid e) \triangleq \sum_{g \in \mathcal{G}} \mathbb{P}(g) \cdot \mathbb{I}(X \mid g, e) \tag{1}$$

where $\mathbb{P}(g)$ is a distribution over $\mathcal{G}$ denoting the probability that strategy g will be triggered based on historic frequency data.

4 Virtual Institutions

This work is done on collaboration with the Spanish Governments IIIA Laboratory[2] in Barcelona. Electronic Institutions are software systems composed of autonomous agents, that interact according to predefined conventions on language and protocol and that guarantee that certain norms of behaviour are enforced. Virtual Institutions enable rich interaction, based on natural language and embodiment of humans and software agents in a "liveable" vibrant environment. This view permits agents to behave autonomously and take their decisions freely up to the limits imposed by the set of *norms* of the institution. An important consequence of embedding agents in a virtual institution is that the predefined conventions on language and protocol greatly simplify the design of the agents. A Virtual Institution is in a sense a natural extension of the social concept of institutions as regulatory systems that shape human interactions [10].

Virtual Institutions are electronic environments designed to meet the following requirements towards their inhabitants:

1. enable institutional commitments including structured language and norms of behaviour which enable reliable interaction between autonomous agents and between human and autonomous agents;

2. enable rich interaction, based on natural language and embodiment of humans and software agents in a "liveable" vibrant environment.

The first requirement has been addressed to some extent by the Electronic Institutions (EI) methodology and technology for multi-agent systems, developed in the Spanish Government's IIIA Laboratory in Barcelona [10]. The EI environment is oriented towards the engineering of multiagent systems. The Electronic Institution is an environment populated by autonomous software agents that interact according to predefined conventions on language and protocol. Following the metaphor of social institutions, Electronic Institutions guarantee that certain norms of behaviour are enforced. This view permits that agents behave autonomously and make their decisions freely up to the limits imposed by the set of norms of the institution. The interaction in such environment is regulated for software agents. The human, however, is "excluded" from the electronic institution.

The second requirement is supported to some extent by the distributed 3D Virtual Worlds technology. Emulating and extending the physical world in which we live, Virtual Worlds offer rich environment for a variety of human activities and multi-mode interaction. Both humans and software agents are embedded and visualised in such 3D environments as avatars, through which they communicate. The inhabitants of virtual worlds are aware of where they are and who is there — elements of the presence that are excluded from the current paradigm of e-Commerce environments. Following the metaphor of the physical world, these environments do not impose any regulations (in terms of language) on the interactions and any restrictions (in terms of norms of behaviour). When this encourages the social aspect of interactions and establishment of networks, these environments do not provide means for enabling some behavioural norms, for example, fulfilling commitments, penalisation for misbehaviour and others.

Technologically, Virtual Institutions are implemented following a three-layered framework, which provides deep integration of Electronic Institution technology and Virtual Worlds technology [11]. The framework is illustrated in Figure 5. The Electronic Institution Layer hosts the environments that support the Electronic Institutions technological component: the graphical EI specification designer ISLANDER and the runtime component AMELI [12]. At runtime, the Electronic Institution layer loads the institution specification and mediates agents interactions while enforcing institutional rules and norms.

The Communication Layer connects causally the Electronic Institutions layer with the 3D representation of the institution, which resides in the Social layer. The causal connection is the integrator. It enables the Electronic Institution layer to respond to changes in the 3D representation (for example, to respond to the human activities there), and passes back the response of the Electronic Institution layer in order to modify the corresponding 3D environment and maintain the consistency of the Virtual Institution. The core technology — the Causal Connection Server, enables the Communication Layer to act in two directions. Technically, in direction from the Electronic Institution layer, messages uttered by an agent have immediate impact in the Social layer. Transition of the agent between scenes in the Electronic Institution layer, for example, must let the corresponding avatar move within the Virtual World space accordingly. In the other direction, events caused by the actions of the human avatar in

Fig. 5. The three layer architecture and its implementation

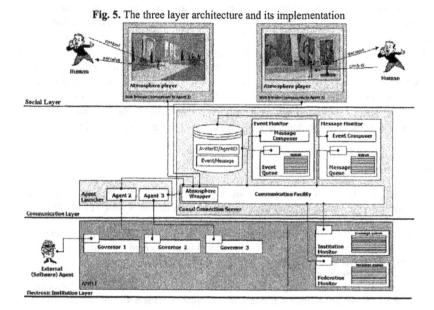

the Virtual World are are transferred to the Electronic Institution layer and passed to an agent. This implies that actions forbidden to the agent by the norms of the institution (encoded in the Electronic Institution layer), cannot be performed by the human. For example, if a human needs to register first before leaving for the auction space, the corresponding agent is not allowed to leave the registration scene. Consequently, the avatar is not permitted to open the corresponding door to the auction (see [11] for technical details of the implementation of the Causal Connection Server).

5 Conclusions

A demonstrable prototype e-Market system permits both human and software agents to trade with each other on the World Wide Web. The main contributions described are: the broadly-based and "focussed" data mining systems, the intelligent agent architecture founded on information theory, and the abstract synthesis of the virtual worlds and the electronic institutions paradigms to form "virtual institutions". These three technologies combine to present our vision of the World Wide Web marketplaces of tomorrow.

The implementation of the three components is described in greater detail on our e-Markets Group Site[1]. The implementation of the data mining systems is notable for the way in which it is integrated with the trading agents — this enables the agents to dynamically assess the integrity of the various information sources. The implementation of the trading agents is greatly simplified by the assumption that preferences for each individual issue are common knowledge and are complementary for each a pair of traders. This assumption, together with the use of coarse discrete representations of continuous variables, reduces the number of possible worlds and simplifies the minimum relative entropy calculations. The implementation of the virtual institutions is an on-going research project with jointly with IIIA[2]. We have built a prototype with a proprietary game engine, and are now moving to modify an open source engine in an attempt to achieve acceptable performance. The whole project is at the 'demonstrable prototype' stage — although we are greatly encouraged by the performance observed. Much work remains to be done, notably implementing a scalable virtual institution.

References

1. Simoff, S., Debenham, J.: Curious negotiator. In M. Klusch, S.O., Shehory, O., eds.: proceedings 6th International Workshop Cooperative Information Agents VI CIA2002, Madrid, Spain, Springer-Verlag: Heidelberg, Germany (2002) 104–111
2. Debenham, J.: Bargaining with information. In Jennings, N., Sierra, C., Sonenberg, L., Tambe, M., eds.: Proceedings Third International Conference on Autonomous Agents and Multi Agent Systems AAMAS-2004, ACM (2004) 664 – 671
3. Sierra, C., Debenham, J.: An information-based model for trust. In Dignum, F., Dignum, V., Koenig, S., Kraus, S., Singh, M., Wooldridge, M., eds.: Proceedings Fourth International Conference on Autonomous Agents and Multi Agent Systems AAMAS-2005, Utrecht, The Netherlands, ACM Press, New York (2005) 497 – 504
4. Zhang, D., Simoff, S.: Informing the Curious Negotiator: Automatic news extraction from the Internet. In: Proceedings 3'rd Australasian Data Mining Conference, Cairns, Australia (2004) 55–72
5. Reis, D., Golgher, P.B., Silva, A., Laender, A.: Automatic web news extraction using tree edit distance. In: Proceedings of the 13'th International Conference on the World Wide Web, New York (2004) 502–511
6. Ramoni, M., Sebastiani, P.: Bayesian methods. In: Intelligent Data Analysis. Springer-Verlag: Heidelberg, Germany (2003) 132–168
7. Zhang, D., Simoff, S., Debenham, J.: Exchange rate modelling using news articles and economic data. In: Proceedings of The 18th Australian Joint Conference on Artificial Intelligence, Sydney, Australia, Springer-Verlag: Heidelberg, Germany (2005)
8. Faratin, P., Sierra, C., Jennings, N.: Using similarity criteria to make issue trade-offs in automated negotiation. Journal of Artificial Intelligence 142 (2003) 205–237
9. Debenham, J.: Auctions and bidding with information. In Faratin, P., Rodriguez-Aguilar, J., eds.: Proceedings Agent-Mediated Electronic Commerce VI: AMEC. (2004) 15 – 28
10. Arcos, J.L., Esteva, M., Noriega, P., Rodríguez, J.A., Sierra, C.: Environment engineering for multiagent systems. Journal on Engineering Applications of Artificial Intelligence 18 (2005)
11. Bogdanovych, A., Berger, H., Simoff, S., Sierra, C.: Narrowing the gap between humans and agents in e-commerce: 3D electronic institutions. In Bauknecht, K., Pröll, B., Werthner, H., eds.: E-Commerce and Web Technologies, Proceedings of the 6th International Conference, EC-Web 2005, Copenhagen, Denmark, Springer-Verlag: Heidelberg, Germany (2005) 128–137
12. :   (Electronic   institution   development   environment: http://e-institutor.iiia.csic.es/)

Modeling Travel Assistant Agents: a graded BDI approach

Ana Casali[1], Lluís Godo[2] and Carles Sierra[2]

[1] Depto. de Sistemas e Informática
Facultad de Cs. Exactas, Ingeniería y Agrimensura - UNR
Av Pellegrini 250, 2000 Rosario, Argentina.
acasali@fceia.unr.edu.ar

[2] Institut d'Investigació en Intel·ligència Artificial (IIIA) - CSIC
Campus Universitat Autònoma de Barcelona s/n
08193 Bellaterra, Catalunya, España.
{godo, sierra}@iiia.csic.es

Abstract. In this paper, we use a graded BDI agent model based on multi-context systems to specify an architecture for a Travel Assistant Agent that helps a tourist to choose holiday packages. We outline the theories of the different contexts and the bridge rules and illustrate the overall reasoning process of our model.

1 Introduction

Nowadays, an increasing number of multiagent systems (MAS) are being designed and implemented. Several theories and architectures have been proposed to give these systems a formal support. Among them, a well-known intentional formal approach is the BDI architecture proposed by Rao and Georgeff [12]. This model is based on the explicit representation of the agent's beliefs (B), its desires (D), and its intentions (I). Indeed, this architecture has evolved over time and it has been applied, to some extent, in several of the most significant multiagent applications developed up to now.

On the other hand, knowledge representation and reasoning under uncertainty is an important traditional AI research field. In the recent past, approximate reasoning models have been used to help knowledge based systems to be more flexible and useful for real applications. In the frame of multiagents systems, i.e. in a distributed platform of autonomous, proactive, reactive and social agents, we wonder how the ideas underlying approximate reasoning could be extended and applied to these systems to enhance their knowledge representation capabilities. Actually, most of agent architectures proposed do not account for uncertain or gradual information. There are a few works that partially address this issue and emphasize the importance of graded models. Notably, Parsons and Giorgini [11] consider in the BDI model the belief quantification by using Evidence Theory. They also set out the importance of quantifying degrees in desires and intentions, but this aspect is not addressed in their work.

Please use the following format when citing this chapter:

Casali, A., Godo, L., Sierra, C., 2006, in IFIP International Federation for Information Processing, Volume 217, Artificial Intelligence in Theory and Practice, ed. M. Bramer, (Boston: Springer), pp. 415–424.

We consider that making the BDI architecture more flexible, will allow us to design and develop agents potentially capable to have a better performance in uncertain and dynamic environments. Along this research line we are concerned with developing a general model for Graded BDI Agents, specifying an architecture able to deal with the environment uncertainty and with graded mental attitudes, see [2, 3] for first results. In these works, belief degrees represent to what extent the agent believes a formula is true. Degrees of positive or negative desires allow the agent to set different levels of preference or rejection respectively. Intention degrees give also a preference measure but, in this case, modeling the cost/benefit trade off of reaching an agent's goal. Then, agents having different kinds of behavior can be modeled on the basis of the representation and interaction of these three attitudes. The graded BDI model we have developed is based on the notion of *multi-context system* (MCS) introduced by Giunchiglia et.al. [5] in order to help in the design of complex logical systems. This framework allows the definition of different formal components and their interrelation. In our approach, we use separate contexts to represent each modality and formalize each context with the most appropriate logic apparatus. The interactions between the components are specified by using inter-unit rules, called *bridge rules*. This approach has been used previously to model agent architectures as in [10], as a framework where the different components of the architecture and their interactions can be neatly represented.

Recently, the Artificial Intelligence community has made a great effort in the development of recommender systems and intelligent agents to help users confronted with situations in which they have too many options to choose from. These systems assist users to explore and to filter out their preferences from a number of different possibilities, many of them coming from the Web. A complete taxonomy of recommender systems can be found in [9]. Between their potential applications, the tourist domain seems to be a good candidate as the offers of tourism products are in constant growth. In this paper, using the graded BDI agent model presented in [2] and extended in [3], we propose an specific architecture for a Travel Assistant Agent, a recommender agent that helps a tourist to choose holiday packages in Argentina. For this purpose, we present the necessary theories for the different contexts and some of the bridge rules. In particular, we introduce some changes in the previously proposed Intention context [2, 3]. In order to evaluate the intention degree of a formula, other variables are taken into account and a set of more flexible functions is defined. In [3] we introduced a Social Context to filter the agent's incoming information, considering the trust in other agents. In this paper, we also extend this Social Context in order to represent the trust needed to decide whether or not to delegate some plans in other agents. By means of this recommender agent, our aim is to illustrate how our model can be used to specify particular agents that operate with graded attitudes and also to illustrate the overall reasoning process of our model.

This paper is organized as follows. In Section 2, the Graded BDI agent model is introduced. In Section 3 we specify the Travel Assistant Agent and in its different subsections, its contexts and some of the main bridge rules are described. Finally, in Section 4 we present some conclusions and future work.

2 Graded BDI agent model

The architecture proposed is inspired by the work of Parsons et.al. [10] about multi-context BDI agents. The MCS specification of an agent contains three basic components: units or contexts, logics, and bridge rules, which channel the propagation of consequences among theories. Thus, an agent is defined as a group of interconnected units: $\langle \{C_i\}_{i \in I}, \Delta_{br} \rangle$, where each context $C_i \in \{C_i\}_{i \in I}$ is the tuple $C_i = \langle L_i, A_i, \Delta_i \rangle$ where L_i, A_i and Δ_i are the language, axioms, and inference rules respectively. When a theory $T_i \in L_i$ is associated with each unit, the specification of a particular agent is complete. The deduction mechanism of these systems is based on two kinds of inference rules, internal rules Δ_i, and bridge rules Δ_{br}, which allow to embed formulae into a context whenever the conditions of the bridge rule are satisfied. In our model, we have *mental* contexts to represent beliefs (BC), desires (DC), intentions (IC), and a social context (SC) which represents the trust in other agents. We also consider two *functional* contexts: for Planning (PC) and Communication (CC). In summary, the BDI agent model is defined as: $A_g = (\{BC, DC, IC, SC, PC, CC\}, \Delta_{br})$.

The overall behavior of the system will depend of the logic representation of each intentional notion in the different contexts and the bridge rules. Figure 1 shows the graded BDI agent proposed with the different contexts and some of the bridge rules relating them.

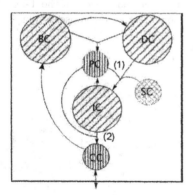

Fig. 1. Multicontext model of a graded BDI agent

In order to represent and reason about graded notions of beliefs, desires and intentions, we use a modal many-valued approach [7] where uncertainty reasoning is dealt with by defining suitable modal theories over suitable many-valued logics. For instance, let us consider a Belief context where belief degrees are to be modeled as probabilities. Then, for each classical formula φ, we consider a modal formula $B\varphi$ which is interpreted as "φ is probable". This modal formula $B\varphi$ is then a *fuzzy* formula which may be more or less true, depending on the probability of φ. In particular, we can take as truth-value of $B\varphi$ precisely the probability of φ. Moreover, using a many-valued logic, we can express the governing axioms of probability theory as logical axioms involving modal formulae. Then, the many-valued logic machinery can be used to reason about the modal formulae $B\varphi$, which faithfully respect the uncertainty model chosen to represent the degrees of belief. To set up an adequate axiomatization for our belief context logic we need to combine axioms for the crisp formulae, axioms of Łukasiewicz logic for modal formulae, and additional axioms for B-modal formulae according to the probabilistic semantics of the B operator. The same many-valued logic approach is used to represent and reason under graded attitudes in the other mental contexts. The formalization of the adequate logics for the different contexts are described in [2, 3].

3 A Travel Assistant Agent

We have designed a Travel Assistant Agent (T-Agent) as an example of recommender agent using our graded BDI agent model. The T-Agent will be in charge of looking for different holidays plans in Argentina, in order to satisfy the desires of a tourist. The plan the T-Agent is expected to offer must be the best choice among the tourist packages supplied by a set of operators. The T-Agent will decide which plan to recommend, taking into account the interests of the tourist, the expected satisfaction of the preferences by the plan, its cost and the trust in the plan supplier. A schematic view of the T-agent and its interaction with the different tourist operators and the user is illustrated in Figure 2.

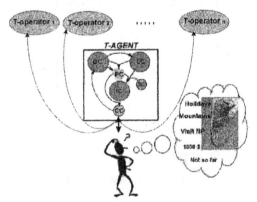

Fig. 2. The multiagent environment of the T-Agent

In the following subsections we outline the particular characteristics of the different contexts, specifying the necessary theories to complete the multicontext specification of the T-Agent.

3.1 Belief Context

The purpose of this context is to model the agent's beliefs about the environment. In order to represent beliefs, we use modal many-valued formulae, following the above mentioned logical framework and considering probability theory as its uncertainty model. In order to define the base (crisp) language, we extend a propositional language L to represent actions, taking advantage of Dynamic logic [2]. These actions, the environment transformations they cause, and their associated cost must be part of any situated agent's belief set. The propositional language L is thus extended to L_D, by adding to it action modalities of the form $[\alpha]$ where α is an action or plan. The interpretation of $[\alpha]\varphi$ is *"after the execution of α, φ is true"*. We define a modal language BC over the language L_D to reason about the belief on crisp propositions. To do so, we extend the language L_D with a (fuzzy) unary modal operator B. If $\varphi \in L_D$, the intended meaning of $B\varphi$ is that *"φ is probable"*. Then the B-modal formulae are built from elementary modal formulae $B\varphi$, and truth constants, using the connectives of Lukasiewicz many-valued logic ($\rightarrow_L$, &). In this logic, modal formulae of the type $\bar{r} \rightarrow_L B\varphi$ express that the probability of φ is at least r and will be denoted as $(B\varphi, r)$.

The theory for the BC of the T-Agent contains:

- General knowledge about the tourism and Argentinian regions and destinations, the geographic characteristic of each region, activities allowed in each place, among others. We structure this knowledge inspired by existing tourism ontologies.
- Information about the tourist plans that the different operators provide. The plans are tourist packages and include the supplier, the cost and description of itinerary. They are structured as follows:

$$package ::= (ID, Operator, Cost, [travel_1, stay_1, ..., travel_n, stay_n, travel_{n+1}])$$

where $travel_i$ is a description of the travel characteristics (e.g. type of transportation, travel length, etc.) and $stay_i$ includes destination, number of days, type of accommodation and activities. Each $travel_i$ and $stay_i$ is considered as atomic sub-plans of a set Π_0, amenable to satisfy desires. Packages P are therefore modeled as composed plans, $\alpha_P \in \Pi$, alternating travel and stay sub-plans.

- Beliefs about how possible desires D (e.g. going to a mountain place or making rafting) are satisfied after executing different plans $\alpha \in \Pi$. Following the model presented, the truth-value of $B([\alpha]D)$ is the probability of having D after following plan α. For instance, the formula *(B[Atuel7]rafting, 0.9)* expresses that the probability of satisfying the goal of making rafting as a consequence of the execution of the plan *Atuel7* is greater than 0.9.

If a package P is composed by a number of subplans $\alpha_i \in \Pi_0$, that is $\alpha_P = \alpha_1; ....; \alpha_n$, the truth-value r of $B([\alpha_P]D)$ will depend on the probabilities r_i of having D after the execution of the sub-plan α_i. Depending on the user's preferences of having the satisfaction of his desire in all the sub-plans, in at least one of them, in most of them, ..., we include the following axiom in this context to model these possible preferences: $(B([\alpha_1]D), r_1) \wedge ... \wedge (B([\alpha_n]D), r_n) \rightarrow (B([\alpha_P]D), \oplus_{i=1,n} r_i)$, where $\oplus$ is an appropriate aggregation operator.

3.2 Desire Context

In this context, we represent the agent's desires. Desires represent the agent's *ideal* preferences regardless of the agent's current perception of the environment and regardless of the cost involved in actually achieving them. Inspired by the works on bipolarity representation of preferences by Benferhat et.al. [1], we suggest to formalize agent's desires also as positive and negative. Positive desires represent what the agent would like to be the case. Negative desires correspond to what the agent rejects or does not want to occur. Both, positive and negative desires can be graded. As for the BC language, the language DC is defined as an extension of a propositional language L by introducing two (fuzzy) modal operators D^+ and D^-. $D^+\varphi$ reads as "φ is positively desired" and its truth degree represents the agent's level of satisfaction would φ become true. $D^-\varphi$ reads as "φ is negatively desired" and its truth degree represents the agent's measure of disgust on φ becoming true.

In this context the tourist's desires will be expressed by a theory containing quantitative expressions about positive and negative preferences, These formulae express in different degrees what the tourist desires, e.g. $(D^+(mountain), 0.8)$ or $(D^+(rafting), 0.6)$, or what it rejects, e.g. $(D^-(northregion), 0.9))$. These desires are the proactive elements of the recommender T-Agent and they start a chain of intra and inter-context deductions in order to determine which is the best touristic plan to recommend to the user.

3.3 Social Context

The aim of considering a Social Context (SC) in the T-agent architecture is to model the social aspects of agency. To do so, a key issue is the modeling of the agent's trust on other agents. In an agent community different kinds of trust are needed and should be modeled [4]. In [3] we used the notion of trust to asses the quality of the information received from other agents. Here, we consider the trust in the touristic package suppliers that interact with the T-Agent in order to evaluate the risk of touristic plans. Assuming we have a multiagent system scenario with a finite set of agents: $\{agent_i\}$, $i \in I_{AG}$, the language for this context is a basic language L extended by a family of modal operators T_{ij}, where $i, j \in I_{AG}$. We consider the trust of an $agent_i$ toward an $agent_j$ about φ, $T_{ij}\varphi$, may be graded taking values in [0,1], to express different levels of trust. Like in the other contexts, we use a many-valued approach for trust modelling. When the agent holding the trust is clear from the context we remove its subindex, that is, $T_{ij}\varphi$ becomes $T_j\varphi$. As for the modal formulae, we follow the intuition that the trust of $\varphi \wedge \psi$ may be taken as the minimum of the trusts in φ and in ψ, hence we interpret the trust operator T_{ij} as a necessity measure on non-modal formulae, adding the corresponding axiomatics. The theory for SC in the T-Agent has formulae like $(T_j[\alpha]\varphi, t)$ expressing that the trust of the T-Agent toward an $agent_j$ about a plan α directed to a goal φ, has degree greater than t. For this application, we consider that the trust depends only on the kind of touristic plan that the operator offers. Hence, we have proposed a plan classification based on a tourism ontology. For instance, we consider the region of the country as a classification element, since there are tour-operators that are good for plans in a particular region, but not in others. We believe that the trust in a provider $agent_j$ is fundamental for the T-Agent to evaluate the risk in endorsing a plan α offered by $agent_j$. Then, as it was mentioned in the IC description, we introduce the trust degree as another variable that must be weighted in the computation of the intention degree. In previous works as in [8], it was considered that the plan quality could be computed as a weighted sum of a *standard rating* (combination of the benefit obtained by the plan execution and its cost) and a *cooperative rating* (evaluated from the trust in the agents involved). For the T-Agent, we propose a weighted combination of the different variables that is formalized in a bridge rule (see (1) in subsection 3.6).

3.4 Intention Context

This unit is used to represent the agent's intentions. Together with the desires, they represent the agent's preferences. However, we consider that intentions cannot depend just on the benefit of reaching a goal φ, but also on the world's state and the cost of transforming it into one where the formula φ is true. By allowing degrees in intentions we represent a measure of the cost/benefit relation involved in the agent's actions towards the goal. Moreover, when the execution of a plan involves the delegation of some actions to other agents, there is some risk that must be contemplated. We present two kinds of graded intentions, intention of a formula φ considering the execution of a particularly plan α, noted $I_\alpha\varphi$, and the final intention to φ, noted $I\varphi$, which take into account the best path to reach φ. Then, for each $\alpha \in \Pi$ we introduce a modal operator I_α, and a modal operator I, in the same way as we did in the other contexts. The intention to make φ true must be the consequence of finding a *feasible* plan α, that permits to achieve a state of the world where φ holds.

A theory for IC in the T-Agent represents those desires the user can intend by different feasible plans. Using this set of graded intentions, the T-Agent derives the final intention and the best recommended touristic plan. This theory is initially empty and will receive from a suitable bridge rule formulae like $(I_\alpha\varphi, i)$ for all the desires φ and for all the feasible plans α that the Planner context PC finds (see subsection 3.5). We consider that the degree of the intention is a function of different variables: the degree d of the desire that intents to satisfy $(D^+\varphi, d)$, the degree of belief r of having the desire after the execution of the plan $(B[\alpha]\varphi, r)$, the normalized cost of the plan c, and the reputation of the tourist supplier o of the plan $(T_o[\alpha]\varphi, t)$. The intention degree is computed as some weighted average $i = f(d, r, c, t \mid w_d, w_r, w_c, w_t)$ by a bridge rule (see (1) in subsection 3.6) that gathers the different degrees d, r, c, t from the appropriate units and their corresponding weights w_d, w_r, w_c, w_t are set to match the tourist's requirements and constraints. For instance, a tourist with little money will increase the weight of the minimum cost criterion and a distrustful user will give more importance to the trust factor. Different functions will define distinct behaviors of the T-Agent. Moreover, for a particular function f, by choosing diverse set of weights the T-Agent can reach different degrees of intentions for a goal φ by a plan α. This allows the T-Agent to take more flexible decisions modeling the user's needs.

3.5 Planner and Communication Contexts

The nature of these contexts is functional and they are essential components of our model. In this work we only draft their functionalities in relation with the mental contexts presented. The Planner Context (PC) has to look for feasible plans in a repository of the touristic packages offered by the different supplier agents. All the touristic plans offered are introduced in the PC via the Communication Context. Within this context, we propose to use a first order language restricted to Horn clauses, where a theory of planning includes at least the following special predicates:

- *plan(α, P, A, c)* where $\alpha \in \Pi$ is the touristic package, P is the set of preconditions; A are the postconditions and $c \in [0, 1]$ is the normalised cost.

- *fplan(φ, α, P, A, r, c)* representing the feasible plan α towards the goal φ, where r is the belief degree of actually achieving φ by performing plan α.

- *bestplan(φ, α, P, A, r, c)* similar to the previous one, but only one instance with the best feasible plan is generated.

Each plan in order to satisfy a goal φ must be feasible, that is, the current state of the world must satisfy the preconditions, the plan must make true the positive desire the plan is built for, and cannot have any negative desire as post-condition. These feasible plans are computed within this unit using an appropriate planner that takes into account beliefs and desires injected by bridge rules from the BC and DC units respectively.

The Communication unit (CC) makes it possible to encapsulate the agent's internal structure by having a unique and well-defined interface with the environment. The theory inside this context will take care of the sending and receiving of messages to and from other agents in the multiagent society where our graded BDI agent lives.

3.6 Bridge Rules

For our T-Agent, we define a collection of basic bridge rules to set the interrelations between contexts. In this Section we comment the most relevant rules and we give an overview of how the T-Agent works.

As already mentioned in the previous section, there are bridge rules from BC and DC to PC that, from the positive and negative desires, the beliefs of the agent regarding what the user can or cannot achieve through a particular plan, generate predicate instances in the PC unit that are used by the planner program to build the feasible plans.

Regarding intentions, there is a bridge rule that infers the degree of $I_\alpha\varphi$ for each feasible plan α that allows to achieve the goal φ. The intention degree is thought as a trade-off among the benefit of reaching a goal, the cost of the plan and the trust in its provider. The following bridge rule computes this value from the degree of $D^+\varphi$, the degree of belief $B[\alpha]\varphi$, the cost of the plan α and the trust t in the tourist supplier o:

$$\frac{DC:(D^+\varphi,d),PC:fplan(\varphi,\alpha,P,A,r,c),SC:(T_o[\alpha]\varphi,t)}{IC:(I_\alpha\varphi,f(d,r,c,t))} \tag{1}$$

Different functions f allow to model different agent behaviors. For instance, if we consider an *equilibrated agent* the function might be defined as a weighted average, where the different weights w_i are set according to the user's interests: $f(d,r,c,t) = (w_d d + w_r r + w_c(1-c) + w_t t) / (w_d + w_r + w_c + w_t)$

The information supplied by the above bridge rule to the IC unit allows this unit to derive, for each goal φ, a formula $(I\varphi, i)$ where i is the maximum degree of all the $(I_\alpha\varphi, i_\alpha)$ formulas, where α is a feasible plan for φ. The plan α_b that allows to get the maximum intention degree i to φ will be set by the PC unit as the *best plan*. Finally, we also need rules to establish the agent's interaction with the user, meaning that if the T-Agent intends φ at degree i_{max}, then the T-Agent will recommend the plan α_b −*bestplan*− that will allow the tourist to reach the most intended goal φ:

$$\frac{IC:(I\varphi,i_{max}),PC:bestplan(\varphi,\alpha_b,P,A,c)}{CC:C(recommends(\alpha_b))} \tag{2}$$

3.7 Implementation

We are now implementing a prototype of this T-Agent in a multi thread version of prolog. Following previous work on implementation of BDI agents [6], we are implementing each mental unit (BC, DC, IC and SC) as a prolog thread, equipped with its own meta-interpreter. The meta-interpreter purpose is to manage inter-thread communication, i.e. all processes regarding bridge rule firing and assertion of bridge rule conclusions into the corresponding contexts. For efficiency reasons, the PC is implemented in the same thread than the BC as they have fluid information interchange when looking for feasible plans. The Communication unit is planned to be implemented in Java as a graphical user interface. This unit will be also in charge of the interchange of messages with the touristic supplier agents.

4 Conclusions and Future Work

We have presented a Travel Assistant Agent specification using our graded BDI agent model. This model allows us to define architectures that explicitly represent the uncertainty of beliefs, graded desires and intentions. Using this framework we defined the T-Agent, a recommender agent for touristic plans in Argentina. The user's profile is incorporated in the T-Agent by introducing his preferences (positive and negative) and the importance he gives to the different variables that weigh in the selection of the plan. This profile together with the touristic information, constitute the knowledge base for the T-Agent's reasoning. With the specification of this concrete agent we aim at showing that our general model is useful and flexible to define particular recommender agents. As for future work, we are working to complete the implementation of the T-Agent architecture presented. This will also allow us to implement a number of particular agents of the T-Agent's family. These specific instances will be obtained by modifying different elements of the model, as the uncertainty model used in the mental contexts or the function that determines the intention degree, among others. This implementation will allow us to experiment and validate the formal model proposed.

Acknowledgments

The authors acknowledge partial support of the Spanish projects AECI PCI-Iberoamérica A/3541/05, TIN2004-07933-C0301 and TIC2003-08763-C02-00.

References

1. Benferhat S., Dubois D., Kaci S. and Prade, H. Bipolar representation and fusion of preferences in the possilistic Logic framework. In *KR-2002*, 421-448, 2002.
2. Casali A., Godo Ll. and Sierra C. Graded BDI Models For Agent Architectures. J. Leite and P. Torroni (Eds.) *CLIMA V, LNAI* 3487, 126-143, 2005.
3. Casali A., Godo Ll. and Sierra C. Multi-Context Specification for Graded BDI Agents. Proceedings of *CONTEXT-05*, Research Report LIP 6, Paris, 2005.
4. Castelfranchi C. and Falcone R. Social Trust: A Cognitive Approach, in *Trust and Deception in Virtual Societies*, Kluwer Academic Publishers, 55-90, 2001.
5. Ghidini C. and Giunchiglia F. Local Model Semantics, or Contextual Reasoning = Locality + Compatibility *Artificial Intelligence*,127(2):221-259, 2001.
6. Giovannucci A. Towards Multi-Context based Agents Implementation. IIIA-CSIC Research Report, 2004.
7. Godo, L., Esteva, F. and Hajek, P. Reasoning about probabilities using fuzzy logic. *Neural Network World*, 10:811–824, 2000.
8. Griffiths N. and Luck M. Cooperative Plan Selection Through Trust. In Proceedings of MAAMAW-99, 162-174, Spain, 1999.
9. Montaner M., López B. and de la Rosa L. A Taxonomy of Recommender Agents on the Internet. In *Artificial Intelligence Review* 19: 285-330, Kluwer, 2003.
10. Parsons, S., Sierra, C. and Jennings N.R. Agents that reason and negotiate by arguing. *Journal of Logic and Computation*, 8(3): 261-292, 1998.
11. Parsons, S. And Giorgini P. On using degrees of belief in BDI agents. In Proceedings of *IPMU-1998*, Paris, 1998.
12. Rao, A. And Georgeff M. Modeling Rational Agents within a BDI-Architecture. In *KR-92*, 473-484 (ed R. Fikes and E. Sandewall), Morgan Kaufmann, 1991.

e-Tools: An agent coordination layer to support the mobility of persons with disabilities.

Cristian Barrué[1], Ulises Cortés[1], Antonio B. Martínez[1], Josep Escoda[1],
Roberta Annicchiarico[2], and Carlo Caltagirone[2,3]

[1] Universitat Politècnica de Catalunya. cbarrue,ia@lsi.upc.edu
[2] IRCCS Fondazione Santa Lucia.
r.annicchiarico,c.caltagirone@hsantalucia.it
[3] Università di Roma "Tor Vergata"

Abstract. This paper outlines the development and integration of an agent coordination layer with a robotic platform to support senior citizens or persons with disabilities. This platform is situated in a given context (such as a Hospital) and it is intended to enhance user's mobility and autonomy. This objective is performed in a safe and sound fashion that meets the sets of laws, norms or protocols which rule the selected context.

1 Introduction

Disability is usually defined as the degree of difficulty or inability to independently perform basic Activities of Daily Living (ADLs) or other tasks essential for independent living, without assistance. It is generally recognized, however, that disability is not merely a function of underlying pathology and impairment, but involves an adaptive process, which is subject to a host of individual (psychosocial) and ecologic (environmental) factors. Currently we define this complex syndrome as Functional Disability (FD)[1]. In fact, FD has to be intended as the result of the interaction of different individual components of compromised functions: physical, emotional, and cognitive aspects usually interact to produce a comprehensive disability which is more than the simple addition of the single impairments, affecting the patient's global function and his self-dependency [2].

Subjects with FD and affected by chronic diseases or outcomes of acute events, such as Parkinson disease, dementia, stroke, accidents, etc. represent a heterogeneous category of individuals: each user may be affected by at least one of these symptoms: ambulatory impairment, memory loss, staggering gait, ataxia, visio-spatial dysfunction, aphasia. In other words, each and every one of these features can be combined differently and with different severity in individual users, impairing their self-dependency and worsening their quality of life. To solve a complex syndrome as FD a number of approaches have been proposed, the most comprehensive being represented by the rehabilitative team. In recent years the introduction of new technologies has been proposed. Assistive

Please use the following format when citing this chapter:

Barrué, C., Cortés, U., Martínez, A.B., Escoda, J., Annicchiarico, R., Caltagirone, C., 2006, in IFIP International Federation for Information Processing, Volume 217, Artificial Intelligence in Theory and Practice, ed. M. Bramer, (Boston: Springer), pp. 425–434.

technologies (AT) may be defined as *devices and techniques that can eliminate, ameliorate, or compensate for functional limitations. They help people with disabling conditions interact more efficiently and effectively with their social and physical environment* [3].

The growing attention given to these citizens creates a need for deploying new types of services to sustain independence and preserve quality of life. Many of those services need to have access to personal data, *e.g.*, user's clinical data or the continuous tracking of that person in a given environment (inside a hospital or a house). These services not only need to be efficient but must also comply with the laws and norms which apply in a country or a region as well as the protocols that rule in a hospital and user or condition specific rules.

One of the most featured tools used by our target population is the wheelchair; unfortunately it is one of the most difficult devices to be autonomously used (requiring control, physical interaction and also planning/ strategy for navigation or obstacle avoidance). One possible solution is represented by the use of power wheelchairs, but the extreme difficulty persons with severe disabilities are taught to manoeuvre them is an example of difficult interaction with AT: nearly one half of the users unable to control a power wheelchair by conventional methods would benefit from an automated navigation system. This indicates a need, not only for more innovation in steering interfaces, but for entirely new technologies for supervised autonomous navigation [4].

In this paper, we present an assistive device realized for a person with disabilities who - due to different pathologies - is no longer able to independently provide to his own self-care [5], and who needs the support of a second person to perform even the simplest every-day activities, referred to as ADLs. The aim is the integration of agent technology with other technologies to build specific *e*-Tools for the target group. *e*-Tools stands for Embedded Tools, as we aim to embed intelligent assistive devices in hospitals, homes and other facilities, creating ambient intelligence environments to give support to users and caregivers. However, according to the type of pathology, the impairment of physical and/or cognitive abilities restricts the possibility of precisely defining the control or maintaining it over a long period of time. Following these remarks, the intelligent platform can provide assistance by suggesting the preferred direction (for example, direction that the user is used to take) so that the user does not have to redefine the control during motion.

In §2 we describe the *e*-Tools project and its current architecture. In §3 we explain the approach followed to design the *agent coordination* layer to coordinate interaction between the software agents, the robotic platform(s) and the environment, and in §4 we present some conclusions.

2 *e*-Tools PROJECT

In order to provide proper healthcare management (embedded monitoring and diagnosis functionalities) and to ease the relation of users with other people and the environment we propose to build an integrated system in which the environment (a home, a hospital) and the people inside it (users, carers) are connected. This approach integrates Ambient Intelligence (sensors, automatic dialers, automatic cooling and heating system) with solutions related to Multi-Agent Systems (MAS), machine learning and other AI techniques, affective computing, wireless devices and robotics. The typical environment considered is a hospital for the neuro-motor rehabilitation, referring to a real institution represented by IRCCS S. Lucia Foundation, located in Rome.

Our target population is characterized by different profiles of FD. That means that an electric-powered wheelchair should be flexible to the needs of different users; at the same time, the wheelchair has to be flexible to the needs of the same user in different times: users go a pathway of changing (dys) functionality - possibly improving - during their illness. The robotic platform we propose (see figure 2b) can be used to support the mobility of senior citizens or persons facing a disability that have a standard wheelchair [5]. That is the platform will be able to drive any standard wheelchair and to provide services through its interface. In this case, wheelchairs will be driven, in an indoor environment, by the robotic platform, supporting the mobility of the person. The platform has to show complete autonomy in tasks such as path planning and location in the environment, and at the same time pay attention to the user's needs and requests. Although the robotic platform will be functioning in a well-known environment, structural elements like corridors, rooms, or halls may differ. The autonomous platform for persons with FD can be considered as an intelligent vehicle whose main feature is moving in areas that are time-dependent and well-known but changing. When a person with disabilities moves in such a platform, he must have the impression that he is in control of the vehicle at all times.

In order to achieve such complex and adaptive behaviour, the system will combine the wheelchair hardware of the robotic platform with a MAS that controls and adapts the behavior of the chair, monitors the state of the user and interacts with him/her through a flexible interface that provides more or less assistance in navigation, depending on the user's individual capabilities. Navigation should be autonomously controlled by the MAS most of the times, to relieve the user from tedious low-level decision-making tasks. To make this possible, the platform will be wirelessly connected to the environment, where an agent-based coordination layer will provide extra information to the robotic platform MAS. To support the agent-based coordination layer and to connect it with the robotic platform MAS, active landmarks will be placed. These active landmarks are small wireless machines installed in some strategic places of an area to transmit local information to the mobile entity. In order to filter all the information received from the sensors and send only relevant information to a given platform, each room must be monitored and controlled by a MAS. This agent-based controller can proactively make decisions about room conditioning, or process sensor signals in order to extract meaningful information (*e.g.* to track a given person in the room).

These elements can be structured into the architecture (see figure 1a) as it was introduced in [3].

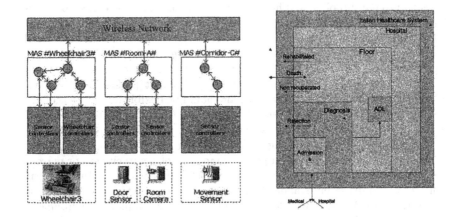

Fig. 1. a) (left) the system levels, b) (right) IRCCS Sta. Lucia organizational simplified model

3 Designing the *e*-Tools Coordination Layer

To deploy *e*-Tools in a real, complex environment such as the IRCCS Santa Lucia, the design and implementation of the agents in the agent-based coordination layer should be done taking into account not only the organizational structures and internal regulations of the IRCCS itself, but also any external requirement defined by the context of IRCCS. In order to introduce all these factors in the design of the multi-agent architecture, we will use the *HARMONIA* approach, introduced in [6]. The idea is to define the agent-based coordination layer as an electronic institution, where not only coordination between the users, the medical staff and the *e*-Tools is provided but also safety mechanisms are included to ensure that the behaviour of the system as a whole and of each individual agent is both *legal* and *acceptable* from the institutional perspective. The institutional model and the concrete role definition was introduced in [7].

The aim of assistive MAS is to provide a series of services to complement and enhance user's autonomy, in many cases severely constrained by their own *FD*, and to give support in rehabilitation tasks. In the other hand the MAS will be collecting information for the medical users like medical data, behavioural data, driving performance, that will be used in medical studies to support diagnosis and treatment.

3.1 The Procedure Level: IRCSS agent-based coordination layer

The Procedure Level focus on the implementation of the Virtual IRCSS by means of an agent-based coordination layer. At this level the main activity is the definition of the agents that will (a) enact the roles defined in the Concrete Level and (b) meet the norms and rules defined in the Concrete Level.

Our MAS has the following basic agents. First, we have a **Patient Agent** (pa), for each client, that could be integrated into the platform or connected to it, for example, using a PDA. This agent enacts the *Patient* role and, therefore, it should provide all the available and permitted services to the user and it should take care of his/hers personal security. Once in a floor, each accepted patient p_i is provided with a personal agent pa_i that allows her to use all the available and authorized agent-based services. Each pa_i is personalized to its owner so its identity is linked to her and makes it unique. Each pa provides a personalized way of interaction with the user and therefore users could use it to ask for help or to ask the platform to drive her/him to a given place into the permitted space or to ask the system to show a possible path to the destination. It should ensure that the user is aware of the activities he (the user) is expected to perform, the pa should augment the likelihood that he will perform at least the compulsory activities such as taking medicines). An important task is however to prevent the user being overly reliant on the system. Also, the pa takes responsibility for auditing the user's biometric signals and acting as a consequence.

The **Medical Agents** (ma) enact the *Caregiver* role, or, (to be more precise), one on the subroles of *Caregiver*, depending on the staff member it is representing and its position in the organizational structure of IRCSS. The ma will be situated in the PCs belonging to the caregivers as well as in their individual PDA. The ma is in charge of managing all the user's request messages. It also serves all caregivers' requests for user information (e.g., a caregiver could use his *Medical Agent* (ma) to ask for: *Tell me Patient$_i$'s (corporal) Temperature* or *Give me the Patient$_i$'s (actual) Status* or *Tell me where Patient$_i$'s is*). Also, the ma notifies the caregiver of any anomaly in the user's biometric signals and it will generate a request for help, if needed. A range of emergency situations can be avoided with such systematic data collection (*e.g.* user's catastrophic reactions). A special task to be performed is to initialize the daily activities for each user, as well as any constraints on, or preferences regarding, the time or manner of their performance. This schedule may then be modified in several ways: (a) the user or a caregiver may add new activities (*e.g.* add a new session at the gym), (b) the user or a caregiver may modify or delete activities already in the schedule, (c) the user performs one of the scheduled activities; or (d) as time goes the schedule is automatically up-dated (*e.g.* changes in priorities).

The **Sensor Network Agent** (sna) undertakes responsibility for the network of sensors. It enacts the *Environment Sensors Manager* role, and its basic target is to distribute the information from all available sensors to all the agents that maybe interested and avoiding to send irrelevant information. Also, it has to report problems and failures in the network. The list of current sensors for this space include: movement, landmarks, cameras, presence, etc.

Finally, the **Main Agent** (MAA) enacts the *Coordinator* and *Information Manager* roles. Therefore, the MAA should keep the coherence of all clients' schedules. MAA is responsible for the protection of all the clients' personal data (this fact is expressed as an Obligation, for example in equation 3). If needed for scalability reasons, the *Coordinator* role can subsequently be distributed in several MAA's which should coordinate among themselves in order to ensure that clinical standards can always be met with certainty. All these agents share an ontology that allow them to exchange information for carrying out their activities. This ontology contains the description of the elements of the physical environment as well as those of the conceptual world that the agents need to know. Also, it contains the actions and propositions that give support to the communicative acts that put them in contact.

3.2 Study

In a controlled experiment carried out at the IRCCS outdoor facilities we got some real users to use a prototype of the MAS controlled platform. This MAS was equiped with prototypes of *pa ma* and the *sna* that allowed users to choose a path to be followed autonomously by the platform in the garden.

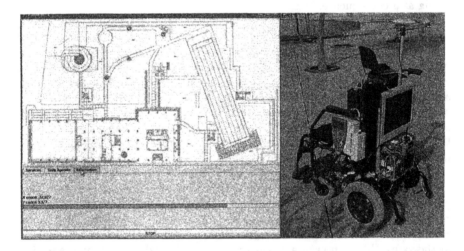

Fig. 2. a) (left) a screen capture of the *pa* monitoring a plan execution, b) (right) The outdoors robotic wheelchair

Figure 2 shows a *pa* capturing the route that the platform is executing on the user's request. It shows the map of the garden indicating the updated platform's position.

Another test was designed to enhance user's autonomy and to evaluate their response to the shared control. For this a specific path was designed and marked on the ground so the users could follow it. An error threshold was established in 30cms from the center line of the given path, when the user drove the platform away of the threshold the MAS got the control returning the platform to the center of the path with the proper orientation. After that, the MAS returned the manual control to the user.

3.3 Virtual Hospital

In figure 1b we show a simplified model of IRCCS Sta Lucia's actual organization and explain some of the scenes that occurs in a hospital to show HAR-MONIA's power to model the agent-mediated interaction in an e-organization.

Patient's are derived into the IRCCS Sta Lucia either by their doctor or from a Hospital to be rehabilitated – to rehabilitate patients from neurological accidents is one of the Sta Lucia's main objectives – there a diagnosticated and either sent to a floor or rejected. Once in a floor, each accepted patient is provided with a personal agent pa_i that allows her to use all the available and authorized agent-based services. Each pa_i is personalized to its owner so its identity is binded to her and makes it unique.

In the following, we will describe typical scenes where pa_i interacts with other agents to accomplish some generic tasks.

Requesting a Plan Here we will illustrate the treatment given to the creation of a plan for a given agent pa_i willing to go from her actual position to a new one X. In our scenario there are two different ways to start this process. Either a user p_i requests the system for a plan to go to X –using her pa_i– or the agent itself initiates the request. We assume that if the pa_i or a_i wants to go to X has the goal to go there $G_{a_i}\mathrm{go}(a_i, x)$. This goal is state in expression 1.

$$G_{a_i}\mathrm{go}(a_i, x) = D_{a_i}\ \mathrm{go}(a_i, x) \wedge \neg B_{a_i} in(a_i, x)$$
$$\wedge\ B_{a_i}\mathrm{achieve}(in(a_i, x)) \tag{1}$$

Once the request arrives into the system we find that the system (sl) has the obligation to find out if pa_i has the necessary permissions to go X before it creates and delivers a plan. Expression 2 depicts all this process.

$$O_{sl}\ (\ \mathrm{check}(sl, P_{a_i}\mathrm{go}(a_i, x))$$
$$< \mathrm{send}(sl, a_i, \mathrm{Plan})) \tag{2}$$

In a hospital or an assisted living facility there are places to which access is forbidden for several reasons to different users. One special case are stairs and lifts. The system should assure that if pa_i is not allowed to change floor she will not use the chairs nor the lifts. Also, in the case of a platform they cannot be used to try to reach the stairs.

Requesting Status A normal action in the daily activity of a healthcare giver is to collect information about a user. In our context this can be achieved using the e-Tools facilities. For example, a caregiver could use his *Medical Agent* (ma) to ask for: *Tell me Patient$_i$'s (corporal) Temperature* or *Give me the Patient$_i$'s (actual) Status* or *Tell me where Patient$_i$ is?* again, before to receive that information the system has the obligation to verify if the requesting ma_k has the appropriate permissions and it will write down the transaction in an special audit file, if finally it decides to deliver the data. This is expressed in expression 3.

$$O_{sl} \ (\text{register}(sl, log,$$
$$\text{personal\_data\_request}(status, ma_k, a_i))) \tag{3}$$

this is because the system should respect the Law on Personal Data Protection [8].

An exception occurs in the case of an emergency. If the system acknowledge that a pa_i is involved in an emergency and this user's *clinical history* (HC) is requested by a caregiver's agent ma_k the system will deliver the information without creating an entrance to the audit files but it will create an obligation in ma_k such that after the end of the emergency it should create an entrance to the audit files as expressed in equation 5. Then, IF Context = Emergency the O_{sl} is created, see expression 4.

$$O_{sl}(\text{inform}(sl, \text{access}(ma_k, \text{HC}(p_i)))) \tag{4}$$

$$O_{ma_k}(\text{declare\_access}(ma_k, \text{HC}(p_i)) > \text{Emergency=NIL}) \tag{5}$$

Help Request Manager When a gethelp request arrives into the system a new situation arises. The system starts to play as Help Request Manager. This request could be originated from two different sources: In the first the a_i decides that her owner is in *problematic* situation and it decides to send a request for help (see equation 6). In the second case is the user himself who calls for help (see equation 7).

$$G_{a_i}\text{gethelp}(p_i, cg_j) = D_{a_i}\text{gethelp}(p_i, cg_j) \qquad G_{p_i}\text{gethelp}(p_i, cg_j) = D_{p_i}\text{gethelp}(p_i, cg_j)$$
$$\wedge \neg B_{a_i}\text{helpattend}(cg_j, p_i) \qquad\qquad \wedge \neg B_{a_i}\text{helpattend}(cg_j, p_i)$$
$$\wedge B_{a_i}\text{needhelp}(p_i) \quad (6) \qquad\qquad \wedge B_{a_i}\text{needhelp}(p_i) \quad (7)$$

When the system sl gets a request as the ones depicted in equations 6 and 7 it should notify it to all the available ma_j and verify that this p_i has not pending requests. This behaviour is defined by equation 8

$$O_{sl}(\text{check}(\neg \text{ wait\_attend}_{p_i})) \ < \text{notify}(sl, ma_k, \text{request}_{p_i})$$
$$\wedge \text{ wait\_attend}_{p_i}) \tag{8}$$

4 Study and Conclusions

An experiment was performed consisting on the pursuit of a simple straight line drawn on the floor using a wheelchair in three different scenarios. The test evaluates the performance of the user navigation using first a conventional wheelchair, secondly a standard electric powered wheelchair manually controlled and, then an autonomous wheelchair prototype with shared control. These tests were all designed to measure the interactions among physical and cognitive capabilities to perform this simple task with more or less assistance. In our experiments, the wheelchairs have been tested by a group of 24 neurological and orthopaedic inpatients who needed a daily use of wheelchair - 10 males (41.7%) and 14 females (58.3%); mean age 67.7 years - during a four-week period. Exclusion criteria were: patients bedridden, patients walking autonomously, presence of global aphasia and blindness. Each subject underwent a structured clinical evaluation and assessment of cognitive, emotional and functional abilities. This entire procedure was performed by a trained physician.

Of all the 24 persons involved in the experiment, 14 finished correctly the first test, while only 12 were able to finish the second. The third test, though, was successfully completed by all 24 persons.

Assistive technologies [9] open a new option to show the versatility and robustness of agent systems on a large scale, reducing the fragility of the conventional software bringing an infrastructure constructed with tolerance to the uncertainty, the inconsistency and different points of view. Technology will never alleviate all problems that aged population and persons with disabilities face, in special those that require a human interaction. e-Tools may also alleviate caregivers from routine tasks and could improve also their quality of life diminishing their degree of distress.

Our main effort is to develop e-Tools capable to supply different levels of disability and to satisfy the needs of each user through its flexibility. We focused on one of the most common problems assistive devices are adopted for: mobility limitations and their correlates. To date, we have developed a) a fully-functional intelligent robotic platform for wheelchairs [5], along with 2) the software to enable to install the agent layer, and 3) a first prototype of the agent coordination layer, following the role structure and objective division defined in §3, but still we have to develop the second layer and to integrate the whole architecture at the IRCCS Santa Lucia in Rome.

Our approach proposes a real integration of heterogeneous technologies to serve to disabled and senior citizen in a non-intrusive way and securing the personal information of the users, working towards an integral solution beyond existing efforts that try to solve subsets of problems. The e-Tools philosophy puts a lot attention in create tools to help users to recover their autonomy in as much as possible. In this sense, our tools are meant not to override any of the personal capabilities of the user if s/he can solve a situation on their own.

References

1. Guralnik, J., Land, K., Blazer, D., Fillenbaum, G., Branch, L.: Educational status and active life expectancy among older blacks and whites. The New England journal of medicine **329** (1993) 126–127
2. Fehr, L., Langbein, W., Skaar, S.: Adequacy of power wheelchair control interfaces for persons with severe disabilities: A clinical survey. Journal of Rehabilitation Research and Development **37** (2000)
3. Cortés, U., Annicchiarico, R., Vázquez-Salceda, J., Urdiales, C., Cañamero, L., López, M., Sànchez-Marrè, M., Caltagirone, C.: Assistive technologies for the disabled and for the new generation of senior citizens: the e-Tools architecture. AI Communications **16** (2003) 193–207
4. Urdiales, C., Bandera, A., Pérez, E., Poncela, A., Sandoval, F. In: Hierarchical planning in a mobile robot for map learning and navigation. Physica-Verlag, Heidelberg (2002)
5. Martínez, A., Escoda, J., Benedico, T., Cortés, U., Annicchiarico, R., Barrué, C., Caltagirone, C.: Patient driven mobile platform to enhance conventional wheelchair, with mul- tiagent system supervisory control. In: Multi-Agent Systems and Applications IV: 4th International Central and Eastern European Conference on Multi-Agent Systems, CEEMAS 2005. Volume 3690 of Lecture Notes in Computer Science., Springer-Verlag (2005) 92–101
6. Vázquez-Salceda, J.: The Role of Norms and Electronic Institutions in Multi-Agent Systems: The HARMONIA Frameworks. Whitestein Series in Software Agent Technologies (2004)
7. Barrué, C., U.Cortés, Martínez, A., Vázquez-Salceda, J., Annicchiarico, R., C.Caltagirone: An e-institution framework for the deployment of e-tools to support persons with disabilities. (In: 3rd Workshop on Agents Applied in Health Care. 19th International Joint Conference on Artificial Intelligence (IJCAI-05)) 6–15
8. : Directive 95/46/CE of the European Parliament and of the Council of 24 october 1995 on the protection of individuals with regard to the processing of personal data and of the free movement of such data (1995)
9. Mittal, V., Yanco, H., Aronis, J., Simpson, R., eds.: Assistive Technology and Artificial Intelligence: Applications in Robotics, User Interfaces and Natural Language Processing. Volume 1458 of Lecture Notes in Artificial Intelligence. Springer-Verlag, Berlin (1998)

Conceptualization Maturity Metrics for Expert Systems

Ovind Hauge, Paola Britos and Ramón García-Martínez

Norsk Teknisk Naturvitenskapelig Universitet. Norway
Software & Knowledge Engineering Center. Graduate School. Buenos Aires Institute of
Technology. Argentine
Intelligent Systems Lab. School of Engineering. University of Buenos Aires. Argentine
rgm@itba.edu.ar

Abstract. Metrics used on development of expert systems is not a well
investigated problem area. This article suggests some metrics to be used to
measure the maturity of the conceptualization process and the complexity of the
decision process in the problem domain. We propose some further work to be
done with these metrics. Applying those metrics makes new and interesting
problems, concerning the structure of knowledge to surface.

1. Metrics

In software development measurement is used to provide some type of quantitative
information to a decision making process, in many cases related to a development
project [Ford, 2004; SEI, 2004]. The measurement can be on the production process
or on the product it self. A metric should have different qualities to be applicable. It
should as said be quantitative, but also objective, easy to find and well defined with a
defined domain. The process of developing software is not trivial and measurement is
done with relatively high uncertainty, but there are several metrics that are widely
used today.

2. Suggested Metrics

In this section we propose some metrics that will examine the problem domain in
expert system development context [García-Martinez & Britos, 2004, Firestone,
2004]. We will give interpretations of the metrics and will describe the expected
development of the metrics throughout a development project. A metric should as
mentioned have certain qualities as simplicity to be applicable. In the representations
of knowledge there are several things that have these qualities. Rules, concepts,
attributes and levels of decomposition are easy to count, they are objective and they
are easy to find [Menzies,1999; Menzies & Cukic, 1999; 2000; Pasan & Clifford,
1991; Kang & Bahieel, 1990]. These things are therefore good candidates to be
included in a metric. Then our suggested metrics are based on rules, concepts,
attributes and number of decomposition levels [Nilsson, 1998].

Please use the following format when citing this chapter:

Hauge, O., Britos, P., Garcia-Martínez, R., 2006, in IFIP International Federation for Information Processing, Volume 217,
Artificial Intelligence in Theory and Practice, ed. M. Bramer, (Boston: Springer), pp. 435–444.

2.1. Number of Concepts, Number of Rules or Number of Attributes

These are a very simple metrics. It is just to count the concepts, rules and attributes. But simplicity is good and these could tell us something about the complexity of the domain. we expect these metric to be increasing all the way throughout the project and converge to an unknown number at the end of the project. Since their values will increase all the way throughout the project it is hard to use them as a metric for maturity. But it could be an indication of maturity when their numbers converge. The table 1 shows the interpretations of these metrics.

Result	Cause
Low Few known concepts, rules or attributes	• The problem area is simple • We do not know many of the concepts in the domain yet
High Many known concepts, rules or attributes	• The domain is complex with many concepts • We have good knowledge about the domain

Table 1. Interpretations of results from "counting metrics"

These metric could be more useful if the results are compared to history from other projects in the same stages. When comparing to history data it could get an indication of the complexity of the project. These metrics will also be combined to others in the following sections.

2.2. Number of Concepts in a Rule / Number of Concepts

The number of concepts in a rule is the concepts that are already included in a rule. If you have 10 concepts and 7 of them are included in one or more rules the ratio will be 0.7. We believe this metric should converge to 1 when the project matures. The value will of course vary when you find new rules and new concepts. The value of this metric will decrease when we discover new concepts and increase when we include a new concept in a rule. If the value of this metric does not converge to 1 we either miss knowledge about relations between concepts in the domain or we have concepts in our knowledge base that are not used and most likely uninteresting. These concepts should therefore be removed. The interpretation of this metric is shown in the table 2.

Result	Cause
Low Many concepts not included in a rule	• We miss knowledge about the concepts and the relations between concepts • We have many concepts that are uninteresting in our knowledge base
High Most concepts included in a rule	• We have good knowledge about the concepts • We have few uninteresting concepts in the knowledge base • There are many relations in the domain

Table 2. Interpretation of results from "concepts in rule/concepts"

This metric will give a measure of the maturity of the knowledge base. If the value is close to 1 this it an indication that the knowledge base is mature. But pay attention to those cases where there are many relations in the domain. If there are a plenty of relations this metric can give a high value without a mature knowledge base as well.

This metric is therefore best to use for simple projects or together with a metric for complexity.

2.3. Number of Attributes in a Rule / Number of Attributes

This metric is similar to the previous one but we expect it to be easier to discover the concepts that the attributes. Because the attributes may not be discovered before we need them it is a bit difficult to use them as a measure of maturity. But if we have unused attributes we may miss something or we have included attributes that are unnecessary. If this is the case we should look at the reason and especially if the value of this metric is low. This metric could therefore be used as an indicator or alarm.

2.4. Number of Concepts / Number of Rules

This metric shows the development of the number of rules compared to the number of concepts. We expect that most concepts contribute to the creation of at least one or most likely several rules. And with good knowledge about the relations in the domain this metric will in most cases decrease below 1.0. In highly related problem domain will the value be much lower than 1.0. This metric can still have a high value at the same time as we have a mature knowledge base. In the cases where the domain only contains a small set of very complex relations the number of rules will be low, but the number of concepts will be high. we recommend combining this metric with some metric for complexity of the domain. Interpretation of the metric is found in Table 3.

Result	Cause
Low Many rules	• We know the relations of the domain and have a mature rule-base • The domain is mature • Complex domain with many relations • Redundant rules
High Few rules	• We do not know the rules of the domain well enough • The domain is not very mature. The relations in the domain are not known. • We have too many uninteresting concepts • Many concepts are only included in one or few, very complex rules.

Table 3. Interpretation of "concepts/rules"

2.5. Average Number of Attributes per Concept

This metric is an indication of the complexity of the domain. A high value means that each concept has several related attributes and this indicates a more complex domain. It can also be used as a metric for maturity. We expect the value to vary during the project as we discover new concepts and new attributes. In the start of the project it is most likely that we find the most important concepts which have the highest number of related attributes. As the project develops new concepts will be found. We believe that the concepts found in the latter parts of the project will have fewer related attributes than then ones found in the start of the project and the value will therefore decrease. It will converge at the end of the project, when no new concepts and attributes are found. This indicates that the knowledge base is maturing. The Table 4 shows our interpretations of the metric. As we see a different number of concepts could give this metric different outcome or value.

Result	Cause
Low Few attributes per concept	• The problem domain is simple and each concept have few interesting attributes • There are many concepts with few attributes • We do not know the problem domain well, we have not discovered all the necessary attributes
High Many attributes per concept	• The domain is big and complex • There are few concepts with many related attributes • We have good knowledge about the problem domain

Table 4. Interpretations "Average attributes/concept"

2.6. A*(Number of Concepts) + B*(Average Number of Attributes Per Concept)

To get a better indication of the complexity of the project we suggest combining the number of concepts and the average number of attributes per concept. This will remove the different outcomes in average number of attributes per concept that was caused by the number of concepts. To be able to get a reasonable result the two metrics must be weighted by the factors A and B. To be able to find values for these factors we propose using history data. This is not within the scope of this paper and will therefore not be done here.

2.7. Average Number of Levels in Decision Tree

For the tasks that are decomposed this average will most likely increase throughout the project and stabilize to the end of the project. The metric is calculated by just counting the levels of the decision trees, add them, and divided the sum on the number of trees. Given the example in Figure 1 we will get the following result: (4+3)/2=3.5.

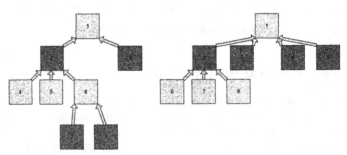

Fig. 1. Decision trees

The Table 5 shows our interpretations of the metric. A high degree of composition can indicate high complexity but also a high degree of understanding of the decision.

Result	Cause
Low Few levels of decomposition	• The domain is simple • We have not decomposed the decisions • We do not have complete knowledge about the domain • We have discovered all decisions but not decomposed they yet
High Many levels of decomposition	• The domain is complex • We have good knowledge about the domain • We totally miss information about some decisions in the domain, which would have decreased the average.

Table 5. Interpretation of results "Average levels in decisions"

2.8. Average Number of Concepts Included in Each Rule

Each rule contains one or more concepts. The number of concepts included in a rule could be a measurement of the complexity of the problem. We expect this number to be increasing as we discover more complex relationships within the problem domain. At the end of the project we suggest that the value converges to a constant. This convergence could be an indication of maturity of the knowledge base. The table 6 shows our interpretations of this metric. We see that the number of rules and the degree of decomposition affects the outcome of this metric, but if the average is high it is likely that we have a complex domain.

Result	Cause
Low Few attributes per concept	• The problem domain has low complexity • We do not have completed knowledge about the rules for a concept and interrelations between concepts • Several rules are not complete/mature and they miss one or more concept to be completed • Many simple rules and few complex rules • Rules are decomposed into more rules
High Many attributes per concept	• High complexity • The rules are completed • We have good knowledge about the domain • There are very few but very complex rules • The rules are not decomposed or at least not at a high degree

Table 6. Interpretations "Average concept in each rule"

2.9. Average Number of Attributes Included in Each Rule

This metric will be similar to the last one but it could give a better measure of the complexity of the domain especially in those cases where many rules are dependent of many attributes of few concepts. This metric will then indicate a high complexity where the previous one indicated low complexity. This metric will unfortunately still be dependent of the number of rules and the degree of decomposition.

2.10. A*Average Number of Attributes in Rule + B*Number of Rules + C* Average Number of Decomposition Levels

To try to remove the dependencies from the previous metric we would suppose to combine attributes, rules and decomposition levels into one metric to better understand the complexity of the domain. The constants A, B and C must be found with use of historical data.

2.11. Average Number of Rules Each Concept Is Included in

One concept could be included in one but most likely more than one rule. The average number of rules a concept is included in could give us an indication of complexity. We expect it to increase throughout the project as more rules are made. If there is found a lot of new concepts it may decrease a bit. But in the end of the project we think it is more likely to find more rules than new concepts. If the number of concepts is very high the number of rules could be low and we could still have a very complex domain. At the end of the project we believe this metric should converge and thus it could be used as an indication of maturity. The table 7 shows our interpretations of this metric.

Result	Cause
Low Each concept is included in few rules	• The domain is simple • The concepts of the domain is not strongly related • The knowledge about the problem area is sparse • We know all or may of the concepts of the area but we do not know all the relations yet • There are a lot of concepts without many rules
High Each concept is included in many rules	• The domain has many relations and it is complex • We have good knowledge about the domain • We may totally miss some concepts of the domain

Table 7. Interpretations "Average rules each concept is in"

2.12. A*Average Number of Rules Each Concept Is Included in*B*Number of Concepts

To remove the dependency of the number of concepts from the last metric we would propose to combine the previous metric with the number of concepts. The constants must, as mentioned, be found by use of history data.

2.13. Average Number of Rules Each Attribute Is Included in

We expect this metric to have a similar development during the project as the previous one with concepts. But we think it is more likely to discover more new attributes throughout the project than new concepts, so the value could vary a bit more than what we saw in Figure 6. We expect this value to converge at the end of the conceptualization phase as well. The table 8 shows our interpretations of this metric.

Result	Cause
Low Each attribute is included in few rules	• The domain is simple • We do not have a mature knowledge base • The domain is not strongly related • We do not have a lot of knowledge about the domain
High Each attribute is included in many rules	• The domain is strongly bound together • We have good knowledge about the domain • We miss many attributes which would decrease this average. • We have good knowledge about just parts of the domain.

Table 8. Interpretations "Average rules each attribute is in"

2.14. For all Levels (Number of Decisions at Level i*i) / Total Number of Decisions

This metric will give an indication of the tree width of the decision trees. If the main decisions consist of many different decisions of if the decisions and the end of the tree are very detailed. We expect that the value of this metric will be increasing throughout the project and stabilize at some point between 1.0 and the depth of the tree. To better understand the metric please see example 1 in Figure 2 and example 2 in Figure 3.

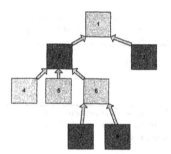

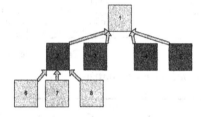

Fig. 3. Example 2: wide tree

Fig. 2. Example 1: deep tree

With the number of decisions at a level, times the level, for instance 2 decisions at level 4 in Figure 8 will give 2*4. The two examples in Table would give these results respectively:

Example	Result
1	$\dfrac{(1*1+2*2+3*3+2*4)}{8} = 2.875$
2	$\dfrac{(1*1+4*2+3*3)}{8} = 2.25$

Table 9. Result from examples

We see that the results indicate that the first tree is deeper than second one. We think this can help to show how the decisions in the problem domain are. This metric could give an indication of what kind of decision trees we have on thus what kind of complexity we have. The table 10 shows our interpretations of this metric.

Result	Cause
Low Most decisions at a high level	• The decisions are based on many decisions at a high level (close to the root of the tree). • The decision process is not very complex • We have not yet decomposed the tree
High Many decisions are taken at a low level	• Few decisions are based on simple decisions. Most decisions contain many decisions at a low level. • We have decomposed the tree • The decision process is complex

Table 10. Interpretations "Sum of Decision levels/number of decisions"

3. Applying the Metrics to Real World

To evaluate our metrics, we have used data from two finished expert systems. They were developed as part of the author's master thesis at ITBA (see Tables 11 and 12).

System 1 Work Accidents

Reference	*Help Assistant on Work Risks in Argentinean Law.* (in spanish). Master Thesis on Knowledge Engineering. School of Computer Science. Politechnic University of Madrid. 2001.
Author	Paola V. Britos
Description	This system should help the user to search in the Argentinean laws for material regarding occupational accidents. A lot of time is spent by the lawyers to search for the right material and this system is meant to help them in their search.

Table 11. Description of system 1

System 2 Airport Control

Reference	*Expert System for Decission Making Training in an Information & Control Air Traffic Center.* (in spanish). Master Thesis on Software Engineering. Graduate School. Buenos Aires Institute of Technology. 2002.
Author	Jorge Salvador Ierache
Description	The system described in this thesis is a decision support system for airport control towers.

Table 12. description of system 2

4. Some Results

We will here present the results from the expert systems described in the last section.

Number of Concepts, Number of Rules or Number of Attributes

System number	1	2
Number of Concepts	17	20
Number of Attributes	81	126
Number of Rules	472	155

These metrics are used as basis for other metrics. But they can also give an indication of the size of the system we have. We see that system 1 has quite many rules. This is because the system contains several simple rules concerning selection of the right document or right law to look up.

Number of Concepts in a Rule / Number of Concepts

System number	1	2
Number of Concepts in a Rule	7	19
Number of Concepts	17	20
Result	0.41	0.95

This metric indicates that system 1 has several concepts that are not related to anything and the knowledge engineer should therefore start working with those concepts.

Number of Attributes in a Rule / Number of Attributes

System number	1	2
Number of Attributes in a Rule	50	121
Number of Attributes	81	126
Result	0.62	0.96

We see the same indication here as we did with the last metric. System 1 needs to focus on those concepts and attributes not included in any rule or at least find the explanation of the result.

Number of Concepts / Number of Rules

System number	1	2
Number of Concepts	17	20
Number of Rules	472	155
Result	0.04	0.13

These resulting numbers are very small and it is hard to give some conclusions based on these numbers. But it could be interesting to follow the development of this figure throughout a project.

Average Number of Attributes per Concept

System number	1	2
Number of Attributes	81	126
Number of Concepts	17	20
Average	4.76	6.3

The number of attributes per concept can give us an indication of the complexity of the concepts in the domain. We observe that the result indicates that system 2's domain is more complex.

Average Number of Levels in Decision Tree

System number	1	2
Decomposed decisions	NA	NA
Average	NA	NA

Decision trees were not used to represent knowledge in these projects. The structure of the knowledge lead to omitting the application of this and other metrics concerning decomposed decisions.

Average Number of Concepts Included in Each Rule

System number	1	2
Average	1.24	1.64

We see that system two has more concepts included in a rule. This is an indication that system 2 may have a more complex domain.

Average Number of Attributes Included in each Rule

System number	1	2
Average	2.17	2.81

This metric is very similar to the previous one and it indicates the same. The domain of system 2 is more complex than the one of system 1.

A*Average Number of Attributes in Rule + B*Number of Rules + C* Average Number of Decomposition Levels

System number	1	2
Attributes in rule	2.17	2.81
Number of rules	472	155
Average decomposition levels	NA	NA
Sum	NA	NA

We will use all the constants set to 1 since we do not have any historical data from previous projects.
Decision trees were as mentioned above not used in any of the projects. Because of that we omitted applying this metric.

A*Average Number of Rules each Concept Is Included in*B*Number of Concepts

System number	1	2
Average rules each concept is in	34.5	15
Number of concepts	17	20
Sum	586.5	300

We have also used 1 for the constants in this metric since we do not have any historical data so far.
These results indicate that domain 1 is a bigger domain with several relations.

Average Number of Rules each Attribute Is Included in

System number	1	2
Result	12.6	3.45

We see the same here as we did in the two last metrics. System 1 has more relations between the attributes then system 2.

Average Number of Rules Each Concept Is Included in

System number	1	2
Average	34.5	15.0

We see that system 1 has more discovered rules in average that system 2. This could be an indication of fewer relations in domain 2.

For all Levels (Number of decisions at level i*i) / Total Number of Decisions

System number	1	2
Result	NA	NA

Decision trees were unfortunately not used and applying this metric was omitted.

5. Conclusions

The intention of this paper was examining the problem domain and showing the need for metrics in this domain. The metrics were suggested with a theoretical background to create a discussion around use of metrics in the conceptualization phase of an expert system development. We applied most of the proposed metrics to two different expert systems. This is not a large enough data set to draw any statistical conclusions. At this point the metrics serve as indicators and the trend seems to be that system 2 has a more complex domain that system 1. This seems reasonable enough. System 2 is an airport control system and system 1 is a system for finding the right law or text concerning accidents at work. The metrics also show concepts which are not included in any rule. This should alert the knowledge engineer and tell him to focus on these concepts. The application we made can also guide the knowledge engineer in finding unused concepts, attributes or rules where no attributes was found and tell him to review these rules.

6. Referentes

Firestone, J. 2004. *Knowledge Management Metrics Development: A Technical Approach.* Published on-line by Executive Information Systems, Inc. http://www.dkms.com/ at: http://www.dkms.com/papers/kmmeasurement.pdf, downloaded 2004-10-02

Ford, G. 2004. *Measurement Theory for Software Engineers*, Published on-line by R.S. Pressman & Associates, Inc. http://www.rspa.com/ at: http://www2.umassd.edu/SWPI/ curriculummodule/em9ps/em9.part3.pdf, downloaded 2004-09-24

García Martínez, R. & Britos, P. 2004 *Expert System Engineering*, Nueva Librería Ed. Buenos Aires

Kang, Y. & Bahieel, T. 1990. *A Tool for Detecting Expert Systems Errors.* AI Expert, 5(2): 42-51.

Menzies, T. & Cukic, B. 1999. *On the Sufficiency of Limited Testing for Knowledge Based Systems.* Proceedings of the 11th IEEE International Conference on Tools with Artificial Intelligence, Pages 431-440.

Menzies, T. & Cukic, B. 2000. *Adequacy of Limited Testing for Knowledge Based Systems.* International Journal on Artificial Intelligence Tools 9(1): 153-172.

Menzies, T. 1999. *Critical success metrics: evaluation at the business level.* International Journal of Human-Computer Studies, 51(4):783-799.

Nilsson, N. 1998. *Artificial Intelligence: A New Synthesis*, Morgan Kaufmann Publishers

Pazzani, M. & Clifford, A. 1991. *Detecting and Correcting Errors in Rule-Based Expert Systems: An Integration of Empirical and Explanation-Based Learning.* Knowledge Acquisition 3 :157-173.

SEI. 2004. *Software Metrics, SEI Curriculum Module SEI-CM-12-1.1,* Carnegie Mellon University - Software Engineering Institute, December 1988, ftp://ftp.sei.cmu.edu/pub/ education/cm12.pdf, downloaded 2004-09-22.

Toward developing a tele-diagnosis system on fish disease

Daoliang Li[1*], Wei Zhu[1], Yanqing Duan[2], Zetian Fu[1]

1 Key Laboratory of Modern Precision Agriculture system Integration, P.O. Box 121, China Agricultural University, Beijing, 100083, P. R. China

2 Luton Business School, University of Luton, LU1 3JU, UK

Abstract. Fish disease diagnosis is a complicated process and requires high level of expertise, an expert system for fish disease diagnosis is considered as an effective tool to help fish farmers. However, many farmers have no computers and are not able to access the Internet. Telephone and mobile uses increase rapidly, so, the provision of call centre service appears as a sound alternative support channel for farmer to acquire counseling and support. This paper presents a research attempt to develop and evaluate a call center oriented Hybrid disease diagnosis & consulting system (H-Vet) in aquaculture in China. This paper looks at why H-Vet is needed and what are the advantages and difficulties in the developing and using such a system. A machine learning approach is adopted, which helps to acquire knowledge when enhancing expert systems with the user information collected through call center. This paper also proposes a fuzzy Group Support Systems (GSS) framework for acquiring knowledge from individual expert and aggregating knowledge into workgroup knowledge by H-Vet in the situation of difficult disease diagnosis. The system's architecture and components are described.

Keywords machine learning; Group Decision Support System, expert system, call centre

1 Introduction

In China, Aquaculture plays a very important role in agricultural structure adjustment and generating farmers' income (Guo, 2001). However, fish diseases have become one of the most devastating threats to the survival of many Chinese fish farms. Fish disease diagnosis is a complicated process and requires high level of

* Corresponding author. Tel: +86-10-62336717; Fax:+86-10-62324371.
Email address: li_daoliang@yahoo.com or dliangl@cau.edu.cn (D. Li)

Please use the following format when citing this chapter:

Li, D., Zhu, W., Duan, Y., Fu, Z., 2006, in IFIP International Federation for Information Processing, Volume 217, Artificial Intelligence in Theory and Practice, ed. M. Bramer, (Boston: Springer), pp. 445–454.

domain knowledge, this pose a major challenge for any attempts to provide accurate and timely diagnosis and treatment.

Advances of Internet technologies have offered new opportunities for enhancing traditional decision support systems and expert systems (Power, 2000). With the development of Expert Systems (ES) and multimedia, computers are able to mimic many important roles that normally require human actions. A number of Web-based expert systems are reported in the literature (Grove, 2000; Potter et al., 2000; Riva, Bellazi, & Montani, 1998; Sedbrook, 1998).

Developments in high performance global communication technologies have also accelerated cooperative image-based medical services to a new frontier. Traditional image-based medical services such as radiology and diagnostic consultation can now be fully enhanced by multimedia technologies to provide novel services, such as tele-medicine. Telemedicine can be defined as medical practices across distance via telecommunications and interactive video technology. It can be used in remote areas or across great distances on the globe (Lim, Pang, & Tan, 2001). It also covers any form of communication between health workers and patients through electronic equipment from remote locations. Similar to tele-medicine, a tele-diagnosis system has been developed to support the diagnosis of various types of problems in China (Duan, et al.,2003), which provide a farmer-to-vet communication in diagnosis.

However, many farmers have no computers and are not able to access the Internet. At the same time, telephone and mobile uses increase rapidly, especially in rural area of China, there are 0.24 billion telephone users, 40% of them are farmers, so, the provision of call centre service appears as a sound alternative support channel for farmer to acquire counseling and support in disease diagnosis in China.

This paper reports a research effort to integrate call center with web-based expert system and tele-diagnosis system in fresh water fish disease diagnosis in China. The system is being developed by Key Laboratory of Modern Precision Agriculture System Integration, China Agricultural University, and was funded by Huo Yingdong foundation in China. The system has emerged as a result of the use of a Web-based expert system called Fish-Expert and tele-diagnosis system called T-Vet. It helps to overcome the limitations and enhance the functionality of traditional ESs. One of the strengths of the system is that it can facilitate computer-not-owned users and knowledge remote acquisition. This research attempts to use this pilot system as a research vehicle to experiment in applying, and to evaluate the usability of, the system with potential users. Feedback collected from the demonstration and evaluation of the Fish-Expert and T-vet has provided valuable insights into the issues related to the development and implementation of H-Vet in China.

2   System architecture and components

Based on the user's needs analysis, a call center oriented tele-diagnosis system, called CORDIS, were developed and integrated to Fish-Expert and T-Vet, H-Vet allow fish farmers and technicians get online help in any situations, the system st

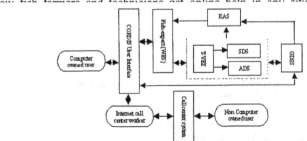

Fig. 1. Structure and Subsystem in H-Vet

To best meet the different needs of fish farmers and vets, 5 subsystems have been designed and developed in H-vet, they are Web-based Expert System Fish-Expert (WES), Call Center System (CCS), Tele-diagnosis System (T-VET), Group Decision Support System (GDSS), and Knowledge Acquisition System (KAS).

As more details about web-based expert system Fish-Expert and tele-diagnosis system (T-VET) are described in Li, et al. (2002) and Duan, et al. (2003), Fish-Expert and T-vet will be described very shortly. More contents will cover the CCS, GDSS, and KAS.

2.1 Web-based expert system Fish-Expert (WES)

The Fish-Expert system mimics the diagnosing process of human experts and has over 300 rules and 400 images and graphics for different types of diseases and symptoms. It is able to diagnose 126 types of diseases amongst nine species of primary freshwater fish. When using the expert system, various information needs to be provided following different diagnosing steps, such as pond inspection, fish inspection and anatomization, water quality examination, and microscopic examination. A final verdict for the type of the disease and its treatments and prevention will be produced based on the system's knowledge base.

2.2 Tele-diagnosis system T-Vet

T-vet is an add-on subsystem to overcome the limitation of the expert system and was integrated to the Fish-Expert. It includes a synchronous tele-diagnosis subsystem (SDS) and an asynchronous diagnosis subsystem (ADS) (Duan,et al., 2003)

A synchronous tele-diagnosis subsystem has been developed and can be used in situations where an urgent diagnosis is required, but it is impossible for the fish vet to visit the site, and the Web-based expert system is not able to solve the problem. To facilitate the tele-diagnosis, a number of functions have been developed and integrated into the system, such as web-calling, a virtual diagnosis room, Computer Supported Cooperative Work (CSCW) module, video/audio conferencing module, and online help module. An asynchronous diagnosis system (ADS) has been developed, which acts as a practical platform for sending and receiving messages between a fish farmer and a vet. Three support modules—user symptom submission, vet diagnosis and email communication are designed to facilitate asynchronous diagnosis process.

The ADS and the SDS act as good complementary tools to the expert system. The integration of the expert system, synchronous and asynchronous systems complements each other and is able to solve most of the problems fish farmers may encounter.

2.3   Call Center System (CCS)

The Call Center System CSS is an add-on subsystem to overcome the limitation of the current low computer owned level. It can provide a bridge between the computer-not-owned fish farmer and Fish-expert, T-Vet through call center agent,. There are 3 main models in the system, such as queuing models to capture the impact of congestion, customer arrival statistics and data collection model, telecommunications resource allocation and telephone-agent staffing model.

As call centers have grown in number and in size, more firms have tried to improve their management by focusing on resource utilization and service levels. This has led to a series of studies dealing with the problem of staffing phone centers, many of which have made use of queuing models to capture the impact of congestion (Aksin & Harker, 2003). So queuing models should be designed to capture the impact of congestion.

Customer arrival statistics and corresponding data collection model is used to evaluate the performance of the service system under study, given customer arrival statistics, servers, buffers, and a shared resource that impacts processing times, to collect all disease case which will be used to acquire fish disease diagnosis knowledge.

Another model take a different approach to telecommunications resource allocation and telephone-agent staffing, a similar approach is taken to determine staffing levels for a multiple class inbound call center.

CCS not only provides a bridge between the computer-not-owned fish farmer and Fish-Expert, but also provides a tool for collecting fish disease diagnosis case which plays a very important role in Fish-expert.

2.4   Group Decision support System (GDSS)

Globalization, virtual corporations, telecommuting, empowerment of teams, reduced cycle time and the need to frequently make decisions quickly makes it necessary for groups to work together while the participants may be in different locations (Tung & Turban, 1998). Distributed Group Decision Support System (DGSS) is a technology that can help groups to overcome some of the difficulties associated with being in different places and sometimes in different time zones (Bendoly & Bachrach, 2003).

Fish disease diagnosis is a rather complicated process in aquaculture production activities. The disease commonly resulted from nutritional and environmental problems as well as infections by parasites, viruses, bacteria and fungal agents. Some rare diseases or new diseases normally can't be identified by one fish vet only, and most of them need to be diagnosed by group work, as result, a Group Decision Support System (GDSS) is essential needed to solve the rare disease diagnosis.

Most of the previous research regarding computer support of groups was related to the decision room environment, where a group of participants meet face-to-face, working on a common task (Stohr & Konzynski, 1992). This paper focuses on the technology to support group work in the framework of 3 situations, such as same-time same-place group work, different-place same-time and different-time different-place group work.

Both same-time same-place group work and different-place same-time group work are belong to synchronous GDSSs, the same-time same-place group work is a face-to-face communication work mode for the decision support. This kind of group work has no any limitation of the work environment, the fish vet can discuss together, how ever the shortcoming of this kind of group work all famous vet must be collected together in call center, and answer the user's questions for some rare disease diagnosis.

Different-place same-time group work is synchronous GDSSs allow distributed participants to interact with one another in a 'real time' mode, i.e., they interact with one another at the same time. The participants are distributed across multiple sites linked by various communication technologies. Some of the supporting technologies are screen sharing, whiteboard, audio-conferencing, and various types of video-conferencing. These technologies can be carried on the Intranet, Internet, corporate or public networks, or VANs. Some major issues here include: the loss of face-to-face contact and the ability to manage the group process.

Asynchronous DGSSs allow distributed participants to log into the same meeting but at different times. Participants can log in and catch up with what is going on in the meeting, enter comments if necessary, and log out of the meeting at various times. E-mail, voice-mail, and workflow management systems such as in Lotus Notes are some of the supporting technologies. The issues here are more than just time and distance barriers. For example, the control of the participants and the participation, and the delayed response time could play an important role. Therefore, attention must be given to the coordination of group members to ensure that they stay on task and track and meet the decision deadlines, as well as it is necessary to encourage timely participation by everyone.

As the rare fish disease cases are very short in the fish disease case base of the web-based expert system, all result of group decision will be acquired by the KAS.

2.5 Knowledge Acquisition System (KAS)

Call center system, Fish-expert, T-vet, and GDSS can provide plenty of successful fish disease cases and solutions, these cases and solutions are very important for the Fish-Expert, so how to integrate them together and make them cooperate together, and then get a best effect for the whole system poses a serious challenge.

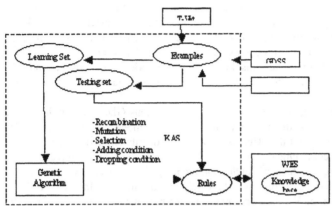

Fig. 2. The Structure of KAS

Case-based reasoning system is a system that solves current problems by adapting to or reusing the used solutions to solve past problems. In case-based reasoning, the study about case adaptation can be divided into two areas. One is about adaptation method and adaptation knowledge that are used at adaptation stage. The other is to reduce the necessity of case adaptation by extracting the most appropriate case for current problems. The former focuses on how to acquire case adaptation knowledge, and the latter focuses on the necessity about case adaptation.

However, the bottleneck phenomenon in acquiring knowledge may be caused in case-based systems. To resolve the bottleneck at the case-based reasoning, a research that automatically acquires knowledge needed for case-based reasoning by using the technologies of machine learning or data mining has been studied (Fig. 2.)

To achieve this intention, we propose a Knowledge Acquisition System (KAS) of adaptation knowledge from derived cases. That is, we construct case base by acquiring cases from Call Center, T-Vet, GDSS automatically acquire adaptation knowledge exploiting data mining concept, and deduce the bottleneck of acquiring adaptation knowledge used at the case adaptation stage of case-based reasoning systems.

3   The diagnosing process

There are 4 kinds of users in the H-Vet, such as computer-not-owned fish farmer, computer- owned fish farmer, vet, and call center agent, the work process for all kinds of users can be seen in fig. 3.

For computer-not-owned fish farmer, he or she can describes the symptoms of their fishes' disease to the call center agent by telephone, and the call center agent inputs all these symptoms into the Fish-Expert interface, and tell the fish farmer the diagnosis result based on the web-based expert system if there is a same disease case in the case base, meantime, this case will be input in the knowledge acquisition system as an successful case. the agent also can ask some questions to the fish farmer based on the web-based expert system, which can add some useful information for fish disease diagnosis.

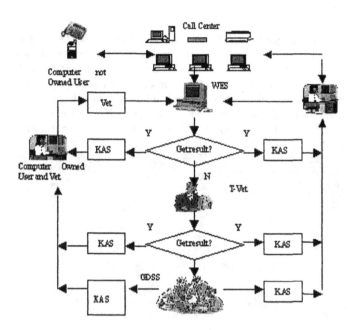

Fig. 3. The work process of H-Vet

The agent can login on the T-Vet (synchronous tele-diagnosis subsystem) interface get as on line help from the vet, and then tell result to the fish farmer, at the same time, this case will be input into the knowledge acquisition system as an successful case. If the agent can't reply the agent's question, the agent will login the GDSS, and submit the question the GDSS, and reply the fish farmer's question base don the GDSS's diagnosis, at the same time the question and the result will be input the knowledge acquisition system as a successful disease diagnosis case.

For computer-owned fish farmer, he/she can login the web-based expert system directly, and use to the Fish-Expert to solve his or her question, if the Fish-Expert can't answer the farmer's question, the farmer can login T-Vet system and get a on-line help from vet or get a synchronous tele-diagnosis help, he can login the GDSS system if T-vet can't help him/her. All successful disease diagnosis will be input the knowledge acquisition system as a successful case during the whole work process.

For call center agent, the main task is to wait computer-not-owned fish farmers' call, and answer their questions base on the Fish-Expert, T-vet and GDSS, the interface and work process for agent same as computer-owned fish farmer.

For Vet, the main task is to answer the questions which the expert system can't solved, there are 2 interfaces for them, one is T-Vet, another is GDSS, the participation of the vet will provide many practical disease diagnosis, which will be added to the case base.

4   Implementation

System tests, such as logic tests, debugging, rule checking and sample field tests were carried out by system developers. This was to ensure the system would work correctly before it was distributed to farmers. After the system testing, H-Vet available for pilot implementation in North China, in cities such as Beijing, Tianjin, and Shandong provinces. User feedback was gathered by conducting interviews and collecting information through the system's built-in visitor feedback form. In general, the system has been an effective aid to fish farmers, fishery experts and a reference system to fish vets. Some interfaces are as follows. (Fig. 4.-7)

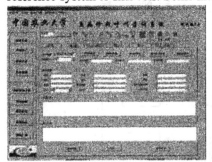

Fig. 4 Interface of Call Center   **Fig. 5** Interface of Agent

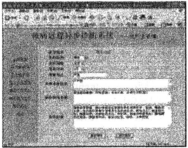

Fig. 6 Interface for Computer Owned User   **Fig. 7** Interface of T-Vet

5   Conclusions

This paper reports a research attempt in developing a hybrid tele-diagnosis system in aquaculture, the system provides a tool for computer and Internet not owned user using web-based expert system, for knowledge automatically acquisition. The research provides some new ideas to solve the bottleneck of traditional expert system.

The wide spread of Internet, Intranet, call center, telecommunication infrastructures and intelligent software will facilitate the work of hybrid tele-diagnosis system, the frame work proposed in this paper and the specific issues list in section 3 and 4 cover the major topics perceived by the researchers as warrant further investigation. As our H-Vet knowledge base increase, more research issues will undoubtedly be added.

The next phase in our research could be the refinement of the framework and testing its value by researchers and practitioners. Also, the identification of software tools that will enhance the multi-site and interorganizational meeting process, and the development of procedures and training methods that will help organizations take advantage of the benefits of using a DGSS need to be researched. The data-mining algorithm will be a key work in the future research, which will play a very important role in knowledge refining and acquisition.

The DGSS environment offers many potential areas for investigation,. The research framework and issues raised in this paper are intended for researchers and practitioners who are interested in looking at the impact of the DGSS environment on fish farmers, vet groups, and call center agents.

Acknowledgement

The research was funded by the Huo Yingdong foundation in China (project number: 94032). We would like to thank many domain experts from the Beijing Aquaculture Science Institute, Aquaculture Department of Tianjin Agricultural College, Aquaculture Bureau of Shandong province, for their co-operation and support. Our special thanks should also go to Prof. Kezhi Xing, Mr Yongjun Guo at Tianjin Agricultural College for his valuable suggestions and comments on the system.

References

1. Aksin, O. Z., Harker, P.T.(2003). Capacity sizing in the presence of a common shared resource: imensioning an inbound call center. European Journal of Operational Research 147, 464• 483

2. Bendoly, E., Bachrach, D. G., (2003). A process-based model for priority convergence in multi-period group decision-making. European Journal of Operational Research 148 (2003) 534• 545

3. Duan, Y., Fu, Z., Li, D. (2003). Toward developing and using Web-based tele-diagnosis in aquaculture. Expert System with Applications, 25, 247–254

4. Grove, R. (2000). Internet-based expert systems. Expert Systems, 17(2), 129–135.

5. Guo, Z (2001). Analysis and prospects for China's aquatic market in 2000. www.ifishery.com/jrdd/2001060601.htm

6. Li, D., Fu, Z., & Duan, Y. (2002). Fish-expert: A web-based expert system for fish disease diagnosis. Expert System with Applications, 23(3), 311–320.

7. Lim, S. S., Pang, Y. K., & Tan, H. S. (2001). Telemedicine VSATapplications: Temasek polytechnic experience. International Telehealth Symposium, 14 March, Bangkok, United Nations Conference Center.

8. Magrabi, F., Lovell, N. H., & Cellar, B. G. (1999). A Web-based approach for electrocardiogram monitoring in the home. International Journal of Medical Informatics, 54, 145–153.

9. Potter, W. D., Deng, X., Li, J., Xu, M., Wei, Y., Lappas, I., Twery, M. J., & Bennett, D. J. (2000). A Web-based expert system for gypsy moth risk assessment. Computer and Electronics in Agriculture, 27(1–3), 95–105.
10. Power, D. J. (August 10–13 2000). Web-based and model-driven decision support systems: Concepts and issues. Proceedings of Americas Conference on Information Systems (AMCIS 2000), Long Beach, California.
11. Rajani, R., & Perry, M. (1999). The reality of medical work: The case for a new perspective on telemedicine. Virtual Reality Journal, 4, 243–249.
12. Riva, A., Bellazzi, R., & Montani, S (1998). A knowledge-based web server as a development environment for Web-based knowledge servers. IEE Colloquium on Web-based Knowledge Servers (Digest No.1998/307).IEE. 1998, 5/1-5. London, UK
13. Sedbrook, T. A. (1998). A collaborative fuzzy expert system for the Web. Data Base for Advances in Information Systems, 29(3), 19–30.
14. Tung, L., Turban, E. (1998). A proposed research framework for distributed group support systems. Decision Support System, 23, 175-188
15. Stohr, E.A., Konzynski, B.R. (1992) Information Systems and Decision Process, IEEE Computer Society Press, Los Alamitos, CA.

A new method for fish-disease diagnostic problem solving based on parsimonious covering theory and fuzzy inference model

Jiwen WEN [1], Daoliang LI [2], Wei Zhu [2] Zetian FU [2]

1 Economics and Management department, Beijing Forestry University, Beijing, China, 100083

2 China Agricultural University, Key laboratory for modern precision agriculture integration, Ministry of Education, Beijing, China, 100083

Abstract. There are three kinds of uncertainty in the process of fish-disease diagnosis, such as randomicity, fuzzy and imperfection, which affect the veracity of fish-disease diagnostic conclusion. So, it is important to construct a fish-disease diagnostic model to effectively deal with these uncertainty knowledge's representation and reasoning. In this paper, the well-developed parsimonious covering theory capable of handling randomicity knowledge is extended. A fuzzy inference model capable of handling fuzzy knowledge is proposed, and the corresponding algorithms based the sequence of obtaining manifestations are provided to express imperfection knowledge. In the last, the model is proved to be effective and practicality through a set of fish-disease diagnostic cases.

Key words Fuzzy set theory, Parsimonious covering theory, Fish-disease diagnosis

1 Introduction

In this paper, the well-developed parsimonious covering theory based probability model is extended. A alternative fuzzy inference model capable of handling fuzzy knowledge for fish-disease diagnostic problem solving is proposed, and the corresponding algorithms based the sequence of obtaining diagnostic information are provided. This model can deal with degrees of manifestations simultaneously and sequences of obtaining diagnostic information.

Firstly, PCT and its probability model are introduced into fish-disease diagnosis domain. Secondly, the best probability criterion is determined on through analyzing fish-disease's characteristic, then the plausible function is calculated and the best solution is founded by thoroughly enumerate strategy and the biggest probability criterion. Thirdly, the limitation of the probability model of PCT solving fish-disease diagnosis is pointed out. So that, fuzzy set theory is introduced to represent degrees

Please use the following format when citing this chapter:

Wen, J., Li, D., Zhu, W., Fu, Z., 2006, in IFIP International Federation for Information Processing, Volume 217, Artificial Intelligence in Theory and Practice, ed. M. Bramer, (Boston: Springer), pp. 455–464.

of manifestations and the diagnostic problem is newly defined. Finally, responding algorithm is proposed to deal with the imperfection of diagnostic information.

PCT (Parsimonious Covering Theory) based on probability model is extended in such a way that it is integrated with fuzzy set theory and corresponding sequence algorithm in this paper. The new model is applied into fish-disease diagnosis domain to deal with three-uncertainty knowledge's representation and reasoning. In the last, the model is proved to be effective and practical through a set of fish-disease diagnostic cases.

2   The fish-disease diagnostic model based on parsimonious covering theory

2.1   Parsimonious covering theory

Parsimonious covering theory (PCT) uses two finite sets to define the scope of diagnostic problems. They are the set D, representing all possible disorders d_i that can occur, and the set M, representing all possible manifestations m_j that may occur when one ore more disorders are present. The relation C, from D to M, associates each individual disorder with its manifestations. An association $< d_i, m_j >$ in C means that d_i may directly cause m_j. To complete the problem formulation we need a particular diagnostic case. We use M^+, a subset of M, to denote the set of observations, which are manifestations present in a particular diagnostic case.

Definition 1. A diagnostic problem P is defined as a quadtuple $<D, M, C, M^+>$, where:

D is a finite, non-empty set of elements, called disorders; and M is a finite, non-empty set of elements, called manifestations;

C is a binary relation between disorders and manifestations, called causation; it represents with a matrix form. A nonzero element c_{ij} means the probability that d_i may directly cause m_j;

M^+ is a subset of M, and it identifies all observed manifestations.

Definition 2. The set $D_I \subseteq D$ is the cover of $M_J \subseteq M$ if $M_J \subseteq Effect(D_I)$

Definition 3. A set $D_I^* \subseteq D$ is an explanation of M^+ for a diagnostic problem if D covers M^+, and satisfies a given parsimony criterion: simple, minimal, irredundant, and relevant criterion.

Definition 4. The solution of a diagnostic problem P is the set of all explanations of M^+ and it must satisfy a given parsimony criterion.

The abductive inference model is based upon the notion of parsimoniously covering a set of observed manifestations, M^+. The premise of the parsimonious covering theory is that a diagnosis hypothesis must be a cover of M^+ in order to account for the presence of all manifestations in M^+. On the other hand, not all covers of M^+ are equally plausible as the hypotheses for a given problem. It must be satisfy a given parsimony criterion: simple, minimal, irredundant and relevant criterion.

2.2 Decision about parsimony criterion in fish-disease diagnostic model

The key to solve disease diagnostic problem is to select a preferable parsimony criterion combined with diagnostic practice. In practice, if the diagnosis objective is different, parsimony criterion is too different.

(1) If the restriction of diagnostic object is single disorder, a cover D_I of M^+ is an explanation if it contains only a single disorder, a single disorder principle should be adopted.

(2) If diagnostic object is a many-disorder system, parsimony criterion is adopted on the characteristic of disorder occurrence: relevancy, a cover D_I of M^+ is an explanation if it only contains the disorders that causally associate with at least one of the manifestations in M^+; irredundancy, a cover D_I of M^+ is an explanation if it has no proper subsets which also cover M^+ or, in other words, removing any disorder from D_I results in a noncover of M^+; minimality, a cover D_I of M^+ is an explanation if it has the minimal cardinality among all covers of M^+, i.e. it contains the smallest possible number of disorders needed to cover M^+.

So, we must firstly analyze the characteristic of fish-disease occurrence, it is summed as follows:

(1) The relationship between fish-disease and fish-disease is various: Two diseases may repel one another, and two diseases may be interrelated. If the relationship of two fish-diseases is interrelated, one disease may be occur directly, indirectly or along with another disease.

(2) The cause of one fish-disease is different in different environment: Many factors, such as intrinsic body, extrinsic environment and man-made management, will result in fish-disease. In the condition of modern intensive breeding, these factors are more easier to result in fish-diseases occurrence more than before.

(3) The diffusion of fish-diseases is various and interrelated: Any original fish-disease is likely to arise other fish-diseases in many potential ways. Any fish-disease likely arises another disease and is likely aroused by another disease too.

In diagnostic practice, two status, many-disease occurrence and simple disease occurrence, are in existence, so irredundancy criterion is adopted to define the scope of diagnostic solution.

2.3 The limitation of PCT's probability model

If the set of observed manifestations, M^+, is known, plausible function of these solution, disease sets which can explain M^+, can be found by probability theory, the best solution can be calculated by thoroughly enumerating strategy and the biggest plausible criterion. Plausible function $L(D_I, M^+)$ represents as follow:

$$L(D_I, M^+) = \prod_{m_j \in M^+} (1 - \prod_{d_i \in D_I} (1 - c_{ij})) \prod_{d_i \in D_i} \frac{p_i}{1 - p_i}$$

The limitation of PCT's probability model in the process of diagnosing fish-disease is summed as follow:

(1) The probability of d_i, $p(d_i)$, is supposed to be a known numeral in diagnostic model, in fact, the value of $p(d_i)$ is affected by many factors; it transforms along with factor's variation.

(2) Degrees of cause-and-effect relation, c_{ij} , is supposed to be known in diagnostic model, in fact, the value of c_{ij} is different if the diagnostic expert is different, so it need to statutes.

So, fish-disease diagnostic knowledge must be pretreated before the diagnostic model is applied into fish-disease diagnostic domain.

2.4   Pretreatments with fish-disease knowledge

Because fish-disease diagnostic system is complex, the factors that arise disease are different, but also the knowledge that experts hold is different because their diagnostic experience and the cognition degree of fish disease is different, so the diagnostic knowledge come from different channels constantly differs. It is necessary to foreclose this fish-disease knowledge in some statistic methods before it is introduced into PCT's probability model.

2.4.1 Decision about the scope of fish-disease

In this paper, fresh water fish-diseases occur in Tianjin is illustrated as examples. Some constantly occurring fish-diseases are summed up according to data provided by Tianjin aquatic company, and the occurring frequency is classified into four levels: 1) frequently; 2) often; 3) infrequently; 4) nonoccurrence. We defined the scope of fish-disease by which occurring frequency is bigger than 0.2.

2.4.2 Decision about the foresight probability of fish-disease

We consider that some factors are interrelated with fish-disease by analyzing a lot of investigation data; they are fish-kind, fish-age, occurring season, occurring area and pool-depth. The foresight probability can be decided by firstly confirming these environmental factors.

1. The first factor is fish-kind: If fish-kind is different, kinds of occurring fish-disease are too different. For example, some disease occurs in carp would not occurs in silver carp. We classify fish-kind into six kinds, such as grass carp, silver carp, variegated carp, carp, crucian carp and so on. Variable k_i represents the corresponding kind; function $cause(k_i) = \{d_j \mid j = 1,2,...,n\}$ represents disease sets when fish-kind is k_i .

2. The second factor is fish-age: If fish-age is different, kinds of occurring fish-disease are too different. For example, some disease occurs in parent fish would not occur in fish-breed. We classify fish-age into four phases, such as fry, fish-breed, grow-up fish, parent fish and so on. Variable a_i represents the corresponding age, function $cause(a_i) = \{d_j \mid j = 1,2,...,n\}$ represents disease sets when fish-age is s_i .

3. The third factor is season: If season is different, kinds of occurring fish-disease are too different. For example, some disease occurs in spring would not occur in summer. We classify occurring season into: spring, summer, autumn and winter four phrases, variable s_i represents the corresponding season, function $cause(s_i) = \{d_j \mid j = 1,2,...,n\}$ represents disease sets when occurring season is s_i .

4. The fourth factor is area: If area is different, kinds of occurring fish-disease are too different. For example, some diseases occur in certain area will not occur in other area. Variable pl_i represents corresponding area name, function $cause(pl_i) = \{d_j \mid j = 1,2,...,n\}$ represents disease sets when occurring area is of pl_i.

5. The probability of fish-disease, p_i, can be calculated by algorithm as follow:

F_1^+ : A subset of F^+, it defines factors, such as fish-kind (k_i), fish-age (a_i), occurring season (s_i), occurring area (p_i) and so on;

D_I : Disease sets that can explain the observed manifestations;

The beginning state is that $F_1^+ = \Phi, D_I = D$; the terminating condition is that $F_1^+ = F^+$, $F^+ = \{k_i, a_i, s_i, p_i\}$. Diagnostic algorithm can be described as follow:

(1) input k_i from F^+;

(2) $F_1^+ = F_1^+ \cup k_i$;

(3) $D_I = D_I \cap cause(k_i)$;

(4) $F_1^+ = F_1^+ \cup a_i$;

(5) $D_I = D_I \cap cause(a_i)$;

(6) $F_1^+ = F_1^+ \cup s_i$;

(7) $D_I = D_I \cap cause(s_i)$;

(8) $F_1^+ = F_1^+ \cup p_i$;

(9) $D_I = D_I \cap cause(p_i)$;

(10) extract D_I and the number of disease in D_I ;

(11) the probability of each disease should be $p_i = \frac{1}{I}$ 。

2.4.3 Decision about degrees of cause-and-effect relationship c_{ij}

In the process of diagnosing fish-disease, degrees of cause-and-effect relation should keep to principles as follow:

1) Because each disease can represent many manifestations, they are classified three levels: necessarily appearing, constantly appearing and occasionally appearing, the level of manifestation should be confirmed at first.

2) Necessarily appearing manifestation plays a decisive role in disease diagnosing, so the value of c_{ij} is defined as 1.0;

3) Constantly appearing manifestation frequently appears in process of certain fish-disease occurring, which can affect the reliability of diagnostic solution, so the value of c_{ij} is defined between 0.3 and 0.9;

4) The specialty of occasionally appearing manifestation is probably occurring; the value of c_{ij} should be between 0 and 0.2.

The equation is $\overline{c_{ij}} = \frac{1}{n}\sum_1^n c_{ij}$ by analyzing questionnaires of 24 experts in Tianjin.

In the process of diagnosing fish-disease, there are three uncertainties: probability, fuzzy and imperfection. The model describing as up can deal with probability, but degrees of manifestation and the imperfection and sequence of diagnostic information are not taken into account. So we must improve on this model.

3   Diagnosis model based on fuzzy theory and diagnosis algorithm

3.1   Diagnosis model based on fuzzy theory

If degrees of observed manifestation are introduced into parsimonious set covering, diagnosis problem is redefined as follow:

Definition 5 "manifestation-disease" diagnosis problem is defined as a quadtuple (D,M,R,M^+), where: $M^+ = \{m_1,m_2,......,m_k\}$ is a fuzzy subset of M, and it identifies the observed manifestations. To each $m_j \in M^+$, $\mu(m_j) \in [0,1]$ is the observed degree of m_j.

In accordance with the diagnostic problem definition written as up, plausible function of diagnostic solution is defined as follow:

Definition 6 $L(D_l,M^+)$ expresses the degree that D_l explains the set of manifestations M^+, and the equation is tenable:

$$L(D_l,M^+) = \prod_{m_j \in M^+} \mu(m_j)(1 - \prod_{d_i \in D_l}(1-c_{ij})) \prod_{d_i \in D_l} \frac{p_i}{1-p_i}$$

The plausible function is in keeping with the fact: $\mu(m_j)$ gradually increases along with degrees of manifestation augments. If the possibility that one manifestation is observed is big, the possibility that one disease can explain the manifestation is comparatively big.

3.2   The selection on fuzzy degree of manifestation

In diagnosing practice, ordinary fishery technicians and fisher folks are accustomed to adopt fuzzy language to describe degrees of manifestation. Each manifestation description is classified five levels, they are "absolutely same, close, relatively close, not same, different", then corresponding fuzzy value is present to make user easy to describe the observed manifestation.

3.3   The algorithm of diagnosis model

The process of fish-disease diagnosis is to find disease sets that can explain a set of observed manifestations through correlative diagnostic knowledge. It behaves as a repetitious process: preparatory examining- first diagnosis- examining again- diagnose again----make a definite diagnostic solution. In the process, old hypothesis is excluded and new hypothesis is brought up. The circulation repeats again and again until the best solution is brought up. On the basis of analyzing diagnostic process, the corresponding algorithm is present. The basic idea of the algorithm is that the original manifestation set is provided; a trial disease hypothesis can be brought up to explain these manifestations, then current hypothesis can instruct us to find more information for the best solution.

Before introduce the algorithm, we must firstly make some definitions:

M_1^+ is a subset of M^+, and it identifies the set of observed manifestations;

$D_l, cause(M_1^+)$, it identifies disease sets that can explain observed manifestations;

S is trial solution sets of observed manifestations;

" $\times$ " represents Descartes accumulation, and the original state is $M_1^+ = \Phi, D_1 = \Phi, S = D$, the terminate condition is $M_1^+ = M^+$, in another word, all observed manifestations have been inputted into the model.

The algorithm of diagnosis can be described as follow:

(1) Input m_j from M^+;

(2) $M_1^+ = M_1^+ \cup m_j$;

(3) $D_I = D_I \cup cause(m_j)$;

(4) $S'' = S' - S, S' = S , S = S \cap cause(m_j)$

(5) IF $S = \Phi$ THEN;

$\{ S_1 = S' \times cause(m_j)$

IF $\left(effect(s'') \cup effect(\{d_i \mid d_i \in cause(m_j)\})\right)$ is the smallest

covering set of M_1^+

THEN $S_2 = \{d_i\} \times S''$

ELSE $S_2 = \Phi$

$S = S_1 \cup S_2\}$

(6) IF $M_1^+ = M^+$ THEN end

ELSE go to (1)

After all probable diagnostic solutions have been found, the plausible function of S can be calculated and the best solution can be found by thoroughly enumerating strategy and the biggest plausible criterion.

4 Test results

Two sample studies are served for testing the developed fuzzy inference model, and the description of each example and some of the test results are given below.

Table 1 d_i and effect (d_i)

Number	effect (d_i)	Number	effect (d_i)
d_1	m_{11} m_{46}	d_{12}	m_{24}
d_2	m_{10} m_{30} m_{33}	d_{13}	m_{02} m_{11} m_{18}
d_3	m_{14} m_{15} m_{43}	d_{14}	m_{04} m_{15} m_{19} m_{25} m_{32} m_{34}
d_4	m_{45}	d_{15}	m_{07} m_{23} m_{29}
d_5	m_{12}	d_{16}	m_{09} m_{27}
d_6	m_{05} m_{33}	d_{17}	m_{15} m_{16} m_{17} m_{41} m_{42}
d_7	m_{37} m_{38}	d_{18}	m_{04} m_{18} m_{19} m_{28} m_{31} m_{41}
d_8	m_{13}	d_{19}	m_{41}
d_9	m_{10} m_{33}	d_{20}	m_{04} m_{15} m_{16} m_{21} m_{28} m_{30} m_{41} m_{44}
d_{10}	m_{01} m_{03} m_{20} m_{35}	d_{21}	m_{08}
d_{11}	m_{11} m_{15} m_{18} m_{19} m_{26} m_{28} m_{30}	d_{22}	m_{04} m_{19} m_{22} m_{25} m_{36} m_{39} m_{40}

Two example is from Jingwu aquatic product breeding factory in Tianjin. After four factors such as k_i = grass carp, a_i = fish-seed, s_i = summer and pl_i = Jinghai are confirmed, disease sets that can explain these factors can be calculated, it is D_I =22, in another word, the probability of each fish-disease is p_i =1/22. Which contains 22 disorders and 44 manifestations. The cause-and-effect relationship between disease and manifestations is shown in matrix. More than 20 test cases have been carried out for this example. Only two test cases are illustrated below for saving space.

4.1 Test case 1

If $M^+ = (m_{15}, m_{16}, m_{42})$, degrees of manifestation separately is: $\mu(m_{15}) = 0.8$, $\mu(m_{16}) = 0.5$, $\mu(m_{42}) = 0.3$, the transformation of disease set in the process of diagnosis is described as Table 2.

Table 2 the diagnosis result of algorithm for test case 1

Manifes-tations	Original state	m_{15}	m_{16}	m_{42}
M_i^+	Φ	$\{m_{15}\}$	$\{m_{15},m_{16}\}$	$\{m_{15},m_{16},m_{42}\}$
D_1	Φ	$\{d_{03},d_{11},d_{14},d_{17},d_{20}\}$	$\{d_{03},d_{11},d_{14},d_{17},d_{20}\}$	$\{d_{03},d_{11},d_{14},d_{17},d_{20}\}$
S'	Φ	D	$\{d_{03},d_{11},d_{14},d_{17},d_{20}\}$	$\{d_{17},d_{20}\}$
S''	Φ	Φ	$\{d_1,d_{02},d_{04},.....,d_{19},d_{21},d_{22}\}$	$\{d_{03},d_{11},d_{14}\}$
S	D	$\{d_{03},d_{11},d_{14},d_{17},d_{20}\}$	$\{d_{17},d_{20}\}$	$\{d_{17}\}$

1) When manifestations observed is $\{m_{15}\}$, diagnostic model will diagnose that disease set is $\{d_{03},d_{11},d_{14},d_{17},d_{20}\}$, user can be instructed to choose other manifestation to obtain the diagnostic solution according to known disease set.

2) When manifestations observed is $\{m_{15},m_{16}\}$, diagnosis system will diagnose that disease set is reduced to be $\{d_{17},d_{20}\}$, user can be instructed to choose other manifestation explained by $\{d_{17},d_{20}\}$.

3) In the case of manifestation set observed being $\{m_{15},m_{16},m_{42}\}$, disease set is $\{d_{17}\}$.

Finally, the last answer $S = \{d_{17}\}$, in another word, when $M^+ = (m_{15},m_{16},m_{42})$, the result of diagnosis is enteritis. It is obvious that the process of fish-disease diagnosis is a process of seeking more perfection answer 'step by step' based on "hypothesis -test" circulation. In the process of diagnosis, part known manifestation is imported, corresponding disease set will be obtained through diagnosis system. The method can instruct user to collect more manifestation expressed by disease set, the scope of disease will gradually reduced to perfect diagnosis result.

5 Conclusion

(1) Because of three kinds of uncertainty, such as randomicity, fuzzy and imperfection, being in existence in the process of fish-disease diagnosis, the degree of manifestations is sufficiently taken into account, a new method for fish-disease diagnostic problem solving based on parsimonious covering theory and fuzzy inference model is constructed in this paper. According to the sequence of diagnosis process, a 'step by step' seeking answer algorithm based on "hypothesis -test" circulation is proposed.

(2) The diagnosis model proposed in this paper is an efficient attempt to solve the fish-disease diagnosis problem, and realizes the integration probability inference

with fuzzy set theory. Fish-disease can be diagnosed more reliably and practically by means of this model.

(3) The advantage of parsimonious covering model based on fuzzy set theory is analyzed through a great quantity cases. It not only can prompt user to collect more diagnostic information, but also can provide more perfect diagnostic outcome accord with the specialty of fish-disease.

Acknowledgement

The research was funded by the Huo Yingdong foundation in China (project number: 94032). We would like to thank many domain experts from the Beijing Aquaculture Science Institute, Aquaculture Department of Tianjin Agricultural College, Aquaculture Bureau of Shandong province, for their co-operation and support. Our special thanks should also go to Prof. Kezhi Xing, Mr Yongjun Guo at Tianjin Agricultural College for his valuable suggestions and comments on the system.

Reference

1. Chinese academy of aquaculture science, strategies for the aquaculture development in the 21 century of China, Beijing,, 2001
2. Wen Ji-wen. A Knowledge-based Fish Diseases Diagnosis Reasoning and Expert System: [D] . Beijing, china agriculture university, 2003
3. Glover F. Tabu search: part 1 ORSA Journal on Computering. 1989,01:190-206
4. Glover F. Tabu search: part 2 ORSA Journal on Computering. 1990,02:4-32
5. Glover F . Future paths foy integer programming and links to artificial in intelligence. Computer and Operations Research.1986.13: 533-549
6. WEN Ji-wen, FU Ze-tian, LI Dao-liang. The Process Imitation and Construction of Reasoning Model of Fish Disease Diagnosis. Aquaculture (In Chinese), 2003(2).

Effective Prover for Minimal Inconsistency Logic

Adolfo Gustavo Serra Seca Neto and Marcelo Finger

Computer Science Department
Institute of Mathematics and Statistics
University of São Paulo
[adolfo,mfinger]@ime.usp.br

Summary. In this paper we present an effective prover for **mbC**, a minimal inconsistency logic. The **mbC** logic is a paraconsistent logic of the family of logics of formal inconsistency. Paraconsistent logics have several philosophical motivations as well as many applications in Artificial Intelligence such as in belief revision, inconsistent knowledge reasoning, and logic programming. We have implemented the KEMS prover for **mbC**, a theorem prover based on the **KE** tableau method for **mbC**. We show here that the proof system on which this prover is based is sound, complete and analytic. To evaluate the KEMS prover for **mbC**, we devised four families of **mbC**-valid formulas and we present here the first benchmark results using these families.

1 Introduction

In this paper we present new theoretical and practical results concerning paraconsistent logics. On the theoretical side, we have devised a **KE** tableau method for **mbC**, a minimal inconsistency logic, and proved that this proof system is correct, complete and analytic. And on the practical side, we have implemented a theorem prover based on the **mbC** **KE** proof system and proposed a set of benchmarks for evaluating **mbC** provers.

Paraconsistent logics are tools for reasoning under conditions which do not presuppose consistency [3]. These logics have several philosophical motivations as well as many applications in Artificial Intelligence such as in belief revision [12], inconsistent knowledge reasoning [8], and logic programming [1].

The relevance of reasoning in the presence of inconsistent information can be seen in the following example[1]. Suppose we are working with classical logic and we have a theory (which is a set of formulas) Γ such that $\Gamma \vdash A$ (i.e. from Γ we can deduce A) and also $\Gamma \vdash \neg A$. That is, this theory allows us to reach two contradictory conclusions. Suppose also that $\Gamma \vdash B$. In classical logic, from $\Gamma \vdash A$ and $\Gamma \vdash \neg A$ we can derive $\Gamma \vdash C$ for any formula C. In particular, $\Gamma \vdash \neg B$.

---

[1] We assume familiarity with the syntax and semantics of propositional classical logic.

Please use the following format when citing this chapter:

Neto, A.G.S.S., Finger, M., 2006, in IFIP International Federation for Information Processing, Volume 217, Artificial Intelligence in Theory and Practice, ed. M. Bramer, (Boston: Springer), pp. 465–474.

In classical logic, a contradictory theory is also trivial, therefore useless. Paraconsistent logics separate these concepts: a contradictory theory needs not to be trivial. Therefore, in a paraconsistent logic such as **mbC**, one can have $\Gamma \vdash_{mbC} A$, $\Gamma \vdash_{mbC} \neg A$ and $\Gamma \vdash_{mbC} B$ without necessarily having $\Gamma \vdash_{mbC} \neg B$. Therefore, in paraconsistent logics one can have an inconsistent theory and still draw interesting conclusions from it.

There have been some implementations of paraconsistent formalisms [1, 4], but we do not know of any implementation of a special class of paraconsistency logics: logics of formal inconsistency (**LFIs**) [3]. This class internalizes the notions of consistency and inconsistency at the object-language level. We have extended the KEMS prover [11], originally developed for classical propositional logic, to deal with **LFIs**. The first version of this extension implements a tableau prover for **mbC**, one of the simplest representatives of this class of logics. The KEMS prover for **mbC** is implemented in Java and AspectJ. Java is a well established object-oriented programming language and AspectJ is the major representative of a new programming paradigm: aspect-oriented programming. Its source code available for download in [10].

The KEMS prover is a **KE**-based Multi-Strategy theorem prover. The **KE** system, a tableau method developed by Marco Mondadori and Marcello D'Agostino [7], was presented as an improvement, in the computational efficiency sense, over the Analytic Tableau method [13]. A tableau system for **mbC** had already been presented in [3], but this system is more similar to analytic tableaux than to **KE**: it has five branching rules, which can lead to an ineffecient implementation. And although this system is sound and complete it is not analytic. Therefore, to implement the KEMS prover for **mbC** we devised an **mbC KE** system and obtained a sound, complete and analytic tableau proof system with only one branching rule.

To evaluate our prover correctness and performance, we needed some families of **mbC** problems. As we do not know any family of valid formulas elaborated specially for **mbC** or any paraconsistent logic, we devised four families of **mbC**-valid problems for evaluating **mbC** provers. These families are not classically valid, since all of them use the non-classical consistency connective. With these families we obtained the first benchmark results for the KEMS **mbC** implementation.

1.1 Outline

In section 2 we present the **mbC** logic. The **mbC KE** system is exhibited in section 3. There we also prove its analyticity, soundness and completeness. In section 4 we show the problem families we devised to evaluate **mbC** provers and in section 5 we present the results obtained with the KEMS prover for **mbC** using these families as benchmarks. Finally, in section 6 we draw some conclusions and point to future work.

2 The mbC Logic

The **mbC** logic is a member of the family of logics of formal inconsistency [3]. Logics of formal inconsistency are a class of paraconsistent logics that internalize the notions of consistency and inconsistency at the object-language level. Paraconsistent logics are tools for reasoning under conditions which do not presuppose consistency [3]. Formal characterizations of paraconsistent logics and logics of formal inconsistency can be found, respectively, in [9] and [3].

The logic **mbC** is the weakest[2] **LFI** based on classical logic presented in [3]. It uses the same set of connectives as propositional classical logic (the binary connectives $\wedge, \vee, \rightarrow$, and the unary connective $\neg$), plus a new one: the unary *consistency* ($\circ$) connective. The intended reading of $\circ A$ is 'A is consistent', that is, if $\circ A$ is true, A and $\neg A$ are not both true. In **mbC**, $\circ A$ is logically independent from $\neg(A \wedge \neg A)$, that is, $\circ$ is a primitive unary connective, not an abbreviation depending on conjunction and negation, as it happens in da Costa's C_n hierarchy of paraconsistent logics [5]. Its axiomatization is shown below:

Axiom schemas

$A \rightarrow (B \rightarrow A)$
$(A \rightarrow B) \rightarrow ((A \rightarrow (B \rightarrow C)) \rightarrow (A \rightarrow C))$
$A \rightarrow (B \rightarrow (A \wedge B))$
$(A \wedge B) \rightarrow A$
$(A \wedge B) \rightarrow B$
$A \rightarrow (A \vee B)$
$B \rightarrow (A \vee B)$
$(A \rightarrow C) \rightarrow ((B \rightarrow C) \rightarrow ((A \vee B) \rightarrow C))$
$A \vee (A \rightarrow B)$
$A \vee \neg A$
$\circ A \rightarrow (A \rightarrow (\neg A \rightarrow B))$

Inference rule

(Modus Ponens) $\dfrac{A, A \rightarrow B}{B}$

Now we present the formal definition of satisfiable and valid formulas in **mbC** [3]. Let $\mathbf{2} \stackrel{\text{def}}{=} \{0, 1\}$ be the set of truth-values, where 1 denotes the 'true' value and 0 denotes the 'false' value. An **mbC**-*valuation* is any function $v : For \longrightarrow \mathbf{2}$ subject to the following clauses:

$v(A \wedge B) = 1$ iff $v(A) = 1$ and $v(B) = 1$;
$v(A \vee B) = 1$ iff $v(A) = 1$ or $v(B) = 1$;
$v(A \rightarrow B) = 1$ iff $v(A) = 0$ or $v(B) = 1$;
$v(\neg A) = 0$ implies $v(A) = 1$;
$v(\circ A) = 1$ implies $v(A) = 0$ or $v(\neg A) = 0$.

A formula X is said to be *satisfiable* if truth-values can be assigned to its propositional variables in a way that makes the formula true, i.e. if there is at least one valuation such that $v(X) = 1$. A formula is a *valid* if all possible valuations make the formula true. For instance, the formula $\neg(A \wedge \neg A \wedge \circ A)$ is a valid in **mbC**, while $\neg(A \wedge \neg A)$ is satisfiable.

---

[2] It is the weakest because all other **LFI**s presented in [3] prove more theorems.

3 A KE System for mbC

The *Analytic Tableau* method is probably the most studied tableau method. It was presented in [13] as "an extremely elegant and efficient proof procedure for propositional logic". The **KE** System, a tableau method developed by Marco Mondadori and Marcello D'Agostino [7], was presented as an improvement, in the computational efficiency sense, over the Analytic Tableau method. It is a refutation system that, though close to the Analytic Tableau method, is not affected by the anomalies of cut-free systems [6].

In [3], a sound and complete tableau proof system for **mbC** is presented. It was obtained by using a method introduced in [2]. This method is a generic method that automatically generates a set of tableau rules for certain logics. For **mbC**, the rules obtained for its binary connectives are the same as that from classical analytic tableaux. The system also has a branching rule (called R_b) similar to **KE** PB rule, as well as rules for negation ($\neg$) and consistency ($\circ$). In total, this tableau system has 5 branching rules.

$$\frac{\begin{array}{l} \text{T } A \vee B \\ \text{F } A \end{array}}{\text{T } B} \;(\text{T} \vee 1) \qquad \frac{\begin{array}{l} \text{T } A \vee B \\ \text{F } B \end{array}}{\text{T } A} \;(\text{T} \vee 2) \qquad \frac{\text{F } A \vee B}{\begin{array}{l} \text{F } A \\ \text{F } B \end{array}} \;(\text{F} \vee)$$

$$\frac{\begin{array}{l} \text{F } A \wedge B \\ \text{T } A \end{array}}{\text{F } B} \;(\text{F} \wedge 1) \qquad \frac{\begin{array}{l} \text{F } A \wedge B \\ \text{T } B \end{array}}{\text{F } A} \;(\text{F} \wedge 2) \qquad \frac{\text{T } A \wedge B}{\begin{array}{l} \text{T } A \\ \text{T } B \end{array}} \;(\text{T} \wedge)$$

$$\frac{\begin{array}{l} \text{T } A \to B \\ \text{T } A \end{array}}{\text{T } B} \;(\text{T} \to 1) \qquad \frac{\begin{array}{l} \text{T } A \to B \\ \text{F } B \end{array}}{\text{F } A} \;(\text{T} \to 2) \qquad \frac{\text{F } A \to B}{\begin{array}{l} \text{T } A \\ \text{F } B \end{array}} \;(\text{F} \to)$$

$$\frac{\begin{array}{l} \text{T } \neg A \\ \text{T } \circ A \end{array}}{\text{F } A} \;(\text{T} \neg) \qquad \frac{\text{F } \neg A}{\text{T } A} \;(\text{F} \neg)$$

$$\overbrace{\qquad\qquad}^{} \;(\text{PB})$$
$$\text{T } A \qquad \text{F } A$$

Fig. 1. mbC KE tableau expansion rules

As explained in [6], branching rules lead to inefficiency. To obtain a more efficient proof system, we devised an original **mbC** **KE** system using signed formulas (see Figure 1). A *signed formula* is an expression $S\,X$ where $S \in \{\text{T}, \text{F}\}$ is called the *sign* and X is a propositional *formula*. The symbols T and F, respectively representing the truth-values true and false, can be used as signs. The *conjugate* of a signed formula T A (or F A) is F A (or T A). The mbC (T ¬) rule is a **LFI** version of classical propositional logic (T ¬) [6]. It states clearly that in mbC we need T ¬A and T ∘ A to obtain F A. In classical logic, we can obtain F A directly from T ¬A.

3.1 Analyticity, Correctness and Completeness Proof for the mbC KE system

An mbC KE proof enjoys the *subformula property* if every signed formula in the proof tree is a subformula of some formula in the list of signed formulas to be proved. Let us call *analytic* the applications of PB which preserve the subformula property, and the *analytic restriction of* mbC KE the system obtained by restricting PB to analytic applications. Given a rule R of an expansion system **S**, we say that an application of R to a branch θ is *analytic* when it has the *subformula property*, i.e. if all the new signed formulas appended to the end of θ are subformulas of signed formulas occurring in θ. According to [6], a *rule R is analytic* if every application of it is analytic. It is easy to notice that all mbC KE rules except (PB) are analytic.

We prove here that the mbC KE system is analytic, sound and complete (some proofs were omitted due to lack of space). It is easy to show a procedure that transforms any proof in the original tableau system for mbC ([3]) in an mbC KE proof, thus proving that mbC KE system is also sound and complete. We will not do this here. Instead, we will demonstrate that even the analytic restriction of mbC KE is sound and complete. That is, when performing a proof we can restrict ourselves to analytic applications of PB, applications which do not violate the subformula property, without affecting completeness.

The proof will be as follows. First we will redefine the notion of downward saturatedness for mbC. Then we will prove that every downward saturated set is satisfiable. The mbC KE proof search procedure for a set of signed formulas S either provides one or more downward saturated sets that give a valuation satisfying S or finishes with no downward saturated set. Therefore, if an mbC KE tableau for a set of formulas S closes, then there is no downward saturated set that includes it, so S is unsatisfiable. However, if the tableau is open and completed, then any of its open branches can be represented as a downward saturated set and be used to provide a valuation that satisfies S. By construction, downward saturated sets for open branches are analytic, i.e. include only subformulas of S. Therefore, the mbC KE system is analytic. As a corollary, it is also sound and complete.

Definition 1. A set of signed formulas DS is *downward saturated* if

1. whenever a signed formula is in DS, its conjugate is *not* in DS;
2. when all premises of any mbC KE rule (except PB) are in DS, its conclusions are also in DS;
3. when the major premise of a mbC KE rule is in DS, either its auxiliary premise or its conjugate is in DS.

For mbC KE, item (3) above is valid for every rule except (T ¬). In this case, if T ¬X is in DS, either T ∘ X or F ∘ X is in DS only if ∘X is a subformula of some other formula in DS.

We extend valuations to signed formulas in an obvious way: $v(\mathsf{T}\,A) = v(A)$ and $v(\mathsf{F}\,A) = 1 - v(A)$. A set of signed formulas L is satisfiable if it is not empty and there is a valuation such that for every formula $SX \in L$, $v(SX) = 1$. Otherwise, it is unsatisfiable.

Lemma 1. (Hintikka's Lemma) Every downward saturated set is satisfiable.

Proof. For any downward saturated set DS, we can easily construct a valuation v such that for every signed formula SX in the set, $v(SX) = 1$. How can we guarantee this is in fact a valuation? First, we know that there is no pair $\mathsf{T}\,X$ and $\mathsf{F}\,X$ in DS. Second, **mbC KE** rules preserve valuations. That is, if $v(SX_i) = 1$ for every premise SX_i, then $v(SC_j) = 1$ for all conclusions C_j. And if $v(SX_1) = 1$ and $v(SX_2) = 0$, where X_1 and X_2 are, respectively, major and minor premises of an **mbC KE** rule, then $v(S'X_2) = 1$, where $S'X_2$ is the conjugate of SX_2. For instance, suppose $\mathsf{T}\,A \wedge B \in DS$, then $v(\mathsf{T}\,A \wedge B) = 1$. In accord with the definition of downward saturated sets, $\{\mathsf{T}\,A, \mathsf{T}\,B\} \subseteq DS$. And by the definition of valuation, $v(\mathsf{T}\,A \wedge B) = 1$ implies $v(\mathsf{T}\,A) = v(\mathsf{T}\,B) = 1$.   □

Theorem 1. DS' is a set of signed formulas. DS' is satisfiable *if and only if* there exists a downward saturated set DS'' such that $DS' \subseteq DS''$.

Corollary 1. DS' is a unsatisfiable set of formulas if and only if there is no downward saturated set DS'' such that $DS'' \subseteq DS'$.

Theorem 2. The **mbC KE** system is analytic.

Proof. The **mbC KE** proof search procedure for a set of signed formulas S either provides one or more downward saturated sets that give a valuation satisfying S or finishes with no downward saturated set. If an **mbC KE** tableau for a set of formulas S closes, then there is no downward saturated set that includes it, so S is unsatisfiable. If the tableau is open and completed, then any of its open branches can be represented as a downward saturated set and be used to provide a valuation that satisfies S. By construction, downward saturated sets for open branches are analytic, i.e. include only subformulas of S. Therefore, the **mbC KE** system is analytic.   □

Corollary 2. The **mbC KE** system is sound and complete.

4 Problem Families

We present below the problem families we devised to evaluate **mbC** theorem provers. We had two objectives in mind. First, to obtain families of **mbC**-valid problems whose **mbC KE** proofs were as complex as possible. And second, to devise problems which required the use of many, if not all, **mbC KE** rules. These families are not classically valid, since all of them have formulas with the non-classical consistency connective.

4.1 First family

Here we present the first family (Φ^1) of valid sequents for **mbC**. In this family all **mbC** connectives are used. It is easy to obtain polynomial **mbC KE** proofs for this family of problems. The sequent to be proved for the n-th instance of this family (Φ_n^1) is:

$$\bigwedge_{i=1}^{n}(\neg A_i), \bigwedge_{i=1}^{n}((\circ A_i) \to A_i), [\bigvee_{i=1}^{n}(\circ A_i)] \vee (\neg A_n \to C) \vdash C \tag{1}$$

The explanation for this family is as follows. Suppose we are working with a database that allows inconsistent information representation. A_i means that someone expressed an opinion A about an individual i and $\neg A_i$ means that someone expressed an opinion $\neg A$ about this same individual. For instance, if A means that a person is nice, $\neg A_3$ means that at least one person finds 3 is not nice, and A_4 means that at least one person finds 4 nice. Then $\circ A_i$ means that either all people think i is nice, or all people think i is not nice, or there is no opinion A recorded about i. $\circ A_i \to A_i$ means that if all opinions about a person are the same, then that opinion is A.

For a subset of individuals numbered from 1 to n, we have $\neg A_i$ and $\circ A_i \to A_i$ for all of them. From the fact that either $\neg A_n \to C$ or for one of them we have $\circ A_i$, we can conclude C.

4.2 Second Family

The second family of problems for **mbC** (Φ^2) is a variation over the first family whose proofs are exponential in size. The sequent to be proved for the n-th instance of this family (Φ_n^2) is:

$$\bigwedge_{i=1}^{n}(\neg A_i), [\bigwedge_{i=1}^{n}[(\circ A_i) \to ([\bigvee_{j=i+1}^{n} \circ A_j] \vee ((\neg A_n) \to C))]],$$

$$[\bigvee_{i=1}^{m}(\circ A_i)] \vee (\neg A_n \to C) \vdash C$$

This family is a modification of the first family where instead of a conjunction of $\circ A_i \to A_i$, we have a conjunction of $\circ A_i \to ([\bigvee_{j=i+1}^{n} \circ A_j] \vee ((\neg A_n) \to C))$ meaning that for every person numbered 1 to n, if all opinions about a person are the same, then either all opinions about some other person with a higher index are the same or $(\neg A_n) \to C$ is true.

4.3 Third Family

With the third family of problems we intended to develop a family whose instances required the application of all **mbC KE** rules. To devise the third family (Φ^3), we have made some changes to the second family trying to make it more difficult to prove. The n-th instance of this family (Φ_n^3) is the following sequent:

$$U_l \wedge U_r,$$
$$\bigwedge_{i=1}^{n}(\neg A_i),$$
$$\bigwedge_{i=1}^{n}[(\circ A_i) \rightarrow ((((\neg A_n) \wedge U_l) \rightarrow C) \vee \bigvee_{j=i+1}^{n} \circ A_j)],$$
$$(\bigvee_{i=1}^{n} \circ A_i) \vee ((U_r \wedge (\neg A_n)) \rightarrow C)$$
$$\vdash C' \rightarrow (C'' \vee C)$$

4.4 Fourth Family

This is the only of these families where negation appears only in the conclusion. The n-th instance of this family (Φ_n^4) is the following sequent:

$$\bigwedge_{i=1}^{n}(A_i), \bigwedge_{j=1}^{n}((A_j \vee B_j) \rightarrow (\circ A_{j+1})), [\bigwedge_{k=2}^{n}(\circ A_k)] \rightarrow A_{n+1} \vdash \neg\neg A_{n+1}$$

Note: if $n \leq 2$, $[\bigwedge_{i=2}^{n}(\circ A_i)]$ in $[\bigwedge_{i=2}^{n}(\circ A_i)] \rightarrow A_{n+1}$ is replaced by the $\top$ formula.

This family formulas can be explained as follows. We have two formulas to represent two types of opinion: A and B. First we assume A_i for every i from 1 to n. Then we suppose for all j from 1 to n that $(A_j \vee B_j)$ implies $\circ A_{j+1}$. And finally we assume that for every k from 2 to n the conjunction of A_k's implies A_{n+1}. It is easy to see that from these assumptions we can deduce A_{n+1}. So we can also deduce its double negation: $\neg\neg A_{n+1}$.

5 Evaluation

Theorem provers are usually compared by using benchmarks. We have extended KEMS prover [11] to prove **mbC** theorems and evaluated it using as benchmarks the problem families presented in section 4. In Table 1 we show some of the results obtained. The tests were run on a personal computer with an Athlon 1100Mhz processor, 384Mb of memory, running a Linux operating system with a 2.26 kernel.

Problem	Time spent (s)	Problem size	Proof size	Tree height
Φ_4^1	0.06	47	197	4
Φ_7^1	0.046	80	491	7
Φ_{10}^1	0.08	113	911	10
Φ_4^2	0.071	77	570	7
Φ_7^2	1.54	164	7350	13
Φ_{10}^2	21.964	278	116037	19
Φ_4^3	0.058	94	706	6
Φ_7^3	1.097	187	5432	9
Φ_{10}^3	17.595	307	52540	12
Φ_4^4	0.007	47	181	3
Φ_7^4	0.013	83	433	3
Φ_{10}^4	0.023	119	793	3

Table 1. KEMS results for **mbC**

From these results it is clear that the second and third families are much more difficult to prove than the other two. And interestingly enough it was easier to prove the third than the second family.

6 Conclusion

We have presented an effective prover for **mbC**: a minimal inconsistency logic. The **mbC KE** system it implements was proven to be sound, complete and analytic. Besides that, it has only one branching rule. We devised some families of valid problems to evaluate our prover correctness and performance. These families can be used to evaluate any **mbC** theorem prover. The KEMS prover for **mbC** obtained the first benchmark results for these problem families.

In the future we intend to design different KEMS strategies for **mbC**. For instance, we want to implement a strategy that uses some derived rules not presented here. After that, we want to extend the KEMS prover to deal with C_1, the first logic in da Costa's C_n hierarchy of paraconsistent logics [5].

This paper has been partially sponsored by FAPESP Thematic Project Grant ConsRel 2004/14107-2.

References

1. H. A. Blair and V. S. Subrahmanian. Paraconsistent logic programming. *Theor. Comput. Sci.*, 68(2):135–154, 1989.
2. Carlos Caleiro, Walter Carnielli, Marcelo E. Coniglio, and Joao Marcos. Two's company: "The humbug of many logical values". In *Logica Universalis*, pages 169–189. Birkhäuser Verlag, Basel, Switzerland, 2005.
3. Walter Carnielli, Marcelo E. Coniglio, and Joao Marcos. Logics of Formal Inconsistency. In *Handbook of Philosophical Logic*, volume 12. Kluwer Academic Publishers, 2005.
4. Newton C. A. da Costa, Lawrence J. Henschen, James J. Lu, and V. S. Subrahmanian. Automatic theorem proving in paraconsistent logics: theory and implementation. In *CADE-10: Proceedings of the tenth international conference on Automated deduction*, pages 72–86, New York, NY, USA, 1990. Springer-Verlag New York, Inc.
5. Newton C. A. da Costa, Décio Krause, and Otávio Bueno. Paraconsistent logics and paraconsistency: Technical and philosophical developments. *CLE e-prints (Section Logic)*, 4(3), 2004.
6. Marcello D'Agostino. Tableau methods for classical propositional logic. In Marcello D'Agostino et al., editor, *Handbook of Tableau Methods*, chapter 1, pages 45–123. Kluwer Academic Press, 1999.
7. Marcello D'Agostino and Marco Mondadori. The taming of the cut: Classical refutations with analytic cut. *Journal of Logic and Computation*, pages 285–319, 1994.
8. Sandra de Amo, Walter Alexandre Carnielli, and Joao Marcos. A logical framework for integrating inconsistent information in multiple databases. In *FoIKS*

'02: Proceedings of the Second International Symposium on Foundations of Information and Knowledge Systems, pages 67–84, London, UK, 2002. Springer-Verlag.

9. Itala M. Loffredo D'Ottaviano and Milton Augustinis de Castro. Analytical Tableaux for da Costa's Hierarchy of Paraconsistent Logics $C_n, 1 \leq n \leq \omega$. Journal of Applied Non-Classical Logics, 15(1):69–103, 2005.

10. Adolfo Gustavo Serra Seca Neto. KEMS - A KE-based Multi-Strategy Theorem Prover, 2006. Retrieved February 01, 2006, from http://gsd.ime.usp.br/~adolfo/projetos/KEMS.zip.

11. Adolfo Gustavo Serra Seca Neto and Marcelo Finger. Implementing a multi-strategy theorem prover. In Ana Cristina Bicharra Garcia and Fernando Santos Osório, editors, Proceedings of the V ENIA, São Leopoldo-RS, Brazil, July 22-29 2005, 2005.

12. G. Priest. Paraconsistent Belief Revision. Theoria, 67:214–228, 2001.

13. Raymond M. Smullyan. First-Order Logic. Springer-Verlag, 1968.

Identification of Important News for Exchange Rate Modeling

Debbie Zhang, Simeon J. Simoff and John Debenham

[1] Faculty of Information Technology,
University of Technology, Sydney, Australia
[2] {debbiez, simeon, debenham}@it.uts.edu.au

Abstract. Associating the pattern in text data with the pattern with time series data is a novel task. In this paper, an approach that utilizes the features of the time series data and domain knowledge is proposed and used to identify the patterns for exchange rate modeling. A set of rules to identify the patterns are firstly specified using domain knowledge. The text data are then associated with the exchange rate data and pre-classified according to the trend of the time series. The rules are further refined by the characteristics of the pre-classified data. Classification solely based on time series data requires precise and timely data, which are difficult to obtain from financial market reports. On the other hand, domain knowledge is often very expensive to be acquired and often has a modest inter-rater reliability. The proposed method combines both methods, leading to a "grey box" approach that can handle the data with some time delay and overcome these drawbacks.

1 Introduction

Until recently, most of exchange rate models are empirical models based on macro economic data. While these models performed reasonably well in predicting long term trends, they have little success in predicting short to middle term movements. Recent research has discovered that irrationality of the market participants, bubbles, and herd behavior are the main driven forces of the short term instability. Many market participants make their decisions before the economic data are announced, trying to beat the market. Their decisions are based on their observations and prediction of market trends. They adjust their investment strategy again after the data announcement according to the differences between their expectation and the actual data. Unarguably, news play an important role in creating such market dynamics. Recent research has confirmed that news has statistically significant effects on daily exchange rate movement. Ehrmann and Fratzscher [1] have evaluated the overall impact of macro news by analyzing the daily exchange rate responses using regression models with news variables. Three key results were found. Firstly, the news about fundamentals can explain relatively well the direction, but only a much smaller extent to the magnitude of exchange rate development. Secondly, news about US economy has a larger impact on exchange rates than news about the euro area. Thirdly,

Please use the following format when citing this chapter:

Zhang, D., Simoff, S.J., Debenham, J., 2006, in IFIP International Federation for Information Processing, Volume 217, Artificial Intelligence in Theory and Practice, ed. M. Bramer, (Boston: Springer), pp. 475–482.

higher degree of market uncertainty will lead to more significant effects of news releases on exchange rate movements. Prast and De Vor [2] have also studied the reaction of investors in foreign exchange markets to news information about the euro area and the United States on days of large changes in the euro-dollar exchange rates. Unlike the traditional models, daily news about economic variables as well as relevant political events in the United States and Europe were used in the regression model, which is:

$$E_t = \alpha + \sum_{i=1}^{8} \beta_i D_i + \varepsilon \qquad (1)$$

where E_t is the percentage daily change in the euro-dollar exchange rate; D_{1-8} represent the following variables: 1 - real economy, euro area; 2 - inflation, euro area; 3 - change in official interest rate, ECB; 4 - statements/political events, euro area; 5 - real economy, United States; 6 - inflation, United States; 7 - change in official interest rate, United States; 8 - statements/political events, United States. It has been found that there is a strong correlation between exchange rate daily movement and the market participants' responses to the daily economy news and political events.

Motivated by their findings, Zhang, Simoff and Debenham [3] proposed a method to automate the exchange rate prediction process using text mining techniques. Nowadays, news retrieval using a computer program is effective and efficient as news data are widely available from the internet. However, to develop a program to understand the news articles and make the correct decision according to the news content is still an extreme difficult task. In this approach, the problem was broken down to multiple text classification problems and a regression modeling problem using numerical data. Relevant news are firstly identified and then being classified into the "good", "bad" or "no effect" news categories, which would have dramatically different impact on the market behaviors. "good" or "bad news" in this application are defined as the news that indicate the US dollar is destined to appreciate or depreciate versus Euro respectively. A regression prediction model is built based on these effects. Since the classification approaches are used, the training data are required to be pre-classified before the training process. The pre-classified training data contains the underlying knowledge of how data is being classified. Therefore, classification of training data is critical in any classification projects. However, many papers ignore this issue and provide no details of the methodology used in this step. This paper proposed a semi-automatic approach to assist the manual classification process.

2 News classification using a rule-based system

The training news data are required to be classified into one of the categories as shown in Figure 1 to incorporate their effects into the exchange rate model. This step can be done automatically or manually.

The automatic approach can be done by linking the news events with the changes in the exchange rate data if precise data are available. The exchange

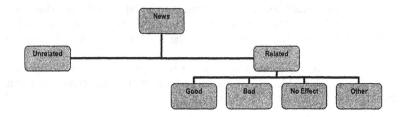

Fig. 1. News categories

rate data are recorded regularly over a time period, often referred to as "time series". At the same time, news about the events that may cause the data fluctuation are also recorded. The correlation between these two observations plays an important role in developing the prediction models. Methodologies like: Apriorilike Discovery of Association Rules, Template-Based Mining for Sequences, and Classification of Temporal Data can be used to discover their correlations. Recently, Ting etc [4] proposed an approach to classify the company announcements into three categories according to changes of the share prices. Lavrenko etc [5] also presented a method for identifying news stories that influence the behavior of financial markets using language models. However, these approaches require precise data which are recorded with high sampling frequencies [6]. Testing the influence of the information requires precise data on both the information available prior to a public announcement and the actual released information. Recording the information flow accurately can be very difficult, particularly for the exchange rate data. Although the times at which scheduled macroeconomic releases are available, identification of the pre and post announcement market behavior is often very difficult. This is due to the decentralized nature of currency exchange market and leaking of inside information to some of the market participants. Delays in publication of the announcements on the internet news sources further contribute to the difficulty. These are the typical issues in the data retrieved from online news web sites including www.bloomberg.com, which are used in this study. At the time the news is published on the web site, some market operators already have the information and have reacted correspondingly.

More common approaches of data sorting relies on analysts' knowledge of the domain. News data are manually classified into several categories according to a set of rules that are specified by the domain experts. Rule based systems such as expert systems can be employed to help collecting and maintenance of the rules. However, the knowledge acquisition and rule generation process from domain experts is time consuming, expensive, and sometimes has only a modest inter-rater reliability. The rules derived from the domain experts can only a good starting point. It would be a sensible approach to use the data patterns to improve the rules. Therefore, a "grey box" method using domain knowledge in conjunction with time series features of exchange rate data to refine the rules is proposed. The domain knowledge to form the initial rules is the white part of the model. However, these rules are not complete and can only be used to describe the data partially. Therefore, the rules need to be fine tuned using the data.

The intention of rule-based classification is to apply a validated, fully disclosed and understandable set of rules to perform the classification. The classification algorithm includes following steps:

- Specify a set of rules that reasonable to experts.
- Associate the text data with the exchange rate trends and classify the news according to the tread.
- Refine the rules if they are contradictive to the classified data in the previous step.
- Reclassify the data according to the new rules.

2.1   Obtaining Information for Developing Rules

Without an on-site domain expert, rules can be developed using published models that represent economists' understanding of the system. The rules used in this paper were developed using regression models provided by [1] and [2]. According to the regression result tables in the literature, the independent variables represent the factors that affect the exchange rate. The sign on the coefficient (positive or negative) indicates the direction of the effect. Although the size of the coefficient for each independent variable gives the size of the effect that variable is having on the exchange rate, they are ignored in the rules as they are highly sensitive to the data sets. It is difficult to quantify how the information is assessed by market participants since they have different responses for the same set of data when they have different expectations.

2.2   Association the News Data with the Exchange Rate Data

Each news item can also be classified according to its association with a particular trend in the exchange rate data. Considering most of the news web sites have time delay in publishing latest news and their refreshing frequency is about twice a day, the time window is set to 12 hours before and 12 hours after the exchange rate data. Figure 2 illustrates the alignment.

The trends are then aligned with news stories for classification. The results are used to examine the rules derived in Section 2.1. Adya etc [7] developed and automated heuristics to detect six features of the time series based on statistics: outliers, level shifts, change in basic trends, unstable recent trends, unusual last observation and functional form. However, to simplify the analysis process, only the upward trend and downward trend are identified. The exchange rate changes of each day are calculated. The days with large changes are selected, such as t1, t2 and t3 shown in Figure 2. The news articles that associated with these days are also selected and put into either "good" news or "bad" news categories

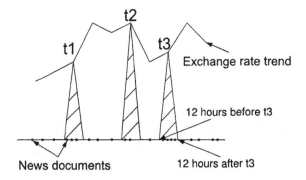

Fig. 2. News Alignment

according to their associated trend. At this stage, both categories contain many unrelated news since many news items of that day may have no impact on the exchange rate.

2.3 Refining the Rules and Classification Results

The rules derived in the section 2.1 can be validated by the classification results obtained in the section 2.2. The news in the "good" or "bad" categories are examined and summarized manually. Some simple heuristics are used to refine the rules. For example, if a rule describes an event has positive impact on the exchange rate, but in the data, both "good" and "bad" news contains multiple times of this event, it suggests that this event has no impact in the exchange rate at least within the period the data were collected. The rule should be removed. If multiple news items in the same category indicate that an event has impact in the exchange rate data, a new rule is added to link the event to the exchange rate movement. After the rules are being refined, the whole data set is manually classified according to the rules. In the final classification results, both "good" and "bad" news items may occur in the same day. This is reasonable as the changes of exchange rate are modeled as the the combined effect of multiple news items.

3   Experiment results

The experiment was conducted using the news articles and the US dollar versus Euro exchange rate data, both collected from www.bloomberg.com between 7/2/2005 to 4/7/2005.

Rules are derived from Ehrmann and Prast's models (see [1] and [2]), which are summarized in Table 1.

Their models also include "statements/political events", the area in which the rules are mainly expanded.

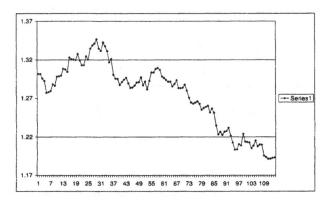

Fig. 3. News Alignment

Table 1. Summary of Ehrmann and Prast's models of positive and negative factors

	Positive factors	Negative factors
US announcement surprised	Inflation, Retail sales Nonfarm payrolles, Industrial production, N.A.P.M, Trade balance, Advance GDP, Average workweek Consumer confidence	Unemployment rate, Housing starts, CPI, PPI
German announcement surprises	CPI, Unemployment rate	Ifo Business Climate Industry production Manufacturing orders Retail sales Trade balance Business confidence PPI

To align trends with news data, a predefined threshold is used to define the trend. If Δg, which is defined in equation , is within the positive and negative range of the predefined threshold, it is considered that there is no changes in the price.

$$\Delta g_t = \frac{p_t - p_{t-1}}{p_{t-1}} \times 100\% \qquad (2)$$

where, Δg_t denotes the change of the exchange rate of day t, p_t and p_{t-1} denotes the exchange rate of day t and t-1.

In the experiment, the threshold of 0.1% is used. Within the experiment period, there were 40 days of upward trend and 49 days of downward trend. The news were compared on a daily base manually. Data have shown that Greenspan has profound inferences in the exchange rate. Although this is a well known fact, the original rules do not include this due to the models' limitation. Therefore, Greenspan's indication of positive or negative economic trend becomes one of the rule. The other rule worth to mention is the effect of U.S. 10 year treasury. The news of U.S. 10 year treasury appear very often. The first thought was that it could be an indicator of the rate trend. After carefully examining the data, no direct association was found. The final classification results using the refined rules are listed in Table 2.

Table 2. Classification results

Total number of News: 2589
    Number of "Unrelated" News: 1885
    Number of "Related" News: 704
        Number of "Good" News: 200
        Number of "Bad" News: 113
        Number of "No_Effect" News: 230
        Number of "Other" News: 161

As the experiment is still in an early stage, having data collected in a longer period would be better to evaluate the rules. More data are being collected using a program that can retrieve news data regardless the news web page format [8]. However, the preliminary results show that this approach provides better classification results than the classification solely based on the domain knowledge.

4   Conclusions

Exchange rate prediction using news article requires high quality training data. To achieve this, the news articles that have impact on exchange rate should be correctly associated with one of its trends, namely the upward and downward trends. Classification solely based on time series data requires precise and timely data, which are difficult to obtain for this application. On the other hand, domain knowledge is often very expensive to be acquired and often has a modest inter-rater reliability. The proposed method combines both methods, leading to a "grey box" approach, which well suits this particular application.

References

1. Ehrmann, M., Fratzscher, M.: Exchange rates and fundamentals: new evidence from real-time data. Journal of International Money and Finance **24** (2005) 317–341
2. Prast, H.M., de Vor, M.P.H.: Investor reactions to news: a cognitive dissonance analysis of the euro-dollar exchange rate. European Journal of Political Economy **21** (2005) 115–141
3. Zhang, D., Simoff, S., Debenham, J.: Exchange rate modelling using news articles and economic data. In: 18th Australian Joint Conference on Artificial Intelligence. (2005)
4. Yu, T., Jan, T., Debenham, J., Simoff, S.J.: Incorporate domain knowledge into support vector machine to classify price impacts of unexpected news. In: Australasian Data Mining Conference. (2005)
5. Lavrenko, V., Schmill, M., Lawrie, D., Ogilvie, P., Jensen, D., Allan, J.: Language models for financial news recommendation. In: Ninth International Conference on Information and Knowledge Management (CIKM), Washington (2000) 389–396
6. Hautsch, N., Hess, D.: Bayesian learning in financial markets - testing for the relevance of information precision in price discovery. Journal of Financial and Quantitative Analysis (2005)
7. Adya, M., Collopy, F., Armstrong, J.S., Kennedy, M.: Automatic identification of time series features for rule-based forecasting. International Journal of Forecasting **17** (2001) 143–157
8. Zhang, D., Simoff, S.: Informing the curious negotiator: Automatic news extraction from the internet. In: Australasian Data Mining Conference, Cairns, Australia (2004)

Autonomous Search and Rescue Rotorcraft Mission Stochastic Planning with Generic DBNs

Florent Teichteil-Königsbuch[1] and Patrick Fabiani[2]

[1] florent.teichteil@cert.fr
[2] patrick.fabiani@cert.fr
ONERA-DCSD
Toulouse, France 31055

1 Introduction

1.1 Motivation

This paper proposes an original generic hierarchical framework in order to facilitate the modeling stage of complex autonomous robotics mission planning problems with action uncertainties. Such stochastic planning problems can be modeled as Markov Decision Processes [5]. This work is motivated by a real application to autonomous search and rescue rotorcraft within the RESSAC[1] project at ONERA. As shown in Figure 1.a, an autonomous rotorcraft must fly and explore over regions, using waypoints, and in order to find one (roughly localized) person per region (dark small areas). Uncertainties can come from the unpredictability of the environment (wind, visibility) or from a partial knowledge of it: map of obstacles, or elevation map etc. After a short presentation of the framework of structured Markov Decision Processes (MDPs), we present a new original hierarchical MDP model based on generic Dynamic Bayesian Network templates. We illustrate the benefits of our approach on the basis of search and rescue missions of the RESSAC project.

1.2 Factored Markov Decision Processes

MDPs [5] are a classical model for decision-making under uncertainty. A MDP is a tuple $\langle S, A, P, R \rangle$ where S is the set of agent's states, A is the set of its actions, P and R respectively are the markovian probability and reward transitions between states for each action. A solution of a MDP is a mapping $\pi : S \to A$ named *policy*, that can be iteratively computed on the basis of the Bellman's equation [5].

Factored Markov Decision Processes (MDPs) [1, 3] are an extension of MDPs where the state space S is defined as a cartesian product of n subspaces V corresponding to an equal number of state variables $S = \otimes_{i=1}^{n} V_i$. State variable transitions are defined using Dynamic Bayesian Networks (DBNs) [1]. For each

---

[1] http://www.cert.fr/dcsd/RESSAC/

Please use the following format when citing this chapter:

Teichteil-Königsbuch, F., Fabiani, P., 2006, in IFIP International Federation for Information Processing, Volume 217, Artificial Intelligence in Theory and Practice, ed. M. Bramer, (Boston: Springer), pp. 483–492.

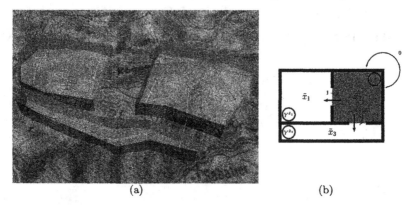

                    (a)   (b)

Fig. 1. (a) Search and rescue autonomous rotorcraft mission: 3 persons must be rescued in the 3 regions of the navigation subspace (software screenshot). (b) Local policy defined in the region $\tau(\pi) = \tilde{x}_2$. Stochastic outcomes are regions $\zeta(\pi) = \{\tilde{x}_1; \tilde{x}_3\}$.

action, a DBN represents the stochastic dependencies between *post-action* state variables $(X_i')_{i=1}^{n}$ and *pre-action* state variables $(X_i)_{i=1}^{n}$ (see Figure 6.a).

For each post-action state variable X_i, a probability tree encodes the stochastic distribution of X_i' values (tree's leafs) knowing the other state variables values (nodes), as shown in Figure 6.b. The reward transitions are encoded as a single decision tree for each action. Classical MDP optimization algorithms are generalized in structured algorithms [1, 3].

1.3 A hierarchical approach

Modeling autonomous robotics problems with factored MDPs remains difficult. In the very simple search and rescue mission of Figure 1.a, with 5 actions: west, east, north, south, statio, and 4 state variables: the rotorcraft's localization and the status of the 3 persons to rescue, the localization variable has 24 possible values (as many as the number of waypoints), that must be enumerated in any decision tree containing a waypoint node. More complicated missions can have hundreds of waypoints, which makes it a burden to model *by hand* the problem because the trees' sizes are polynomial in the arity of state variables.

Our hierarchical model allows to tackle larger state spaces by reducing the size of the decision trees used to model the problem. We use state abstractions in order to decompose the problem with respect to its variables of highest arity: in the search and rescue example of Figure 1, the localization variable (24 positions) is decomposed into a region variable of arity 3.

2 Hierarchical factored MDP

2.1 State subspace splitting

Let X_p be a state variable with a large arity. The state subspace generated by X_p (navigation subspace) is a graph V_p that can be partitioned into smaller weakly coupled abstract subgraphs $\tilde{V}_p$. The partition can be either a mission input, or the result of an automatic partition process [6]. The resulting abstracted states can be considered as the values of a new abstracted state variable $\tilde{X}_p$, which is an abstraction of the original state variable X_p. The abstract state space of the factored MDP becomes $\tilde{\mathcal{V}} = (\otimes_{i \neq p} V_i) \times \tilde{V}_p$. Let us consider the mission of Figure 1: whereas a X_p node would have 24 subtrees, the corresponding $\tilde{X}_p$ node only has 3 subtrees.

2.2 Local policies

Actions need to be abstracted correspondingly into macro-actions. At the region level, abstract actions correspond to local policies defined and applied within the regions of the partition $\tilde{V}_p$. Let π be such a local policy, defined in a region $\tilde{v}_p$. Let Π_p be a set of local policies defined on each region of the partition $\tilde{V}_p$. A minimal set of local policies can be automatically generated [2, 4], in such a way that an optimal policies can be obtained as a combination of such local policies in the regions. Extra local policies can be added by other methods.

Unfortunately, in both cases, the number of local policies can be very large. In theory, the maximum number of local policies is $\sum_{\tilde{v}_p \in \tilde{V}_p} |\mathcal{A}|^{|\tilde{v}_p|}$, each of which should have a corresponding DBN encoding for the dependencies between the pre- and post-action variables.

In order to keep a substantial benefit from the decomposition, it is useful to notice that in most problems, all the local policies DBNs share a common structure. It is indeed possible to define a single DBN structure, where the corresponding local policy, the region where it is applicable, and the reachable regions appear as parameters that can be automatically instantiated when the local policies are computed.

3 Abstract generic Dynamic Bayesian Network

In this section, we present the syntax of our abstract generic DBN for modeling factored stochastic autonomous robotics problems. Our generic DBN is parametrized by a local policy $\pi \in \Pi_p$. Since a local policy is defined for a single region of the reduced variable $\tilde{X}_p$, we can define the mapping $\tau : \Pi_p \to \tilde{V}_p$ between local policies and the region where they are each one defined.

We illustrate our approach with a small academic instance of a search and rescue autonomous rotorcraft mission (see Figure 1.b). The decomposed subspace matches the localization variable, whose arity is 24, abstracted in 3 regions ($\tilde{X}$). We will consider a local policy π defined in the second region $\tilde{x}_2$, that consists in going out towards the regions $\tilde{x}_1$ and $\tilde{x}_3$ with respectively the probabilities $1 - p$ and p. Last but not least, each region contains a person to rescue: these subgoals are represented by 3 binary state variables $\left(Y^{\tilde{x}_i}\right)_{1 \leqslant i \leqslant 3}$ indicating if each person was already rescued or not.

3.1 Reduced state variable modeling

Let us consider a decision tree (probability tree or reward tree) containing a node of the reduced variable $\tilde{X}_p$. The local policy π is only defined in $\tau(\pi)$ so that the node $\tilde{X}_p$ only has two abstract subtrees: one corresponding to the value $\tau(\pi)$, and one other representing the other values where the policy is not applicable, noted $\overline{\tau(\pi)} = \tilde{V}_p \setminus \{\tau(\pi)\}$.

Since π is only applicable over $\tau(\pi)$, the $\overline{\tau(\pi)}$-subtree of any $\tilde{X}_p$ variable in probability trees is symbolically represented as a nil leaf. Instead of defining these nil leafs inside each probability tree, it is better to define a binary mask tree that indicates where the local policy is applicable. This mask tree should contain at least a node of the state variable $\tilde{X}_p$, as shown in Figure 2.

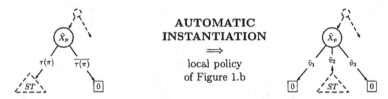

Fig. 2. Generic mask tree example and one of its instantiations

The function that automatically instantiates the subtrees of a $\tilde{X}_p$ node in any decision tree is presented in Algorithm 1. It calls the function `InstantiateTree`, that instantiates the $\tau(\pi)$-subtree of the generic node T (see Algorithm 6). The $\overline{\tau(\pi)}$-subtrees are nil leafs (*nil_leaf*).

Algorithm 1: Function `InstantiateXpSubtrees`

Data: T (generic node), T^π (instantiated node), π, τ, ζ, $[\tilde{v}'_p = -1]$
Result: T^π (instantiated tree)
begin
    $subtree \leftarrow T.son(\text{`}\tau(\pi)\text{'})$;
    for $\tilde{v}_p \in \tilde{V}_p$ **do**
        if $\tilde{v}_p = \tau(\pi)$ **then** $T^\pi.sons().push(\text{InstantiateTree}(subtree, \pi, \tau, \zeta, \tilde{v}'_p))$;
        else $T^\pi.sons().push(nil\_leaf)$;
    return T^π;
end

The treatment of a $\tilde{X}'_p$ node is slightly different from a $\tilde{X}_p$ node. Let ζ : $\Pi_p \to \tilde{V}_p$ be the mapping from a local policy to its reachable regions. It means that π transforms $\tau(\pi)$ into $\zeta(\pi)$. In our small instance depicted in Figure 1.b, only the regions $\tilde{x}_1$ and $\tilde{x}_3$ are reachable with π : $\zeta(\pi) = \{\tilde{x}_1; \tilde{x}_3\}$.

A $\tilde{X}'_p$ node can only have 2 abstract subtrees: one for the value $\zeta(\pi)$ and one other for the value $\overline{\zeta(\pi)} = \tilde{V}_p \setminus \zeta(\pi)$. Each subtree must be transformed into as many subtrees as the cardinality of the corresponding abstract value (see Figure 3 and Algorithm 2).

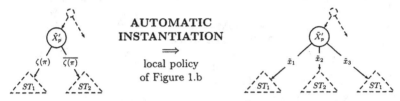

Fig. 3. Example of a decision tree containing a $\tilde{X}'_p$ node and one of its instantiations

---

Algorithm 2: Function `InstantiateXppSubtrees`

Data: $\mathcal{T}$ (generic node), $\mathcal{T}^\pi$ (instantiated node), π, τ, ζ
Result: $\mathcal{T}^\pi$ (instantiated tree)
begin
   $st_1 \leftarrow \mathcal{T}.son('\underline{\zeta(\pi)}')$;
   $st_2 \leftarrow \mathcal{T}.son('\overline{\zeta(\pi)}')$;
   for $\tilde{v}'_p \in \tilde{V}_p$ **do**
      if $\tilde{v}'_p \in \zeta(\pi)$ **then** $\mathcal{T}^\pi.sons().push(\mathtt{InstantiateTree}(st_1, \pi, \tau, \zeta, \tilde{v}'_p))$;
      else $\mathcal{T}^\pi.sons().push(\mathtt{InstantiateTree}(st_2, \pi, \tau, \zeta, \tilde{v}'_p))$;
   return $\mathcal{T}^\pi$;
end

3.2 State variables depending on the reduced state variable

We can take advantage of our abstract model to introduce state variables that are defined for each value of the reduced state variable. In the case of our small exploration mission (Figure 1), let us consider a person to rescue in each region of the navigation subspace. Each value $\tilde{v}_p$ of the abstract navigation state variable corresponds to a subgoal to achieve, represented by a binary state variable $Y^{\tilde{v}_p}$ (see Figure 1.b).

Only can be achieved the subgoal corresponding to the region where the unknown local policy of our generic DBN is defined. The other subgoals can not be realized with this local policy, since it is not applicable inside the regions where they are enclosed. Therefore, for each set $\left(Y^{\tilde{v}_p}\right)_{\tilde{v}_p \in \tilde{V}_p}$ of variables depending on the reduced variable, the generic DBN defines 2 abstract variables: the variable $Y^{\tau(\pi)}$ defined for the abstract value $\tau(\pi)$, and the variable $Y^{\overline{\tau(\pi)}}$ representing all the variables defined in the regions $\tau(\pi)$.

Figure 4 depicts the decision trees of $Y^{\tau(\pi)}$ and $Y^{\overline{\tau(\pi)}}$ and an instance of their automatic instantiation for a given local policy. A decision tree containing a $Y^{\tau(\pi)}$ node is illustrated too.

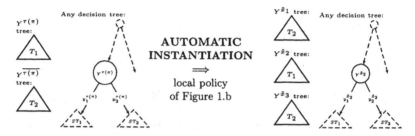

Fig. 4. Example of the decision trees of $Y^{\tau(\pi)}$ and $Y^{\overline{\tau(\pi)}}$, and of a decision tree containing a $Y^{\tau(\pi)}$ node. An automatic instantiation is presented.

Algorithm 3 details the automatic instantiation of the two abstract probability trees $\mathcal{T}_{Y^{\tau(\pi)}}$ and $\mathcal{T}_{Y^{\overline{\tau(\pi)}}}$. Since a node of any decision tree can be an abstract $Y^{\tau(\pi)}$ node (primed or not), it must be analyzed before being instantiated, as done in Algorithm 4.

Algorithm 3: Function `InstantiateYpTrees`

Data: $\mathcal{T}_{Y'^{\tau(\pi)'}}$, $\mathcal{T}_{Y'\overline{\tau(\pi)}'}$, π, τ, ζ

Result: $\left(\mathcal{T}^{\pi}_{Y^{\tilde{v}_p}}\right)_{\tilde{v}_p \in \tilde{V}_p}$

$\mathcal{T}^{\pi}_{Y^{\tau(\pi)}} \leftarrow$ `InstantiateTree`$(\mathcal{T}_{Y'^{\tau(\pi)'}}, \pi, \tau, \zeta)$;

for $\tilde{v}_p \in \tau(\pi)$ do $\mathcal{T}^{\pi}_{Y^{\tilde{v}_p}} \leftarrow$ `InstantiateTree`$(\mathcal{T}_{Y'\overline{\tau(\pi)}'}, \pi, \tau, \zeta)$;

3.3 Abstract leafs of the generic probability trees

Due to action uncertainties, the outcome of a local policy is not deterministic. Let us consider for instance the local policy depicted in Figure 1.b: starting from region $\tilde{x}_2$, the local policy can lead to regions $\tilde{x}_1$ and $\tilde{x}_3$ with respectively probabilities $1 - p$ and p. Let $\tilde{\mathcal{P}}^{\pi}$ be the abstract probability transition distribution over the partitioned subspace $\tilde{V}_p$ for the local policy π: this distribution is the stationary probability distribution of the markov chain resulting from application of the local policy π inside $\tau(\pi)$ [2].

Algorithm 4: Function `InstantiateNode`

Data: n (generic node), π, τ
Result: n^π (instantiated node)
begin

    if $n = Y'^{\tau(\pi)'[']}$ then $n^\pi \leftarrow Y^{\tau(\pi)[']}$;

    else $n^\pi \leftarrow n$;

    return n^π;

end

The probabilities of obtaining the different values of any state variable may depend on the local policy probability distribution. These state variable probabilities are stored in the leafs of their probability trees. We suppose that they can be expressed as functions of 2 abstract local policy probabilities:

- $p^{\tau(\pi)}$: probability of staying in the region $\tau(\pi)$
- $p^{\varsigma(\pi)}$: if the reduced post-action state variable $(\tilde{X}'_p)$ is a parent node, probability of going to the value of the parent reduced state variable

An example of abstract probability leaf and one of its possible instantiations are shown in Figure 5. The abstract leaf is a formal algebraic expression of $p^{\tau(\pi)}$ and $p^{\varsigma(\pi)}$. Given the abstract probability transition distribution $\tilde{\mathcal{P}}^\pi$ over the partitioned subspace $\tilde{V}_p$ for the local policy π, Algorithm 5 computes the probability of an instantiated leaf. It calls the function `Evaluate` from the computer algebra library to assess the leaf. If $\tilde{v}'_p \neq -1$, it means that $\tilde{X}'_p$ is a parent node of the leaf l, and l belongs to the $\tilde{v}'_p$-subtree of the $\tilde{X}'_p$ parent node.

Fig. 5. Generic probability leaf example and one of its instantiations

3.4 Abstract leafs of the generic reward tree

Local policy transition probabilities are associated with local policy transition rewards. Let $\tilde{\mathcal{R}}^\pi$ be the transition rewards defined for the local policy π over the reduced state variable subspace. These reward transitions can be computed on the basis of the local policy transition probabilities just defined.

Algorithm 5: Function `InstantiateLeaf`

Data: l (generic leaf), π, τ, ζ, $[\tilde{v}'_p = -1]$
Result: l^π (instantiated leaf)
$p^{\tau(\pi)} \leftarrow \tilde{\mathcal{P}}^\pi(\tau(\pi), \tau(\pi))$;
if $\tilde{v}'_p \neq -1$ **then** $p^{\zeta(\pi)} \leftarrow \tilde{\mathcal{P}}^\pi(\tau(\pi), \tilde{v}'_p)$;
$l^\pi \leftarrow$ `Evaluate`$(l, {}^{\backprime}p^{\tau(\pi)\prime} = p^{\tau(\pi)}, [{}^{\backprime}p^{\zeta(\pi)\prime} = p^{\zeta(\pi)}])$;

As for the local policy transition probabilities, we suppose that the local policy transition rewards are formal algebraic expressions of:

- $r^{\tau(\pi)}$: average reward obtained if staying in $\tau(\pi)$
- $r^{\zeta(\pi)}$: if the reduced post-action state variable $(\tilde{X}'_p)$ is a parent node, average reward if going to the value of the parent reduced state variable

Figure 5 still is a good example of a generic reward tree and its instantiation for the local policy of Figure 1.b, with the proviso of replacing p by r. In the same way, Algorithm 5 presents the automatic reward leaf instantiation algorithm, with the proviso of replacing p by r and $\tilde{\mathcal{P}}$ by $\tilde{\mathcal{R}}$.

3.5 Main automatic DBN instantiation algorithm

Algorithm 6 automatically instantiates a decision tree for a given local policy. The version of our algorithm presented in this paper is recursive. It is called from functions `InstantiateXpSubtrees` and `InstantiateXppSubtrees`, when instantiating the subtrees of the nodes $\tilde{X}_p$ and $\tilde{X}'_p$ (see Algorithms 1 and 2). Notice that the optional argument $\tilde{v}'_p$ is not an input of `InstantiateXppSubtrees`: otherwise, it would mean that $\tilde{X}'_p$ is a parent node of itself, what is impossible.

4 Application to a search and rescue mission

We applied our generic MDP model to search and rescue missions described in section 1.1. We tested our generic model with 4 state variables (see Figure 6):

- R : regions of the environment (stands for $\tilde{X}_p$)
- $O.$: person to rescue in the region where the unknown local policy is defined (stands for $Y^{{}^{\backprime}\tau(\pi)\prime}$)
- O_- : persons to rescue in the other regions (stands for $Y^{\overline{{}^{\backprime}\tau(\pi)\prime}}$)
- A : rotorcraft's autonomy (binary variable, **full** or **empty**)

In '$O.$' probability tree leafs, $Lp.$ stands for '$p^{\tau(\pi)}$' and $Lp_- = 1 - Lp. = \overline{p^{\tau(\pi)}}$.

Table 1 shows the elapsed time comparison between automatic instantiation and optimization stages, when increasing the sizes of both the state and action spaces. Note that **the same generic DBN** was used to model all of the tested

---

Algorithm 6: Function `InstantiateTree` (recursive)

Data: $\mathcal{T}$ (generic decision tree), π, τ, ζ, $[\tilde{v}'_p = -1]$
Result: $\mathcal{T}^\pi$ (instantiated decision tree)
begin

    if $\mathcal{T}.root().type() = leaf$ **then** $\mathcal{T}^\pi \leftarrow$ `InstantiateLeaf`$(\mathcal{T}.root(), \pi, \tau, \zeta, \tilde{v}'_p)$;

    else

        $\mathcal{T}^\pi \leftarrow$ `InstantiateNode`$(\mathcal{T}.root(), \pi, \tau)$;

        switch $\mathcal{T}.root()$ **do**

            case $\tilde{X}_p$: $\mathcal{T}^\pi \leftarrow$ `InstantiateXpSubtrees`$(\mathcal{T}.root(), \mathcal{T}^\pi, \pi, \tau, \zeta, \tilde{v}'_p)$;

            case $\tilde{X}'_p$: $\mathcal{T}^\pi \leftarrow$ `InstantiateXppSubtrees`$(\mathcal{T}.root(), \mathcal{T}^\pi, \pi, \tau, \zeta)$;

            otherwise

                for $subtree \in \mathcal{T}.root().sons()$ **do**

                    $\mathcal{T}^\pi.sons().push($`InstantiateTree`$(subtree, \pi, \tau, \zeta, \tilde{v}'_p))$;

    return $\mathcal{T}^\pi$;

end

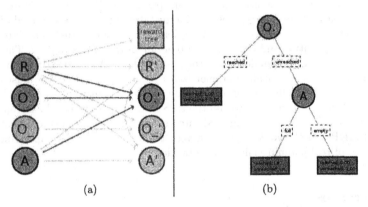

      (a)   (b)

Fig. 6. (a) Generic DBN and (b) O. generic probability tree (software screenshot)

Nb of enume-rated states	Nb of regions (states per region)	Nb of generated local policies	DBNs instan-tiation time	MDP optimi-zation time
82944	9 (9)	21	0.01	0.12
746496	9 (81)	61	0.01	16.77
58982400	17 (9)	69	0.03	1621.62
530841600	17 (81)	117	0.06	> 1 hour

Table 1. Elapsed time comparison between instantiation and optimization stages, for growing size search and rescue missions (in seconds, with a P4-2.8GHz processor)

instances. First, it appears that the number of states exponentially grows with number of regions, so that unstructured enumerated models of MDP would have been very tedious and quite impossible to model. Second, the number of generated local policies (automatic generation algorithm of [4]) is round 100, what means that usual factored MDP models would have required to manually input a hundred or even more DBNs, in order to define our real search and rescue missions. On the contrary, our generic hierarchical DBN model enables to define **only one DBN** for the whole mission. Third, the automatic DBNs intanciation time is insignificant compared to the optimization time ($< 1\%$): it confirms the modeling and effectiveness benefits of our approach.

5 Conclusion

In this paper, we proposed an original generic hierarchical framework for modeling large factored Markov Decision Processes. Our approach is based on a decomposition into regions of the state subspaces engendered by the state variables with large arity. The regions are macro-states of the thus abstracted MDP. Local policies can then be computed (or defined by other means) in each region of the decomposition and taken as macro-action of the abstract MDP. The factored MDP model is then defined at the abstract level. A generic DBN template can be defined, symbolically parametrized by the local policies. We illustrated and showed the significance of our method on real instances of search and rescue aerial robotics missions (within the RESSAC project) where the navigation subspace can easily be decomposed into regions: the use of classical unstructured MDP models would have been very tedious and perhaps impossible for the kind of real planning missions we tackle.

References

1. Craig Boutilier, Richard Dearden, and Moises Goldszmidt. Stochastic dynamic programming with factored representations. *Artificial Intelligence*, 121(1-2):49–107, 2000.
2. Milos Hauskrecht, Nicolas Meuleau, Leslie Pack Kaelbling, Thomas L. Dean, and Craig Boutilier. Hierarchical solution of markov decision processes using macro-actions. In *Proceedings 14th UAI*, pages 220–229, San Francisco, CA, 1998.
3. Jesse Hoey, Robert St-Aubin, Alan Hu, and Craig Boutilier. Optimal and approximate stochastic planning using decision diagrams. Technical Report TR-2000-05, University of British Columbia, 10 2000.
4. Ron Parr. Flexible decomposition algorithms for weakly coupled markov decision problems. In *Proceedings 14th UAI*, pages 422–430, San Francisco, CA, 1998.
5. Martin L. Puterman. *Markov Decision Processes*. John Wiley & Sons, INC, 1994.
6. R. Sabbadin. Graph partitioning techniques for markov decision processes decomposition. In *Proceedings 15th ECAI*, pages 670–674, Lyon, France, July 2002.

Solving multi-objective scheduling problems—An integrated systems approach

Martin Josef Geiger

Lehrstuhl für Industriebetriebslehre, Universität Hohenheim, D-70593 Stuttgart, Germany, mjgeiger@uni-hohenheim.de

Abstract. In the past, numerous approaches have been formulated either for approximating Pareto-optimal alternatives or supporting the decision making process with an interactive multi criteria decision aiding methodology. The article on the other hand presents an integrated system for the resolution of problems under multiple objectives, combining both aspects. A method base of metaheuristics is made available for the identification of optimal alternatives of machine scheduling problems, and the selection of a most preferred solution is supported in an interactive decision making procedure.

As the system is aimed at end users, a graphical interface allows the easy adaptation of metaheuristic techniques. Contrary to existing software class libraries, the system therefore enables users with little or no knowledge in the mentioned areas to successfully solve scheduling problems and customize and test metaheuristics.

After successfully competing in the finals in Ronneby (Sweden), the software has been awarded the *European Academic Software Award 2002* (http://www.easa-award.net/, http://www.bth.se/llab/easa_2002.nsf).

Key words: Multi-Objective Optimization, Multi-Objective Metaheuristics, Decision Support System, Scheduling

1 Introduction

In general, the resolution of multi-objective problems is twofold. First, optimal solutions need to be identified by means of some algorithmic approach. For a given problem Π having a set of feasible alternatives $\mathcal{X}$ and a set of optimality criteria $G(x) = (g_1(x), \ldots, g_k(x)), x \in \mathcal{X}$, optimality of alternatives is in the light of conflicting optimality criteria here understood in the sense of *Pareto-optimality* [20] as further described in Definition 1 and 2. Without loss of generality, a minimization of the objective function values is assumed here.

Definition 1 (Dominance). *An objective vector $G(x), x \in \mathcal{X}$ is said to dominate a vector $G(x'), x' \in \mathcal{X}$ if and only if $g_i(x) \leq g_i(x') \; \forall \, i = 1, \ldots, k \wedge \exists i \mid g_i(x) < g_i(x')$. The dominance of $G(x)$ over $G(x')$ is denoted with $G(x) \prec G(x')$.*

Please use the following format when citing this chapter:

Geiger, M.J., 2006, in IFIP International Federation for Information Processing, Volume 217, Artificial Intelligence in Theory and Practice, ed. M. Bramer, (Boston: Springer), pp. 493–502.

Definition 2 (Efficiency, Pareto-optimality, Pareto set). *An objective vector $G(x), x \in \mathcal{X}$ is said to be* efficient, *if and only if* $\neg \exists x' \in \mathcal{X} \mid G(x') \prec G(x)$. *The corresponding alternative x is called* Pareto-optimal, *the set of all Pareto-optimal alternatives the* Pareto set P.

The second step of the resolution of multi-objective problems is the selection of a most preferred alternative $x^* \in P$, involving a single human decision maker or even a group of people.

Search and *decision making* can be combined in three general ways [6].

1. A priori: The decision maker states his/her preferences allowing the construction of a utility function and the successive resolution of the resulting mono-criterion problem of maximizing the overall utility.
2. Interactive: The resolution of the problem alternates between search and decision making, successively revealing the preferences of the decision maker.
3. A posteriori: The choice of a most preferred alternative is performed after the determination of all optimal solutions.

Over the years, numerous concepts have been proposed to support both aspects of search and decision making. Most interactive methods are based on goal programming [13] or reference point approaches [23] and allow the successive refinement of the decision makers' preferences. An overview is e. g. given by VINCKE [21].

Besides methodological progress, implementations of algorithms have been made freely available on the world wide web. For genetic algorithms for example, an archive is maintained under http://www.aic.nrl.navy.mil/galist/src/. The particular case of multi-objective optimization has been addressed by several researchers, and an overview about implemented source code is maintained by COELLO COELLO on the EMOO webpage, http://www.lania.mx/ ~ccoello/EMOO/EMOOsoftware.html. Unfortunately however, most implementations require a throughout understanding of the underlying methodologies and techniques in order to be reused and adapted to particular problem domains. This can impose a problem in teaching and demonstration work, when non-experts are required to interact with the computer programs. Here, implementations are required similar to established computer user interfaces with which the users are familiar. Only very recently, components are being developed that allow the visualization of the outcomes of multi-objective optimization problems, one example being GUIMOO by CAHON, VAN DEN HEKKE and SEYNHAEVE. Integrated systems however, combining both search *and* decision making are to our knowledge not freely available yet.

The paper is organized as follows. Section 2 presents an integrated system for multi-objective optimization and decision making, using the example of scheduling under multiple objectives. The problem is well-known from operations research and computer science and is of high practical value with applications in many areas [15]. Results obtained with the system are presented in Section 3, and conclusions and discussion are given in Section 4.

2 A metaheuristic system for multi-objective scheduling

2.1 The addressed problem

Machine scheduling considers in general the assignment of a set of resources (machines) $\mathcal{M} = \{M_1, \ldots, M_m\}$ to a set of jobs $\mathcal{J} = \{J_1, \ldots, J_n\}$, each of which consists of a set of operations $J_j = \{O_{j1}, \ldots, O_{jo_j}\}$ [4]. The operations O_{jk} typically may be processed on a single machine $M_i \in \mathcal{M}$ involving a non-negative processing time t_{jk}. Usually, precedence constraints are defined among the operations of a job, reflecting its technical nature of processing. Other important aspects that frequently have to be taken into consideration are release dates and due dates of jobs.

A solution $x \in \mathcal{X}$ to the problem, a so called *schedule*, assigns start and end times for the operations with respect to the defined constraints of the problem.

While first approaches to machine scheduling consider optimality of schedules for a single objective function, multi-objective formulations of the problem have become increasingly of importance in the last years [18]. As these criteria are often conflicting, not a single but a whole set of solutions may be regarded as optimal in the sense of Pareto-optimality, introduced earlier in Definition 2, and the resolution of the problem lies in the identification of all $x \in P$.

Various optimality criteria are based on the completion times C_j of the jobs J_j in the schedule. The most prominent to mention is the minimization of the maximum completion time (makespan) $C_{max} = \max\{C_1, \ldots, C_n\}$. Another objective is the minimization of the sum of the completion times $C_{sum} = \sum_{j=1}^{n} C_j$. Both measures implicitly try to optimize cost of production by minimizing the production time of the jobs.

In many situations, due dates d_j are present for each job J_j which define a preferable or required time of job completion. It is here possible to compute due date violations in the form of tardiness values $T_j = \max\{C_j - d_j, 0\}$. Usual optimality criteria based on this consideration are the minimization of the maximum tardiness $T_{max} = \max\{T_1, \ldots, T_j\}$, the minimization of the total tardiness $T_{sum} = \sum_{j=1}^{n} T_j$, and the minimization of the number of tardy jobs $U = \sum_{j=1}^{n} U_j$ where $U_j = 1$ if $T_j > 0$, 0 otherwise.

In terms of machine efficiency, idle times I_i of the machines M_i may be considered up to the completion of the last job on M_i. Possible optimality criteria are therefore the minimization of the maximum machine idleness $I_{max} = \max\{I_1, \ldots, I_m\}$, and the minimization of the total machine idleness $I_{sum} = \sum_{i=1}^{m} I_i$.

An important factor for the resolution of the scheduling problem is the *regularity* of the functions [5]. It is here possible to represent an optimal schedule as a permutation of operations, corresponding to the position of the job in the sequence of production. An interpretation of the permutations is possible by computing a schedule with respect to the given job sequence, assuming earliest possible execution of the operations [7].

2.2 Components

For the resolution of multi-objective production scheduling problems, the integrated system *MOOPPS* has been implemented. As illustrated in Figure 1, the system consists of different components for the resolution of the problem.

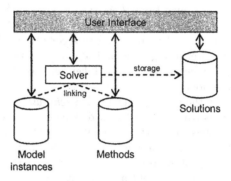

Fig. 1. System architecture.

A *method database* contains a set of heuristics approaches for solving multi-objective scheduling problems:

1. Priority rules [12], based on the early work of GIFFLER and THOMPSON [11] for generating active schedules.
2. Local search neighborhoods [16] within a multi-point hillclimber.
3. Multi-objective evolutionary algorithms [1], incorporating elitist strategies and a variety of crossover neighborhoods like e.g. uniform order based crossover, order based crossover, two point order crossover, and partially mapped crossover.
4. The 'MOSA' multi-objective simulated annealing algorithm of TEGHEM et al. [19].
5. A module based on the 'AIM' aspiration interactive method [14] for an interactive search in the obtained results.

The *model instance database* stores the data of the problem instances that have to be solved. General job shop as well as flow shop scheduling problems can be formulated. Besides newly generated data sets, well-known test instances from literature [3] have been included. Solutions are obtained by linking model instances with methods and stored in a solution database. This allows the reuse of specific metaheuristics for a range of problem instances as well as the comparison of results obtained from different heuristic approaches.

A graphical *user interface* links the modules described above into a single system. Besides the construction of model instances and the definition of metaheuristic search algorithms, an interactive decision making procedure enables the user to select a most preferred schedule. Visualization of alternatives is available in alternative space and in outcome space. The alternatives as such are presented as Gantt charts [10], their outcomes as plotted Pareto fronts.

2.3 Visual interface

The user interface is a key aspect of the implemented system as it is designed for end users. It brings together visual components to store, retrieve and modify problem instances, configure metaheuristic methods, execute them and manage the obtained results. All components like for example crossover/mutation operators and their corresponding application probabilities are available. New configurations of metaheuristics can be derived from predefined and implemented techniques by simply changing the attribute values of the methods. Also, the progress of the metaheuristics while optimizing a particular problem instance can be monitored by storing the currently best alternatives after definable intervals of evaluations.

After executing methods on problem instances, solutions are obtained that need to be further investigated. As mentioned above, two visualizations are of importance. First, a two-dimensional outcome space plot visualizing the Pareto front. Here, a direct interaction is possible by allowing the user to select alternatives. Second, a visualization of the alternatives as such using job-oriented or machine-oriented Gantt charts [24]. The detailed starting times of the operations can be monitored here, and an indication whether a job is tardy or not is easily available.

In order to allow a widespread use of the software, the graphical user interface is available in English, French, German, Hungarian, Italian, Polish, and Spanish language. Also, a 103-pages printed documentation is available.

2.4 Optimization and decision making

The resolution of multi-objective scheduling problems is supported by a two-stage a posteriori procedure as described in Section 1. First, Pareto-optimal alternatives or an approximation P_a of the Pareto set P are computed using the chosen metaheuristics. Second, an interactive search in the obtained results is performed by the decision maker.

During this interactive decision making procedure, aspiration levels $A = \{a_{g_1}, \ldots, a_{g_k}\}$ for each of the optimized objective functions $G(x) = (g_1(x), \ldots, g_k(x))$ are chosen. As shown in Figure 2, the elements of the approximation P_a of the Pareto set P are accordingly divided into two subsets, the subset P_{as} of the alternatives fulfilling the aspiration levels $(g_i(x) \leq a_{g_i} \forall i = 1, \ldots, k)$ and the subset $P_{\neg as}$ of the alternatives that do not meet the aspiration levels. It is obvious that $P_{as} \cup P_{\neg as} = P_a$ and $P_{as} \cap P_{\neg as} = \emptyset$.

The initial values of the aspiration levels a_{g_i} are set to the worst values in P_a: $a_{g_i} = \max_{x \in P_a} (g_i(x)) \forall i = 1, \ldots, k$ and as a consequence, $P_{as} = P_a$. The decision maker is allowed to modify the values of the aspiration levels and successively reduce the number of elements in P_{as} until $|P_{as}| = 1$. The

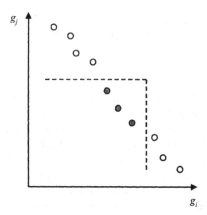

Fig. 2. Decision making component. A cone in outcome space divides the set of alternatives into alternatives fulfilling the aspiration levels (grey background) and alternatives outside the cone (white background).

remaining alternative in P_{as} is the desired compromising solution x^* as the fixed aspiration levels are met by this alternative.

Another interpretation of the method can be seen in a moving cone in outcome space that contains all alternatives fulfilling the current aspiration levels. While the visualization of the outcome space provided by the system is limited to two dimensions at a time, the decision making procedure as such can accommodate higher dimensions without any further problems. The procedure here allows the arbitrary change of the aspiration levels a_{g_i} in any direction, enlarging or reducing them. This is important as the situation in which $P_{as} = \emptyset$ appears, an adjustment of at least one aspiration level a_{g_i} is necessary in order to allow the identification of a most preferred alternative x^*.

3 Computational results

Different configurations of the implemented metaheuristics have been tested on benchmark instances of multi-objective machine scheduling problems taken from literature [1, 2], ranging from $n = 20$ jobs on $m = 5$ machines up to $n = 100$ jobs on $m = 20$ machines. Using various configurations of evolutionary algorithms, close approximations of the true Pareto fronts or the best known solutions could have been obtained.

Algorithm 1 gives the pseudo-code of the applied evolutionary method. It can be seen, that two sets are maintained during search. First, a population POP_i of n_{pop} individuals, and second, an archive P_a of alternatives which are currently not dominated by any other known alternative. After termination of the optimization runs, P_a is returned as an approximation of the true Pareto set

P. This strategy allows the evolvement of the population POP_i while keeping the best found alternatives in P_a, implicitly implementing an elitist strategy.

Algorithm 1 Multi-objective evolutionary algorithm

1: Set $i = 1$
2: Set $P_a = \emptyset$
3: Initialize: Compute starting population POP_i with n_{pop} individuals
4: Update P_a with POP_i
5: **repeat**
6:   **repeat**
7:     Select alternatives $x_1, x_2 \in POP_i \cup P_a$
8:     Compute x_1', x_2' using crossover neighborhood $\mathbf{N}_c(x_1, x_2, z)$
9:     Apply mutation $\mathbf{N}_m(x, z)$ with probability p_{mut}
10:    Test new alternatives x_1', x_2' for acceptance in POP_{i+1}
11:   **until** number of elements in $P_{i+1} = n_{pop}$
12:   Update P_a with P_{i+1}
13:   Set $i = i + 1$
14: **until** termination criterion has been met
15: Return P_a

When selecting two alternatives x_1, x_2 for reproduction, the union of both sets POP_i and P_a forms a mating pool. Selection is done with respect to the Pareto-ranking-based approach of FONSECA and FLEMING [8]. Crossover operators tested include partially mapped crossover PMX, order based crossover OBX, uniform order based crossover UOBX, and two-point crossover TPOX [22]. New alternatives are generated until a new population POP_{i+1} has been formed which replaces the old population POP_i. Step 10 of Algorithm 1 ensures that no duplicates are added to the succeeding population POP_{i+1}.

The length of the test runs has to be chosen depending on the size of the problem instances. Good termination criteria turned out to be 1,000,000 evaluated alternatives for instances with $n = 20$, 5,000,000 evaluations for instances with $n = 50$, and 10,000,000 for $n = 100$.

For the instances proposed by BASSEUR et al. [2] on the basis of TAILLARD [17], the approximations came close to the best known alternatives of which most have been identified. Unfortunately it was not possible to improve any of them. It may be mentioned however, that for the smaller instances the known results are already proven to be optimal and therefor not further improvable.

New alternatives have been identified dominating the previously reported best known solutions for the instance of BAGCHI [1] with $n = 49$ jobs on $m = 15$ machines. The considered objective functions of this instance are the minimization of the maximum completion time C_{max}, the minimization of the average completion time of all jobs $\frac{1}{n}C_{sum}$, and the minimization of the average tardiness of all jobs $\frac{1}{n}T_{sum}$.

Figure 3 gives a plot of the results in outcome space. The best solutions obtained with a multi-objective evolutionary algorithms using the fitness as-

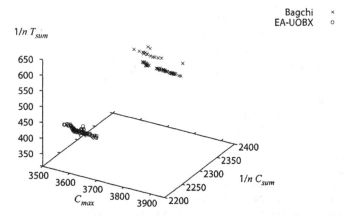

Fig. 3. Comparison of obtained approximation for the problem instance from [1] with previously known best solutions.

signment of FONSECA and FLEMING [8] and a uniform order based crossover UOBX are compared with the results reported by BAGCHI. It can be seen, that all alternatives of [1] are dominated. In particular with respect to the objective of minimizing the average tardiness of jobs, significant improvements have been obtained.

When closer investigating the results, it can be observed that the obtained alternatives are in rather close proximity to each other. The schedules share significant similarities both in outcome space, see Figure 3, and in alternative space. This indicates that Pareto optimal alternatives are closely concentrated in the search space of feasible alternatives $\mathcal{X}$ and helps to explain to some extend how metaheuristic search may work. As qualitatively good alternatives are typically close to other alternatives of high quality, this information may be exploited when computing neighboring alternatives using crossover or mutation operators.

4 Conclusions and discussion

A decision support system for multiple objective scheduling problems has been presented. It incorporates a set of metaheuristics that can be adapted to specific problem instances. As the user interface is highly visual, non-experienced users are able to solve scheduling problems under multiple objectives with comparably little knowledge.

Computational results have been gathered for benchmark instances taken from literature. It has been possible to observe the effectiveness of the implemented methods, even in comparison to the best known results of the test instances. While the results are satisfying with respect to that aspect, a further development and improvement of the methods is unfortunately not permitted to the end user as the source code is not accessible.

After an approximation of Pareto-optimal alternatives has been obtained, an interactive decision making module based on the aspiration interactive method allows the identification of a most preferred schedule. The system may also be used to compare different approximation results of various metaheuristic approaches in terms of their approximation quality. It is therefore suitable for demonstrating the use, adaptation and effectiveness of metaheuristics to complex combinatorial optimization problems using the example of machine scheduling under multiple objectives.

The system successfully competed in the *European Academic Software Award*, a biannual contest of academic software in research and higher education. In this context, it has been evaluated by an international panel of experts. As it is aimed at end users who are not necessarily experts in the relevant field of metaheuristics or scheduling, its' realized concept differs from existing implementations. Rather than being generic like know software class libraries, it is specific. This bears the disadvantage of a potentially difficult adaptation to other problems than scheduling. On the other hand however, as it presents a closed system with no need of adapting and recompiling source code, it may also be used as a demonstration and learning tool in higher education. Based on the experiences gathered, we believe that it is able to stipulate the understanding and use of modern metaheuristics in research and higher education, and contribute to the further development and distribution of modern heuristics.

Acknowledgements

The author would like to thank Zsíros Ákos (University of Szeged, Hungary), Pedro Caicedo, Luca Di Gaspero (University of Udine, Italy), and Szymon Wilk (Poznan University of Technology, Poland) for providing multilingual versions of the software.

References

1. Tapan P. Bagchi. *Multiobjective scheduling by genetic algorithms*. Kluwer Academic Publishers, Boston, Dordrecht, London, 1999.
2. Matthieu Basseur, Franck Seynhaeve, and El-ghazali Talbi. Design of multiobjective evolutionary algorithms: Application to the flow-shop scheduling problem. In *Congress on Evolutionary Computation (CEC'2002)*, volume 2, pages 1151–1156, Piscataway, NJ, May 2002. IEEE Service Center.
3. J. E. Beasley. Obtaining test problems via internet. *Journal of Global Optimization*, 8:429–433, 1996.
4. J. Błażewicz, K. H. Ecker, E. Pesch, G. Schmidt, and J. Węglarz. *Scheduling Computer and Manufacturing Processes*. Springer Verlag, Berlin, Heidelberg, New York, 2. edition, 2001.

5. R. W. Conway, W. L. Maxwell, and L. W. Miller. *Theory of Scheduling.* Addison-Wesley, Reading, MA, 1967.
6. Richard L. Daniels. Incorporating preference information into multi-objective scheduling. *European Journal of Operational Research,* 77:272–286, 1994.
7. Richard L. Daniels and Joseph B. Mazzola. A tabu-search heuristic for the flexible-resource flow shop scheduling problem. *Annals of Operations Research,* 41:207–230, 1993.
8. Carlos M. Fonseca and Peter J. Fleming. Genetic algorithms for multiobjective optimization: Formulation, discussion and generalization. In Stephanie Forrest, editor, *Proceedings of the Fifth International Conference on Genetic Algorithms,* pages 416–423, San Mateo, CA, 1993. Morgan Kaufmann Publishers.
9. Tomáš Gál, Theodor J. Stewart, and Thomas Hanne, editors. *Multicriteria Decision Making: Advances in MCDM Models, Algorithms, Theory, and Applications,* volume 21 of *International Series in Operations Research & Management Science.* Kluwer Academic Publishers, Boston, Dordrecht, London, 1999.
10. Henry L. Gantt. Efficiency and democracy. *Transactions of the American Society of Mechanical Engineers,* 40:799–808, 1919.
11. B. Giffler and G. L. Thompson. Algorithms for solving production-scheduling problems. *Operations Research,* 8:487–503, 1960.
12. R. Haupt. A survey of priority rule-based scheduling. *Operations Research Spektrum,* 11(1):3–16, 1989.
13. Sang M. Lee and David L. Olson. Goal programming. In Gál et al. [9], chapter 8, pages 8.1–8.33.
14. V. Lotfi, T. J. Stewart, and S. Zionts. An aspiration-level interactive model for multiple criteria decision making. *Computers & Operations Research,* 19(7):671–681, 1992.
15. Michael Pinedo. *Planning and Scheduling in Manufacturing and Services.* Springer Verlag, Berlin, Heidelberg, New York, 2005.
16. Colin R. Reeves. Landscapes, operators and heuristic search. *Annals of Operations Research,* 86:473–490, 1999.
17. Eric Taillard. Benchmarks for basic scheduling problems. *European Journal of Operational Research,* 64:278–285, 1993.
18. Vincent T'kindt and Jean-Charles Billaut. *Multicriteria Scheduling: Theory, Models and Algorithms.* Springer Verlag, Berlin, Heidelberg, New York, 2002.
19. E. L. Ulungu, J. Teghem, P. H. Fortemps, and D. Tuyttens. MOSA method: A tool for solving multiobjective combinatorial optimization problems. *Journal of Multi-Criteria Decision Making,* 8:221–236, 1999.
20. David A. Van Veldhuizen and Gary B. Lamont. Multiobjective evolutionary algorithms: Analyzing the state-of-the-art. *Evolutionary Computation,* 8(2):125–147, 2000.
21. Philippe Vincke. *Multicriteria Decision-Aid.* John Wiley & Sons, Chichester, New York, Brisbane, Toronto, Singapore, 1992.
22. Darrell Whitley. Permutations. In Thomas Bäck, David B. Fogel, and Zbigniew Michalewicz, editors, *Handbook of Evolutionary Computation,* chapter C3.3.3, pages C3.3:14–C3.3.20. Institute of Physics Publishing, Bristol, 1997.
23. Andrzej P. Wierzbicki. Reference point approaches. In Gál et al. [9], chapter 9, pages 9.1–9.39.
24. James M. Wilson. Gantt charts: A centenary appreciation. *European Journal of Operational Research,* 149:430–437, 2003.